P9-EMC-284

Making the Arab World

Making the Arab World

Nasser, Qutb, and the Clash That Shaped the Middle East

Fawaz A. Gerges

PRINCETON UNIVERSITY PRESS
Princeton & Oxford

Published by Princeton University Press,
41 William Street, Princeton, New Jersey 08540

In the United Kingdom: Princeton University Press,
6 Oxford Street, Woodstock, Oxfordshire OX20 1TR

press.princeton.edu

Jacket photograph: Burning of the Muslim Brotherhood's headquarters in Cairo, Egypt, in retaliation for an attempted assassination of President Gamal Abdel Nasser, October 27, 1954 / AP Photo

Jacket design by Faceout Studio, Charles Brock

ISBN 978-0-691-16788-6

Library of Congress Control Number: 2018930051

British Library Cataloging-in-Publication Data is available

This book has been composed in Miller Text

Printed on acid-free paper. ∞

Printed in the United States of America

10 9 8 7 6 5 4 3 2 1

AS ALWAYS, FOR NORA

Contents

Preface

THIS BOOK SETS OUT to explain how the opposing forces of Arab nationalism, spearheaded by the military, and the Islamists, led mainly by the Ikhwan (the Muslim Brothers), have shaped the development of postcolonial Arab politics. It does so by focusing on two seminal, and interconnected, figures: Gamal Abdel Nasser and Sayyid Qutb.

Far from being diametrically opposed, the movements that Nasser and Qutb represent have had critical commonalities with each other. The book aims to break down the established and misleading dichotomy of two monolithic ideas that has dominated conventional thinking on Middle Eastern politics. Through a detailed historical, sociological, and personality-based approach the book shows that Arab nationalism and Islamism are constructed in large part through interaction with each other, and also that each group has "ideational fluidity," shifting from one mode of thinking to another. In so doing, the book avoids reductionist and ahistorical viewpoints that frequently stereotype both Arab nationalists and Islamists.

The history pinpoints the rise of nationalist forces—both religious nationalists and more secularly oriented nationalists—starting in the nineteenth century. Although the narrative traces the gradual emergence of nationalists and Islamists as sui generis political forces to the beginning of the twentieth century, lasting until the 1940s, it focuses particular attention on the successful July 1952 coup d'état in Egypt by the Free Officers, a moment that represents the official rupture of the nationalist movement into two separate strands. Egypt was initially the main battlefield, but the confrontation between nationalist (Arabist) and Islamist spread to neighboring countries, undermining the development of nascent postcolonial states. This prolonged confrontation, between the two most powerful social and political movements in the region, has left a deep, indelible scar on Arab states, societies, and economies. Today, the deep divide between nationalists and Islamists is invested with profound existential meanings that far outstrip those at its genesis.

Moreover, in order to relate the story of the titanic clash between the Arab nationalist and Islamist movements, the book is framed as a dual biography of Gamal Abdel Nasser, Egyptian president and highly charismatic Arab popular leader, and Sayyid Qutb, master ideologue of revolutionary Islamism. Based on extensive interviews with their contemporaries, as well as on archival sources, the biographies of Nasser and Qutb present fresh readings of both men who have been mythologized by their enemies but also, tellingly, by their disciples. Nasser thus emerges as more a pragmatist than an ideologue and as more open to Islam than his secular image would suggest. Qutb comes out as a more complex and multidimensional personality than has usually been presented, whose legacy is often deliberately misinterpreted by Islamists themselves. Avoiding "clear-cut divisions," the double biography provides valuable and much-needed nuance on Nasser's and Qutb's lives and on their troubled times.

The rift between the nationalists and the Islamists created a significant political fault line in Egyptian political life and remains a part of political life throughout the Arab world and the Middle East. However, far from being a binary and inevitable division—as it is too often depicted by both participants and analysts—the struggle between nationalists and Islamists is far more complex. The focal point of the struggle is the state, its power, and its position as custodian of the public sphere, not ideology.

One of the key goals of this book is to reconstruct the history of this deadly encounter between nationalists and Islamists and to shed further light on its effects on state and society in Egypt and neighboring Arab countries. These two movements formed a duality defining sociopolitical life, and the study argues that their interaction—both as a fierce rivalry and as a symbiotic cooperation—was so profound that neither can be properly understood if viewed as a separate historical agent. There is a large library of books dealing with Nasser and Egyptian and Arab nationalism and another large library of books on Qutb, the Muslim Brotherhood, and Islamist movements in general. A remarkable aspect of this scholarship is the degree to which these two libraries present separate pictures and are not integrated across time and space. Studies of Nasserism and nationalism mention Qutb and the Muslim Brotherhood, but such observations tend to be marginal to the main lines of analysis. In a similar vein, books on Qutb and political Islam pay remarkably little attention to the evolution and continuing popular support for populist nationalism as articulated by Nasser. While studies of Islamism note populist opposition to elitist secularism, there tends to be little recognition that the nationalist movement in Egypt did not involve a rejection of Islam, even in some of its more "traditional" forms. In contrast, this analysis presents a distinctive synthesis of the two existing libraries and concentrates on the dynamic interaction between nationalism and Islamism from the late nineteenth century till the present, though focusing specifically on the period since the early 1950s.[1]

I have worked on this book intermittently since 2006, spending two years on field research in various Arab countries, which enabled me to conduct scores of in-depth interviews with leading activists, public intellectuals, politicians, and civil society leaders. Utilizing historical sociology and a historical-thematic approach, the book takes human agency seriously by focusing on collective action, hidden internal struggles, clashes of personalities, and pivotal watershed moments. It is rich with ethnographic details, including personal testimonies of old men who have since died and middle-aged ideologues who have been at the forefront of the confrontation.

On a personal note, I have been engaged in these debates for many years, and the book is an attempt to make sense of the prolonged divide that has hindered political transition and evolution in the region. For example, the durability of this clash was shown in 2013, when the Egyptian military overthrew the elected government of President Mohamed Morsi of the Ikhwan. Many observers were surprised by the depth of popular support for Abdel Fattah al-Sisi's clampdown in 2013 against a democratically elected government led by the Ikhwan so soon after the massive Tahrir demonstrations that had overthrown the military regime of Hosni Mubarak. The book provides an analytical and empirical framework for understanding the current turmoil in Egypt and neigboring Arab countries—as a continuation of the long-standing interaction between nationalism and activist Islamism—and also a framework for making sense of the complexities of the groups involved.

Framed as a dialogue in Arab politics, the book is based mainly on ethnography, exhaustive primary sources, and one-on-one interviews with and personal testimonies of those who have been at the forefront of a fierce and prolonged power struggle between their two respective Arab nationalist and Islamist camps. In important ways, this book represents a valuable resource as a document in oral history. It carefully provides context for views expressed by the historical figures being interviewed, giving a direct personal dimension for understanding how the movements actually operated and developed.

Particularly rewarding were my conversations with most of Qutb's surviving contemporary disciples and ardent supporters who joined his underground network, al-Tanzim al-Sirri, or the Secret Organization, and spent years by his side in and out of prison. His followers draw an intimate portrait of the radical Islamist theorist. While Qutb's writings have been debated by scholars,[2] his life in prison and in the underground has not been fully and critically examined. The prison years are pivotal. It is behind the bars of Nasserist jails that Qutb constructed a theoretical repertoire about the revolutionary Islamist project and attempted to put it into practice. Having spent years with him in the solitude of prisons and outside, Qutb's disciples are best positioned to clarify the background, intentions, and implications of some of his controversial terms and his vision in general. According to their testimonies, Qutb spent countless hours discussing his ideas and further elaborating on various themes. He trusted them completely and confided in them by sharing his dreams and his apocalyptic interpretations of them. They hand-copied most of his manifestos and books in prison and spread his call inside and outside. This small circle of followers were his eyes and ears and would have sacrificed their lives for him, as they have indicated.

Over a two-year period, I spent countless hours attentively listening to Qutb's contemporary disciples, reminiscing about their past moments with him. They confided what had transpired behind closed doors. They told me about Qutb's antipathy to Nasser and his desire to rid Egypt of its *faroun* (tyrant) and the social and political structure that had given rise to secular Arab nationalism and Westernization in general. I have extensively relied on these firsthand interviews, recollections, and memoirs of Qutb's contemporaries to reconstruct his life journey—from a public intellectual with a secular mentality to a revolutionary Islamist. My uninhibited access to Qutb's most inner circle and that of the Ikhwan's old guard and younger activists provides a unique window into a shadowy, secretive universe, allowing this book to zero in on these years and trace Qutb's footsteps and actions, thus filling a major gap in the literature.

Initially, most of his disciples were reluctant to talk to a stranger about their past history and trauma, their subversive activities and years in prison camps. They feared that I, as an outsider, had a "hidden agenda," but beyond this, what they feared just as much was to face some painful memories. Most had served almost a decade in jail, and despite their advanced age, they were still under surveillance by the security services; their telephones were bugged and their daily movements monitored. I labored hard to convince them of my academic balance and commitment to reconstructing the story of Qutb, particularly during his prison years. I stressed the importance of their perspective and testimony in the reconstruction of this early and pivotal chapter of revolutionary Islam. I urged them to narrate the story in their own words, to tell their version of events, and to document the extent of their role and participation in Qutb's al-Tanzim al-Sirri. There remain few survivors of the Qutbian generation, I reminded them—the gatekeepers of his secrets and direct witnesses to his innermost thoughts. I implored them to share their insights on Qutb's fateful journey into the revolutionary underground and his rationale for leading al-Tanzim al-Sirri. I cautioned that unless recounted, the story of Qutb's al-Tanzim will die with them; the official narrative that portrays Qutb and his followers as terrorists will prevail. They owed it to their mentor, Qutb, I argued, to set the record straight.

I do not regret my supplications as these survivors proved to be the key to unlocking the Qutbian riddle and role in the momentous events of the 1950s and 1960s. Their narratives are of utmost historical significance because they fill a gap in the literature about the internal dynamics and the ideological fissures that the prison years triggered within the Ikhwan. A full decade after our interviews, these fissures have neither healed nor weakened; rather, they have deepened and widened. Thus, ultimately, Qutb's contemporary disciples warmed up to the idea of opening up to me and correcting the historical record. "We should have told our side of the story a long time ago," conceded Ahmed Abdel Majid, eighty years old, six feet tall, and still an ardent Qutbian follower. "It is in our interest to tell the truth about our jihadist endeavor and why we revolted against the Nasser dictatorship. We have nothing to be ashamed of; we risked our lives to defend Islam," insisted Abdel Majid after he got to know me a bit better. "Our silence and inertia harmed our cause and enabled the authorities to portray us as terrorists."[3]

This was the same Abdel Majid who a few months earlier had refused entreaties by a well-known radical Islamist to grant me an interview. Subsequently, he arranged several interviews for me with leading members of al-Tanzim. In addition to furnishing me with precious memoirs and other unpublished manuscripts in Arabic about the Qutbian journey, Abdel Majid spent more than twenty hours walking me step by step through the radicalization and militarization process that took place after the confrontation between the Ikhwan and the Free Officers in 1954. He rarely complained about my intrusive and critical questions, our hours-long meetings that often kept us awake after midnight; instead, he graciously served me sweetened tea, Turkish coffee, and Arabic delicacies. A frail man with breathing difficulties, he appeared to be in a hurry to be relieved of a big historical burden that was weighing him down. He frequently expressed regret and disappointment that few writers have investigated the long war between the Islamists and the nationalists, a confrontation, in his opinion, "between two ideologies, two identities, and two radically opposing ways of life—Islam versus apostasy." He suggested that "a big chunk of responsibility falls on our own shoulders because we were afraid that throwing light on our jihadist journey would benefit the enemies of Islam. We feared that we would open old wounds and rekindle people's suspicions of the Islamist movement. We also did not want to go against the expressed wishes of the Ikhwan to keep silent," he said.[4]

Other leading dissidents conceded that psychology and socialization into a culture of secrecy and the underground had impaired their vision and judgment and made them easy prey to conspiracy theories. "Remember that we [political Islamists] are socialized into a tribal mentality, one that is deeply suspicious of the other," said Ahmed Ra'if, a midlevel member of the Ikhwan underground organization who was imprisoned together with Qutb's followers, and is now an Islamist insider.[5] "We view the world in black and white—*hakimiyya* versus *jahiliyya* [God's sovereignty versus the state of ignorance or unbelief]—and the other as menacing and threatening; we are terror-stricken by any open interaction with strangers and outsiders," explained the vigorous eighty-year-old Ra'if, who was instrumental in arranging some of my interviews with top Qutb contemporaries, including Abdel Majid.[6] Considered the official chronicler and publisher of the Ikhwan and well connected to all Islamist trends,

Ra'if told me that the problem is that Islamists are indoctrinated to blindly obey and to eschew critical thinking; they are conditioned to see enemies lurking everywhere.

My patience was thus handsomely rewarded. I got unfettered access to most of Qutb's disciples as well as to his right-hand men in al-Tanzim al-Sirri. Those old men in their seventies and eighties introduced me to a younger Qutbian generation that seeks to carry the revolutionary torch forward. Time and again, I was told by Qutb's followers that by the late 1950s their mentor was essentially in charge of the Ikhwan and tried to revolutionize the timid Islamist organization. Although in 1966 Nasser hoped to extinguish the Qutbian fire by sending Qutb to the gallows, his "martyrdom" provided the fuel that has powered several jihadist waves, according to his contemporary disciples. Qutb's loyalists say that he knew that his blood would be a curse to haunt Muslim *tawagheet* (tyrants) and to quench the thirst of the *umma* (the global Muslim community) for sacrifice and cultural and political renewal.

In addition to extensive interviews with Qutb's supporters, I also interviewed scores of elderly Ikhwan of the Qutbian generation who said that they resisted his efforts to hijack the Islamist organization and turn it into a revolutionary vanguard. These elderly men distanced themselves from Qutb's subversive ideas and stressed that while incarcerated Qutb did not speak for the Ikhwan, and that the legitimate leadership did not sanction his underground activities. Such claims are hotly disputed by Qutb's followers and detractors alike. Younger Ikhwan activists whom I interviewed have their own axe to grind against the old guard, whose authoritarianism and resistance to change, in their opinion, have frozen the Islamist organization in time, delaying both its evolution and its democratization. The dispute among various Ikhwan constituents shows the persistence of an ideological and generational divide within the Islamist movement. From the onset, the Ikhwan was never a monolith. Rather, the movement was fraught with friction revolving around strong personalities, political ambitions, and ideological differences. Far from the inherent continuity that the Ikhwanist self-view holds to be the historical norm, there was significant divisiveness, even internal revolts carried out by rival factions within the group.

Similarly, I interviewed at length Nasser's surviving Free Officer comrades; top advisers, including his eldest daughter, Huda, who was his private secretary during the last years of his tenure; Mohamed Hassanein Heikal, his closest confidant; and other contemporaries who witnessed his life journey with its twists, turns, and sharp detours. My goal was to understand continuity and change in Nasser's worldview and the most important factors that shaped his character and conduct. The idea was to avoid taking the dominant narrative of Nasser for granted and, instead, to retrace his journey through various phases and watersheds in order to paint a fuller and more complex portrait of the man and his times. Given the tumultuous times that young Nasser inhabited in the 1920s, 1930s, and 1940s, it was not surprising to discover that he, together with other Free Officers like Anwar Sadat, had joined the Ikhwan and had been an active member of its paramilitary network, called al-Tanzim al-Khass (the Special Apparatus).

There is insufficient space to list all of the people who took time from their busy schedules to answer my queries over the last two decades. But this truncated list includes key actors, participants, and public intellectuals who spent countless hours with me reflecting on their life journeys and putting up with my critical and, sometimes, contentious questions. I interviewed them more than once and, I am sure, taxed their patience: Ma'mun Hudaybi; Mohamed Mahdi Akef; Mahmoud Izzat; Sayyid Eid; Mahmoud al-Sabbagh; Ali Ashmawi; Ahmed Adel Kamal; Farid Abdel Khaleq; Ahmed Abdel Majid; Ahmed Ra'if; Abdel Majid al-Shazili; Abdel A'l Aw'd Musa; Abdullah Rashwan; Abu El-Ela Madi; Essam Sultan; Abdel Moneim Abu al-Futuh; Issam al-Iryan; Kamal Habib; Montasser al-Zayat; Al-Sayyed Nazili; Ahmed al-Assal; Hilmi al-Jazzar; Gamal Sultan; "Hassan Karate"; Yasser Saad; Sani Ismail; Mamdouh Ismail; Ibrahim Za'farani; Seif Abdel Fattah; Nadia Mustafa; Mohamed Ama'ra; Mohamed Abdel

Sattar; Adel Abd El-Barri; Mohammed Beshr; Essam al-Haddad; Ibrahim Za'farani; Hesham El-Hamamy; Khaled Mohieddin; Mohamed Hassanein Heikal; Huda Abdel Nasser; Mohamed Fayek; Sami Sharaf; Abdel Ghafar Shukr; Diaeddin Dawoud; Osama El Baz; Hussein Abdel al-Razaq; Tariq al-Bishry; Sayyed Yassin; Adel Hussein; Magdi Hussein; Radwan al-Sayed; Wahid Abdel Majid; Mohamed al-Sayed Said; Sherif Younis; Mustafa Kamel al-Said; Gamal al-Banna, Hassan Hanafi; Hossam Tammam; Hossam Eisa; Salah Abdel Mat'al; Sharif Abu al-Majd; Abed al-Wahab al-Masiri; Ra'fat Sayyid Ahmed; Mohamed Salim; Tawakkol Karman; Saad Din El Otmani; Mohammed El Hamdaoui; Redwan Ziadeh; Ussama Abdel Khaleq; Nabil Abdel al-Fatah; Sayyed al-Qemani; Saad Eddin Ibrahim; Mohamed Al Sayed Said; Galal Amin; Kheir al-Din Haseeb; Bahgat Korany; Ahmed Youssef Ahmed; Walid Kazziha; Ne'mat Guenena; Bahman Baktiari; Samer Shehata; Burhan Ghalioun; Gamil Mattar; Diya' Rashwan; Amr El-Shobaki; Hassan Ahmed Abou Taleb; Ali Fehmi; Ahmed Thabet; Samir Mirkus; Osama Al-Ghazali Harb; Mohamed Salah; Rula Dajani; Mohamed Dajani; Raghid El-Solh; Manar El Shorbagy; Ahmed Sobhi Mansour; Shakir Al-Louibi; Nadia Abu Majid; Hazem Amin; Tewfick Aclimandos; Adel Hamad; Lutfi Ma'moul; Dalal al-Bizzri; Gamal Amer; Yousry Moustafa; Rahil Gharaibeh; Abdul Laif Arabiyat; Muriwed Tell; Tariq Tell; Emile Habib; Nahed Hattar; Mustafa Hamarneh; Laith Shubailat; Mohammed Suleiman; Mohammed al-Yadoumi; Mohammed Qahtan; Khaled Ahmed al-Buhairi; Hamoud al-Hatar; Abdul al-Karim al-Eryani; Nabil Al Sofee; Nasser Yehia; Mohammed Sadiq; Abdel Hamid Barakat; Habib al-Ariqi; Najib Said Ghanem; Ghaleb al-Qirshi; Abdul Wahab al-Ansi;Gamil al-Ansi; Mansour al-Zandani; Hassan Zaid; Abdul Bari Taher; Nasr Taha Mustafa; Umat al-Salam Ali Al-Raja; Abdu Mohammed al-Jundi; Feisal al-Mukarom; Ma'ruf al-Bakhi; Maan Bashour; Massoud Hamed; Hazem Salem; and Jamil Abu Bakr.

These scholars and public intellectuals—Saad Eddin Ibrahim, Bahgat Korany, Gamil Mattar, Sherif Younis, Nabil Abdel Fatah, Mohamed al-Sayed Said, Sayyed Yassin, Gamal al-Banna, Kheir al-Din Haseeb, Farid Abdel Khaleq, Tewfick Aclimandos, and Raghid El-Solh—went above and beyond the call of duty and provided intellectual insights which have strengthened my narrative and arguments. I am deeply appreciative of their critical input.

I am indebted to colleagues at Westerm universities who read the whole manuscript or some chapters and offered critical feedback, including the late Fred Halliday, James Piscatori, Charles Tripp, Hazem Kandil, Jasmine Gani, Avi Shlaim, Mohammed Ayoob, Enid Hil, Nader Hashemi, Jan Wilkens, and Filippo Dionigi.

Although I had begun the research for this book before I joined the faculty at the London School of Economics, in 2009, I have been fortunate to have a group of intelligent and knowledgeable doctoral students at LSE who lent a critical hand in helping to put the final touches on the manuscript. I can't thank enough my research assistant, Anissa Haddadi, for reading the entire manuscript and offering valuable feedback that has enriched the analysis. I could not have asked for a better research assistant than Anissa; and I am looking forward to the completion of her doctoral thesis, "Myths, Norms and the Politics of National Identity in the Egypt of Nasser and Qutb: Society Must Be Desired," which examines themes similar to those of this book, though through a theoretical lens.

I also want to thank Dr. Mike Farquhar, previously a doctoral candidate at LSE, who copyedited most of the following chapters and synthesized them. His superb analytical skills have considerably improved the book. I am very appreciative of Dr. Mustafa Menshawy of the University of Westminster for his diligent search for primary Arabic sources and his immense contribution to this book. For two years Mustafa worked closely with me and filled important empirical gaps in the literature. I owe thanks to Dr. Magdalena C. Delgado, previously a doctoral candidate at LSE, for editing three chapters; to Noor Al-Bazzaz, a doctoral student at LSE, for editing chapter 1; and to Andrea Dessi, a doctoral candidate at LSE, for reading a few sections.

I am appreciative of Eric Crahan, my editor at Princeton University Press, who provided valuable insights which helped me restructure the manuscript and make it flow better. I'd also like to thank Jennifer Lyons, my agent, for her constant support and friendship.

Perhaps inevitably, this book, which is a labor of love, eventually became a burden on my family who were forced to put up with my long absences while I conducted field research and spent countless hours writing. I owe this book to Nora and the children, and I am forever indebted to them for their love and for providing me with the precious time to complete the manuscript. Selfless and supportive as ever, Nora, a political economist, pointed out the importance of the state as a dispenser of public social goods and guardian of the public sphere in the struggle among the social forces and classes in the Middle East. On our long walks, my eldest son, Bassam, who has just completed his law degree at Yale University, reminded me of the need for a comparative global approach in trying to understand the modern history of the Arab world. In his estimation, the violent and bloody struggles in the region are neither unique nor destined to last forever; rather, they are similar to historical patterns of development in other regions. My daughter, Annie-Marie, a postgraduate student of law and gender at SOAS University of London, convincingly argued that my history should have paid more attention to the question of law and gender as critical variables in the struggle for liberation from colonialism as well as patriarchy and male-dominated ruling elite in the post-independence state. Hannah, nineteen, and Laith, sixteen, bemoaned my long absences and my distracted attention. Why do books take so long to write? was their usual refrain. This book is as much theirs as it is mine.

Fawaz A. Gerges
January 16, 2018

Making the Arab World

Introduction

FOLLOWING THE LARGE-SCALE POPULAR uprising that toppled President Hosni Mubarak in February 2011, Egypt witnessed a polarization between Islamist and secular nationalist forces. Ultimately, this contentious dynamic culminated in the military toppling of the country's first democratically elected post-revolution president, Mohamed Morsi of the Islamist movement al-Ikhwan al-Muslimun, better known in English as the Muslim Brotherhood (Ikhwan will be used throughout this book). As soon as it took power, the new military-dominated administration led by Abdel Fattah al-Sisi undertook a campaign of repression, violently breaking up Ikhwan protests, killing a few thousand and arresting tens of thousands more. Remarkably, it did so with considerable support from nationalist secularists and revolutionaries who had earlier protested in their millions against Morsi's tenure and who had initially taken to the streets to denounce the tradition of regime-led oppression in their country.

Even more striking was the extent to which the new military-dominated order and its supporters instantly sought to ground their legitimacy by invoking a historical precedent with great symbolic weight and situating themselves in relation to the legacy of Gamal

Abdel Nasser, Egypt's second president and in many ways the country's founding political figure. Indeed, the then young, charismatic army officer did everything in his power to repress the Ikhwan during his presidency, which lasted from 1954 until his death in 1970. The Sisi administration, state media, and public commentators sought to reclaim Nasser as a powerful symbol who had prevailed against the Islamists in his own day by offering the alternative ideology of secular-leaning Arab nationalism.[1] With no well-defined ideology of their own, contemporary nationalists and secularists filled their ideological vacuum with Nasserist terms and slogans. They depicted the Ikhwan as untrustworthy and dangerous. The Islamist organization had a grand design to hijack and Islamize the identity of the Egyptian nationalist state, they insisted. Huge portraits of Nasser filled Tahrir Square, and anti-Islamist activists drew nostalgia-tinged parallels between the former president and Sisi, an irony conveyed by the *Guardian* correspondent in Cairo, who reported that although Nasser was the man the Ikhwan wanted to forget, he was very much part of the new Egyptian psyche.[2]

The Origins of the Nationalist-Islamist Fault Line

In so many ways, this recent wave of repression echoed earlier efforts by Egyptian regimes to crush the Ikhwan in 1948, 1954, and again in the second half of the 1960s. Although Egypt was initially the main battlefield, the nationalist-Islamist struggle spread to neighboring countries, undermining the development of the fragile postcolonial states in the Middle East. Today, the divide between nationalists, on the one hand, and Islamists, on the other, is a major cleavage not only in Egyptian politics but also across the Middle East and beyond. This division goes so deep that it has come to be invested with profound existential meaning. Writing in the Arabic-language newspaper *al-Hayat*, the Syrian poet Adonis, a prominent secularist and a vehement critic of the Islamists, has gone so far as to argue that the struggle between Islamists and secular-leaning nationalists is more cultural and civilizational than it is political or ideological; it is organically linked to nothing less than the struggle over the future of Arab identity.[3] In a similar vein, the Ikhwan portray the "fascist coup" that removed Morsi from power as an attack on the whole Islamist project, and even as an extension of the Westernized secular ruling elite ideology which targets Islam. For the Islamists, the battle against their secular-leaning opponents is a stark existential struggle between faith and *kufr*, or unbelief.[4] Although both secular and religious nationalists depict their confrontation as a clash of cultures, identities, and even civilizations, what such narratives leave out are the real objects of the struggle: the state, its power, and its position as custodian of the public sphere.

This book traces this profound fault line back in time through decades of contemporary Egyptian history. The rise of both the Islamist and nationalist political forces from the beginning of the twentieth century is located in their common struggle against British colonialism and a domestic political establishment accused of collaborating with the occupying power. In addition, the book places particular focus on the origins of the conflict between these two leading social movements in the aftermath of the July 1952 coup that ousted the monarchy. Far from being either straightforwardly binary or inevitable—as it is often represented by participants and outside observers alike—the struggle between the nationalists and the Islamists involved much ambiguity and complexity. It emerged and was consolidated through a series of contingent events, personality clashes, and workaday political rivalries. Power, not ideology, was the driver. If this is the case, what explains the escalation of the confrontation between the Islamists and the nationalists into an all-out war that has endured to this day? Why did both sides subsequently invest their rivalry with cultural and existential meaning? What does the use of culture as a weapon of choice by the nationalists and the Islamists reveal about the identity and imagination of leading postcolonial social forces? In what ways have they reproduced the structure of Western colonialism, which was filled with the rhetoric of domination and annihilation of the Other? Finally, what are the costs and consequences of this prolonged confrontation for state and society, and to what extent has it impacted the formation of national identity and institution building in Egypt and neighboring Arab states?

The Free Officers and the Ikhwan: A Bittersweet Connection

Before the 1952 Revolution, the Ikhwan and the Free Officers had initially joined ranks to overthrow the British-backed monarchy. Although their union might prove controversial now, contextualizing it allows us to see that early instantiations of these two leading social and political movements displayed much in common. Both dedicated themselves to anti-colonialism and reformation of Arab and Muslim society. At the heart of their programs was the struggle for national liberation and the empowerment of the nation to resist what were seen as alien influences and Westernization. In the first half of the twentieth century, nationalist and Islamist public intellectuals and activists viewed culture—including religion, language, and tradition—as having a pivotal role to play in fueling transformative change. Both deployed it as their weapon of choice, even as each stressed certain aspects and elements of this culture over others. Their goals were intertwined, since there was a consensus that national liberation and empowerment would require a cultural renaissance and an awakening of the masses. *Islah al-fard wa-l-mujtama'*, or reformation of the individual and society, was a prerequisite for the emancipation of the homeland from colonial domination. Sharing a common sociological lineage, both groups understood political deliverance and salvation with reference to questions of identity, social justice, and cultural renewal; they shared suspicions that Egypt faced a conspiracy mounted by international actors in cahoots with an indigenous fifth column. They believed there was an urgent need for strong state actors capable of cleansing the land of corrupt politicians and traitors, and to protect Egyptian society from enemies at home and abroad. Both anointed themselves as the guardian and vanguard of the people, promising the masses freedom and deliverance from hardship and inequity. According to the incisive Egyptian cultural critic Sherif

Younis, the two groups clashed violently not because of radical differences between them but in fact precisely because they were too similar, with each seeing its mission as being to rescue the country from bondage and reset history on the right path. In the words of Younis, who is critical of both groups, "the struggle between the Ikhwan and the Free Officers was over power politics and authority because they shared a similar worldview."[5]

It was not until the late 1950s, after the confrontation between the Free Officers and the Ikhwan, that ideological lines between Arab nationalists and Islamists truly hardened. Before that rupture, the distinction between them was blurred, as both mined Arab and Islamic heritage for ideas and moral capital. Both put a high premium on identity, *asala* (authenticity), and modernity, and diagnosed the challenges facing Egypt and the Arab neighborhood in similar terms. The problem, as they saw it, was how to respond to the domineering colonial West and to inspire and trigger political and economic empowerment and a cultural renaissance. Both viewed Egypt as a spearhead in the struggle to bring about Arab and Muslim renewal and emancipation from Western domination. For example, Hassan al-Banna, the founder of the Ikhwan, embraced Egyptian nationalism as an extension of his Islamic faith. Farid Abdel Khaleq, a disciple and confidant of Banna, recalls the latter saying that there is no contradiction between Islam and love of one's country. "Al-Banna was a religious nationalist who often reminded us that the Prophet cried when he had to migrate from Mecca, and that he would not have left if he had not been forced to do so," said Abdel Khaleq. "For *al-shahid* [martyr] al-Banna, Arab nationalism is an integral part of Muslim culture and Islam encompasses both *al-wataniyya* [territorial or local nationalism] and *al-qawmiyya* [pan-Arab nationalism]."[6] Thus, up until the 1952 Free Officers' taking of power, both the nationalists and the Islamists had long defined themselves in contrast to the colonial "Other." It is this reconfiguration of the old dynamic of anti-colonial "Othering" that in turn contributed to consolidating their split.[7] The war within exceeded the war with the colonizer in brutality. Each side denied the humanity of the Other and portrayed its rival as a traitor or even a *kafir*, an infidel.

Despite their initial union, the Free Officers and the Ikhwan had a complicated business-like relationship. In contrast with the Ikhwan, the Free Officers did not have a social base of their own, and they hoped to utilize the Islamist movement's organized networks to boost their profile. But the Ikhwan, led by the Supreme Guide Hassan Hudaybi following the death of Banna in 1949, endeavored to climb to power on the shoulders of the young army officers. Both groups hoped to inherit the spoils of the old regime and reconstruct state and society in their own image, though they had no preconceived master plan beyond that of seizing power. Soon after the coup, the Free Officers' and the Ikhwan's interests and lofty aspirations collided. The brief honeymoon between the soldiers of God—Hudaybi and the Ikhwan—and the soldiers of the nation—Nasser and the Free Officers—had been short-lived, their marriage of convenience eroded by their thirst for power. Both felt entitled to be at the helm of the new Egypt and to chart its destiny, with each hoping to bring about a coalition in which the other camp would be reduced to a junior partner. Both had felt that the high stakes justified the risks involved in a confrontation of this magnitude. Each had gambled that the other camp would blink and step back from the brink of abyss—but neither did.

It took less than two years for this power struggle to turn these two former allies into bitter enemies. After the Ikhwan threatened Nasser's authority in 1954, they faced the brunt of his fury. He brutally suppressed the movement in the course of the 1950s and 1960s, imprisoning thousands of its members, including top leaders like Hudaybi and Sayyid Qutb. As we will see, this violent confrontation became a defining moment in the political history of Egypt and the wider region. Ultimately, it is that clash, and the Ikhwan's humiliating experience of mass incarceration in prison camps, that triggered and consolidated a long war between the two foes. This extended showdown consumed the energies of the two leading political and social movements in the Arab world and had long-lasting consequences: it deformed the development of postcolonial Arab politics by polarizing and militarizing Arab societies and sowing the seeds for durable authoritarianism.

The rupture between Nasser's Free Officers and Hudaybi's Ikhwan facilitated and expedited the construction of an expansive and intrusive security state apparatus, designed to protect the regime. The violent struggle shaped the identity of *al-dawla al-wataniyya*, or the national state, in two significant ways. First, the new military rulers prioritized securitization, particularly national (internal) security or regime survival, at the expense of formal institutionalization. In the end, internal security took precedence over individual liberty and free political association. The regime's emphasis on both freedom and state security represents one of the most dichotomous aspects of Nasserist politics. As Nasser built a multilayered security apparatus to carry out his ambitious social agenda and protect his "revolution," the security services took on a life of their own in their competition for resources and influence, ultimately emerging as rival power centers. The military itself became directly involved in this bureaucratic rivalry. It established a security branch of its own and focused more on internal rather than external threats. As the security services came to exercise intrusive control over Egyptians' everyday lives, the original military regime established by Nasser and the Free Officers mutated into something sinister and oppressive. Moreover, the securitization and politicization of the Egyptian armed forces, together with a lack of professionalism and transparent decision making, was partly responsible for the country's humiliating defeat in the Six-Day War with Israel in June 1967 and the previous military debacle during the Suez Crisis in 1956.

Second, the rupture between the Free Officers and the Ikhwan—or between Arab nationalists and Islamists, more generally—shaped the moral economy and grand narratives of both movements toward the Western powers and Zionism, but also their developmental road map. Both portrayed themselves as anti-hegemonic, anti-colonial forces with an abiding commitment to achieving social justice and lifting the nation out of abject poverty and cultural decline. Both painted their rivalry as an extension of a greater struggle against external powers and foreign domination, as well as a quest for liberation, authenticity, and dignity. Each camp accused the other of being a crony of outside forces bent on controlling Arab and Muslim destiny and thwarting Arab unity and Islamic solidarity. Although Arab nationalists and Islamists portrayed each other as bitter enemies, their grand narratives and conceptions of both the Self and the Other mirrored one another. A critical upcoming doctoral dissertation from the London School of Economics on the formation of national identity in Egypt notes that the struggle for power that entrapped both movements in social antagonism is a direct result of the contingency of both their identity and their desire to shape Egypt's future on its own terms, with minimal participation or interference from the other.

This reduction of national identity into two "pure" oppositional and exclusive poles was already at play in the colonial framework's Othering of Egyptians as non-modern and in its dissemination of a subjectivity split into two poles: a modern and more European-like elite that stood in opposition to non-modern ordinary Egyptians, who had yet to be *re-formed*.[8] While both the Free Officers and the Ikhwan prioritized action over theory, they had also developed a Gramscian-like understanding of ideology as a powerful tool that could be used to manufacture popular consent, ensure the mobilization of the masses, and also help foster obedience and loyalty among their respective members. In the final analysis, the Free Officers and the Ikhwan became prisoners of their own ideological constructs, which limited their policy options and incurred strategic costs.

Third, Nasser's brutal suppression of the Ikhwan radicalized and militarized an important segment of the Islamist movement. With its members imprisoned en masse in prison camp conditions in the 1950s and 1960s, and facing torture and humiliation, the Ikhwan underwent a metamorphosis and fragmentation which gave rise to a more radicalized type of Islamist activism. Egyptian prisons of this period nurtured a subversive, revolutionary brand of Islamism which justified the use of violence to effect a top-down transformation of state and society. This subversive Islamist current aimed not only at replacing the Nasserist "apostate" state with what was envisioned as a Qur'anic political order but also at transforming the mainstream Ikhwan in its own revolutionary vision. The birth of violent Islamism or jihadism, as it came to be known in subsequent decades, owes its origins and intellectual roots to this episode.

Gamal Abdel Nasser versus Sayyid Qutb

Retracing this contentious episode of Egyptian history naturally entails an examination of two towering figures of Arab politics: Nasser and the man he had executed in 1966, Sayyid Qutb. The story of these two leaders testifies to the rise and formation of a new post-independence elite that went from being united against colonialism to tearing itself apart. In the aftermath of the Ikhwan-Nasserist split, two different camps from within this elite turned to battling one another as fiercely as they had previously battled against the foreign occupiers. While their struggles came to be invested with cultural and existential overtones, the biographies of Nasser and Qutb offered in this book highlight the fundamentally contingent nature of two individuals who could, in principle, have traded places with one another. The political careers of both men were marked by ideational fluidity, including dramatic shifts between different ideological poles. In their younger years, each stood on the side of the aisle that the other would later come to embrace. While Nasser moved in the underground networks of the Ikhwan in the early 1940s, the young Qutb vociferously opposed in the 1920s and 1930s what he understood to be regressive religious, social, and historical conventions prevalent in Egyptian society.

Both men were very much part of the same anti-colonial generation, preoccupied with shared concerns for cultural regeneration and national renaissance. As Nasser and Qutb grew up, the role of culture and civilization as drivers of progress was still being debated in Egypt and beyond. Outside of the Arab world, intellectuals had for a long time emphasized the role of the Enlightenment in bringing about a series of revolutions that led to national renaissance and economic and technological development across Europe. In Egypt, the process of acculturation instigated by the Napoleonic expedition in 1798 had meant that from the nineteenth century onwards the role of culture and religion in modernity was also debated in the country.

This conversation included both Islamic writers such as Jamal-al-Din al-Afghani and Mohammed Abduh and secular Arab thinkers who had found refuge in Cairo and who had called for the separation of state and religion. By the 1940s, however, decades of colonialism and ideological vacuum had triggered a return to religion in literary and political circles and religious activism. Arabo-Islamic culture provided an ideational framework within which post-independence national identity could be projected and reworked in order to foster popular mobilization against the occupation. Anti-colonial nationalists viewed culture as both a tool of domination—a foundation of Western domination—and a means for liberation. On the one hand, the colonial European powers had used culture to assert Western superiority over Arabs and Muslims. On the other hand, anti-colonial nationalists made a conscious choice to utilize their own indigenous national culture as a way to regain agency, self-esteem, and dignity.

In their search for the most effective ways to lift the Egyptian masses out of abject poverty and move beyond the sociocultural decline that, in their opinion, characterized the aftermath of the 1919–1922 revolution, both Nasser and Qutb experimented with different programs and ideas for achieving these ends. Right up until the moment when they parted ways in 1953–1954, they were both in the same ideological trenches, battling the old regime and struggling to replace it with an indigenous-led order. Both were consumed with the question of how to wrest independence from colonial control and protect Egyptian sovereignty. The freedom that they sought implied social and economic development that would rid Egypt of parasitical capitalism, which they both saw as an extension of colonial control.

Nasser's place in history and postcolonial Egypt was assured by his role at the head of the Free Officers movement, which toppled the Egyptian monarchy in a putsch in 1952. The military junta formed a heterogeneous group, but as a co-founder of the movement, Nasser had always been influential. At the beginning, preferring to work from behind the scenes, Nasser had asked Mohammed Naguib, an experienced general with a high profile, to become the official figurehead of the Free Officers. Nonetheless, a fierce rivalry emerged soon between the two ambitious military men. Naguib was beloved by the masses, a development which directly threatened Nasser's control over the Revolutionary Command Council (RCC), the executive decision-making body, and the two officers shared different visions of post-independence Egypt. As the Ikhwan attempted a rapprochement with Naguib, Nasser moved to oust his friend-turned-foe. As chapter 2 shows, after much political wrangling and skirmishing, Nasser eventually succeeded in ousting Naguib as president of Egypt. If at first Nasser had struggled to win over the hearts and minds of the masses, his anti-colonial calls to resistance against imperialism and his promises to overturn the socioeconomic inequalities created by colonial capitalism made him popular. Perhaps what endeared Nasser most to the Egyptian public was his recurrent use of dialectal Arabic in his speeches, especially in addressing ordinary Egyptians. Unlike the political establishment in the old regime, including the Palace, Nasser paid particular attention to his audience and tailored his addresses accordingly, giving the impression that every Egyptian had a place in his thoughts. In a way, he used his vision of society, which included social justice, dignity, and economic development, to cement an organic bond with Egyptians. Nasser's special relationship with the people gave him more control over the state and the reshaping of national identity.

In the second half of the 1950s Nasser articulated an Arab nationalist ideology and a socialist political program, with the goal of consolidating his hegemony inside Egypt and in the Arab neighborhood. His instrumentalization of Arab nationalism was designed to shape the identity of the Egyptian state, an identity embedded in anti-colonial, anti-hegemonic rhetoric, and embodied in authenticity, dignity, and liberation. As Aziz al-Azmeh, an academic critic, notes, far from being mutually contradictory, Egyptianism and Arab nationalism in fact complemented one another: Egyptianism was framed in general nationalist terms rather than specifically in contrast to Arabism, a definition that "rendered it possible for Egyptianism to join up with Arabism and for the two to shade off into one another."[9] Most accounts of Nasser's Arab nationalism focus on the geostrategic advantage accrued by his pursuit of such a politics and its anti-imperialistic dimension. However, his instrumentalization of Arab nationalism also did a great deal to augment his legitimacy at home. In fact, these domestic and geostrategic aspects were mutually reinforcing.[10]

Despite his apparent openness to the masses, Nasser did not tolerate dissent and political pluralism because, in his opinion, they were a luxury that postcolonial Egypt could not afford at that stage. He prioritized the unity of the Egyptian nation and its people, and considered liberal democracy and political parties a threat to social harmony and national unity. During his youth, he had been bitterly disappointed by the political establishment's apathy and subservience to the occupying power. Nasser saw political parties as the root of corruption and the huge economic disparities between the pro-capitalist upper classes and the impoverished masses. He also accused the old political elite of being responsible for the growing fragmentation and de-politicization of the majority of ordinary Egyptians. He sought to cleanse the new system of mainstream political parties as the last remnants of the old regime, fearing that opening up the political sphere immediately after independence would allow the old guard to make its way back into power. Nasser ended up replacing the old elite with a new one. Indeed, the Free Officers monopolized political life and also extended state control over the religious establishment in an effort to radically reconstruct the country's society and economy. Nasser and his comrades, like the Ikhwan, conceived of their role as a vanguard. Once in power, they acted like one, seizing the state and using it as a vehicle to implement their ambitious agenda. Both the pan-Arab nationalists and the pan-Islamists were in this sense fundamentally statist movements, differing only in their ideological orientation. Neither had the vision or the foresight to build new institutions or to restructure the postcolonial state which they had inherited and reform its institutions. Both were more concerned with exercising power than they were with institution building, citizen empowerment, and participation.

Despite Nasser's assertion that he envisioned a popular participatory democracy in Egypt, he mainly focused on monopolizing power. From the outset, Nasser and his supporters among the Free Officers dominated the Revolutionary Command Council and greatly restricted dissenting voices.[11] Moreover, the RCC's marginalization of other political players, including the Ikhwan, set the stage for the Nasserist state to develop along authoritarian lines. Similarly, the Ikhwan's record during and after the coup displayed little evidence that the group would have acted democratically or would have been less authoritarian than the Free Officers. In fact, the next chapters will show that the Ikhwan supported Nasser's anti-democratic measures as long as they received their share of power in the nascent order. In a similar vein, in 2012 the Ikhwan's unwillingness to enter into a dialogue with the country's secular forces and its determination to change the constitution, despite widespread protests, allowed the military to seize power and oust Morsi. Moreover, since recapturing power, the Sisi administration has been decisive in trying to silence the opposition. Thus, in both cases and across different timeframes, nationalists and Islamists alike have reduced the role of the state to a coercive and functionalist tool.

Indeed, from the outset, Nasser systematically eliminated the opposition and moved against all political currents perceived to represent a threat to his rule. He banned all the political parties that had participated in political life under the old regime. He also brutally suppressed independent leftist and progressive voices in the late 1950s, after they had started to organize themselves and to call for popular political participation and more radical reforms of the economy and foreign policy. Nasser's Arab socialism did not include space for independent socialists, many of whom were forced to join the ruling party after spending years in prison. The same can be said of Nasser's relationship with Egyptian communists, who were never included in decision making despite their role in the theoretical outlining of Nasser's Arab socialism. Moreover, under Nasser, and despite his rapprochement with the USSR, the communist movement, which had been greatly repressed during British occupation, was further decimated and most members were imprisoned and sent to forced labor camps.

While the Free Officers thus severely repressed an array of political forces, including communists and independent socialists, Nasser and the secular nationalism that he espoused are too commonly seen as one side of a binary and oppositional pairing with Islamism. This is an established and misleading dichotomy of two monolithic ideas that have dominated conventional thinking on Middle Eastern politics. A major conclusion of this study is that neither nationalism nor Islamism were or are monolithic or ideologically unified movements, but rather that they involve diverse perspectives and distinctive individuals and factions. Nevertheless, despite the wide spectrum of political opponents targeted by the Nasserist state, its repeated persecution of Ikhwan members and the emphasis of the regime on its all-out war against the Islamist organization stand out as a defining feature of postcolonial Arab politics. The year 1954 marked a key turning point. An attempt on Nasser's life by a member of the Ikhwan's underground wing provided the Free Officers with an immediate reason to crack down on the Islamist movement and offered a cover for its effort to neutralize a key player in Egyptian politics. At that time, the Ikhwan were the only oppositional force powerful enough to contest Nasser's rule and challenge his hegemony. The removal of the Ikhwan from the political scene would therefore free his hand in domestic and foreign policy, and allow him to implement his social agenda without outside hindrance. The die was cast for a test of wills between the Free Officers and the Ikhwan.

The Ikhwan's framing of the struggle between the nationalists and the Islamists as an existential, zero-sum conflict gave Nasser further rationale for his brutal repression of the organization. It also allowed him to use the state as a way to monopolize the religious space with the goal of consolidating his dominance. Thus, from 1954 the Ikhwan faced the brunt of a state security apparatus determined to dismantle it and delegitimize it as a credible political alternative. The Nasserist state deployed all of its powers to neutralize the Ikhwan and consolidate its own control of society. This involved physical repression, including the incarceration of thousands of the movement's rank and file. It also involved efforts to accumulate religious capital for the regime itself, by integrating religious institutions into the state framework and mobilizing the religious establishment as a counterweight to the Islamist opposition.

Beyond the human and material costs, the long war that broke out between the pan-Arab nationalists and the pan-Islamists immediately after the end of the colonial moment has derailed the normalization of state-society relations and the articulation of a cohesive national identity. By monopolizing social space, dominating discourse, and militarizing the political, pan-Arab nationalists and pan-Islamists put society on a war footing. The result is that decolonization did not usher in fundamental change either institutionally or sociologically. No rupture occurred in the organization of the state, the restructuring of the military-security apparatus, the aspirations of the elite, and the relationship between the ruler and the ruled.

It was in the context of this long war that, in the Ikhwan, Sayyid Qutb emerged as a figure who would match the strength of Nasser's ideological influence and legacy. Already a prominent writer by the time Nasser came to power, Qutb continued to produce increasingly radical Islamist works of enormous influence even after his imprisonment by Nasser. In addition, from his jail cell Qutb also took over the leadership of an underground paramilitary faction with ties to the Ikhwan, representing an immediate and a clear danger from within to the Islamist movement. In these ways, he competed with the mainstream leadership of the Ikhwan to advance and implement a revolutionary Islamist ideology the reverberations of which are still felt in Egypt and around the world today. Qutb's execution by the Nasserist state in 1966 only served to further cement his legacy.

Ever since, Qutb's memory and manifestos have nourished and inspired most subsequent waves of militant Islamists, although many of the radical religious activists who have modeled themselves on him have misunderstood his call. As a leading former militant, Kamal Habib, who was inspired by the Qutbian call for arms, noted, "We read into Qutb what we wanted to read without understanding the differences in context, social, and political circumstances and the severe prison conditions under which Qutb lived and penned his manifestos." In a way, in the Egyptian and the Arab imagination in general both Nasser and Qutb have become mythical figures or rhetorical devices, but their invoked images often serve political and ideological projects.[12] In contrast to Nasser, whose image allows plural interpretations, Qutb's is more ideologically fixed and divisive. Habib stresses that the endurance of Qutb's legacy lies in establishing once and for all "the charisma of shari'a as a superior way of life, an inspiration for action." It is no longer important to read and interpret Qutb's words because his foundational concept—the charisma of *al-shari'a* (Islamic laws)—opens the way for multiple interpretations by radical religious activists, adds Habib. "Qutb could not be held accountable for the use and abuse of his ideas by young men like me who are dissatisfied with the secular status quo. Each generation invented its own Sayyid Qutb."[13]

The works that Qutb produced during his prison years would eventually come to have an impact far beyond Egypt. After September 11, 2001, his books were dusted off in Western, particularly U.S., libraries, and thumbed by scholars searching for clues to the inspiration and motivations of jihadist groups like Al Qaeda. In addition to Osama bin Laden and Ayman al-Zawahiri, Qutb has become a household name in America as a supposed "philosopher of terror." In this context, too, he has been terribly misunderstood, presented as a caricatured image. What this reflects is the extent to which, far from being confined to the home front, the struggle between Nasser's pan-Arab nationalism and Qutb's pan-Islamism came to be enmeshed in the Cold War rivalry between the superpowers, the United States and the Soviet Union. The two dominant social movements exported their ideas externally and projected their values and worldviews assertively. Nasser's attempt to construct a coalition of Arab states to maximize Egypt's influence regionally and globally pitted him against the United States and, to a lesser extent, the Soviet Union. Viewing Nasser's Arab nationalism as a threat to its vital interests in the region and its local allies, Washington clashed repeatedly with the Egyptian leader and tried to cut him down to size. Ironically, throughout the Cold War, the United States aligned itself with Islamist-based states and movements to counterbalance Nasser's radical secular Arab nationalism, as well as socialism and communism. For Arab nationalists, America's hostility and conspiracy against "the Arab nation" is taken as an article of faith, culminating in Nasser's crushing defeat in the Six-Day War in June 1967, which marked the beginning of the decline of secular Arab nationalism and the rise of Islamism.

In Qutb's own lifetime and throughout the Cold War, despite their own harsh anti-Western rhetoric, his disciples were more actively opposed to Russian communism than to American liberal capitalism. The Islamists and the United States found themselves in the same trenches battling both Nasser's secular Arab nationalism and the expansion of socialism and communism in Muslim lands in general. Although Qutb warned that the confrontation with America was inevitable because of the latter's crusading spirit and imperial design, he prioritized the fight against the enemy within. From the mid-1950s until the end of the Cold War in 1989, with only minor exceptions, Qutb's followers battled radical secular nationalism and socialism of the Nasserist variety. They allied themselves with the United States by default, a realpolitik position culminating in a holy alliance against the Soviet invasion of Afghanistan in 1979. Built on shifting sands, the informal association between militant Islamists and U.S. foreign policy crumbled once the Soviet army retreated from Afghanistan in disarray in 1989. It was only with the end of the Cold War and the emergence of the United States as the unrivaled superpower that the dynamics of the relationship between American foreign policy and Islamists underwent a dramatic transformation, with accommodation and coexistence giving way to a new and deadly zero-sum struggle.

Besieged and under attack at home, a small but critical segment among Islamists—many of them influenced by Qutb's thinking—decided not only to attack U.S. interests worldwide but also to bring war to the American homeland. This was a radical departure from the ways in which anti-colonial Islamist movements had waged their struggles in the past. The fateful decision by militant Islamists to target the U.S. metropolis had major repercussions on global politics, triggering a series of reactions and counter-reactions—a U.S. global war on terror—that has yet to run its course. Ever since, the United States has waged multiple wars against militant Islamists, and the latter have expanded their attacks worldwide against Western interests and pro-U.S. Muslim rulers.

None of this is intended to suggest a straightforward causal link between the confrontation between Nasser and Qutb, on the one hand, and the 9/11 wars, on the other. There is no continuum between Sayyid Qutb and Ayman al-Zawahiri and Osama bin Laden, even though both internalized his worldview. But the 9/11 story shows the bitter and enduring inheritance of the prolonged confrontation between Arab nationalism and Islamism, and how Qutb's ideas and life story have found fertile and receptive soil among young radicalized Muslims who impose their own interpretation on his life and works. Although the radical Islamist wing has mutated and changed focus, targets, and tactics, it has been nourished on the Qutbian diet, its sense of victimhood and injustice and its binary division of the world. This explains why the Qutbian legacy was an important variable in the recent rupture in relations between the Islamists and the United States.

The Qutbian and Nasserist Voices

The prolonged conflict between the nationalists represented in the figure of Nasser and the Islamists represented in the figure of Qutb deserves serious historical attention. Rather than being diametrically opposite, the movements that Nasser and Qutb represent have mirrored each other in three ways: (1) the shaping of their idealized aspirations by postcolonial disappointments; (2) the failure in achieving their strategic goals; and finally (3) the authoritarianism of their movements. The book thus seeks to overcome the simple either-or approaches that have come to dominate the analysis of Arab political and social order and to give concrete and personal form to an Arab nationalist–Islamist dialectic.

The book thus offers an original take on Nasser and Qutb and the movements they represent. The nationalist-Islamist struggle was more about power and the role of the state than it was about competing visions and ideologies. The different personalities engaged in the historical struggle were important elements in shaping the tensions and conflicts, and even the cooperation, between the two movements.

Contrasting sharply with the dominant narrative about Nasser, in this book the portrait drawn by his fellow travelers shows that his politics remained quite fluid and uncertain until after the 1952 coup, and that they only crystallized once he was in power. Nasser's journey was uncharted, and on the way he made discoveries and his views evolved and matured. In interviews with Nasser's contemporaries and confidants, I pressed them on the reasons behind Nasser's change of heart toward the Ikhwan and his subsequent decision to brutally suppress the group. According to Nasser's comrades who were privy to internal debates within the RCC, the executive decision-making body of the nascent military regime, Nasser and the Free Officers were willing to include the Ikhwan as a junior partner but refused to grant them veto power over pivotal decisions. A picture emerges of the young Colonel Nasser, ambitious and determined, who methodically purged potential rivals and gradually consolidated his power. In the first two years after the coup, Nasser might not have had a road map or a blueprint for the future, confidants say, but he never lost sight of his ultimate destination: to solely rule Egypt. "My father was not interested in power for its own sake but to transform Egypt from a colonized and backward nation to a free, modernized, and powerful one," said Nasser's daughter, Huda. "He knew the inhumane conditions under which most Egyptians lived, especially the *fellahin* [peasants], and desired to lift up people out of misery. Yes, he was in a hurry to alleviate the plight of poor Egyptians and end the country's dependency on the West."[14] Nevertheless, there is relative consensus among Nasser's friends and foes that he aimed at building a top-down centralized authoritarian order in which he, together with a small inner circle, was the ultimate arbitrator. From the beginning Nasser was instrumental in launching a systematic campaign to dismantle the formal and representative institutions of the old regime, including the judiciary and the political parties, and to consolidate military rule.

Although Nasser's acquaintances acknowledge that initially the conflict with the Ikhwan was contingent and revolved around power, they insist it morphed into something more ideological and visceral. In this, they take a similar stance to that of Qutb's supporters, who depict the split in similar terms. It is worth mentioning that the relationship between power and ideology, consistent with the larger theme of this book, is fluid. Both variables are relevant and will be highlighted throughout the analysis. For more clarity, the thrust of the argument is that the ideology-power nexus is interactive or mutually constituted but not equal, meaning that ideology matters but is of secondary importance to power. In summary, the confrontation between Arab nationalists and Islamists was more a struggle between two camps vying for influence and political supremacy than one about ideology per se, though as the conflict escalated in the late 1950s and 1960s it took on ideological overtones.

According to the dominant Nasserist narrative, the Ikhwan conspired with "Arab reaction," meaning Saudi Arabia and its allies, to destroy the leader of the Arab nationalist movement—Nasser; they were the spearhead of a reactionary counterrevolution, hatched particularly by the United States and Britain, to replace the defiant Arab nationalist government with a puppet regime. The Nasser camp viewed the confrontation with the Islamists as an extension of a broader and more dangerous struggle with America and its regional allies. Nasser was convinced, said his aides, that the United States was waging a war by proxy against him and deploying political Islamists in Egypt and neighboring Arab states as agents and conspirators. According to Sami Sharaf, Nasser's chief of staff and keeper of his secrets, the Egyptian president sent Qutb to the gallows in 1966 because he said that would deal a fatal blow to the Islamists inside and outside Egypt. Nasser also believed, Sharaf added, that executing Qutb would deliver a hard blow to his foreign enemies: Saudi Arabia and its superpower patron, the United States.[15]

The irony is that Qutb and his followers believed that Nasser was an agent of the unholy Zionist-American alliance tasked with weakening Islam from within and diluting its influence in state and society. I did not meet a single Qutbian who did not subscribe to a variant of this conspiracy theory: Nasser was an agent, a tool of the Americans, and of Soviet communists to a lesser extent. Similarly, the Ikhwan leadership also believed that both the United States and the Soviet Union incited Nasser against the Islamist movement, which, in their calculus, threatened their strategic interests in the Middle East.

Moreover, Arab nationalists note that political authoritarianism undermined the Nasserist state and made it vulnerable to internal and external challenges, culminating, in their opinion, in Israel's crushing defeat of "the most powerful army in the Middle East," in the Six-Day War in June 1967. "Everything revolved around Nasser, who turned into a cult of personality at the cost of building durable institutions," lamented Khaled Mohieddin, a friend of Nasser and a leading Free Officer who participated in the 1952 coup.[16] Nasser "prioritized bread and butter over personal freedom, though the two are not mutually exclusive," acknowledged Mohamed Fayek, one of Nasser's leading aides from the beginning of the revolution until his arrest and imprisonment by President Anwar Sadat in 1971. "A one-party rule and lack of checks and balances and transparency brought ruin to our institutions, particularly the military. Nasser unwittingly ended up presiding over a police state"—strong words uttered by a trusted and loyal member of Nasser's inner circle.[17]

Others contended that Nasser never shed his clandestine sensibility, having spent many years plotting to overthrow the old regime, and ruled Egypt with a bunker mentality. According to Abdel Ghafar Shukr, in charge of ideological indoctrination of the youth, in 1961 Nasser adamantly proposed the establishment of a paramilitary organization to confront reactionary forces in Egypt and neighboring Arab states, a fact that throws further light, in Shukr's opinion, on Nasser's belief in revolutionary action as opposed to formal institutions.[18] Shukr, privy to the internal dynamics of the Nasserist state, said that institutions existed but were systematically degraded by Nasser and his men and that power was concentrated in *al-za'im*'s (the sole leader's) hands. "So when Nasser died from a heart attack in 1970, the Nasserist project fell like a ripened fruit."[19]

Contrary to the dominant narrative that portrays Nasser's defeat in the 1967 Six-Day War as the single most significant variable in allowing Islamists to subsequently consolidate their hegemony in Egypt and elsewhere in the Middle East, my interviews with participants, activists, politicians, and public intellectuals of all ideological colors point to Sadat's coming to power and control of the Egyptian state. Sadat launched a frontal assault against his predecessor's inheritance and legacy. The "pious president," as Sadat insisted on being called, built his own legitimacy on an informal alliance with Islamists and the "petrodollar" in the Arab Gulf and put the power of the state in the service of a drive to bring about a sea change in Egypt's economy, politics, and society. The revolt against Nasser's Arab socialism came from *within* the regime's power structure. Neither the Islamists nor the nationalists were as unified as they would have us believe. The two movements suffered internal dissension and faced rebellion from within. Activists, including Islamists and nationalists, chronicle the steps taken by the Sadat administration, from 1971 onwards, which empowered religiously based groups and fragmented and weakened secular nationalist and socialist forces.

Montasser al-Zayat, a former member of the militant Islamic Group who was a college student in the 1970s and is now a leading Islamist attorney, said that the coming to power of Sadat marked a significant shift in the fortune of religious activists. "Sadat's rule was a golden moment for the Islamist movement. He permitted us to organize and recruit followers on campus and outside and released the Ikhwan from Nasser's prisons and contributed to the religious revival that swept the *umma* in the 1970s," he said.[20] Zayat confessed that his generation had made a strategic error by rising up against Sadat. "If we had patience and forbearance, we could have gradually transformed Egypt into a truly Islamic society." Echoing the same point, Ibrahim Za'farani, an Islamist student in the 1970s and now an Ikhwan leader in Alexandria, said: "Our generation was normal and did not live in fear and underground. We had opportunities that previously our elders never dreamed of because of Sadat's positive approach to the Islamists."[21] Nevertheless, these same religious activists and university students of the 1970s say they never trusted Sadat and they judged him by his deeds. "We knew that Sadat was using religion for political ends," said Seif Abdel Fattah, now an engaged Islamic academic and a politician. "He could not fool us because we were conscious and politicized."[22] Wahid Abdel Majid, a liberal public intellectual, also stressed the pivotal role played by oil, money, power, and globalization in bringing about social and political transformation of Muslim countries during the 1970s. "Sadat played on people's hopes, fears, and greed to bury Nasserism and portray himself as the leader who would bring about salvation," said Abdel Majid, who does not hide his disdain for Sadat. "The name of his game was religion and the manipulation of religious symbols to restructure social and political space."[23]

Nevertheless, evidence shows that Sadat was an enabler who systematically paved the way for the new religious politics and revival to dominate the public space from the 1970s onwards. Not unlike Nasser, who privileged Arab nationalism and empowered it, Sadat cultivated the religious trend. In both cases, the postcolonial, post-independence state propped up ideologies that allowed it to construct a durable hegemony and secure its control.

According to Ikhwan members, the Islamist ascendency in the 1980s, the 1990s, and the first decade of the twenty-first century did not usher in either transformation or reformation of the movement; instead, it continued to feed the civil war between the Islamists and the Arab nationalists. Participants and activists say the Islamist group has been riven by a profound division between an ultraconservative old guard loyal to the memory of Qutb and an energetic group of younger, reform-minded figures. These two internal segments have clashed over substantive political, social, and strategic questions, as well as over the internal practices of the Ikhwan as an organization. The reformers have called for a fundamental restructuring to overcome what they see as the autocracy, patriarchy, and lack of transparency of the old guard.

These reformist voices whom I interviewed at length include senior members like Mohamed Abdel Sattar, a reformist leader of the 1970s generation and a scientist by profession, who knew the Ikhwan intimately from the inside and spent three years in Mubarak's prisons in the second half of the 1990s; Ahmed Ra'if, who belongs to the Ikhwan school of thought but no longer has any formal affiliation with the organization, and who spent years in prison as part of Qutb's Tanzim but who prides himself on thinking outside the Islamist box; and Farid Abdel Khaleq, a former top leader who could not himself be accused of taking sides in the internal power struggle.[24]

There exists a relative consensus among internal critics, such as Abdel Moneim Abu al-Futuh and Farid Abdel Khaleq, that the Ikhwan have not made a clean break with the past and that no rupture has occurred within the Islamist movement either epistemologically or psychologically. According to such prominent figures, the top leadership is still wedded to a worldview nourished on victimhood, fear, and suspicion of the Other.[25]

However, the challenge of leadership is only half the story, reformists say, because the ideological structure of the movement itself also functions as an inhibiting factor. "The structure constantly clones itself through a limited process of selection of recruits and indoctrination," stated Abu al-Futuh. In separate interviews, reformists such as Abu al-Futuh, Abu El-Ela Madi, and Abdel Sattar each argued that the interests of the Mubarak regime and the old guard effectively converged on the issue of keeping the Ikhwan insular and fossilized. On the one hand, Mubarak used the Ikhwan as a *faza'a*, or a threat to internal and external stability, portraying his own political authoritarianism as a necessary evil in order to deter the Islamists. On the other hand, the Ikhwan old guard countered the reformists' demands to open up the workings of the movement by repeatedly claiming that it faced imminent danger due to being targeted and repressed by the authorities. Thus internal critics blame the authoritarianism of the Mubarak regime for reinforcing the culture of secrecy and paranoia within the Ikhwan. At the same time, these dissidents point out that ultraconservative leaders instrumentalized the political repression exercised by the Mubarak regime as a justification for tightening their own grip on the organization.[26]

When confronted with the kinds of charges leveled by the younger reformists, the Ikhwan old guard tend to mount two kinds of defense: on the one hand, denying that some aspects of the picture painted by their critics were in fact accurate; and on the other hand, defending their prerogative to behave in some of the ways described by the reformists. In 1999, during his own tenure in the position, Ma'mun Hudaybi—the son of Hassan Hudaybi, who succeeded the founder Banna as supreme guide (*murshid*)—bluntly told me that members must show obedience to the senior leadership.[27] His successor, Mohamed Akef, was also unapologetic about charges by reformist members regarding the reluctance of the Ikhwan to engage more proactively in opposition to the Mubarak regime in the first decade of the twenty-first century. "I will not risk the future of *al-jama'a* [the group] by defying the Mubarak regime and triggering all-out confrontation."

"Critics who call on us to protest in the streets do not think about the grave consequences. Unlike other small groups, we, as the biggest organization, act responsibly and measure our actions carefully. We will not give the security forces justification to clamp down harder on us. I have to protect the movement."[28] Akef also belittled questions related to the dominance of the old guard and the sidelining of the reformists. "My door is open to all members who are disciplined and who regularly communicate with me. Those who do not have themselves to blame," he said angrily.[29]

Mahmoud Izzat, whose powerful position is akin to chief of staff of the Ikhwan, at the movement's headquarters in the al-Rawda neighborhood in Cairo in late 2006, similarly dismissed reformers as "sore losers," claiming that they "do not speak for the base and have no constituency of their own." In response to the charges of autocracy and lack of transparency, he replied, "The Ikhwan holds regular elections, practices *shura* [consultation], and is transparent. We have our own mechanisms of selection of morally fit candidates, as opposed to those politically ambitious [individuals]."[30] He also disputed the idea that hard-liners of the Qutbian worldview have taken control of the Ikhwan since the 1970s, and that they have retarded the development and evolution of the movement. As an example, he pointed to the presence of a plurality of viewpoints in the Guidance Office, while simultaneously stressing that they were united within the Ikhwan family. He also cited the movement's pacts with non-Islamist parties to run candidates in parliamentary elections in the 1990s. Against charges of stagnation and fossilization, he replied, "You can't stop change because it is *sunnat al-hayat* [life's law] and we have endeavored to embrace good changes; but [we] reject foreign influences that corrupt our faith and culture," Izzat lectured me. "We do not pay attention to detractors who wish *al-jama'a* harm and are envious and full of hate."[31]

Responding to defiant denials by the old leadership, Hesham El-Hamamy, a young centrist and a close ally of reformist leader Abu al-Futuh, acknowledged that the 1980s and the 1990s were two decades of lost opportunity: the Ikhwan did not produce a program or a road map that spelled out their philosophical vision about the identity of the state that they desire or relations between government and society. Instead, the powers that be in the Ikhwan, Hamamy pointed out, resisted efforts and pleas by reformists like Abu al-Futuh, Abdel Sattar, Madi, Mohamed Ali Beshr, and others to translate and codify their scattered pronouncements on various issues into concrete policy proposals.[32] Hamamy suggested that it would take an internal revolution to transform the Ikhwan's power structure. "It is a struggle that has to be fought and won by reformists, even though the odds are against us. For the foreseeable future, the elders will continue to have the upper hand at the cost of stagnation and paralysis for the Islamist movement."[33] The struggle within will determine not only the future of the Ikhwan but also that of Egypt and the Arab region, said Hamamy emphatically. Hamamy's words have proved prophetic in light of what has transpired in Egypt since the ouster of Mubarak, the coming to power of the Ikhwan, and the subsequent violent confrontation with the nationalists led by the military.

The Book Design

The body of this book follows a broadly historical-thematic structure, utilizing historical sociology to illuminate the struggle between the two leading social movements in the Arab world. The study concentrates on the ideas and actions of individual personalities, with the core analysis being a double biography of Gamal Abdel Nasser and Sayyid Qutb, based on interviews with their contemporaries as well as textual sources. The personality-based approach and the extensive utilization of information from interviews with people involved in the nationalist-Islamist struggle present a strong conclusion that neither nationalism nor Islamism was or is a monolithic or ideologically unified movement; rather, they involved complex diversities of perspective and involvement by distinctive individuals and factions. By focusing on collective action, hidden internal struggles, and personality clashes, the book also allows a better understanding of the patterns of contentious politics that have characterized relations between the nationalists and the Islamists since independence. In a way, the book borrows a page from Eric Hobsbawm in treating history as an act of continuance, producing patterns and cycles which can be traced and compared.[34] Unlike the mass corpus of recent literature which is mostly interested in *explaining* or *predicting* events classified under the rubric of ongoing "revolutions," the book is rather a critical attempt to *understand* the modern history of the Arab world. Taken together, the chapters that make up this book move beyond a clear-cut, frozen-in-time binary division of the rift between secular nationalist and Islamist. Rather, what emerges is a picture of flux and complexity; marked by intersections and interactions between the two camps, on the one hand, and internal divisions within each camp, on the other. The violent nationalist-Islamist clash is fundamental to understanding critical aspects of contemporary Arab and

Muslim politics, including the crisis of mistrust and suspicion and the psychology of vendetta that have taken a grip on the Islamist imagination.

Chapters 1 and 2 establish the backstory to the rise of Islamist and nationalist political currents that emerged in Egypt in the 1940s, locating their birth in the collapse of semi-liberal politics that had been, until then, the dominant form of activism. It starts by retracing the impact of the Napoleonic expedition to Egypt and its link to the cultural renaissance of the late nineteenth century, in which religious and secular writers engaged with European political thought, this as they actively became involved in the anti-colonial struggle. These chapters also outline how the consolidation of a liberal political establishment within a colonial framework hampered both its popular legitimacy and its spectrum for action. The main argument of these two chapters is that obstructionism on the part of the British imperialists and the monarchy, along with the failures of the semi-liberal politicians themselves to deliver on their promises, gave rise to a period of frustration, reconfiguration, collective action, and contentious politics. It is against this background that the twin communitarian forces of nationalism and Islamism emerged as critiques of the quasi-liberal order, setting the stage for the political earthquake of 1952.

Chapter 3 focuses on the period which followed the Free Officers coup in 1952 and examines the relationships between the Free Officers and the Ikhwan as well as the internal dynamics of the two groups. Indeed, the two movements were internally divided along a variety of lines and centers of power. Particular attention will be given to the Nasser-Naguib rift and Hassan Hudaybi's struggle for legitimacy and authority over the Ikhwan, as well as to the increasing enmity between the leader of the Ikhwan and the leader of the Free Officers. The personality clash between Nasser and Hudaybi played a crucial role in sowing the seeds of mistrust and resentment that eventually led the two movements to a violent confrontation. Far from predestined, the rupture between the Free Officers and the Ikhwan was the result of the former's unwillingness to share power and the latter's desire to have a significant say in decision making in the aftermath of the revolution. Although their collision could have been avoided, it launched the two movements on a bloody and bitter path.

As chapter 4 shows, following the overthrow of the monarchy, the Nasser-led military regime worked hard at asserting its grip on power, both ideologically and through the development of the state's security apparatus. Moreover, Nasser moved quickly to rid Egypt of all organized political opponents, including the political parties that operated during the old regime, Marxists, and finally the Ikhwan. If the state repression targeted a wide spectrum of political tendencies, Nasser's particularly brutal suppression of the Ikhwan, the most powerful social movement at that time, laid the groundwork for decades of bitter struggle. By the same token, this clash helped to catalyze the emergence of a revolutionary brand of Islamism represented in the figure of Sayyid Qutb. This bloody struggle ultimately created a rift that has shaped the modern Middle East and is still playing out to this day, intermittently plunging the Arab world into a vicious spiral of hatred whose expression is only becoming more and more savage.

Chapters 5, 6, 7, and 8 focus on the two men who are at the heart of the story: Nasser and Qutb. These chapters emphasize that these two individuals in fact each moved through many stages in their respective lifetimes, sympathizing more or less with Islamism or secular nationalism at different points in time. Far from being destined inevitably for the historical roles they would eventually fulfill, each arrived at his eventual destination through a convoluted pathway, shaped in large part by personal ambition and struggle for power amid diverse influences and shifting historical circumstances. In a way, it is not difficult to imagine each of the two men ending up in the other's place.

Chapter 9 explores the relationship between Qutb and the Ikhwan, which he only joined as late as March 1953, and his decision to take over the leadership of a faction of the movement whose members engaged in underground paramilitary activity in the wake of Nasser's 1954 crackdown. This chapter further complicates the standard picture of the nationalists and the Islamists standing at loggerheads over a binary divide, each represented as a homogeneous bloc. In fact, Qutb's relations with the Ikhwan were complex and often fraught. His decision to head the armed wing known as al-Tanzim al-Sirri amounted to a kind of internal coup against the Ikhwan's traditional establishment, spurred by his ambition and determination to move from the realm of ideas to the realm of radical political praxis.

Chapters 10 and 11 examine the period after Qutb's execution in 1966, the overwhelming defeat of Egyptian forces by the Israeli military the following year, and the subsequent transformation of Egyptian and Arab politics. Many scholars in retrospect saw the Six-Day War in June 1967 as marking the death knell of Arab nationalism and providing the space for a wave of Islamist activism which would gather pace in Egypt and the Arab neighborhood in the following decade. In fact, as chapters 10 and 11 argue, the flourishing of politicized Islamist activism in this period—much of it in radical forms inspired by Qutb—was in large part driven by the simple fact of state sponsorship afforded to the Islamists under Nasser's successor, Anwar Sadat, in an effort to shore up his own power base. This shift in momentum within Egypt was bolstered by the newly muscular influence exerted by conservative, oil-rich Gulf monarchies, after the jump in petroleum prices brought about by the 1973 oil embargo.

Meanwhile, chapter 12 explores how the split between Nasser and the Ikhwan in the 1950s and 1960s—particularly insofar as it catalyzed the emergence of the radical current led by Qutb—impacted the Islamist movement itself over subsequent decades. From the 1970s until the present day, an ultraconservative old guard strongly influenced by the memory of Qutb has remained an extremely powerful presence within the Ikhwan, quashing the reformist hopes held by some younger members. In this chapter, centrist and reformist members relate how the old guard that has dominated decision making put the Ikhwan in the freezer for the last three decades and blocked efforts to open up the movement and make it more transparent, agile, and democratic. According to these activists, the movement was intellectually and sociologically impoverished and unequipped to translate its numerical majority into social capital and governance.

This chapter fleshes out the struggle within the Islamist currents and the deepening of the generational, social, and ideological divides among members. It documents the Ikhwan's systemic crisis, which was laid bare after the group gained power in Egypt in 2012. This systemic crisis partially explains the blunders and mistakes committed by the Ikhwan during and after the January 25 Revolution of 2011, which further undermined its standing in the public eye.

Finally, the conclusion situates the recent clash between the nationalists and the Islamists in the aftermath of the January 25 Revolution within the broader historical struggle. It shows how both movements remain captives and prisoners of the past, of their own narratives and conceptions of the Self and the Other. It thus opens with an investigation of the drivers behind the derailing of Egypt's political transition and the 2013 ouster of President Mohamed Morsi, a member of the Ikhwan. Particular focus will be given to the resistance of the deep and wide state dominated by the security services and the military to the new Islamist hegemony. However, as the chapter highlights, the internal divisions that threatened the cohesion of the Ikhwan and hampered its chances of survival in power had surfaced long before it won the elections in Egypt. Firsthand accounts by its leading members expose a rigid and insular movement dominated by a small ultraconservative inner circle that has resisted change and monopolized power. According to these participants, the old guard has never forgotten and forgiven the *muha'n*, or calamities, of the 1950s and 1960s and has harbored hopes of exacting vengeance on their nationalist tormentors. Thus, far from healing the old scars and overcoming the divide, the nationalist-Islamist fault line has deepened and hardened, becoming bloodier and costlier than it was in the 1950s and 1960s. As we will see, battle lines have increasingly expanded from Egypt to neighboring Arab states, including Tunisia, Libya, and Syria, with the struggle getting entangled in a new regional cold war.

In summary, this book examines two major themes and dynamic developments shaping Arab history in the past century and a half: the development of relatively secular nationalism and the evolution of sociopolitical Islam-identified activism. These two movements formed a duality defining sociopolitical life, and the study argues that their interaction—both as a fierce competition and a symbiotic cooperation—has been so profound that neither can be properly understood if they are viewed as separate historical agents.

Chapter 1

Egypt's "Liberal Age"

THE HISTORICAL AND CULTURAL heritage of the territories encompassed by the borders of the modern Egyptian state has long been shaped by three circles of influence: Arab-Islamic, African, and European.[1] However, the occupation of Egypt by Napoleonic France in 1789 tilted the balance of influence northwards towards Europe. More than just a military venture, the Napoleonic expedition was framed as a *mission civilisatrice* that would bring the ideals of the French Revolution—liberty, equality, and fraternity—to the Nile Valley.[2] Although the French occupied Egypt for only four years, they left an indelible impact by overthrowing the Mamluk elite[3] and establishing *diwans* (administrative councils) that were headed by local actors, including the *'ulama* (Muslim religious scholars), judges, and notables. During his time in Egypt, Napoleon asserted his rule through a combination of coercion and ideology, stressing the compatibility of Islamic and republican values and pushing for the establishment of an Islamic republic where politics would be inscribed in a religious framework. Regardless of the propagandistic pronouncements behind Napoleon's policies, his invasion fed the emergence of the question of the "national self" in Egypt. Several developments contributed to this soul searching and the quest for self-definition: the dislocation of Mamluk power in favor of the involvement of local actors, the process of acculturation that followed the invasion, the introduction of the Arabic printing press, and the organization of an official press when the French published a political journal called *Courier de l'Egypte*.

The French defeat was followed by the reign of Muhammad Ali and his dynasty, which enacted a series of reforms, including centralizing state power, building a state bureaucracy, and improving the education system with the establishment of medical and language schools, as well as enacting tax and land reforms. Those policies led to a gradual Egyptianization of the army and the police, in addition to a substantial and consequential rise of nationalist sentiments and a nascent native elite determined to actively participate in state affairs. At the same time, Egypt's formal position as a province of the Ottoman Empire constrained the development of an independent national identity as state officials continued to depict the country as an active member of the Islamic *umma* (the Islamic community). Throughout the Muhammad Ali dynasty, the religious and nationalist discourses continued to mirror each other.

Nonetheless, from the Napoleonic invasion until the coming of Khedive Isma'il's rule—"khedive" was the title of the viceroy of Egypt under Turkish rule—Egypt's national identity formation occurred through a repeated process of interaction and comparison with Europe. The modernization project carried out by Muhammad Ali and his dynasty was primarily based on an attempt to make Egypt more like Europe economically, militarily, and administratively. Yet the deepening involvement by European powers in Egyptian internal affairs culminated in the occupation of the country by the British in 1882, a development that instigated ruptures and dislocations which had lasting ramifications for the emergence of the Egyptian "national self," and subsequently for the articulation of politics in the country.

This chapter retraces those shifts and their manifestation within the British colonial framework. It outlines how the simultaneous opening of the political scene and the consolidation of colonialism impacted the development of liberal politics in Egypt and influenced the processes of national identity formation.

Two arguments are advanced. The first is that the engagement of European powers in the Egyptian economy and the expansion of European colonization in the region caused a shift in the processes of identity formation from one of interaction with the European Other to one of opposition, in which Islam acted as an anchor for the constitution of Egypt's political self. This fusion of nationalism and religion in turn reflected the emergence of the image of a national political community in which the boundaries between the private and public spheres, as well as their role in the constitution of the "national self," had yet to be redefined, debated, and negotiated. The second argument is that despite the dissemination of liberal ideals by both the British and the Egyptian quasi-liberal elite, the fact that the colonial framework was based on authority rather than consensus impeded the constitution of a cohesive but diverse political community where multiple voices could engage in discussion and negotiation.

The National Question: Islam, the Nation, Modernization, and Colonialism

Muhammad Ali and his dynasty adopted a set of policies that ultimately focused on the centralization and modernization of the state, particularly the army, the bureaucracy, and infrastructure, in an attempt to transform Egypt into a European power. Despite Isma'il Pasha's claim that "Egypt is part of Europe," the various modernization processes thus far had only increased encroachment by the two rising European empires—Britain and France—on Egypt's independence and sovereignty. Turning to European financiers and governments to finance their ambitious modernization project, the Ali dynasty miscalculated by borrowing at exorbitant interest rates. Furthermore, endemic corruption left the Egyptian state unable to service or repay its debts. European powers used Egypt's indebtedness to tighten their grip over Isma'il and to weaken the Palace's control over the state apparatus. For example, the Caisse de la Dette, an international commission designed to supervise the repayment of Egyptian state debts to European governments, was instituted in 1876 and was supplemented by a joint Anglo-French financial administration of the country between 1876 and 1882. The khedive's loss of control undermined his legitimacy and authority as the ruler of the country in the eyes of the people.

Egypt's debt crisis also directly impacted the rural community, which contained the bulk of the Egyptian population. While Muhammad Sa'id Pasha, the fourth son of Muhammad Ali, and Isma'il Pasha, his grandson, enacted new laws that ultimately aimed at ending the feudal system, these were rarely implemented. In the 1860s, the American civil war led to a cotton boom in Egypt, but although the elite and village notables profited significantly, the peasantry gained little, especially as land prices increased. The result is that the Turco-Circassian[4] elite and the village notables, together with Europeans who were protected by the Ottoman capitulatory system,[5] bought large land holdings, while peasants found it increasingly hard to keep up with repeated tax increases. In 1878–1879 the country saw a wave of peasant revolts that were brutally repressed by the army. As discontent continued to brew among the population, self-reflecting questions about the nation, the self, and modernity preoccupied Islamic scholars.

While some *'ulama* (religious men of letters) and other writers looked within the Islamic corpus to bring about cultural renewal, others mined the European Enlightenment for sustenance and progress.[6] Seeking to bridge the divide between the two opposing schools of thought, another group of thinkers attempted to marry *asala* (cultural authenticity) with liberal European ideas. They appropriated selectively from Europe, arguing that neither outright emulation nor outright rejection of European political and social models could provide the fuel to power an Egyptian *nahda* (awakening or renaissance). Regardless of the differences in worldview and philosophy among the three schools, all were forward-looking and believed in universal progress, leadership, and agency, viewing the nation-state as the key political organization and the focus of their *nahda* project. This project of cultural renewal was an extension of the acculturation process triggered by Napoleon's invasion and subsequently pursued by Muhammad Ali.

The renewed dialogue between the Middle East and the West in the nineteenth century occurred during a critical moment pregnant with social tensions and struggles. Several intellectuals debated the Industrial Revolution and its adverse effects on society and the working classes. Although Middle Eastern writers praised the progress made in Europe, they were fully aware of the contestation within European societies and growing inequities among the social classes. More and more Egyptian and Muslim public intellectuals began to view modern life on the continent through the lens of leading European critics, including the doctrine of socialism, which highlighted the predicament of the poor and the growing obsessive individualism and personal enrichment of the few, around which liberalism based itself. These Arab writers directly questioned the viability and validity of modernization purely modeled on Europe's blueprint.[7] For instance, the aim of Jamal al-Din al-Afghani and 'Abdullah al-Nadim was to look at Europe's progress and learn appropriate lessons, while at the same time finding a third way that would bring about a social ideal based on dignity and equality. The result was that Muslim writers paid considerable attention to socialist European thinkers such as Saint-Simon, Robert Owen, Pierre Proudhon, and Karl Marx.[8]

Jamal al-Din al-Afghani, in particular, pioneered some of the most innovative ideas informing the debate on national pride and religious regeneration in Egypt.[9] He critically examined the role and place of reason, philosophy, science, religion, and social cohesion in helping to generate cultural renewal. Drawing from both Islamic thinkers such as Ibn Khaldun and French historian and politician Francois Guizot,[10] Afghani contended that Islam was not just a religion, but a civilization that comprised within itself all the necessary elements to fuel a new *nahda*. For Afghani, this renewal entailed a return to the principles laid down by the Prophet and his four caliphs, who lived a modest life in which social justice prevailed over personal enrichment. Afghani notes that the rightful Muslim ruler is not necessarily democratic but is one who struggles for the generation of Islam; in other words, Islam needed a Martin Luther. By discussing Western ideas and Western history, and relating them to the challenges facing the Muslim community, Afghani acknowledged the role of the European Other in the constitution of a renewed Islamic civilization. But he was also ambivalent toward the West, a stance shared by other Muslim intellectuals who played a key role in the rise of nationalism and national consciousness in the twentieth century in the Arab-Islamic world. On the one hand, these writers wanted to emulate Europe's progress and even surpass it. On the other, they affirmed the authenticity of their national identity as a way to break away from their Europeans occupiers.

For Afghani, the West became an image through which Islam could establish itself as ethically and morally superior, albeit in a process of opposition to Europe. His thought is anchored in anti-colonialism, and his support for the Egyptian state's authentic identity is an extension of a belief that the fight against the colonizers could be won through the achievement of independence. Two of Afghani's most important concepts also reflect his stance of opposition to Europe. He used the concept of Islamic civilization to inscribe continuity between Egypt's past and present consciousness and to assert the future national role of the country as the regional leader of the Islamic *umma*. In opposition to the linear view of progress, Afghani asserted a cyclical view of history; the authentic character of Islamic civilization would be reclaimed and even reinvigorated through a dialectical relationship to the European Other and his symbols. The idea was to imitate European progress by identifying Islamic concepts around which the social body would be reorganized.

The process of opposition is again reflected in his concept of *ishtirakiyya al-islamiyya* (Islamic socialism). Afghani saw socialism as the political creed of the Qur'an, an ideology whose principles were articulated by the Prophet himself and his first four successors. He utilized the concept of Islamic socialism to critique materialism and continuously compared Islamic socialism to Western socialism, dismissing the latter as fragile and weak. Afghani argued that this frailty stemmed from the inability of Western socialism to embed itself in Western socioreligious ideals, instead developing as a reaction to socioeconomic developments. In contrast, there existed an organic link between Islamic socialism, Islamic teachings, and Arabic culture, which unlike Western nationalism was an authentic articulation of the social ideal of Islam. Afghani argued that by uncovering and reclaiming its true Islamic identity, Egypt would affirm its own national individuality while at the same time retaining its pivotal role in the *umma*. At the end of the nineteenth century, a shift was taking place in Egypt as national consciousness and anti-colonialism coalesced towards the same goal, but many still viewed Afghani's calls for partition from the Ottoman Empire as radical. If the growing role of both the French and the British made it increasingly difficult for intellectuals to reconcile the role of Europe as a stimulus for progress when European colonialism had so severely impacted the living conditions of ordinary Egyptians, Islam still provided a powerful framework for identity. It is no wonder then that severing all ties with the Ottoman Empire was seen as highly perilous at a time when the struggle had shifted from the Europeanization of Egypt to the liberation of Egypt from its colonial masters.

Such heated debates about how best to modernize Egypt and end British colonialism peaked with the 'Urabi revolution, a term used to refer to a movement of Egyptian-born army officers and notables led by army colonel Ahmad 'Urabi between 1879 and 1882. The indigenous rebels' revolt had three targets: the power held by a small Turco-Circassian elite over the army; foreign control of Egyptian finances and politics; and British military domination.[11] While the protests by the religiously framed *'ulama* against the French occupation after 1798 clearly used Islam as their rallying cry, the 'Urabi revolt both reflected the growing nationalist character of the anti-colonial movement and included tenets of Islam as a basis for social identity. This twin aspirational identity explains why soldiers, police officers, merchants, guilds, and peasants joined in the ʿUrabi revolt and why the *ʿulama* remained divided with both the Palace and the ʿUrabists vying for their support. Although the power of the *ʿulama* had declined since Muhammad Ali, Al-Azhar continued to provide teachers for the whole Ottoman Empire till the end of the nineteenth century. The *ʿulama* still enjoyed a privileged position in society as the representatives and guardians of moral authority. In the face of growing encroachment by European powers in Egypt and the khedive's subservience to them, the continued inclusion of the country in the Ottoman Empire became a contentious point in the debate both within the ʿUrabi movement and in *ʿulama* circles.

For ʿUrabi, an uprising against the khedive also meant questioning Egypt's formal link and attachment to the Ottoman Empire and through that the *umma* as well; it would then openly question Egypt's place in the world, not just in the region. This ambivalence is reflected in the National Party's January 1882 declaration, where the ʿUrabi nationalists asserted their determination to achieve independence and self-government as well as their loyalty to the caliph and most importantly through him to the Islamic *umma*. This document attests to the linkage and interweaving of both the national and the Islamic foundation of Egyptian nationalism. The strategic goals of the actors and social movements converged towards the overthrow of European power and the Palace as well.

Interestingly, the composition of the ʿUrabi group shows the lack of homogeneity within the nationalist movement and the fragmentation of the *ʿulama*. While some senior *ʿulama* continued to support the ʿUrabist revolt, others who initially had been reluctant joined in. In a similar vein, Mohammed Abduh, an Islamist modernist thinker and a fervent disciple of Afghani, and Sheikh ʿIllaish, an ultraorthodox cleric, both became important figures in the ʿUrabi movement. For example, Abduh actively participated in the revolt while promoting and publishing the views of the exiled Afghani. He soon emerged as one of the leaders of the civilian wing of the ʿUrabist nationalist opposition, which called for structural political and social reforms that would give Egyptians a greater role in governing themselves.[12] Despite the heterogeneity of the nationalist movement, religion was the dominant framework for identifying the nascent Egyptian character as a political community. The ultimate goal of these participants in the nationalist movement, a mixture of secularists, semi-secularists, religious modernists, and orthodox clerics, had converged towards the struggle against colonialism. This fight against colonialism overshadowed their different visions of the political articulation of an independent Egypt.

As with other examples of nationalist awakening and activism at the time, the British acted swiftly to suppress the 'Urabists' revolt by authorizing a large expeditionary force, which militarily defeated the rebels at the Battle at Tel el-Kebir in 1882.[13] Colonial Britain attempted to silence and smother the diehard 'Urabists by either exiling or imprisoning their leaders, with 'Urabi himself sent to exile in Sri Lanka. In his memoirs, 'Urabi pointed out that British military intervention was the main cause for the failure of his movement.[14] Although the British claimed that the occupation of Egypt would be temporary, it lasted for another seventy-five years.

Debating Liberalism in the Late Nineteenth Century

One of the first measures carried out by the British to assert their control after the occupation of Egypt was to suspend all newspapers that backed the 'Urabists,[15] targeting both journalists and nationalists.[16] Despite intensifying censorship inside Egypt, the British encouraged a group of Christian secular writers to migrate from Lebanon to Cairo. In 1884, Ya'qub Sarruf and Faris Nimr, who were active in academic and intellectual circles in Lebanon, left for Egypt. In Lebanon, the two, both teachers at the Syrian Protestant College—now known as the American University of Beirut—had set out to publish a journal that focused on modern science and technology. Their magazine faced a serious backlash from the most conservative elements of the intelligentsia, and even their employer had become increasingly unhappy about their secularism. In contrast, the British authorities allowed them to reestablish their magazine, *al-Muqtatal*, when they reached the capital. In 1892, Jurji Zaydan, who also came from the Syrian Protestant College, started another publication, *al-Hilal*. The two magazines consistently advocated the pivotal role of science, instead of religion, in the advancement of civilization. Some of the writers who contributed to the magazines included Shibli Shumayyil, an ardent proponent of Darwinism, materialism, and socialism. In 1897 Farah Antun, a Lebanese journalist and a strong advocate of anticlericalism, left Tripoli for Cairo, where he founded a magazine called *al-Jami'ah* and published French literature by Jean-Jacques Rousseau, Ernest Renan, and others. It is worth noting that Antun was both a friend and an intellectual adversary of Islamist modernists like the Syrian writer Rashid Rida and Mohammed Abduh.

Despite their different nationalities, these writers fostered an inter-Arab dialogue where ideas of secularism would once more question the place of religion in the nation. This in turn led to the consolidation of a national political sphere and community in Egypt. Political debates about the interplay between Islam, nationalism, and progress flourished despite the authorities' repeated efforts to suppress them.

In the first decade of the twentieth century, nationalists found their leader in the charismatic Mustafa Kamil, who was a strong opponent of British imperialism but who had ties to France. His views were intrinsically linked to the geopolitical realities that Egyptian intellectuals faced. Kamil initially found support for his anti-British calls in France and also with Khedive Abbas Hilmi II and Sultan Abdul Hamid, who both materially supported his campaign.[17] As part of his struggle against the British, Abbas Hilmi II had supported the establishment—by Kamil and other Egyptians such as Ahmad Lutfi al-Sayyid—of the Society for the Revival of the Nation, which soon became known as the National Party. In 1900, with government backing, Kamil founded *al-Liwa*, through which he disseminated his group's views. However, following the signing of the Anglo-French Entente Cordiale in 1904, Kamil broke away from the khedive and turned to the Ottoman sultan. He distinguished himself as the leader of an uprising against the khedive and the British-led government in June 1906 following the Dinshawai Incident, in which a fracas between residents of the village of that name and a group of British officers on a pigeon-shooting expedition resulted in the death of a British soldier. The Egyptians involved were dragged before a British military tribunal, resulting in the hanging of four illiterate peasants and the flogging and imprisonment of many others. The brutal repression of the peasants by the British provoked anger throughout the country, a reminder of the constant humiliation of the Egyptians by their foreign tormentors. Kamil used the international press to vent his anger and frustration with the colonial administration and published a virulent letter in the French newspaper *Le Figaro* on July 11, 1906, exposing the brutality of colonialism and openly mocking the lack of judicial independence during the trial. This episode and the far-reaching reaction to it "accomplished more for the Egyptian nationalist movement than Kamil had been able to gain in the twelve years he had spent traveling and haranguing."[18] A key feature of the revolution led by Kamil is that it was peaceful, built around a campaign mobilized in his newspapers, including the Arabic-language *al-Liwa*, which put forward the National Party's views, and two other English and French publications. As a result of outrage by European liberals at the Dinshawai Incident the liberal government in Britain "announced a new policy designed to prepare Egyptians for self-government as quickly as possible."[19] In May 1907, Lord Cromer, a fierce colonialist, retired as the consul general of Egypt. Justified by ill health, Lord Cromer's departure was partly connected to the Dinshawai Incident and the subsequent controversy. Kamil and other nationalists hailed as a triumph the exit of this long-standing enforcer of the British colonial order.[20]

Political parties rose in this time of flourishing liberal and nationalist politics, partly facilitated by the semi-liberal ideology of Lord Cromer's successor, Eldon Gorst. Although Gorst's policies were cleverly designed to consolidate British control, they also allowed for simultaneous political-constitutional and radical administrative reforms, such as integrating more Egyptians into government posts.[21] In 1907 alone, the same year that Lord Cromer left his post, nine parties were formed,[22] including al-Hizb al-Watani, al-Umma, al-Islah 'ala al-Mabadi al-Dusturiyya, al-Ahrar, al-Nubala', al-Masri, al-Jumhuri, and al-Ishtraqi al-Mubarak; three of these would dominate Egyptian political life for almost half a century. Despite being elitist with a narrow social constituency, these parties' agendas varied greatly with respect to the core concerns facing many Egyptians, particularly how to deal with the British occupation. The changing political landscape in Egypt reflected economic developments that benefited a new rising middle class. The aftermath of the British occupation saw a sharp increase in taxes, but threatened with mass revolts from both increasingly landless peasants and dissatisfied landholding families, the British colonial regime of Evelyn Baring (subsequently known as Lord Cromer) maintained low taxation. This allowed the consolidation and gradual rise of a new middle class made up of landholding families that gradually transformed themselves into agrarian capitalists and entrepreneurs. After the Dinshawai Incident, the British also took a more conciliatory position towards the growth of nationalist sentiments and included a few Egyptians in ministries, where they were allowed to push for controlled reforms.

By the first decade of the twentieth century this new Egyptian middle class had developed a vested interest in the colonial system, and its nationalism had been muted by a conviction that independence could be attained by pushing for liberal reforms in the fields of education, administration, and Islamic law. A case in point was Mohammed Abduh's and Sa'ad Zaghloul's positions in the British-controlled government and Rashid Rida's accommodating stance towards the British until the mid-1910s.

The first of the three most influential parties to emerge was al-Umma (the Nation), founded in September 1907 by a group of wealthy notables, prominent government officials, and young intellectuals. Al-Umma's agenda found supporters in the landowning Egyptian elite and also attracted prominent intellectuals, who were often rebel members of al-Azhar, including Ahmad Lutfi al-Sayyid, Taha Hussein, Muhammad Hussein Haykal, and Mustafa Abdel

Raziq. Al-Umma communicated its program through its official mouthpiece newspaper, *al-Jarida*, which called for cooperation with the British, rejection of pan-Islamism, and discreet opposition to the khedive. It also stressed the need for Egyptians to rely on themselves rather than any other country in achieving independence.[23] The party pursued a liberal and Westernizing agenda that focused on building up the country, promoting national unity, encouraging trade and industry, freedom of education and the press, rights for women, and democracy. Its chief spokesman, Ahmad Lutfi al-Sayyid, was editor of *al-Jarida*. He unambiguously rejected the idea of a continuing Egyptian political bond with the Ottoman Empire[24] and explicitly advocated secular nationalism by "banishing Islam from the public sphere." Egypt's modernization, Sayyid argued, should be modeled "on the Greek and Roman classics just as Europe had done."[25] Al-Sayyid's position contrasted with that of Mohammed 'Abduh, who sought a compromise between the religious sphere (Islam) and the secular sphere (modernity).

Hizb al-Watani (National Party) was the second party that built a social base and gained momentum. It was established in October 1907 by Mustafa Kamil, who proclaimed "the independence of Egypt" as the foundation or mandate of the National Party.[26] Its key goal was to bring about the evacuation of British troops from Egyptian soil and secure the granting of a constitution by the khedive which would limit his extensive powers. The National Party advocated stronger ties with Istanbul, a policy grounded in the conviction that ending the British occupation would require the support of the Ottoman Empire.[27] Although Kamil's nationalism possessed an Islamic identity, his disciples included Copts like Wisa Wasif and Murqus Hanna, and he called on Egyptian Christians to join Muslims under the national banner.[28]

The third important party, usually referred to as Hizb al-Islah 'ala al-Mabadi al-Dusturiyya (the Constitutional Reform Party), was formed in December 1907 as a Palace organ loyal to the khedive. Led by Sheikh 'Ali Yusuf, with a newspaper called *al-Mu'ayyad* as its mouthpiece, its program dismissed ties with the Ottomans and focused instead on securing fulfillment of the "pledges and promises made by Britain when it had occupied Egypt."[29]

Other minor parties, such as the Hizb al-Watani al-Hurr (the Free National Party), were even more outspoken than al-Umma and the Constitutional Reform Party in their calls for closer ties with the British occupier, as part of a politics framed around slogans such as reform, education, and Westernization. Identifying with British policy in Egypt, Hizb al-Watani al-Hurr's newspaper, *al-Muqattam*, opined that a stable administration influenced and checked by an advanced European power was the best road to reform.[30] Established in 1908, Hizb al-A'yan (the Party of Notables) represented the remnants of the Turkish community in Egypt and called for closer links with both the Ottomans and the British occupiers. Meanwhile, Hizb al-Misryyin al-Mustaqillin (the Independent Egyptians' Party), whose members were mostly Copts, called for the separation of religion and the state, the unification of Egypt and Sudan, and greater protection for foreigners and minorities.

The flourishing of a liberal and open society in Egypt was severely curtailed by restrictions imposed by the British colonial authorities. After a brief moment Gorst abandoned his lenient policy in favor of a harsher one, using emergency measures and laws to silence the nationalists by censoring their media outlets and pressuring the party leaders.[31] Legislation enacted in March 1909 empowered the interior minister to suspend or close newspapers without resort to the judiciary.[32] Another law stipulated that journalists could be tried in the Criminal Court rather than in the lesser Felony Court. These laws paved the way for the closure of newspapers associated with the National Party and the imprisoning of their publishers. Ahmed Helmi of *al-Qutr al-Misri* was a famous case in point.[33]

The colonial authorities clamped down hard on socialist parties. In 1908, as soon as a socialist party called al-Hizb al-Ishtiraki al-Mubarak (the Blessed Socialist Party) was founded, the British sealed it off. Similarly, in 1914 the colonial rulers shut down a socialist magazine, *al-Mustaqbal*, established by Salama Musa, a journalist and writer born into a wealthy Coptic family. Influenced by both

Farah Antun and Shibil Shumayyil, Musa had also founded a socialist society in Cairo. Even the political parties that were legally tolerated faced limitations on access to legislative powers and were never allowed to secure any access to executive authority, which was fully controlled by colonial Britain,[34] despite the vast popularity of such parties.[35]

Restrictions on freedom of speech gave rise to two new features in Egyptian political life: first, the appearance of underground secret societies, with twenty-seven such organizations reportedly existing by 1911; and second, the emergence of the politics of exile as a means to sustain the struggle against British colonialism as exemplified by the decision of the leader of the National Party, Muhammad Farid, to move to Turkey.[36]

Therefore in the first decade of the twentieth century, the political parties that flourished in Egypt reflected the heterogeneity of the elite's attitude towards the Palace, the British, and the Ottoman Empire, though they developed no common vision and there existed no national consensus on what the identity of an independent Egyptian nation would be. The dissemination of secularist ideas, often backed heavily by the British, the suppression of Islam as a potential anchor for nationalism, and the weakening of the Ottoman Empire all significantly contributed to the growth of parties which promoted liberal values without possessing a meaningful political ideology beyond a belief in capitalism as a vehicle to reach modernity. In a way, those parties' raison d'être revolved more around the ideal of individual enrichment than around a cohesive national ideal.

The Secular-Liberal Wafd in the 1920s

The vibrancy and diversity which characterized the Egyptian political scene in the first two decades of the twentieth century culminated in a third popular revolution, led by Sa'ad Zaghloul, between 1919 and 1922. The result was the 28 February 1922 Declaration, which gave Egypt limited independence. Enacted a year later, a new constitution set the terms for a period in which Zaghloul's liberal Wafd party dominated Egyptian politics. Indeed, the period from 1922 until 1953, the year when the new Free Officers issued a decree dissolving all political parties, is often referred to as the "Liberal Era" in modern Egyptian politics.[37] This label, however, is a simplification of the more complex and illiberal reality of the British occupation. Despite nominal Egyptian independence, the capitulatory system and Mixed Courts, which inscribed the superiority of Europeans in law, persisted until the negotiation of the Anglo-Egyptian Treaty of 1936. For all the optimism and dynamism associated with this period, the ongoing autocracy of the Egyptian Palace, not to mention of the British, ensured that the semi-liberal project was doomed to fail from the start. The inherent failure and eventual collapse of the quasi-liberal moment paved the way for the rise of far-right nationalist and Islamist groups from the late 1930s onwards.[38]

Zaghloul's popular revolution in 1919 stood against British domination and the economic hardships and miseries experienced under colonial rule during World War I. Not unlike 'Urabi's revolt and Kamil's uprising, Zaghloul's revolution aimed at greater political independence and a measure of economic equity. However, Zaghloul's revolution was led by a new generation of nationalist leaders who subscribed neither to the "Pan-Islamic pro-Ottoman sentimentalism" that emerged at the turn of the century nor to the "romanticism" of Mustafa Kamil's National Party.[39] Rather, the Zaghloul generation adopted secular liberal ideas.[40] By 1918, the new nationalist leadership had collectively come to the realization that as landowners, financiers, and industrial or commercial entrepreneurs, they had a vested economic interest in political independence.[41] The British authorities clamped down hard on this new nationalist leadership when Zaghloul and his supporters sought to collect signed depositions from a range of organizations in the country in order to form a delegation authorized to negotiate Egypt's independence with British officials in the series of peace conferences that followed World War I. The British military authorities prevailed upon the Ministry of Interior to prevent the circulation of these depositions. The British also prevented the Wafd and any other delegation from traveling to London or Paris, and forced Zaghloul into exile in Malta and the Seychelles. After the British confiscated the depositions and denied travel permissions, the Wafd successfully escalated its campaign, organizing demonstrations across the country, strikes by transport workers, judges, and lawyers, and even violent attacks on British military personnel. Faced with a widening upheaval, the British authorities eventually acceded to the demand of Zaghloul and his cohorts that they be treated as sole representatives and spokespersons for the Egyptians in negotiations for independence.[42] This victory was symbolized in the 28 February 1922 Declaration, in which the British government recognized Egypt in principle as an independent sovereign state, albeit with qualifications that in practice allowed colonial Britain to continue to intervene in the country's internal affairs.

The Wafd grouping around Zaghloul formally organized itself as a political party in September 1923, calling for complete independence from Britain, constitutional government, the protection of civil rights, and Egyptian sovereignty over the Sudan and the Suez Canal.[43] Although the Wafd would become the dominant force in Egyptian politics for more than two decades, from the start it faced serious obstacles to achieving its goals. These included a constitution which concentrated power in the hands of the king and thereby facilitated his autocratic tendencies, along with ongoing obstructionism by the British. In principle, the promulgation of the constitution in April 1923 heralded a new era in Egyptian political life, a foundational document without precedent. Although the Basic Law passed in 1882 had been an important political milestone, formalizing the separation of powers between the cabinet and the Parliament, and guaranteeing the independence of members of Parliament, it had not included a constitution and it failed to address individual rights or obligations. In contrast, the 1923 constitution insisted on such liberal measures as dedicating twenty-one articles to the rights and duties of Egyptians, including privacy of communications and freedom of belief, religion, and speech.[44]

However, the 1923 document proved to be profoundly flawed because it invested extensive powers in the king, including the power to select and appoint the prime minister, to dismiss cabinets by royal fiat, to reject legislation promulgated by the Chamber of Deputies, to appoint the president of the Senate and one-fifth of its members, and most importantly, to dissolve the elected Parliament.[45] The opening session of the Parliament in 1925 reflected both the tensions between the Palace and the Wafd and the inherent defects of the constitutional arrangement. At the end of the ten-hour opening session, the king dissolved the Wafdist-dominated assembly, which had responded to his opening speech with chants of "Long Live Zaghloul!" The king asserted his supremacy and made a mockery of a constitution that he had always detested.[46] He also resented the document because, although it gave him considerable power, it empowered the Egyptian public, paving the way for elections that forced him to allow Wafdist candidates, whom he detested, to form a government. Another contentious point was that the 1923 constitution reaffirmed the superiority of foreigners' rights in Egypt, which clearly showed the sway of colonial authority.

In the next two decades, the viability of the constitutional experiment was constantly menaced by the Palace's persistent efforts to establish a royal autocracy. Moreover, despite granting Egypt truncated independence in the 1920s, the British residency did not relax its iron fist towards its former colony. British intervention, particularly on behalf of the Palace, exacted a heavy toll on the legitimacy and sustainability of the constitutional moment. Colonial Britain felt threatened by the Wafd's nationalist agenda, broad popularity, and significant capacity for popular mobilization.[47] The result is that throughout the 1920s, much of British involvement in Egyptian politics aimed at curtailing the Wafd's influence by adopting repressive measures that included imposing martial law, imprisoning Zaghloul and other nationalist leaders, and time and again deploying gunboats and tanks to dictate terms to the Egyptian elite. The British preferred to deal with a non-Wafdist cabinet unless they needed to negotiate an Anglo-Egyptian treaty, which only the Wafd could deliver.[48] For example, in November 1924 the British intervened against the Wafdist cabinet because, in line with the 1923 constitution, the Zaghloul government had begun to "Egyptianize" state institutions as a manifestation of genuine independence.[49] This Egyptianization directly undermined the authority of British officials, who presented Zaghloul with an ultimatum forcing him to resign.[50] The British framed the move against the Zaghloul government as providing an opportunity for "reasonable Egyptians to assert themselves."[51] Once again the British intervened in 1926 and forced Zaghloul to decline the premiership of a newly formed cabinet despite his party's win in the general election held that year. To convince Zaghloul of the seriousness of their threat, the British ordered battle cruisers towards Alexandria, which brought the message home to Zaghloul and his supporters.[52] Colonial Britain intervened for a third time in 1927, following the Parliament's push for greater autonomy in running the military, the appointment of an Egyptian commander to replace the British leadership, better training for Egyptian cadets, and expansion of the fighting units. Under duress, the Wafdist-supported cabinet of Abdel Khaleq Tharwat accepted the extension and entrenchment of existing arrangements, ensuring supervision and control of the Egyptian army by a British inspector general.[53] Yet it was not until the fourth flagrant British intervention, against the Wafdist cabinet of Mustafa Nahhas in 1928,[54] that Lord Lloyd, the British resident in Egypt, became convinced of the "unsuitability" of parliamentary arrangements as a means for governing Egypt.[55] Lord Lloyd not only urged the king not to endorse the legislation in question if it was passed by the Parliament but also increasingly favored the dissolution of the Parliament. He recommended a course of action that would not "restrain his majesty from taking any steps he thinks necessary to break up the Wafd before it is in a position to dictate its terms to him and incidentally to put up against us an opposition which could only be overcome by the use of considerable force."[56]

The goal of protecting British interests directly resulted in the dilution of Egyptian independence and sowed the seeds of conflict with a succession of Egyptian governments.[57] In sum, the British and the king, the two most powerful political forces in Egypt, played a fundamental role in the failure of the constitutional moment. From the outset, both regarded constitutionalism as a menace to their hegemonic influence, and they spared no effort to curtail its advance and entrenchment in society. More than any other factor, the British authorities and the maverick king sacrificed constitutionalism on the altar of their narrow interests, a point worth mentioning when pondering the question of why democracy has not taken hold on Arab soil.

Disillusionment with Politics and Economy and the Struggle for Liberation in the 1930s and 1940s

Although the Wafd had initially been vocally critical of the vast powers invested in the king by the 1923 constitution, it played by the rules of the game and did not attempt either to limit the king's constitutional prerogatives or to challenge the Palace's repeated violations of the document. In the end, the Wafd's political shortsightedness and self-serving pursuit of power also undermined the constitutional process. Zaghloul sought to benefit politically from the arrangements wrought by the new constitution. He even applauded the document, the drafting of which he had initially criticized, for embracing "modern principles" and for declaring the source of all powers to be "the Umma."[58]

The year 1936 saw the signing of the Anglo-Egyptian Treaty, which in theory fettered British hands and limited their military presence mostly to the Suez Canal Zone. The treaty formalized years of negotiations between the British and the Egyptian delegation led by Wafdist prime minister Mustafa Nahhas, following the granting of the country's nominal independence in 1922. The Wafd and its leadership celebrated the treaty as conferring genuine independence. However, nationalist critics of all persuasions pointed out that the document sanctioned infringement of Egyptian sovereignty, with Britain reserving the right to intervene in the country's internal affairs whenever it perceived a threat to its primary interests. In fact, the treaty deepened and widened the divide among the Wafd's supporters, many of whom viewed it as compromising the nationalist agenda that had initially been the party's raison d'être. The credibility of the Wafd continued to be undermined by its failure to address the interests of industrial laborers and the rural population, or to address the rising cost of living during the interwar period.

The buoyant mood which had followed the Zaghloul revolution in the early 1920s had by the late 1930s given way to dark premonitions of a nation and a people in servitude. Egypt was not seen as a master of its own destiny, politically or economically. The British residency kept a stranglehold on Egyptian politics by backing the Palace against legitimately elected representatives and parties, thus annulling the will of the people. Britain's frequent interventions in the country's internal affairs, together with its violent assault against protesters and dissidents, were a constant reminder to Egyptians from all walks of life that they should resist and possibly expel its influence from their country even by force. A relative consensus emerged that a corrupt political class had failed Egypt by being pliant and shying away from defending Egyptian national interests.

In the past, Egyptian entrepreneurs and bankers had stimulated economic activities in Egypt, placing the objective of national development at the heart of their strategies. However, over time the self-serving political network allowed foreign interests to continue to dominate the country's economic life. This occurred at the expense of a comprehensive national development program based on land reforms and expansion of local manufacturing, which might have improved the well-being of citizens and lifted the *'ummal* (urban working classes) and *fellahin*[59] out of abject poverty and misery. The prospects for such reforms were limited because most of the leading liberal parties belonged to the land-owning bourgeoisie. During the interwar period, with the rise of industry and the growth of the financial sector, the bourgeoisie developed interests in these new areas of the economy. Concerned as they were with their own vested interests, it is perhaps unsurprising that no Wafd government ever adopted or carried out any fundamental agrarian reforms or passed any legislation bolstering the rights of the embryonic working class.[60]

Historically, Egypt served as a producer of raw materials and commodities for a capitalist world system, but at the risk of oversimplification, it is fair to say that most Egyptians neither owned the means of production nor enjoyed its fruits, with the exception of a small upper segment of notables, landlords, and businessmen. In his important book *Party Politics in Egypt*, Marius Deeb notes that foreign corporations tended to employ resident foreigners, while "Egyptians had little chance of being employed in business houses."[61] This meant a high level of unemployment among the population, despite the tripling of enrollment in state secondary schools and the doubling of enrollment at Cairo University.[62] Unemployed and with no economic prospects, both the rising *effendiyya* (urban middle classes) and the *'ummal* felt excluded and marginalized. By the 1930s and 1940s the growing divide between the universe of the colonized and that of the colonizers was illustrated by the spatial restructuring of Cairo. The capital was a segregated city, with the wealthiest and most developed areas inhabited by the Europeans and resident foreigners, while the poorest and least developed zones housed Egyptians.[63]

The plight of the *'ummal* and the *fellahin* was particularly grim. A collapse in cotton prices in the early 1920s, which saw a tenfold drop from an index figure of 200 at the end of 1920 to only 20 in March 1921,[64] led to a 10 percent decline in per capita national income, which hit peasants particularly hard. As workers' conditions became equally hard in the 1930s due to the Great Depression, the country faced a social crisis that resulted in "severe economic contraction."[65] Egypt's exports lost more than a third of their value between 1928 and 1933, partly because of a drop in the world price of cotton from USD26 to USD10 per qantar.[66]

Instead of passing legislation to ameliorate the dismal conditions of poor urban laborers, the ruling political elite squeezed the emerging trade unions in an effort to further weaken the growing working-class movement. Throughout the 1920s and 1930s, the organization of trade unions saw little advancement in its fortunes for three major reasons. First, the political parties "sought to control industrial labour by organizing their own unions as adjuncts of their party political machines."[67] For example, in December 1930 the Wafd formed a trade union under the leadership of Prince Abbas Hilmi, a member of the royal family. After Hilmi "detached his union from the Wafd in 1933–1934 and formed the Egyptian Labour Party,"[68] the Wafd then formed another trade union in 1935. Likewise, the Liberals formed their own union, which was led by Dawoud Ratib. Even the unpopular Ismail Sidqi government opened a Labour Bureau.[69] Second, these trade unions were not representative of workers because agricultural laborers, who made up the vast majority of Egypt's workforce, were excluded from membership. For two decades the Wafd continued to control the vote of agricultural workers through their provincial representatives and appointees, as well as village headmen.[70] Third, the Wafd enacted new laws which restricted the activities of trade unions. The first Wafd government strengthened the 1923 Law of Associations (Assembly) in order to combat activities by trade unions, and it had earlier amended parts of the Penal Code to allow the authorities to act effectively against the labor movement, which was seen as spreading subversive, anarchist, communist, and anti-constitutional ideas. Disciplinary measures, including prison sentences, were introduced against strikes by government officials and employees of public utilities and transport services.[71]

The Wafd's position after it gained power contrasted sharply with its previous initiatives towards labor organizations which sided with the workers against discriminatory conduct by foreign management, often acting as a mediator between the workers and the government.[72] In response to the disgruntlement of middle- and lower-class members, the Wafd enacted social reforms, though these "did not go beyond measures to widen opportunity for individuals within the capitalist elite system."[73] For example, the Wafd founded an agrarian bank to provide urgent credit to small and medium-sized landowners, but still, "agricultural workers were not permitted to unionize and land reform, which had become the great social issue of pre-revolutionary Egypt, was given, at best, lip service."[74]

The convergence of a deepening political divide with dismal socioeconomic conditions produced a severe crisis of authority and utterly discredited the ruling elite, including native capitalists who had originally aimed to challenge foreign enterprise and capital. In the eyes of ordinary Egyptians, the political and financial elites had sacrificed national sovereignty on the altar of narrow and parochial self-interest.[75] While Egyptian entrepreneurs and bankers had earlier stimulated economic activities at home through projects such as Misr Group and Banque Misr, they in the end fell victim to avarice and expediency, and colluded with foreign capital to enrich themselves at the expense of a more inclusive national development strategy. By pursuing self-destructive policies and failing to adopt a new wider and more inclusive agenda, the Wafd proved to be its own worst enemy. Support for the party decreased and the Wafd slipped into internal strife, which led to the expulsion of leading members, who then went on to form their own parties. This internal rivalry was in turn exploited by the king.[76] Finally, the inflationary hardship caused by World War II further radicalized opinion and continued to erode the Wafd's credibility. As a result, new groups with a more radical tone appeared on the political scene and found a support base in an increasingly disaffected population.

Instead of expanding the Wafd's own societal base, particularly among the growing urban, educated middle class known as the *effendiyya*, the urban working classes, and the *fellahin*, the party thus lost its moral compass, became detached from the pulse of nationalist sentiment, and squandered its political capital. Many within its ranks were unscrupulous and corrupt. In the mid-1930s and the 1940s the Wafd collaborated with the British at the expense of Egyptian sovereignty and dignity. Its popularity consequently waned and its claims to represent the "conscience of the nation"[77] ceased to resonate with the wider population. The Wafd's intent to press ahead with this course of action, even as its political project was increasingly undermined by conflict with the king, eventually led to a profound backlash against the liberal constitutionalism that it represented. By rallying around the authoritarian framework of the colonial system and allowing itself to become the representative of one particular class interests, the Wafd and the rest of the ruling political elite, along with the British and the Palace, contributed to the stifling of the political space, as well as the nascent political community. The governing elite failed to articulate the demands of the people or to establish a real dialogue between the different strata of the social body with a conception of Egypt as a political rather than just as a national imagined community. As Egyptians lost faith in the liberal spirit at the heart of the constitutional process, they increasingly turned to slogans of *asala* (authenticity) and revolutionary action as a more viable alternative for bringing about change.

Chapter 2

The Anti-colonial Struggle and the Dawn of Underground Politics

THE GROWING DISENFRANCHISEMENT OF the population under colonial domination led to the emergence of underground politics as a tool and a weapon in the liberation struggle. This development prompted the two leading Islamist and nationalist parties to collide, a collision that has fundamentally divided Egypt and has left deep scars on the country's contemporary identity and politics. Two important conjectures can be drawn from this rupture, which unfolded between the late 1940s and the early 1950s. First, the failure of liberal constitutionalism in Egypt deepened the divide between the pro-British old regime and the people. It also contributed to the politicization of the private space as exemplified by the emergence of revolutionary underground movements or paramilitary organizations. Second, the unresolved dichotomies between Self/Other, state/people, and public/private inscribed at the heart of the imagination of the Egyptian political community were reflected by the rupture within the anti-colonial nationalist movement between a military and a religious pole, which set the scene for the July 1952 coup and the subsequent bitter and violent conflicts that followed.

The Struggle for Liberation in the 1940s

During World War II, despite various treaties stipulating Egyptian sovereignty, the British continued to prioritize their vital imperial interests over those of Egypt. As thousands of British and Allied troops flocked to Cairo, Egyptians were further reminded of their unfulfilled hopes and aspirations: despite guaranteed nominal independence, the country was not the master of its own destiny, and its governing elite was either pliant or subservient to foreign powers, particularly colonial Britain. The status quo was no longer tolerable or acceptable, and as trust in establishment parties like the Wafd dissipated, widespread support for radical alternatives spread throughout society. The Ikhwan (the Muslim Brothers) and Young Egypt (Misr al-Fatat) were two examples of radical alternative politics. The Ikhwan movement was established by a primary schoolteacher, Hassan al-Banna, in 1928. Young Egypt first appeared as an association launched by Ahmed Hussein, a lawyer, in 1933, before developing into a militant political party in 1938. Of the two groups, Young Egypt reflected the emergence of a measure of sympathy within Egyptian society for European fascism and a growing acceptance of the use of violence in the service of political ends. It promoted a mixture of extreme nationalism and anti-colonialism under the motto "God, Fatherland, and King." Young Egypt also set up a paramilitary organization called al-Qumsan al- Khadra' (the Green Shirts) in an attempt to enforce its anti-colonial stance and extremist religious worldview, firmly basing it around a belief in the necessity of violence and self-sacrifice.[1] Young Egypt found inspiration and motivation in the rising Nazi and fascist movements in Europe, establishing concrete connections with these movements and participating in the 1936 Nuremberg Rally in Germany.[2] Although Young Egypt emphasized religion as the sole moral force that could effect cultural renewal and glory in Egypt, its approach differed from that of the Ikhwan.

In contrast to the enlightened Islamic vision promoted by Mohammed Abduh, the Ikhwan proposed a radical Islamist project that called for the establishment of a Qur'anic-based state and rejected the colonial framework as a vehicle of reform.[3] Although in the early years of the Ikhwan, Banna was willing to work within the political system, as witnessed by his letters to the Palace, which often called for reforms, the king repeatedly dismissed his ideas and vetoed his participation in the state. Angry at the corrupt political elite and the Palace, Banna soon adopted a supranational approach and refused to pigeonhole the organization into any conventional political category. Insisting on the apolitical nature of the Ikhwan, he presented the group as a "benevolent" society seeking to create through the Qur'an a "new spirit" that would scatter the "darkness of materialism" through the "knowledge of God."[4] Throughout the 1930s and 1940s, the Ikhwan grew from strength to strength, surpassing the Wafd in popularity, membership, and class representation. The failure of the Wafd had meant the disintegration of the social coalition between the urban *effendiyya* (professionals, government employees), the middle-landowning notability, and the more nationalistic elements of the great landed aristocracy.[5] This alliance had guaranteed social and political harmony in which all these groups and classes participated in demonstrations, strikes, and votes. Religious minorities such as the Copts had also been included in this "nationalist" project, and the Wafd's influential secretary, Makram 'Ebeid, was himself a Copt. Feeling threatened by the Ikhwan's program and ideology, the Copts viewed the organization as alienating and hostile. Accordingly, Coptic leaders launched a campaign to "revive the Coptic nationalism to counter the radically Islamist thought of the Ikhwan."[6] Parochialism and local *asabiyya* (religious social cohesion) invaded the Egyptian social fabric, an indication of the slow "death of liberalism" in the country. Religious values replaced liberal and nationalist sentiments amidst a general sense of disillusionment which would have long-term repercussions on Egyptian political development.

The emergence of authoritarian social movements and parties reflected an increasing shift towards radical religious discourse in the politics of the 1930s and 1940s. Radical religious and political thought, and violence, were themselves by-products of a period in which Egyptian constitutionalism had been constantly abused and undermined by the king, the British, and the dominant political parties. Consequently, ambitious revolutionary and anti-hegemonic groups filled the void.[7] Some of these radical currents showed sympathy towards European fascism, though it was a passing temptation and ultimately fascism remained a marginal phenomenon. In a similar vein, the radicalization and increasing utilization of religious discourse by public intellectuals from diverse backgrounds was directly related to the concurrent historical circumstances. The early twentieth century witnessed the rise of Islam as an object of inquiry in both Western and Middle Eastern scholarship, as a direct result of the emergence of Orientalist studies in the West in the late eighteenth century and their gradual influence on Islamic scholars in the late nineteenth and early twentieth century. Another factor was the use of colonial missionaries in order to "reform" the colonized. Authors like Afghani and Rida validated their conceptualization of Islam as a motor for cultural renewal and modernization by arguing that religion had played a pivotal role in the constitution of European civilization and identity as well as in the rise of European scientific, military, and economic superiority. Moreover, the fragmentation of Islamic authority after the disintegration of the Ottoman Empire allowed various social movements to compete for a redefinition of Islam along their own particular lines. For the Arab population of North Africa and the Middle East, World War II caused increased economic hardships, a situation that contributed further to a growing emphasis on Islamic norms and values as an appealing framework within which to understand and engage with Egypt's social and political conflicts.

The result of this changing mood is that leading modernist thinkers and the Wafd began to use Islamic symbols and rhetoric in their discourse. In a sharp departure from an earlier epoch in which modernists like Taha Hussein, Abbas al-Aqqad, and Muhammad Hussein Haykal had promoted European culture and disparaged traditional values, these same thinkers adopted a romantic retreat towards the epic early golden days of Islam. Retreating from his earlier critical approach to religious heritage, Taha Hussein drew an emotional interpretation of the Prophet's life in *'Ala hamish al-sira* (On the Margin of the Prophet's Tradition).[8] Similarly, Haykal, the leading constitutionalist, produced a series of books on the Prophet and the first caliphs, in which he emphasized—using inflammatory language—that the motivation behind his portraits was to expose the plots against Islam "by the church leaders and the Western colonisers." He also said he hoped that humanity could find "the new civilisation it looks for" in Islam.[9] Similarly, Aqqad focused on the crowning days of Islam by writing volumes on *'abqariyyat* (geniuses), in which he highlighted the glory of early Islam and accentuated exceptional, charismatic leaders in Islamic history.[10] These apologetic works by modernist writers reinforced the worldview of religiously based social movements like the Ikhwan and prepared the ground for radical groups calling for the adoption of a purely Islamic model as the only vehicle for change in Egypt. As a Western academic noted, "the intellectuals surrendered their previous bearing—rationalism and Western cultural orientation—without being able to produce any viable Muslim-inspired alternative."[11]

Strikingly, from the 1920s onwards, both the Wafd, whose nationalism had been secular, and the king exploited traditional religious institutions to outbid each other. When in 1927 the then Wafd-dominated Parliament passed legislation transferring control over religious schools and institutes from the rector of al-Azhar to the Ministry of Education, the king backed the Azharis, whose rallying cry against the new law was "Down with the Parliament." After the fall of the Wafd government in 1930, the king appointed his own man, Sheikh Mohammed al-Zawahiri, as rector of al-Azhar, an institution that found itself in the crossfire of the Palace and the Wafd in the 1940s. The king and his allies recognized the significant role that the religious establishment could play in their struggle against the Wafd and the constitutional arrangement.[12] King Farouk, for instance, had long been known for his drinking and womanizing, yet after February 4, 1942, when he was humiliatingly forced to appoint Mustafa Nahhas as prime minister after British tanks encircled his palace, Farouk grew a beard and regularly attended Friday prayers. Although his motives were unclear, Farouk's newly displayed piousness seemed either an empty defiance of the British occupiers or a reactionary shift following his humiliation by both the secular Wafd and a hegemonic foreign authority. Despite Farouk's use and abuse of the sacred, the religious establishment retained the will and capacity to challenge the Palace. This was demonstrated clearly following Farouk's divorce from his wife, Princess Farida of Egypt, in 1945, when he asked Sheikh Mustafa al-Maraghi of al-Azhar to issue a fatwa forbidding her to remarry, and al-Azhar's sheikh infuriated the monarch by rejecting the request.[13]

Another significant development transforming Egyptian politics at this time was the increasingly tense situation in Palestine, which fueled the rise of radical communitarian politics and brought the Arab question to Egypt just as pan-Arabism was taking root abroad in the Fertile Crescent. More than any other single regional or international development, the loss of Palestine shattered the legitimacy of the incumbent authorities in Egypt and further radicalized the country's political scene. Arabism—which had initially been employed as a rebuttal to the Ottoman Empire's control over Arab populations—slowly gained momentum as a device to be used against the colonizers and to affirm Egyptian identity vis-à-vis imperialism.

As clashes between Zionists and Palestinians intensified in the 1920s and 1930s, the reverberations were felt in all of the neighboring Arab countries. The Palestinian tragedy resonated with Arabs of all persuasions, reminding them of Europe's enduring colonial legacy. For Arabs, as well as many non-Arab Muslims, Palestine represented yet another injustice perpetrated by colonial Europe against a vulnerable community. Ordinary Egyptians, fearing the Zionists' conquest of the land and its holy sites, identified with the Palestinians, with many volunteering to fight alongside them and die on the battlefield. Moreover, Egyptian dissidents and the opposition in general established from the beginning a link between emancipation from colonialism at home and the liberation of Palestine. Many were convinced that only once Egypt had broken its colonial chains would Palestine be freed.

Yet despite this, official Egyptian backing for the Palestinians was limited. Neither the mainstream political parties nor the Palace invested major social and material capital in the Palestinian question. In the 1920s Egyptian politicians focused more on the domestic political struggle which aimed at ending the lingering British presence than on the affairs of neighboring Arab and Islamic countries.[14] Thus the Egyptian government did not actively engage in Palestine in the 1920s, though it did more so in the 1930s.[15] In July 1938, "Wafdist youths held a meeting with Palestinian youths and adopted resolutions calling for Islamic and Arab unity on behalf of Palestine."[16] The Liberal Constitutionalists also developed a pro-Palestine stance. One of the party's leaders, Muhammad Hussein Haykal, chairman of the Egyptian Senate, warned in 1937 of "the inherent danger of setting up a Jewish state in Palestine."[17] Notwithstanding these pronouncements, the Egyptian ruling elite was too consumed by jockeying for political advantage at home to show interest or to fully engage in the Palestinian struggle. In his diaries, Haykal best explains the indecision and hesitance of the political elite towards the Palestinians:

> Politicians of Egypt of different partisan colours found in this negative position [towards Palestine] the apex of unparalleled wisdom. The problem of Egyptian-British relations and organising these relations required Egypt's full commitment and efforts. These efforts, if directed to Palestine or another issue, would weaken the Egyptian case for independence. Sa'ad Zaghloul Pasha and other politicians declared this position frankly.[18]

On the whole, the political ruling elite hoped to shield Egypt from contentious developments in Palestine and to prevent opposition groups from using the plight of the Palestinians as a weapon against the government. When in the 1920s protests erupted in Jerusalem between Arabs and Jews over the status of the Western Wall, the Liberal Constitutionalist government went as far as to censor anti-Zionist articles in the Egyptian press, lest the coverage inflame public opinion at home. Prime Minister Ismail Sidqi even ordered the expulsion of many Palestinians who had fled to Egypt following clashes in Palestine.[19]

Against this background, successive governments responded haphazardly or recklessly to unfolding events in Palestine, and took half measures that were designed to appease public sentiments at home and counterbalance other Arab states. At a time when the Egyptian public was enraged at the suggestion made by the British Peel Commission in 1937 that Palestine be partitioned, Prince Mohamed Ali, head of the Regency Council, avoided a confrontation with the British. Instead of taking a more active role and engaging directly with the Palestinians, the prince sent letters to the British Foreign Office and to the British high commissioner in Palestine suggesting that Britain establish an Arab-Jewish federation.[20]

Faced with the apathy and paralysis of the ruling political establishment on Palestine, a range of actors in Egyptian society, including Islamists, nationalists, feminists, student groups, writers, and young army officers, acted independently, rallying support for the Palestinians and exerting pressure on the government to do the same. The National Party, which was not part of the ruling political establishment, declared wholehearted support for the Palestinian cause and joined other groups in calling for a sixteen-hour strike in Alexandria on 16 September 1947, to protest the impending United Nations partition resolution. These groups also heeded a call by the Arab Higher Committee[21] to observe a general strike day throughout the Arab world on 3 October against the UN resolution. Crowds of youths filled al-Azhar mosque and whipped up popular support for the strike.

Among the most consistent champions of Palestinian rights was the Egyptian Feminist Union, led by Huda Sha'rawi in 1923, which focused on women's issues such as suffrage, education, and freedom of dress.[22] Sha'rawi and others subsequently extended their agenda to broader nationalist causes, including confronting the British occupation. When the first instance of serious Palestinian resistance materialized with the General Strike of 1936, the Feminist Union immediately called for public donations, and committees of women actively collected funds.[23] In addition, telegrams were sent to British officials and the League of Nations, and international women's organizations were contacted to join the Egyptians in condemning Zionist immigration to Palestine.[24]

The political establishment's failure to directly engage with the situation in Palestine created opportunities for the new, radical political actors that had appeared on the scene in Egypt. Young Egypt was among the first groups to call for the collection of private donations for the Palestinian national cause. The party also called for a boycott of Zionist goods and for the rejection of the Peel Commission's partition plan. The proposed partition, wrote the founder of Young Egypt, Ahmed Hussein, aimed at separating Arab countries from the rest of Asia in order to impede economic and cultural cooperation between Egypt and its neighbors.[25] When the UN voted in November 1947 to partition Palestine and establish a Jewish state there, Hussein called for the formation of armed groups to fight in Palestine. He even organized a brigade of volunteers staffed by his party that traveled to Syria as Palestine's first line of defense.[26]

More than any other opposition group, the Ikhwan spearheaded the fight in support of the Palestinian cause. The Ikhwan mobilized Egyptian public opinion against the Zionist threat and deployed their underground organization, al-Nizam al-Khass (the Secret Apparatus), as a weapon of choice in Palestine. Actively participating in the armed struggle in Palestine, the Muslim Brothers earned a reputation for steadfastness and courage. They collected aid for Palestinian victims and recruited fighters to travel to Palestine. The Secret Apparatus even attacked Jews and their businesses in Egypt, failing to distinguish between legitimate resistance and violent actions against civilians. Later, after the Secret Apparatus gained notoriety for terrorist attacks against Egyptian politicians and foreigners inside Egypt, top Ikhwan leaders asserted that the paramilitary organization had originally been founded to defend the Palestinians;[27] this was an acknowledgment of the significance of the Palestinian cause, although—as will be discussed later—there was much more to the establishment and expansion of the Secret Apparatus than the war for Palestine.

When Egypt did eventually take some more concrete steps with regard to Palestine, this was in large part a Palace-led attempt to outmaneuver radical groups such as the Ikhwan and Young Egypt because the king was keen to be seen as keeping pace with them.[28] Thus in 1946 the Palace called for a meeting of the Arab heads of state, after which it issued a communiqué robustly criticizing the recommendations that had been made that same year by the Anglo-American Committee of Inquiry regarding the acceleration of Jewish immigration to Palestine.[29] Farouk also ordered his minister of war, Mohamed Haydar, to prepare the army to enter Palestine. He did so without informing the prime minister, Mahmud Fahmi al-Nuqrashi, who initially had adamantly opposed Egypt's military intervention in Palestine.[30] The Egyptian leadership did not appreciate the strength of the Jewish armed forces although it had received several reports dispatched by the Egyptian consul in Jerusalem describing the organizational superiority of Jewish troops.[31] After Haydar received orders to send the army to Palestine, he naively told the cabinet that "the Egyptian military is capable on its own of occupying Tel Aviv, the capital of the Jews, in fourteen days, without assistance from the other Arab states."[32] Neglect, hubris, and ignorance were the hallmarks of the official Egyptian position towards Palestine, which exacted a heavy toll on the credibility and legitimacy of the constitutional order.

Moreover, following in the footsteps of his father, King Farouk dreamed of becoming the undisputed leader of the Muslim world. It is worth mentioning that Farouk's father, King Fu'ad, aspired to resurrect the caliphate and to anoint himself a caliph, thus playing a major role in convening the Cairo Conference of 1926 to make his dream come true. In a similar vein, King Farouk hoped to exploit the Palestinian cause as a means to advance his greater ambitions as an Arab and Islamic leader and to outmaneuver the kings of Transjordan and Saudi Arabia, who also vied for the same strategic prize. King Farouk feared the regional ambitions of King 'Abdullah of Transjordan, particularly his designs on Greater Syria, which included Lebanon and Arab Palestine. In fact, one of the major reasons behind Farouk's intervention in the 1948 Palestine War was his desire to "contain 'Abdullah and prevent him from gaining further influence and power in the Arab arena."[33]

Prime Minister Nuqrashi had both political and military reasons for opposing Farouk's decision to intervene militarily in Palestine. He argued that following a hoped-for British withdrawal from the Suez Canal Zone, Egypt should not reveal that it had a weak army through military intervention in the Palestine War.[34] In order to convince his prime minister of the merits of participation in the conflict, Farouk promised he could guarantee sufficient weapons, hinting that Britain would help in the provision of arms and ammunitions. These assurances made by the young Egyptian king—who was derisively referred to in official British correspondence as "the boy"—were baseless.[35]

The 1948 war in Palestine was disastrous, fueling anger and disillusionment with the Egyptian political establishment because it woefully exposed the weakness of the army and the lack of commitment to build an effective military institution. In a way, the king and the government committed political suicide by sending troops to Palestine knowing full well that the army was not equipped and prepared to do real battle. They underestimated the effects that the war would have on the psychology and imagination of young army officers who felt humiliated by irregular Jewish forces on the battlefield in Palestine. Before Egyptian troops had returned home, young army officers concluded that the real battle was inside Egypt, and they became more determined than ever to take ownership of their country. One of those soldiers in the Palestine war was Gamal Abdel Nasser.

Nasser and his peers directly experienced the reckless policies of the Egyptian political class with fatal consequences. After his return from Palestine, Nasser declared that his participation in the Palestine war had convinced him, together with his army comrades, that the "greatest jihad is in Egypt," not abroad.[36] For these young officers, to "save the homeland" from the grip of "wolves" became a personal mission and a strategic priority.[37] Many held both the monarchical regime and the British colonial power responsible for their humiliation at the hands of the newly born Jewish state. These nationalist officers, together with the Ikhwan and other radical activists, began to clandestinely plot to overthrow the British-backed monarchy. From the ultraright to the ultraleft, the opposition turned to subversive and revolutionary methods to topple the old regime. A critical point to highlight is that the interwar years witnessed the depoliticization of the political space by a shortsighted elite that focused more on capitalist modes of power and self-aggrandizement than on the aspirations, concerns, and will of the people. By not laying out a forward-looking, inclusive political vision, the governing establishment unwittingly created an ideological vacuum that was filled by underground, paramilitary groups. Constitutionalism lay in ruins.

Nasser and the Ikhwan in Collusion

Two groups in particular—the Ikhwan and disgruntled nationalist army officers—spearheaded plots against the monarchy and organized underground cells which colluded with one another. Although differences existed between Islamists and nationalists when pressed on questions of sovereignty—specifically the sovereignty of God versus that of the state—there was a striking resemblance between their ideas on such key issues as the role of the state, the nation or the *umma*, development and welfare, and political autonomy. They shared a similar social genealogy and class background, belonging mainly to the petite bourgeoisie and the aspiring middle classes, a rising social class aimed at capturing the state. The imagined differences between them were greatly outweighed by similarities and commonalities, particularly the struggle against both colonial control and the subservient monarchy. From the late 1940s until the early 1950s, Islamist activists and national army officers joined ranks in a successful campaign to rid Egypt of the liberal-leaning political establishment and the constitutional arrangement. Their interests momentarily converged and both bided their time, waiting for an opportune moment to strike a fatal blow to the old regime.

By the end of the 1940s, the Ikhwan had emerged as a formidable political and social movement. This was significantly aided by a vast expansion in membership and in finances, collected through membership fees, legacies, and the profits from the group's economic enterprises.[38] In his seminal work, *The Society of the Muslim Brothers*, Richard Mitchell notes that "it seems clear that the Society did receive contributions from wealthy or well-to-do Muslims who saw some value in its work."[39] Those contributors had political and economic interests in common with "the avowed aims of the Society itself, hostility to communism for instance."[40] Furthermore, the Ikhwan's *da'wa* (religious call) and their dissident message resonated among a pious middle class of merchants and urban artisans, chipping away at the social base of grand old parties like the Wafd. As its membership and societal presence increased, the Islamist organization's political appetite expanded.

Throughout the 1940s, Hassan al-Banna, the founder of the Ikhwan, labored hard to strengthen the organization and ensure that it was well positioned to defend itself in case of political repression at home and that it would have the capacity to go on the offensive if necessary. Banna had built the elite Secret Apparatus (al-Gihaz al-Khass or al-Nizam al-Khass), which he kept secret from his closest aides. Within it he had also established another unit called the Special Apparatus (al-Tanzim al-Khass), which comprised army officers who either belonged to the Ikhwan or shared commonalities with them.[41]

The Ikhwan, along with others in the broader Islamist movement at that time, invested considerable time and effort in the co-optation of army officers and the penetration of the military as an institution. Both mainstream and radical Islamist leaders considered a putsch by the military the most effective means to seize power and transform society. To deliver a decisive blow against their common enemy, the Ikhwan and the army conspirators needed each other. The Special Apparatus included dissident army officers from the Free Officers. At one point, members of the Special Apparatus also included such luminaries as Nasser himself and Anwar Sadat who swore *bay'a* (fealty) to Banna. As the architect of the Secret Apparatus, together with the Special Apparatus, Banna naturally expected the young army officers who joined its ranks to heed his orders.

The relationship between the Ikhwan and dissident army officers strengthened in the course of the Brothers' repeated clashes with the pre-1952 monarchical regime. In December 1948, Prime Minister Nuqrashi ordered that the Ikhwan be disbanded. The decision cost him his life when he was assassinated later that same month by a conspirator, a member of the Secret Apparatus. Although Banna denied any link or connection with the killing of Nuqrashi—asserting that "those who carried out the assassination are neither Brothers nor Muslims"—the die had already been cast for all-out confrontation between the Ikhwan and the authorities. One of the main responsibilities of Ibrahim Abdel Hadi, Nuqrashi's successor as premier, was to oversee the killing of Banna in revenge. Banna was assassinated in February of the following year, in an operation planned and carried out by the Iron Guard, a secretive body formed on the orders of King Farouk by his private physician, Yusuf Rashad, under the supervision of the commander of the ministers' guard, Muhammed Wasfi Bek.[42]

Far from isolated incidents, the assassinations of Nuqrashi and Banna occurred at a moment when both the Ikhwan and King Farouk were increasingly resorting to violence as a tactic for advancing their respective political projects. In addition to killing Banna, the king's Iron Guard had targeted other politicians, such as Amin Othman, who was assassinated in October 1944 in connection with his efforts to help bring the Wafd back to power.[43] Despite the killing of Banna, the Ikhwan persisted in their efforts to fill the power vacuum left by the failure of the king and the dysfunctional political process led mainly by the Wafd, which remained the most popular party despite growing public disillusionment with its performance. The Ikhwan pursued a successful lawsuit that resulted in the cancellation of the order to disband their movement. Since the interior minister had the power to veto and overrule the legal finding in their favor, the Ikhwan also launched a public relations campaign to ensure that there could be no objection to the court ruling.[44] Interior Minister Fuad Serajeddin—an influential voice within the Wafd and a confidant of its leader, Mustafa Nahhas—agreed to the revocation of the order disbanding the Ikhwan on the basis of a pragmatic calculation. He hoped to use the Ikhwan to counterbalance the rising influence of the communists and to play the two dissident groups off against each other: Preoccupied with battling one another in the streets, the Ikhwan and the communists would be distracted from devoting important resources to attacking the government.[45] The Wafdist administration in power at that time agreed to coexist with the Ikhwan.

The nationalist army officers looked to the Ikhwan for support because of its large power base and because both shared a strategic goal of independence from colonial hegemony. The young officers viewed the Islamists as natural allies in the nationalist struggle for liberation and recognized their ability to field an effective fighting force if and when the need arose. They were impressed with the Ikhwan's military performance and daring during the Palestine war, as well as their armed resistance against British troops in the Suez Canal Zone. As will be explored further in subsequent chapters, this brief flirtation between the Ikhwan and the army officers accelerated the overthrow of the monarchy in 1952.

Built on a fragile foundation, the constitutional order disintegrated entirely that year, beginning with a fire that burned Cairo on 26 January 1952, including hundreds of luxury establishments that were symbols of European power, and then the July coup which put an end to the monarchy. As the old order collapsed, its foreign masters displayed a remarkable degree of weakness. After the Cairo fire, the king urged the American ambassador to Egypt, Jefferson Caffery, to intervene and "put the brakes" on any attempt by Britain to intervene militarily in Cairo and the Delta.[46] At the same time the king called for British and American intervention to prevent the coup. Once the coup occurred, Farouk insisted that the U.S. ambassador guarantee his safety and accompany him while he left Egypt.[47] In broad terms, the coup marked the rise of American political influence at the expense of the enervated British power.

Both the Free Officers who carried out the putsch and the Ikhwan who backed it claimed its leadership and ownership of the revolution. Nevertheless, the removal of the liberal-leaning political establishment paved the way for the rise of a new nationalist and Islamist elite, which had a radically different worldview and sensibility from that of its predecessor. In contrast to the old regime, this nativist elite—which encompassed nationalists, Islamists, and leftists alike—prioritized decolonization, social justice and development, and communitarianism rather than individual freedoms and constitutional rights. The new nativist elite resented the unholy alliance between foreign power and capital, on the one hand, and the ruling political class at home, on the other, and wanted to seize the state to ensure a clean break with the past. Driven by resentment and ambition, the first priority of the Free Officers and their allies was to rid Egypt of the old regime—its ideology, symbols, institutions, and power structures—and replace it with a nativist government. A reinvigorated deep state would spearhead national renewal, independence, and modernization. The constitutional arrangement would be replaced with a revolutionary order that dispensed with checks and balances, or legal and institutional requirements. The 1952 coup was also about restoring the army's power, prestige, and credibility after its humiliation in Palestine in 1948 and its subsequent emasculation by the British-dominated monarchy.[48] There is no wonder that by 1954, as will be shown in chapters 2 and 3, the Free Officers had "crushed or froze every political opposition in the country and moved towards a military dictatorship."[49]

For the Ikhwan, the coup brought them a step closer towards realizing Banna's dream of reconstructing a new state in which the Islamic law would be the law of the land, as it had been in the early days of Islam.[50] The different projects of those two movements reflect the unresolved dichotomies between self/other, state/people, and public/private that were inscribed at the heart of the imagination and actualization of the political community during Britain's occupation of the country.

Chapter 3

The Free Officers and the Ikhwan

AFTER NASSER AND THE Free Officers came to power in 1952, they set about consolidating their grip on the reins of government. The military junta initially maintained cordial relations with the Ikhwan. Far from being diametrically opposed, the Islamist movement and the Free Officers who carried out the coup had much in common and might easily have found ways of cooperating in governance. Most importantly, both movements stood united in their aspirations for an independent Egypt, their disillusionment with the political establishment, and their opposition to British occupation. Beyond these practical considerations, however, the Free Officers and the Muslim Brothers, along with the nationalist movement at large, never reached a consensus on a common and inclusive vision of what postcolonial Egypt would be. Distrust and enmity between the two groups surfaced immediately in the aftermath of the Free Officers' coup, not before. Although there had existed ideological differences between the two movements, they came to blows over questions of power and decision making. In particular, it was the stubbornness and miscalculation on the part of the Ikhwan leadership and their refusal to act as a junior partner in a coalition with Nasser that led to the breakdown of their relationship.

In addition, the increasing acrimony between Nasser and Hassan al-Banna's successor, Hassan al-Hudaybi, as well as the internal divergences within both camps, fed the split further. As the rift between the two groups deepened, Nasser struggled to establish his dominance first over competitors within the military and then against other rivals across the political spectrum. Only then did Egypt's new military leader take advantage of this newfound stability to move against the Ikhwan and try to crush the Islamist movement by imprisoning thousands of Ikhwan members, including its top leaders. In charting stage by stage the evolution of the relationship between the Free Officers and the Muslim Brothers from 1952 onwards, it becomes apparent that realpolitik and the thirst for power and recognition, not ideology, are the source of the decades-long conflict that has continued to shape the identity of the postcolonial, post-independence state in much of the Arab world.

The Free Officers: Lack of a Revolutionary Road Map

On 23 July 1952, a covert military formation known as the Free Officers led a successful coup and overthrew a monarchy that was increasingly seen across the country as a colonial pawn. While they managed to seize power with relative ease, Nasser and his army comrades had no preconceived master plan beyond this point. The lack of a clear and established post-coup strategy was confirmed by Mohamed Hassanein Heikal, a journalist who subsequently became Nasser's confidant and the official chronicler of his rule. Having spent countless hours with Nasser and other Free Officers immediately after the coup, Heikal said that although the young army men were motivated and quick learners, they lacked a road map and were "clueless" about the future; although the Free Officers had no detailed agenda, the 23 July coup gradually transformed into a thoroughgoing revolution. The coup had been a success but the revolution now needed to take form. Nasser in particular was determined to set out a clear plan for the revolution: "Nasser was keen to chart a blueprint, a vision, for the future," Heikal told me.[1] He recounted how they had brainstormed together about the philosophy of the revolution and the road ahead. Heikal had previously insinuated that he was the man behind Nasser's *Philosophy of the Revolution*,[2] but when pressed on the issue, he said he only helped Nasser organize his thoughts and craft the narrative. On his ninetieth birthday in 2013, Heikal left no doubt about the lack of theoretical grounding of the Free Officers' revolution, telling a journalist that it "had had no programme at all. There was a dream to remove the royal ruler [the king] on the basis that he is the root of all evils, and the rest was transcendental hopes."[3]

Recently released official British and American documents also show that indecision was clear from the first day of the coup. The solitary goal of coup leaders was to "cleanse the army" of corrupt officers,[4] but that was where the consensus ended. Even when faced with the key question of whether or not the incumbent prime minister should resign, Mohammed Naguib, the nominal head of the Free Officers movement, showed uncertainty and hesitancy.[5] With each passing day after the coup, the junta's demands expanded from initially securing the resignation of the king's corrupt associates to overthrowing the king himself.[6] Thus, what primarily united the Free Officers was strong nationalist sentiment and the desire to take control of the country and increase its regional role. However, once they had seized power a bitter struggle between Naguib, the formal leader of the Officers, and Nasser, the informal mastermind of the coup, threatened to rip the military formation apart. The aim had by then moved to a new goal: consolidating the power of the revolutionary command. One question remained unanswered, however: around what ethos would this new revolutionary command articulate itself?

Although it took the Free Officers a while to put their house in order and consolidate their authority following the coup, the ethos of the new revolutionary order rapidly became clear—top-down and authoritarian. In the aftermath of the coup, unity gave way to distrust and military games were replaced by political ones. After a rocky and uncertain start, Nasser emerged as the strongman, and with methodological precision, he moved to neutralize his rivals and opponents both within and outside the Free Officers movement. Whatever their long-term goals with regard to securing Egypt's independence from colonial domination and its place in the Arab world, prominent Free Officers led by Nasser were concerned primarily with consolidating their power and control. Nasser first favored the consolidation of military rule and the purging of the old regime's representatives, large landowners, bankers and businessmen, and their foreign allies. Egyptian critics contend that the Free Officers movement was self-enclosed and secretive, an extension of communitarian and identity politics that emerged in the 1930s and dominated the scene in the 1940s. "The Free Officers inherited the Royal Sarayya,"[7] asserted cultural critic and historian Sherif Younis.[8] In a way, the monarchy was not structurally overthrown because the Free Officers embraced its underground, paramilitary autocratic culture, Younis pointed out. Sociologically, noted the young Egyptian critic, no rupture existed between the old regime and the new regime.

As Nasser and his followers started to move decisively against forces within the military, the autocratic culture gradually came to dominate the Free Officers group. From then on, Free Officers who were seen as a threat to Nasser and his followers would be targeted. Many members of the formation held diverse views on key issues, and the question of the role that the military ought to play in Egypt's political life proved particularly divisive. While one camp wanted the military to surrender power to an elected civilian government and return to its barracks, another insisted it ought to directly guide the transition to a new order. According to Khaled Mohieddin, one of the Free Officers and a friend of Nasser's, there was no consensus on how to proceed, especially with regard to the extent of the social and political transformation that ought to be undertaken. While it has often been said that Nasser rapidly managed to muster a clear majority on his side and that dissenters were a tiny minority, Mohieddin refrains from making such a clear-cut division.[9]

Caught up in internal rivalries and power-consolidation tactics, the new leaders of Egypt failed to establish a clearly defined vision for the country's post-coup political regime. The lack of ideological grounding and set principles around which the new political order ought to be built proved problematic and, here again, exposed the heterogeneity of the military revolutionaries. The main ideological schism among the Free Officers has often been described as one between a democratic camp led by Naguib and an anti-democratic one led by Nasser, but it is important to stress that neither of them was interested in democratization. Despite their respective revolutionary and conservative stances, Nasser and Naguib were not ideologically different from one another. Nasser's close allies testify that he did not believe in democracy. Rather he aimed to establish a dictatorship under his control that would allow him to engineer social reforms and change.

Time and again in the course of this research project I was told by his former close allies among the Free Officers that Nasser was not a democrat and had never claimed to be one. He had been socialized into an underground, authoritarian culture, and believed that liberal capitalist democracy, synonymous with European colonialism, was unsuitable for Egypt. Given the dismal social conditions in the country, he was convinced that local and foreign capital would purchase votes and hijack the revolution. Although Nasser called for fundamental changes in Egypt's social and political system, Naguib did not put up stiff resistance to land reform, a priority for Nasser and the Free Officers.[10] Moreover, Naguib did little to push for a democratic system. For example, although in February 1953 he promised to hold elections, in January 1954, he issued a statement announcing the disbanding of all political parties and confiscation of their properties and funds. He justified his decision by saying that the parties were creating dissent, collaborating with foreign governments, and misusing freedom by turning it into chaos and partisan politics.[11] He also reinstated the press censorship that had been lifted in August 1952 and announced a three-year transitional period from the military to a civilian government, thus postponing the transfer of power to civilian authority. In fact, there were hardly any democrats among the Free Officers. The Free Officers acted systematically to dismantle the multiparty system and the power structure of the old regime, such as the passage of Qanoun Tanzim al-Ahzab (the Law for the Organization of Political Parties), formalized by the cabinet on 9 September 1952. Although they had promised that the party law would be judicially executed under the supervision of the State Council, they never respected their pledge.[12] In his autobiography, Naguib laments that decision by the State Council as marking a descent toward political authoritarianism, and he acknowledges that the law was designed to disinherit the old social classes and liquidate political rivals, particularly the Wafd, which remained the biggest and most popular political party.[13] Upheld by the State Council, this law went into effect even though Yusuf Siddiq and Khaled Mohieddin, two members of the Revolutionary Command Council (RCC), opposed it.[14] A week after dissolving all political parties, the RCC formed Hay'at al-Tahrir (Liberation Rally), a propaganda outfit designed to act as an alternative to the disbanded traditional parties, or a framework for political action. In reality, Hay'at al-Tahrir embodied an early attempt by the Free Officers to found a vanguard one-party system.[15] Formally headed by Naguib and dominated by military figures, especially those officers who had experience with political action, the Liberation Rally attracted disgruntled members of other parties and demagogues who joined for ulterior motives. Although Naguib was the rally's top figurehead, Nasser was the power broker and driver behind it.[16]

Far from focusing on building a freer political space and reforming institutions, the Free Officers' priorities lay instead in decolonization, independence, and tackling the huge social and economic inequities that existed in Egypt, especially in the rural areas. Although they disagreed about who should be in charge and about the extent to which it was necessary to purge the country of the old classes, empowerment, social development, and land reforms, not liberalization, were the common denominators within their ranks. This change was evident in the interim constitution proclaimed on February 10, 1953, which avoided mention of all the checks and balances of the preceding, mostly liberal constitution of 1923. According to professor of law

Tharwat Badawy, the most remarkable feature of the new constitution was "bringing legislative and executive powers into one hand, and freeing [this hand] from all restrictions so that it could act freely and easily to realize the goals of the revolution."[17] Thus while the Free Officers had a vision of the society they wanted to establish, one where social justice, equality, and dignity would prevail, their vision was not anchored in a set of ideological principles. As a result, the revolutionary command failed to break away from the authoritarianism and political asphyxiation that characterized the colonial regime, and just like its predecessor, it became dominated by power politics and internal struggle.

The Naguib-Nasser Struggle: Realpolitik and the Quest for Power

As dissension continued to grow and threaten the new revolutionary command, Naguib and Nasser's relationship continued its downward spiral. A biographer of Nasser narrates the evolving personal and professional rivalry between Nasser and Naguib: "The man who personified the revolution and who had the people behind him stood for nothing. But sensing his strength on the street level and the consequent weakness of Nasser and his young comrades, Naguib tried to get rid of them."[18] The two leaders' intense rivalry divided members of the Free Officers into camps supporting one or the other, which eventually led to deep internal rifts. One key instance of intra-army struggles occurred in January 1953 when the RCC announced the detention of thirty-five officers from the artillery regiment who stood accused of a conspiracy against the new regime.[19] Hurriedly set up, a revolutionary court swiftly convicted the detained officers and imprisoned them. They were released in March 1954 in order to put down another alleged revolt mounted by the cavalry regiment which sided with Naguib against Nasser in their power struggle. Leading Free Officers fought bitterly against one another and co-opted military comrades in an effort to tip the balance of forces in their favor. Historian Ahmed Hamroush, a former Free Officer himself, points out that although calls for democracy were a rallying cry in the internal infighting among the Free Officers, the struggle was mostly about power and personality.[20] As the internal power struggle became fierce, the RCC was ruthless in clamping down on rivals. The words of one officer, Mohamed Hegazi, who had confronted Nasser during a stormy meeting with the Fursan officers, or cavalry, and who had opposed extending the transitional period of army rule, proved prophetic:

> The constitution is suspended. The Parliament is suspended, public rights are restricted, the press is under censorship, the Revolutionary Council unanimously takes over authority without consulting with anyone. No one even consults with the Free Officers who made this revolution. This means that we are on the road to military dictatorship.[21]

Those within the military who felt the wrath of the new regime included some of its erstwhile closest allies. For example, Colonel Yusuf Siddiq, who had himself been hailed for his pivotal role in the success of the Free Officers coup, was targeted together with his supporters for calling for the return of the army to its barracks and the revival of parliamentary life. Subsequently, Siddiq resigned from the RCC in February 1953 and lived in exile in Switzerland.[22] After he secretly returned to Egypt in August that year, he was summarily put under house arrest. In March 1954 he wrote an open letter to Naguib asking him to form a coalition government which would be entrusted with organizing new parliamentary elections, but this did little to improve his situation. He was detained for a year in a military prison, then held under house arrest along with his wife for two years.[23] Gamal Hammad, who had written the first post-coup Free Officers statement, subsequently asserted that Siddiq had "paid a heavy price" merely for "supporting democracy."[24] Democracy or not, Siddiq was not the only officer to be persecuted for airing a viewpoint in opposition to Nasser's. Another member of the Free Officers, Ahmed Shawqi, second-highest-ranking officer after Naguib, was sentenced to ten years in prison after publishing a newspaper article in March 1954 in which he scathingly accused the RCC of dictatorship and interfering in politics. He concluded his piece with the terse instruction, "Go [back] to your barracks." As a result, Shawqi was put on trial before Mahkamat al-Thawra (the Court of the Revolution), which lasted from October 1953 until April 1954, on charges of "causing *fitna* [dissent] in the army and putting the *watan* [the nation] in danger."[25] Officers perceived as rivals of the RCC faced detention and exile and torture as well. For example, Hosni al-Damanhouri was severely tortured by RCC member Salah Salim after he had been falsely accused of sowing strife within the military.[26] "We became like fish eating each other," confesses Naguib in his memoirs, a symbolically accurate description of this early phase of the military regime.[27]

Eventually, in 1954, having moved against comrades who disagreed with the way he controlled the RCC and who sided with Naguib, Nasser took steps to expel the president. Naguib meanwhile did not intend to go down without a fight and established contact with the Ikhwan in a bid to outmaneuver the young colonel. While the Ikhwan and the Free Officers had established contact and cooperated in the months leading up to the coup, their relationship had rapidly deteriorated after the officers seized power. The Ikhwan had hoped to have a political role in the aftermath of the coup but had found themselves increasingly marginalized by Nasser and his supporters. With Naguib they had now found an unlikely ally. The general and the Islamist group shared a hatred of communism and socialism in general.[28] Moreover, the interests of both converged: the Ikhwan thought that Naguib would be easier to deal with than the shrewd and aggressive Nasser, while Naguib recognized the power base of the Ikhwan and their ability to mobilize the streets. From 1953 until early 1954, members of the Ikhwan sided with pro-Naguib protesters, who battled Nasser's followers on an almost daily basis throughout the country. Naguib also sought the support of the Wafd and met with Mustafa Nahhas, who had been granted amnesty on the understanding that he would undertake no political activity.[29]

Infuriated by Naguib's treachery, Nasser tried to neutralize his elderly rival. According to Ahmed Hamroush, a member of the

RCC even suggested that Naguib be assassinated, though the idea was struck down after Abdel Latif al-Baghdadi, an influential Free Officer, voiced his objection.[30] In February 1954, army units loyal to Nasser put Naguib under house arrest after he resigned from the RCC because of insults, harassment, and marginalization by Nasser's allies.[31] As massive pro-Naguib protests broke out in the streets of Cairo, facing off against pro-Nasser demonstrators who were fewer in number, the cavalry rebelled. The RCC backpedaled and reinstated Naguib in March. In a countermove, Nasser promptly appointed himself prime minister and his closest ally, Abdel Hakim Amer, commander of the armed forces. As new rounds of demonstrations resumed, the RCC accepted a "democratic transition."[32] Although Nasser issued the "March 25" declaration advocating the return of the army to its barracks, he filled the cabinet with reliable members of the RCC.[33]

Naguib proved to be no match for the steely Nasser, who bided his time and awaited an opportune moment to deliver a decisive blow. Mobilizing his allies within the RCC and the trade unions and temporarily making amends with the Ikhwan, as will be discussed further below, he eventually subdued Naguib and had him put under house arrest once again. This signaled the beginning of Nasser's hegemonic moment. He had not only defeated his main rival but had also sidelined other officers who objected to his dictatorial ways. By 1954, after a two-year struggle, Nasser had firmly asserted his control of the RCC.

In my two lengthy interviews with him in 2006, Khaled Mohieddin described a driven and paranoid leader who systematically removed rivals from positions of authority, as well as officers who disagreed with him. Mohieddin, who died in May 2012, was one of them. "Nasser did not tolerate any person who could threaten his hold on power," he told me.[34] It had taken two messy years for Nasser to rid himself of imagined and real rivals within the officer corps and to place his own supporters and protégés within the RCC and key army units. He had also used those two years to hone his voice, to distinguish himself from his fellow officers, and to ingratiate himself with the Egyptian public. On more than one occasion, he nearly lost his equilibrium and had to recalibrate his tactics in order to keep his opponents at bay. He could easily have lost the struggle and been put under house arrest himself or even killed. However, he was shrewder and luckier than those around him and the intra-army struggles only emboldened him and strengthened his resolve. With each crisis, Nasser emerged more determined than ever to reshape Egypt in his own image and to sideline his detractors and critics. In my conversations with his close friends and allies among the Free Officers, they recalled how they had been surprised by his single-mindedness, doggedness, and will to dominate. He kept his cards close to his chest and outmaneuvered friends and foes alike.

In addition to carrying out these intra-army purges, the leading Free Officers sought to tear down the old regime and clamp down on rivals from across the political spectrum. From the outset, Nasser knew that he would face resistance and opposition from the old social classes and their allies, who were deeply entrenched in the state apparatus. He became convinced that the Free Officers would not be able to carry out their revolution and transform Egypt without breaking up the power structure of these classes and dismantling their networks and institutions. Consequently, the RCC acted swiftly against the centers of power and figureheads of the old regime, appropriating their wealth and assets and proscribing their participation in the political space. Leading politicians of the old regime who had not fled the country were incarcerated and tried in military courts with minimal due process. In September 1952, for example, military police arrested forty-three figures associated with the old order, including Naguib al-Hilali, who was prime minister on the night of the July 23, 1952, coup, as well as his interior minister, Murtada al-Maraghi. Other prominent detainees included Ibrahim 'Abd al-Hadi, the leader of the influential al-Hayaa al-Sa'diyya party.[35] The Revolutionary Tribunal sentenced 'Abd al-Hadi to death in October 1953 on charges of "betraying the homeland and the principle of the revolution by deliberately communicating with foreign bodies for the purpose of harming the regime and the supreme interests of the country."[36]

Although the sentence was subsequently reduced to life imprisonment by Naguib, who was then president, the court issued another five death sentences, of which three were subsequently carried out. Other senior politicians who were detained by the regime included six Wafdist leaders led by Fuad Serajeddin, a confidant of the party's spiritual leader, Mustafa Nahhas. Members of Rejaal al-Sarayya (Men of the Palace), who worked closely with the king, were also detained, including King Farouk's press officer, Kareem Thabet; the head of the royal court, Hafiz Afifi; and Abbas Helmi and Said Haleem, who were members of the royal family. Meanwhile, Nahhas was put under house arrest together with his wife, facing charges of espionage, dealing with foreign powers, and spreading false rumors about the new military authorities.[37] Again the trials of these politicians of the old regime all lacked due process. They were held behind closed doors and the charges were read to the defendant for the first time with no legal investigation or inquiry.[38] Ahmed Hamroush, the official chronicler of the July 23, 1952 coup, noted that the Qur'anic verse gracing the door of the courtroom said: "And kill them wherever you overtake them."[39] This verse, whose remaining part is "and expel them from wherever they have expelled you," clearly shows the trials were an act of revenge against the old guard. Hamroush agrees that these trials, in which only the prosecutors and the accused were allowed to attend, "targeted the Wafd and the other political parties and groupings."[40]

Led by Nasser, the RCC also targeted the institutional backbone of the old regime, particularly the judiciary and the bureaucracy, systematically replacing independent judges and technocrats with army officers or other pliant and loyal individuals. The most publicized clash occurred between the RCC and a prominent, pioneering lawmaker, Abd al-Razzaq al-Sanhouri, who had generally supported the Free Officers and had been on good terms with them. Sanhouri hated the Wafd and had even convinced the Free Officers that the party would win the next elections, thereby preventing them from carrying out the fundamental change they so wanted.[41] Things took a turn for the worse, however, when the lawmaker's criticism targeted the military regime. He criticized the Free Officers' abolition of the 1923 constitution, which he defended as being more democratic in essence, and expressed opposition to other subsequent autocratic measures enacted by the Free Officers. Just like the Wafdists, Sanhouri would now pay the cost of his affront, which earned him the officers' wrath and abuse. In a violent scene that symbolized a direct and sustained attack on the judiciary and the institutional fabric of society, thugs beat up Sanhouri and humiliated him before his colleagues in daylight, a development etched in public memory as marking a rupture with the old institutions and ways of doing things.[42]

The Free Officers and the Ikhwan: A Struggle for Power

In sharp contrast with the old regime, the Free Officers initially took a relatively conciliatory attitude towards the Ikhwan. Yet, although the two factions had worked together in the years leading up to the coup, their collaboration did not survive the Free Officers' seizure of power. Each camp had different agendas and goals. Hudaybi and his advisers wanted to have a significant say in decision making and demanded that the Free Officers grant them a veto over pivotal decisions. "Hudaybi thought that Nasser and other officers were his boys because they had sworn *bay'a* [fealty] to al-Banna and were members of al-Nizam al-Khass," a senior Ikhwan member in the know confided. "We naively believed we owned the revolution. We could guide these inexperienced young officers and show them the right way."[43] On the contrary, Nasser had no interest in sharing power, either with the Ikhwan or with other political groups, especially the former, who, in his view, threatened his political ambitions and weakened his hold on the reins of power. Given their will to power and clashing interests, the Ikhwan and the Free Officers were bound to come to blows in a power struggle which would pivot on the issue of authority, not ideology.[44] "Hudaybi and his inner circle could have postponed the inevitable by bending with the powerful wind and swimming with the storm," said senior al-Nizam al-Khass commander Mahmoud al-Sabbagh, who was part of al-Nizam's inner circle. "But they miscalculated by underestimating Nasser and the young officers and overestimating their own strength."[45]

The important meetings the two camps held in preparation for the coup on July 18 and 19, 1952, attest to their divergences. Representing the Free Officers were Nasser and Abdel Hakim Amer, while Salah Shadi, Abdel Qader Helmi, and Hassan Ashmawi were there for the Ikhwan.[46] In the first meeting, on July 18, Nasser and Amer updated Shadi, Helmi, and Ashmawi on the coup and only spoke in general terms, providing minimal details, while asking for the Ikhwan's support for the putsch, including their members in the army. The meeting left the Ikhwan delegation divided over whether they should support the officers. As they left the meeting, Helmi, Shadi, and Ashmawi voiced conflicting views:

> Abdel Qader (Helmi): You should know, Salah, that we are not part of them [the Free Officers].
>
> Salah (Shadi): They [the Free Officers] are the ones who are part of us [the Ikhwan].
>
> Abdel Qader (Helmi): Why can't we act as two separate parties and cooperate?[47]

The conversation exemplifies the confusion and uncertainty that the Ikhwan felt about their relationship with the Free Officers, and particularly Nasser. Ikhwan officials offer different takes on Nasser, contradicting each other and exposing the existence of rival centers of power within the Islamist organization. In my many interviews with Muslim Brothers who were contemporaries of Nasser, the fervor displayed by the pro-Nasser and anti-Nasser camps was surprising, even though the latter held a decisive majority. The Ikhwan were split between those who mistrusted Nasser and the Free Officers in general, including Hudaybi, the supreme guide, and those who sought to outmaneuver the young officers and wield power from behind the scenes. A minority in the paramilitary wing known as al-Nizam al-Khass or the Secret Apparatus lobbied hard to join the Nasser caravan and reserve a front seat in the nascent political order. For example, Salah Shadi asserts that Nasser was an active member of the Ikhwan and that his Free Officers group had been first founded as an affiliate of the paramilitary Ikhwan network, al-Gihaz al-Khass, in the army.[48]

Meanwhile, Hussein Hamouda, an Ikhwan member of the Free Officers, claims that most of the ninety-nine Free Officers were Ikhwan.[49] The reality is more complex than this one-sided narrative, however. The Free Officers numbered between 290 and 340, and many were former members of the Ikhwan, including Nasser and Mohieddin, who had quit the organization between 1947 and 1950 over ideological differences and conflict over strategic priorities. But Hussein al-Shafei, a Free Officer who participated in the coup, argued that the Ikhwan's support to the Free Officers was minimal.[50] While there is room for debate between these two positions, it is certainly the case that several members of the Special Apparatus (al-Tanzim al-Khass) were involved in the 1952 coup. After his return from Palestine in the late 1940s, Nasser distanced himself from the Ikhwan's Special Apparatus and dedicated himself to building up the Free Officers movement as his own underground network within the military, known as Tanzim al-Dubat al-Ahrar. This separation was strategic because he believed that establishing an underground group in the military would bring together members with a broader range of religious and political affiliations, including independents, socialists, and communists such as Yusuf Siddiq. Nasser no longer needed the Ikhwan's paramilitary network to do his bidding. He kept tight control over the army conspirators, including officers who belonged to the Ikhwan, and did not reveal his game plan to his former allies, despite preserving his clandestine links with them. The ambitious young colonel became the driver behind a new conspiracy to overthrow the status quo.

The Ikhwan never forgave Nasser for what they viewed as deceptive and treacherous behavior on his part. "Nasser used and abused the Ikhwan for his own selfish interests," said the senior Ikhwan leader Farid Abdel Khaleq, giving voice to widespread sentiments among the organization's base. "He not only violated his *bay'a* to the

Ikhwan but also hijacked the Free Officers movement and eliminated officers who belonged to the Islamist group. Nasser leveled everything that stood in his way to capture power."[51] Abdel Khaleq's opinion is a mild indictment of Nasser, who is vilified in much stronger terms by hardliners for reneging on his oath and stabbing the movement in the heart.

Immediately after Nasser and the Free Officers carried out the coup in July 1952, Ikhwan leaders considered Nasser one of their own. In their first meeting with Nasser, top Ikhwan leaders, including Supreme Guide Hudaybi, discovered to their dismay that Nasser was his own man, ambitious and unwilling to defer to their authority. From the outset, the old men of the Ikhwan were fooled by Nasser, a junior officer who brilliantly manipulated both friends and foes in order to dominate decision making. In his early encounters with Ikhwan figures after the coup, Nasser insisted he was only prepared to include them as junior partners in the cabinet, without the veto power over pivotal decisions that Hudaybi had demanded. Nasser, together with the Free Officers, was determined to concentrate power in his own hands and exclude potential rivals, particularly the Ikhwan with its significant social base and potent paramilitary force. Political mistrust between Nasser and the Ikhwan developed shortly after the coup, deepening and widening in the year that followed. When Nasser did eventually split with the Islamist group once and for all in 1954, the Ikhwan framed his actions as duplicitous. In numerous interviews, the Ikhwan chiefs all expressed resentment of Nasser for stabbing the movement in the back and betraying his oath of *bay'a* to Banna. "Nasser was a traitor who violated his *bay'a* to the martyr al-Banna and sold his soul to Caesar on the altar of his political ambitions," said Abdullah Rashwan, the Ikhwan's legal counselor who represented top Islamist lieutenants both in the courts of the monarchical regime and in those of Nasser, Sadat, and Mubarak. "Nasser repressed the Ikhwan in order to monopolize power in his own hands at the cost of displeasing God and his Prophet."[52]

In contrast, Nasser and his comrades denied the Ikhwan's assertion and insisted that the group's role in the coup was minor. The

Muslim Brothers subsequently used their limited connection with the Free Officers to try to hijack "our revolution," some of Nasser's comrades said. Analyzing the claims by both sides, Zuheir Mardini, an independent researcher, notes that Nasser had informed the Ikhwan about the coup's timing and the master plot as well as future plans to dissolve the constitution, hold general elections, and abolish the monarchy.[53] In addition, following the repressive legal moves against political parties in September 1952, Nasser took the Ikhwan Supreme Guide Hudaybi to meet Interior Minister Sulayman Hafiz in order to find a "legal way out" to avoid imposing draconian measures on the movement.[54] During the meeting the two camps agreed on a "way out" and the Ikhwan avoided being subjected to the same legal restrictions which had been placed on all other political parties. The Free Officers did not have a social base of their own and they hoped to utilize the organized networks of the Islamist movement to fill the vacuum of public support. In a similar vein, the Ikhwan led by Hudaybi endeavored to climb to power on the shoulders of the Free Officers.

From the onset, then, each of the two camps was interested in using the other for accessing power. In this sense, the relationship was doomed to fail. As Tewfick Aclimandos, who has extensively researched this chapter of relations between the Ikhwan and the Free Officers from the late 1940s until the early 1950s, explains: "Confrontation was inevitable because both sides had differing agendas and priorities and there existed no trust between them. The odds were against coexistence because the seeds of conflict had existed before the coup, though both needed each other and avoided a confrontation at all costs."[55] Once Nasser had rid himself of Naguib and other rivals among the Free Officers, he turned his full attention to this key political rival. Compared with elements of the old regime like the Wafd, the Ikhwan presented Nasser with a more daunting challenge and a more significant threat to his political ambitions. Long before the coup, Nasser and other Free Officers were shocked by the Ikhwan's backing for the unpopular Ismail Sidqi government because, in the words of Khaled Mohieddin, that showed "they are double-faced, double-tongued, and untrustworthy."[56] Nevertheless, Nasser was willing to co-opt the Ikhwan and accommodate them in the nascent military regime as long as they played by his rules.

In later years, both the Ikhwan and Nasser framed their clash in ideological terms. The Ikhwan retrospectively accused Nasser of authoritarianism and portrayed themselves as victims and defenders of pluralism and constitutionalism. Nasser, on the other hand, claimed that Hudaybi had demanded that the new government intervene in the citizens' private lives and impose a strict moral code consistent with Islamic norms. Following his split with the Ikhwan, Nasser also accused them of using religion as "a means to deceive people" and would label them traitors and collaborators "with backwardness," a reference to the Saudi regime, which he accused of using religion as a political tool against secular Arab nationalism.[57] Hussein al-Shafei, a member of the nine-member Free Officers Command, which formed the RCC, suggested in retrospect that the biggest mistake of the Ikhwan was that they had sought to establish a monopoly over the true meaning of Islam and to define who is a real Muslim.[58]

However, such ideologically framed narratives of the clash were in fact largely propagandistic and mythmaking. Both Nasser and the Ikhwan were more concerned with scoring political points against each other than with critically and faithfully taking stock of the past. Both overlooked the tensions and contradictions that had existed within their own ranks and the mutual interests that had existed between their two respective camps. The ideological fault lines between the Ikhwan and the Free Officers were initially blurred. Both had similar social origins and shared a common goal of dismantling the old semi-liberal-leaning regime and replacing it with political authoritarianism. The two camps saw eye to eye on the fundamental question of doing away with constitutionalism and excluding the former political establishment from politics. Although there had existed divergences between the two camps in terms of outlook, political priorities, goals, and even agenda, these were not very pronounced and they had common foes. Both viewed the political in terms of black and white, right and wrong, anointing themselves as overseer to rid the country of traitors and evildoers. They saw themselves as historical agents with a divine mission to rescue Egypt and change the course of history. Their blind ambition ultimately pitted them against each other in a brutal power struggle, a struggle that spiraled out of control in 1954.

For all their subsequent efforts to portray themselves as defenders of pluralism and victims of Nasser's authoritarianism, the Ikhwan had initially been quite prepared to cooperate with the Free Officers as long as it seemed to be in their interest to do so. Their conduct after the coup raises many questions about their supposed commitment to an open society and democratic politics. Far from defending political diversity and inclusiveness, the Ikhwan backed the abolition of the 1923 constitution and sided with the military in its suppression of suspected dissidents. Initially, they partnered with the Free Officers to cleanse the system of the old political classes and to divide the spoils between themselves. According to Khaled Mohieddin, who was a member of the RCC, in the immediate wake of the coup the Ikhwan encouraged the military officers to stay in power and to abolish the parliamentary system. By removing rivals from the political process, the Ikhwan hoped to "contain the revolution and steer it according to their own ambitions," Mohieddin noted in his memoirs.[59] Hussein al-Shafei, another member of the RCC, points out that the Free Officers had to act swiftly to prevent the Ikhwan from seizing "custody of the revolution" and "grabbing power." "The revolution has the right to preserve itself," stated Shafei.[60] Depicting the power struggle between the Free Officers and the Ikhwan, he writes:

> They [the Ikhwan] believed that we took something from them. We did not take anything from them. They had wished to capture power but then the revolution occurred with its courageous and risky measures. Now they want to take over [this revolution] without having taken any risks.[61]

According to Shafei, the Ikhwan had let the young officers take all the risks associated with overthrowing the monarchy but still hoped to inherit the revolution on a silver platter, this despite waiting a few days before publicly announcing their support for the coup. Although senior sources close to the Ikhwan, like the respected Sheikh Ahmad Hassan al-Baquri, noted that Nasser had said that "the Ikhwan were one of the main backers of the revolution prior to its execution,"[62] their reluctance to publicly support it after the coup came as a shock to the Free Officers. However, according to Aclimandos the Ikhwan's support was more negative than positive. "Although the Ikhwan did not expose the secret of the coup and did not exploit the subsequent security vacuum afterward, they refrained from active participation and bided their time till the dust settled on the battlefield."[63] Nonetheless, the Ikhwan's thirst for power despite their procrastination over their public stance vis-à-vis the coup particularly angered the Free Officers, who saw themselves as the custodians of the revolution. It is worth noting that a similar feeling gained popularity among Egyptians after the January 25, 2011, Arab Spring revolution. Just as the Ikhwan had waited for about a week before publicly siding with the July 1952 coup, it took them three days to publicly come out in support of the January 2011 revolution. Neither the Free Officers in 1952 nor many Egyptians after 2011 forgave the Ikhwan for trying to lead from behind and reap the benefits from the sacrifice of others.

These tensions did not prevent the Ikhwan from fully supporting some of the repressive measures carried out by the Free Officers, especially when these helped the Brothers eliminate political rivals. Immediately after the coup, Sayyid Qutb—who had already been close to the Ikhwan, though he only formally joined the Islamist organization in 1953—vocally and publicly called on the Free Officers to do away with representative democracy and to replace it with a just dictatorship. The Islamist group's harsh stance against protesting workers in Kafr al-Dawar city in the Nile Delta in August 1952 is a case in point. The Brothers launched a massive campaign to have those behind the strike sentenced to death as traitors.[64] Protesting against low wages and corruption in their textile factory, two workers—Mohamed Mustafa Khamis and Mohamed Hassan al-Baqri—were sentenced to death and eleven others received up to fifteen years in prison. The Kafr al-Dawar massacre is universally interpreted as the moment when the Free Officers with the support of the Ikhwan crushed a potentially serious challenge by the left before it could blossom into a full revolt.[65]

Hudaybi and Nasser: A Clash of Personalities

The power struggle between the Ikhwan and the Free Officers was further exacerbated by a clash of personalities between the leaders of the two camps. According to close aides, following their first encounter, Nasser and Hudaybi distrusted and expected the worst from each other. A few days after the army takeover in July 1952, Hudaybi and senior aides had met with Nasser and other Free Officers to draw a road map of their future relations. According to Hudaybi's confidant and second in command, Farid Abdel Khaleq, who was present at the meeting, Hudaybi expected Nasser to deal with the Ikhwan as an equal partner in the new government and show deference to his authority as the leader of the most powerful organization in Egypt. Indeed, as mentioned previously, just a few days before the coup, Nasser had met with members of the Ikhwan to let them know about the Free Officers' plan. However, according to Farid Abdel Khaleq, the first encounter between the top leaders of the Ikhwan and the Free Officers embittered Hudaybi against Nasser and poisoned the wells of trust between them. After Hudaybi demanded that the Ikhwan be consulted in advance on all key decisions, Nasser retorted, "I will not accept guardianship of the revolution from any party." A shocked Hudaybi turned to one of his allies, Hassan Ashmawi, and demanded, "Had you not already agreed on a partnership?" to which Ashmawi replied, "Yes, we did."[66]

Khaled Mohieddin corroborates the minutes of that first defining meeting between Nasser and Hudaybi. According to him, Nasser replied to Hudaybi that he had never agreed on a power-sharing formula and that while he was willing to inform the Ikhwan about major decisions, he was unwilling to consult with them in advance.[67] As he left the meeting, Hudaybi confided to his team, "This man [Nasser] cannot be trusted. He rescinded earlier promises and agreements, and lied about that. Nasser does not share our Islamist vision, and at most the Free Officers movement is reformist, not Islamist. Nasser has taken us for granted. We must be on our guard."[68] For his part, Nasser said the Ikhwan was trying to dominate decision making and to hijack the Free Officers movement.[69] That fateful meeting colored the attitudes of Nasser and Hudaybi towards each other, with the two of them subsequently developing a visceral hatred for one another. What transpired in that first encounter between Hudaybi and Nasser set the stage for a series of missteps and miscalculations, which would culminate in a violent confrontation between the Free Officers and the Ikhwan.

At the heart of the conflict between the two organizations lies confusion about what understandings and agreements had been reached between the two sides before the 1952 coup. Increasing evidence suggests that Hudaybi's aides did not fully inform him about what assurances, if any, the Free Officers had provided to the Ikhwan regarding power sharing. While there are conflicting accounts about the precise nature of these understandings, one point is clear: as mentioned earlier, during the July 18 and 19 pre-coup meetings, Nasser did not commit to a specific set of policies beyond a general promise of cooperation with the Ikhwan. He remained vague and did not reveal his cards to either Salah Shadi, Hassan Ashmawi, or other Ikhwan members who were present. Yet, without going into further details, Shadi and Ashmawi had told Hudaybi that an agreement had been reached with the Free Officers. This explains Hudaybi's shock during his first meeting with Nasser, when the latter refused to accept a power-sharing arrangement with the Ikhwan.[70]

Previous accounts insufficiently scrutinize the great extent to which this clash between Hudaybi and Nasser became bitterly personal. The clash of personalities was exacerbated by televised speeches, in which the young colonel mocked Hudaybi and denigrated his authority, leadership, and self-respect, giving an idea of just how visceral and personal the conflict was:

> I met the Supreme Guide of the Ikhwan [Hudaybi], and he made a number of demands; the first of which is to impose hijab in Egypt, for every woman walking in the street to wear tarha [hijab]. I told him, if I make this a law, they will say that we have returned to the days of al-Hakim bi-Amr Allah, who forbade people from walking at day and only allowed walking at night. And my opinion is that every person in his own house decides for himself the rules. And he replied: "No, as the leader, you are responsible." So I told him: "Sir, you have a daughter in the School of Medicine, and she is not wearing a tarha. ... If you are unable to make one girl who is your daughter wear the tarha, how do you want me to put the tarha on 10 million women, by myself?"[71]

In the course of the struggle to secure leverage from the Free Officers after the 1952 coup, the Ikhwan paid dearly for specific instances of political miscalculation and ill judgment. As a scholar notes, "Hudaybi misjudged Nasser and underestimated him, ending up crushed by the young colonel. Before and after the coup Nasser, together with other officers, acted as if he had nothing to lose—kill or be killed."[72] Especially disastrous was Hudaybi's decision to lend his backing to Naguib in the power struggle with Nasser. This estranged Nasser even further, bitterly turning him against the supreme guide and the political wing of the movement. As the Ikhwan could not rescue Naguib's sinking ship, taking sides put them squarely in Nasser's firing line.

The Fracturing of the Ikhwan: A Mutiny by al-Nizam against Hudaybi

The struggle for power between the Free Officers and the Ikhwan came at an inopportune time for the Islamist group. In the aftermath of the assassination of their founder, Hassan al-Banna, by the state security services in 1949 and the proscription of the organization, the Ikhwan had already suffered a severe crisis of authority and identity. Sheikh Ahmad Hassan al-Baquri, a religious scholar and

Ikhwan leader, depicted the impact of Banna's loss in stark terms as "the absence of the father from his children who were terribly dependent on him ... We were orphaned by his disappearance."[73] Riven by internal divisions and open revolts, the Islamist organization had spent several years in a state of disequilibrium and internal turmoil. Although in 1951, Hudaybi, who was a judge, was selected as the group's *murshid*, many members questioned his Islamic credentials and saw him as an outsider to the movement. They also directly doubted his leadership capabilities by insisting he would be unable to heal the growing internal rift that had developed between the open political wing and the Secret Apparatus (al-Nizam al-Khass) of the organization. Hudaybi lacked Banna's charisma and oratorical skills, which had proved so crucial in mobilizing popular support. Baquri expressed the sentiment of many Muslim Brothers:

> Ikhwan members, especially the young men, looked forward to having a new supreme leader, an orator for the masses, an adviser for young men—exactly as his predecessor had been—but [Hudaybi] was a judge above all. He measured every word carefully. The Ikhwan were not satisfied by this reserved position. They needed someone who would lead and lay out a road map for the future of the movement and explain to officials what they should do.[74]

Indeed, from the beginning of his leadership Hudaybi was less in tune with the aspirations of the movement's base. Only one month after he assumed office in 1951, he angered many Ikhwan and other political factions by visiting the Palace and attempting to normalize the relationship between the two camps. He naively described his move to journalists as a "generous visit to a generous king." This phrase became notorious and would subsequently be cited derisively by his critics on innumerable occasions. For Fathi al-Asal, then the general inspector of the Ikhwan's headquarters, Hudaybi's visit and his conciliatory tone toward the king proved that he was the "*murshid* (teacher) of the Palace and not that of the Ikhwan."[75]

The leaders of al-Nizam or Secret Apparatus were particularly mistrustful of Hudaybi and viewed his selection as a threat to the very survival of their paramilitary apparatus. Their suspicions were not unfounded. The election of a former judge to head the Ikhwan signaled a new era, one intended to lend respectability to the Islamist group; to allay the fears of the Egyptian political establishment with regard to the Ikhwan's resort to political violence in the second half of the 1940s; and to rehabilitate the organization's image. More importantly, one of Hudaybi's key goals was to infiltrate the Secret Apparatus with men who were loyal to him. He viewed the underground wing as a liability rather than an asset and profoundly distrusted it. This was, however, easier said than done because in the years before Banna's assassination, even the founder of the movement had lost control of the paramilitary group. Indeed, the underground organization had increasingly taken action into its own hands, carrying out attacks that threatened the survival of the open political wing. Ultimately, Banna paid with his life for the recklessness and hubris of the armed apparatus that he had himself established.

As Hudaybi tried to consolidate his leadership, he struggled to find internal allies, and the Ikhwan remained divided over how to deal with the Free Officers. The political wing's old guard refused to exert pressure on the Secret Apparatus because of disagreements over how the movement should deal with Nasser. Almost one-third of the constituent board of the Ikhwan sided with Nasser; and so did senior members of the Secret Apparatus, including its commander in chief, Abdel Rahman al-Sanadi. Members of al-Nizam felt that Hudaybi was risking the organization's future by confronting Nasser. Hudaybi's defiant stance particularly angered operatives who had played a key role in his selection as a nominal leader of the Ikhwan. Moreover, other members felt that Hudaybi was overstepping his authority. He might have been chosen as the supreme guide, but upon assuming his position, he had been reportedly and bluntly told: "We want nothing from you; you need not even come to the headquarters. We will bring the papers for you to sign or reject as you will."[76] In his seminal book, *The Society of the Muslim Brothers*, Richard Mitchell notes that the internal bickering had "released the specter of an organization bound by fundamental rules of disciplined obedience to leadership without a leadership."[77]

The rivalry between Hudaybi and the Secret Apparatus was so deep that some al-Nizam insiders place responsibility for the Ikhwan's internal turmoil squarely on Hudaybi's shoulders. Mahmoud al-Sabbagh, who was second in command of al-Nizam when the mutiny against Hudaybi occurred, contended that Banna's successor did not have his finger on the pulse of the Islamist movement:

> Hudaybi was for the king when the majority of Ikhwan members and Egyptians opposed the royal regime which disgraced itself by its subservience to colonial Britain. He bungled a special relationship with the Free Officers with whom we had joined ranks to overthrow the monarchy and gain our independence. Hudaybi single-handedly antagonized Nasser, leader of the revolution, and ruined a promising alliance that could have gradually ushered in an Islamic authority.[78]

When asked how and why Hudaybi provoked Nasser, Sabbagh went on:

> Hudaybi treated Nasser as a subordinate and demanded that the Ikhwan be granted a veto power over major decisions taken by the Revolutionary Command Council. Not showing sensitivity to the young army officers, who were proud and terribly jealous of their independence, Hudaybi unnecessarily poisoned the wellsprings of goodwill and trust between the Ikhwan and the new military rulers. He squandered more than a decade of joint collaboration and planning between al-Nizam and the Free Officers who carried out the successful coup.[79]

In a claim which has never before been publicly articulated, Sabbagh argued that "what Hudaybi did not grasp is that those army officers were our men, an extension of our underground network. Many officers swore *bay'a* [fealty] to al-Nizam, including Nasser, the mastermind of the coup, and in a sense, the revolution was ours, a prayer came true."[80]

Sabbagh, Ahmed Adel Kamal, and other al-Nizam lieutenants asserted that eight army officers out of the thirteen members of the RCC had formally joined their paramilitary network, a development which, they say, shows the extent to which al-Nizam had succeeded in co-opting and infiltrating the junior corps of the armed forces. Although close comrades of Nasser who were interviewed for this book warned of a tendency among the Ikhwan to exaggerate their role in the coup and to overstate the number of Free Officers who had joined al-Nizam, they conceded that several of them—including Nasser—had done so.

Sabbagh suggested that Hudaybi overplayed his hand with the Free Officers. The *murshid*, he opined, "should not have pressed Nasser to relinquish his decision-making authority immediately after the revolution and he should have refrained from being hostile to the new rulers." He stressed that the Ikhwan should have been content to participate in the government formed by Nasser, "which was offered on a silver platter, and should have showed patience and political shrewdness."

Here Sabbagh refers to a pivotal moment in the relationship between the Ikhwan and the Free Officers. Indeed, soon after the coup, using multiple direct and indirect channels, Nasser had informed Ikhwan leaders that they could join his cabinet as long as they avoided testing or challenging his authority. He had also warned them that should they overstep their boundaries, he would go over their heads and appoint members of the Islamist group who had accepted his mandate as the undisputed leader. RCC member Mohieddin later confirmed in his memoirs that it was Nasser who had suggested appointing members of the Ikhwan to the new post-coup cabinet.[81] Far from bringing the two organizations together, the move only drove them further apart. In response to Nasser's proposition, Hudaybi named two candidates, Sheikh Baquri and Ahmed Hosni, whose appointment to the cabinet was agreed to by the Free Officers. However, things turned sour when, without consulting the military junta, Hudaybi sent two different members to take the oath to join the cabinet.[82] The move was not well received by the Free Officers and only escalated tensions between Hudaybi and Nasser. The two men's struggle for authority was once again clear for all to see. According to Mohieddin, the Ikhwan's decision to appoint different members to the cabinet was part of its effort "to show its authority towards us and that it can play us over, so we refused to change the two ministers."[83] Hudaybi's decision also alienated him from some members of the Ikhwan, who were at a loss trying to fathom his intentions. When pressed about this troubling episode, Sabbagh's response was direct. "What do you call that move, smart or dangerous? A slap in Nasser's face, which led him to believe that under Hudaybi's leadership the Ikhwan was a rival vying for power, unwilling to be a junior partner." He said it had been an "open secret" that Nasser and other Free Officers had "impressed on some of us that Hudaybi had to go in order to normalize relations with the revolution and restore trust. ... But we [al-Nizam] stressed to Nasser that we would have nothing to do with overthrowing our political leadership, even though we felt strongly that Hudaybi was a liability and could not steady the Ikhwan ship at this rocky moment," he recalled.[84] The Free Officers declined Hudaybi's new list but retained the two previous nominations. Hudaybi remained defiant and ordered Baquri to decline the appointment. When Baquri disregarded his command and joined the cabinet as a minister of *awqaf* (endowments), Hudaybi retorted by expelling him from the Ikhwan.[85] As a member of the Irshad office, which was the highest executive authority within the Ikhwan, Baquri owed loyalty to the group's supreme guide. By accepting the cabinet position without consulting Hudaybi, he had betrayed the *bay'a* and blatantly defied the authority of his leader.

This latest division within the Ikhwan aggravated the group's crisis of leadership, causing further animosity, chaos, and confusion among members. Although Hudaybi had forced Baquri to resign from the Ikhwan, he subsequently still called on him to help mediate and broker a settlement between the Ikhwan and Nasser.[86] This example shows that in the struggle between the Ikhwan and the Free Officers, political interests and personality clashes mattered much more than ideology, identity, and hierarchy. "Contrary to what the pro-Hudaybi faction claims, we did not conspire with Nasser to forcefully remove him from power," Sabbagh said. While there had been a serious internal revolt against Hudaybi's authoritarian rule, he argued that it had not been led by al-Nizam but by "the old guard among the Ikhwan ... who had feared that the *murshid* [teacher or guide] was not qualified to navigate the ship into safe harbor." Many Brothers feared that Hudaybi "had maneuvered the Ikhwan into a collision course with the Free Officers, with catastrophic repercussions," Sabbagh said. "They felt strongly that Hudaybi must be stopped before he brought ruin to the Islamic movement."[87]

Having interviewed senior members of the Ikhwan's open political wing who stated that Nasser used al-Nizam to engineer an internal coup and replace Hudaybi with a pliant successor, I confronted Sabbagh with this widespread conviction. Did al-Nizam members allow themselves to be manipulated by Nasser? Did they thereby violate their oath to Hudaybi and threaten the unity and the survival of the Islamist movement? His response was clear:

> Listen, our relationship with Nasser and the Free Officers was warm and close and we do not deny it. We were not fooled. We believed that Nasser was a genuine son of our Islamic movement and that the revolution would ultimately bring about an authentic government based mostly on shari'a laws.[88]

According to Sabbagh and other al-Nizam lieutenants, the Hudaybi camp's portrayal of al-Nizam as a Nasserist tool was used to downplay the gravity of the internal revolt against Hudaybi's authority and dismiss it as an insidious plot by a few rogue elements in cahoots with Nasser. "Although we opposed Hudaybi's hostile approach to the Free Officers, we did not conspire with Nasser to unseat him," reiterated Sabbagh. "Many Ikhwan, not just al-Nizam, wanted to replace Hudaybi with an experienced, charismatic figure from the founder's inner circle, one who fully grasped the challenges and opportunities facing the Islamic movement. We [al-Nizam] only supported the emerging consensus among the Ikhwan."[89] Conscious of posterity's verdict and anxious to set the record straight, Sabbagh was oblivious to the implications of his account: al-Nizam's top lieutenants felt that it was Nasser, not their own Supreme Guide Hudaybi, who had inherited the mantle of the Islamic revolution and thus deserved their loyalty. This shows the depth of the rift which had opened up within the Ikhwan and the extent to which Nasser was able to manipulate the internal ambitions, contradictions, and divisions among various Ikhwan constituencies in order to destabilize the Islamist organization.

Hudaybi's al-Nizam Gamble

Amid growing dissension that endangered both the unity of the Ikhwan and his leadership, Hudaybi became convinced he had to cleanse al-Nizam of its pro-Nasser elements. He was especially concerned by the close relationship between Nasser and the paramilitary branch's commander in chief, Abdel Rahman al-Sanadi, and his followers. Sanadi had known Nasser through the latter's association with al-Nizam in the years leading up to the Free Officers' coup, and the two had remained on very good terms. In November 1953, Hudaybi decided to make a move against Nasser's supporters within the Ikhwan and sacked Sanadi, together with other members of the Secret Apparatus. Although Hudaybi intended to consolidate his grip on the Ikhwan, his decision ultimately backfired. Made aware of Sanadi's dismissal, Nasser saw a window of opportunity and persuaded Sanadi and his lieutenants to engineer a coup in retaliation and force Hudaybi out. By instigating the coup, Nasser pitted the armed branch of the Ikhwan against its open political wing. Some of Sanadi's lieutenants told me that they viewed Nasser as one of their own, and that their political leadership should have wholeheartedly embraced the new revolution. "We played a big part in the success of the July revolution," a commander of al-Nizam said proudly, though he insisted on remaining anonymous. "The revolution had realized the goals set by the founding father [Banna]." Thus, despite the previous denial of Sanadi's second in command, Sabbagh, that al-Nizam never tried to force Hudaybi out, a rushed bid was made to sideline Hudaybi once and for all.

In a poorly planned and desperate attempt, some members of al-Nizam met with Hudaybi to demand his resignation. One of those in attendance brandished a gun in the leader's face in an effort to compel him to resign; a humiliating gesture for a *murshid* whose followers were expected to show him absolute obedience.[90] The coup failed and Hudaybi remained in charge of the organization. It also put Sanadi and his men at risk since they now openly threatened Hudaybi's leadership. Although Sanadi and his men lost the battle against Hudaybi, al-Nizam's rebellion fractured the Ikhwan in several ways. First, it fragmented its political wing, and second, it deepened the existing rift between the paramilitary and the political branches of the movement. After expelling Sanadi and his lieutenants from al-Nizam, Hudaybi remained determined to assert his control and purged leading political rivals from the executive bureau. However, while the infighting left the organization more vulnerable in its power struggle with Nasser, it still maintained a large popular base and effective institutions, making it more resilient than Nasser had anticipated. His divide-and-rule tactics did not produce the desired ends as Hudaybi and his supporters won a resounding victory and retained control over the Ikhwan political machine. Sanadi and his men were discredited, demoralized, and marginalized. Nasser was running out of options, and it was shortly thereafter that Nasser and his close allies decided to dissolve the Islamist organization.

On the Ikhwan side, internal fragmentation further deepened following the assassination of Sayed Fayez, a senior member of the Secret Apparatus appointed by Hudaybi, in an operation allegedly plotted by Sanadi and carried out by his operatives.[91] Fayez was killed after Hudaybi had appointed him to replace Sanadi and overhaul the Secret Apparatus. Despite this setback, Hudaybi remained intent on remodeling and restructuring al-Nizam by putting his loyalists in top positions. He thus nominated Yusuf Tal'at to replace Fayez. Tal'at had been a member of the first generation of the Ikhwan under Banna and was a well-known lieutenant within al-Nizam. The *murshid* also appointed an advisory committee to assist him in reconstructing the paramilitary network and purging its ranks of "criminality" and "terrorism." The forced exit of Sanadi and his associates, who had run al-Nizam like a tribal fiefdom, left a vacuum: a lack of skilled, mid-level operational managers and a steady hand to guide and coordinate the disparate elements within the network. However, far from disappearing quietly into the sunset, Sanadi and his lieutenants erected obstacles to hamper Tal'at's efforts to reform al-Nizam. These obstacles culminated, as we will see in the following section, in the attempted assassination of Nasser in what is known as the October 1954 Manshiya incident.

Following his appointment as the head of al-Nizam, Tal'at faced stiff opposition from members who were still loyal to Sanadi. Having failed to consolidate his authority within the paramilitary organization, Hudaybi embarked on building a parallel network to counterbalance the influence of Sanadi's men. As relations deteriorated between Hudaybi and Nasser in 1953 and 1954, Tal'at went on a spree recruiting from the ranks of the Ikhwan, favoring quantity over quality. By the time of his arrest for his role in the assassination attempt against Nasser in October 1954, Tal'at had established underground cells throughout the country, each composed of seven men. This new architecture had many holes and weaknesses and contained the seeds of its own destruction. Recruits were neither properly vetted nor adequately trained. Tal'at wanted al-Nizam to be open to all members of the Ikhwan and was prepared to take "every Muslim who is ready to join in jihad." This attitude paid insufficient heed to the status of al-Nizam. As a paramilitary force it required unique skills and a rigorous set of checks and controls to instill discipline, respect for authority, and the prevention of foolish and reckless actions.[92] By failing to establish a reliable and effective command-and-control structure, Tal'at committed grave mistakes, which ultimately led him into a similar trap as his former nemesis, Sanadi. In the past, Tal'at had indirectly criticized Sanadi for taking action into his own hands without prior approval from the supreme guide and the political leadership. Although upon his nomination he promised a clean break with his predecessor, when faced with a crisis he repeated the same mistakes.

As the crisis intensified in the summer of 1954 between the Ikhwan and the Free Officers, Tal'at met with senior associates and dissident army officers who belonged to the Ikhwan in order to brainstorm about how to incite a popular uprising against Nasser. Some hardliners advocated killing Nasser and his close allies within the RCC by carrying out a daring armed assault on the Free Officers' headquarters. According to participants, this proposal was deemed impractical and as a result did not gain traction. Instead, the consensus was that al-Nizam would wage a systematic propaganda campaign against Nasser to mobilize the public and trigger a popular uprising. The Ikhwan would go on the offensive only once the people had risen up against the Free Officers. Hudaybi counseled caution and instructed Tal'at to time his actions with breaking developments on the ground. Lacking experience and a strict hierarchy of leadership, Tal'at's branch waged a scorched-earth propaganda war against Nasser by distributing secret pamphlets on Cairo streets, often without the consent and prior knowledge of Hudaybi. Al-Nizam literarily turned a political battle into an existential struggle, in which it observed no red lines in its attacks on Nasser and his supporters among the Free Officers. Written by Sayyid Qutb, who was in charge of the Ikhwan propaganda arm, the leaflets accused Nasser of treason and portrayed him as a treacherous, bloodthirsty closeted Jew.

A senior Ikhwan official said that he and others had complained bitterly about al-Nizam's all-out propaganda war against Nasser and had warned of dire repercussions.[93] They demanded that the leaflets be terminated and that the Ikhwan stop burning bridges with the new military rulers. "Despite our repeated warnings, the distribution of inflammatory leaflets continued," said Farid Abdel Khaleq, who was part of the Ikhwan inner circle. As the ideological struggle launched by Tal'at's revived al-Nizam intensified, Hudaybi went into hiding, informally putting Tal'at and his men in charge of the Ikhwan during his absence. "When the *murshid* went into hiding, al-Nizam and Qutb were put in charge while the political leadership was sidelined. We could not contact the *murshid* except through al-Nizam and other secret branches which knew his whereabouts, an intolerable situation fraught with danger," Abdel Khaleq continued.[94] The strategy chosen by Tal'at and acquiesced in by Hudaybi proved counterproductive and deadly. Two officers close to Nasser told me that the smear campaign enraged Nasser and convinced him that Hudaybi and his supporters within the Ikhwan ought to be neutralized.[95] Ultimately, al-Nizam's bellicose tactics served only to hasten the showdown with the Free Officers. Members of al-Nizam conceded that they felt confused about the unfolding crisis. There was hardly any coordination or communication between the top leadership of the Ikhwan and the various underground cells and units, who were left to their own devices and itching for a fight.

In early 1954 Nasser was thus facing the crisis of his political life. In addition to the internal rift within the RCC, pitting him against Naguib, the popular hero of the revolution, he was now also directly targeted by Tal'at and his operatives. This did little to slake his ambition for total control. "In two or three years I hope to press a button and move Egypt forward, press another button and bring the country to full stop," Nasser acknowledged on one occasion, in the context of a heated argument with a group of Ikhwan leaders.[96] From 1952 to 1954, Nasser had sought to convince the leadership of the Ikhwan to abandon its independent political ambitions and join en masse his newly established Liberation Rally, but he had met with rejection from Hudaybi and his allies. With his fragile regime enjoying little public support and facing a rebellion from within the military, Nasser could no longer tolerate the existence of a defiant Islamist political organization, not even one weakened by his divide-and-rule tactics and internal fighting among Ikhwan power centers. Sanadi's failed coup attempt against Hudaybi after his dismissal, coupled with the increasing ideological struggle launched by Tal'at and his men, was the last straw. In January 1954, Nasser and the Free Officers decided to dissolve the Ikhwan and dismantle this last oppositional fortress to their authority. On January 13, 1954, the cabinet issued a decree declaring the Ikhwan a political party and therefore subject to the 1953 law abolishing political parties, from which it had previously enjoyed an exemption. The decree accused Hudaybi and "his clique" of plotting to "overthrow the present form of government under the cover of religion."[97]

After removing Naguib from the scene, Nasser ordered a mass crackdown on the Islamist movement. Again, this involved violent coercion alongside efforts to split the Ikhwan and co-opt some of its members. Hudaybi was detained along with 450 other members, and the government initiated a press campaign designed to personally discredit the *murshid*. Among those arrested were key leaders, like Abdel Qader 'Awda and Omar al-Telmessany, who had earlier been freed by the Free Officers in the hope that they might be won over. Nasser had especially been keen to co-opt the charismatic 'Awda because he had wanted him to replace Hudaybi in the event of a successful coup against the *murshid*.[98] Once this plan failed, however, both were detained and even allegedly tortured.[99]

Nasser's scheme against the Ikhwan did not improve his popular support. Just two months later, in March 1954, despite his attempt to sideline Naguib, the two officers were still involved in a power struggle and Nasser faced a popular uprising against his repressive measures. Accordingly, he made a tactical retreat. The RCC announced the reinstatement of Naguib in the presidency and the restoration of normal parliamentary life. The Nasserist regime rescinded its decision to dissolve the Ikhwan and other political parties; released the incarcerated members of the Ikhwan, including Hudaybi; and lifted censorship of the press. In a move to defuse the crisis and gain time, Nasser and the Free Officers announced that the revolution would come to an end, and promised a new era of freedom. Reaching out to the Ikhwan, Nasser sent his information minister, Muhammed Fuad Jalal, to attempt a reconciliation with Hudaybi and through him with the group as a whole. He had still not given up on trying to co-opt the Islamist organization in his ongoing power struggle with Naguib.[100] Nasser sought to persuade the Ikhwan against siding with Naguib again, as they had in February 1954.[101] He thus agreed to all of the conditions laid down by Hudaybi, releasing detained Ikhwan members and visiting Hudaybi at home upon the latter's release.[102] However, the resolution of the March 1954 crisis was short-lived. Nasser merely bided his time and waited until he had organized his forces sufficiently for a counterattack against Naguib, the opposition in general, and Hudaybi in particular. To realize its grand design, the Nasserist revolution was consuming its children, former allies, and political rivals as well.

As a result of Nasser's maneuvering in March 1954, Naguib was once again unseated later that month. This time the Ikhwan kept silent and relations with Nasser remained cordial, though this did not last long. Deeply suspicious of one another, Nasser and Hudaybi were bound to come to blows. A final reckoning between the Free Officers and the Ikhwan was inevitable, driven by a clash of personalities, priorities, and interests. Although after his release in March 1954 Hudaybi had pledged his organization's "support" for the Nasserist regime, his allegiance was not shared by the reconstituted Secret Apparatus. Still embittered by the dissolution of the Ikhwan and the arrest of its leadership in early 1954, the new paramilitary branch led by Tal'at initiated a rigorous recruitment campaign and reverted to its old ways, drawing contingency plans for sabotage and assassination. Without consulting Hudaybi, al-Nizam embarked on a perilous journey, one that threatened to embroil the political wing in a fatal confrontation with the Nasser regime. It was a reckless replay of the bloody events of the late 1940s, which had culminated in the assassination of Banna and the dissolution of the Islamist organization.

The Showdown between Nasser and Hudaybi

By this time, influential voices in both the Nasser camp and al-Nizam were beating the drums of war, actively planning for an all-out conflict. The spark that triggered the confrontation was related to the negotiation of the evacuation agreement settling Anglo-Egyptian relations. While the Egyptian government was negotiating with the

British for the settlement of the Suez dispute in 1954, Hudaybi and senior aides met independently with British officials and allegedly concluded a "secret treaty" in which, according to the government, they made treacherous concessions.[103] "In our eyes, Hudaybi's action bordered on treason," Nasser's chief of staff, Sami Sharaf, intimated. "By secretly meeting with the British, the Brothers weakened our negotiating position and stabbed us in the back."[104] In his autobiography, Sharaf, at that time working in military intelligence, detailed the Ikhwan's attempts to impose its own views on the technical as well as the procedural matters of the negotiations and any possible consequent agreement with the British.[105] His account implied that Nasser and his comrades viewed the Ikhwan as a quasi-state seeking to impose its own *wisaya* (custodianship) on the country. This sense of threat grew as networks of Ikhwan were found to be active within the military and the police, aiming to control these vital state institutions.[106]

In another gamble, while on a tour of Arab countries in July 1954, Hudaybi publicly rejected the Anglo-Egyptian evacuation agreement signed by Britain and Egypt, describing it as a capitulation and questioning the authority of a non-elected government to conclude and ratify treaties with foreign powers. Hudaybi's criticism made headlines in the Arab world and terribly embarrassed the army officers back home. According to Khaled Mohieddin—Nasser's closest friend until he criticized Nasser's authoritarian style of governance—the fact that al-Nizam members were dropping anti-Nasser pamphlets on Cairo streets denouncing the government for its "betrayal" of the national cause was "the straw that broke the camel's back." Mohieddin told me, "What Hudaybi did was unacceptable because he politicized national security. Hudaybi played with fire and should have expected to be burned."

At the end of August 1954, the Nasser regime retaliated by launching a propaganda offensive directed primarily at Hudaybi with the aim of discrediting him. The press campaign reminded Egyptians that Hudaybi had allegedly negotiated a "secret treaty" with the British and had made more damaging concessions than the government. In response, Hudaybi drafted a letter to Nasser, which was also distributed as a pamphlet on the streets of Cairo on August 22. In it, he denied the government's charge that he had conducted unilateral talks with the British and pleaded with Nasser to give the Ikhwan an opportunity to inform the public of their position. Addressing a large group of Ikhwan at the traditional weekly meeting two days later after the pamphlet distribution, Hudaybi was calm but unyielding. He reassured his excited and angry audience that he was prepared "for whatever comes" and reiterated a basic foundational principle of the Ikhwan that "death in the path of God is the noblest of our wishes."[107]

That dramatic end was not lost on those assembled, who readied themselves for a final showdown with Nasser and the Free Officers. During the speech, one attendant shouted, "Death to the traitors." Soon after that address, also in August 1954, Hudaybi and his closest partisans disappeared from public view. The Tuesday assembly was the last time Hudaybi was seen by members of the Ikhwan until he was arrested and brought to trial a few months later. Hudaybi was detained on October 30, a few days after the assassination attempt on Nasser.[108] The senior leadership of the Ikhwan convinced Hudaybi to go into hiding lest he be assassinated or arrested. "We hoped that things would calm down and that the storm would pass without wrecking our *gama'a* [community]," said Farid Abdel Khaleq, a close confidant of Hudaybi. "The *murshid* said he would delegate authority and absent himself to diffuse the crisis and appease Nasser. We were wrong because Nasser wished the destruction of *al-gama'a* and the removal of Hudaybi," he said, gesturing excitedly with his hands.[109]

Hudaybi's sudden disappearance hastened the confrontation with Nasser. Fearing for his life, Nasser also briefly stopped appearing in public. With Hudaybi and his closest advisers in hiding in Alexandria, fissures and rivalries within the Ikhwan started to resurface with a vengeance; Hudaybi's opponents struggled to gain greater control over the Guidance Council and the Consultative Assembly. Meanwhile Nasser stoked the flames of dissent and mutiny within the Ikhwan's political wing and pressed for a leadership alternative to Hudaybi. During the two months of Hudaybi's absence, infighting almost tore the Ikhwan apart. More alarming were plans made by the Ikhwan to assassinate Nasser, despite the fact that in an open letter to the prime minister, Hudaybi had assured him that "you may walk without guard day or night in any place without fearing that the Ikhwan will raise one hand against you."[110] This did little to alleviate Nasser's fears. He asserted that he was "fed up with the Brothers who had gone altogether too far in their vendetta" against him.[111]

Nasser's instincts proved right as Yusuf Tal'at and his followers had decided to target him after he signed the evacuation treaty with Britain. For Nasser and the British, the treaty had been a win-win situation. Anthony Nutting, who negotiated the treaty and later got to know Nasser well, said that while Egypt obtained the withdrawal of British troops, Britain got what it needed in the way of base facilities in the Suez Canal Zone.[112] The Ikhwan, on the other hand, opposed the treaty. In a conversation with Nutting, Nasser expressed his continued anger with the Islamist organization, warning that they "gave me the broadest of hints that it would not be very long before a final show-down took place with Naguib and his fanatical bed-fellows."[113] The showdown came one week later and provided an "opportunity [for] which Nasser had been waiting."[114] The leadership of al-Nizam had chosen Mahmud Abdel Latif, a tinsmith from the Embaba district of Cairo, to carry out the hit against Nasser. Testifying subsequently in court, Abdel Latif said he accepted the mission because Nasser was committing an "act of treason" in signing the treaty, which "gave away the rights of the nation."[115] He said he was given a pistol by a Cairo section leader of al-Nizam, Hindawi Duwayr.[116] The orders were clear: Kill Nasser during his speech in al-Manshiya in downtown Alexandria.

On October 26, as Nasser addressed a huge throng of supporters and workers who had been brought in to shout approval, Mahmud Abdel Latif forced his way to the front of the crowd and fired eight shots at him at point-blank range. In an historic moment that captured the imagination of Egyptians, the unharmed Nasser delivered a defiant impromptu speech to the crowd. That moment of drama and courage was broadcast and rebroadcast over the radio to the Arab world and became etched in the popular imagination:

> Oh ye people ... Let everyone remain in his place ... my life is yours, my blood a sacrifice to Egypt. I speak to you with God's help after the mischievous tried to kill me. Gamal Abdel Nasser's life is your property; I have lived for you and will do so until I die, striving for your sake.[117]

Although the Ikhwan's political leadership asserted that the Nasser regime orchestrated the assassination attempt as a pretext to crush their organization, al-Nizam operatives in the know concede that a rogue unit plotted the assassination. Subsequent testimony by Abdel Latif and al-Nizam lieutenants showed that the top echelon of al-Nizam had sanctioned the killing of Nasser.[118] Other elements of al-Nizam advocated storming the cabinet with a commando group and murdering pro-Nasser ministers. Tal'at himself admitted that he had considered assassinating Nasser and other army officers. He also told the court that he had given a suicide belt of dynamite to a Cairo section leader, Ibrahim al-Tayyib, a few days before the attempt on Nasser's life, although he denied that he had given final authorization to kill Nasser.

There was overwhelming evidence of foul play by al-Nizam cells. Even if Abdel Latif and his cohorts in al-Nizam had not been given official blessing by Hudaybi, they had been exposed to his discursive provocation. When Nasser signed the treaty, Hudaybi called him a "traitor to the national cause."[119] Hudaybi's inflammatory rhetoric—accusing Nasser of treason and calling on members of the Ikhwan "not to succumb to colonizers" and not to give up the right of Egypt "to secure the full evacuation [of British forces] from all of its land," as Nasser had failed to do—provided possibly legitimate justification for die-hard al-Nizam operators to attempt to kill Nasser.[120] In addition, Tal'at said that he had faced threats from the old guard within al-Nizam, particularly Sanadi loyalists. The latter labeled the new al-Nizam chief a "traitor" to Banna's cause because, in their eyes, he was there to do Hudaybi's bidding and was stealthily trying to shut down al-Nizam. According to Tal'at and Mohamed Fargali, the head of the advisory committee, many al-Nizam operators refused to cooperate with Tal'at and remained faithful to Sanadi. Tal'at even told the court that he was shocked to find out that many members were more loyal to Sanadi than they were to the Ikhwan. He added that he could not exercise control over them and was incapable of forcing them out. His account is refuted by members of the organization's old guard. "We resolved to keep a watchful eye on Tal'at but we never threatened or actively opposed him," said Sanadi's right-hand man, Mahmoud al-Sabbagh. "Hudaybi got rid of us but he did not know what to do with al-Nizam and his new men were not qualified to lead such a complex organization."[121] At that point, the internal situation within the Ikhwan had grown so bad that Hudaybi's men feared retaliation by Sanadi's operatives, which could have prompted an open civil war within the paramilitary network. While Tal'at's narrative during the trial was self-serving and intended to distance him from the attempt on Nasser's life, his account tallies with the power struggle that raged within the ranks of al-Nizam. In their own defense in the courtroom in 1954, Tal'at and his men portrayed al-Nizam as a train without brakes, which they were powerless to stop or even slow down. They wanted to convince the court that they were passive bystanders in an unfolding violent drama, unable to alter for better the direction of events.

The Manshiya incident allowed Nasser to sweep the slate clean of his rivals.[122] Nineteen fifty-four resembled 1948, when al-Nizam had acted recklessly and endangered the very survival of its parent organization, the open political wing. Regardless of whether Hudaybi and his advisers had known in advance about the assassination plot, they failed to exercise control over al-Nizam. Instead, Tal'at had built a bloated underground force numbering approximately 20,000 men with hardly any military training or strict organizational checks and safeguards. While Sanadi's force was highly selective and elitist, Tal'at's men were ordinary members of the Ikhwan who joined al-Nizam en masse. In a sense, the political leadership of the Ikhwan was ultimately accountable for al-Nizam's actions since the assassination attempt was carried out by Tal'at's faction. Both in 1948 and in 1954 the paramilitary branch fulfilled its duties as understood by its commanders: protecting the Islamist movement and battling its enemies. In both cases, al-Nizam operatives carried out assassinations and sabotage, and said they believed that senior political leaders like Banna and Hudaybi had authorized these actions. In both cases, Banna and Hudaybi disputed these claims and painted themselves as innocent of the spilled blood. Something had gone terribly wrong: the political leadership—formally and officially in charge of the military wing—either was not fully in control of al-Nizam or turned a blind eye to its use of violence, actually condoning its actions. Since al-Nizam's inception in the late 1930s, its operatives had had no inhibitions about using violence in the service of politics. From the start, its raison d'être had been armed resistance against the British colonial presence in Egypt and then against Zionism in Palestine. Banna had conceived of al-Nizam as an elitist, clandestine military arm of the Ikhwan with little institutional or political oversight. Hudaybi's initial half-hearted effort to reform al-Nizam had failed dismally because of lack of commitment and strong leadership, the heightening of tensions with the Free Officers' regime, and internal resistance by hardliners within the paramilitary branch. Nasser's heavy-handedness, coupled with Hudaybi's disappearance and the ensuing battle for supremacy within the Islamist organization, had caused disarray in its ranks, as well as calls for armed action against the movement's tormentors. The hardliners had taken matters into their own hands and decided to kill Nasser.

"Under Hudaybi, *al-gama'a* [the community] was paralyzed and splintered, and there was no one who could have applied the brakes on al-Nizam and prevented the violent collision with Nasser's regime," suggested a former al-Nizam commander who opposed confrontation with Nasser. "The Manshiya incident was a reckless and suicidal mission." Indeed, the attempt on Nasser's life amounted to a death knell for the Ikhwan, and a God-sent gift for Nasser. The continuing existence of the underground network had long been a sore point in relations between the two strongmen. Nasser's chief of staff, Sharaf, told me that his boss suspected that Hudaybi's paramilitary group—that is, Tal'at's faction of al-Nizam—had infiltrated the army and set up cells that plotted subversion and assassination: "Nasser never believed Hudaybi's claims that he had disbanded al-Nizam al-Khass and had not hired its assassins."[123] In interviews, Sanadi's men revealed that Nasser had an "irrational" fear of Hudaybi's al-Nizam and had recruited members of the Sanadi faction to spy on members of Tal'at's faction, keeping an eye out for potential assassins while traveling in the country. Nasser believed, I was told, that al-Nizam operatives would easily be able to recognize their newly activated counterparts, Tal'at's men.[124]

Indeed, the Nasser regime crushed the Ikhwan with utmost speed and urgency. On the same day the attempted assassin was positively identified as a member of the movement, organized mobs began ransacking and torching the Ikhwan's Cairo headquarters and other district branches throughout the country. In the following days crowds composed mainly of government workers attacked shops and offices owned by Ikhwan supporters, under the gaze of the police and the National Guard and even in some cases with their direct participation. Shouts of "Death to the traitors!" and "Death to the Ikhwan of the Devil!" filled the air. On October 29, 1954, just three days after the attempt on his life, addressing thousands of supporters in Maydan al-Gumhuriyya (Republic Square) in downtown Cairo, Nasser declared all-out war on Hudaybi and the Ikhwan. He pledged that "the revolution shall not be crippled; if it is not able to proceed white, then we will make it red," suggesting that, if necessary, blood will be shed for the sake of the revolution. The following day, Hudaybi was arrested. The government launched a two-month propaganda offensive against Ikhwan leaders, who were denigrated as "merchants of religion," accused of using and abusing Islam and manipulating the trust of their followers. In particular, the official propaganda machine focused on alleged plots hatched by al-Nizam to topple the government and impose a "theocratic state" in Egypt. Rekindling Egyptians' memories of the period following Nuqrashi's assassination in December 1948, the Ikhwan were depicted as extremists prone to terror and violence. Branded as enemies of the nation, they faced the brunt and fury of the Nasserist state. By the end of November 1955, the government announced the arrest of a thousand Ikhwan members, including top leaders in the political and military wings; among them were Hudaybi's leading partisans and all members of the Guidance Office, as well as Tal'at and most of his lieutenants.[125] Nasser's efforts to crush the Ikhwan were made easier because he "already knew the Ikhwan one by one."[126]

Nasser's key objective was to break the back of the most powerful Islamist organization in Egypt and the Muslim world. He established a People's Tribunal and appointed three army officers, rather than jurists, to conduct trials of Ikhwan members. Among them was Anwar al-Sadat, who would succeed Nasser as president in 1970. The tribunal, which was designed more to collectively punish the Ikhwan than to establish individual guilt and bring about justice, conducted political trials in which defendants enjoyed little due process. "This military tribunal made a travesty of law and brought the Ikhwan public empathy," said a prominent Egyptian jurist, Tariq al-Bishry, who did not share the Islamist organization's vision. "The court acted as prosecutor and executioner and therefore delegitimized the government case."[127] Initially broadcast daily on radio with transcripts printed in the press, trial proceedings stooped so low that the government was forced to heavily censor press accounts of the hearings and stop broadcasts. Subjected to insults and ridicule by the court and the audience, defendants were confused and frightened. Legal decorum was not observed, and the proceedings were dominated by theatrics. When he was displeased with testimony offered by Ikhwan members, the chief "judge," Gamal Salem, a Free Officer and a close ally of Nasser, put words into their mouths and forced the answers that he desired to hear. The truth was the first casualty of these revolutionary trials. The rule of law suffered a fatal blow, with significant ramifications for state-society relations.

This is not to say that al-Nizam did not carry out the attempted assassination of Nasser or that it did not plot sabotage and insurrection. As mentioned, the accused Abdel Latif confessed that he had attempted to kill Nasser, and he provided specific details of the conspiracy. Other section leaders of al-Nizam also confessed and corroborated his story. This was in addition to a trail of evidence implicating the top echelon of al-Nizam. However, there was little evidence tying the conspiracy to the mainstream political leadership of the Ikhwan. Yet the government claimed that Hudaybi and his "gang" had planned the assassination as a first shot in a "bloody insurrection" designed to overthrow the Nasser regime. The trial afforded Nasser an opportunity to crush Hudaybi and his inner circle and to eliminate Naguib, his only rival for the leadership of Egypt. According to Mohieddin, a RRC member, "Nasser used the assassination attempt on his life to eliminate the Ikhwan from political life and silence his critics among the Free Officers."[128] Naguib's political fate was sealed after his name was mentioned very early in the legal proceedings against Ikhwan members. He was dismissed as president and placed under house arrest. Although the extent of the Naguib-Ikhwan connection was unclear, it brought him ruin. Barely a month after the trial began, the People's Tribunal passed sentences of death by hanging on Hudaybi and six members of the Ikhwan. Seven defendants received sentences of life imprisonment, while another two were sentenced to fifteen years. Friends of the government were acquitted. Not wanting to make him a martyr, the Free Officers commuted Hudaybi's death sentence to life imprisonment with hard labor. They swiftly sent the remaining six on death row to the gallows, heedless of the long-term repercussions that this move would have at home and the protests that it would inspire in neighboring Arab countries. There was no immediate public backlash, either in relation to Naguib's removal or in relation to the draconian measures taken against Ikhwan. Although Sanadi and his cohorts supportive of Nasser escaped the latter's wrath, they ceased to exist as an underground group. In one stroke, Nasser purged Egypt of his rivals and foes and anointed himself kingmaker. But the last words of the executed foretold future trouble. According to observers at the hangings, the charismatic, vocal leader Abdel Qader 'Awda, Hudaybi's right-hand man, ended his life with a curse on the Nasserist state: "Praise be to God that He has made me a martyr and may He make my blood a curse upon the men of the revolution."[129] 'Awda's defiance before his executioners turned him into a heroic figure among younger Ikhwan members, who pledged to avenge his "martyrdom." Ironically, 'Awda had been the intermediary who initiated contacts between Nasser and the Ikhwan. The chants of "martyrdom" were repeated by other members of the Ikhwan who were either sentenced to death or to lengthy prison terms.

Conclusion

The period following the Free Officers coup witnessed the emergence of an intense power struggle between the Ikhwan and the new military regime set up by Nasser and his allies. This confrontation was never truly ideological; rather, it was a political rivalry between two camps vying for influence and power. In December 1953, the Ikhwan adamantly refused the return of parliamentary life by siding with military rule. The Ikhwan leaders were against ending emergency rule and opposed the return of the army to its barracks. At this stage, the interests of the Ikhwan and the Free Officers converged, allowing them to maintain relatively cordial, or at least ambivalent, relations, and both positioned themselves to dominate the political space. It was only later, when the political landscape changed, that the Ikhwan protested what it now described as the dictatorial presence of the military in power and demanded that the very same military officers return to their barracks.

As in any battle, there was a winner and a loser. Nasser came out on top. This outcome was due to the Ikhwan's weakness and Nasser's strength. He maintained a honeymoon period with the Ikhwan for almost two years, from 1952 until 1954, till he cleansed the system of rivals within the RCC. In early 1954, the Nasser regime then took legal steps to dissolve the Islamist group, detaining Hudaybi, only to release him shortly afterwards so that he might be co-opted to the Nasserist camp in order to remove Naguib from power.

The violent confrontation between the Ikhwan and the Free Officers helped shape Egyptian politics for years to come. Once the Free Officers had locked up their adversaries, their appetite expanded so that they no longer tolerated any form of political dissent. Nasser and his comrades were determined to bring about fundamental change from the top down and swiftly, without having to deal with institutional, ideological, and political constraints and checks and balances. They steadily dispensed with all democratic pretenses and set up a populist dictatorship, a self-enclosed decision-making body that concentrated power in few hands. Nasser emerged as the undisputed leader of the revolution, and by 1956 he had purged the political arena of potential opponents and consolidated his monopoly over decision making. He also enshrined secular Arab nationalism, or Arabism, as the official ideology of his regime. What began as squabbling over power distribution and control between Hudaybi's Ikhwan and Nasser's Free Officers hardened into a bigger ideological struggle between pan-Islamism and pan-Arab nationalism, a struggle that has defined the modern Middle East.

The die was thereby cast for a long war between the two most powerful social and political movements in the Arab world—the Islamists versus the army officers, who became fervent nationalists and offered an alternative secular-leaning vision. This struggle, which has ebbed and flowed from 1954 till the present, has shaped the identity of the postcolonial, post-independence state and its conduct towards its citizens and the outside world.

This nationalist-Islamist schism also reveals an unresolved issue related to the question of liberation and post-independence identity. As Muhammad Hussein Haykal noted, despite the growth of nationalism in Egypt, something resembling a common Egyptian thought only started to emerge after World War I, just as calls for independence grew more vocal. Haykal's point is important because it draws attention to the colonial context where the development of nationalism is not synonymous with a homogenization of national identity. As a result of British occupation, national identity in Egypt became gradually grounded in a dialectical process of total opposition to the Other (the occupiers), while the national rhetoric projected the Egyptian people as forming a united and a homogeneous bloc. Thus, despite their internal heterogeneity, which reflected the fragmentation of Egyptian society, both the Free Officers and the Muslim Brothers insisted that they represented the beating heart of the Egyptian nation.

The reality was more complex than the claims of either camp. If before the 1952 revolution Islamists and semi-secular nationalists came together over their common definition of "Egyptianness"—fighting against British occupation and foreign influence—this is where the consensus ended. Moreover, although most Egyptians were united by their desire to gain total independence, the differences between the groups that had come together under the banner of nationalism were largely ignored by the nationalist discourse. Consequently, the crystallization of nationalism around an expression of Egyptianness as sameness and of foreignness as difference delegitimized political claims, which by their nature are based on social and economic distinctions. Nationalism thus inscribed identity as unitary rather than as a relational process. Identity became synonymous with "being against" something rather than as "belonging together" in a constituted ensemble.

While both the Ikhwan and the Free Officers saw the history of Egypt as a constant struggle against injustice and despotism, they ultimately failed to shed the ethos of authoritarianism that had been institutionalized by the colonial experience. Moreover, as a consequence of national identity being equated with sameness, the imagined communities inscribed at the heart of the Ikhwan's and the Free Officers' rhetoric did not include a firmly determined role for the different social sections of society within the political sphere. Instead, both movements believed that unilateral actions remained the only effective means to effect real change, though at the expense of the people they claimed to represent. For more than half a century the Islamists and the nationalists have continued to maintain their monopoly on the social and political space in Arab countries and have stifled other voices and ideological orientations. Time and again the two warring movements have colluded with each other to prevent institutionalized or organized dissent from establishing a popular base.

Another important factor to stress is that despite their claim to power, both the Ikhwan and the Free Officers did not lead a popular struggle as the FLN did in Algeria. In Egypt the revolution had to be manufactured, and to this end, both the Free Officers and the Ikhwan had to create their own revolutionary subjectivities to appeal to their popular base. Perhaps the biggest mistake committed by the Free Officers and the Ikhwan is their failure to include in their ideal of the political a concept of the people as a construct whose main role is to open up a civic space for wider participation. Instead, their conception of *al-shaab*, or the people, only served to produce social subjectivities whose main characteristic was to remain subservient to their movements' hegemony, sacrificing both the civic and the political sphere.

Chapter 4

The Birth of the Deep State and Modern Radical Islamism

ULTIMATELY, HASSAN HUDAYBI'S DEFEAT in the struggle with Gamal Abdel Nasser had disastrous consequences for the Ikhwan and contributed to setting the terms of the relationship between the Islamist movement and the Arab nationalists spearheaded by Nasser. Having destroyed the monarchy, the Free Officers' lofty aspirations had crashed at the altar of political ambition and realpolitik. The honeymoon between the soldiers of God (Hudaybi and the Ikhwan) and the soldiers of the nation (Nasser and the Free Officers) had been short-lived. Theirs was a marriage of convenience, subsequently eroded by the temptations of power. Both felt entitled to be the leader of the new Egypt and to chart its destiny, with each hoping to rule unilaterally with the other camp accepting the role of a junior partner. Both felt that the high stakes involved justified taking risks in a confrontation of this magnitude. Each gambled that the other would blink and step back from the brink of abyss, but neither did. The growing antagonism between the two Islamist and nationalist movements led to radicalization and politically based violence. This increasingly violent struggle ultimately created a rift that is still playing out on the Arab streets today, intermittently plunging the Arab world into a vicious spiral of hatred whose expression is only becoming more and more savage.

In less than two years, the business-like relationship between the Ikhwan and the Free Officers turned into an intense political struggle over the future of Egyptian identity and the state. The former allies became bitter enemies, setting the stage for a clash that became a defining moment in the political history not only of Egypt but also of the wider region. Egypt and the Arab neighborhood have since witnessed a prolonged confrontation between Islamists and secular-leaning Arab nationalists. What happened in Egypt was, in many respects, the beginning of a civil war that continues to reverberate across the contemporary Arab world more than half a century later. By threatening Nasser's authority, the Ikhwan courted a harsh and largely indiscriminate backlash from the new Nasserist state. Throughout the 1950s and 1960s, Nasser brutally suppressed the Islamist movement, imprisoning thousands of its members, including the top leadership like Hudaybi and Sayyid Qutb, the latter of whom only formally joined the Ikhwan in 1953. This clash, and the Ikhwan's humiliating experience of mass incarceration and torture, triggered the beginning of a bloody struggle between the two rivals.

The Rise of the Deep State

The violent and drawn-out confrontation consumed the two leading political and social movements of the Arab world. By polarizing and militarizing Arab politics, and increasing feelings of insecurity and mistrust between rulers and ruled, the effects of this conflict led to the consolidation of political authoritarianism in the Arab world's most populous and influential country, Egypt. Although centered in Egypt, the nationalist-Islamist struggle quickly spread across the region, weakening and undermining the fragile development of the postcolonial state. The rupture between Nasser's Free Officers and Hudaybi's Ikhwan facilitated the construction of an expansive and intrusive security state, a feature of the Arab state system that has been repeatedly highlighted ever since. As political authorities became more and more fearful of their populace, security apparatuses were expanded and their powers increased. Political, ideological, and personal survival became the primary objective of the new authorities.

This violent struggle was to shape the identity of the state system in two significant ways. On the one hand, the new military rulers would prioritize internal security and regime survival at the expense of formal institution building and the rule of law. This, in turn, would have far-reaching implications for state-society relations, contributing to the durability of authoritarianism and the gradual emergence of the so-called deep state or the police state in Egypt. Instead of promoting individual freedoms and recognizing the right of political association, this confrontation early in the life of the post-independence state would strengthen a trend of regime insulation from and mistrust of its populace. If prior to the violent clash with the Ikhwan Nasser had demonstrated certain reservations about the desirability of establishing a dictatorship in Egypt, this collision with a powerful social movement equipped with an underground apparatus convinced him of the need to do so. The roots of political authoritarianism date back to this fateful moment in the early 1950s.

As Nasser built a multilayered security apparatus, the various security services took on lives of their own in their competition for resources and influence, and emerged as rival power centers. As early as 1952, the Free Officers issued a law regulating cooperation between the armed forces and the police in matters of internal security. Veteran judge Tariq al-Bishry described the legislation as opening the door to an increasing role for the military in civilian life, "either to keep internal security, enact emergency rule, or to set up emergency courts."[1] The original regime of military rule established by Nasser and the Free Officers rapidly morphed into something more sinister and oppressive, a deep and wide state. Soon enough these new security services came to exercise intrusive control over Egyptians' everyday lives. The military itself became directly involved in this bureaucratic rivalry by establishing a security branch of its own and focusing more on internal rather than external threats. Security bodies were created or revamped for the purpose of facing up to these perceived menaces, including al-Mukhabarat al-'Amma (the General Intelligence Service [GIS]), founded in 1954, the same year in which Nasser's conflict with both Naguib and the Ikhwan peaked.[2] Nasser took direct charge of the creation of the internal security body.[3] He maintained control over the rest of the security apparatus, in order to guarantee both loyalty and efficiency in realizing designated targets. Strikingly, Nasser insisted on keeping the powers and prerogatives of these bodies overlapping, and asserted his control by being the only one to decide plans and missions.

For example, if there was a plot to assassinate Nasser, he himself would—ironically—have to take the decision regarding which body led the investigation.[4] These bodies were extended in staff and in powers and regulated under the law. These measures massively inflated what Egyptian sociologist Anouar Abdel-Malek labeled the "senior officers caste" in the "Officers Republic" of Egypt, which dominated most civilian institutions, not just the press.[5] All newspapers founded after the revolution were edited by members of this "caste." For instance, Anwar Sadat was the editor of *al-Gumhouria* (which literally means "the Republic") in 1955–1956, and Hamroush and Tharwat Okasha edited *al-Tahrir* (Freedom) magazine. Nasser and the Free Officers treated these newspapers as an "ideological state apparatus" that should remain under the control of the regime.[6]

As discussed in the previous chapter, the Free Officers' revolution had to be manufactured. By forming an integral part of the regime's propaganda arm, these newspapers and journals helped disseminate the Nasserist nationalist ideology and its vision for the army as well as the idea that Nasser was the rightful custodian of both the state and the nation. The development of a conception of "Egyptianness" as sameness and unity against the occupier meant that the junta increasingly came to think of itself as the only representative of the Egyptian nation and its authentic core as well. The Free Officers had become the People and Egypt could not be Egypt without them. In turn, the classification of this new "military caste" as the only legitimate national Self implied the continuation of a state-people relationship characterized by the subordination of the people to the state. Thus national identity increasingly became conceived of as a unitary entity embodied by the military junta rather than as a relational process between social classes. The tightening grip of the military caste over the security apparatus was concomitant with its growing hold over the ideological arms of the state.

This aspect of Nasser's use of the state to propagate its ideological message is extremely important because it shows the challenge faced by the new rulers, that of manufacturing consent. In the political landscape, this tendency was further exemplified by the continuation of the void that had been synonymous with the colonial regime. After crushing the Ikhwan, the Free Officers allowed other ideological groups to barely exist under the patronage of the Nasserist state.[7] The key goal of the Nasserist state was to consolidate its own hegemony and eliminate organized and institutionalized opposition such as the Ikhwan and the communists.[8]

Moreover, the rupture between the Free Officers and the Ikhwan in Egypt—and more generally, between Arab nationalists and Islamists—impacted the moral economy and grand narratives of both movements towards the Western powers, Zionism, and modern development. Both movements portrayed themselves as anti-hegemonic, anti-colonial, and with an abiding commitment to social justice and economic development. Both framed their rivalry as an extension of the greater struggle against external and imperial domination, as well as a quest for liberation, dignity, and a rediscovering of "true" Arab-Muslim identity. Each accused the other of being subservient to outside forces bent on controlling Arab and Muslim destiny while working to thwart plans for Arab unity and Islamic solidarity. In so doing the Free Officers and the Ikhwan became prisoners of their respective ideological constructs. The gradual effect of this ideological straitjacket, which was designed to increase their legitimacy and popularity at home while countering their rivals, was to limit policy options, at significant long-term strategic cost to both movements.

Although the two movements conceptualized each other as bitter enemies, their grand narratives and conceptions of the Self and the Other mirrored one another. A critical thesis from the London School of Economics notes that the struggle for power that trapped the Islamists and the secular-leaning nationalists repeats another deep-seated and unresolved narcissistic breach. The collapse of the caliphate in 1924 and its replacement by a colonial system left a tear in the Arabo-Islamic epistemological space as new and old norms were presented as mutually exclusive. In practice this symbolic breach was illustrated by the actual antagonistic split between a more secular-oriented and an Islamist elite over the question of who should be the rightful leader of the newly constituted system. This in turn only repeated "an original rupture that is constitutive of Arabo-Islamic subjectivity: that of the original Shia-Sunni divide following the death of the Prophet Muhammad. In both cases the violent social antagonism that opposed the two camps took place over the question of power and succession and led to a redefinition of Islam and its role as driver of societal and political norms."[9]

In a similar vein, had Hudaybi been willing to compromise in 1952–1954 and accept Nasser's terms for the Ikhwan to participate as a junior partner in his ruling coalition, the structure and identity of the state would have been substantially different; it might well have been less intrusive, authoritarian, and deep. The long history of close ties and common ground between Nasser and the Islamists is such that this counterfactual question is not far-fetched. Their disagreement after the 1952 coup was a product of miscalculation, excessive ambition, and overreaction, a power struggle that spiraled out of control. There was nothing inevitable about the rupture in relations between the Free Officers and the Ikhwan between 1952 and 1954. Testimonies by contemporary participants on both sides testify to the role of contingent and political factors behind this breakdown of relations.

According to Farid Abdel Khaleq, a senior leader of the Ikhwan, Nasser decided to purge the Ikhwan after they challenged the hegemony of the Free Officers and insisted on a dominant role in the post-monarchy regime. "In our meetings immediately after the 1952 coup, Hudaybi asked that the Ikhwan be consulted on major domestic and international decisions by the Free Officers and that a partnership be set up between the two factions," recounted Abdel Khaleq. "Nasser retorted by saying, 'I do not accept any *wisaya* [oversight]' and that the revolution would act independently and freely."[10] As a gathering storm loomed at the beginning of 1953 Abdel Khaleq said he met one on one with Nasser and implored him to prevent the descent into war between their two respective movements. "I told him, 'Brother Nasser, our common interests lie in cooperation, not confrontation, and we must be frank with each other and resolve our differences.'" Nasser's response was shocking, said Abdel Khaleq, because he used a term that implied sinful behavior. "Brother Farid, you are *usat* [disobedient]. I called on you to join the cabinet and you refused. I called on you to merge with Hay'at al-Tahrir [Liberation Rally, the regime's new propaganda arm] and you refused. This is defiance and rebellion." Abdel Khaleq went on: "I beseeched him not to judge our refusal to participate in his nascent regime or merge our movement into his Hay'at al-Tahrir as *maasiya* [disobedience]; instead, let us cooperate together, while preserving our separate identities."[11] Abdel Khaleq pointed out that it took Ikhwan leaders only one month to learn that the Free Officers were not trustworthy and that they were uninterested in sharing power. "Accordingly, we decided against joining the government and instead would offer advice [opposition] from outside, though we never intended to militarily confront the Free Officers," he insisted.[12] Implicit in this insider's account is that power politics and power distribution lie at the heart of the breakup between the Ikhwan and the Free Officers, even though Abdel Khaleq accuses the Free Officers of power grab and deception: Nasser is portrayed as the driver behind the conspiracy to corner the Ikhwan and to force them to either accept limited participation in the new cabinet or face the wrath of the Free Officers. Also implicit in Abdel Khaleq's account is that Hudaybi and his inner circle called Nasser's bluff and paid dearly for their miscalculation.

A parallel narrative by Nasser and his supporters of the 1954 split asserts that the Ikhwan leaders overplayed their hand by underestimating the young army colonel and by thinking that they could outmaneuver him and rule from behind the scenes. Nasser subsequently portrayed the Ikhwan as cynical, devious, and untrustworthy, regularly repeating the mantra *al-ikhwan laysa la-hum iman* (the Ikhwan cannot be trusted). "The Ikhwan were not interested in sharing power; they wanted to hijack the revolution," said Sami Sharaf, Nasser's chief of staff and gatekeeper. "Hudaybi had mistakenly reckoned that he could control the revolution from behind the curtain, and that Nasser and his comrades were not tough enough to stand up to him."[13] This was a simple case of a political gamble backfiring, Sharaf said, and the refusal of the Ikhwan to recognize this reflects nothing but blind ambition and denial. Mohamed Heikal—a shrewd journalist who was witness to Nasser's journey and became one of his closest confidants—recalled that Nasser was of the opinion that Hudaybi and his inner circle wanted to be in the driver's seat, with a view to engineering a program of ultraconservative religious transformation in Egypt. In his first few meetings with Hudaybi and his circle, Nasser developed a sense of what they had in mind in terms of imposing their Islamist worldview on Egyptian society. According to Heikal, Nasser, whose piety reflected the moderate Islam of most Egyptians, could not stomach the Ikhwan's severe and rigid interpretation of the faith. He suspected them of using religion for ulterior and politicized reasons. "Nasser was not ideologically opposed to the Ikhwan," added Heikal. "Nasser was a Muslim-Arab patriot and viewed his nationalist identity and Muslim faith as compatible, not mutually exclusive."[14]

Khaled Mohieddin, who was privy to the internal debate within the RCC, also downplayed the role of ideology—specifically, the

Ikhwan's Islamic vision for Egyptian society—as a decisive factor in the deterioration of its relations with the Free Officers. "Nasser was not opposed to the ideology of the Ikhwan; he feared the left more than the religious right and the first thing he did was to purge the government of socialist and leftist-leaning comrades who questioned the creeping authoritarianism of the Free Officers," he stated emphatically. "The Ikhwan fully supported the dismantling of parliamentary life and Nasser's purging of progressive, leftist forces. Blinded by political ambitions, the Ikhwan were willing to do whatever it took to exercise power, including acquiescing in the suspension of parliamentary life. The poor creatures [the Ikhwan] did not realize that if they challenged Nasser, he would crush them in the same way he had crushed others. He bluntly warned Ikhwan leaders that the Free Officers would not take risks governing while the Ikhwan enjoyed the fruits of power from behind the scenes."[15]

Regardless of what drove the rupture in relations between the two movements, there is little doubt that Nasser's brutal suppression of the Ikhwan led to the radicalization and militarization of a small but increasingly vocal segment of the Islamist movement. As a result of this brutal clampdown, including the mass imprisonment of Ikhwan members in abysmal prison camp conditions during the 1950s and 1960s, the Islamist movement itself split into two camps. While, on the one hand, many of its members internalized the reasons for their failure by musing that they had not been "radical enough," on the other hand, many more Muslim Brotherhood members reached the opposite conclusion: "we were too radical." During this period of incarceration, the Ikhwan experienced significant division and fragmentation. Some members underwent a metamorphosis, embracing a more radicalized understanding of Islamic activism. Egyptian prisons of the period harbored this new revolutionary brand of Islamism, which increasingly justified the use of violence as a means to bring about a top-down transformation of state and society. The ultimate objective became that of replacing the Nasserist "apostate" state with what was envisioned as new, more righteous Qur'anic political order. The birth of revolutionary Islamism or jihadism, as it came to be known in subsequent decades, owes much of its origin and roots to this episode and epoch.

The Birth of Qutbism or Revolutionary Islamism

Prisons are, of course, notorious for catalyzing radical change and producing charismatic leaders, thinkers, and theorists; they are incubators of revolutionary ideas no matter the historical and intellectual context in which imprisonment takes place. The many examples of this dynamic include the case of the theologian Dietrich Bonhoeffer, a staunch opponent of the Nazi regime in Germany who was involved in plotting to assassinate Adolf Hitler. Already intellectually active in the 1930s, Bonhoeffer continued his activity when detained in Nazi prisons and eventually in a concentration camp, where he was executed. The texts written by Bonhoeffer during detention, including letters to his fiancée,[16] are considered among the most influential contemporary texts on faith-based resistance to oppression and dictatorial rule.[17] The case of Antonio Gramsci is perhaps even more popular. Gramsci's *Prison Notebooks*, written during his arduous imprisonment for opposition to the fascist Italian regime, have become a key point of reference in Western political theory, well beyond the Marxist tradition which informed his own thinking.[18] Just as imprisonment was for Gramsci an experience both of suffering and of intellectual growth, so it was also a crucial experience for Nelson Mandela and other members of the African National Congress (ANC). During his time in detention, Mandela developed political strategies and exchanged ideas with fellow prisoners, including members of other organizations engaged in the same battle. In the words of one biographer, "Robben Island, with hundreds of political prisoners serving long sentences, provided a more sustained opportunity to sharpen political ideas with dialectic and polemic to put the struggle in a wider context."[19]

Though each detainee has a different experience of captivity, imprisonment—far from discouraging intellectuals—frequently nurtures their imagination and creativity. Qutb and his fellow Ikhwan detainees in the 1950s and 1960s were no exception to this rule. However, an examination of the evolution of Qutb's intellectual thought during his prison years from 1954 till 1964 reveals that he developed a normative ethics which partially crystallized around the concept of politically driven violence. With Qutb, violence is not only used as a tool of opposition to the state, it de facto becomes an identity marker that helps differentiate real Muslims from the rest. His growing calls for offensive jihad turn armed activism against corrupt leadership into an obligatory duty of Muslims. In this sense, in Qutb's worldview materialism and immaterialism progressively become entangled in a dialectical relationship. With the concept of offensive jihad, the body becomes the material site of opposition to the established order, while the possibility of its disappearance (through imprisonment, torture, or death) marks the affirmation of true faith and thus a return to an authentic (imagined) and idealized self. The Egyptian prison camps triggered a feeling of existential crisis among the Ikhwan, insofar as they posed a stark threat both to their own individual being and also to that of the Islamist movement as a whole. The majority decided to bide their time and lick their wounds with a view to ensuring the survival of their group and seeking to outmaneuver Nasser in the longer term, while a minority led by Qutb acted otherwise.

Qutb was in many ways an unlikely candidate to become a militant Islamist theorist, having begun his career as a secular literary critic. He had published poems extensively and explicitly tackled themes such as love and the homeland. He had even written a poem commemorating Zaghloul, the founder of the Wafd party, which was such a bitter rival of the Ikhwan. He started one of his poems by comparing the tomb of Zaghloul with the Kaaba, the shrine at the heart of the Grand Mosque complex in Mecca which is the most sacred site for Muslims the world over.[20] His other poems on the theme of love included titles such as "I Love You," "Why I Love You?," and "Kiss."[21] Qutb's transformation from a literary semi-liberal critic into a revolutionary Islamist has to be given historical context.

Qutb's shift from secular literary criticism towards a worldview strongly informed by religious discourse was part of the fashion of the times. Many secular intellectuals pursued comparable trajectories in the 1930s and 1940s. The prominent author Tawfiq al-Hakim, for example, published in 1933 *Ahl al-kahf* (The People of the Cave), a play based on the Qur'anic story of the same name. This was followed by *Awdat al-ruh* (Return of the Spirit) in 1934, *Muhammad* in 1936, and *Al-rebat al-muqadas* (The Sacred Bond) in 1944. Muhammad Hussein Haykal, who held a PhD in law from the Sorbonne and was appointed leader of the Egyptian senate in 1945, wrote *The Life of Muhammad*. For Haykal, Islam was a valid way of life and rational for the modern era.[22] He also wrote other works, including *Al-Siddiq Abu Bakr* and *Faruq Umar* (the two caliphs who took over after the death of Muhammad). While strongly informed by religious discourse, Haykal believed in the impossibility of returning to an Islamic system and establishing Islamic rule on earth, *al-hukm islami*, in our time due to "different conditions" and the "intellectual and scientific progress" achieved in the last fourteen centuries.[23] Other literary figures, such as Abbas al-Aqqad and Ahmad Amin, also shifted focus to Islamic themes in their writings, which led a literary critic, Ali Shalash, to describe this new trend as a "rebellion against literature."[24]

Moreover, some public intellectuals utilized Islamic and modern themes in an attempt to formulate an alternative political vision for the future of Egypt. Khalid Muhammad Khalid is a case in point. In 1950 he published his first book, *Min huna nabda'* (From Here We Start), which was influential and controversial as well. Khalid, who became an adviser to Nasser after the 1952 coup, promoted representative government and socialist policies, including placing limitations on private property and the nationalization of the means of production.[25] Arguing that Islam was a religion, not a state, Khalid angered the old regime, which banned his book and imprisoned him. But the Egyptian courts refused to ban the book and delivered a verdict that nullified all the accusations leveled by the government against the author. Similarly, an influential text by the Syrian author Mustafa al-Siba'i, *Ishtirakiyyat al-islam* (The Socialism of Islam), published in 1960, is said to have been inspired by Khalid's book.[26] A common thread that runs through the writings of these authors is a call for some degree of adaptation and reconciliation between Islam and modernity; they argue for an understanding of Islam broadly in line with many aspects of their former humanistic and modernist commitments.

Qutb was thus just "one of those who began to combine writings on Islam with a concern for and awareness of challenges faced by Egypt as a nation at the time."[27] This tendency can be traced to the 1936 Anglo-Egyptian Treaty, which officially signaled the end of the formal British occupation of Egypt and initiated a new outlook and a perspective among public intellectuals who confronted the task of debating Egypt's future and Egyptians' place in the world.[28] That was a time marked by growing disillusionment with the West in both its capitalist and communist incarnations, a lack of trust in liberal capitalism and constitutionalism, and frustration with the failure of political parties to deal with acute social problems.[29] Egyptians became disillusioned with the political establishment that had embraced the normative values of the European middle class but continued to marginalize the population at home, thus failing to foster a climate of tolerance and openness. The construction of national identity in Egypt developed through an articulation of the Self as "being against," with the result that Islam gradually established itself as a determinant characteristic of the "New Egypt." The fight for a "New Egypt" allowed a new generation of activists in the 1930s and 1940s to differentiate themselves from both the Egyptian and the European political establishment. Islam also provided a resource for opposing the normative values disseminated by colonialism and an anchor of the revolution in what was then seen as a more authentic and autochthonous system of values.

Qutb's transformation took a more radical form for a number of reasons. His stay in the United States between 1948 and 1950 increased his disillusionment with Western civilization and further deepened his conviction that the Islamic way of life was mankind's only salvation from godless capitalism and communism.[30] Qutb criticized the moral corruption which he considered to have proliferated within both the Egyptian state and society at large, leading to individual and national decay.[31] He also attacked both the state and intellectuals, including the religious hierarchy in Egypt, for having been indifferent to these conditions and failing to adopt an authentic Muslim approach to cleanse state and society of moral corruption.[32] His book *Ma'arakat al-islam wa al-ra'simaliyya* (The Battle of Islam and Capitalism), first published in 1951, represented a shift in his thinking towards a strongly religiously influenced discourse. Qutb called for Islam to be adopted both as a way of life and as a ruling system, not just confined to a private sphere of worship. His reasoning is that the state system had failed to bring about cultural renewal.[33] Going beyond questions relating specifically to the Egyptian state, in *Ma'arakat al-islam wa al-ra'simaliyya*, Qutb emphasizes the Palestinian tragedy in the 1948 war and the creation of Israel: "We experienced in Palestine that neither the eastern bloc nor the western bloc cares about the principles that they call for."[34] Elsewhere, Qutb emphatically declares that the experience of "using the ready-made constructs which we begged to have" had proven to be an abject failure.[35]

The Islam presented in Qutb's writings gradually becomes a total ideal portrayed as the only way to heal the identity split caused by colonization and furthered by the continued authoritarianism of the Free Officers' regime. In a way, his Islamic ideal acts as a kind of narcissistic plaster that allows Egyptian society to return to its authentic Self, thereby erasing the ontological shock created by modern European occupation.[36] His emphasis on an original temporality—through its call for a return to the Islam practiced by the Prophet and the four caliphs who succeeded him—also represents a way to actualize in praxis the quest for the authentic Egyptian. He provides a different temporality to that of Western modernity, which Islamists such as Qutb increasingly came to associate with the continued alienation of Muslim societies.

In Qutb's view, the solution is a return to *asala*, which loosely translates as authenticity or a search for identity and which he found in Islam. Accordingly, he argues that the shari'a should be implemented as an all-encompassing system of law governing personal, political, penal, civil, and commercial affairs. He presents Islam as a realistic solution to "basic problems," such as lack of social justice, not just a spiritual remedy.[37] More importantly, he sees Islam as an alternative to nationalism both at the level of the Egyptian polity and at the pan-Arab level. At both levels, in his opinion, nationalism had failed to prevent the partition of historic Palestine, to resist British occupation, and to tackle social ills like corruption and underdevelopment; in contrast, Islam provides for a collective pan-Islamic solidarity while at the same time being alert to issues at the level of the individual state, such as the need to bring about social justice.[38]

Although Qutb's books like *Ma'arakat al-islam wa al-ra'smaliyya* reflected an important shift in his thinking by the early 1950s, his prison experience from 1954 till 1964 was transformative. While spending time in Nasser's jail, Qutb began to advocate the use of violence to bring about God's kingdom on earth. In his book *Ma'lim 'ala al-tariq* (Milestones), first published officially in 1964, Qutb described not only non-Muslims but also contemporary Muslims as *jahili*, a term which literally translates as "ignorant" and evokes Arabian society prior to the advent of Islam. By using the term *jahili* to point to the ignorance of Muslims and non-Muslims alike, Qutb achieved three things. First, this language reminded Muslims of the early days of Islam, when the Prophet Muhammad and his companions fought *jahili* people with word and sword and prevailed. Second, the term *jahili* provided a justification for confronting the Nasser regime and his successors, Anwar Sadat and Hosni Mubarak, on both political and religious grounds: Nasser, Sadat, and Mubarak were not only political tyrants but also unbelievers. Third, Qutb's description of society as *jahili* extended the category of people that Muslims should battle beyond the military and political elite to include ordinary people who must be brought back into Islam by either co-option or coercion.

Qutb's appeal found receptive ears particularly among young members of the Ikhwan, both inside and outside jail, who were clamoring to exact vengeance against Nasser for his clampdown on the movement. These religious activists also sympathized with Qutb's ambitious and broader call for a revolutionary Islamist alternative to that of the mainstream religious establishment and that of the Ikhwan as well. His revolt targeted formal, traditional authority in all its religious, political, and epistemological manifestations. He deployed the sacred text—the Qur'an—as an effective weapon of choice and invested his revolutionary call with legitimacy, thus inspiring members of the Ikhwan over the heads of their established leaders. Qutb, who had no religious training or credentials, dismissed fourteen centuries of interpretations and counter-interpretations of the religious canon through his direct and unfiltered reading of the Qur'an. His call for the creation of a vanguard which would Islamize society from the top down, by force if necessary, clashed with the Ikhwan's ideology. In contrast, the worldview of the organization's leadership emphasized the need for strategic patience and perseverance in the face of persecution and the role of *da'wa* (religious call) and reform as means of effecting social and political change. Once again, to understand Qutb's emphasis on the role of a revolutionary vanguard, it is important to take note of the broader context in which his ideas were formed, including transnationally. Qutb's notion of vanguard is close to that advocated under the same rubric by the communist pioneer Vladimir Lenin.[39] While it is difficult to draw any direct line between Lenin and Qutb, historian John Calvert notes that Qutb's diagnostic plan and his call to action bear resemblance to Lenin's call for the formation of a vanguard to change society even by violent means.[40] The Indian Abul A'la Mawdudi, from whom Qutb borrowed heavily, was himself directly influenced by Lenin's writings regarding the role of the revolutionary vanguard, the state, and its organization.

The Struggle within the Ikhwan

Qutb's preaching and his success in recruiting followers caused a major breach in the ranks of the Ikhwan. For ten years, beginning in the late 1950s, an intense struggle raged among Ikhwan members in Nasser's prisons. On one side stood an old guard whose primary goal was survival and the prevention of the disintegration of the organization. On the other hand, a small dissident contingent led by Qutb challenged the quietist attitude of the old guard. Top Ikhwan leaders were alarmed not by Qutb's call to arms against Nasser but by his description of contemporary Muslim society as *jahili*, a label which they viewed as a recipe for *fitna* (sedition) among believers.

Far from being a purely academic and theoretical dispute, the Qutbian revolt had serious implications for the Ikhwan and their relations with the Nasserist state. While in prison, Qutb guided and spearheaded a paramilitary group known as al-Tanzim al-Sirri, the Secret Organization, which comprised hundreds of dedicated young men who clandestinely organized themselves into small, decentralized cells all over Egypt (see chapter 6 on al-Tanzim al-Sirri).[41] Qutb conceived of al-Tanzim's operatives as a vanguard that would struggle to reestablish God's authority and sovereignty on earth. He instructed the members of this vanguard to sever their loyalty to *jahili* society and to *jahili* leadership: "The group must separate itself from the *jahili* society and become independent and distinct from the active and organised *jahili* society."[42] I was told by surviving members of al-Tanzim that the manifesto called *Milestones* was in fact a compilation of individual writings leaked out to them while Qutb was in jail. Qutb hoped that these writings would guide the incipient organization in its deliberation, helping its operatives to jell into the vanguard that he had conceived.[43]

Qutb's rousing manifestos, which he penned in prison from 1954 until 1964, provided ideological and theological nourishment and sustenance to dedicated followers both inside and outside Egyptian prisons. His story and ideas have also inspired subsequent generations of young Muslims battling Muslim rulers because of their failure to apply Qur'anic laws in state and society. The Nasserist regime banned *Milestones* six months after its publication, though by that time the work had already gone through five printings.[44] The Egyptian authorities were slow to comprehend the extent of both the Qutbian revolutionary call and its popular appeal.

It was the threat posed by Qutb's al-Tanzim which led Nasser to send him to the gallows in 1966. As Zeinab al-Ghazali, a close contemporary and confidante of Qutb, argued, *Milestones* is the manifesto that caused the execution of Qutb.[45] Unlike Banna's underground group, al-Nizam al-Khass (the Secret Apparatus), Qutb's paramilitary organization was more ideologically ambitious and daring, though less effective and potent. Qutb hoped to topple the Nasserist state and fundamentally restructure Egyptian society from the top down. He anointed himself the chief interpreter of Islam's sacred text—the Qur'an—and assigned the task of transformation of society and polity to a vanguard which he indoctrinated. While Banna had always taken the position that the Ikhwan should not seek political power until the Egyptian people were sufficiently re-Islamized to accept an Islamic order, Qutb approached the problem of political power differently, arguing that all barriers to Islam's rule must be cleared even if by force. Since oppressive regimes had in his view come to separate their subjects from Islam, they were one of the key obstacles to be forcibly removed:

> Islam does not force people to accept its belief, but it wants to provide a free environment in which they will have the choice to believe. What it wants to abolish is those oppressive political systems under which people are prevented from expressing their freedom to choose whatever beliefs they want, and after that it gives them complete freedom to decide whether to accept Islam or not.[46]

Clearing the way for this freedom has to be by *jihad bi-l-sayf* (jihad by the sword), added Qutb.[47] Banna's religious call for *da'wa* was more Gramscian in strategy; although there is no evidence that Banna had read the Italian author, his establishment of the secret apparatus is evocative of Gramsci's concept of war of maneuver. Banna's reliance on a process of indoctrination, whereby a set of concepts, systems, and practices—rather than force—would be used to control the minds of human beings, is reminiscent of the concept of war of position and of Gramsci's conception of ideology. Accordingly, Banna encouraged his disciples to focus on winning hearts and minds, shaping the educational system, and targeting intellectuals as key means of effecting change.[48] He had envisaged three steps for the delivery of his message: (1) propagation and preaching; (2) lobbying and mobilization; and (3) execution.[49] Although Banna had not excluded jihad to realize the goals of the *da'wa*, including the use of force, he had stressed the need for peaceful means to start with and warned against aggression.[50] It is true that Banna oversaw the creation of the armed Nizam al-Khass alongside the open political wing within the Ikhwan. But the weight of evidence shows that his first priority had been armed struggle against the British colonial presence in Egypt and then Zionism in Palestine, even though al-Nizam al-Khass did carry out terrorist attacks against Egyptian politicians and civil society in the 1940s. In contrast, Qutb's core concern was Egypt itself, and he called for bold radical initiatives, arguing that efforts to effect long-term social and ideological transformations were "futile" due to the oppressive nature of the state.

Even after Qutb was executed by the Nasserist state in 1966, his revolutionary project lived on.[51] In 1965, Qutb's ideas were seen as the key driver inspiring some Ikhwan members to plot coups and assassinations against state officials. His influential disciples included Zeinab al-Ghazali, who was also imprisoned for six years beginning in 1965. In her memoirs, published fifteen years later, she reiterated the same creed as Qutb's with apparent pride and without expressing any regrets. Moreover, she dedicated her book to "the blood which was shed to act as massive waves pushing generations across history forward to the road of God."[52] In the introduction, Ghazali argued that "'the societies of *jahiliyya*' distracted mankind from the righteous path and strayed away from the path of God."[53] Even an activist-author like Ghazali, who had spent years in prison and suffered humiliation and torture, struck a defiant note on the first page of the book's introduction: "the prison cells and the torture ... had only made those loyal propagators of *da'wa* and the builders of its school of thought stronger, steadier, and more patient to push this *batel* [falseness] away and uproot it."[54] Throughout her memoirs, Zeinab al-Ghazali reminded religious activists of the core concepts which had emerged out of Qutb's writings, particularly the idea that sovereignty belongs to God or *al-hakimiyya*, not to humans or *al-jahiliyya*. Asked under imprisonment and torture about her political ambitions, she asserts that she replied that she hoped to "set up Qur'an and Sunnah" or an Islamic system of governance. She argued retrospectively that "there is no rule except for God." Addressing her detractors, she contended that "when we build our Qur'anic state, your political structures will collapse and your myths will be shattered."[55]

Although Qutb's subversive ideas continue to echo into the present, it would be misleading to assert a direct causal link between his revolutionary Islamism and that of Al Qaeda or the Islamic State. Rather, if Qutb's revolutionary Islamist ideal still resonates with a small portion of the Muslim population, it is because the identity split embodied by the Islamist/semi-secularist nationalist struggle is still unresolved. His internal distinction between authentic and inauthentic Muslims is being reappropriated by Salafi-jihadists such as the Islamic State and deployed effectively in an effort to impose a redefinition of mainstream Sunni Islam that serves their own interests. Qutb's Manichaean vision of a world divided between a *jahili* society and a dignified, just, and noble Islamic society is also constitutive of Salafi-jihadist discourse. By stressing the effects of colonization and the consequences of the Sykes-Picot agreement on the geographical divisions of Muslims and their spiritual fragmentation, the Islamic State draws from the unresolved internal identity rupture that Qutb placed at the center of his discourse. However, it is worth mentioning that, in contrast to the armed rebellion by Ayman al-Zawahiri, Osama bin Laden, and Abu Bakr al-Baghdadi against both the far enemy and the near enemy, Qutb never called for transnational jihad, and it is important to take into account changing historical and sociological circumstances. Nevertheless, these transnational revolutionaries were certainly inspired by Qutb's ideas, his defiance of formal authority, and his martyrdom. Over the last half century Qutb has served as a model for most jihadist waves in Muslim lands. He has not only been used and abused by radicals like Zawahiri, who invoke his name in an effort to secure legitimacy for their own radical ideas, he has also been misunderstood by young men who take his words and apply them to moments in time and space which differ from the context in which he himself was living and writing.

I have encountered scores of Islamist dissidents and activists who concede that they misread Qutb. The reason for this misunderstanding is that Qutb's ideas were not seriously contested or deconstructed by the Ikhwan leadership. With the exception of the Ikhwan old guard's indirect rebuttal in the 1960s of Qutb's indictment of Muslim society as *jahili*, the dominant wing within the Ikhwan has avoided deconstructing his concepts and has treated him with deference and respect, routinely referring to him as al-Shahid al-Hayy (the living martyr). While these mainstream Ikhwan knew that Qutb's ideas were socially destructive, they refrained from seriously critiquing them because his popularity was such that they feared doing so would undermine their own credibility. It is an open secret that there also remains an influential Qutbian contingent within the Islamist organization, and his legacy coexists uneasily with Banna's. He holds pride of place among ultraconservatives, and his writings form part of the Ikhwan curriculum for educating and indoctrinating members. Centrist members of the Ikhwan would not dare to launch a direct attack on Qutb, and any negative reference to al-Shahid would elicit a swift rebuke by senior leaders, as has been the case. There is no evidence that Hudaybi himself ever directly disavowed Qutb's call for violence in *Milestones*. Hudaybi certainly saw chapters of the book, having been given them by Qutb's sisters, Hamida and Amina, and by Zeinab al-Ghazali, who acted as intermediary between Hudaybi and Ikhwan members in the underground. Although Hudaybi was well aware of Qutb's radical and potentially incriminating revolutionary overtones, he was impressed with aspects of the work and its vigorous defense of Islam, and so gave it his blessing. As Ghazali recalls in her memoirs:

> I know that *al-Murshid* [the supreme guide] viewed these parts of the book and approved for Qutb to publish them. When I asked him ... he said ... *fi Baraketallah* ... God Bless him ... I read and read [the book].[56]

Despite claims that Hudaybi only called for peaceful measures, it was probably with implicit knowledge that Ghazali and other members of the Ikhwan went about putting Qutb's violent radical concepts into practice on the ground. Although Hudaybi was wary of some of Qutb's key ideas and distanced himself from Qutb in public, the fight against the Nasserist state was a priority which trumped all others. My interviews with Ikhwan officials over the years have convinced me that Hudaybi might have tacitly allowed Qutb to get on with militant activism because it seemed a useful measure that would aid his own struggle against Nasser.

Banna and Hudaybi belonged to a different school of thought than Qutb. They subscribed to a gradualist, peaceful approach to Islamizing society, while Qutb instilled in his followers a revolutionary methodology to bring about a rupture in state and society, a fundamental change. Hudaybi's tacit backing of the Qutbian project must be seen in the context of the bitter struggle with Nasser and Hudaybi's anxiety about the survival of the Ikhwan. Several members of al-Tanzim say that Qutb sought and obtained Hudaybi's approval to lead al-Tanzim. In her memoirs, Zeinab al-Ghazali says that Qutb and the Ikhwan obtained Hudaybi's blessing for an educational program that would span thirteen years in the name of the "age of *da'wa* in Mecca" with a "base of the Islamic nation who are brothers committed to Sharia and its rules ... a base which has all the features of a proper Islamic nation ..."[57] Ghazali, who was a pivotal intermediary between Qutb and Hudaybi, had read *Milestones* and pushed for its approval by the *murshid* and then its publication.

It is no wonder, then, that it took Hudaybi, together with other Ikhwan leaders, a long while to criticize Qutb's ideas, since they had earlier given them their blessing. Hudaybi also sent notes and letters to members of the Ikhwan, which were later collected in a book published after his death in 1977 under the title *Du'at la Qudat* (Preachers, Not Judges). In his book, Hudaybi refuted Qutb's subversive claim that Muslims could be atheists, *jahili*, even if they believe in God and Muhammad.[58] It was not until the 1990s, with the escalation of armed clashes between Arab governments and Qutbian disciples, that a few religious scholars close to the Ikhwan began to critique Qutb's manifestos as misguided, based on misinterpretation, simplification, and even distortion of the holy texts. A prominent mainstream scholar, Yusuf al-Qaradawi, who is known for his informal links to the Ikhwan, has published a number of articles refuting Qutb's ideas on *jahiliyya*. The voices of Hudaybi and Qaradawi remained a minority, however, and the critique—such as it was—came too little and too late. There is as yet no resolution to this contestation, and the Ikhwan as an organization has failed to come to terms with the Qutbian inheritance and legacy within its ranks. The unwillingness of the Ikhwan to publicly address Qutb's place within the group testifies to the existence of a generational divide, between a powerful, conservative segment within the old guard that idealizes al-Shahid and a younger segment that prefers to steer the group away from Qutbian influence. The current leaders of the movement are reluctant to open old wounds and remind the public of that controversial and painful chapter in its history, preferring to sweep it under the carpet, knowing that this could have serious consequences for the future of the Islamist movement. Mohamed Ama'ra, an Islamist public intellectual close to the Ikhwan, said that he and others have urged Ikhwan leaders to resolve the dialectical tensions and contradictions that exist between Banna's and Qutb's schools within the movement. According to Amara, the Ikhwan do not distance themselves from Qutb because they do not want to upset their base. "It is easier for intellectuals than the organization to deconstruct Qutbian ideas and we have already begun to do so," he told me.[59]

Finally, it is worth underscoring that the propagation of these radical ideas would not have been possible had it not been for the weakness and inefficiency of the Ikhwan leadership under Hudaybi. Hudaybi never exercised the degree of control over the movement that Banna had enjoyed. These deficiencies on the part of the Ikhwan leadership were only exacerbated by Nasser's efforts to stir up internal dissent and rifts. The fault line within the prison walls in the late 1950s and the 1960s has left deep scars on the Ikhwan's evolution and structure. Ever since that period, the Islamist movement as a whole has been torn, pulled and pushed in two dramatically different ideological directions; one militant and the other far more conservative. Contrary to what Islamists and their detractors claim, the unity of the Islamist movement is a myth, a political construction. Like other social agents, Islamists are divided along ideological, generational, personality, and socioeconomic lines. Although a minority, the revolutionary bloc has attempted to hijack the movement, and its violent actions have spoken louder than the majority's quietist posture. The Qutbians have had greater influence on the Islamist movement than their small numbers warrant. In addition to the revolutionary wing, the Qutbians are entrenched within the top echelons of the Ikhwan and exercise considerable influence over decision making. Ironically, reformist members lament that these old guard Qutbians wage a relentless struggle to preserve their status within the Ikhwan and stubbornly oppose any attempt to transform the Islamist organization. "Qutb would turn in his grave if he had known what his disciples have done with his legacy," said Hassan Hanafi, a philosopher who posits a contrarian interpretation of the Qutbian narrative anchored in Third World progressive socialism.[60] In a sweeping indictment of the Ikhwan, Mohamed Habib, a former second in command who became disillusioned with the organization and was forced out in January 2010, points out that both current Ikhwan leaders and rank-and-file members have internalized Qutb's subversive ideas of *hakimiyya* and *jahiliyya*, postponed violence, and dismissed democracy as un-Islamic, and that this has had disastrous consequences for the movement. "My direct knowledge of Ikhwan leaders over the years indicates that they are not self-critical and do not acknowledge errors and sins before or after they gained power in the wake of the [Arab Spring] revolution."[61]

Conclusion

If the Ikhwan and the Free Officers had cemented their informal alliance and cooperated in building the institutions of the postcolonial, post-independence state, the face of the Arab Middle East would have been radically different. Instead, the deepening authoritarianism of the Nasserist state and its gradual exclusion of the Ikhwan only fed the growing antagonism between the two movements. With the Nasserist state, the military became a hegemonic political class that functioned with increasing independence of its social and economic base. In this sense, Nasser paved the way for the political and economic dominance of the army in Egypt. The military's firm control over both the security and ideological apparatus of the state antagonized and angered the Ikhwan further. al-Hudaybi's refusal to accept a junior role in the newly formed revolutionary cabinet set the stage for a hostile relationship between the two movements. The brutalization and humiliation of the Ikhwan by the Nasserist state, including prison camps and torture, was ultimately responsible for the radicalization of a minority of Muslim Brothers. As the Nasserist state failed to provide a space where the Ikhwan's subjectivity could be articulated, Qutb's ideas, developed in a Nasserist prison, ended up projecting death as the only space where "the living together" could be imagined. This retrenchment of the Qutbian discourse in the imaginary through its emphasis on life after death allowed young Muslims who felt persecuted by the revolutionary regime to escape a temporality that had simply become too difficult to bear.

Neither political authoritarianism nor religious messianism and nihilism would have become deeply entrenched in Arab and Muslim soil if the two movements had been able to work together. The clash between Nasser's and Qutb's supporters, reflected particularly starkly in the hanging of Qutb in 1966, caused a rupture in the nascent Arab political system and pitted powerful social forces against each other. Seething with anger and aching for vengeance ever since, the Qutbian vanguard(s) have waged trench warfare against the enemies of Islam near and far. In a way, the nationalist-Islamist vendetta tribalized and militarized Arab politics. Hero-worshipped and canonized by their respective followers, Nasser and Qutb set a powerful example of a cult of personality that has infected and poisoned Arab political culture. The sole-leader model has become the norm, not the exception, in the region.

Secular-leaning Arab nationalists have been left awaiting deliverance by another messiah like Nasser, only to be rewarded with third-rate successors, such as the late Muammar Qaddafi and Saddam Hussein. Although promising salvation and glory, those relatively secular dictators erected police states that prioritized security at the expense of rights and individual freedoms; they sucked the blood out of the veins of Muslim civil societies. Revolutionary Islamists have glorified Qutb as the father of all martyrs. Standing tall in the face of tyranny, Qutb is portrayed as a morally courageous believer who sacrificed his life for Islam. "Al-Shahid al-Hayy"—"the living martyr," as he is called—is set apart from other contemporary religious figures and theorists because he lived a virtuous life and did not compromise his principles. A well-known Egyptian writer, Adel Hamouda, noted that "because he [Qutb] was executed, he has become a hero ... a role model ... a master ... a mentor ... and an exceptional human being."[62]

Islamists and nationalists say that the painful era is behind them, though the aftermath of the Arab Spring popular uprisings in 2011 shows clearly that the wounds have not yet healed. Although in 2011 and 2012 supporters of both camps united briefly against secular authoritarian rulers, such as Ben Ali of Tunisia, Hosni Mubarak of Egypt, Qaddafi of Libya, Ali 'Abdullah Saleh of Yemen, and Bashar al-Assad of Syria, that moment proved to be fleeting. Once the dictators were removed, Islamists and nationalists fought it out on the streets, reviving images and symbols of a painful and distant past. The current confrontation between nationalists led by the military and Islamists spearheaded by the Ikhwan has turned out to be as bloody and costly as the struggle between the Free Officers and the Ikhwan in the 1950s and 1960s. It is all-out war. Far from being deconstructed, the ghosts of the past still haunt nationalists and Islamists, both of whom remain prisoners of their entrenched narratives.

Chapter 5

Young Gamal Abdel Nasser

NASSER'S STATUS AS THE leader of secular-leaning Arab nationalism—or, as he was later known, "the lion of the Arabs"—was by no means preordained. Rather, the politics and ideals for which he came to be known only crystallized over the course of a tumultuous lifetime and career and exposed him to a range of competing ideologies, which were more complex and ambiguous than often portrayed. Nasser's life also serves to emphasize that the challenge for scholars exploring the history of this period is to avoid viewing it through clear-cut divisions. The different social and political orientations which he flirted with or embraced throughout his life reveal the different facets of both Nasser the man and Nasser the president. A biography underlines the fluidity of the positions that he adopted along the way; proving that he was more of a pragmatist than an ideologue.

Nasser has become an international icon and his legacy has been reinterpreted and reappropriated in Egypt, the Arab world, and beyond. Adulated by supporters and loathed by detractors, Nasser has been called a defender of secular nationalism, a betrayer of the Islamic cause, a hero, and a dictator.[1] On balance, in the Egyptian and the Arab imagination Nasser is mythologized, becoming "a rhetorical device," whose image connotes plural interpretations and nonsectarianism.[2] While the endurance of the Nasserist symbol and benign image can be explained by the social reforms and ideals for which Nasser is known, there is a darker and more brutal side which involved large-scale repression and violence against political opponents. The durability of Nasser's legacy lies in what is still seen as his defiance, his belief in the dignity of everyday Egyptians, and his commitment to lift them out of poverty and illiteracy as well as his love for Egypt, which was greatly reciprocated by the masses.

Nasser's Birth and Childhood Years

Most autobiographies of Nasser trace his childhood to Bakos, a suburban district of Alexandria, where he was born on January 15, 1918. A remarkable feature of Nasser's childhood is that he lived all over Egypt. Moving around the country exposed him to the many facets of the Egyptian nation. It also allowed him to witness firsthand inequity and abject poverty. Nasser was just three years old when his father, a postal clerk, was reassigned to Asyut in Upper Egypt. Asyut was dominated by a population mostly made up of illiterate, poor farmers, but a third of the inhabitants in the area were also Copts. There, the young Nasser heard stories of his father getting on well with the Christians and of him owing them massive favors. Although a town of forty thousand inhabitants, Asyut had no primary public school, but Nasser was one of the Muslim pupils admitted to Muharram Bek, a school organized by the Christian community there.[3]

In 1923–1924, when he was five years old, Nasser moved to Khatatba, where he attended a primary school for the children of railway employees until he was sent to live with his paternal uncle in Cairo and attend El-Nahassin primary school. There, Nasser lived in a working-class neighborhood, and his school was near Khan al-Khalili market, in the vicinity of al-Azhar mosque in Old Cairo, the oldest religious and educational Muslim institution in the world. These "colourful surroundings, where jewellers, goldsmiths, tinkers and carpenters made and sold their goods in small shops lining a maze of noisy narrow streets," was the young Nasser's first "serious schooling."[4] During his stay with his uncle, Nasser exchanged letters with his mother, with whom he had a deep bond, and visited the family during school holidays. However, in 1926, the letters from his mother stopped. Nasser was only told of her passing away, during the childbirth of his third brother, months later, following a holiday visit to the family. This indelible shock left an emotional scar in the young Nasser.[5] Aged eight, he moved again and was sent to a little village near Suez overlooking the Red Sea. He subsequently resettled in Damanhur, one of the largest cities in the Nile Delta, before moving back to Alexandria in 1928 to stay with his maternal grandfather. In Alexandria, he spent his fourth year of primary school at the El-Attarin School before being sent in 1929 to a boarding school, the Helwan High School, where he stayed for one year. After his father joined the postal service in Alexandria, Nasser subsequently moved back to Alexandria and attended the Ras el-Tin High School. It is in this school that Nasser's nationalist feelings were nurtured. In 1930, the 1923 constitution, a result of the 1919–1922 revolution, was abolished by the government, provoking mass protests by Egyptians and students who demanded the restoration of the constitution and the end of the British occupation. Although he was too young to fully understand the reasons behind the demonstrations, Nasser joined in the protests and got beaten by the police. Recounting this fateful moment, he explained:

> While crossing the Manshiya Square in Alexandria, I noticed clashes between some demonstrating students and the police, I did not hesitate: I immediately joined the demonstrators not knowing anything about the cause of demonstration for I found no reason to ask. At the beginning it seemed that the demonstrators had the upper hand, but soon the police forces were backed with two trucks stuffed with policemen, turning the tables once more. I remember attempting to throw some stones but was immediately caught and, on trying to escape, I was struck by a blow on the head by a police baton followed by another blow until I fell down. All drenched in blood, I was driven to prison along with a group

> of students who failed to escape. It was at the police station, while receiving treatment for my head injuries, that I learned that the demonstration was an anti-government protest led by the "Misr al-Fatat" (Young Egypt) society.[6]

Nasser would subsequently and briefly join Young Egypt, marking a shift from being a supporter of the monarchy to a more radical vision.

In 1933, at fifteen years old, Nasser attended the El-Nahda Secondary School at the El-Zaher district of Cairo after his father was reassigned to the capital. There, Nasser's family first stayed in a house owned by Jewish folks with whom the "young Gamal seems to have gotten along well ... [to the extent that] he even took meals" with them.[7] Nasser's early experience of religious coexistence and cooperation would be later reflected in his conduct of developing good relations with members of other faiths, by showing flexibility and tolerance towards other communities. He encouraged his own children to donate toward the construction of the main cathedral in Cairo.[8]

The El-Nahda school's curriculum seems to have had a particularly important impact on the shaping of Nasser's nationalist sentiments. His favorite subject was history, and he read widely beyond the set syllabus, with encouragement from his teachers. Historical works that he read included books on Napoleon Bonaparte, Alexander the Great, Gandhi, Jean-Jacques Rousseau, and Voltaire. Nasser also read literary works like Victor Hugo's *Les Misérables* and Charles Dickens's *Tale of Two Cities*, both of which discussed the idea of revolt against tyranny and unjust laws.[9] He even penned an article in the school magazine titled "Voltaire, Man of Liberty," in which he expressed admiration for the French thinker because he had maintained his independence from the ruling authority and "paved the way for the French Revolution."[10] However, it was Julius Caesar who was Nasser's favorite icon, serving as a hero for his first historical essay—not least because he had conquered the British![11] In 1935, at the age of sixteen, Nasser played the dictator in Shakespeare's eponymous play.[12] He was keen on Arab literature, and his favorite readings included books by the renowned Egyptian poets Ahmed Shawki and

Hafez Ibrahim. Shawki's poems and plays shifted from religious to patriotic and historic. While on a scholarship in France, Shawki had formed an anti-British group that called for the end of British occupation, and he was a close friend of nationalist leaders like Mustafa Kamil. Similarly, Ibrahim's writings highlighted the abject poverty of Egyptians and the politics of British occupation. Like Shawki, Ibrahim was close to the leaders of the 1919–1922 revolution. Other literary works included novels and plays by Tawfik Al-Hakim, especially his 'Awdat el-Rouh (Restoration of the Spirit), which envisions the rise of an Egyptian leader who will unite Egyptians and inspire them to fight for their freedom and the revival of the national spirit. Other Arabic books on Nasser's reading list included the life of the Prophet Muhammad and other influential Islamic figures, as well as manuscripts on influential Egyptian political leaders like Mustafa Kamil.

The early formative years, together with other experiences, shaped Nasser's character, sensibility, and worldview and instilled in him a sense of cultural tolerance and moderation. According to Heikal, Nasser's diverse readings added historical evidence to his conviction that the army could serve as the solution to Egypt's problems. Moreover, his love for Arabic and European texts on military strategy and leadership stayed with him throughout his life as he continued to read such works as *Governor of Egypt* by Charles Roux and *The River of War* by Winston Churchill.[13]

Nasser as a Youth: All about Nationalism

If education, readings, and experiences in various cities had a decisive impact on the emergence of Nasser's nationalist sentiments,[14] the sociopolitical context which he inhabited had a greater weight on the development of his character. To identify the many facets of what has come to be known as Nasserist politics, it is necessary to understand the environment in which Nasser's own identity evolved and consolidated. Nasser's formative years occurred at a critical time in the development of Egypt's national identity. He was born just a year before the 1919–1922 revolution. By then, the expansion of modern state institutions and colonial capitalism had instigated a redefinition of "Egyptianness." By the early twentieth century more and more Egyptians had migrated to urban centers in the hope of a better life. As a result, foreigners, the emerging educated middle class, and the working class, including former peasants, now all lived together in cities. Consequently, the long-held conception of Egyptian subjectivity as divided between city and country became less and less relevant and a vision of Egypt as an indivisible political and economic entity emerged.[15] The result is that "the literate culture increasingly placed peasant and city dweller alike into the same socio-political and indeed moral category."[16] Mustafa Kamil's defense of the peasants and opposition to the khedive following the Dinshawai incident in 1906 was a direct reflection of this shift.[17] The nationalist leaders' new focus on the *fellah*, or Egyptian peasant, helped legitimize their political aspirations and allowed them to expand their social base of support among the masses. By the time Nasser was born, the nationalist discourse had already made use of the *fellah* as one of the defining images of the Egyptian national self.[18] In this sense, the pivotal role given to the *fellah* in the Nasserist discourse crystallized the development that had taken place within the larger nationalist rhetoric in the years leading up to the Free Officers' coup.

In the 1930s, this shift in the conception of Egyptians as a national people was accompanied by the weakening of Egyptian territorial nationalism and a turn to a more ethnocentric nationalism.[19] Two writers call this "integral nationalism," flourishing as a counter-reaction to the colonial parliamentary system and the Westernized mode of values that the political elite of the 1910s and 1920s had adopted.[20] The mood in the 1930s darkened as a result of the Great Depression and its negative effects on the Egyptian economy. Complicating matters were repressive measures by the Sidqi government and the Wafd's inability to exercise power independently and without interference from the Palace and the British. The hopes and aspirations of the 1920s gave way to disillusionment and bitterness. For Egyptians, nominal independence had done little to improve their life and access to the country's economy and polity.

Nasser came into contact with a broad spectrum of opinions, including student organizations, socialist and leftist groups, revolutionaries, and the Ikhwan. As Egypt witnessed a period of severe economic crisis, political repression, and polarization, anti-government strikes repeatedly rocked the country. For instance, in 1930 Nasser joined a student protest against the Sidqi government's abolition of the 1923 constitution and its replacement by a more authoritarian document. In 1935, following the government's unwillingness to accede to popular demands, several political groupings coalesced into a united front, calling for the restoration of the 1923 constitution.[21] Far from a passive observer of the political tumult which engulfed Egypt during this period, Nasser actively participated in civil disobedience and protests. In a letter to a friend, at the age of just seventeen, he expressed his growing disillusionment and anger at the political establishment: "The situation today is critical; Egypt is in a precarious state," he wrote before lamenting the dying nationalist spirit of Mustafa Kamil:

> Mustafa Kamil has said, "Even if my heart moves from my left to my right, even if the pyramids move, even if the current of the Nile changes direction, I will never change my principles." Everything which has happened up to now is a long introduction to a greater and more important task. Several times we have said that we would work together, to wake our nation out of its sleep, to arouse the forces hidden deep inside the people. But alas, up to now nothing, no, nothing has yet been accomplished.[22]

Nasser wrote just as fondly of the revolutionary commitment that had prevailed in the years leading up to the 1919–1922 revolution:

> Where is the patriotism which in 1919 ignited a fire in our breasts? ... Where are those who can bring up a new generation enabling the Egyptian, now weak, humiliated, and silent on the usurpation of his [her] rights ... to be so strong and high-headed enough to struggle for the quest of independence and freedom ... ?[23]

In this letter, Nasser also notes the endemic corruption of the political establishment and mourns the loss of *al-karama* or "dignity," a term he would turn into a powerful symbol of his mass politics.[24] Decades later, *al-karama* would become the rallying cry of the millions of Arabs who revolted against authoritarian rulers during the large-scale popular uprisings which shook the region between 2010 and 2012. This is a reminder of the durability of Nasser's legacy, even if there is nothing specifically Nasserist about the political invocation of the idea of dignity, as some Arab nationalists would have it. Nasser's criticism of the national mood and situation in Egypt mirrored that of many Egyptian intellectuals. An increasing number of writers and thinkers—including Tawfiq al-Hakim, Muhammad 'Awad Muhammad, the Misr al-Fatat (Young Egypt) leader Ahmad Hussein, and the Coptic journalist and pioneer of Arab nationalism Salama Musa—criticized the parliamentary system and party politics, which they viewed as responsible for *hizbiyya* (factionalism).[25] As two academics note, *hizbiyya* "embodied the transformation of Egyptian politics into an arena for personal and factional power struggles devoid of any higher purpose." It came to be viewed as an incurable sickness in the body politic, "the sickness of factionalism [*marad al-hizbiyya*] [...] by the 1930s it was becoming a widely accepted term in the Egyptian political lexicon, a symbol of the bankruptcy of Egyptian public life."[26] Once again, there is continuity between Nasser's subsequent rejection of representative parliamentarianism and party politics and the intellectual and sociopolitical environment in which he had grown up.

It is in this context that in 1936 Nasser attempted to join the military academy, but his application was unsuccessful and he instead enrolled at Cairo University's law faculty. He tried again in 1937 and this time he was accepted.[27] In addition to their political and economic grievances, many Egyptians were infuriated at the predominance of foreigners in the military. In a bid to qualm social discontent, a more inclusive army policy had been included in the 1936 Anglo-Egyptian Treaty, which benefited Nasser and his generation.

His decision to join the military was not random: he saw the institution as intimately bound up with the hopes and prospects of nationalist politics. As public disillusionment with mainstream political parties increased, many Egyptians looked to the army as the only body capable of changing the toxic conditions in which they found themselves. This widespread public sentiment still holds today: the military is seen as a unifying, nonpartisan symbol of the nation. According to his confidant and official biographer, Mohamed Hassanein Heikal, Nasser subsequently acknowledged that he had viewed the military as a spearhead that could awaken Egypt's population from its malaise and subservience to foreigners.

Nasser's comrades who spent time with him in the military academy recalled that he was already highly politicized and deeply anxious about the strangulation of the nation by colonial domination and the subservience and corruption of the ruling political elite. During a two-year military posting to Sudan in 1939, which was then part of Egypt, Nasser witnessed how Britain attempted to wrest Sudan away from Cairo's control. This augmented Nasser's anti-British stance. As Anthony Nutting noted, Nasser "could not but feel slighted by the continued British rejection of Egypt's claim to sole sovereignty in the Sudan which had been voiced by the first prophet of modern Egyptian nationalism, Mustafa Kamil."[28] Those early experiences thus cemented Nasser's resolve to expel Britain from Egypt and attain real independence. He shared these sentiments with other officers in his circle of trusted friends at that time, including Khaled Mohieddin, Abdel Hakim Amer, and Anwar Sadat, all three of whom he met when they served together in Sudan. In an interview, Khaled Mohieddin recalled that his friendship with Nasser developed during their service in Sudan. The two found common ground in their aspirations for the liberation of the country from British colonialism and for lifting Egyptians out of severe poverty, he added.[29]

During this period Nasser remained strongly committed to the idea that an independent Egypt, ruled by King Farouk, would be a viable system of governance. Nutting persuasively argues that "far from being directed against the throne, his [Nasser's] initial object was, so he subsequently told me, to try to put some stuffing into the King and, by creating a militant opposition within the army, to strengthen Farouk's resistance to further encroachments on Egypt's sovereignty."[30] While he viewed the monarch as corrupt, he still considered him "for better or worse, the symbol of Egypt's nationhood."[31] Nasser was an Egyptian patriot, an Egyptian nationalist, and he saw the king as the symbol of the nation. At this stage, Nasser also does not appear to have had a radical vision for Egyptian society. According to Mohieddin, he was not socially and ideologically a revolutionary and his key goal was to liberate the homeland from British colonialism and give Egypt back to the Egyptians: "Like his generation, Nasser was more concerned about *al-tahrir wa-l-tamsir* [Egyptianization and liberation from colonial rule] than *al-hurriyya* [freedom] or *al-dimuqratiyya* [democracy]."[32] Nasser's position seems to have echoed that of his comrades in the military, whose key goal was also gradual, limited change. Recalling the views of the circle of friends which included Nasser and Mohieddin, Sadat, speaking in the mid-1950s, summarized their worldview:

> The problem was to ... turn [Egypt] from a semi-feudal country into a modern, ordered, viable state, while at the same time respecting the customs of the people. On this last point, respecting the customs of the people does not mean chaining them to a dead past, it means respecting the essential and the invisible continuities in a national life. We would conserve everything that did not impede the real process of the community.[33]

The 1942 Palace Siege: Nasser's Shift to a More Radical Vision

If in his teens Nasser had been a proponent of the monarchy, his relatively conservative politics gradually evolved and turned more radical. Increased unemployment in the 1930s and the 1940s, coupled with the rise of an educated Egyptian middle class, led to persistent calls by nationalists to invest in the local economy and engineer

Egyptian industrialization.[34] The nationalist movement turned more and more to nativism as Egyptian youth continued to feel excluded from state institutions and suffer from lack of employment opportunities. Calls for Egyptian "authenticity" became more vocal and popular. As Omnia el-Shakry notes, the colonial context meant that Egyptian intellectuals "grounded their sociology of knowledge in the particular and the local. Such a foundation was not a simple valorization of the local over the universal; it was, rather, the registering of a more radical epistemological difference from the West—a difference based on the rejection of universal anthropocentric (or secular) history and universal taxonomies of civilization."[35]

Two developments in particular fed Nasser's radicalization: first, the besieging of the palace by British tanks in February 1942, an act designed to force King Farouk to appoint Wafd leader Mustafa al-Nahhas as prime minister; and second, the 1948 war in Palestine. The former was particularly important. According to Buthayna Abdel Rahman al-Tikriti, the palace siege triggered talk of revolution among Nasser and his comrades.[36] As Nasser himself subsequently explained, the siege planted the seeds of revolution inside him and made him realize that "there is a dignity to be defended."[37] Other army officers felt that they, together with the nation, had been directly targeted by the British humiliation of their king. As the future Egyptian president Mohamed Naguib noted in his memoirs, "The king allowed them to snatch his authority. When I saw all of that I felt humiliated and disgusted by my military uniform. I offered my resignation because I could not stand wearing my military uniform while walking among people."[38] The British ultimatum to the king stirred anger at a system which made it possible for the colonialists to humiliate Egypt and its top ruler. This incident enflamed nationalist sentiments among army officers and reinforced Nasser's commitment to effecting political change through military action.[39] Nasser thus had undergone a gradual evolution which would over time see him becoming increasingly opposed to the British-dominated monarchy, a dramatic shift in his worldview. The palace siege also served to demolish what little faith Nasser had had in the Wafd party, the dominant force in

Egyptian nationalist politics. He developed a visceral hatred of the Wafd, which culminated in his subsequent decision to proscribe the party after the July coup in 1952. Once again, Nasser's shifting views vis-à-vis the Wafd reflected a broader disillusionment with political parties across Egyptian society.

Nasser and the Ikhwan

Accounts of Nasser's life often emphasize his secular nationalist philosophy and exclude other influences that shaped his worldview, depicting a sense of coherence and perhaps even inevitability in his career. This dominant narrative fails to take into account his gradual evolution as a political actor, and the complexity and diversity of influences that informed his trajectory, including his association with the Ikhwan in the 1940s and early 1950s.

Like many other young and disillusioned Egyptians Nasser flirted with nativist and authoritarian alternatives. He first joined Young Egypt (Misr al-Fatat),[40] but soon left the group as he strongly disagreed with its adoption of principles associated with the politics of European fascism.[41] It was after abandoning Young Egypt that Nasser turned to the Ikhwan. Senior Ikhwan official al-Demerdash al-Aqaly has retrospectively drawn a direct link between Nasser's more radical shift and his recognition of the urgent need to "make a change" after the 1942 palace siege and his subsequent decision to join the Islamist organization.[42] The Nasser-Ikhwan connection could also be explained by Nasser's assignment in Sudan, where politics and religion had been mixed since the Mahdi Revolution.[43] His experience there probably convinced him that religion could play a positive role in ridding the Nile Valley—comprising Egypt and Sudan—of colonial occupation and backwardness.[44] Once again Nasser's shift in the 1940s paralleled a growing tendency in Egypt's intellectual circles. As noted earlier, this period and the subsequent decades witnessed a rise of literary religious production. Many writers, some of whom had previously taken a secular stance, devoted their attention to religious and Islamic subjects. This literary shift included books on the life of the Prophet Muhammad and on early Islamic history and civilization; a return to Islamic imagery and history was also reflected in many periodicals and magazines.

Despite the historical context in which Nasser flirted with Islamic groups, this time of his life remains controversial as conflicting narratives have emerged. While Ikhwan officials exaggerate the significance of his connection with their movement in order to sow doubts about his moral character, Nasserists and Arab nationalists dismiss the episode as propagandistic Ikhwan nonsense. On the one hand, Ikhwan members claim that Nasser was a fully fledged member of the organization, particularly its paramilitary networks, and that his subsequent desertion amounted to treason.[45] On the other, Nasserists argue that Nasser was a born-again nationalist, drawing his political journey as a straightforward line of ideological continuity and consistency. Al-Sayyed Yassin, a leading public intellectual who himself made the transition from the Ikhwan to secular Arab nationalism in the mid to late 1950s, asserts that Nasser was a child of the 1940s, when Arab nationalism gained momentum. "Nasser fought in the 1948 Palestine war and felt that the future of Egypt was organically linked to its Arab neighbors," Yassin reminded me. "Nasser did not discover Arab nationalism in the 1950s and 1960s; he was a son of the Egyptian nationalist movement, which was at the forefront of the anti-colonial struggle in the Arab nation, including Algeria and Palestine."[46]

Most biographers of Nasser also minimize his role in the Ikhwan. His image as a secular pan-Arab leader seems incompatible with his participation in the pan-Islamic organization. Although they are correct to characterize Nasser's early affiliation with the Ikhwan's al-Nizam al-Khass as purely tactical and utilitarian, they are wrong to insist that the Ikhwan's Islamist agenda was alien to his secular nationalist mind-set. These narratives tend to suggest that his temporary collaboration with the Islamic organization even after the 1952 coup was inherently unsustainable because of their fundamentally differing ideologies and philosophies.[47] A Western representative of this viewpoint is Jean Lacouture, who paints a portrait of Nasser and the Ikhwan as having intrinsically incompatible worldviews.[48] The reality is more complex. Nasser's politics remained quite fluid and uncertain until after the 1952 coup, and they only crystallized once he was firmly in power. Nasser's journey was uncharted. As he confronted life, Nasser made discoveries and his views evolved and matured accordingly. According to Heikal, who was in the know, the politically inexperienced Nasser and his comrades were pulled and pushed in different directions, with both the Ikhwan and the communists trying to hijack the revolution. "Nasser was baptized by blood and fire and learned politics through trial and error," Heikal said in an interview in his office overlooking the Nile in Cairo. "For Nasser, experience and action were more important than theory and ideology, and his worldview evolved gradually after 1952."[49]

Moreover, it is worth mentioning that the schism between secular and religious nationalists had not taken place yet. Both nationalists and religious activists cooperated with each other in their attempt to redefine a modern national Egyptian culture. The two world wars in Europe and the Great Depression in the 1930s did not inspire confidence in liberal capitalism and democracy among many Egyptians within the rising middle class. As anger against the paralysis of the domestic political establishment continued to ferment, the Ikhwan's activist outlook resonated with Egyptians regardless of its political-religious agenda. In contrast with mainstream political parties, the Islamist organization took initiatives that appealed to public sentiments. For example, following the British occupation, European missionaries had been allowed to control most of the orphanages in the country. When scandals emerged regarding the harsh conditions of children in those facilities, including violence and forced conversion, the Ikhwan came out strongly in defense of Egyptian orphans. By the 1940s, the group had begun to co-opt both the working class and the rising middle class, instigating contacts with unions which protested against the government and organizing sports activities and cooperative economic ventures. It is also worth noting that in its early decades, the Ikhwan's largest constitutive members were professionals and educated *effendis*, not primarily the *'ulama* and imams.

Seeing the Ikhwan as the social and organizational force most likely to prove helpful in bringing about a far-reaching transformation in Egypt, Nasser and other army officers—including Abdel-Moneim Abdel Rauf, Abu al-Makarem Abdel Hay, and Mohamed Labib—formed the Special Apparatus (al-Tanzim al-Khass). The Special Apparatus was itself a branch of al-Nizam al-Khass, the Secret Apparatus founded by Hassan al-Banna in 1938 and led by Abdel Rahman al-Sanadi.[50] Its aim was to organize the ever-increasing number of military recruits like Nasser and to create a critical mass within the armed forces to deploy when necessary.

In existing accounts, including Nasser's own memoirs,[51] this important chapter in his life has been treated as a minor footnote rather than being critically explored. No one is better placed to shed light on this early phase of Nasser's relationship with the Ikhwan than Khaled Mohieddin, a fellow officer and a close friend of Nasser who joined him in plotting and executing the 1952 coup. In his aristocratically furnished Cairo apartment, Mohieddin confirmed that in 1947 he and Nasser had traveled to Banna's residence, where Nasser swore the *bay'a* (fealty) on a pistol and a copy of the Qur'an to both Banna and Sanadi. Mohieddin also insisted that Nasser and he had belonged to the Special Apparatus. "We joined al-Tanzim al-Khass and took an active role in training its new recruits," he recalled. According to Mohieddin, it was Nasser who recruited him to join al-Tanzim al-Khass, and both trained young Ikhwan members to use firearms and bombs to harass British troops in the vicinity of the Suez Canal Zone in order to make it costly for Britain to stay in Egypt.[52] "Nasser was ecstatic about joining the Ikhwan's al-Tanzim al-Khass because that allowed him to train a group of dedicated young men to defend the homeland," he added. In interviews, Ikhwan leaders confirmed Mohieddin's story. A senior Ikhwan leader, Farid Abdel Khaleq, a confidant of the first two supreme guides, Hassan al-Banna and Hassan al-Hudaybi, told me that "Nasser was one of us and he had trained Ikhwan youth on how to use firearms. I saw him with my own eyes."[53] Although Nasser subsequently dismissed his early flirtation with the Islamic organization as trivial, his affiliation with the

Ikhwan's underground apparatus was a consequential act. From the 1940s until 1953 he kept close company with Ikhwan figures, including Hassan al-Banna and Sayyid Qutb. After the Free Officers came to power, he even offered the Ikhwan a junior partnership in the new cabinet.[54]

So why do Nasserists categorically deny his connection with the Ikhwan, while the latter claim him as one of their own? Mohieddin suggested that on the one hand, Nasserists seek to project an image of their hero as having a flawless character while on the other hand, Ikhwan members use Nasser's *bay'a* to their supreme guide to portray his subsequent persecution of the group as a sinister betrayal. For Mohieddin, Nasser's joining the Ikhwan did not mean he ever shared their pan-Islamic orientation. Rather, he insisted that the young officers were shopping for means and tools to free Egypt from the clutches of British imperial control. "We paid more attention to the efficacy of the group than to its ideology," he said. "We did not mind if it was nationalist or religious because the strategic goal was one and the same—resistance against the British,"[55] Mohieddin told me. "Neither Nasser nor I was bothered by the religious character of the organization; the fight against British colonialism and its internal capitalist clients dominated our being and took priority over everything else."[56]

According to Mohieddin, Nasser was pragmatic: as the Ikhwan was the most powerful and organized social force in the country, he saw it as having the capacity to bring about the changes that Egypt so badly needed. Indeed, he was convinced that the Ikhwan's well-organized underground network was ideally placed to carry out attacks against British troops in the Suez Canal Zone and to plot for the eventual overthrow of the British-backed monarchy. Thus the Nasser-Ikhwan connection points more to a tactical, utilitarian calculation on Nasser's part than an ideological affinity with the Islamic movement. Moreover, Mohieddin emphasized that at the time, resistance forces had not pigeonholed themselves along nationalist, Islamist, or socialist lines. Even if many activists subsequently subscribed to a specific ideology—Marxism, in Mohieddin's case—the political and social space was fluid, and inter-ideological fertilization was very common. As he put it, in the social and political context of the 1930s, 1940s, and early 1950s, liberating Egypt from colonial domination topped everything else:

> We believed that as long as our country was enslaved, Egyptians would remain underdeveloped and unable to rejuvenate their society and restore their glorious past. Liberation of the homeland was the key to our survival and rebirth as a great nation, and armed resistance was the most effective means to reclaim our land and spirit.[57]

Again, Mohieddin reiterated that it was the anti-colonial struggle that had primarily motivated the young officers' links to Ikhwan:

> Regardless of what you think of the Islamic movement now, in the 1940s and early 1950s we [army officers] saw the Ikhwan's secret wing as the standard-bearer of the nationalist resistance against a foreign occupier, not a subversive, illegitimate group as it is characterized today. We joined the Ikhwan underground because it was the only potential paramilitary network that could carry out effective attacks against the British.[58]

Mohieddin added that Nasser had been especially open to cooperation with the Ikhwan and was drawn to Banna because he recognized the "thirst and hunger" for a new order in Egypt, and acknowledged that only the military could bring about thoroughgoing political change. Nasser was not alone among army officers in his belief in the Ikhwan as a potent force for change. Mohieddin recalls how as a young officer he was also drawn to the Ikhwan due to their strong belief and discipline, while at the same time immersing himself in Marxist theory.

Mohieddin's account corroborates the view that many Egyptians, including the Free Officers, saw the Ikhwan as a social force whose broad base of support allowed it to gather various political tendencies within its ranks, all united by anti-British sentiments and desire to affirm Egyptian sovereignty. Accordingly, in joining the Ikhwan, Nasser was searching for an anchor and a base of support that would allow him to harass British troops stationed in Egypt and plot his next move against the monarchy. As a soldier and a man of action, he was more interested in solutions and capacity building than in abstract philosophical ideas.

Finally as explained earlier, at that time, the lines were blurred between religious nationalism of the Ikhwan type and secularly oriented nationalism. It was not till the mid-1950s that the Egyptian nationalist movement splintered along secular nationalist and religious lines. Even after this rupture, the Nasserists and the nationalists never shed their piety or downplayed the role of religiosity in their lives. A common mistake made by observers of Nasserism and Arab nationalism is to view the movement as "hard secular" or nonreligious instead of "soft secular" or neutral.

Despite his flirtation with the Ikhwan Nasser soon became disappointed and eventually left the group, just as he had done with political parties such as the Wafd and Young Egypt. He was not alone, as others, including Mohieddin, shared his disillusionment. In one of my interviews with Mohieddin the former Free Officer acknowledged that although he initially thought the two ideologies had much in common, his infatuation with the Ikhwan lasted less than two years.[59] He added that the Free Officers soon came to see the Ikhwan as having a parochial and backward-looking agenda that could not unify Egyptians or lift them up from misery and poverty. "Every time I talked to Mohamed Labib [an officer and a member of the Ikhwan's Special Apparatus] about the Ikhwan's blueprint and political vision, he would say that shari'a [Islamic law] is our constitution and that it has all the answers to our problems," recalled Mohieddin. "So what does shari'a have to say about agricultural reforms, poverty alleviation, and industrialization? I met Hassan al-Banna in 1947 and he told me that he preferred not to have a program and to leave everything open to Muslims, who would decide."[60]

The Palestine War and Its Implication

If the 1942 palace siege precipitated Nasser's turn to radicalism, his combat experience in the 1948 Palestine war had an even more dramatic impact on him and more broadly on the junior officer corps. The reverberations of that watershed development echoed in every Arab society, not just on Egyptian streets. The defeat of the Arab armies, the mass expulsion of Palestinians and the loss of historic Palestine—which came to be known as the Nakba (catastrophe)—turned loyal junior officers like Nasser and Sadat into subversives and revolutionaries. They held the incumbent ruling classes accountable for the humiliation they suffered at the hands of irregular armed Jewish groups as well as for the defects of their military equipment. Nasser's generation saw the corrupt and cowardly political establishment as having sacrificed the armed forces and national security and the fight against Zionist aggression on the altar of its own narrow interests. They returned home determined not only to expel the British imperialists but also to overthrow the quasi-liberal political system in Cairo. By stripping the constitutional order of its fragile legitimacy, the conflict in Palestine proved to be its death knell.

Nasser's own memoirs of the war in Palestine are replete with expressions of despair at the inadequate provision of supplies for Egyptian troops, their sense of betrayal, and the perceived weakness and duplicity of the political establishment in Cairo.[61]

> In the tragedy which we witnessed in Palestine, the nightmare continued for six long and dark years.[62] ... There is a criminal who should be held accountable for the defeat.[63] ... The army did not commit the crime of Palestine but someone else did.[64] ... It was just a political war?[65] ... We suffered from a destructive lack of information.[66] ... The night of 20 May [1948] was the most depressing of all my entire life as I was in the Gaza military hospital surrounded with beds of soldiers injured on the battlefield ...[67]

The impact of the Palestine debacle on the agenda of the Free Officers is extremely important. Until the war, they primarily focused on reforming the military and expelling the British from Egypt: (1) ending the British occupation; (2) reforming the army and purging it of corrupt elements; and (3) pushing for the formation of a national government.[68] However, Nasser's experience in Palestine appears to have been a significant driver in his shift towards a radical nationalist commitment to overthrowing the old regime. He was especially traumatized by the loss of his own soldiers and comrades. Upon hearing the news of the death of his fellow officer Ismail Mohieddin, Nasser, who is universally described as stubborn, ardent, and rugged, admitted: "I lost control of my emotions and burst into tears. I cried profusely unlike any other occasion in my life. I cried over a brave and strong fellow officer."[69] The war also convinced Nasser that the "near enemy"—the king and the British occupier—had to take priority over the "far enemy"—Israel—since fighting the former could ultimately lead to victory over the latter. As an Egyptian writer noted, Nasser's secret plans for a regime change at home crystallized while he was besieged by Jewish militants at the Palestinian district of Falluja four years before the 1952 coup.[70]

If the Palestinian experience led Nasser to rethink the Free Officers' strategy, it also affected him ideologically. Although from the mid-1910s to the mid-1940s, Arab nationalists had found refuge in Egypt and promoted Arab nationalism in the press and called on Egypt to play a greater role in Arab affairs, Nasser's diaries contain few references to this cause. Significantly, he does not mention it as a driving force behind his commitment to fight in Palestine. Instead, his focus is a sense of loyalty to the army in which he served, an army which symbolized the Egyptian homeland.[71] Heikal, whose relationship with Nasser went as far back as the Palestine war, argues that Nasser saw Palestine through a typical traditional Egyptian nationalism lens: for him, it first represented a strategic territory linking Egypt with Syria and the Red Sea with the Mediterranean.[72] Upon his return from Palestine, Nasser said that his experience there—especially the long and costly siege in the battle of Falluja—convinced him that there was an umbilical cord between Egypt and its neighboring Arab countries. Thus the Palestine conflict bolstered his commitment to Arab nationalist principles and led him to move away from his previous association with the Ikhwan. Khaled Mohieddin confirmed this point, telling me: "After we returned from the Palestine war, Nasser and I left the Ikhwan and organized our own independent Free Officers movement within the military. We were no longer enamored with al-Tanzim al-Khass."[73] Nonetheless, even after his own personal split from the Ikhwan in the late 1940s, Nasser maintained an institutional link with their paramilitary networks in order to advance the cause of his own secret group—the Free Officers movement.

Mohieddin noted that the Palestine war reminded Egyptian officers, including Nasser, of the ties that bind the Arab countries together strategically and culturally. When asked why he and his comrades had not seen it as an experience of fighting alongside a diversity of Muslims from different parts of the Islamic *umma* (the global Muslim community), as opposed to a diversity of Arabs from across the Arab world, he retorted: "We did not go to Palestine to wage a religious war; we were defending a neighboring Arab country whose loss would have had an impact on our own security." The Free Officers saw the occupation of Palestine as a reflection of a catastrophe that affected the rest of the Arab nations. The replacement of British occupation forces by Jewish settlements only strengthened their anti-colonialist and anti-imperialist attitudes. The humiliation of the Arab armies and the despair and chaos in which Palestinians were plunged mirrored their own experience with colonialism. Thus the army officers, including Nasser, fought in Palestine to protect Egyptian national security, Mohieddin insisted.

In his autobiography, Nasser expresses similar feelings. Reminiscing on the eve of the outbreak of the war and in its aftermath, he wrote:

> When the Palestine crisis loomed on the horizon I was firmly convinced that the fighting there was not fighting on foreign territory. Nor was it inspired by sentiment. It was duty imposed by self-defense. After the siege and the battles in Palestine I came home

> with the whole region in my mind one complete whole. The events that followed confirmed this belief in me ... An event may happen in Cairo today; it is repeated in Damascus, Beirut, Amman, or any other place tomorrow.[74]

In this excerpt, if Nasser refers to Palestine as part of *Arab* territory, not foreign territory belonging to the Palestinians, it is because he makes a direct parallel between the occupation of Palestine and the colonial occupation of other Arab countries. In Nasser's worldview, the similarities resulting from the oppression of these Arab populations by colonial forces outweigh the differences. Nasser sees Palestine as another manifestation of the colonial emasculation of the indigenous Arab; thus the liberation of Palestine coalesces with the liberation of Egypt. His experience in Palestine consolidated his subjective inclusion of the Egyptian national self in the framing of a wider collective Arab self. If before the Palestine war Nasser viewed it as a duty of the Egyptian army to defend another Arab territory, in its aftermath he had become convinced that the Arab territories were united by their similar experience of colonialism in both practical and subjective domination. His own lived experience in Palestine left indelible marks in his mind. Upon returning home in September 1948, he brought with him a bloodstained shirt and handkerchief and told his wife that he had been wounded by a bullet which hit a few centimeters from his heart.[75] He kept these clothes at home as a grim reminder.

Conclusion

Nasser has been portrayed as a dyed-in-the-wool secular Arab nationalist whose politics were steered and defined by this strong ideological leaning. Yet, as this chapter shows, he was exposed to and experimented with an array of political orientations in the course of his lifetime. Despite Nasser's populist rhetoric, his politics were strongly informed by pragmatic calculations rather than by a priori ideological principles. People who knew Nasser and worked with him in the 1950s and 1960s draw a portrait of a man less driven by ideology than by pragmatic political calculations. Time and time again during our interviews, his former collaborators and close associates reiterated to me that his nationalist discourse lacked a clear ideological structure and content. Instead, they asserted that it was designed mainly for constructing a new social constituency and emasculating the old classes that had dominated life in Egypt. One of the key points highlighted in this chapter is that although Nasser eventually became known as the undisputed leader of Arab nationalism, this does not take into account the complexity of his worldview and conduct. Moreover, Nasser's ideological formation was neither predetermined nor fixed. Given his bourgeois middle-class background and the volatility of Egyptian politics of the time, Nasser's journey was erratic and unpredictable. Like his generation in the colonized world, he was preoccupied, even haunted, with the anti-colonial struggle and the quest for national liberation, independence, and economic empowerment. His pursuit led him first to experiment with nationalism, Islamism, and then Arab nationalism, all of which are modern, reformist, and anti-hegemonic ideologies. One constant never changed: first and foremost, Nasser was a patriot and an Egyptian nationalist. Although his institutional socialization and patriotism naturally disposed him to nationalism, there was nothing predestined about it. The key variable was Nasser's political ambitions and will to power, which found an effective outlet in the military as an institution.

The war in Palestine played a major role in convincing Nasser that political change in Egypt could only come about by a military coup. After his flirtation with various political tendencies, Nasser had lost faith in the ability of the country's political leadership to free Egypt from the clutches of colonialism and to regain its freedom, power, and glory. In Cairo, another young Egyptian, Sayyid Qutb, who was as disillusioned with the political establishment, would soon turn out to be one of Nasser's early important allies and then his greatest domestic enemy.

Chapter 6

Young Sayyid Qutb

SAYYID QUTB'S LIFE JOURNEY from childhood in a small village in Upper Egypt, through his young adulthood in Cairo, to the time of his split with the Nasserist state in 1953 spanned and was informed by a remarkable diversity of social contexts: the traditional religiosity of his village; the nationalist fervor of the 1919 revolution and its aftermath; the secular literary circles of 1920s Cairo; his enthusiastic flirtation with Nasser's Free Officers; and a gradual integration into increasingly radical modes of Islamist political activism.[1] The portrait that emerges is not one of a consistently religious radical who aims to fulfill his God-given mission. Nor is it one of a Road to Damascus conversion from a secular critic to a leader of Islamist militancy, as Qutb is often portrayed by his biographers. Rather, what emerges is an account of a life in which nationalist and religiously informed politics were in constant dialogue and at times in conflict, with Qutb himself often pulled in the direction of one school of thought or the other by the distinctly practical, everyday circumstances of his own experiences and relationships. Far from following a straightforward line, Qutb's journey was full of sharp twists and turns. And contrary to the portrait drawn by biographers, it is doubtful whether Qutb had a clear and linear vision of where his journey would lead and end.

A crusader at heart, he battled his way through life championing a variety of different causes—not unlike Nasser, whose path was equally uncertain and eventful.

Growing Up: Qutb's Childhood in Upper Egypt

Sayyid Qutb Ibrahim Hassayn Shadhili was born in 1906 in Musha, a village in the Asyut governorate. Although Qutb and Nasser came from the same governorate, their early years were very different. Unlike Nasser, whose peripatetic childhood was spent largely in urban environments like Cairo and Alexandria, Qutb spent the first fourteen years of his life in rural Musha, surrounded by his family. Qutb's father, Ibrahim, a farmer, and his mother, Fatimah, came from wealthy rural backgrounds, though the family experienced financial problems when Qutb was just ten years old.[2] His father had to sell several land parcels, which directly impacted the family's social status in the village. In his memoirs, Qutb recalled the family's economic problems as a shock that shattered his otherwise peaceful childhood and put an abrupt end to his time of innocence.[3]

Just like Nasser, Qutb was very close to his mother, who considerably influenced his character and sensibility. The fact that two of her brothers had studied at al-Azhar gave his family "scholarly stature" in rural Egypt, and she was herself praised for piety.[4] Qutb's mother was determined to give her son the best possible education. The family was initially divided over whether to send him to a *madrasah*, a modern school, or a traditional *kuttab* (Qur'anic school), though after much debate, Qutb attended a *madrasah*, which he loved and in whose modernist curriculum he took pride. He described it as a "holy place," comparing it with the *mihrab*, an alcove located in mosques to indicate the direction of prayer. In contrast, he saw the *kuttab* as merely standing for outdated ritual and idle convention.[5] After experiencing both schooling systems—he, together with other children from the village, was sent to the traditional Qur'anic school for a short period—Qutb confided that he loathed his time at the *kuttab*. His experience and disdain for the *kuttab* and its teachers were recounted in his quasi-autobiographical book *Tifl min al-qarya* (A child from the village). He portrays his second-grade teacher, a Qur'an reciter called Sheikh Ahmad, as a backward man, who railed against modern education, telling lies to parents about the *madrasah*'s curriculum: "the government wants to obliterate the Qur'an by neglecting its memorization in the schools!" After Qutb had returned to the *madrasah*, he and other students formed a Qur'an memorization team and organized contests against students from the *kuttab* to prove the rumors wrong. By the end of his fourth school year, Qutb says he had memorized the Qur'an in its totality. He performed well in all his classes, excelling particularly in Arabic. As a ten-year-old, Qutb would read the newspapers to villagers who would come to his father's house to hear the latest news. School had become his refuge, a sacred place, reflecting his passion for learning and consciousness.

Qutb's love for reading and learning paralleled Nasser's. An avid reader, Qutb purchased books from "uncle Salih," an itinerant bookseller who visited the village, eventually acquiring a collection of twenty-five texts. Two of his books particularly impressed the villagers: *Kitab Abi Ma'shar al-falaki*, on astrology, and *Kitab shamhurash*, on traditional folk rituals and magic. At the villagers' demand, Qutb even undertook fortune-telling and other services for those who sought his support for happiness and good luck.[6] Other favorite readings included *One Thousand and One Nights*, Sherlock Holmes novels, and Bukhari's canonical collection of hadiths.[7] Qutb's childhood readings were consistent with his relatively conservative milieu, which mixed religiosity and traditional folklore. His thirst for learning was a direct reflection of the responsibilities placed on his shoulders. His mother insisted that he, as the oldest child, was the best placed to succeed professionally and help the family regain both its wealth and its social status. The result was that Qutb grew up an ambitious young man determined to excel in life, one with a strong sense of discipline. He remained convinced that he was destined for greatness and that he was the answer to his family's problems.

The family's financial decline reflected a much deeper problem affecting the rural population. The expansion of liberal capitalism in the early twentieth century had made a growing number of peasants landless, with many of them falling into abject poverty. From the late 1910s onwards, the country witnessed increasing social and political turmoil, and inhabitants from both urban and rural areas participated in popular revolts, which ultimately led to the 1919–1922 revolution.[8] Qutb was aware of the deepening political upheaval engendered by Egyptian nationalist opposition to the British presence in the country. He first heard of the Wafd founder Sa'd Zaghloul from his school headmaster and attended meetings at home, where his father and neighbors whispered that "new sacred name" with reverence and awe. Qutb recalled a patriotic speech by his school headmaster in which he announced that the school would be closed indefinitely as part of the national strikes in 1919, and that he and the *effendi*s would join the "revolution." That in turn inspired the then thirteen-year-old Qutb to compose his own first patriotic speech, which he delivered in celebration of the sacred revolution on various occasions in the village.[9] His father was himself a delegate to Mustafa Kamil's National Party and subscribed to the party journal *al-Liwa*.[10] Carried via popular culture like songs of famous artists such as Sayyed Darwish, Zaghloul's revolt resonated with Egyptians like Qutb's father, neighbors, and teachers primarily because it was about resisting foreign domination and calling for independence.[11]

If in his youth Nasser dreamt about the 1919 revolution and the potent revolutionary spirit that had inspired it, Qutb was old enough to experience and vividly recall the events. They left a deep impression on his imagination, and he would subsequently evoke them to rally young Egyptians to the nationalist cause. The national upheaval had allowed him to transcend the confines of his village to imagine himself as part of an Egyptian nation, a community made up of believers and patriots, traditionalists and modernists. As explained in the previous chapter, at this stage Egyptians did not conceive of a divide between their religious faith, on the one hand, and their love of their national community and country, on the other. Qutb was to become part of a new elite, raised in a traditional environment steeped in an Islamic frame of reference but socialized into modernist and nationalist symbols of collective identity, progress, and reform.[12] Although his memoirs acknowledge tensions between modernizing and traditionalist tendencies, as we will see, these conflicting feelings emerged after his move to the capital. There is a natural tendency among Qutb's biographers to search for signposts in his early years which might foreshadow his subsequent transformation into a revolutionary Islamist. While Qutb attended mosque prayers from an early age, this attests more to his quest to show that he was mature enough to fulfill his mother-given mission of restoring the family's wealth and social respectability than to anything else. Moreover, writings such as *Tifl min al-qarya*, first published in 1946, did not prioritize Islam as a point of reference.

Although *Tifl min al-qarya* is Qutb's memoir, the biographical elements are at times intertwined with fictional undertones. The aim was to narrate an authentic account of Qutb's life in a Nile Valley village at the turn of the twentieth century, a similar undertaking to Taha Hussein's classic modern autobiography, *Al-ayyam*.[13] Thus, although Qutb's memoirs retrace his childhood, some points might have been emphasized to compare and contrast with Hussein's vision of Egypt and its future. Indeed, the two autobiographies share a theme of transcendence and criticism. Both Hussein and Qutb critiqued the traditional establishment for perpetuating a status quo which was unjust, reactionary, and detrimental to progress; just as both shed light on the struggle to climb the social ladder from humble beginnings, as well as aspects of class struggle and the role of education in advancing modernization in Upper Egypt. Scattered throughout the two narratives are examples of the dialectic which was underway between modernity and traditionalism, as well as their coexistence. However, while Hussein wholeheartedly embraced European ideas as a model of development and civilization,[14] Qutb navigated the two universes with ambivalence. While hailing Hussein as a brilliant thinker, he was critical of Hussein's call for Europeanization and Westernization, which Qutb saw as misguided and alien to the Eastern heritage and culture to which Egypt and the Arab world belonged.[15] In contrast with Hussein's book, Qutb's autobiography paints a more romantic portrait of village life and offers more details about rural Egypt in general.[16]

Rather than offering early signposts of Qutb's subsequent religious radicalization, *Tifl min al-qarya* provides insights into his consciousness and the impact of his socioeconomic environment on the development of his identity. As he acknowledges, "everything around him made him feel as if he belonged in some place other than the village."[17] From a young age Qutb clearly felt that the village was intellectually and socially constraining, and that there was a greater destiny awaiting him beyond its confining walls. In contrast with Nasser, whose living experiences in various cities made him feel at home in his own country, Qutb often felt out of place, an alien that did not belong. In this sense, his mission to reestablish his family's lost financial mini-fortune and social status can be compared with another grand mission that he would later champion: restoring Egypt's true authentic Self by reestablishing a true Islam over the state of *jahiliyya* (ignorance).

Exchanging the Village for the Big City: Qutb's Move to Cairo

Qutb departed Musha in 1921 in order to attend secondary school in Cairo, where he lived with a journalist uncle, Ahmed Othman. The move was designed to ensure professional and social success: Qutb's education would allow him to firmly establish himself within the new rising *effendiyya* class. He arrived in the capital just a year prior to the end of the revolution and the granting of formal independence to Egypt. Nationalist fervor filled the air and Qutb was swept up in the powerful tide of collective identity, pride, and visions of progress, making him an ideal candidate to join the new nationalist generation which was emerging in Egypt at that time.

After completing his secondary education in 1929, Qutb attended the teacher-training institution Dar al-Ulum, whose syllabuses married the traditional education of al-Azhar with that of the modern university. During his time there, his wide-ranging studies spanned disciplines including history, geography, literature, English, sociology, education, math, physics, philosophy, and religion.[18] He maintained his excellence in Arabic language and literature and began to compose poetry and write essays. At the age of nineteen, Qutb's first published poem, in which he attacked British policies and defended Zaghloul, appeared in the pages of the daily *al-Balagh* (Proclamation), which had been founded in the 1920s.[19] His works subsequently appeared in Cairo publications such as *al-Hayat al-Jadida* (The New Life).[20] Just like Nasser, Qutb was an activist, though at that time, his activism was geared more towards cultural change than political. He founded a student organization aimed at strengthening relations between Egyptians and other "Eastern" students.[21] He was also active in advocating for curriculum changes, such as introducing English-language instruction and artistic criticism, as well as expanding Arabic-language and religious studies and Hebrew education in a proposed preparatory year at the college.[22]

Upon graduating from Dar al-Ulum in 1933, Qutb taught for six years before taking up a variety of posts at the Ministry of Education, where he would remain until shortly after Nasser and the young Free Officers overthrew the monarchy in 1952. From the 1920s until the 1940s, he belonged to a secular nationalist literary circle in Cairo, one engaged in battles against writers who relied on religion to advance or rationalize their arguments. A cursory review of his writings from this time, together with interviews with his contemporaries, indicates a secular outlook deeply suspicious of mixing religion and politics. Initially, unfettered by identity politics and pan-Arab or Islamist sentiments, he even went as far as to suggest that Islam and the Arabic language were alien to the Egyptian temperament and character. He also openly questioned the capacity of the Arabic language to cope with the swift changes of the contemporary age, arguing that Western languages were better equipped to accommodate science and modernity. In a series of articles in the 1930s, he took aim at tradition and called for a wholehearted embrace of modernity. Drawing a distinction between his preferred Egyptianism and the Arab-Muslim heritage, Qutb depicted the past as an impediment to progress in science and the arts.[23] Instead, his fundamental concern was to move away from the past in order to bring about a leap forward that would allow for a progressive reformation of state and society.

Qutb's growing ambivalence towards Islam during his first decade in Cairo was further illustrated by his call for separation of religion from literature.[24] While he clearly was not an atheist, such views are nonetheless indicative of Qutb's complex personality and worldview. Like many of his young peers, he engaged in soul-searching about the meaning of life and the afterlife and wanted to draw from Western ideas in order to marry modernization and the preservation of Arab traditions.[25] Qutb's early ambivalence towards religion and the role of tradition helps explain the varying, and sometimes contrasting, sketches drawn by his biographers that range from portraying him as irreligious to being merely spiritual and philosophically idealist.[26] According to Abbas Khadir, his closest friend at that time, Qutb experienced a period of doubt. Khadir recalls Qutb confiding to him that "religion was necessary to guide and lead the human herd who otherwise would be unruly and anarchic"—a utilitarian, even Machiavellian, view of the function of religion in society.

Inasmuch as Qutb's criticism of Arabic, the language of the Qur'an, showed a skeptical and dissenting disposition towards religion's role in Egypt, he gave voice to the small literary circle to which he belonged. This collective of authors championed critical theory and rational thought, eschewing conformity and blind obedience to tradition. Throughout much of this period, Qutb's literary and intellectual mentor was Abbas Mahmud al-Aqqad, a renowned writer and public intellectual who was known for his nationalist writings during the 1919 revolution and was one of the leading secular voices of the first half of the twentieth century.[27] Qutb was introduced to Aqqad through his uncle, Ahmed Othman. Aqqad distinguished himself as an outspoken partisan of a new school of poetry known as the Diwan group. Seemingly greatly influenced by English writers such as Hazlitt, Coleridge, Macaulay, Mill, and Darwin,[28] this school rejected all classical trends which insisted on the unity of each *bayt* (line or verse) within any given poem, and instead emphasized the organic unity of the poem as a whole. Its members also emphasized the need to draw upon all sources of inspiration, both traditional and foreign, as these broadened and deepened the poet's perception and sensibility.[29] Beyond this reformist literary stance, the pioneers of the Diwan group advocated social change and displayed firm faith in scientific progress and rationalism.[30] For many years, Qutb faithfully followed in the footsteps of Aqqad, deploying his pen in defense of the latter's secular, liberal school of thought and ridiculing rivals who called for a discourse steeped in religious authenticity.

Until the early 1940s, Qutb was also an active member of the Wafd party and a supporter of parliamentary government and its institutions, the antithesis of an Islamist public intellectual. In contrast with Nasser, even when in the late 1940s Qutb eventually did become disillusioned with Egyptian rulers and their corrupt politics, he held back from claiming membership in any political party, including the Ikhwan, and did not at first veer either to the ultraright or to the left. Ideologically, he remained a centrist with a critical sensibility. Even after Qutb subsequently migrated towards a greater concern with authenticity and Islam in the mid to late 1940s, he was at first more concerned with cultural renewal and development than with an ideologically based Islamist project. He could not be considered an Islamist by any stretch of the imagination. It is only after he formally joined the Ikhwan in 1953 that we can authoritatively use that affiliation to mark an epistemological change in his worldview.

The contradictions, ambiguities, and shifts in Qutb's thinking from this period belie the various oversimplified narratives of his life that have often been advanced by interested parties. The old guard within the Ikhwan has promoted a portrait of the young Qutb as a wild hedonist influenced by decadent Western fads and values. Such narratives allow the Ikhwan to take credit for Qutb's subsequent spiritual reawakening and to portray the organization as the group that saved his soul and oversaw his rapid transformation into a born-again Islamist activist. Such narratives have been advanced by Mahmoud Abdel Halim, the official chronicler of the Ikhwan, who penned three volumes on its history. Abdel Halim claimed that in 1934, Qutb published an editorial in the leading newspaper *al-Ahram* in which he advocated nudity on the beaches and insisted that bikini-clad women would "not trigger *fitna* [sedition] ... but artistic admiration."[31] Enraged by Qutb's supposed call for public nudity, Abdel Halim asserts that he planned on writing a rebuttal in the same newspaper, before he was stopped by Hassan al-Banna himself. Banna, Abdel Halim asserted, found it counterproductive to publicly embarrass the young Qutb and insisted the latter would ultimately rediscover the truth and return to the Islamic fold of his own accord.[32] Abdel Halim's account built up Banna's foresight and emphasized Qutb's impiousness prior to his embrace of the Islamic call.[33] Perhaps unsurprisingly, neither I nor other researchers, including Sherif Younis, who spent years studying Qutb's life and ideas,[34] have been able to unearth Qutb's alleged pro-nudity op-ed in *al-Ahram*. Qutb was raised by a pious family in rural Egypt. Nothing in his background and youth indicates that he would have advocated nudity or, as suggested earlier, that he might have denied the existence of God. It is quite clear that the young Qutb was neither a hedonist nor an atheist.[35]

In contrast to the mainstream Ikhwan, Qutb's own surviving disciples tend to dismiss his early literary career as an inconsequential footnote—a detour from his true sacred calling. Qutb's "lost years," as his followers describe the early part of his career, are a painful reminder of the young man whom they want to banish from memory, a man who did not live up to their expectations of spiritual purity, piety, and absolute certainty. In scores of interviews, Qutb's contemporary disciples consistently steered the discussion away from his early career, preferring instead to focus on his Islamist phase in the 1950s. Time and again, my inquiries about the young Qutb were dismissed as irrelevant and detracting from the real Qutb: "The Qutb I know is of *Al-zilal* [In the Shadow of the Qur'an] and *Ma'alim* [Signposts], not of poetry or anything else," roared Abdel Majid al-Shazili, a senior member of Qutb's al-Tanzim al-Sirri who is now a leading Qutbian theorist. "As far as we are concerned, the earlier, young Qutb never existed because al-Shahid plucked [his former self] out by the roots and joined the Qur'anic generation."[36] Like Qutb's other impassioned followers, Shazili genuinely believes that the young man of letters vanished after Qutb's conversion to Islamism. While Qutb's disciples reluctantly concede his earlier dissolute period, they see the later Qutb as having consciously overcome his own decadence.

Conclusion

In their own ways, both the mainstream Ikhwan and Qutb's die-hard disciples refuse to acknowledge the complexity and diversity of his life, reducing him to a caricature of himself. The complexity of Qutb's journey is also glossed over by analysts who view him mainly through the lens of the revolutionary Islamism he embraced and developed in the 1950s and 1960s. In contrast, it would not be an exaggeration to argue that the young Qutb was a postmodern man par excellence, exhibiting doubts and contradictions throughout most of his journey, and only later arriving at ideological certainty. In particular, the contrast between Qutb's village roots and the urban lifestyle that he came to adopt in these years seems to have caused an identity crisis that stayed with him, professionally and personally, throughout his adult life until his death. In fact, Qutb's identity conflict was so strong that literary critic Ali Shalash refers to it as *qalaq wugudi* or existential anxiety.[37] Qutb's own writings point to this internal conflict. In his novel *Ashwak* (Thorns), which was published in 1947 and represents an autobiographical account of a failed love story, the main protagonist is torn between the urban principles which Qutb associated with his life in Cairo and the rural roots of his upbringing in a small village.[38]

Despite the claims of Qutb's radical disciples, his intellectual and ideological ambiguity and fluidity shows he felt caught in between two worlds. He turned to religious literary themes belatedly in the 1940s after failing to make a name for himself in the secular literary circles which he had revered for so long. Qutb's embrace of the Ikhwan came even later, at the end of the 1940s and in the early 1950s, a transition that signaled a hardening and deepening polarization of the Egyptian political and social scene. The writer's love for words would soon be overshadowed by a thirst for power.

The path of Qutb and another young man of his generation and temperament, Gamal Abdel Nasser, would briefly converge in the early 1950s and then violently collide. Ambitious and resembling each other in many ways, both were in a hurry to transform Egypt in their own image and leave their mark on the country's history. Qutb made the mistake of his life in 1953 by joining Nasser's foes, the Ikhwan, after the two sides came to blows over power sharing in the nascent political order being erected after the toppling of the pro-British monarchy on July 23, 1952. The young colonel, Nasser, turned against the public intellectual and radical activist, Qutb, with a vengeance. He sent Qutb, together with the leadership of the Ikhwan and thousands of its members, to prison camps. In one stroke, he sought to crush the only remaining viable opposition to his rule. Qutb would resist Nasser's hegemony to the end, offering a revolutionary Islamist alternative. He would spearhead resistance to Nasser from behind the prison walls.

Chapter 7

The Lion of the Arabs

Nasser's Arabism: Between Ideology and Realpolitik

If the Palestine war gradually pushed Nasser towards a more pan-Arab nationalist way of thinking, it was in part because of his personal experience. The feelings of despair and humiliation shared by both the Arab military officers and the Palestinian population bolstered his sense of identity as a member of an Arab political community.[1]

After 1948, Nasser identified more with Arab nationalist symbols of language and belonging than he did with religious rituals and forms of identity. As he later stressed in his memoirs, the Arab nation, not the Islamic *umma*, "is the most important and the most closely connected with us. Its history merges with ours. We have suffered the same hardships, lived the same crises; and when we fell prostrate under the spikes of the horses of conquerors, they lay with us."[2] While Nasser's own rhetoric implies that his pan-Arab vision is deeply rooted in ideology, his actions tell otherwise. Rather, his use of Arab nationalism or pan-Arabism—whether at this stage in his life or later—was never purely a matter of principle and sentiment. It was not conceived as just an idealist political project but rather as a product of realist calculations taken within the parameters of the particular set of circumstances in which he found himself.

A closer look at Nasser's use of Arab nationalist ideology shows that it was not innate but rather incidental and contingent. In fact, there is no single driver that explains Nasser's championship of Arab nationalism. The nationalization of the Suez Canal in 1956 is a case in point. It marked a turning point in Nasser's evolution and recognition of the importance of Arab nationalism and non-alignment, though this ideological orientation was a means to an end. Instead, it represented a strictly Egyptian, eminently nationalistic act accomplished with a view to purely Egyptian interests, which was then framed as anti-colonial defiance and as linking Nasser to the Arab world and "making him finally the tribune of its mute masses, from Bassorah to Khartoum."[3] It was thus regional and international developments as well as Egyptian national interests in the early and mid 1950s that led Nasser to conclude that Egypt must deploy all elements of its power to counterbalance Western efforts, which were trying to build up local rivals to his country. Moreover, Arab nationalism or pan-Arab nationalism provided Nasser with a powerful mobilizational tool against external threats, including Western-orchestrated defense pacts, the U.S. refusal to provide arms to the Egyptian military and financial aid to build the Aswan Dam, and Israel's costly and humiliating attacks on Egyptian troops. Although in the 1956 Suez crisis Nasser used the mosque and nationalist pride as a two-pronged mobilizational strategy against the tripartite invasion, his aides recall Suez as a tipping point in Nasser's conversion to Arab nationalism.

Nasser's Arab nationalism never stood in the way of bitter rivalries with other pivotal Arab countries like Iraq and Saudi Arabia. From the mid-1950s onwards Nasser also wielded Arab nationalism as an effective weapon to counterbalance his local rivals and maximize his bargaining power regionally and internationally.[4] According to Heikal, Nasser's biographer and confidant, the widespread outpouring of support for Egypt throughout Arab countries, including Egypt's rivals in Iraq, Saudi Arabia, and Jordan, convinced him that the destinies of Egypt and the Arab world were intertwined; the Arab arena provided Egypt with strategic depth, a force multiplier. "While the Palestine war in 1948 persuaded Nasser of the imperative of Arab collective security, Suez converted him to the cause of Arab nationalism as a shared destiny and identity," recalled Heikal. "Of the three circles listed by Nasser, the Arab circle was the most important, and he saw Egypt's destiny as inextricably linked to the Arab neighborhood."[5]

Heikal's argument must be placed in context. Mohieddin argues that Nasser's embrace of Arab nationalism was a gradual response to international and regional developments that underlined his drive to play a leadership role in the Arab arena. The Cold War, particularly the aggressive designs and defense schemes of the United States, motivated Nasser to build a coalition of Arab countries unified around the ideology of Arab nationalism. As the leader of this coalition, Egypt would resist America's new colonialism and play a bigger role regionally and globally, said Mohieddin. When I pressed him on the question of whether Nasser instrumentalized or really believed in Arab nationalism, Mohieddin said that Nasser did not see any contradiction between his belief in Arab nationalism and his utilization of this powerful ideology to advance Egyptian national interests. "Indeed, Nasser was an Egyptian patriot and nationalist, but he also adopted Arab nationalism as a strategic choice to counterbalance Western hegemonic designs in the Arab world and committed himself and the nation to pursuing it."[6]

According to Mohieddin, Heikal, and others, there existed no contradictions between Nasser's Egyptian patriotism and his promotion of Arab nationalism: Nasser prioritized Egyptian nationalism, while simultaneously advocating pan-Arab solidarity, not Arab unity or the creation of a pan-Arab state. The unity between Egypt and Syria between 1958 and 1961 which came to be known as the United Arab Republic (UAR) was the exception to the rule. Time and again, I was told by Nasser's inner circle that Nasser had been skeptical about the merger of Egypt and Syria but the bickering Syrian ruling elite had presented him with a stark choice: either a union between the two countries or Syria descending into chaos. Syrian politicians offered their country to Nasser on a silver platter, hoping that the popular Egyptian leader would bring them stability and order. Against his good judgment and instincts Nasser agreed to the merger, asserted Heikal, in order to save Syria and to make sure that this first Arab unity experiment succeeded and spread to neighboring Arab states.

Heikal acknowledged that 1958 marked a watershed in Nasser's worldview and conduct: it caused him to think the unthinkable, that pan-Arab unity was no longer a dream but a reality. His coronation by the Syrian masses on his first visit there after the establishment of the United Arab Republic was inspirational and had a colossal psychological effect on Nasser's character, according to close aides. On arrival in Damascus, Nasser was celebrated like legendary Salah al-Din al-Ayyubi, the victorious Islamic warrior who expelled the Crusaders from Jerusalem in 1187, and was carried directly from the airport to the tomb of Ayyubi, a powerful symbolic act that could not have been lost on Nasser. Like Ayyubi, who after defeating the Crusaders established a powerful empire in Syria and Iraq ruled by the Ayyubi dynasty, Nasser must have dreamed of a greater glory by creating the United States of the Arab world—unifying all the Arab states in a single pan-Arab union. Indeed, from 1958 till 1961, Nasser inscribed pan-Arab unity as an important goal of his political discourse and action and pressured other Arab leaders to join the United Arab Republic. Revisiting this period, it is evident that pan-Arab nationalism led by Nasser, or Nasserism, seemed unstoppable, bound to prevail over the fragile old regimes. Nasser, together with like-minded pan-Arab nationalists in Syria, Iraq, and Lebanon, prematurely penned the obituaries of the pro-Western monarchies, including Saudi Arabia, Iraq, and Jordan. Even independent observers and scholars agreed that the old regimes were swimming against the tide of history, ultimately bound to sink.

Although the Iraqi monarchy could not withstand the violent storm and was blown to a million pieces by Nasser's fellow army officers, others like Saudi Arabia and Jordan proved more viable and resilient than their foes had hoped. Nasser's pan-Arab nationalist moment was fleeting, lasting for only three years. In the final analysis, Egypt's political union with Syria was a risky gamble. As Patrick Seale, a keen observer of Syria and Arab affairs, noted, "Nasser agreed to bind Egypt to a country he has never seen. This was a measure of his leap in the dark."[7] Attributing Nasser's decision to embrace the union with Syria to his overambitiousness, Seale suggested that Nasser was "seduced by the boldness and magnitude" of the project and "trapped by his role as a champion of Arab rights and arbiter of its destiny."[8] Others, including Nasser's confidant Heikal, contended that Nasser's adventure was more strategic than personal—safeguarding Syria and the Arab region from external threats and subversive ideologies like communism.[9] The need for solidarity in the face of outside interference was particularly strongly felt after the declaration of the Eisenhower Doctrine, according to which the United States promised military aid to any country threatened by "international communism."[10] The U.S. move was interpreted as an attempt to "overthrow progressive nationalist rule in Syria and contain the national role of Egypt," an explanation for the Syrian-Egyptian unity as a "self-mechanism."[11]

Nonetheless, the UAR project proved to be disastrous, surviving for only three tumultuous years prior to its dissolution in 1961. Even if their ideologies appeared quite similar at first glance, the honeymoon between the Egyptian and Syrian regimes was short-lived. Nasser and the Syrian leaders came to blows not only over ideological issues but also over governance and the political structure of the union. Each accused the other of untrustworthiness and even betrayal. Syrians criticized Nasser for failing to respond to Israeli provocations against Syria and for attempting to "Egyptianize" the country. Nasser suspected that the radical Arab nationalists from the Baath party in Syria were trying to sabotage the union and seize power. He was also aware that the Baath party, plagued with internal rifts, did not have a broad social base of support inside Syria.[12] For example, when Egypt and Syria formed the United Arab Republic in 1958, the Baath party voluntarily dissolved itself as a contribution to ensuring the success of the union. Yet the decision led to disputes among party members and further internal splits.

If 1958 represented the height of the pan-Arab nationalist (unionist) project, 1961 was a turning point in Nasser's conduct, a realization that the journey is littered with minefields. From 1961 till his death of a heart attack in 1970, Nasser would no longer entertain ambitious pan-Arab unity proposals by his Arab counterparts and instead insisted on coordination and collaboration or what he called the solidarity of Arab ranks. The high hopes vested in the union between Egypt and Syria crashed on the rocks of territorial nationalism and the entrenched interests of Egypt's and Syria's ruling elites. Moreover, by delivering a hard blow to Nasser, the breakdown of the United Arab Republic intensified inter-Arab rivalries and led Nasser to lash out angrily against what he labeled "reactionary" Arab regimes like Saudi Arabia, which he accused of conspiring against the Egyptian-Syrian union. In fact, his decision to militarily intervene in Yemen in the 1960s and back the Yemeni Free Officers led by Ali Abdel Ghan against the rule of Imam Ahmed bin Yehia Hamideddin was partly motivated by opposition to Saudi Arabia for its alleged role in the breakup of the UAR. The Yemen debacle exacted a heavy toll on the Egyptian state, particularly by overextending its military and undermining Nasser's credibility. Yemen became a killing field where Arabs shed each other's blood and the Arab cold war spiraled out of control. Nasser's costly Yemen venture was a significant contributing factor in the defeat of the Egyptian army in the June 1967 war with Israel, a watershed marking the decline of Arab nationalism.

Thus promoting a pan-Arab platform served Nasser's own purposes of maximizing Egypt's bargaining power regionally and internationally. In contrast to the pan-Arab nationalist project in the Mashreq (the Arab east)—Syria, Iraq, Lebanon, Palestine, and Jordan—which entailed the merger of the Arab states in a pan-Arab unified state, Nasser believed only in cooperative Arab nationalism or Arab solidarity, not pan-Arab unity. The idea of Arab nationalism as a framework for the construction of a project of Egyptian domination of regional politics remained a theme throughout Nasser's career. When pressed by interviewer Jacques Benoist-Méchin on exactly this question in 1957, Nasser denied that it was his intention to replace European and American imperialism in the Middle East with a new form of Egyptian imperialism. However, his musings on the nature and extension of the Arab nation appeared to clearly belie his protestations. "I have an exact knowledge of the frontiers of the Arab nation," he told Benoist-Méchin. "I do not place it in the future for I think and I act as though it already existed. These frontiers end where my propaganda no longer rouses an echo. Beyond this point, something else begins a foreign world which does not concern me."[13]

The argument has also been made, by Lacouture among others, that Nasser's pan-Arab nationalism was motivated by another set of pragmatic considerations: Egyptian economic interests. In an interview with the *Christian Science Monitor* in 1959, Nasser exquisitely linked pan-Arab nationalism with materialistic pragmatic considerations:

> When I was teaching in our staff college, I delved into the problems of the Mediterranean basin," he continued. History, I found, showed quite naturally that when the Arab countries were united they rid themselves of invaders ... From this reading of history I saw that those things which should have been our strengths, such as our geographical position, or the oil of the area, were used as justification for occupying us. Instead, they should have been sources of strength and the protection to us ... So I began first by working to build an Arab nationalism which applies to all the Middle East. A vacuum had to be filled, as I have said, Egypt in the Middle East is not playing the role of an invader, but as a supplier of ideology. [14]

Other contemporaries of Nasser traced his vigorous focus on the idea of Arab economic potential and its profit-earning capacity to his readings at the military academy.[15] Nasser referred to these economic concerns in an interview with Lacouture in late 1953. Asked about possible plans for Arab unification, Nasser suggested that the rivalry between the Saudis and the Hashemites made this impractical. A more modest form of integration might begin "through economic and defense agreements like those which you have in Europe," he suggested.[16]

Nasser's Use of Islam

In contrast with Nasser's nationalist ideology, his recourse to the Islamic repertoire and use of religion tends to be glossed over in the literature. His struggle for power against the Ikhwan has often been portrayed as an indication of Nasser's secularist predisposition. However, the growing divide between the Ikhwan and the Free Officers did not mean that the latter were firm or hard secularists who profoundly believed in the separation of the state and religion. Rather, as Mohieddin told me: "My friend, Nasser, could have ended up a religious nationalist [like the Ikhwan] as opposed to a pan-Arab nationalist."[17] For a long time, the Ikhwan propagated a self-serving claim that Nasser had moved away from the Islamist movement in the late 1940s as a result of becoming less religious and tilting towards communist groups. However, recollections by his close aides and personal details show that Nasser remained religious throughout his life. Sami Sharaf, Nasser's chief of staff, dismisses the Ikhwan assertion as self-serving and notes that like Egyptians Nasser was pious and took solace in the Prophet Muhammad as his "great model."

Heikal offered a more nuanced account of Nasser's relationship with Islam. He said that Nasser knew the significance of the sacred in Egyptian life and counseled being cautious and refraining from confrontation with religion. "When I was writing *al-mithaq* [the social charter declared by Nasser in May 1962], Nasser advised me against confronting the role of religion in the public sphere because it is a lose-lose exercise," said Heikal. "Nasser knew the power of the religious imagination and its peril and thus sought to co-opt it." Heikal recalled Nasser's recommending a strategy of positive engagement with the religious question and avoidance of any negative utterances.[18] Adding an important footnote, Heikal acknowledged that after the Six-Day War in June 1967 Nasser instrumentalized religion in order to motivate the military and inspire sacrifice for the homeland.[19] Contrary to the Ikhwan narrative, Nasser was not a secularist and did not try to secularize state institutions; he never lost an opportunity to affirm his faith and showcase his religious values.[20]

Long before the Six-Day War, the Nasserist state incorporated religious institutions and symbols partly in order to deny the Ikhwan an outlet for social mobilization. Strikingly, Nasser also used religion proactively as a means to extend state power and achieve and sustain social cohesion. For example, he regarded al-Azhar, one of the oldest religious and educational institutions in Islam, as an influential tool in shaping and promoting his regime's domestic and foreign policies. Again, here Nasser's pragmatism and realpolitik calculations seem to have been the driving factor behind his utilization of religion and religious institutions like al-Azhar. Moreover in the mid-1950s, in his struggle with religious political activists and rivals such as the Ikhwan, Nasser instrumentalized the sacred imagination to show that he was as religious as his Islamist foes, if not more so, in order to consolidate his own legitimacy and hegemony. He used the pulpit of al-Azhar to drive the point home to the public. When Britain, France, and Israel attacked Egypt during the 1956 crisis, Nasser traveled to al-Azhar on two consecutive Fridays and addressed the nation after *jumaa* (Friday) prayers, assuring citizens that Egypt would resist the invaders and would emerge victorious. In a symbolic act marrying religion and politics, Nasser affirmed this discursive mixture in a speech on November 2, 1956:

> If Britain considers itself a Great Power, if France considers itself a Great Power, we are *Shaab Mu'men* [a nation of believers]. Our slogan would be Allahu Akbar [God is Great]. Allah will help us. Allah will make us victorious. We depend on Allah and on ourselves. We will make jihad, struggle and fight. We will win with Allah's will. Allahu Akbar Allahu Akbar. *Wa Salamu Aleikum wa Rahmat Allah* [Peace be upon you].[21]

Nasser sought to guarantee al-Azhar's loyalty and avoid any potential for independence or rebellion by its scholars, as had been historically the case when al-Azhar scholars like Omar Makram and

Mohammed Abduh resisted Napoleon and Khedive Tawfiq respectively. In order to do so, he imposed financial and political restrictions which limited the ability of al-Azhar sheikhs to play an independent role.[22] Under his regime, reforms therefore included Law 103 of 1961, which reorganized and placed al-Azhar, along with its endowments, under the jurisdiction of the Ministry of Religious Endowments. This motion allowed Nasser to appoint both the minister of religious endowments, the sheikh of al-Azhar, and al-Azhar's undersecretary, thereby extending state control over the most important religious institution in the country as well as corollary institutions such as Mujamaa al-Azhar.[23]

Subsequently, the Nasserist state utilized the authority of al-Azhar as a counterweight to both internal and external foes who wrapped their opposition to Nasser in religious terms, such as the Ikhwan, the Salafis, and Saudi Arabia.[24] Islamist activists were barred from joining mainstream state-run institutions of the al-Azhar variety. For example, when the director of Al-Azhar University, Mohamed al-Bahy, attempted to appoint Mohamed Suleiman as the university's undersecretary, his request was rejected twice on claims that Suleiman was a member of the Ikhwan.[25] In his memoirs, Bahy, a close functionary of the Nasser regime who was appointed as minister of religious endowments, revealed that the intelligence services established Islamic bodies and forums in order to "trace, collect information and clamp down on Islamist groups through different means, including hearsay and rumors."[26] The Nasserist state also used al-Azhar to discredit and attack Islamist groups and to gain legitimacy at home as well. Sheikh Mahmoud Shaltout, appointed the sheikh of al-Azhar in 1958, called Nasser *al-shab al-mu'men* (the young believer).[27] The ruling authorities also appointed army officers to al-Azhar's affiliated agencies and boards, thereby entangling the religious institution with the "Officers Republic." Those army officers sought to shape al-Azhar's role in society by establishing new forums designed to shape the agenda of popular consciousness in the religious domain. For example, Colonel Abdullah Te'ima founded the Supreme Council for Islamic Affairs and linked it to al-Azhar, providing financial assets to the council by purchasing nationalized buildings from the Ministry of Religious Endowments.[28]

Egypt was not the only postcolonial, post-independence state to harness traditional elements, particularly religious capital, to shape the agenda of popular consciousness and influence which ideas prevailed in society. Seyyed Vali Reza Nasr points out that the continuity of traditional elements is a product and an extension of colonialism which left the state apparatus with superior identity and encouraged interventionist attitudes and a desire for hegemony. Many postcolonial states adopted paternalistic practices in governance in the form of neopatrimonialism and abused religious symbolism to compensate for the weakness of formal institutions and lack of legitimacy. In his investigation of the politicization of Islam in Pakistan and Malaysia, Nasr shows that the process was not only bottom-up but also state-led. In both countries, he notes that the postcolonial ruling elite incorporated religion in state institutions, an exercise which greatly benefited the Islamization of society. The instrumentalization of religion by the postcolonial state aimed at filling a moral and ideological vacuum after achieving independence and at gaining legitimacy and social cohesion.[29] Additionally, guided by the imperatives of revenue extraction, legitimation, hegemony, and economic growth, the incorporation of religion allows the state to extend its power not only to the public sphere but also to the private, thus consolidating its hold on society. Nasr further argues that "state-led Islamization is in essence the indigenization of the postcolonial state embedding it in the local value systems"; thus, it is an effective tool to project state power to the masses.[30]

According to Colin J. Beck and Nasr, the incorporation of Islam nourishes Islamization because the state channels ideological and material resources to religious institutions, as well as simultaneously opening up a political space for dissidents by framing the ideological base for social movements. In a way, religion and Islam can often be the only legitimate space for civil action in authoritarian contexts because other feasible channels of political expression may not be tolerated or available.[31] Despite Nasser's constructed image as a secular nationalist, he, just like so many post-independence leaders, used religious imagery and rhetoric to legitimate and consolidate both his power and his grip on the state.

Indeed, ideas are an efficient means to impose power or at minimum to facilitate control and manage society; the cultural base from which support is derived is decisive.[32] Therefore, reintegrating religious values has the potential to incorporate society at large, strengthen legitimacy, and expand control. In his quest to create a new hegemony and a new modernity beyond colonial modernity, Nasser utilized a grand narrative of popular sovereignty, Arab cultural renaissance, and Islamic heritage. Far from distancing his ideological project from religion, Nasser wrapped it around traditional elements and extended state control over religious institutions, thus ensuring continuity with the past. He often reiterated his commitment to Islam as the spiritual anchor of state and society and did not cut the umbilical cord with the religious imagination. In this context, it becomes apparent that Anwar Sadat's more extreme and direct use of religion was inscribed in the continuity of what Nasser had started, albeit in a more radical form.[33]

Nasser's Anti-imperialism

To the extent that Nasser's politics were ideologically driven, the fundamental principle from which they stemmed was neither Arab nationalism, nor Islamism, but anti-imperialism. Nasser's anti-colonial rhetoric was part of his desire to project a new political imagination that sought a rupture with colonial modernity. While the drive to rid Egypt of its British overlords had long motivated Nasser, as we have seen in previous sections, his experience in Palestine reinforced and reinvigorated his anti-colonial struggle and fed his search for an alternative political framework. Nasser saw Israel as nothing more than a creature of imperialism, considering that Zionism would have remained a "foolish idea" if its adherents had not succeeded in recruiting Britain as their colonial sponsor. For him, battling Israel was equivalent to fighting the forces of international imperialism[34] and the campaign in Palestine was "self-defense."[35] This did not mean that Nasser always adopted a purely confrontational stance vis-à-vis Israel. Instead, at times, he also pursued a more conciliatory approach.

Furthermore, contrary to widespread Arab and Western accounts, Nasser's anti-imperialism did not amount to anti-Westernization. He never conflated imperialism with Western culture or saw Western society as an enemy. Likewise, he did not consider the anti-colonial struggle in cultural and religious terms. Nasser aide Mohamed Fayek corroborates this view and emphasizes that Nasser was not anti-Western. "Nasser often reminded us that the West is not an intrinsic enemy of Egypt and the Arab world, and that it is important to engage the Western powers and find ways and means to cooperate," Fayek told me. "Even after the 1967 war, Nasser recommended that we develop our links with France further in order to counterbalance the rupture of diplomatic relations with America."[36] (Egypt severed relations with the United States after the Six-Day War.) This measured approach also extended to Nasser's staunch enemies, such as Egypt's former colonial power, Great Britain. In a 1964 speech, Nasser asserted his willingness to work with the British, this despite all past and present disagreements. "We are ready to work in all possible ways to build solid and good relations with Britain because our concern is not to make problems flare up and fight with the English," he said.[37] Rather, Nasser's generation of anti-colonial nationalists deployed universal concepts of self-determination, popular sovereignty, popular democracy, resistance, and anti-hegemony as effective weapons. "Throughout his life Nasser never believed in a clash of civilizations between East and West. [Rather], he viewed the anti-colonial struggle through ideological and strategic lenses," said Heikal, in a conversation in his Cairo study. "At the height of the attacks on Egypt by Western powers in 1956 and 1967, Nasser recognized the strategic and political calculations behind their actions and was not blinded by culture," he said.[38] "Trained as an officer and widely read in strategy and politics, Nasser believed that national interests drive policy, including [that of] the great powers," Heikal told me in a serious tone. "Unlike the religious right, he was a realist and pragmatist. His combat experience in the Palestine war reinforced his belief that the Arabs should harness all elements of power to resist imperialism," he concluded.

Indeed, in *The Philosophy of the Revolution*, Nasser reminded Egyptians that national weakness only constitutes a recipe for perpetual subjugation and domination by foreign powers. He adopted views comparable to those of Frantz Fanon, based on the realization that the problem of colonization includes not only the interrelations of objective historical conditions but also the subjective social environment in which colonized people were forced to live; culture plays a role both as an object of subjugation of the colonized and as a tool for their liberation, as well as the role of agency in confronting these conditions.[39] The two men also shared a vivid critique of the elite and educated classes. As Fanon warned in *The Wretched of the Earth*: "The unpreparedness of the educated classes, the lack of practical links between them and the mass of the people, their laziness, and, let it be said, their cowardice at the decisive moment of the struggle will give rise to tragic mishaps."[40] Another parallel between Nasser and Fanon involves the role of culture as an emancipatory force. While Fanon stressed that cultural traditions could help the colonized free themselves from the colonial framework's representation of their culture as backward, he also warned that idealism alone would not bring about real liberation. Instead, Fanon encouraged a materialist conception of the nation based on political agency and collective direct action to dismantle the political-economic foundation of colonial rule.[41] Nasser's celebrated slogan—"Raise your head, my brother; the era of oppression has ended"—had powerful cultural currency and appeal. By reinstating the agency of Egyptians, Nasser aimed to project a political subjectivity that radically broke away from the one imposed by the British colonial system. He established a direct correlation between his coming to power and the beginning of a new era, one of liberation, where the former colonized can regain their dignity and with that their agency. However, as we will see in later sections, Nasser ultimately failed to break away from the institutionalization of authoritarianism that had been an integral part of the colonial framework. Nonetheless, Nasser's rhetoric and speeches were populist; they were practical and liberating, destined to motivate and inspire Egyptians and Arabs in general to take action against their occupiers. For Nasser the redefinition of Egyptian national subjectivity was a means to an end: to consolidate his legitimacy and control of the political system and to mobilize the masses against these rivals that the Nasserist state saw as enemies of the nation.

Nasser utilized realism and ideational reasoning to great effect, seeing no contradiction between the two concepts. Echoing the realists, he pointed out that any power vacuum and weakness would likely be filled by colonialism, conceived as an expansionist force:

> If ever imperialism knew that there were Egyptians ready to shed their blood and to meet force by force it would withdraw and recoil like a harlot. This, of course, is the state or habit of imperialism everywhere.[42]

Nasser's realism is also exemplified by his initial pragmatism in his dealings with the United States, Israel, and other world powers. Quite apart from the possibility of enlisting American aid to evict the British from the Suez Canal Zone, he also hoped early on that Washington would supply Egypt with modern weapons. As early as September 1952, Nasser held informal talks with the then U.S. ambassador to Egypt, Jefferson Caffery. During their meeting, he explained the goals of the revolution and the importance he attached to equipping the military with new arms. He assured the ambassador that Washington need not fear that Egypt would use American weapons to attack Israel for, as he put it, "I do not believe in war as an instrument of policy."[43] A month later, Nasser met with William Foster, the American assistant secretary of defense, who agreed to recommend that Washington accept a list of Egypt's requirements to a total value of $100 million.[44] Despite these optimistic openings, relations with the United States soon deteriorated. By fall 1952 it had become clear to Nasser that Caffery's sweet words and Foster's prompt acceptance of Egypt's arms requirements did not reflect the real intentions of the U.S. government, which made its arms assistance conditional on Egypt joining its regional defense pacts.[45] Mohieddin confirms that until the mid-1950s Nasser hoped to be on good terms with the Americans and did not want to rock the boat, even after Washington let him down. "In contrast to some of us who had sought to align Egypt's international relations with the socialist camp, Nasser viewed the United States as a natural ally," he explained. "At the beginning, Nasser believed that America could be a force for good in Egypt. At heart he was enamored with the American success story," he added.[46] Heikal also notes that Nasser was not an ideologue and was genuinely interested in developing mutual relations with the United States, which he saw as capable of counterbalancing Britain's domineering role in Egypt. According to Heikal, Nasser's early hopes were dashed because the United States forced him to choose between being "with us or against us," and he was bluntly told that there is no neutrality between good and evil.[47]

Echoing Moheiddin's and Heikal's testimony, Mohamed Fayek, a senior aide to Nasser who worked in his presidential office and also served as a minister, said that in the beginning Nasser and other Free Officers had thought that the United States could be a friend of Egypt. Relations with Washington deteriorated, he said, because of Egyptian unwillingness to join its defense schemes in the Middle East as well as Egypt's leadership role in the Non-Aligned Movement. "The U.S. refused an independent role for Egypt in the region," added Fayek, "and implicitly warned Nasser that non-alignment was a red line. Our interests diverged as we charted an independent course in international relations."[48]

The evidence shows that Nasser, who expressed a desire for cordial relations with the United States on several occasions, did not take an ideological position against the global Western superpower, despite growing resentment among his fellow officers. Indeed, his pragmatic stance put him at odds with some hawkish Free Officers around him. Members of the Revolutionary Command Council (RCC) were angered by what they considered to be the gross impertinence of the U.S. government, which refused to supply Egypt with arms, yet reserved the right to tell them that they should not seek weapons elsewhere. Some army officers even recommended that Egypt ought to break off diplomatic relations with Washington and that protests should be organized against the American embassy in Cairo. They wanted to show the Americans the strength of Egyptian sentiments against efforts by Secretary of State John Foster Dulles to pressure the Free Officers to take sides in the global East-West rivalry and to join U.S.-led regional defense pacts against Soviet communism. Nasser talked his colleagues out of such hotheaded action.

As relationships with the United States hardened, in 1955 Nasser met President Tito of Yugoslavia. Putting on a show, the two leaders cruised the Suez Canal on board an Egyptian naval training ship. From this most skillful diplomatic tightrope walker, who not only managed to get substantial aid from the West but also became the only leader of a communist state to receive payment from Moscow in U.S. dollars, Nasser learned with fascination how to play the two rival Cold War superpowers off against each other. As Tito told him, the golden rule in this great powers game was to maintain all possible contacts with both sides. With this in mind, Nasser remained intent on maintaining relations with the United States. He was not going to let the RCC push him into breaking relations with a potentially useful partner out of irritation over an impertinent intervention by Dulles. Nasser also knew that "he held all the cards" in this dispute and that "the only way the United States could strengthen its hand would be to reverse the decision to refuse to arm Egypt." It was thus clear that "the storm would either blow itself out or would bring him some benefit."[49] According to Mohieddin, Nasser admired and trusted Tito greatly because he was an independent socialist. He never lost sight of Tito's golden rule, even after U.S.-Egyptian relations subsequently reached a low point. Throughout his rule, Nasser preserved his contacts with both superpowers and successfully played them off against each other to maximize his bargaining position and extract rent and foreign aid.[50] His pragmatism toward Washington, despite its pronounced hostility to Nasser's pan-Arab nationalist project, was on display in the late 1950s and 1960s. In a speech before Parliament in November 1964, Nasser insisted that

> there have never been direct problems between us and the U.S. We might disagree on some issues such as the U.S. support for Israel, the U.S. position on Congo, and the use of force policy adopted in some areas. Nevertheless, we try in all ways to have *'ilaqat saleema* [unblemished relations] with the U.S.[51]

Meanwhile, Nasser's relations with the Soviet Union were complicated. Although the two countries had had no relations before 1955, as Nasser lost confidence in the United States in the mid-1950s, he turned increasingly to Moscow for military and diplomatic backing. Egypt progressively developed warm ties with the Soviet Union, with Russian leaders frequently reminding Egyptians that Russia provides their country with weapons and wheat unconditionally.[52] Explaining his relationship with a communist state, Nasser emphasized Egypt's independence: "As the Soviet Union is a communist state and as we are not a communist state, does this [fact] have an impact? Of course not."[53] As he made such statements, the Nasserist state continued to imprison and persecute communists at home,[54] a fact that testifies to the primacy of *raison d'état* in Russian-Egyptian relations.

In a similar vein, Nasser initially even showed pragmatism towards Israel, despite the bitter taste that the Palestine war had left in him. At the Guildhall in London on November 9, 1955, British prime minister Anthony Eden suggested that both Israel and the Arabs should be willing to compromise over the question of borders in order to reach a peace settlement. He hinted that the eventual solution should lie somewhere between the existing borders of the territory which Israel had gained by conquest in the 1948 war and the lines agreed to in the United Nations partition plan. Israeli prime minister David Ben Gurion immediately rejected Eden's proposal. In contrast, Nasser welcomed Eden's idea as marking the first occasion when a major Western leader had made a constructive statement on the Palestine conflict.[55] This example clearly shows that at the outset of his administration Nasser was disposed to reaching a peaceful settlement with Israel regarding its permanent borders with a Palestinian state, recognizing Israel's right to exist and also its security. Throwing light on Nasser's conduct and worldview during his first two years in office offers a comparative lens through which to understand continuity and change in his policies in subsequent years as well as the drivers behind them. Although Nasser turned more radical in the late 1950s and 1960s, he did not shed his realist-pragmatic sensibility in regional and global affairs, where he displayed a measure of moderation. Historically, Nasser has been misunderstood because his populism and vocal rhetoric have been taken as evidence of a revolutionary disposition and sensibility. A closer look at his policies from the early years till his death in 1970 indicates a more complex, fluid, and pragmatic pattern. As this chapter demonstrates, despite Nasser's populism, more often than not his choices were driven by the reality of the anti-colonial fight, Cold War politics, and Egyptian socioeconomic interests. While Nasserism owes its durability and continued appeal to the power of the social ideals and the denunciation of colonialism and capitalism in which Nasser anchored his rhetoric, in practice he was guided by political pragmatism and the imperative of Egyptian national interests, not ideology.

Nasser and Socialism

From early on Nasser prioritized social justice and economic development, particularly nationalization of big businesses, land reforms, and the eradication of monopolies. As examined previously, Nasser's social reforms were integral to the strength and the durability of the Nasserist ideals in Egypt and beyond. He correlated the destruction of the colonial-capitalist framework directly with the improvement of the socioeconomic conditions of Egypt's impoverished masses. As a consequence, one of his primary socioeconomic priorities was to lift Egyptians out of abject poverty and give the population access to public education. His policies particularly benefitted the lower and middle classes, not just the poor. Despite the strength and breadth of Nasser's social reforms, it is important to note that when he first seized power in the early 1950s, he lacked a distinct ideological anchor and social base of support. Furthermore, his turn to socialism did not take place until 1961. The result is that he was left to learn the challenges of governance by trial and error. Given the severe economic and social conditions in Egypt which Nasser inherited in the early 1950s, his emphasis on social justice and development makes considerable sense. One common feature of the pre- and post-socialist phase of Nasserism was the progressively radical social agenda that appealed to the masses—providing medical care, education, and employment. Immediately after the coup, Nasser took initiatives to address the dismal socioeconomic conditions in the country, promising equitable social development. Notwithstanding his ideological fluidity, he had his finger on the pulse of public opinion. He had understood that the urgent task was to give Egyptians hope and a stake in the nascent order by making a concrete commitment to empowering the lower and middle classes.

The Nasserist social ideal did not include the domination of a new class over another. His vision of a society articulated around the concept of "social justice" meant the dissolution of classes and was opposed to the domination of any class over another.[56] This opposition to class dictatorship, including the domination of the proletariat, provides one of the clearest distinctions between Nasser's Arab socialism and Marxist politics. Critics point out that Nasser's vision encompasses an inclusive society where all the forces of the nation could work together in harmony. He aimed to establish a society that allowed for equal opportunities for all citizens so that every Egyptian could "determine his place in society by his own work and his own effort."[57] According to Mohieddin, as soon as he gained power, Nasser adopted the demands of the Egyptian nationalist movement, which revolved around two key political and social demands: liberation from colonialism and independence, and social justice.[58] For example, the 1956 constitution lists six principles of the revolution, which Nasser condensed into two broad categories: (1) to restore political freedom to the nation and its citizens; and (2) and to ensure social freedom to the nation and its citizens.[59]

Further dismissing Nasser's alleged tilt toward communism, Sami Sharaf, his chief of staff, notes that Nasser imprisoned communists and forced them to distance themselves from their superpower patron, the Soviet Union.[60] Indeed, Mohieddin, Nasser's Marxist friend from their days at the military academy, recalls that there was no love lost between Nasser and Marxism. "When I asked Nasser if Marxist officers could join the Free Officers movement, Nasser responded, 'You could do so individually, not as an organization, and your loyalty should be to the revolution.'"[61] There is a consensus among Nasser's comrades that by the mid-1950s, he embraced the aspirations and goals of the Egyptian nationalist movement, which invested his administration with popular-revolutionary legitimacy and allowed him to engineer top-down social change. "Nasser's priorities were those of the Egyptian [and Arab] nationalist movement, which earned him massive public support and turned him into a hero," said Mohamed Fayek. "But his style of governance was authoritarian, [he was] a strongman."[62] Mohieddin shared similar views, telling me when I pressed him: "Nasser was ideologically neutral. He was not committed to social transformation of society along Marxist lines, only to changing the old system of social inequities and expanding economic and educational opportunities."[63]

Nasser's Authoritarianism

Just as Nasser's pan-Arab ideals were ultimately rooted in considerations related to the economy and Egyptian national interest, so was he equally pragmatic when it came to using coercion as a means for bringing about the kinds of political change he desired. This includes his interactions with the Free Officers themselves. According to Mohieddin and others, there existed three disparate groupings within the Free Officers. One camp consisted of a small group of young socialist and Marxist officers like Mohieddin. According to the latter, this progressive camp was not deeply rooted in the military and was unwilling to carry out a putsch to eliminate rivals, though it represented a highly motivated social constituency. A second camp was aligned with the Ikhwan and included key officers with leadership skills and organizational and operational assets. More important, this camp was part of a larger social base that included nearly half a million sympathizers. Consequently, the Ikhwan-aligned officers were the most coherent group and were a serious threat to Nasser's political ambitions. Nasser himself was located within a third camp of officers with far less clear ideological leanings and no social foundation. This camp was made up of gradually radicalized officers who hoped to achieve a thoroughgoing socioeconomic restructuring using the military and technocrats as an instrument of top-down change. Nasser saw the Ikhwan-aligned and the Marxist camps as a potential threat to his domination of the RCC and of the larger social spectrum. Strikingly, these two camps constituted the most ideologically driven groupings among the Free Officers. Nasser never recoiled from using violence against anyone who could prove to be an obstacle to his power, even if it meant targeting other nationalists, irrespective of their political orientation. As chapter 2 showed, Nasser got entangled in an internal power struggle with Naguib and his supporters and ultimately put Naguib under house arrest for good.

Moreover, in the initial organization of the Free Officers, the movement included a unit known as Lagnet al-Irhab (the Department of Terrorism),[64] whose purpose was "liquidating those who are against the nationalist movement."[65] Nasser himself held that political assassinations were "an inevitable positive task."[66] Of course, these moves by Nasser and his comrades did not occur in a vacuum. Instead, they took place at a time of political ferment in Egypt, when a variety of groups embraced political violence as part of what had become a zero-sum struggle for survival and will to power, under circumstances which impressed upon these agents the sense that only violence could bring about the required change.[67]

Soon after the coup Nasser's relationship with the Ikhwan went from conciliatory to antagonistic. The final straw was the Ikhwan-led attempt on Nasser's life in October 1954, which prompted him to brutally suppress the movement. Although Sayyid Qutb is the most famous example of Nasser's persecution of the Islamists, thousands were imprisoned and tortured by the Nasserist security apparatus. This violent schism marked the start of a long and bloody struggle between the Islamist movement and the Nasserist state. "Look, Egypt paid a heavy price because of the power struggle between Nasser and the Ikhwan, which culminated in the establishment of a dictatorship," Mohieddin said. "Although Nasser had good intentions and the right policy priorities, the top-down authoritarian system established by Nasser weakened society and ravaged political life, ultimately allowing Islamists to revive and dominate Egypt. Nasser prioritized social justice at the expense of open society and constitutionalism, though I often made the case that social justice and political diversity are not mutually exclusive," explained Mohieddin. He nonetheless added that he and his wife were fond of Nasser, his old comrade, despite their disagreement over the direction of the revolution. "Politically ambitious, Nasser was in a hurry to enact social change without being hindered by checks and balances," said Mohieddin, who, unlike Nasser, came from a firmer social background and opposed Nasser's monopoly on power and politicization of the military.[68]

Heikal disagrees with Mohieddin up to a point. Calling Nasser neither a democrat nor a dictator, he argued that Nasser ruled Egypt by "popular consent" rather than "participation."[69] Nasser, Heikal contended, won the hearts and minds of Egyptians because of his egalitarian and forward-looking revolutionary social agenda and programs and his defense of the homeland against foreign powers. The public overwhelmingly supported Nasser's decisions and trusted him as a leader. Heikal argues that Nasser's popular legitimacy shielded him against accusations of monopolizing power. "Nasser did not hoard power either for its own sake or to enrich himself and his business cronies as his successors have done," insisted Heikal. "Rather, he invested all capital at his disposal in modernizing Egypt and meteorically expanding the middle class. Nasser also lifted millions of Egyptians up out of poverty and rescued them from destitution."[70] "Nasser fundamentally transformed the social classes in Egypt," stated Heikal. "He gave Egypt back to the Egyptians and made them feel proud of their nation."[71] His testimony as Nasser's confidant and official biographer provides a colorful, expansive window into the Nasserist worldview, though some critics would say a distorted one. Indeed, in his zeal to defend Nasser, Heikal overlooks a key critical point raised by comrades of Nasser like Mohieddin and Fayek: that top-down authoritarianism exacted a heavy toll on state and society, and ultimately undermined the Nasserist progressive social agenda. According to Mohieddin, Nasser's conscious choice of top-down authoritarianism as a system of governance was counterproductive and harmed the revolution's strategic goal, which was to fuel a renaissance.[72]

Mohieddin is not the only one to take such view. The historian Sherif Younis dismisses Heikal's point about popular legitimacy and asserts that Nasser manufactured consent and legitimation by proscribing all political parties and controlling civil society, including labor unions and non-governmental professional associations. In seeking to establish a new constituency and a technocratic elite that owed its loyalty to the new regime, Younis argues, the Free Officers offered a political and social program anchored in social justice, expansion of the educational system, land reforms, nationalization of the private sector, and disinheriting the old urban and rural elite. "Unfortunately, rationality and sound economic planning was sacrificed at the altar of populism and gaining public trust," lamented Younis. "Nasser transformed Egypt from a multiparty political system to corporate militarism and clientelism. A small inner circle of aides trusted by Nasser formulated domestic and foreign policies behind closed doors."[73] Younis cited the case of Heikal himself, whose editorials used to be dissected by both Egyptians and foreigners for clues about the regime's thinking. A top-down closed system of governance produced catastrophic decisions, such as the May crisis in 1967 that led to the June Six-Day War, a war that hastened the end of the Nasserist project, if not the Nasserist state.

Younis nevertheless added that Nasser and the Free Officers were not bad and did not represent a rupture with Egyptian modern history. "Nasser was an Egyptian patriot who desired to rebuild and strengthen social and political life in the country on a more solid foundation," he said. "His ideas were not born out of a vacuum but were an extension of those of the authoritarian intelligentsia from Muhammad Ali in the nineteenth century until the 1940s. Like their distant predecessors, the Free Officers believed that capturing power would allow them to institute fundamental change and that reliance on a pliant technocratic elite would be safe and effective. What this entails is the demise of politics," he concluded.[74] Although the new elite filled the vacuum left by the dismantling of political parties and groups, it did not lay the ground for a new political space or formal institutions. Nasser and the Free Officers prioritized their ambitious social agenda over broad political participation. Nasser did not tolerate organized dissent of any persuasion lest it abort or undermine his expensive social reforms. Therefore, in practice, Nasser maintained the authoritarian character of the colonial system. His realist and pragmatic calculation was designed to minimize dissent at all cost, even if that meant reproducing the violence that had been integral to the British occupation.

On the one hand, Nasser's uplifting rhetoric provided Egyptians with a strong and valorizing ideational space, where agency, dignity, and an ideal vision of the future anchored in solidarity and equality were repeatedly projected. On the other hand, the political space remained under the tight grip of the Nasserist regime. A divide between the state and the people was objectively maintained: the state's subjective power was contingent on its objective power over the population.

Conclusion

Throughout his career, one of Nasser's primary goals was to cleanse Egypt of the old corrupt ruling elite and imperial control. He labored hard to build a new legitimacy and hegemony inscribed in an ambitious social vision—a radical social agenda which marked a rupture with the liberal capitalist economy of the old regime. Even Nasser's detractors credit him with transforming Egypt from backwardness to a modernized state with a big middle class. Despite the ideals of social justice, equality, and dissolution of classes around which Nasserism anchored its vision, the reforms passed by the government, especially the Five Year Plan (1960–65), directly benefitted the middle class. These reforms allowed the state to dominate all the sectors of the economy, and as a result the public sector became the largest employer of educated and skilled young university graduates and professionals. This greatly enlarged the middle class and allowed Nasser to create a new elite which he could use in his struggle against the upper classes. The middle and lower classes were given a stake in the state, and in return they had to back the government's policies. Nasser's progressive policies lifted millions of Egyptians out of abject poverty and misery. By restructuring the education system and passing land reforms and setting up subsidies, the Nasserist state did more to help the working classes than all of its predecessors and successors alike.

Despite such impressive achievements, in many ways, what defined Egyptian politics both during Nasser's lifetime and afterwards was corporate militarism, or a corporatist sociopolitical system in which the military is one of the major corporate groups involved in organizing society, on the basis of shared interests with various other corporate groups.[75] Both Arab nationalism in the 1950s and 1960s and Islamism in the 1970s gained prominence because corporate militarism instrumentalized them as semiofficial ideologies. There can be little doubt that Arab nationalism would not have gained widespread traction and popularity in Egypt and neighboring Arab countries were it not for Nasser and the Egyptian state. Similarly, Nasser's successor, Anwar Sadat, promoted religion and piety as an alternative ideology to secular Arab nationalism and used state institutions, together with the oil revolution in the Gulf, to tip the balance of social forces in favor of religious activism and Islamism. In other words, ideologies were subordinated to corporate militarism and personalities, such as Nasser and Sadat. It was Nasser who institutionalized and legitimized the role of corporate militarism in Egyptian politics, even though nationalist intellectuals like al-Sayyed Yassin dispute the notion that Nasser militarized the state or relied on army men in critical cabinet portfolios. This corporate militarism also included the building up of a vast and complex security apparatus, which laid the foundation for the further institutionalization of repression.

Nasser's turn to authoritarianism mirrors that of Sayyid Qutb, who shifted from literary criticism to Islamic orthodoxy and activism in a short period of time. Equally convinced that he had a decisive role to play in the future of Egypt, Qutb found in the Ikhwan the audience and the public he had always craved. Coincidentally, his transformation from an average writer to a revered figure in Islamist circles would also be the beginning of a prolonged and deadly confrontation and growing obsession with Nasser.

Chapter 8

The Accidental Islamist?

QUTB'S MIGRATION TO THE religious right in the early 1950s marked a watershed moment, a dramatic departure in his thinking and conduct. Depending on their ideological persuasion, Arabic-language biographers offer differing explanations of Qutb's belated shift to revolutionary Islamism, but they have in common a tendency to raise more questions than they provide answers.[1] Most such biographies either celebrate Qutb's journey and discovery of the truth culminating with his martyrdom; or they portray the man as a misguided demagogue who anointed himself a religious authority and ex-communicated Muslim rulers and ordinary citizens alike. As explained previously, Qutb's disciples insist that his change of heart and mind testifies to Islam's transformative power and dynamism.[2] They are sure that his turn to the Ikhwan helped him discover the inner beauty and power of Islam, and its capacity to offer a solution to human suffering and freedom from material slavery.

Qutb Shifts towards Islamic Activism

In offering this account, Qutb's disciples are undoubtedly repeating what they learned from the master himself. In his widely read popular manifesto, *Signposts*, written while incarcerated in Nasser's prisons between 1954 and 1964, Qutb stated he had found the truth in Islam after much experimentation with and attraction to other alien, false values. He blamed Western philosophies and theories of knowledge for leading him astray, away from Islam to *jahiliyya* (a state of unbelief and ignorance). He used the details of his own experience to caution Muslims to shun Western social sciences lest they be corrupted and tricked into *jahili* (ignorant) beliefs and traditions as he himself had been. It is worth citing Qutb at length to show how he explained his shift from secularism to religiosity and radical religious activism:

> The person who is writing these lines has spent forty years of his life in reading books and in research in almost all aspects of human knowledge. He specialized in some branches of knowledge and he studied others due to personal interest. Then he turned to the fountainhead of his faith. He came to feel that whatever he had read so far was as nothing in comparison to what he found here. He does not regret spending forty years of his life in the pursuit of these sciences, because he came to know the nature of jahiliyya, its deviations, its errors and its ignorance, as well as its pomp and noise, its arrogant and boastful claims. Finally, he was convinced that a Muslim cannot combine these two sciences—the source of Divine guidance and the source of jahiliyya—for his education.[3]

Qutb said that through his return to religion, he had effectively cleansed himself of all foreign, materialistic philosophies and influences. These claims by Qutb help rationalize his shift from secularism to radical Islam rather than represent critical reflection on his trajectory. They seem clearly intended to wipe the slate of the past clean, assigning four decades of intellectual output and advocacy to the rubbish heap of history. Qutb wanted his supporters and detractors alike to forget this phase of his journey, which included most of his adult life. He told his disciples that he would have liked to burn all of the books and articles that he had written in this *jahili* stage of his trajectory.

Despite their neatness and attractiveness, the simple narratives offered by Qutb and his disciples inevitably fail to capture the complexity and versatility of human experience and identity formation as well as the shifts and turns that come with it. Several drivers—rather than just religious inspiration—lie behind Qutb's eventual shift towards radical religious activism. To begin with, it is worth reiterating that his embrace of political Islam was gradual; there was no single tipping point, no single factor that triggered a rupture. Rather, Qutb's trajectory was bound up with a host of contingent variables including the challenges of a career as a secular litterateur, a shifting cultural and political climate in Egypt, his emotive and intellectual evolution, and a disappointing bid to achieve recognition and responsibility under the umbrella of the Free Officers' regime.

Qutb's literary career brought him neither financial success nor the public recognition that he desperately craved. In the interwar period, the literary scene in Egypt was saturated with popular, grand writers like Qutb's mentor Abbas Mahmud al-Aqqad. For many precious years Qutb struggled to be taken seriously as a man of letters but his books never gained traction. Regardless of how many battles he waged on behalf of his mentor and how prolific he was in his own literary output, neither Aqqad nor other prominent writers bothered to review any of his works. This was especially hard on Qutb as he confessed that the motivation behind many of the literary fights in which he had been engaged in defending Aqqad were "ignoble" and "disgusting."[4] Qutb reportedly resented the lack of reciprocity and recognition from the literary establishment, particularly his own mentor. "He felt that the literary luminaries stabbed him in the back," according to his contemporary confidant, al-Sayyed Yassin. "They did not accord him equal treatment or recognize him as an original talent, which was a hard blow to his pride and ambition."[5]

Qutb formally inaugurated the split from his erstwhile secular mentors and his transition towards a greater reliance on religious discourse with the publication of an article full of bitterness and regret, published in *al-Thaqafa* magazine in 1951. In it, Qutb openly accused Aqqad and his generation of selfishness and shortsightedness.[6] He charged that "the old writers," as he dismissively labeled them, had failed to invest any time or effort in mentoring him and his young contemporaries, or in sharpening their literary skills. They only cared about their own self-interest and careers, Qutb insisted. He cited his own case, and his relationship with Aqqad, as an illustrative example and deplored the fact that he had been forced to chart his own literary journey alone, without a helping hand from the leading writers. This generation of literary luminaries had "forfeited its duty not only towards the youth but also towards the nation, society, and humanity," he claimed. Qutb's rebellion was part of a general alienation felt by the young generation of writers against their mentors and elders, including more well-known literature figures of the time such as Naguib Mahfouz, who openly wrote about it.[7] In Qutb's case, however, his indictment of his former mentor was particularly virulent and scathing, and he did not hesitate to declare an all-out war on the elders.[8] He painted the portrait of a self-indulgent and greedy elite that was more concerned with its own material welfare than with calling for an end to the suffering and hunger of millions of Egyptians.[9] He even went so far as to accuse prominent intellectuals of lacking nationalist fervor, of collaborating with the occupiers, and of succumbing to moral corruption, including lust, greed, and alcohol. He claimed that said literary figures "authored their works after the war while sitting in brothels, surrounded by naked thighs and dirty talk."[10] Not only were they egocentric but they had also lost their conscience and lived an immoral lifestyle, he contended.[11]

Qutb insisted that he had severed all ties with his former mentors in the literary establishment, because, having failed his scrupulous moral test, they were no longer worthy of imitation or respect. According to his contemporaries, however, as a proud and ambitious man, Qutb had felt slighted and had never forgiven them for their snub.[12] The precise circumstances of Qutb's transformation from a close supporter and disciple of Aqqad to an arch-opponent remain unclear. Some critics, such as Ali Shalash, argue that the key factor in this shift was Qutb's own "mediocre" literary production. "It was clear that the pioneers of the literary institution were not satisfied with

Qutb's literary standards. They did not find any original features," Shalash noted.[13] While it is true that other young authors—including Naguib Mahfouz, who would subsequently win the Nobel Prize for Literature—were also not acclaimed or supported by the literary figureheads of the era, Shalash explains that Qutb's exceptionally severe reaction to the snub was rooted in his own excessive ambition, restlessness, and emotionalism.[14]

Be that as it may, Qutb's indictment of his former mentors and his concomitant shift away from avowedly secular values fit with the mood of the age, a time in which the cultural and political landscape in Egypt was beginning to radically change. As mentioned in chapters 1 and 3, in the 1940s Egypt witnessed further decay of the quasi-liberal governing coalition and an ideological shift toward both the religious and secular far right. This transformation was driven by the failure of successive governments to free the country from the clutches of British hegemony and to improve the quality of life for Egyptians.[15] It contributed to the rise of various modes of authoritarian politics, including an increasingly influential Islamist presence. In this context, many public intellectuals and opinion makers, including not only Qutb but also many of his former secular mentors, began to migrate to these newly fertile religious pastures, penning obituaries for the sick liberal order. Rather than exceptional, Qutb's increasing flirtation with religious discourse around this time reflected a broader intellectual pattern in Egyptian society.

As noted, Nasser had also flirted with nativist politics in the 1940s. The growing popularity of alternative modes of radical politics was a response to what had come to be viewed as excessive secularization, liberalization, and Westernization by a corrupt and subservient political elite. Thus it is in keeping with the mood of the day that Qutb gradually came to reject Western values and political theory, including democracy and the rule of law. Like Nasser, Qutb also left the Wafd and ferociously turned against the party because, in his opinion, it failed to stand up to colonial Britain and was accessory in the repression of Egyptians.[16] In 1948, three years prior to writing that scathing article against literary intellectuals, Qutb had already written an article in which he had called on young people to stay away from "parties and depend rather on themselves."[17] According to an Egyptian biographer of Qutb, Hilmi al-Namnam, there is a clear correlation between Qutb's disillusionment with the political establishment in general and his turn towards Islam as an alternative approach to achieve social and political change.[18] It also paralleled a change that had been taking place within Egypt's charged political environment: a shift away from territorial nationalism (*wataniyya*) to an ethnically Arab one intertwined with a religious frame of reference called *qawmiyya* or supranationalism.[19]

In addition to the change in Egypt's political mood in the 1940s, the turn in Qutb's journey around this time also coincided with the popularity and success of religiously oriented books and pamphlets in Egypt and neighboring Arab countries. This was partly due to the resurgence of political Islam, which was embodied most prominently in the charismatic figure of Hassan al-Banna, the founder of the Ikhwan, and his followers. Thus by the mid-1940s, Qutb had found a literary niche in religious writing that allowed him to bask in the limelight and enjoy the sweet taste of public success. In 1945 he published a book titled *Artistic Imagery in the Qur'an*, which focused on highlighting the linguistic particularities and the specific artistic aspects of the Qu'ran in order to reveal its beauty to the general public. Prominent writers like Aqqad, Taha Hussein, and Muhammad Hussein Haykal turned to Islamic writings, inaugurating a trend that gained popular momentum in the coming decades.[20] Despite their respective crises of orientation as well as lack of internal political and social cohesiveness, both the Ikhwan and the nationalist intelligentsia were aware that they faced a common enemy: colonial domination.[21] Thus this vision of religious nationalism had the special attraction that it "promises a future that cannot easily fail: its moral and spiritual goals are transcendent and not as easy to gauge as are the more materialistic promises of secular nationalists."[22] This appeal to Islam by many Egyptian public intellectuals is a reminder of the Durkheimian functionary role that religion can play in society.[23]

In 1949, however, Qutb turned another corner with the publication of his book, *Social Justice in Islam*, a critical commentary on the social, economic, cultural, and educational conditions and policies of the Egyptian state in the interwar period. In it, Qutb laid down a theoretical framework for proper conduct in social, legal, and political affairs. His main goal was to dissect socioeconomic and political challenges and to propose a solution based on what he called "genuine Islam," an ideal type, which could act as a holistic system to manage the affairs of society. Rooting his argument in Qur'anic verses and seeking along the way to discredit other religions and ideologies, especially Christianity and communism, Qutb underscored the significance of Islam as a comprehensive alternative that can "impose the rules of social justice, and can guarantee the rights of poor people to live in dignity."[24] *Social Justice in Islam* was much closer to a political tract than *Artistic Imagery in the Qur'an*, and it earned Qutb further visibility and recognition.

From the late 1940s into the early 1950s, Qutb gradually came to embrace a progressive interpretation of religion as offering a solution to Egypt's deteriorating social and economic conditions. This period marked the beginning of a radical shift in Qutb's thought, although it is important to stress that at this stage he was not yet a revolutionary Islamist. Instead, he now looked to Islam as a complete way of life in harmony with the masses, a divine system capable of providing salvation and renewal, as well as the means to reform and to modernize Arab societies. As a prominent scholar on Islam put it: "This conceptual shift reflects a deep ideological alteration in Qutb's thought that took place in the late 1940s and left him more committed to the plight of peasants and workers."[25] At the heart of this transformation was Qutb's new belief, articulated in *Social Justice in Islam*, that "genuine" or "true" Islam could more effectively address questions of social injustice and inequity than laissez-faire capitalism or Marxism.

If less than two decades earlier Qutb had dismissed the Islamic heritage as an impediment to progress, he was now mining the distant past for answers; he unapologetically offered the stored-up

Islamic tradition as a way out of the current social malaise. Qutb's embrace of religion as a frame of reference was not unique among his generation; what was unique, however, was that a committed social activist and public intellectual was now identifying himself with *al-mustad'afun* (the wretched of the earth), particularly Egyptian peasants, and was speaking their religious language. He offered a radical and progressive vision of Islam that set him apart from the *'ulama* (the clerics or men of letters), whom he had attacked for their privileges and for their static, traditionalist, and conservative interpretation of the faith.

"Qutb pioneered a leftist, progressive Islamic discourse that challenges the dominance of reactionaries and ultraconservatives," pointed out Hassan Hanafi, an Egyptian philosopher, who coined the term *al-yassar al-Islami* (the Islamic left). "His works lay the foundation of the Islamic left, an egalitarian spirit that shows the fundamental role that justice plays in Islam. Qutb reminded Muslims of the most important moral message of Islam—social justice and freedom," Hanafi added during this author's interview with him in the imposing library at his home in Cairo. In response to my suggestion that Qutb was in effect a religious Marxist, Hanafi shot back, "No, Qutb was a progressive leftist, not a Marxist. The left had existed long before Marx, who had no monopoly on progressive politics. ... Qutb's genius lies in showing that 1,400 years ago, long before Marx and Marxism, Islam had provided a comprehensive philosophical system and an ideal that prioritized social harmony and justice as a way of life. Qutb disseminated Islam's progressive tenets."[26]

By this stage in his career, Qutb's religious writings had secured him a receptive audience among Egyptians and turned him into an acknowledged public intellectual. In particular, his *Social Justice in Islam* was a big hit among young Ikhwan members. In fact, many of them mistakenly thought that Qutb was one of them and had written the book with them in mind. "Qutb reminded my generation of the beauty and humanity of Islam, and that our duty was to strive for a moral and just society in harmony with Allah's message," recalled Ahmed Assal, now in his eighties, who then was a young Ikhwan sympathizer. "After I read *Al-'adala al-ijtima'iyya fi-l-islam* [Social Justice in Islam], I thought that only an Ikhwan thinker could have written such a powerful treatise expressing the true spirit of Islam. Many Brothers felt the same way, though we had not heard of Qutb before."[27] When I asked Farid Abdel Khaleq, a top Ikhwan leader who got to know Qutb well, about the reasons for the popularity of *Social Justice in Islam* among members of the Ikhwan, his response was clear: "His book filled a conceptual vacuum left by the assassination of *al-murshid* [the supreme guide Banna], and it examined a basic Islamic principle—social justice," he said. "What mattered most to young Ikhwan was the subject matter and not the writer himself. Qutb was not well known to the Brothers and he had no relationship to or affiliation with our movement until 1953."[28]

The growing admiration for Qutb's works within the Ikhwan came despite his continuing distance from Islamist circles. He lived his life freely, reportedly even occasionally visiting a local bar called al-Liwa, where, according to a journalist who worked with him, he enjoyed a little cognac.[29] It was not until after Qutb returned home in August 1950 from an almost two-year study tour in the United States that he drew closer to the Ikhwan, though he did not formally join the movement until 1953. His stay in America was decisive in reinforcing and consolidating his new religiosity and worldview. Much has been written on his observations of the United States, which he recorded in letters and commentaries to colleagues and friends in Egypt.[30] His journey to America crystallized in Qutb's imagination a stark binary between Islam's abundant spiritualism and the West's obsessive materialism. Soulless America sharpened his consciousness of the Islamic moral economy and heritage and bred in him a lifelong abhorrence of and antagonism to the materialistic culture of both liberal capitalism and Soviet Marxism. He saw in America (and the West by extension) a jungle in which people battled for money and profit and sexual gratification. In contrast, the spirituality of Islam allowed individuals to escape material temptation and free themselves from the prison of the self. Seeing the East and West as essentialist, monolithic categories, Qutb returned from America convinced of the moral superiority of Islam and the cultural decline of the West. After that his views only hardened.

In the interim, he contributed editorials to newspapers and magazines of differing ideological persuasions. Throughout this period, a dualism in Qutb's thinking was reflected in his journalistic articles on the one hand and the books that he published between 1950 and 1953 on the other.[31] In the former, he called for cooperation with Egyptian communists in the struggle to oust British occupiers, while in *Ma'rakat al-islam wa-l-ra'simaliyya* (The battle of Islam and capitalism), published in 1950, he attacked communism as an ideology that focused on materialism as opposed to striving for the good life.[32] Qutb contended that communism was inherently opposed to "freedom of speech and freedom of intellect"[33] and that adopting either communism or capitalism would bring Egyptians and Muslims nothing but confusion and identity crisis.[34] According to Sherif Younis, Qutb's dualism reflects his division of labor between his short-term objective of bringing an end to the British colonial regime and his long-term goal of creating an Islamic moral economy.[35] Indeed, Qutb's anti-colonial mission took a pragmatic rather than a radical approach. In 1951, for example, he called for a single front uniting communists, nationalists, and the Ikhwan in the fight against the British occupiers and in the struggle against "autocracy, feudalism, and capitalism, as they are all an extension of colonialism."[36] On another occasion, he also advocated a "guerrilla war" in which "all parties and groups," along with loyal independents, would join forces to form brigades or launch a boycott campaign.[37] Qutb's call for unity in the face of occupation reflects a shift in the public mood and the political landscape in Egypt whereby several movements collaborated against the British despite their ideological heterogeneity. The Ikhwan–Free Officers connection is a case in point.

Qutb himself had established a relationship with the Free Officers before and after they carried out the successful coup against the monarchy in July 1952. Although his prior relationship with the young army officers is not well documented, evidence exists that Qutb was the only civilian to have known about the coup in advance; he was also the only civilian who attended the meetings of the Revolutionary Command Council (RCC) and had a close relationship with Nasser.[38] Nasser's close friend and fellow army conspirator Khaled Mohieddin recalled that immediately after the revolution Qutb was one of the most vocal of those publicly urging the officers to cleanse Egypt of elements of the old regime, even if that required establishing a dictatorship. "His articles were noteworthy because of the extent of his support for our revolution and his belligerent and fanatical policy recommendations," Mohieddin told me. "Qutb was one of few writers who publicly advocated the suspension of the liberal constitution and rule by the bayonet, an insanely dangerous idea that fed the ambitions of some of us," he added.[39]

In an article published two weeks after the expulsion of King Farouk and addressed to the head of the Free Officers, General Mohammed Naguib, Qutb gently reproached the "hero and his heroic assistants" for having stopped at toppling the king and for preparing to retreat to their barracks before purging politicians associated with the old regime. "In the name of millions," Qutb insisted, "we will not allow you to return to the barracks because your mission is not over yet and your duty is to complete it."[40] Qutb advised Naguib and his comrades to strike mercilessly against reaction. He revived the notion, once popular with Muslim reformers, of the "just dictator" as a panacea to the country's problems. According to Adnan Musallam, whose doctoral thesis was on the formative stages of Qutb's intellectual career, Qutb made the case that "the RCC must strike with iron fist against all those trying to abort the revolution."[41] Musallam cited the open letter which Qutb sent to Naguib to illustrate his case. Qutb explicitly demanded the establishment of a "just dictatorship for six months to conduct a comprehensive cleansing which deprives corrupt politicians of their constitutional rights and permits only trustworthy figures to participate in political life.[42]

Writing as an independent, Qutb's voice added urgency and legitimacy to the unfolding debate in Egypt after the 1952 coup about whether or not the young, inexperienced, and ambitious army officers should surrender power to civilians and retire to their garrisons. No, Qutb insisted, because Egypt's future depended on the swift actions of the military rulers, the knights of the nation. In addition to his calls for ongoing military rule, Qutb was one of the first writers to lend legitimacy to the coup by calling it a "revolution" and insisting that it spread to all aspects of Egyptian life.[43] He was also one of the few writers to lay the theoretical foundation for the popular legitimacy of the social revolution as opposed to that of constitutional or liberal democracy. Qutb, along with others, provided Nasser and his comrades with the rationale to suspend the relatively progressive 1923 constitution all in the interest of a "just" dictatorship.[44] Like Nasser, Qutb argued that constitutional democracy and revolution were mutually exclusive and inherently contradictory. In his articles he used the powerful Arabic word *tathir* (cleansing) to describe the course of action that the military junta ought to take in order to subdue the old ruling class. There could be no coexistence with reactionary politicians, as he saw it, because they did not believe in the revolution and would never accept it.[45] In his article "Hazehi al-ahzab gheir qabela leil-baqaa" (These parties are unviable), Qutb backed the proscribing of political parties.[46] Echoing the pro-Nasserist camp, he asserted that they were an extension of the corrupt and reactionary old regime and therefore they were untrustworthy and could not be reformed. The task was to get rid not only of a few fraudulent personalities within these political organizations, he added, but of the whole rotten and corrupt structure. In his own words, "These parties are beyond reformation and incapable of reconstitution and adaptation to the revolutionary order; they have outlived their usefulness."[47] In another editorial, Qutb yet again cautioned the military rulers against attempts to reach a compromise with the leaders of the political parties: "That would be the most dangerous conspiracy that the revolution must guard against ... These parties are intrinsically hostile to the revolution. They will only submit to its instructions until the storm passes and then stab it in the back and destroy it." He assured the Free Officers that the task of separating friends from foes must be executed even at the cost of collateral damage to innocents: "Oppressing ten or twenty innocents is better than endangering the survival of the revolution."

In reality Qutb advocated the removal from the political process of the entire social stratum which constituted the old regime, which he viewed as a monolith and an existential threat to the revolution. He criticized the first post-coup prime minister, Ali Maher, for appointing ministers to his cabinet who could not be trusted to execute the will of the people because they were part of the old regime. Half measures and tinkering with the system would not do, Qutb insisted, only real revolutionaries who take decisive action against reaction. A few days after Qutb's call, Maher tendered his resignation. The Free Officers had forced Maher out because, in their opinion, he was not sufficiently forceful and swift in purging the old regime and he had opposed land reforms, a high priority for the military rulers. On the same day, Naguib formed a new cabinet and inaugurated a campaign of repression against civil society leaders who were accused of obstructing and impeding the cleansing of the political process. Scores were arrested. Qutb's wishes were further fulfilled when Naguib issued the January 1953 decree banning political parties, confiscating their assets, and laying out a road map for a three-year period of transition to civilian rule.

After reading the articles Qutb published in the first year following the coup, one gets the impression that Qutb was either one of the Free Officers or a firm public advocate and a believer in their cause. This notion is given further credence by the stance that Qutb adopted toward a labor dispute which occurred on August 12, 1952, when protesters in Kafr al-Dawar rioted and violently clashed with the security forces over wages and dismal working conditions. One might have expected the author of *Social Justice in Islam* to defend the workers or at least offer moral support for their cause. However, Qutb urged the new military rulers to physically suppress labor protests at all costs. Three days after the confrontation in Kafr al-Dawar, in his article *Harakat la tukhifana* [Tactics do not scare us], Qutb portrayed the workers who were protesting as political hooligans doing the bidding of the old regime, in a desperate and final effort to resuscitate a dying order.[48] He stated that the struggle had been won and that the march forward was unstoppable. Echoing the Free Officers, Qutb blamed evil-minded communists for exploiting the Kafr al-Dawar workers in order to trigger chaos, seize power, and abort the revolution. In a dangerous precedent, a military court was set up and two workers were sentenced to death for their alleged participation in the protests, becoming the first political casualties of the new military regime. Mohamed Hafiz Diab, a sociologist and an authority on Qutb, claims that Qutb pushed the RCC to send the two communist workers to the gallows.[49] Another writer, Sanaa al-Misri, further noted that Qutb was an adviser to Abdel Mon'im Ibrahim, one of the military court chairs and a member of the RCC that issued the rulings that included the execution of the two workers who participated in the Kafr al-Dawar protests.[50]

It would be misleading to credit Qutb with the harsh clampdown by Egypt's new military rulers against the opposition, but he was undoubtedly one of the leading public advocates for repression of elements of the old order and for the suspension of constitutionalism. Qutb also reportedly served as an assistant to Nasser, becoming the secretary general of Hay'at al-Tahrir (Liberation Rally), the propaganda arm of the Free Officers established on January 23, 1953.[51] Although Qutb stayed in this position for only a month, elections were cancelled and parties were dissolved during those four weeks.[52] According to Mahmoud Al-'Azab, an Egyptian officer belonging to the Ikhwan, the Free Officers revered Qutb as the "father of their revolution."[53]

As with everything else, Qutb actively supported the Free Officers against big landowners who resisted land redistribution and new taxes on their income. Writing in the popular magazine *Rose al-Yusuf*, he advised the landowners to submit to the revolution and accept land redistribution or face disinheritance and catastrophic consequences.[54] He reminded Egyptian feudalists of the bloodbath that had been visited upon their Russian counterparts during the Bolshevik revolution and warned them that they would face a similar fate if they persisted in their resistance. "For a fleeting moment

Qutb thought that the young army officers would cleanse Egypt of the pro-British monarchy and establish an authentic political order as well," said Ahmed Ra'if, a former senior Ikhwan member who knew Qutb and who published chronicles and memoirs of Ikhwan members in Nasser's prisons. "Qutb viewed the revolution as divine intervention, a miracle, and he fully backed it without reservation and heedless of the consequences," this reflective eighty-year-old told me, straining not to offend his former Islamist cohorts.

In the first year after the revolution, Qutb not only supported the Free Officers but also developed a good relationship with Nasser and Naguib. Nasser and his comrades frequently visited Qutb in his home in Helwan, a suburb outside Cairo. They spent hours in his spacious study and garden, discussing politics, educational reform, literature, and poetry.[55] In return, Qutb frequented the headquarters of the Free Officers and attended the meetings of the RCC.[56] His name often appeared in the news in connection with regime politics, and he reportedly even had an office in the junta's headquarters.[57] Although Nasser's Free Officer friend Mohieddin does not recall if Qutb actually had a space in the headquarters, he acknowledged that Nasser and his comrades were in contact with him. "Qutb's unwavering support for the revolution was welcomed and appreciated," he told me.[58] Qutb also briefly collaborated with the Free Officers in the field of education, serving as undersecretary of state in this area.[59] According to an Egyptian biographer, the Free Officers put him and another person in charge of reforming the country's educational system.[60] The RCC also reportedly appointed him cultural adviser, and Qutb also instructed army officers on the theology of liberation in Islam and the meaning of revolution.[61] Ikhwan members have acknowledged this close relationship between Qutb and the Free Officers, suggesting that he had even been nominated for the post of minister of education,[62] though he was never appointed to this post. Qutb himself—in his final testimony before his execution in 1966, *Limaza 'adamuni* [Why they executed me]—stated that he had spent twelve hours a day working with the Free Officers.[63] "They trusted me and offered me key positions," he revealed.[64]

Thus, immediately after the 1952 coup Qutb nurtured a close relationship with Egypt's new military rulers as well as with the Ikhwan, although he was not yet a formal member of the latter. He did not consider the two connections to be mutually exclusive because his primary focus was defending the revolutionary order. Throughout this period, he participated in the public debate as an independent public intellectual who had at least as much in common with the soldiers of the nation as he did with the soldiers of God. When Qutb did eventually join the Ikhwan in March 1953, the move was a clear sign of his disillusionment with the Free Officers and the end of the love affair. As discussed in chapter 2, although the Ikhwan was the only organization to have escaped the first round of repression associated with the junta's controversial January 1953 decision to proscribe political parties, rivalries and mistrust between the Free Officers and the Muslim Brothers had by then clearly started to emerge.

So why did Qutb jump ship in March 1953 and formally join the Ikhwan? What brought about his rupture with the new military rulers and his formal embrace of the Islamists? In *Why They Executed Me*, Qutb said that he had stepped down from his role in the Liberation Rally so soon after his appointment because of differences that he had with the Free Officers. Although he did not elaborate on this point, he insinuated that the issue at stake was Nasser's crackdown on the Ikhwan and his own failure to mediate between the two rival camps.[65] Qutb said he felt the Americans had poisoned the minds of the Free Officers against the Ikhwan, and that it was Washington, "Zionism, and colonial *salibiyya* [the Crusaders]" that had incited the former to "destroy the Ikhwan."[66]

Qutb's disciples echo this conspiratorial narrative, similarly blaming the United States for infiltrating the young revolution and co-opting Nasser and his comrades to its sinister cause. According to this view, Nasser was an evildoer who betrayed the trust of the people and mortgaged the future of Egypt to Western, particularly American, interests, while Qutb refused to compromise the original values of the revolution. Such accounts are informed by Qutb's own post facto justification of his split with the military rulers. While they leave many questions unanswered, one reason for Qutb's defection to the Ikhwan was tied to the affinity between the latter's agenda and elements of his own thinking, particularly about the religio-political relationship.

In an article published on July 28, 1952, months before his split from the Free Officers, Qutb argued that the Ikhwan were the ones capable of introducing a proper system of "Islamic education," which he believed should stand at the epicenter of efforts to create his envisaged "Islamic society."[67] In another article, published in April 1952, Qutb hailed the uniqueness of Islam as a "sociopolitical project" that shuns "the myth of separation between religion and politics," a position which subsequently moved Qutb closer to the Ikhwan, according to Sherif Younis.[68]

Qutb's followers and members of the Ikhwan assert that Qutb initially embraced the junta only as a way to establish a Qur'anic-based state. Time and again, I was told that Qutb did not see any contradiction between Arab nationalism and Islam as long as nationalism was viewed as a temporary transition facilitating the establishment of God's sovereignty on earth. For Qutb, the Arab world was part of the Islamic world and Arab nationalism was only one subset, one component of Islam; in contrast, Islam, understood holistically, superseded all provincial loyalties, including nationality, ethnicity, sect, and tribe. According to the Qutbian narrative, before the Free Officers seized power, Qutb had contributed to their education and had tried to guide their worldview along an Islamic framework. "But al-Shahid, a man who only fears God, underestimated the wickedness of Nasser and his subordinates who, as soon as they consolidated their grip on power, stabbed Qutb in the back and held him captive," claimed Abdel Majid al-Shazili, one of Qutb's most zealous disciples.[69] "As soon as Qutb discovered that the army conspirators were not applying Qur'anic laws, he severed all links with them," insisted Ahmed Abdel Majid, a top lieutenant in Qutb's underground organization who was sentenced to death with his mentor in 1965 but escaped execution by a presidential decree.[70] "Qutb joined the Ikhwan because he saw them as the only effective Islamic movement in Egypt."

While such ideology probably informed Qutb's decision to shift his loyalties from the Free Officers to the Ikhwan, it is likely that more mundane considerations were at play simultaneously. As had been the case in his relationship with the secular literary establishment earlier in his career, Qutb's enthusiastic support for the Free Officers was never properly rewarded. While cabinet posts and other official appointments were distributed among the officers themselves, Qutb was holding out for two posts: either minister of education (for which he was reportedly considered) or head of state media.[71] Once again, he felt out of place, his talents not fully recognized. This clearly did not fit with the ambitious vision that had been instilled in him since childhood. It was after he had failed to secure either of these two titles that he joined the Ikhwan as head of its *da'wa* (indoctrination) department; his shift towards the Ikhwan therefore seemed to be motivated by calculation and self-interest.[72]

Qutb's final breakup with the Free Officers and union with the Islamists had as much to do with his own pride and ambition as it had to do with politics, theology, or ideology per se. One of Qutb's friends, Abbas Khadir, recalled that Qutb had been embittered by the decision to eventually give the leadership of the ministry of education to a person related to Nasser. The offer of the second-tier position of undersecretary of state did not assuage Qutb's wounded pride and vanity. As Khadir bluntly put it, "His fierce ambition would ultimately bring about his ruin." To add insult to injury, Qutb had resigned his earlier position as a supervisor in the office of the ministry of education in October 1952 to join the new administration either as a minister or as head of state media; only to be passed over in favor of colleagues who he felt were not as qualified as he was. The Free Officers had let him down and did not recognize his significant contribution to the revolution. They were thus no different from his literary mentors who had declined to reciprocate his devotion or from the old corrupt political establishment that relied on clientelism and nepotism.

Moreover, Qutb's growing role in the Ikhwan took place at a time where the movement was undergoing a period of disarray and internal rifts. Many Muslim Brothers felt their new *murshid*'s leadership paled in comparison to Hassan al-Banna's charisma and ambitious ideological vision. When Nasser launched a full-blown propaganda campaign against the organization via the state's official press, a small number of Brothers became convinced that the Ikhwan should respond more aggressively against the government. They also insisted that it was urgent to move beyond Hudaybi's conservative outlook, searching for a new revolutionary vision. It is during this period of ideological vacuum that Qutb formally joined the Ikhwan. In July 1954 Qutb was appointed the editor of the Ikhwan's newspaper, *al-Ikhwan al-Muslimun,* though he only held the post for eight weeks because Nasser closed it down. A few months later, Qutb was sentenced to fifteen years in prison for his alleged involvement in the attempt on Nasser's life. As the next chapter will make clear, the more direct ideological decision-making role that Qutb played within the organization coincidentally took place while he was cut off from it, incarcerated in Nasserist prisons. While in jail, Qutb recruited fellow Ikhwan members with the aim of creating his own Islamic revolutionary vanguard against the wishes of Hudaybi and the rest of the Ikhwan establishment. Although Qutb had sided with Hudaybi in the latter's struggle against Nasser in 1953, he did not hesitate to bypass his superiors within the Ikhwan to achieve his more ambitious goal. This presented the group with the most important internal challenge it had faced.

In offering a narrative whereby Qutb temporarily allied with the Free Officers and then split with them for ideological reasons, Qutb's followers overlook the input of more worldly considerations. They omit the extent to which he was motivated by ambition and pride. In reality, when the military regime eventually claimed revolutionary legitimacy as a basis for its 1954 crackdown on the Ikhwan, Qutb ended up being a victim of what he himself had pushed for when he urged the Free Officers to cleanse Egypt of their opponents even at the cost of collateral human loss. Although his supporters subsequently idealized him as a martyr and a hero who had little interest in worldly affairs and dedicated his life to making God's word supreme, the accurate characterization of Qutb is that he was an amateur in the political sphere. His gamble to play politics and back the Ikhwan misfired badly, and he himself was consumed in the aftermath.

After he severed his relationship with the Free Officers and formally joined the Ikhwan in 1953, Qutb found himself immediately caught in the crossfire between two powerful, strong-willed men: Nasser and Hudaybi, the Ikhwan's supreme guide. Instead of keeping his distance, Qutb closely aligned himself with the Hudaybi camp and spearheaded the fight against Nasser. Insofar as this move served to alienate the ambitious young officer, turning him into a bitter enemy, it proved to be a colossal blunder that would ultimately cost Qutb his life. In the annals of revolutionary moments worldwide, the pattern of Qutb's tragic story is all too familiar and only adds to the list of revolutionaries who have ended up being consumed and often assassinated by the very forces that they themselves had helped to mobilize. Maximilien Robespierre was executed by the French revolutionary forces in the chaotic aftermath of 1789. Leon Trotsky's intellectual disagreements with other figureheads of the Bolshevik revolution of 1917 resulted in his exile and assassination at the hands of his former comrades. The Irish national hero Michael Collins was murdered by a splinter faction of the IRA. Thomas Sankara, the Burkinabé revolutionary Marxist, was eventually killed by a commando unit led by one of his former comrades. In Algeria, Ahmed Ben Bella was toppled by Houari Boumediene, an army strongman and a close friend of his, just as in Egypt, Naguib was ousted by Nasser; the list goes on and Qutb's case figures as only one of many.

Conclusion

Biographers of Qutb who stress continuity throughout his life, just like those who posit a sharp rupture in his thinking from the 1950s onwards, fail to recognize the extent to which all along his path was characterized by ambivalence, contradictions, contingency, and an interplay of diverse influences. These features were perhaps inevitable given the wide variety of the social contexts that he navigated, ranging from the conservative environment of an Upper Egyptian village to the elite literary circles of Cairo to cooperation with the Free Officers' nationalist republican regime, all of which culminated in his gradual embrace of Islamist politics and the Ikhwan.

Far from being the inevitable antithesis to Nasser in all that he said and did, by sentiment and sensibility Qutb could have championed pan-Arab nationalism as enthusiastically as he subsequently fought for pan-Islamism. The stories of Nasser and Qutb are intertwined. Both were influenced by the sociopolitical environment in which they lived and both traveled a familiar journey, flirting with a broad range of ideologies. The two men briefly collaborated with each other before and in the aftermath of the Free Officers' coup, even forging a personal relationship. When Nasser and his comrades seized power in July 1952, Qutb was one of the most vocal public intellectuals who backed the "revolution" and its military rulers. From July 1952 until February 1953, he published scores of newspaper and magazine articles in which he showered praise on Nasser and the army officers who carried out the revolution, imploring them to suspend constitutional checks and balances and establish a "just" military dictatorship. Like Nasser, Qutb was in a hurry to transform Egyptian society from the top down, as opposed to seeking incremental change through a constitutional process. Like Nasser, Qutb saw the military, particularly the young officers, as the vanguard best equipped by temperament, sensibility, and patriotism to enact transformative change. He had little faith in either the old constitution-based order or the corrupt politicians who milked the system and who had no appreciation for the gravity and urgency of the severe problems facing Egypt. Prior to resigning his official duties in the Liberation Rally and formally joining the Ikhwan in 1953, Qutb had trusted the new Egyptian knights to right the colonial wrongs of the past and create a better future.

Ultimately, like Nasser, Qutb was a creature of his times, internalizing and responding to social challenges which he, along with his countrymen, faced. Ironically, Nasser and Qutb's vision of building a different future for Egypt is what eventually turned them into bitter enemies. Personality matters too. Rather than being merely a totem for one ideology or another, Qutb was first a human being whose trajectory was steered in part by questions of pride, ambition, and the workaday circumstances of his existence. It is only through tracing the various stages of his journey that a full portrait of the man and his ideas emerges and we see how the accumulated effects of his repeated disillusionments brought about his subsequent radicalization. Although Qutb had backed the 1919–1922 revolution, in the 1940s he became bitterly disappointed with the establishment elite. His critique of the literary elite is a direct consequence of the larger socioeconomic context that had developed in Egypt, where the youth felt slighted by an *effendiyya* which they saw as primarily concerned with their own welfare. Similarly, Qutb believed in the 1952 revolution only to be subsequently estranged from the Free Officers because they did not grant him a senior post in the nascent order and they traveled a different road from his. In both cases, Qutb felt used and abused by those whom he had helped achieve recognition and influence; he sought to play an important role and to have his voice heard. It is in this context that Qutb formally joined the Ikhwan in 1953 and embraced Islam as an all-encompassing way of life. The success of his Islamic writings had made him popular among young Muslim Brothers, gaining a receptive audience and a stage on which to perform his newly discovered crusading mission.

Chapter 9

Qutb's al-Tanzim al-Sirri

THE FREE OFFICERS' CRACKDOWN on the Ikhwan morphed into an armed clash between the Arab nationalist project represented by the Nasserist state and an emergent radical Islamist current led by Qutb. Al-Tanzim al-Sirri, a paramilitary organization, was established by Ikhwan members after Nasser's suppression of the movement in 1954. Qutb played a pedagogical-ideological role but also provided practical guidance and supervision to a relatively large number of the dedicated young religious activists both outside and inside Egypt's prisons who joined al-Tanzim al-Sirri. After Egyptian authorities discovered this underground group in 1965, they referred to it as al-Tanzim al-Sirri (the Secret Organization). Although this name was not used by its members themselves, it is applied as the most convenient label.

Interviews with al-Tanzim's key lieutenants illuminated Qutb's role in the organization and his contribution to its activities. They were in direct and indirect contact with Qutb himself between the 1954 crackdown on the Ikhwan and Qutb's death by hanging in August 1966. Throughout my interviews, these activists narrated their stories in their own words, recounting their version of events and the extent of their participation in al-Tanzim. As they were direct witnesses to Qutb's innermost thoughts and to his titanic clash with the Nasserist state, I challenged them to set the record straight about Qutb and his rationale for going underground. What pushed him to the brink of the abyss? How important was torture and the experience of the prison camps in embittering this frail critic and activist? What was the extent of his ideological transformation between 1954 and 1965? What did he hope to achieve by confronting the powerful Egyptian state? What did he instill in members' consciousness regarding Islam's internal and external enemies? Did he in practice sanction the use of violence to reestablish God's sovereignty on earth or what he called *al-hakimiyya*?

Moreover, I urged Qutb's contemporaries to elaborate on the relationship between al-Tanzim and the mainstream Ikhwan, particularly its supreme guide, Hassan al-Hudaybi. Did Qutb act alone, or did he obtain a mandate from Hudaybi to establish and command a paramilitary group? Who recruited al-Tanzim's members and how was it done? How were clandestine cells structured, organized, trained, and indoctrinated? While Qutb was imprisoned, how did his ideas, manifestos, and directives reach al-Tanzim's lieutenants and foot soldiers in the field? Why, during this period of mass incarceration, did the Ikhwan split into two clashing factions, the rejectionists aligned with Qutb and the accommodationist old guard? And to what extent has that rift haunted the Ikhwan in the decades since?

These illuminating conversations highlight what has been a mysterious presence in discussions of the relationships between the Muslim Brotherhood and the Nasserist state, but more importantly they offer a new dimension to understanding the influence of Qutb and the transformation that he underwent during the prison years from 1954 till 1965.

The Structure of the Ikhwan and the First Wave of Nasserist Repression

In the early 1950s, the Ikhwan represented the largest social force in Egypt, its leadership having labored for more than three decades to build the movement and to extend its influence across Egypt. The simultaneously complex and flexible organizational structure that the group developed over that period, and which has been described as a "federated structure of authority,"[1] allowed it to withstand several waves of government repression. In the mid-1930s, Banna outlined his long-term vision for the movement, which was articulated around three levels of membership: (1) *musa'id* (assistant); (2) *muntasib* (related); and (3) *'amil* (active).[2] At the first level, members were merely required to contribute a small sum of money and put their signature to a membership card. Advancement to the next two levels required deepening commitment and active support for the group. To be promoted to the status of "related" member, a Brother needed to be someone who "proved his mastery of the principles of the movement, attended regular meetings, and committed himself to absolute 'obedience.'"

To achieve the status of "active" membership, an even greater commitment was required, including "physical training, achievement in Qur'anic learning, and fulfillment of Islamic obligations such as pilgrimages, fasting, and contributions to the *zakat* treasury." Finally, the highest form of membership—*mujtahid*—was more exclusive, "open only to a select handful of the most dedicated," and, according to scholar Richard Mitchell, it was "probably related to the roots of the secret apparatus."[3] Ikhwan members were bound to the movement by an oath of brotherhood (*bay'at al-'ukhuwwa*),[4] and at the grassroots level, the movement was organized into small units, each known as a family (*usra*).

Ikhwan members were thus linked by horizontal and personalized ties which helped guarantee confidence and obedience, both of which were guiding principles of the movement. This flexible and graded membership system helped ensure that the group would never run short of members and facilitated its spread across the whole of Egypt. By 1949 the Ikhwan had over 2,000 branches comprising between 300,000 and 600,000 active members, making it the largest organized social and political movement in the country.[5] When Banna originally established the Ikhwan in the late 1920s, the membership was minuscule—a few hundred members only.

In addition to the meteoric increase in Ikhwan membership, its members spanned a wide spectrum of ideological, social, and professional backgrounds. Precise information on the socioeconomic distribution of membership is difficult to amass since the group kept such information secret. However, some hard, albeit random, statistical evidence can be deduced from the court records of cases that involved the Ikhwan. For example, one scholar concluded that, of the fifteen defendants who appeared in court in connection with the assassination of Prime Minister Mahmoud al-Nuqrashi in 1948, six were students, five were civil servants, three were small-business men, and one was an engineer.[6] The available statistical evidence suggests that the Ikhwan drew its membership from most sectors and classes of society. Similarly, declassified U.S. State Department files from that period indicate considerable diversity in occupation among Ikhwan members. From this evidence, the bulk of Ikhwan members and supporters came from the most Westernized and modernized segments of society, but they also included workers, farmers, police officers, and religious functionaries.[7]

The Ikhwan's broadly based membership makes sense when one looks at the organization's activities, including recruitment, propagation, and training, which penetrated a wide range of social spaces. In the early days the Ikhwan existed mainly outside Cairo and was confined to mosques, which were deemed the most effective platform for recruitment, propagation, and training activities.[8] In the 1930s the group spread to larger towns and cities and increasingly moved out of the mosque setting into urban areas. It also shifted away from its earlier, primarily theological framing and drew on the input of members from such professional fields as law, economics, education, engineering, and chemistry to advance what was presented as a more "scientific" understanding of Islam.[9]

Given the effectiveness of the Ikhwan's modes of recruitment as well as its internal cohesiveness, the Egyptian state had never succeeded in destroying the organization. Even after the government sought to dissolve the movement in 1948, the U.S. State Department received reports of secret mass meetings and pamphleteering across Egypt. In 1951, the group was still active and capable of mobilizing three thousand people on less than twenty-four hours' notice.[10]

The Stirring of Militant Currents from the Ruins of the Ikhwan

Thus, when the Nasserist state launched its first wave of mass arrests against the Brothers in mid-January 1954 and dissolved the organization, it only took the Islamist group a short while to get up and running again despite the imprisonment of thousands of its senior leaders and members.[11] By June of that year, there were already reports of a revival of Ikhwan activism.[12] Divided and exhausted by two years of rivalry with the Free Officers, the leadership of the Ikhwan was ill equipped to directly challenge the Nasserist state, though it remained intent on its own survival. The Islamist movement had suffered a crippling blow, but it soon became apparent that the Free Officers' brutal suppression could neither eliminate it from the social and political landscape nor wipe out its underground networks.

In the midst of the 1954 clampdown, the dominant view among the Hudaybi-led Ikhwan was that the organization should endeavor to absorb the shock of the attack and bide its time until political conditions changed and the balance of power shifted against Nasser. The goal was survival: the primary objectives were to weather the violent storm and preserve internal cohesion. With thousands of junior members and senior chiefs caught up in Nasser's dragnet, including most of the organization's key actors, there was little else that the Ikhwan leadership could do. Meanwhile, in prisons, Ikhwan members reflected on their predicament and plotted their next moves against the Nasserist state. A divide between the traditional leadership and the lower-rank members was now gradually developing. The

Brothers were angry and bitter because they felt betrayed by Nasser. They were aware that without the organization's support, the Free Officers would have been able neither to successfully stage the 1952 coup nor to obtain the support of the population. As far as they were concerned, the Ikhwan were being persecuted by the very movement that they had empowered. As frustration deepened among some imprisoned Ikhwan members, their resentment increased against their own leadership for its quietism and unwillingness to strike back at the Nasserist government. The prisons thus became a key forum for activism, where the Brothers would argue over how to pick up the pieces and what changes, if any, ought to be instituted within the organization in order to bolster its resilience against external elements.

Moreover, those who had not been caught up in the crackdown did their best to continue their activities under the oppressive new conditions. One of them was Ahmed Abdel Majid, who was both a member of the Ikhwan and an officer in the Egyptian military intelligence service during the prison years; unknown to the authorities, he helped from the outside.[13] After several colleagues intervened on my behalf, I was able to meet him and ask him about the prison years. "After the Nasser regime dismantled the Ikhwan and imprisoned its members in 1954, we—young men, on our own—brainstormed about ways and means to assist our brethren's pressed families and to keep the Islamic flame lit. We sought to absorb the shock and plot our next moves," he confided. When I pressed him on his double-agent role working for both the state and the Ikhwan, he insisted he did not see any contradictions between his loyalty to the Islamist group and his official duty as a military man. By persecuting his cohorts, he suggested, Nasser and the Free Officers had acted unjustly and had lost legitimacy. "Initially, there existed no centralized authority," he said, expanding on his account of the Ikhwan members' efforts to remain active in the earliest days after the suppression of the movement in 1954. "Each unit did its own thing. Ours prayed together and talked politics. We read the Ikhwan's publications, particularly the letters of *al-shahid* [the martyr] Hassan al-Banna, and we discussed how to augment our members and link up with other sympathizers in hiding. In the first two years, we kept a very low profile and refrained from recruitment outside our closest circles," he explained.[14] Although similar efforts were under way elsewhere, they remained organic and dispersed. "We had no idea that throughout the country other young Egyptians had organized themselves in similar cells and shared our goal of reviving the Islamist movement and defying Nasser. We were in the dark; separated from one another by a barrier of fear," added Abdel Majid, who was a founding member of al-Tanzim, headed al-Tanzim's intelligence committee, and was in charge of units in Upper Egypt.[15]

Just like Abdel Majid, Ahmed Adel Kamal, another Ikhwan member who acted as a lieutenant of al-Tanzim, told me that soon after the clampdown, he had acted on his own to secretly assemble together a group of Ikhwan. His aim was to revive al-Nizam al-Khass (the Secret Apparatus), which, as seen in chapter 2, had been created by Banna as part of the Ikhwan's opposition to the British and the monarchy. The organization was dissolved after an al-Nizam operator killed Prime Minister Nuqrashi in December 1948. In the early 1950s Hudaybi had sought to revive it but the group was once again swiftly crushed by the state.[16] Adel Kamal continued his efforts to re-create a paramilitary group until 1959, when he realized that he was under surveillance by the security services. Adel Kamal and Abdel Majid were not the only politically radicalized religious activists who responded to the arrest of thousands of Ikhwan by seeking to build clandestine paramilitary structures. I came across many people who engaged in such efforts.

Therefore, the repression exerted by the Nasserist state only hardened attitudes among some sections of the Ikhwan's membership, both inside and outside the prisons. The consolidation of these new, increasingly militant currents within the Ikhwan ranks was facilitated by the movement's complex organizational structure because the senior leadership was insulated from the foot soldiers at the bottom. The imprisonment of the leadership allowed and motivated lower-ranked members to develop new ideas, which in turn created spaces for dissent within the movement itself.

Sayyid Qutb Assumes Leadership of the Revolutionary Current

More than anyone else, Sayyid Qutb took ownership of this newly emerging revolutionary current. In this repressive context, his project was especially attractive to Ikhwan members because it differed radically from the views and praxis of the mainstream Ikhwan and offered an alternative to it. His ideas differed markedly from those of Banna, who had until then always been the bedrock and intellectual foundation of the Ikhwan. Unlike Banna, Qutb eschewed gradualist political engagement and social mobilization in favor of nourishing a subversive vanguard that would spearhead the institution of a new Islamist utopia. Although Banna had founded the original chapter of the Secret Apparatus (al-Nizam al-Khass), he aimed to keep its role limited. Following the assassination of Nuqrashi in 1948, Banna disowned the assassins and demanded that the group's operators show self-restraint and patience.[17] Banna's emphasis on the use of newspapers, magazines, and public lectures to spread the message of the Ikhwan also stood in stark contrast to the grand narrative advanced by Qutb and those around him. Qutb and his cohorts dismissed politics and activism as ineffectual and instead prioritized the armed struggle and subversion against Nasser, whom they labeled the *taghut* (tyrant). It was this set of ideas and narratives that facilitated the crystallization of a new paramilitary wing within the ranks of the imprisoned Ikhwan and its supporters on the outside. An important difference between Banna's and Qutb's strategy revolved around the former's willingness to challenge the strict top-down hierarchical structure of the Ikhwan. Banna had been the founder and spiritual guide of the organization when he created the paramilitary wing, while Qutb had no formal affiliation with the Islamist organization when he revived the underground apparatus and took control of it. Complicating the story is that Hudaybi's supporters assert that Hudaybi was unaware of Qutb's underground operation, while others in the know point out that Hudaybi had been informed about the new organization and had even given it his tacit acquiescence.

By 1953 Qutb had split with the Free Officers and become a full-fledged member of the Ikhwan. Nonetheless, it was ultimately his experience in the prison camps that radicalized and militarized him by convincing him of the urgent need to overthrow the secular order and replace it with a system firmly grounded in the Qur'an. While incarcerated he crafted a blueprint for revolutionary change, referred to by his disciples as the *fiqh al-harakah* (the operational and actionable approach). Designed to indoctrinate and inspire religious activists to action, Qutb's prison writings represented a complete break with his earlier works as a social critic and literary writer. As one of Qutb's jail companions, Sayyid Eid, put it, "The prison years transformed Qutb's thinking and writing. He turned his pen into a deadly weapon against the *tawagheet* [tyrants] and aimed at awakening the *umma* from its prolonged slumber."[18]

From November 1954, when he began a fifteen-year sentence, Qutb worked on radical amendments to his multiple-volume commentary on the Qur'an called *In the Shadow of the Qur'an.*[19] Qutb's amended edition differed very significantly from the original, parts of which he had written between 1952 and 1954, a period when Nasser remained on relatively good terms with the Ikhwan. If originally the series had focused on the aesthetic and intellectual aspects of the Qur'an and Islam, which Salah al-Khalidi, a Qutb biographer, called *al-muftah al-gamali* (the aesthetic key), the book now prioritized mobilization, *al-muftah al-haraki* (the operational key). This new and firmly ideological outlook emphasized revolutionary Islam and the inevitability of the confrontation with *jahiliyya.*[20] Now, Qutb saw the Qur'an as a revolutionary text that was the key to the transformation of primitive seventh-century Arabia into an urban civilization. As such, it represented the most powerful weapon in Islam's arsenal in the unfolding battle between Islam and its manifold enemies, particularly local renegades like Nasser and his nationalist officers.

Qutb's ultimate goal was to once again bring about a fundamental transformation of society in order to institute *hakimiyya*, God's sovereignty on earth. He made a correlation between the Egypt in which he lived and the environment in which the Prophet Muhammad had first spread the message of Islam. It is this analogy between the era of the Prophet and contemporary Egypt that allowed Qutb to bring Qur'anic evidence to bear in the development of his resolutely absolutist perspective. To this end, he took a radical step in categorizing contemporary Egyptian society as *jahili*, a term historically used to capture the spiritual ignorance of Arabian society prior to the arrival of Islam. Qutb drew a direct line between "the old *jahiliyya* of the Arabs" with what he called *al-jahiliyya al-haditha* (modern *jahiliyya*).[21] From his prison cell, he argued, "We are also surrounded by *jahiliyya* today, which is of the same nature as it was during the first period of Islam, perhaps a little deeper."[22] Qutb defined *jahiliyya* as a deviation from the worship of One God and the way prescribed by God—as a society which derives its systems, laws, regulations, habits, standards, and values from a source other than God. Drawing from this definition, Egyptian society, he insisted, could only be seen as a *jahili* society: "Our whole environment, people's beliefs and ideas, habits and art, rules and laws—is *jahiliyya*, even to the extent that what we consider to be Islamic culture, Islamic sources, Islamic philosophy, and Islamic thought, are also constructs of *jahiliyya*."[23]

Insofar as *jahiliyya* amounted to servitude of humans to other humans, Qutb thus noted, it stood for the replacement of *hakimiyya* with man-made laws. Instead, according to him, true Islamic life involves total submission to God and rejection of all modes of *jahili* life, whether ancient or modern: "The Islamic society is, by its very nature, the only civilized society, and the *jahili* societies, in all their various forms, are backward societies." In this titanic struggle between good and evil, he opposed any compromise or coexistence, instructing his followers that "Islam cannot accept or agree to a situation which is half-Islam and half-*jahiliyya*."[24]

Qutb's vision of history was reduced to that of an eternal struggle between truth and falsehood. Qutb preached that Islam would ultimately prevail and would rule the earth, a Manichaean struggle, acknowledged his disciples. He made it clear, however, that the triumph of Islam would not occur simply by virtue of its revelation by God but rather through agency: "It is brought into being by a group of people understanding the task, believing in it completely and conforming to it as closely as possible ... striving to this end with all they possess."[25]

Qutb called for the creation of a believing generation or a Qur'anic generation, which would act as a vanguard "duty-bound to carry the greatest burden, to point out the road of salvation to humanity, and to build the road as well."[26] As noted in chapter 5, Qutb contended that he had cleansed himself of Western and decadent secular influences; now he sought to cleanse his followers' minds of anything that could corrupt and dilute this pure Islamic doctrine. According to his jail companion, Sayyid Eid, Qutb demanded that all converts systematically reject previous distortions of the Islamic doctrine and rely only on the Qur'an itself.[27]

The concept of the Qur'anic generation was developed by Qutb in *In the Shadow of the Qur'an,* in which he stipulated that this generation would be subject to the authority of the holy book itself, not to human laws or persons. Once again, the emphasis was on a conception of the Qur'an as an active constitution or a road map capable of guiding men to the right path. Members of this Qur'anic generation, Qutb insisted, ought to live in isolation from others to preserve their purity and avoid moral corruption; the most important life is to "live for the Qur'an and live by the Qur'an,"[28] a vision which broke away from the mainstream Ikhwan ethos of gradualist propagation. According to Eid, "Al-Shahid taught us that society was corrupt and that we must have as little contact as possible with the outside world."[29] In his commentary on the Qur'an, Qutb reminded Muslims that just like important Islamic figures such as Abu Bakr and Abdullah ibn Massoud, who had endured cruel torture at the hands of the leaders of the unbelievers, the Qur'anic generation would also have to pay a heavy price for its godly aspirations.[30] In private he also warned his disciples that the path to salvation and liberation and the reestablishment of a divine kingdom on earth is paved with toil and blood, said Eid, who spent almost a decade in prison with Qutb and was one of his most loyal disciples.[31] Nonetheless, his vision also held out hope for victory, since despite the tortures they endured, these early Muslims had ultimately prevailed.

From the late 1950s until his execution in August 1966, Qutb clandestinely worked at instilling his understanding of *'aqida* (Islamic creed) to a select group of young believers inside and outside prison. He saw them as the inheritors and vanguard of his mission and vision in this life and, after his death, the ones who would shoulder the historic and sacred task of re-Islamizing knowledge, society, and government both at home and abroad. "Qutb taught us that *'aqida* is a force multiplier; it is our secret nuclear weapon," explained Ali Ashmawi, a founding member of al-Tanzim who also served as its field commander. "By arming ourselves with *'aqida* we feel superior to adversaries and go on the offensive,"[32] he continued before adding, "He told us we were living in similar circumstances to those experienced by the Prophet and his companions and early Muslims in seventh-century Arabia. [...] Al-Shahid wanted us to walk the same path as the first Muslim generation and shoulder our responsibility in reestablishing the Islamic order."[33]

The idea of *jahiliyya* also had profound implications for how the Egyptian state and ordinary citizens figured in Qutb's vision for the transformation and future of Egyptian society. Disillusioned and embittered with fellow Egyptians who had failed to lift a finger to defend persecuted Ikhwan members like himself, Qutb viewed them with contempt. In multiple interviews, his supporters and former Ikhwan detainees shared similar sentiments. "How could fellow Muslims forsake us and be passive in the face of injustice exacted on us?" wondered Eid. The experience of the prison camps left deep scars on the imagination of many members, shattering their attitudes about the sanctity of the Muslim community and its duties and responsibilities. The repression triggered soul-searching among the imprisoned

Ikhwan about what had gone wrong and where they ought to go from there. Instead of critical self-reflection and reassessment of past conduct, a critical segment led by Qutb blamed the Nasserist state, along with foreign powers—particularly the United States, the Soviet Union, and Israel—for their calamity. Nasser, along with the rest of the ruling establishment, came to be viewed by the Ikhwan generally as an evil force that had hijacked the revolution and corrupted some of the Islamist movement's own sons. Far more significantly, Qutb designated the elites *kuffar* (unbelievers or disbelievers), claiming that they had in practice renounced Islam. More radically still, Qutb was prepared to argue that even ordinary Egyptians had ceased to be Muslims. For Qutb, there was no gray area: "It is either the rule of Allah or the rule of *jahiliyya*," he wrote.[34] Qutb's excommunication of state officials and lay Egyptians—grounded in his understanding of the concept of *jahiliyya* as applicable to contemporary society—had major implications for the use of violence as a political tactic: it offered a way around religious prohibitions against shedding Muslim blood.

Even Qutb's disciples, who insist against credible evidence that Qutb did not excommunicate ordinary Muslims, concede that their mentor taught them that Nasser and his supporters were renegades from Islam. "Yes, I won't deny that al-Shahid instilled in us a belief that Nasser and his cronies were tyrants and apostates, and that we had a religious obligation to bring them to the right path," acknowledged Abdel Majid al-Shazili, a follower of Qutb who was sentenced to life in prison in 1966 and is now a top theorist and keeper of his legacy. "Qutb exposed Nasser's camp of unbelief and he did not mince any words or shy away from the truth," he added.[35] These feelings were echoed by Eid, who told me: "Qutb taught us that Nasser was a manifestation of the moral corruption, secularization, and Westernization of society. [...] While getting rid of the *taghut* [tyrant] was a priority, Qutb impressed on us the need to overthrow the whole system and cleanse it. For as long as Islam was banished from all aspects of life, the likes of Nasser would spread the moral filth in our lands."[36]

Qutb's brutal indictment did not stop there. He also challenged the traditional *'ulama*'s (religious establishment) authoritative hold over the masses by insisting that their interpretation of Islamic doctrine was anachronistic. Just like Qutb had done with his literary mentors in his younger years, and subsequently with Nasser, he launched a direct attack on Muslim scholars, portraying them as prisoners of blind imitation and out of touch with the real conditions of ordinary Muslims and their daily struggle. These "defeated scholars," Qutb contended, "are ignorant of the nature of Islam and of its function as given by God, and that it has a right to take the initiative to bring about human freedom."[37] Instead of appreciating the value of Islam as a dynamic, revolutionary force for universal emancipation, Qutb contended that the *'ulama* had essentially accepted the Western understanding of religion as a private endeavor with no relationship to practical life.[38] Going for the kill, he railed against what he had always depicted as an unholy alliance between the rulers and the professional men of religion. The latter, he argued, were parasites, collaborators, and exploiters. They had sold their souls and legitimized the oppressive status quo, including colonialism.[39]

It was only by discrediting the professional men of religion that Qutb could hope to offer an alternative revolutionary interpretation of Islamic doctrine through direct appeal to the *umma*. He recognized that subverting the two most important institutions—political authority and religious orthodoxy—would have profound personal consequences. "All along Qutb knew he was bound to be martyred for his beliefs," recalled Sayyid Eid. "I remember vividly that he frequently marveled at why they let him live as long as they did."[40] Qutb's subversive ideas have been internalized by waves of radicalized religious activists who see the *'ulama* as subservient to the oppressive political authority. This interpretation helps to explain why the religious establishment has been ineffective in countering the narrative of *takfiri* groups like Al Qaeda and the Islamic State.

If the Ikhwan's earlier experience of repression in the late 1940s had sowed the seeds of *takfiri* (excommunication) ideology, the tragedy of 1954 caused a rupture in its members' collective consciousness and gave rise to a full-blown *fiqh al-takfir* (jurisprudence of excommunication), which would spiral out of control in the subsequent decades. While Qutb's defenders blame overzealous radicals for misinterpreting his thought, detractors assert that he was instrumental in popularizing *takfiri* ideology. Both groups agree that since the late 1960s, proponents of *takfiri* ideology uniformly reference Qutb's writings and sayings. Qutb had lit the spark, and *takfiri* ideology spread like wildfire, first in Egyptian prisons, then in top Arab universities and beyond.

During his time in jail, from 1954 till 1965, Qutb also penned his widely read and most controversial manifesto, *Signposts*, which was a synopsis of his more extensive commentary, *In the Shadow of the Qur'an*. In *Signposts*, he continued to develop his ideas on the role that the Qur'anic generation was to play as a vanguard responsible for bringing about the restoration of Islam:

> How must this Islamic resurrection begin? A vanguard must resolve to set it into motion in the midst of the *jahiliyya* that now reigns over the entire earth. The vanguard must be able to decide when to withdraw from and when to seek contact with the *jahiliyya* that surrounds it. If the vanguard is to find its way, it needs signposts to point toward the commencement of its long road, to tell it what role it will have to play to attain its goal, to inform it of its real function ... These signposts will likewise tell it what position must be taken towards the *jahiliyya* that reigns over the earth.[41]

In *Why They Executed Me*, written a few weeks before his execution, Qutb suggested that he had given up on peaceful dissent by the mid-1950s. After witnessing the alleged abuse and killing of his prison mates, he said he concluded that Islam and the *umma* (global Muslim community) were being targeted and that it was his personal duty to defend the faith through armed struggle. Therefore, Qutb presented a theological justification for the use of violence by drawing on edicts pronounced by authorities such as the thirteenth-century scholar Ibn Taymiyya, who, just like Qutb, spent time in prison due to his radical views and died behind bars. In his seminal work, *Fi fiqh al-jihad* [The jurisprudence of jihad], Ibn Taymiyya contended that Muslims must kill Muslims if the latter are aggressors, if they are corrupt, or if they are not practicing the *hudud* (rules) of God, because as such they were nothing but an extension of *jahiliyya*.[42] Ibn Taymiyya also expanded the scope of authority to wage jihad beyond the prerogative of the ruler or the state to other groups and individuals in society. This view of jihad as *fard 'ayn* (a task incumbent on every Muslim) stood in contrast to the view of jihad as *fard kifaya* (a collective duty to be carried out by a group of people, historically the army, on behalf of state authority). This paradigm shift called for the militarization of the whole of society.[43]

The Ikhwan Divided: A Rift between Hudaybi's Accommodationism and Qutb's Confrontationalism

From the second half of the 1950s until his temporary release from jail on health grounds at the end of 1964 at the behest of the prime minister of Iraq, Abdel Salam Arif, Qutb embarked on a mission to recruit fellow Islamist prisoners and to rally them to his cause. Having suffered from breathing problems before he was imprisoned, he spent most of his years of incarceration in prison hospital facilities. During a spell in the Tura prison hospital, he interviewed scores of visiting cellmates from various prisons, particularly al-Qanatir, to find out who would be receptive to his revolutionary ideas. He succeeded in recruiting dozens of prisoners to his underground project. Although Qutb's followers were a minority—nearly one hundred members among the incarcerated Ikhwan, who numbered in the low thousands—their very existence shattered the unity of the Ikhwan and exposed internal ideological and doctrinal fault lines. Throughout this time, Qutb never requested authorization from the Ikhwan leadership to recruit imprisoned members to his cause. He went to great lengths to mask his proselytizing efforts from Ikhwan leaders, and when they confronted him, he denied converting detainees. By covertly recruiting Ikhwan prisoners to his revolutionary scheme,

Qutb went against the ethos of absolute obedience to the hierarchy that had long been a core principle of the Islamist organization. He possessed no official function or authority to replace the Ikhwan's worldview with his own interpretation.

Ikhwan leaders were appalled when news reached them that Qutb had been preaching subversive ideas to the rank and file. The most alarming news was his idea of *takfir* (excommunication), including the whole of Egyptian society: the state, ordinary people, and the *ulama*. The accommodationist camp—the part of the Ikhwan leadership which continued to operate according to the pragmatic principles laid out by Banna—was led by Hudaybi's inner circle, including Farid Abdel Khaleq, Salah Shadi, Amin Sudqi, and Lutfi Salim. This inner circle had retained hopes of striking a compromise with the authorities by signing a formal petition of fealty to Nasser and renouncing violence. The accommodationists knew the Ikhwan did not have the capabilities to directly confront the Nasserist state. Moreover, the severity of the repression against them had taken a heavy toll on them and their families. "Experience has taught us an invaluable lesson: refrain from giving the authorities a pretext to persecute us and dismantle our institutions," said Abdel Khaleq, Hudaybi's second in command. "We paid dearly for challenging tyranny. We could not resist the Nasserist state's coercive powers. Nasser's goal was to dismantle the Ikhwan as an organization, using blood and iron to break its backbone."[44] While Abdel Khaleq avoided direct criticism of Qutb, who is still highly revered among most Islamists, he said he had feared that Qutb's *takfiri* ideology would threaten the very existence of the Ikhwan and alienate Muslim public opinion. Faced with this new challenge, the Ikhwan leadership grilled Qutb and demanded that he refrain from spreading *fitna* (sedition): "A *fitna* almost tore apart the ranks of the jailed Ikhwan," acknowledged Abdel Khaleq. But he claimed that "the supreme guide swiftly cautioned Qutb against any unauthorized teaching and preaching, and nipped the *fitna* in the bud."[45] According to Abdel Khaleq, who as Hudaybi's trusted man was privy to the confrontation, Qutb disavowed such heretical views and insisted that he only taught prisoners Qur'anic lessons.[46] "He was agreeable and nonconfrontational, seeking to dispel suspicions that he had gone rogue," Abdel Khaleq said. On the other hand, according to Sayyid Eid, who was in Qutb's camp, Qutb's seemingly conciliatory stance was but an artifice. "We [both sides] put the best face on a dangerously embarrassing situation. Qutb had a low opinion of the tired old men of the Ikhwan who suffered in silence at the hands of Nasser and who willingly refused to resist oppression and injustice. He viewed them as being out of touch with the emancipatory and revolutionary power of *'aqida*," Eid told me.[47] "Sayyid Qutb had contempt for the Ikhwan political leadership, whom he derisively called functionaries," he added.[48] "He dismissed them as stupid and spineless, status quo men." Despite his reassurances to Hudaybi and other Ikhwan leaders, Qutb had unambiguously excommunicated Nasser. According to Eid, Hudaybi's intervention did little to calm the dissidents. "Far from it," he said. "Dozens of Ikhwan members, including myself, were steadfast in their support of Qutb's defiance of the Nasser regime and the need to build a vanguard to carry out an Islamist revolution."[49]

In prison Qutb enlisted Ikhwan members over the heads of their "legitimate" leaders and drove a wedge into the heart of the Islamist movement. Those who looked up to him for inspiration and guidance distanced themselves from the formal institutions of the mainstream Ikhwan, which caused a serious rift between Qutb's men and other Ikhwan prisoners. According to Ahmed Ra'if, a well-placed Ikhwan member who was in contact with both camps at that time, the internal divide even poisoned the atmosphere in more than one jail.[50] The two sides bickered so bitterly and intensely that Hudaybi issued a directive from his prison cell calling for a cessation to the hostilities, although neither camp adhered to a ceasefire and skirmishes frequently occurred.

Meanwhile, Qutb continued to disseminate his ideas during daily lessons to the prisoners. According to attendees, these primarily focused on two themes: *'aqida* (Islamic doctrine), and *siyasa* (politics). Qutb reminded his disciples that if they harnessed the hidden power of *'aqida*, they would be emancipated and fearless; they would become closer to God and act as his faithful agents in reinstituting a just and pure Islamic order on earth. "His aim was to transform members from mere religious activists into revolutionaries to confront the internal and external enemies of Islam," confided Eid. "He made new men out of us, armed us with *'aqida* and summoned us to reestablish Islam in its purity and beauty in a similar way to that of the early Muslims."[51] Eid's recollections testify to the power of Qutb's message, written especially for the youth who he hoped would spearhead the coming Islamist revolution. "Unfettered by previous conventional interpretations of the Qur'an, Qutb offered his own interpretation in a straightforward and accessible style and addressed us in captivating language that resonated with all of us," Eid recalled.[52] "My eyes welled with tears when Qutb dictated some passages of his masterpieces, *Signposts* and his Qur'anic exegesis," said Eid, who transcribed books that Qutb dictated to him during their time together in prison. "I and many others felt that he was giving expression to our deepest aspirations and fears about the plight of Egypt and the *umma*, and the threat posed by renegade rulers and their masters—crusaders and Zionists."[53]

The hardening of attitudes among some Ikhwan members translated into a determination to take practical steps to strike violently at the Nasserist state. Some of those who had moved in these circles at that time, whether inside or outside of prison, told me that they had wanted to kill Nasser and his close aides. More ambitious members had visions of overthrowing the regime as a whole and replacing it with a Qur'an-inspired government. A common thread among these newly radicalized recruits was visceral hatred of Nasser and what he represented. Sherif Younis, a cultural critic and a biographer of Qutb, points out that exacting vengeance on the Nasserist state was the key concern of Qutb and his followers; they wanted to teach Nasser a lesson that would not be lost on rulers who dared to target the Islamist movement.

Younis's views are corroborated by the supporters and former disciples of Qutb's whom I have interviewed. "We wanted to pull Nasser's junta up by its roots and liberate our Ikhwan brethren from captivity," recollected Ali Ashmawi, who took steps to achieve these ends and planned to kill Nasser. "Initially, our aim was to prevent the Ikhwan organization from disintegrating and to prepare the ground for a future uprising against Nasser and his thugs. We wanted organizational continuity but with new blood and fresh faces unknown to the security services."[54] Of all al-Tanzim's lieutenants and foot soldiers, Ashmawi was the most forthcoming about the history of the organization because he had little to lose, having been demonized by the Ikhwan for breaking down under torture following his arrest in 1965 and exposing his co-conspirators. His old cohorts have never forgiven this "human act of weakness and treachery," as he put it, although he assured me that when he found himself sitting next to Qutb in a courtroom some weeks after their arrest, the latter showed empathy for his plight. "I explained to him that the Ikhwan abused me and treated me like a pariah in prison. Qutb reassured me that he understood my predicament and that blaming the victim is wrong. 'Nasser's security men are the villains, not you,' [he] added with a gentle smile on his face," according to Ashmawi.[55]

Ashmawi's narrative is significant for this study as he was present at the birth of al-Tanzim and served as its military field commander. His is the most unscripted, comprehensive, and revealing voice on the issues at stake, and the least constrained by any existing connections with the Ikhwan. Most of Ashmawi's recollections are corroborated by other members of al-Tanzim and independent sources. Others who moved in these circles at the time also confirmed the shift to more militant views that was then under way. "We could not be passive while our brethren were being unjustly abused and oppressed," said Ahmed Abdel Majid.[56] "That would have violated one of the fundamental tenets of our religion; resisting injustice and defying renegade rulers."[57] Beyond the question of vengeance and a perceived duty to defend their oppressed co-religionists, taking action against Nasser under these circumstances was also seen as necessary in order to defend Islam itself. "Once Nasser's regime persecuted the Ikhwan, it became obligatory for us to step forward and defend Islam," said Abdel Majid. Challenged on his implicit assumption that the Ikhwan could be directly equated with Islam per se, he responded that "the

Islamist movement is the guardian and protector of Islam ... If you target its sons, you are harming Islam and hindering its growth."[58]

More and more former disciples of Qutb told me their priority had been to eliminate Nasser: "We concluded that Nasser must go. We wanted to kill the devil and rid Egypt of him," agreed Abdel A'l Aw'd Musa, an intense seventy-six-year-old who was introduced to me by Abdel Majid.[59] The two men knew each other from al-Tanzim and became best friends while in prison. "Blinded by hatred and revenge, many of us pledged to assassinate Nasser and be martyred in the process," added Aw'd, who established one of the first underground cells outside Cairo, which, although initially designed to assist the families of incarcerated Ikhwan members, became tasked with the more ambitious goal of subverting the Nasser regime. "My unit's fundamental goal was to kill Nasser and avenge our persecuted Brethren," he explained. "We recruited between fifty and seventy fit young men, raised one thousand pounds to carry out the operation, and trained and readied ourselves for an opportune moment." The cell selected Alexandria as an ideal location and developed a plan to position three separate assassination teams armed with automatic weapons.

However, as division over whether it would be better to assassinate Nasser or overthrow the regime hardened, the plan never came to fruition. "As we talked to other members who had also organized themselves in small paramilitary units, our plot met with stiff resistance and opposition from senior leaders who warned against rash actions inspired by vengeance and emotion. We were told that killing Nasser would not dramatically change the system and that a like-minded secular dictator would replace him. It was not easy to postpone our short-term goal of punishing Nasser for his crimes, for the greater good of overthrowing the corrupt, decadent regime," explained Aw'd. "While debating the decision with our Brothers, we cried and prayed for inspiration and wisdom. What you need to comprehend is that Nasser hurt us badly and left deep scars in both our souls and our bodies," he emphasized.

Even now, more than half a century on, when pressed on the question of where this hatred for Nasser had come from, Aw'd's voice rose in intensity and anger. Recalling the period of imprisonment which preceded his decision to become involved in paramilitary activities, he said, "We were brutalized and humiliated by Nasser's security thugs and treated worse than animals ... I was nineteen years old when the authorities arrested me in 1955 for helping the pressed families of the imprisoned Ikhwan. They tortured me, together with other members, with electric shocks and they terrorized us using wild-eyed black dogs. For six months we could not shower ... Many days we went without food for twenty-four hours. Nasser's men aimed at breaking our will and humiliating us by calling us female names like *al-'arousa* [bride]." Aw'd said that in his prison there existed several views among the Ikhwan detainees, who numbered around two thousand. He recalled that he belonged to a group that pledged to kill Nasser no matter what; others suggested that they should be more strategically minded and patient, and prepare to oust Nasser's regime. There existed yet another camp which preoccupied itself only with theology and neglected political and operational issues, according to Aw'd. "A year and half later I was released from prison, though I had been sentenced to five years, and I was assigned as a teacher in a young girls' school. As a young man, the authorities wanted to tempt me and corrupt me by having me teach at a girls' school. Instead, I, along with two Brothers who were subsequently executed by Nasser, Abdel Fatah Ismail and Abdel Fatah Sharif, embarked on a journey to revive the dormant Ikhwan and strike at the heart of the beast," Aw'd went on, with an indignant expression.

Throughout Egypt, scores of Ikhwan members and sympathizers embarked on similar journeys. Whether motivated by the desire for vengeance against Nasser or driven by more politically ambitious goals, individual initiative was a common denominator for these various undertakings. Aw'd and his contemporaries said that they acted as if every one of them was individually responsible for the survival of the Islamist movement. "In the absence of the [jailed] Supreme Guide Hudaybi, we acted as substitutes to fill the leadership vacuum and prevent the breakdown of the Islamic organization," Aw'd told me. Equating Islam with the Ikhwan—a common feature among all of the former activists interviewed for this project, without exception—he said that "protecting Islam was a binding individual duty."

Pressed on whether killing Nasser, on the one hand, and preserving the Ikhwan and defending Islam, on the other, were synonymous, Aw'd retorted that "the two goals are not mutually exclusive." He explained: "Nasser was a bitter enemy of the Ikhwan and Islam. The Ikhwan are the vanguard who, in the absence of a state based on Qur'anic laws, always protect Islam and sacrifice blood and treasure to do so." Abdel Majid concurred with Aw'd on this point. "Yes, we wished Nasser harm, though we knew that we had bigger enemies than Nasser," he said.[60] "The military junta proved to be a front and a tool for an unholy global conspiracy against Islam." In this regard, the clash between the Ikhwan and the Nasserist state laid the groundwork for subsequent Islamist militancy not only against pro-Western Arab rulers but also against their Western patrons. More than anyone else, it was Sayyid Qutb who emerged as a key voice promoting this belief to his followers both inside and outside his prison. "Qutb pointed out that Nasser would not have persecuted the Ikhwan without the consent and prodding of the crusading powers," said Sayyid Eid.[61] "Qutb told us that initially the army officers had collaborated with the Ikhwan, until evil-minded America recruited him to the anti-Islamic camp. Nasser sold his soul on the altar of political expediency." In my interviews with Eid and other former conspirators, all spoke of how they had come to view the internal rivalry in Egypt as an extension of a colossal struggle in which they as believers were engaged; with the imperialist and materialistic West, on the one hand, and with godless communism, on the other. Not unlike other nativists and traditionalists in the West, Qutb's revolt against the modern world cast materialism as a present and immediate danger to Islam's transcendental truth.

In the words of Eid, however, "Qutb instilled in us a heightened consciousness of the West's ceaseless efforts to colonize and subjugate Muslims and to subvert our religious values."[62] Extending his critique of Christianity and the West to encompass local actors whom he viewed as U.S. clients, Qutb cautioned Muslims to be wary of the "Americanized Muslims" who controlled the most sensitive posts in society and served the interests of their imperialist masters. According to Qutb, a litany of American-owned institutions, including publishing houses and media outlets, were engaged in propagating a liberal and submissive interpretation of Islam: even the professional men of religion, custodians of Islam's heritage, had succumbed to American patronage and bought into their narrative. Qutb believed that, in conformity with American interests in the Cold War context of the time, the pliant religious and intellectual establishment had rejected an Islam that resists imperialism and oppression and opted instead for an Islam that resists communism; this spiritual and intellectual colonialism allowed Washington to field an army of collaborators and to firm up its grip over Muslims without firing a shot:

> The Free World does not fight us with tanks and guns except for limited periods of time. Instead, it wages a battle against us with tongues and pens. It also fights through philanthropic societies and organizations it establishes, revives, and supports for the sake of controlling the most sensitive centers in our land.[63]

Although Qutb stressed that both capitalism and communism were bankrupt materialistic ideologies, while in prison he taught his supporters that America posed a graver threat to Islam than the Soviet Union. In addition to using American Islam as an ideological tool against Soviet communism, the United States had another sinister goal, Qutb suggested. They wanted to strike at the heart of Islamic doctrine (*'aqida*) and to raise doubts in Muslims' minds about their religion. Instead of seeing America's two-pronged goals as mutually exclusive, Qutb saw them as fitting together as part of an integrated design to tame and domesticate Islam:

> This army of collaborators is instructed to shake the foundation of *'aqida* in the soul by all means. [This] has taken the form of research, science, literature, art, and journalism. The intent is to

belittle the importance of *'aqida* and the shari'a, to interpret it in an unsuitable manner, to emphasize its "reactionary character," and to call for discarding it.[64]

Qutb thus viewed the struggle between Islam and the West in apocalyptic and existential terms. He was one of the first Islamist activists to note the shift of global power away from Europe to America and to claim that the United States possessed an ambitious hegemonic worldview vis-à-vis Muslim countries. His account of the role played by America in the plight of the Ikhwan members in Nasser's prisons resonated particularly among his disciples on the grounds that he knew the country well, having lived and traveled there for almost two years.[65] Many praised him for resisting the temptation of materialistic culture and preserving his religious purity and authenticity during his time in the United States. Qutb's study tour in America lent credibility and authority to his critique of the country and endeared him to the radical religious dissidents who fell under his spell. "Unlike others who sold their soul to the devil, al-Shahid was incorruptible," said Abdel Majid. "Qutb told us that the Americans offered lucrative incentives to bribe him and get him to work for them but he did not succumb to the temptation. Despite promises of riches and power, [he] was steadfast and defiant, unwilling to be a traitor to his religion and country."[66] Eid seconded this: "America could not co-opt al-Shahid and buy him off," he said, also recalling Qutb's saying that U.S. intelligence services had indirectly attempted to recruit him. "Qutb's firsthand experience with America and its machinations reinforced his suspicions that the Western superpower aimed at dominating and conquering the lands of Islam ... [He] wrote to friends and colleagues back home warning of the new rising threat on the horizon."[67]

Qutb's tale that U.S. spooks had tried to recruit him while he was studying in America was taken at face value by his supporters and gained wide public currency. Admiring biographers, such as Salah Abdel Fatah al-Khalidi,[68] reference the story as an example of his prominence and moral courage, which they contrast with the "weakness" of other Muslims who lacked Qutb's "resilience and steadfastness" and were recruited by the superpower.[69] Qutb's story is cited as an indictment of evil-minded Americans who would spare no expense to corrupt Muslim thinkers and intellectuals and infiltrate their society; it is even used to attack other Islamists who show any acquiescence in their position towards the West.[70]

While Qutb's study tour in America had heightened his awareness of the country's rising status, his disciples suggest that a more important factor in his hostility to the United States was the pivotal support given by Washington to the partition of Palestine and the establishment of a Jewish home in the heart of the Arab and Islamic world. Nonetheless, Qutb's critique of America was visceral, encompassing both U.S. foreign policy and the American way of life. There was something instinctual, hurtful, and irrational about the America that Qutb knew. For the rest of his life, he never wavered from his conviction that America was the prime enemy, along with local tyrants and intellectual slaves, and that Muslims are obliged to resist American imperialism. "Al-Shahid was prophetic about America's imperial designs on the Muslim world," said Shazili during one meeting in his apartment in Alexandria.[71] "Long before anyone else, Qutb pointed to America as the chief enemy of Islam and Muslims," he added. Pressed on the question of why the United States—as an enemy of Islam—should have taken actions such as opposing the British-French-Israeli invasion of Egypt over the nationalization of the Suez Canal in 1956 and forcing them to withdraw their troops, Shazili responded that "America did it because it wanted to replace Britain and France as the dominant hegemon in the area. [...] The Suez crisis was a godsend for the Americans, who used it as a vehicle to expel their European partners from the Middle East and to deceive gullible Arabs into thinking that America was a friend," [72] he explained before exclaiming, "Do not tell me that Eisenhower had Egypt's interests at heart. You do not buy this lie. In 1956 the Americans rewarded Nasser for his brutal suppression of the Islamic movement. Qutb believed that Nasser was America's point man in Egypt, carrying out its design to neutralize Islam." During our meeting, Shazili repeatedly emphasized that he and all of Qutb's disciples had been wholeheartedly committed to this hypothesis.[73] Again, pressed on questions such as why America—as a supposed co-conspirator with the Free Officers—should have turned against Nasser and been instrumental in causing his military defeat by Israel in the June 1967 war, Shazili had a conspiratorial retort for every twist in the story. "Long before the Jews humiliated Nasser in 1967, Qutb had predicted that the Americans would use him and then abuse him," he said, laughing loudly.[74] "Qutb told us that the Americans would spit Nasser out once they squeezed the juice out of him. Al-Shahid knew America from the inside out. America has no moral scruples and is blindly driven by an unquenched thirst for power," he said, relating Qutb's worldview as his own.[75] "What you do not understand is that for the Americans, by the end of the 1960s Nasser had outlived his usefulness," he said. "Once he killed Qutb and his friends and locked the sons of Islam behind bars, Nasser became too powerful and dangerous and had to be cut down to size. [So] America gave the Jews the green light to clip Nasser's wings."[76] He added that "our tyrants kid themselves into believing that if they do the West's bidding at home, they will be indispensable to their foreign masters. Neither Nasser nor Saddam Hussein expected America to stab them in the back after all the services they had provided."[77] He suggested that Arab rulers are too "blinded by ambition, hubris, and ignorance" to recognize their role as "insignificant pawns in a great power game."[78]

Such narratives, advanced by Shazili and many of his fellow travelers, illustrate how—under the influence of Qutb—the profound hostility that they felt towards Nasser was inseparably bound up with their hostility towards an America that they saw as controlling and micromanaging Arab and Muslim politics. The world according to Qutb revolved around America's constant drive to intellectually and mentally colonize Muslims and enslave them. He saw America's hand behind every misfortune that had befallen Islam since the "rape" of Palestine. Withstanding the test of time, the Qutbian inheritance of anti-Americanism came to color the views of Islamists and became part of their grand narrative. It was against this background that Qutb's contemporaries came to see that the task of rescuing Islam had fallen to an elite Islamist vanguard, whose chief responsibility would be to protect the Islamic creed against falsehood and apostasy at home and to pave the way for the establishment of their vision of a Qur'anic-based system. However, Qutb's disciples made it clear that he never directed them to battle America directly, instead advising them to focus their energy on the enemy within. "Qutb's priority was America's agents within Muslim societies, not America per se," recalled Eid.

Although Qutb and his supporters' feelings were the result of the harsh humiliation and violence they had to endure at the hands of the Nasserist security services, their thirst for vengeance overshadowed the spiritual aspects of religion. It was power they were after, albeit this time in the name of God. According to Sherif Younis, who has written extensively on the Nasserists and Islamists, "Qutbism represented a rupture within the Ikhwan because it prioritized power over *al-din* [religion]. Qutb cancelled *al-din* for the sake of *al-siyasa* [politics]. [...] For Qutb and his disciples, *al-din* became synonymous with power."[79] Even Abul Hasan Ali al-Nadwi, the Indian scholar who pioneered the key concepts which Qutb drew from, like *hakimiyya* and *jahiliyya*, criticized both Qutb and his mentor, Abul A'la Mawdudi,[80] for reducing the believer's relationship with God to that of blind obedience and downplaying the relationship of love that exists between the believer and God. Nadwi lamented that Qutb abandoned the spiritual and human aspect of Islam, stressing only obedience and fear.[81]

The Emergence of al-Tanzim

This context is important to understanding the emergence of al-Tanzim. Its crystallization as an organization came about quite organically. It formed out of units created by some of those who had remained at liberty after the 1954 clampdown and who were determined to continue their armed activism. Gradually, al-Tanzim developed into a somewhat coordinated paramilitary operation, concentrated in urban areas like Cairo and Alexandria, although its secret and dispersed paramilitary cells lacked heavy arms and ammunition. While in the mid-1950s, young angry activists had been primarily concerned with exacting vengeance on Nasser, in the late 1950s, as various cells began to link up with one another, they soon realized they needed to put forward a clear vision or road map for the future. As operatives brainstormed about tactics and strategy, the leading figures in al-Tanzim decided to devise a long-term plan for revolutionary change.

There is no denying that al-Tanzim members' particular understanding of religion factored prominently in their decision to go underground and defend "Islam against its enemies," as they put it to me. Religious ideas, as they understood them, shaped their imagination and worldview, and conditioned their conduct. While politics was the focal point in the conflict between the Ikhwan leadership and the army officers, religious socialization and fervor were the driving force behind these youngsters' march to war. They stressed the unity of Islam and its revolutionary character, and that there is no distinction to be made between faith and other areas of life, including politics. A widespread sentiment among them was that whenever there is *zulm*, or injustice, ardent religious activists would rise up to put things right.

Al-Tanzim's beginnings were humble. With the dismantling of the Ikhwan's institutions and networks, followers and supporters had lost their political equilibrium and they sensed danger. In both urban and rural areas, Islamist social networks were activated by neighbors and friends who knew each other well and trusted one another. Time and again, I was told by activists who lived through this period that they felt like a wrecked ship in a stormy sea with no captain, no navigation equipment, and no control over the ship's direction and destiny. Al-Tanzim is a case study of the ingenuity and resourcefulness of these grassroots religious activists, and their capacity to build a complex underground network against great odds. Undeterred by the Nasserist state's concerted effort to destroy the Ikhwan, and with hardly any financial backing or military experience, these young activists took great risks in an uncertain bid to unseat Nasser. The power of ideas is key to understanding their self-conscious action, regardless of how reckless and suicidal it may seem to outsiders. The lesson we can draw from al-Tanzim is still relevant to understanding the rise of paramilitary Islamist groups today, insofar as it speaks to the marrying of radical religious ideas and ideologies with a sense of injustice, victimhood, and persecution.

Recounting his experiences in several interviews in his small town about two hundred kilometers from Cairo, Ashmawi explained that the trick was secrecy, patience, and meticulous planning. "As youngsters, we felt it our duty to organize ourselves into small cells and to preserve the spirit and infrastructure of the Ikhwan. We kept our endeavor secret from our fathers, mothers, and families. We feared for their safety and for our own security," he said.[82] He explained that in its early days "no one in particular" was in charge of the emergent movement. "It was an individual effort by small circles of trusted friends. Young religious activists sought each other out and recruited their best friends to join their own separate cells."[83]

When al-Tanzim initially acquired a leader, that person was Abdel Aziz Ali, a former army general and minister who was one of the heroes of the 1919 revolution against the British colonial presence. However, he was still very much wedded to the old ways of thinking and acting employed in the anti-colonial struggle, characterized by hit-and-run tactics and gradual escalation. Al-Tanzim's lieutenants, in contrast, were ambitious, impatient, and daring, and they were determined to pursue a riskier strategy of confronting the Nasserist state head-on. They thus searched for a charismatic *emir* (leader) with the capacity and the temperament to make their nascent organization more effective. "We were dying to join the fray and prove ourselves," said Ashmawi with a loud laugh. "We had contempt for conventional views and trusted only our instincts and our hearts."[84]

After their brief, disappointing experience with Abdel Aziz Ali, in the late 1950s the founding members of al-Tanzim—who included Abdel Fatah Ismail, Ashmawi, and Abdel Majid—contacted Farid Abdel Khaleq, the Ikhwan's second in command, and asked him to be their leader. "I was blunt with them," Abdel Khaleq told me during multiple interviews in his flat in an up-scale neighborhood in Cairo.[85] He said he warned them that the path they were pursuing "would provide the Nasser regime with a rationale for brutalizing the sons of the Islamic movement further and for perpetrating more bloodshed." He added, "I also warned them that I would inform the supreme guide and have him take appropriate [punitive] measures if they proceeded with their project," indicating a complex relationship between al-Tanzim and the Ikhwan leadership, which will be discussed in greater detail later in this chapter.[86]

It was at this stage, having become disillusioned with Abdel Aziz and having been turned down by Farid Abdel Khaleq, that members of al-Tanzim began to put out feelers to Qutb. "The key word was 'inspiration.' We searched for a leader who would inspire us and educate us about the duties and responsibilities of jihad," said Ahmed Abdel Majid, who was head of al-Tanzim's intelligence committee. "We were less interested in military and intelligence drills, and more so in theological and ideological renewal and transformation. Sayyid Qutb was an inspirational role model who could empower our nascent *jama'a*."[87]

Qutb's story, his reputation for defiance in the face of hardship, and his rejection of Egypt's secular order resonated among these young firebrands, whose thirst for heroism and martyrdom was unquenchable. He reminded them of heroic and charismatic Islamic figures in early Muslim history who had sacrificed blood and treasure to defend the *umma*. They saw him as a potential demolisher who could blow the whole system up. However, they recalled that initially they did not know how to reach Qutb and were not confident that he would be willing to risk his life by accepting leadership of this nascent group. "We were skeptical as to whether al-Shahid would take our *jama'a* seriously and agree to take charge of it," admitted Abdel Majid.[88]

To their delight, al-Tanzim's lieutenants were able to get in touch with Qutb in the late 1950s via two women who acted as intermediaries: Qutb's sister Hamida and the audacious Ikhwan activist Zeinab al-Ghazali. Having thus made contact with Qutb, al-Tanzim's operatives pleaded with him to be their leader and pledged to swear *bay'a* to him. "We were elated when word reached us that Qutb had consented to our request," recalled Aw'd, who was then in his twenties. Qutb's agreement to lead al-Tanzim remains controversial as he, along with some of his defenders, denied it was a paramilitary organization aimed at overthrowing the Nasserist regime. However, in all my interviews with al-Tanzim's surviving lieutenants, they were clear that he had agreed to lead the underground organization and transform it into an effective vanguard.

"That new development qualitatively transformed our endeavor from a fringe underground faction to a potentially potent force," Aw'd further asserted. What he and his cohorts meant is that ideas are at least as important for an organization like al-Tanzim as numbers.[89] The importance of ideas is emphasized in social movement theory (SMT), a conceptual framework which has become increasingly central in recent scholarship as a means for understanding Islamism.[90] Al-Tanzim needed the support of Qutb in order to offer an ideational basis that might inspire its members to assume great risks, including imprisonment, torture, and even death. Moreover, al-Tanzim needed a charismatic leader like Qutb in order to win over or stand up to the timid Ikhwan leadership, which remained wedded to the pursuit of nonviolent means to break down the Nasserist state.[91]

Qutb provided theological and intellectual firepower and guidance. Before he joined, al-Tanzim had consisted only of disconnected underground units and cells with centralized decision making, and no *emir* to inspire and instill *'aqida* in members. With Qutb at the helm, a coherent and unified organization emerged with a totalitarian Islamist vision that appealed to young religious activists like Aw'd and Abdel Majid. The goal shifted from the ouster from power of Nasser and his inner circle to the transformation of society as a whole by blowing everything up. In sum, Qutb invested al-Tanzim with hegemony, including doctrinal cohesiveness, inspiration, charisma, and daring, enabling it to think the unthinkable.

From Qutb's viewpoint, the decision to offer "guidance," as he noted in his confessions, to the organization's young members bordered on suicidal. Nasser did not tolerate political dissent, let alone armed insurrection. Qutb knew well the costs inherent in confronting the Nasserist state. To avoid entangling all of his disciples in this new venture, he did not even inform Eid and his other prison followers about the underground organization that was taking shape on the outside. Nonetheless, Eid recalled Qutb saying that he fully expected to be killed by the Egyptian authorities because of his revolutionary views. "Al-Shahid acted and behaved as if he was destined to be martyred at any moment," recalled Eid.[92] "Qutb knew that incarcerated Ikhwan members were under constant surveillance by the authorities, even after their release," recalled Shazili, who was in charge of a branch of al-Tanzim in Alexandria during this period. Shazili himself would eventually be imprisoned after al-Tanzim was crushed in 1965; he spent almost a decade behind bars.[93] "He did not want to compromise al-Tanzim by merging the two groups together. Unlike Qutb's prison supporters, al-Tanzim's members were religious activists or Ikhwan members who had not been arrested. They were clean." Shazili also noted that Qutb wanted to have a backup plan, in case one of the two groups was exposed.[94]

"Qutb kept us in the dark," Eid confirmed. "His first priority was to protect the newborn baby and to not compromise our security in case the authorities got wind of it," he said, referring to the security of Qutb's followers in jail. "He wanted to ensure the long-term survival of the Islamist movement, not just al-Tanzim."[95] Eid remained a close follower of Qutb after the latter was released from jail on health grounds at the end of 1964. He recalled meetings with his mentor at Qutb's home in the Cairo suburb of Hilwan. "After my release in 1964 I spent most of my days with Qutb at his home, and I sensed that something big was happening because he frequently met for hours with a group of young men behind closed doors," Eid recalled. "Although I pressed him to include me in the circle, Qutb cut me short and told me not to ask too many questions, saying that we should not put all our eggs in one basket. He said that I, his [younger] brother Mohammed, and others should be able to carry the torch forward, if he fell."[96] "I obeyed al-Shahid because he knew better and I trusted his judgment," said Eid decisively. "He had thought of the future and the need to keep the core of the Qur'anic generation alive."[97]

That Qutb was prepared to face such peril strongly suggests that he viewed taking the helm of al-Tanzim as a game changer. As Shazili and others noted, Qutb was not a traditional critic or a theorist confined to an ivory tower. Rather, he insisted that it is the responsibility of Islamic intellectuals to lead and to take risks in the course of promoting the Qur'anic doctrine. "Qutb reminded his disciples that Islam is an emancipatory and revolutionary force, and that only men of action will harness that powerful force and unleash it," said Eid. "Qutb was a man of action, a firm believer in *al-islam al-haraki* [actionable Islam]."[98] Qutb's politicized and militarized Islam was more ideological than spiritual, resonating particularly among young men from rural areas and small cities, what Egyptian sociologist Saad Eddin Ibrahim called a new intelligentsia.[99] "Qutb did not only theorize about the urgent need for a vanguard but devoted the last decade of his life to building a real vanguard," explained Shazili.[100] Ashmawi echoed this point and told me that Qutb "often reminded us that we were the vanguard tasked with replacing the status quo with an Islamic system. As foot soldiers of Islam, Qutb expected us to march to the battlefield and fight to win over hearts and minds to the divine path."[101] Pressed on the question of whether Qutb sanctioned the use of violent means to effect political change, in practice Ashmawi responded affirmatively. "Yes, Qutb aimed at violently overthrowing the whole social and political order, not only the Nasser regime," he said. "He taught us that all means must be used to change the status quo, including violence, and insisted that we plan strategically before we strike. He trained us to be patient and that, once we go on the offensive, we must deploy overwhelming force to tip the balance in our favor."[102] He added, "We were a paramilitary organization, not a peaceful protest movement. Qutb was a revolutionary Islamist who believed in revolutionary change."[103]

In numerous interviews, Qutb's disciples make it abundantly clear that their "teacher" had abandoned the possibility of bringing about fundamental change by peaceful means. By the late 1950s Qutb had given up on changing the system by persuation and contestation. The Qutb doctrine would be drenched in blood: "Al-Shahid entertained no illusions about what it would take to purify society and cleanse it of alien influences because domestic and foreign enemies would fight to the death," said Shazili. "It would take sacrifice, martyrdom, and, yes, blood, a lot of it."[104] Qutb impressed upon al-Tanzim members, I was told, the need to be fully prepared before militarily confronting the state apparatus. No half measures, no armed skirmishes with the regime, he advised his ardent supporters. "When you take arms against the tyrant, you must hit him hard and break his will," a follower recalled Qutb's directive. "He must not be able to retaliate."[105]

Furthermore, according to Ashmawi, Qutb also played a pivotal role in the education and indoctrination of al-Tanzim's cadres. "Before we connected with Qutb, we were theologically naive, blind and deaf, feeling our way in the darkness," he said, with a loud laugh.[106] "He opened our eyes and ears to the truth and showed us the way." Before his release from prison in 1964, Qutb's role in the indoctrination of al-Tanzim members was facilitated by distribution of the works that he was composing in his jail cell. "Qutb's exegesis of the Qur'an and his *Signposts*, authored in jail and smuggled out to us, nourished our spiritual thirst and hunger," recalled Shazili nostalgically. "We were converted to Qutbian ideas, heart and soul." In this way, Qutb was able to endow al-Tanzim with a theological vision based on his own interpretation of the Qu'ran, and to utilize Islamic doctrine as the constitution for revolutionary change and the transformation of Egyptian society. He preached to his followers the urgency of Islamizing state and society, and their role as an Islamic revolutionary vanguard in facilitating and spearheading this transformation.

The text of *Signposts* was smuggled out of Qutb's prison chapter by chapter by Qutb's own sister Hamida and the activist Zeinab al-Ghazali. They would hand these smuggled writings over to the five men who made up the leadership committee of al-Tanzim, headed by Abdel Fatah Ismail, who would then spend hours clandestinely studying Qutb's words as if they were law. Fearful of exposure and arrest, committee leaders would memorize whole paragraphs and communicate them orally to other cells and units throughout the country. "We carried Qutb's manuscript in the thick of the night and hid it deep inside our clothes," said Aw'd, laughing heartily. "We felt like we were transporting a dangerous weapon. ... We walked in alleyways and back streets, not the main roads, and our hearts beat fast at the sight and sound of a person."[107]

According to Ashmawi, Qutb wrote *Signposts* precisely as a call for action and as a road map for al-Tanzim's members because "he wanted us to comprehend Islam's essence, especially *al-'aqida*." Abdel Majid concurred: "I remember vividly that the first chapter sets out the steps needed to bring about the Islamic revolution, the most important of which was that there should be a vanguard ready to confront *jahiliyya*." Stopping short of identifying himself and his comrades as this vanguard, Abdel Majid nonetheless added, "Qutb knew perfectly well that we were trying to find our way and he provided *Signposts* pointing the road ahead."

Besides smuggling Qutb's writings out of prison, Hamida and Ghazali also played other important roles, including keeping Qutb updated on al-Tanzim's activities and carrying directives back and forth to its members. "We were duped by Zeinab and Hamida," said an officer who insisted on being anonymous; he had been in charge of security in the prison hospital where Qutb resided. "I had no idea that they were trafficking in subversive materials and plotting a revolution in jail." Ghazali, who remained associated with al-Tanzim throughout its existence, also acted as recruiter and financier. Married to a wealthy businessman, she opened her salon and kitchen to dissidents. She raised money at home and abroad for families of incarcerated Ikhwan and partially managed al-Tanzim's finances. She was also the main contact between al-Tanzim and the Ikhwan's supreme guide, Hudaybi, arranging meetings between Hudaybi and al-Tanzim's founder and acting chief, Abdel Fatah Ismail. In her memoirs, she also implicitly acknowledged relaying messages between Qutb and Hudaybi, confirming that the latter was kept abreast of efforts to revive the Islamist organization underground.

All of those interviewed for this book confirmed that Ghazali played a significant part in connecting al-Tanzim's lieutenants with the political wing of the Ikhwan and facilitated meetings for the secret organization in her house. Ghazali's role in al-Tanzim was second only to that of Qutb, and it cost her dearly as she was detained by the Egyptian authorities in 1965 as a conspirator in Qutb's al-Tanzim. In her autobiography, *Days of My Life,* she paints a shocking portrait of her torture ordeal, which included sexual abuse. Prison inmates told me that they saw her being hung upside down, with her feet tied to the ceiling. Ghazali remained defiant throughout. She was sentenced to twenty-five years in prison with hard labor but was eventually released following a presidential decree issued by Nasser's successor, Anwar Sadat, in 1971. She would subsequently reward Sadat by assisting a group of jihadist conspirators who attempted to assassinate him and seize power in 1974.

The Murky Relationship between al-Tanzim and the Mainstream Ikhwan

Although Qutb kept his recruitment of followers inside the prisons hidden from the Ikhwan leadership, Ghazali's role as an intermediary between Qutb and Hudaybi points to some kind of awareness and approval of the existence of al-Tanzim by the group's top leadership. The nature of this relationship nonetheless remains both controversial and politically sensitive. This question goes to the very heart of a broader question regarding whether al-Tanzim was a paramilitary arm of the Ikhwan or an independent venture undertaken by young religious dissidents on their own initiative. From the time of the exposure of al-Tanzim in 1965, the Egyptian authorities launched a propaganda offensive aimed at undermining the Ikhwan as a whole; the official campaign asserted that al-Tanzim was an affiliate of the Ikhwan and that the latter was therefore a terrorist organization. Against this background, Ikhwan officials have repeatedly denied that the broader movement and its leadership played any formal role in al-Tanzim; they have accused the Nasserist state of manufacturing evidence against their organization. Moreover, accusations of close links between al-Tanzim and the Ikhwan have often been used by detractors of the Islamist movement as evidence of its violent character and of its inability to become a trusted political actor. Ikhwan senior leaders would prefer that the story of al-Tanzim be forgotten, swept under the rug.

Those of Qutb's confidants and disciples who dare to speak out say that they are ostracized by the Ikhwan and that their voices are muzzled. "The Ikhwan are allergic to our very existence and want us silent like the dead," said Abdel Majid. "I instantly became a persona non grata once I published my recollections of al-Tanzim, and they treated me like a traitor to the cause." He noted that current Ikhwan leaders, several of whom were themselves active members in the underground organization, view the story as a liability because it reminds the public of a poisonous and destructive chapter of their history. Some contemporary Ikhwan leaders even go so far as to deny the very existence of al-Tanzim as an armed force. "Why do you keep quizzing me about Qutb's al-Tanzim?" Mahmoud Izzat, a seventy-year-old multimillionaire who currently runs the organization in exile in hiding, demanded of me angrily. "The whole thing is a Nasserist construction invented by his intelligence thugs to use as a bludgeon against the Ikhwan. We possessed neither arms nor plans to overthrow the military junta," he assured me. While others claim it is an open secret that Izzat himself in his early teens was one of the youngest members of al-Tanzim, he would not answer questions on the subject. Apparently exasperated with my line of questioning, he interrupted me abruptly. "That subject is not of any real interest to me or to the Ikhwan," he declared. "It is dead."[108] Subsequent efforts to organize a second interview with Izzat were unsuccessful because, in the words of his secretary, "he does not want to talk to you."

Others within the Ikhwan, while acknowledging the existence of al-Tanzim, deny that it ever had the blessing of the leadership. Senior official Farid Abdel Khaleq, who represented Hassan al-Banna's school within the Ikhwan and was his confidant, continually insisted that the senior leadership, particularly Hudaybi, had not sanctioned

Qutb's paramilitary organization. "Hudaybi's hands had already been burned, and he would not let a few well-meaning and excited activists ignite a fire that would destroy the organization. We had nothing to do with al-Tanzim al-Sirri," he insisted.[109] Abdel Khaleq—who had himself declined the request from members of al-Tanzim to take over the leadership of the group in its early days—implied that Qutb's actions had almost brought ruin to the Ikhwan. "We did our best to convince Qutb to disband his group, but we failed. The Ikhwan cannot be blamed for the blunders of others," he added. "To be honest with you, after joining the Ikhwan in 1953, Qutb entertained illusions about steering the entire movement on a radical path," said Abdel Khaleq.[110] "He might have even dreamt of building his own power base. But the truth is that he was not part of the Ikhwan inner circle and he exercised little influence among the top leaders," he added in a whisper, as if afraid of being heard by outsiders.[111] Such narratives distance the open wing of the Ikhwan from Qutb's paramilitary network and often go along with a tendency to blame him for entangling the Ikhwan in another futile fight with the Nasserist state. Qutb, I was told, had his own agenda and did not represent the Ikhwan as an institution; he persisted in his recklessness in contravention of direct orders from the movement's leadership. The implication is that Qutb's al-Tanzim was the work of a rogue element within the Ikhwan, though no senior Ikhwan has dared to say so publicly with the exception of Abdel Khaleq, who was no longer an active member of the inner circle. Qutb's "martyrdom" turned him into a sacred figure among Islamists, deterring those who disagree with him from voicing criticism.

However, such accounts raise more questions than they answer with regard to the relationship between al-Tanzim and the Ikhwan. At the very least, by Abdel Khaleq's own admission, the senior leadership knew that Qutb had organized a paramilitary group. Moreover, despite the efforts of senior Ikhwan figures to deny any involvement, primary evidence suggests that Hudaybi did in fact sanction al-Tanzim. Abdel Majid recalled that after Abdel Khaleq had refused to take charge of the organization and prior to Qutb's acceptance of the leadership role, its members had approached Hudaybi directly to seek his approval.[112] "Abdel Fatah Ismail met with the supreme guide and made the case for al-Tanzim, and he received a legitimate mandate to reassemble scattered Ikhwan members," he said. While the reference here to "reassembling scattered Ikhwan members" reflects the fact that discussions proceeded in general terms, interviewees insisted that everyone involved understood the purpose of al-Tanzim.

In contrast, other former al-Tanzim lieutenants insisted that Hudaybi had agreed to the paramilitary organization and stressed the importance of his backing. "We could not have moved forward without the authorization of the supreme guide because we needed religious legitimation," said Ashmawi. "We sought and promptly received Hudaybi's approval."[113] Both Abdel Majid and Ashmawi said that it was Ghazali and the then acting chief of al-Tanzim, Abdel Fatah Ismail, who had met with Hudaybi and obtained his authorization. Faced with the question of how to explain Abdel Khaleq's claim that Hudaybi had told him that he would not sanction al-Tanzim, Abdel Majid argued that Hudaybi did not tell Abdel Khaleq the truth because he had merely wanted to keep the peace within the Ikhwan and to distance the movement from al-Tanzim in case the authorities discovered its existence.[114] "The supreme guide told Zeinab al-Ghazali, who arranged the meeting with Abdel Fatah Ismail, that the mainstream Ikhwan were no match for Nasser and that only a committed vanguard like al-Tanzim would deliver a hard blow to the Egyptian ruler," he said. "That was the context of why [he] granted Abdel Fatah Ismail authorization in order to counter Nasser's decision to proscribe the Islamist movement."[115]

"Some Ikhwan portray us as rogue elements and illegitimate upstarts, but we are legitimate sons of the organization," said Abdel Majid.[116] "The Supreme Guide Hudaybi sanctioned our endeavor and gave his consent to Qutb as leader of al-Tanzim," he insisted. "As members of the Ikhwan, we had to seek Hudaybi's permission because we had sworn *bay'a* to him. We could not act alone because that would have violated our religious pledge—a blasphemy."

All surviving members of al-Tanzim say that from the outset, Qutb himself had refused to head the underground group unless he obtained an official decree from the supreme guide. In her autobiography, Zeinab al-Ghazali acknowledged that she acted as intermediary between Qutb and Hudaybi. She further asserted that she had obtained the latter's consent.[117] According to her, Hudaybi was even the first to read Qutb's *Signposts* before sanctioning its publication and saying Qutb was "the hope for the *da'wa* [the call] now."[118]

These contradictory internal accounts are unsurprising given that the Islamist organization was in a state of virtual paralysis and that Hudaybi tended to keep his cards close to his chest. He wanted to have it both ways: to shield the political organization against accusations of possessing an armed wing, while keeping his options open with regard to the possibility of militarily confronting the Nasserist state. Upon assuming the leadership of the Ikhwan, Hudaybi had developed an evasive style, frequently saying things that he did not mean and taking decisions in secret that contradicted his previous pronouncements.

The Crackdown on al-Tanzim al-Sirri

In the summer of 1965, Nasser's security forces accidentally discovered al-Tanzim after a member they arrested on unrelated charges exposed the underground organization while being interrogated. While its members had amassed weapons and money, and had undertaken training and planning, al-Tanzim had yet to carry out any military operations. Qutb and his men lost the fight before "firing a single shot," as Ashmawi put it.[119] The authorities acted swiftly and aggressively to dismantle al-Tanzim's cells and to complete the destruction of the Ikhwan as an institution. After al-Tanzim was exposed and its members arrested, interrogated, and tortured, Qutb took full responsibility for his operational role and went beyond the call of duty, trying to shield his disciples and followers. When confronted by the authorities with evidence extracted from other prisoners under torture, which they claimed revealed gaps in his own testimony, such as in the aforementioned case of Ashmawi, Qutb simply said that he had sought to protect his cohorts. In his last testament, *Why They Executed Me,* he implied that during interrogation, his key goal had been to bear the brunt of the burden and to minimize the costs to al-Tanzim's members.

The Egyptian government used confessions extracted under torture from members of al-Tanzim to indict both Qutb and the Ikhwan leadership. Qutb and al-Tanzim's six top lieutenants were sentenced to death by hanging. According to Sami Sharaf, Nasser's chief of staff, in debates among Egyptian officials over whether or not to execute Qutb, Nasser had taken a particularly strong line. "Nasser said that executing Qutb would deal the Ikhwan a mortal blow, as well as any future counterrevolution by religious fanatics," he said. "Nasser believed that Qutb was the head of the snake and only removing the head would keep the poison from spreading." Nasser thus tipped the balance in favor of executing Qutb, not knowing that this fateful decision would have quite the opposite result.

Qutb and his two closest confidants—Mohamed Yusuf Hawash and Abdel Fatah Ismail—were shortly sent to the gallows. Nasser commuted the death sentences of Qutb's other partners—Ashmawi, Abdel Majid, Sabri Arfat, and Majdi Abdel Aziz—to life in prison. Dozens of other members of al-Tanzim received prison sentences ranging from several years to life. Thousands of members of the Ikhwan, including senior leaders, were arrested, reportedly tortured, and given long jail terms. "We wanted to bury the Ikhwan, period," confessed Sami Sharaf. "Our goal was to remove the cancer from the Egyptian body politic."[120] The Nasserist state waged a systematic public campaign to discredit the Ikhwan, portraying al-Tanzim as the armed wing of the Islamist group, part of a sinister conspiracy to destroy state institutions. Seeking to demonize Qutb, the government-controlled media spent weeks painting al-Tanzim as a terrorist organization that plotted attacks against public landmarks and facilities like roads, bridges, and power stations. Qutb, Egyptians were told, directly ordered al-Tanzim to target the civilian infrastructure, with a view to sowing disorder and chaos and destabilizing the country. The authorities also used confessions extracted from al-Tanzim operatives to show that the armed faction had received money and weapons from foreign sources, and that it had shadowy connections with militants and terrorists in neighboring Arab states, particularly Saudi Arabia, which was at that time a rival of Nasser's Egypt. Sharaf still supports these accusations: "Qutb and the Ikhwan leadership conspired to replace the pan-Arab nationalist government with a theocracy," he told me. "We exposed their lies, plots, and foreign connections, and told Egyptians the real story behind these deviants."

For his part, Qutb assured his disciples that his death would in fact serve as a catalyst for his cherished Islamist revolution. "Al-Shahid [Qutb] often reminded us that his blood would transform his words into human bombs that would sweep away Nasser's tyranny," said Shazili, who spent many years at hard labor for his role in Qutb's al-Tanzim. "His martyrdom would be an inspiration for thousands, millions, of young Muslims."[121] Eid agreed, saying that he "believed that Qutb's death would achieve what he could not do while he was alive."[122] There are many accounts of the final hours leading up to Qutb's execution at 3:00 a.m. on August 29, 1966.[123] A common thread that runs through these stories is that Qutb went to the gallows with no hesitation or regret and that, on the night of Qutb's execution, the prison official Hamza al-Bassouni convinced Qutb's sister Hamida, who was also imprisoned, to meet with her brother and try to convince him to confess that al-Tanzim had been "in alliance with a [subversive, anti-government, foreign] force," in return for his release.[124] Qutb immediately and emphatically rejected any suggestion that he might secure his own freedom by confirming this false claim, saying, "I swear by Allah that if this had happened I would have said it, regardless of whatever force stood in my way. This did not happen [i.e., there was no foreign hand behind al-Tanzim] and I would never tell a lie."[125]

From interviews with Qutb's contemporary disciples, a portrait emerges of the man as a crusader who was unafraid to die for his beliefs and in fact welcomed martyrdom. Well versed in Islamic history, Qutb knew better than Nasser the enduring and powerful role that iconic symbols and martyrs have played in Islamic tradition, particularly if they are perceived as righteous and pious individuals who resist injustice and defend the sacred. One of the few images that exist of Qutb on the day of his hanging shows him with a smile on his face, saying goodbye to his prison guards minutes before being led away to the gallows on that hot August night. A serious man with a stern countenance, not known for public joviality, this image of Qutb facing imminent death suggests that he was at peace with himself and prepared to meet his creator without fear or trepidation.

Without a funeral for his relatives and followers to bid him farewell, Qutb was buried in an unmarked grave in al-Qarafa al-Kubra (the Great Cemetery), the site of the mausoleum of the ninth-century jurist Imam Shafi'i. Nevertheless, Qutb remained (and still remains) alive in the minds and hearts of Islamists worldwide, endearingly referred to as al-Shahid al-Hayy (the living martyr). For religious dissidents, Qutb's manifestos have attained a degree of influence greater than that warranted by their substance because they are interpreted through the prism of pain, suffering, and sacrifice. "Qutb's words have a special resonance due to his steadfastness in the face of tyranny," said Shazili. "By practicing and living what he preached, he set an enduring model for future generations of religious dissidents."[126]

Conclusion

The relationship between Qutb and the Ikhwan was fraught with tensions and contradictions. From the outset, Qutb was an outsider and a belated convert to the cause; an accidental Islamist. Only eighteen months after his official joining of the Ikhwan in March 1953, he was arrested and held for a decade behind bars. According to senior Ikhwan members, Qutb never really developed either institutional or informal links within the Islamist movement. A maverick with a volatile character, he was not the type to toe the party line.

According to his disciples, Qutb saw himself as guiding the Islamist caravan in the right direction and rescuing Islam from oblivion.

There was nothing ambiguous about his effort to transform the Ikhwan into a revolutionary vanguard, and to supply the theological fuel to sustain its new mission. He was fully conscious of the task at hand and struggled to nourish it and keep it secret. Qutb's attempted coup against the Ikhwan is important because it shows the extent of his ideological transformation as a revolutionary Islamist theorist and ideologue, and his determination to bring about real change. He aimed at dismantling all existing institutions, including his own, the Ikhwan, and blowing everything up. This fact does not match the emphasis typically placed by Qutb's biographers on continuity over discontinuity, and their tendency to portray Qutb as simply an extension of the Ikhwan institutional family.[127] Such narratives take into account the importance of Qutb's writings and the impact of the prison years but leave out his leadership of al-Tanzim.

While Qutb's disciples, including some of those interviewed for this book, are prepared to speak frankly about Qutb's status as a rebel who possessed his own revolutionary agenda and who advanced his own cause, the Ikhwan and Qutb's biographers ironically consider him a loyal and faithful son of the Islamist movement. This image of Qutb dovetails with popular narratives of the Ikhwan as a unified organization, a well-oiled machine whose various parts act in unison. This ahistorical picture underestimates the existence of conflicting viewpoints and widely publicized splits within the organization, going back even to the lifetime of its charismatic founder, Hassan al-Banna. It also fails to acknowledge that if Qutb's internal coup was the most serious and dangerous of these rifts, it is because it challenged the ideological foundation of the Ikhwan's traditionally conservative mandate.

A more complex interpretation of Qutb's formal affiliation with the Ikhwan shows how his own ambition led him to use that powerful organization to advance his own career and to try to implement his own philosophy. As discussed in chapter 5, Qutb's formal joining of the Ikhwan had coincided with an internal period of crisis as multiple power centers within the group competed with one another for influence. After the assassination of Banna, the appointment of

Hudaybi as *murshid* or supreme guide had from the outset divided the Brothers. His failure to assure a role for the organization within the Revolutionary Command Council (RCC) further delegitimized his authority. By the mid-1950s, the Ikhwan faced an existential crisis: the *murshid* had been put under house arrest and the state launched a massive wave of repression against the organization. With no strong ideological vision to sustain the group in the prison camps, the Brothers were left to their own devices. That was an ideal situation for a strong-minded individual and brilliant agitator like Qutb, who hoped to transform the Islamist group and mold it in his own image.

Qutb stepped up both his recruitment inside prison and his radicalization efforts. If he had helped the Free Officers clearly articulate their ideological vision, he would now do the same for the Brothers, and this time he finally stood a chance to lead the group to the promised land. What emerges from Qutb's formative years and early adulthood was his quest for recognition and deference, no matter which circles he navigated. Though he had been unsuccessful in the literary scene and subsequently with the Free Officers, his new reinterpretation of Islam and the concomitant revolutionary vision that went with it finally won him the recognition for which he had so urgently strived. Moreover, Qutb's analogy between seventh-century Arabia and modern Egypt is one of two analogies he subtly articulated in his writings. In *A Child from the Village* and *Why They Executed Me*, the carefully crafted image of Qutb is that of a prophet-like, selfless man whose total embrace of Islam allowed him to have a vision that seemed to come from God; if operationalized, this vision would finally reestablish the sovereignty of God on earth (*hakimiyya*).

In this context, it is unsurprising that the political struggle between the Nasserist state and the Qutbian Islamists has come to be invested with existential overtones. Feeding this subjective narrative of the conflict was the fact that from 1954 onward, the Nasserist state deployed its security and ideological apparatus to repress the Islamist movement without providing suspects with due process, at the same time portraying the Brothers as the most important threat to Egyptian society. With both camps repeating mirroring narratives of the Other as an existential threat, violence became the norm. Unfortunately, this vision is still a prevalent feature of Arab politics, and has contributed to the rise of waves of radical religious jihadists. This initial framing of the struggle as existential has been recycled and adapted by subsequent generations of religious activists and nationalists. In their quest for power, both the state under Nasser and the Ikhwan laid the foundation for an articulation of politics and of the relationship between ruler and people as strictly unitary and autocratic, thus paving the way for the institutionalization and normalization of one-party authoritarian rule. Furthermore, by instilling the notion that politics is a zero-sum, life-and-death game and that any form of dissent is synonymous with subversion and foreign conspiracy, they have left no space for the emergence of a legitimate opposition.

The worldview of society as being starkly divided into patriots and traitors, the camp of belief and the camp of unbelief (*hakimiyya* versus *jahiliyya*) or between the people and the enemies of the people, that they anchored at the heart of Arab politics could only lead to the securitization of both the state and social movements.

Finally, beyond the impact on Arab politics at large, the events left a profound legacy within the Ikhwan itself which lasts until today. By recruiting Ikhwan members to his secret society behind the back of the leadership and later on by using al-Tanzim to disseminate his own vision, Qutb institutionalized what would become an enduring rift pulling and pushing the Ikhwan in two different directions: towards the gradualism of Ikhwan founder Banna, on the one hand, and towards the revolutionary vanguardism of Qutb, on the other. More than half a century after Qutb's execution, though his disciples' numbers have dwindled, they remain a force to be reckoned with within the Ikhwan. By controlling key positions and committees within the organization, the Qutbians exercise a degree of influence disproportionate to their actual numbers. Although the Ikhwan leadership denies the existence of an ideological divide, time and again centrist and reformist members have accused the Qutbians of resisting efforts to reform and democratize the movement's decision making and of maintaining the autocratic status quo. Ironically, in the 1950s and 1960s it was Qutb and his supporters who defied the old guard with their call for the transformation of the Islamist movement and society in general. Nowadays, the roles have been reversed. Trading places with their former detractors, now the Qutbians have assumed the role of the reactionary old guard within the Islamist movement.

Chapter 10

The Decline of the Nasserist Project

NASSER'S CRUSHING DEFEAT BY Israel in the Six-Day War in June 1967 transformed Arab politics in both the middle and long terms in Egypt and throughout the Arab world.[1] Did the third Arab-Israeli war in itself drive a paradigm shift from pan-Arab nationalism to religious nationalism or pan-Islamism, as many writers assert? The question is not whether the 1967 loss was a turning point in Arab politics—it clearly was. The real question is how, when, and in what ways did the shift from Arab nationalism to Islamism occur?

The dominant narrative presents Nasser's defeat in the Six-Day War as the single most significant event in allowing the Ikhwan and Islamists in general to consolidate their hegemony in Egypt and elsewhere in the Middle East. Specialists too often assume that it was a straightforward tipping point, swiftly bringing about the end of Arab nationalism or pan-Arab nationalism as espoused by Nasser.[2] However, to grasp fully the declining fortunes of Arab nationalism and the consequent resurgence of the Ikhwan and Islamism after the 1967 war, it is necessary to take a longer historical view.[3] Events in Egypt before the defeat by Israel had already gone a long way towards weakening the Nasserist state and undermining Nasser's own standing in Egypt and the Arab neighborhood. Long before 1967, the Nasserist state was already running on empty, suffering one hard blow after another both at home and in the region. These setbacks included the collapse of efforts to unify Egypt with Syria under the banner of the United Arab Republic, severe economic problems, and fierce inter-Arab rivalries culminating in a disastrous Egyptian military venture in Yemen (which escalated after the 1962 Yemeni coup). From the mid-1960s onwards, the Nasserist state was pulled and pushed in different directions by competing social groups, its authority fraying fast. The ideological balance that Nasser tried to maintain was being eroded under mounting domestic, regional, and international pressure.

It was against this background that Egypt experienced the 1967 defeat. On the morning after, no one captured the spirit of the moment better than Naguib Mahfouz, the prominent Arab novelist: "Never before or after in my life had I ever experienced such a shattering of consciousness and shock as I felt at that moment."[4] Most of the critics of the Nasserist regime and its performance in the war at this time were themselves part of the Arab nationalist constituency, not rival Islamist adversaries. The defeat shook the confidence and morale of this constituency to its very foundation but did not destroy its belief in the supremacy of secular nationalist and socialist ideas. Critics took Nasser to task for being a traditionalist-centrist who had failed to break free of his petit bourgeois class and religious affiliation and identity. They called for a radical shift to the left, not the right, and a clean break with the past. Even after the defeat, the secular nationalist and socialist paradigm remained ascendant. The rise of the political Islamists only came later in the 1970s and 1980s, even though religiously based forces had been present in Egypt and other Middle Eastern countries throughout the 1950s and 1960s.

Political and Economic Woes on the Eve of 1967

Long before the 1967 conflict, Nasser had been forced to contend with regional rivalries. His dream of building a united Arab coalition led by Egypt and able to challenge superpower domination had not materialized. The June 1967 defeat proved that Nasser's use of Arab nationalism as a weapon to destabilize his Arab rivals had increased inter-Arab rivalries and fed an internal hegemonic fight for regional leadership. Egypt's short-lived union with Syria between 1958 and 1961 had exposed Nasser's ambivalence towards fully operationalizing a merger between Egypt and another Arab country. This reluctance put him at odds with other pan-Arab nationalists in the Mashreq (the Arab east), who wanted to merge all the Arab states in a union called the United States of the Arab world. It also weakened Nasser's ideological hold over the Arab arena because various strands of pan-Arab nationalism were now competing against his own vision. Following Nasser's move away from the idea of a pan-Arab nation and towards Arab solidarity, Arab nationalists in Syria, Iraq, Lebanon, Palestine, and beyond questioned his revolutionary credentials and accused him of forfeiting the struggle to liberate Palestine. His aim, they asserted, was to prioritize Egyptian interests over those of other Arab countries. Meanwhile, regional foes like the monarchies of Saudi Arabia and Jordan had proven far more resilient and resourceful than Nasser had thought they would. As Saudi Arabia continued to intensify pressure against Nasser, he accused it of being behind the breakup of the United Arab Republic and miscalculated by intervening militarily in Yemen in the 1960s. Yemen became an inter-Arab killing field, showing the limits of Egyptian power and undermining the Egyptian state. The Yemen war also exposed deep cracks in the Arab nationalist project and demonstrated why Nasser and other Arab leaders failed to move towards Arab unity in practice.

Thus ultimately, the intra-Arab-nationalist rivalry played a major role in Nasser's undoing. As a self-styled revolutionary, he could not afford such a blow to his hegemony and his claim to leadership of the "Arab cause."[5] Nasser's relations with the militant Baath party in Syria—officially founded in 1947 with branches in a number of Arab countries, with a platform comparable to Nasser's nationalist project—was a case in point. The Baath party, whose ideology prioritized the establishment of a unitary pan-Arab state as opposed to Nasser's Arab solidarity, challenged the Egyptian leader's revolutionary mantle, calling into question his commitment to pan-Arab causes, particularly Palestine. Like their Islamist rivals, the Arab nationalists bitterly fought with each other over tactics and strategy. Nasser's conflict with co-nationalist Baathists cost him dearly and caused him to blunder monstrously in the May 1967 crisis with Israel, which brought ruin to his army and regime. Trying to outbid the militant Baathists in Syria and Iraq and counter their accusations of cowardice vis-à-vis Israel, Nasser miscalculated by upping the ante with the Zionist state, thus providing a rationale for Israel to preempt the Egyptian army and vanquish it.

What is more, before long even Nasser's more modest ambitions within the Egyptian domestic sphere collided headlong with hard economic realities. By 1965 the Nasserist state had reached a critical deadlock, particularly with regard to its much-touted economic program of "populist *étatisme*" or populist state capitalism. According to John Waterbury, a specialist on Egypt's political economy, far from increasing productivity, the regime's emphasis on using the public sector as an instrument of social and political transformation caused a massive decline: "The crisis that overtook Egypt in 1956–66 ... was caused by the gross inefficiencies of a public sector called upon to do too many things: sell products at cost or at a loss, take on labour unrelated to production needs, earn foreign exchange, and satisfy local demand. It was also caused by the neglect of the traditional agricultural sector which, while taxed, was not reformed so as to become an engine of growth in its own right."[6]

Expansion of educational opportunities for the growing youth population and increasing rural migration to urban Cairo overtaxed the ability of the incompetent bureaucracy to provide jobs and essential services, and threatened to upset the interests of the rising new middle class.[7] Centralized state planning created swollen bureaucracies but sluggish economic performance, thus producing a systemic overload. According to scholar Carl Brown, "reality did not live up to expectations."[8]

A five-year plan put in place by the Nasserist state covering 1960–1965 aimed at increasing investment in the industrial sector and building the Aswan Dam with a view to boosting agricultural and industrial production. During this five-year plan, expectations went up as targets were mostly met as scheduled. Investments increased to almost 18 percent, economic growth rose to 6 percent, and per capita income went up by 30 percent after a long period of stagnation.[9] This rosy economic picture was based on foreign indebtedness, however. By 1965, as the second five-year economic plan was unveiled, frustration had replaced hope. The state began to feel the pinch of debts incurred due to its dependence on loans to finance 30 percent of its investments; commodity imports increased by 48 percent in order to meet the targets of the economic plans. In the words of Galal Amin, a leading Egyptian socioeconomic analyst known for his sympathy towards Nasser, the plan was "over-ambitious."[10] Salah Nasr, the head of Egyptian National Intelligence, who was sent by Nasser to Rome in 1967 to request a $10 million loan from the Italian government, described the economy from the mid-1960s onwards as bleak:

> From 1965 the economic situation suffered from shortage in foreign currency, the burden of foreign debts, and a crisis between Egypt and the Western countries because Egypt had been unable to repay the interest on these debts. This led Nasser to amend the five-year plan into a seven-year plan, before amending the latter into a "three-part achievement plan."[11]

As Egypt lost its main sources of income with the closure of the Suez Canal in June 1967 and the halving of its oil production, the government's ability to secure foreign aid and grants was undermined. The United States, which had provided Egypt with 300 million Egyptian pounds from 1958 until 1965, ceased its aid payments in February 1967. Overall, foreign agencies and countries reduced their aid to Egypt from $200 million between 1961 and 1966 to just $16 million from 1967 till 1969, a qualitative drop that had a major impact on the Egyptian economy.[12]

As populist state capitalism was almost brought to a halt during 1965 and 1966, restructuring became inevitable. The burden of this restructuring fell exclusively on the lower-middle and working classes, whose income and standard of living declined considerably.[13] The poverty rate in urban areas, which had been lowered to 30 percent in 1958–1959, increased to 35 percent in 1965–1970. Similarly, rural poverty went from 35 percent in 1958–1959 to 44 percent in 1965–1970.[14] These painful developments were particularly damaging for a regime whose hegemony depended in part on its populist achievements to maintain the backing of the middle classes, which had always been its key constituency.[15]

The economic disparities were also a reflection of the internal divisions in Egypt that the Nasserist state had been able to mask ideologically but had never been fully able to overcome. Even under Nasser, the country had remained socially fragmented. Professionals, including lawyers, engineers, doctors, and small business owners—who did not feel they had been given a share in the Nasserist revolution—had found in the Ikhwan an alternative through which they aimed to gain a greater voice in the affairs of the country. The economic downturn of the mid to late 1960s gave the Islamist organization an opportunity to expand its constituency, as it could now appeal to the lower and middle classes that had borne the brunt of the economic decline.

Nasser used the state's apparatus to disseminate his socialist ideology, which had allowed socialist unions and student groups to gain political currency. But the failure of Nasser's socialism—or, rather more accurately, the populist state capitalism that had been applied in practice—had left them divided among various leftist ideologies. These internal divisions within the Nasserist camp subsequently helped his successor, President Anwar Sadat, to co-opt the Islamists and successfully turn them against the vestiges of the Nasserist left. With the fragmentation of the left, Marxist intellectuals who had been co-opted by the Nasserist regime, including Lufti al-Khouli, stepped up their criticism of the state's policies. Although Khouli did not launch a direct attack on the Nasserist regime, he used *al-Tali'a*, a magazine that he had set up, to attack the "adverse elements" within Egyptian society who, in his opinion, fought against efforts to implement the revolution as envisioned in the national charter. These reactionary elements, he insisted, had infiltrated the revolutionary state and its apparatus, including the bureaucracy. Khouli called on individuals within Egyptian society, or the revolutionary fighters, as he labeled them, to oppose those elements and launch a phase of self-criticism to evaluate what went wrong. Although Khouli wanted to use *al-Tali'a* to inaugurate his "self-criticism" campaign, the 1967 war put a halt to his plan.

This binary division of Egyptian society into good and bad illustrates the internal divisions that the Nasserist state had tried to hide. It also points to a lack of internal class cohesion. As the regime faced more criticism, the meteoric growth of the bureaucracy had created a massive segment of the population that was dependent on the state and as such subservient to its vision. By failing to construct participatory democracy to anchor his social ideals, Nasser had created a new dependent middle class that did not develop a project of its own for itself and the country; Egyptians feared that opposition to the state or its policies would lead to their financial ruin. Finally, in the midst of internal tensions within the Nasserist state, the capitalists and industrialists from the old regime were biding their time, waiting for an opportunity to strike back. Therefore, in the wake of the June 1967 defeat, Egypt remained a fragmented society held together by a state that had imposed a collective vision on society.

Along with these economic worries at home, the Egyptian state's coffers were further depleted by the ill-fated military venture in North Yemen from 1962 till 1967. Following the toppling of Imam Muhammad al-Badr in a republican military coup in 1962, Nasser immediately dispatched a battalion of Special Forces to support the Yemeni officers who took over in Sanaa. What began as a token commitment of troops a few days after the ouster of the imam turned into a military intervention costly in blood and treasure, with 55,000 Egyptians bogged down in a bloody and intractable guerrilla war which came to be known as "Egypt's Vietnam."

The war in Yemen provided Nasser with an opportunity to establish a foothold on the Arabian Peninsula, a step towards effecting regime change in Saudi Arabia, just across Yemen's northern border, whose conservative rulers had long been a thorn in his side. Yemen was also strategically important for Egypt because it would offer the means of blockading oil supplies to Israel through the Bab al-Mandab Strait, a tactic which would be successfully employed in the 1973 Arab-Israeli war.[16] Nevertheless, these wished-for strategic interests had been framed into an ideological discourse, which distorted the lens through which Egyptian decision makers saw Yemen. According to Sami Sharaf, Nasser's powerful chief of staff, Egypt's position in Yemen "had been part of a continuous battle between the Arab national movement and the world hegemons [regional and global powers]."[17]

The Yemen war served only to sap the strength of the Egyptian state because it evolved into a proxy conflict pitting Nasser against powerful regional and global forces, including Saudi Arabia and its superpower patron, the United States. The Saudis were disturbed by the Yemeni army officers' declared desire to spread their republican revolution to neighboring Saudi Arabia.[18] Wary of the new threat building across their southern border, in 1963 the Saudis spent $15 million to train and arm royalist tribes, hire hundreds of European mercenaries, and establish their own radio station.[19] Remnants of the imam's army also had elements of the Saudi National Guard fighting alongside it.[20] The Americans, for their part, had an economic stake in the conflict, which went beyond their commitment to backing the Saudi monarchy. The Arabian-American Oil Company, more commonly known as Aramco, had built on its foundation in Saudi Arabia to sign a concession with the imam in 1950 which provided for exploration for oil and other natural resources in Yemen.[21] The imam had also granted a lucrative oil exploration concession to another American company, the Yemen Development Cooperation of Washington.[22] Egypt's involvement in the war, and the fact that it undermined U.S. oil interests in Yemen, put Nasser at loggerheads with President Lyndon Johnson and forced him to rely more on the USSR for weapons and aid.[23] Mohamed Heikal even claimed that Israel also took part in the Yemen conflict, making a de facto alliance with Yemeni royalist and Saudi forces.[24] Furthermore, Nasser's announcement in April 1965 that Egypt would support the revolutionary movement in Southern Yemen until the end of the British occupation enflamed tensions with London and internationalized the conflict further.[25]

Egyptian military intervention in Yemen was catastrophic.[26] In addition to depleting the resources of the Egyptian state in the run-up to the 1967 showdown with Israel, it was a hard blow to the prestige of Nasser and the Egyptian military. Although the Egyptian army confronted an array of powerful forces operating behind the scene, it did not distinguish itself on the battlefield. As Anthony Nutting noted, much of the political damage exacted on the Nasserist state by the Yemen war lay in "the shaming evidence that it revealed of the ineptitude and ineffectiveness of tens of thousands of Egyptian troops against a relatively small number of guerrilla tribesmen."[27]

In this fraught context, Nasser lashed out angrily when his intelligence services within Egypt accidentally discovered Qutb's al-Tanzim al-Sirri in 1965. He feared that, far from being weakened, the Ikhwan had been conspiring to unseat him. Nasser felt betrayed by this conspiracy. He told a group of Arab students in Moscow in August 1965 that the Ikhwan's revolt against him came in spite of the fact that "we had lifted martial laws one year ago, had liquidated prison camps, and had issued instructions for the [detainees] to return to their jobs."[28] Faced with this perceived threat, Nasser had recourse to the state's coercive powers. Some members of Parliament demanded harsher punishments, to hit "with an iron hand" these elements that "seek to destroy and corrupt."[29] Nasser even established a new body, the Military Criminal Investigation Office, tasked with investigating the "conspiracy." He put one of his confidants, Shams Badran, in charge of this body and kept a close watch on the progress of the investigation. Amid intense turf warfare, his security services outbid one another,[30] in an attempt to annihilate the Ikhwan and to prove their bureaucratic worthiness. Thus behind the Nasserist state's constructed unitary vision, rival centers of power had emerged. These internal divisions and rivalries within the state were a direct consequence of the absence of a clear road map for the development of the Nasserist state. Nasser's decision to send Qutb to the gallows reflected a real anxiety about the threat that the Islamists represented to his rule at a moment of gathering storms both at home and regionally. It also exposed a failure to realize that his state and the Islamist organization were undergoing similar processes of internal fragmentation. Qutb's al-Tanzim was a product of the inability of the Ikhwan leadership to deal with the various factional and ideological cleavages within the organization. In the second wave of repression against the Ikhwan, Nasser's security services took matters into their own hands by clamping down on arrested Ikhwan members, exposing the failure of the state leadership to control its own security apparatus. In a way, both the state and the Ikhwan had created a monster.

The 1967 Defeat and the Morning After

The earthquake of the 1967 defeat was thus all the more damaging insofar as it came at a moment when the Nasserist state was already reeling. In its wake, a certain number of Arab nationalists continued to stand by Nasser, often suggesting that what had occurred in the conflict with Israel amounted to a betrayal rather than a defeat. In a book published a few months after the war, Amin al-Nafouri, a Syrian army commander and politician, asserted that Nasser was not supported by "sufficient pan-Arab solidarity, which is the first condition for winning a confrontation against Israel."[31] Dedicating his book to the "spirit of the glorious hero and the martyr of Palestine Gamal Abdel Nasser," Mohamed Heikal, a close confidant of Nasser, blamed the defeat on a conspiracy by the United States and Saudi Arabia against Nasser in the Yemen war. The United States had intervened in the Yemen conflict, providing the Saudi government with financial and military aid, in order to weaken the Egyptian military, the only force in the region capable of seriously threatening Israel, Heikal asserted.[32] Ahmad al-Shuqayri, the first head of the Palestine Liberation Organization (PLO), also argued that Nasser had been viciously betrayed by treacherous Arab rulers who stabbed him in the back. Shuqayri accused Saudi King Faisal of hypocrisy for calling for jihad during the 1967 war, while failing to commit troops to the fight.[33]

Nonetheless, the 1967 defeat inflicted a crippling blow on the Nasserist state. "Defeat goes deeper into the human soul than victory," wrote Albert Hourani, the preeminent historian of the modern

Middle East, in his *History of the Arab Peoples*: "To be in someone else's power is a conscious experience which induces doubts about the ordering of the universe."[34] Israel's crushing victory over the Arabs in 1967 was widely regarded as a kind of "moral judgment."[35]

The defeat was painfully personalized and internalized by leading Arab intellectuals, critics, and prominent novelists like Naguib Mahfouz, winner of the 1988 Nobel Prize for Literature, one of the few contemporaries who subtly criticized the Nasser regime at the height of its power.[36] The rupture and psychological trauma that Mahfouz and his generation experienced stemmed from the gravity and totality of the defeat amid a widely held misperception that the Arabs had finally reached a promising historic moment, one of empowerment and renewal. As a cultural critic, George Tarabishi, notes, the 1967 defeat shocked the Arab imagination because there had existed among Arabs a common tendency to overestimate their strength and power and to underestimate that of their enemy.[37] Nourished on illusions of grandeur and an exaggerated sense of self-importance, Arab leaders banished the idea of military defeat from their thinking and planning, promising citizens glorious victories over enemies.

In charged, painful reflections, Tawfiq al-Hakim, a leading dramatist and critic whose earlier writing had influenced Nasser and the "formation of his nationalism,"[38] notes that "the nightmare of the defeat" was a rude awakening from a sweet dream. When the war broke out on June 5, Hakim describes a festive mood on the streets of Cairo where the ruling party, the Arab Socialist Union, had put up signs displaying such victory slogans such as "On to Tel Aviv ..."

It is worth citing Hakim at length—because of his intellectual stature, as well as his harsh criticism of Nasser, which triggered a storm of protests—in order to give the reader a glimpse of the public mood in Egypt and the Arab world on the morning of the outbreak of hostilities:

> The whole atmosphere around us almost convinced us that the entry of our armies into Tel Aviv would not take longer than nine

o'clock in the evening of the same day, June 5, 1967. ... The next few days passed and our forces were in a continuous retreat which resembled a rout.[39]

... It was impossible, intellectually or logically, easily to believe that our armies could be routed in a few days. Years had passed during which the regime emphasized the army's prowess and showed us, whenever there was a revolutionary celebration, military parades which included the newest models of tanks. During those parades we saw the rockets called al-Qahir and al-Zafir and regiments called al-Sa'iqah, which ran snarling a frightening roar; we saw troops who dropped down from the heights, hurdled over walls, and who literally tore up and ate snakes ... We had also heard in speeches about the power of our aircraft which had no equal in the Middle East.[40]

... I sat in front of the television open mouthed like a moron listening to the collapse of revolutionary Egypt—a process which was complete in a few hours. But the drone continued in the accustomed way all around me: patriotic anthems, the songs of singers and songstresses, and company banners: victory, victory, victory, this Victory Company, that Victory Company, Victory Automobile, Victory Manufacture, Victory Store—everything victory on victory on victory. ... But Egypt hardly reasoned and was unconscious of the fact that she had become a laughing-stock through these words and descriptions.[41]

In his controversial testimony, *'Awdat al-wa'i* (The return of consciousness), Hakim paints a grim portrait of political life in Egypt during the 1950s and 1960s when he and other intellectuals lost consciousness and blindly followed the new mahdi or messiah, Nasser, "idolized by people."[42] Hakim said he was reluctant to call Nasser a "true politician" since he "had more of the nature of a dreamy, emotional, artistic writer."[43] Hakim argued that Nasser "stripped us throughout the years of every independent thought and of every strong personality other than his own."[44] According to this respected public intellectual, Nasser's adoption of authoritarianism and Arab nationalism brought ruin to his beloved Egypt: "Verily, the idea of leadership of the Arab world is what has ruined us all and what possessed the thought of 'Abd al-Nasir and made of him a destructive force—destructive of himself, of Egypt, and of the Arabs."[45] Hakim lays the blame squarely at the feet of the Nasserist revolution for the "loss of consciousness of Egypt" through the glitter of fairy tales and false hopes.[46]

Regardless if one agrees with Hakim's damning indictment of Nasser, whom he calls "the absolute ruler," the substance of his critique, if not the tone, was echoed by Egyptian and Arab intellectuals and writers across a broad ideological spectrum. This was particularly the case among ardent and radical supporters of Arab unity and pan-Arabism as well as Marxists. For example, although Khouli had criticized the Nasserist state before the Six-Day War, he saw its tragic outcome as the result of its deviation from a revolutionary path. He blamed the social groups in power for their failure to faithfully implement the social policy of the National Charter and, most importantly, for their unwillingness to share power with the people. In addition to Khouli, the intelligentsia at large poured scorn on the military rulers who promised salvation but delivered defeat and called for a new revolution to liberate Arabs from backwardness, patriarchy, and authoritarianism. In their eyes, the war's shocking denouement was a referendum on Nasser's policies and practices.

In the poem "Hawamish daftar al-naksa" (Footnotes in setback's notebook), memorized by millions of agonizing Arabs and secretly copied and circulated in Egypt after censors refused to allow its publication, Nizar Qabbani, a popular poet who backed Nasser, proclaimed the death of the Arab order and cried for revolutionary change:[47]

1
The old word is dead.
The old books are dead.
Our speech with holes like worn-out shoes is dead.
Dead is the mind that led to defeat.

7
In short
We wear the cape of civilization
But our souls live in the stone age.

12
Our enemies did not cross our borders
They crept through our weaknesses like ants.

14
We spend our days practicing witchcraft,
Playing chess and sleeping.
Are we "the Nation by which God blessed mankind"?

17
If I knew I'd come to no harm,
And could see the Sultan,
This is what I would say:
"Sultan,
When I came close to your walls
and talked about my pains,
Your soldiers beat me with their boots,
Forced me to eat my shoes,
Sultan,
You lost two wars,
Sultan,
Half of our people are without tongues,
What's the use of a people without tongues?
Half of our people
Are trapped like ants and rats
Between walls."
If I knew I'd come to no harm
I'd tell him:
"You lost two wars
You lost touch with children."

18
If we hadn't buried our unity
If we hadn't ripped its young body with bayonets
If it had stayed in our eyes
The dogs wouldn't have savaged our flesh

20
Arab children,
You will break our chains,
Kill the opium in our heads,
Kill the illusions.
Arab children,
Don't read our suffocated generation,
We are a hopeless case.
We are as worthless as a watermelon rind.
Don't read about us,
Don't ape us,
Don't accept our ideas,
We are a nation of crooks and jugglers.
Arab children
Spring rain,
Corn ears of the future,
You are the generation
That will overcome defeat.[48]

Qabbani questions the very foundation of Arab state, society, and even culture. For him, the 1967 rout, like the 1948 defeat, exposed the dismal failure of the Arab political system and showed its backwardness and oppressiveness. Labeling Nasser another "sultan," not unlike his predecessors who had lost the 1948 Palestine war, Qabbani calls on a new generation of Arab children, not tainted or corrupted by power, to smash the existing order and overcome defeat.

The significance of Qabbani's critique is that it came from within the constituency of the Nasserist pan-Arab nationalist elite. Although Qabbani was not actively political, he was a vocal advocate of Arab nationalism and unity. Far from being an enemy of Nasser, Qabbani had publicly supported the Egyptian revolution and celebrated its achievements, particularly its political triumphs in the 1956 Suez crisis and the 1958 union between Egypt and Syria. He acknowledged that he was embittered by the 1967 defeat:

> My grieved country,
> In a flash
> You changed me from a poet who wrote love poems
> To a poet who writes with a knife[49]

Qabbani was the rule, not the exception, among opinion makers and intellectuals who had backed Nasser's Arab nationalist vision. The dominant narrative is that the 1967 defeat was catastrophic, in the words of a nationalist Bahraini writer, Mohammed Jaber al-Ansari, because it has left deep scars on the psychology of Arabs: the defeat was first and foremost "existential," or as Ansari aptly put it, "it was the mother of all defeats."[50]

According to Ansari, on multiple levels the Arabs still have not recovered from the effects of the defeat; their lands are still occupied, their politics and society penetrated by the great powers, and they seem unable to overcome a mind-set of fatalism and impotency. Similar to the loss in the 1948 Palestine war, the 1967 defeat was a turning point that further impeded institutional development in Arab countries and prematurely blocked their quest to achieve genuine self-reliance, independence, and empowerment. That trauma, the unrealized promise, the shattered dreams, still haunts the Arab imagination.[51]

Some zealous Nasserists and pan-Arab nationalists downplayed the significance of the defeat. In his book, *Min al-naksa ila al-thawra* (From setback to revolution), Nadim Bitar, a pan-Arab nationalist scholar-advocate, contended that what had happened in the 1967 war was only a setback, and that despite the pain it caused, "We welcome the *naksa*, and its great challenges." The designation of the outcome of the conflict as a mere setback, or *naksa*, rather than an outright defeat, was adopted in official circles in Egypt and neighboring Arab states. However, it proved to be a difficult sell for skeptical Arabs. In particular, as time progressed and the consequences of defeat persisted, Nasser's declared commitment to "eradicating the consequences of aggression" no longer resonated as strongly as it did initially.

A consensus has emerged among Arabs that in 1967 their society, not just their military, was defeated and that the catastrophe exposed its civilizational and scientific backwardness. The well-known Egyptian writer Ahmed Baha' al-Din argued that the Israeli challenge is more civilizational than military and that the defeat reflected a failure to modernize Arab societies.[52] Therefore, it is essential, as the progressive intellectual Yasin al-Hafiz argued, to situate the defeat within a broader context. In his book *Al-hazima wa al-idiulugiyya al-mahzuma* (The defeat and the defeated ideology), Hafiz bluntly asserted that the 1967 war dealt a devastating blow not just to the Egyptian military but more fundamentally to the pan-Arab nationalist ideology that undergirded the Nasser regime.[53]

Like Hafiz, novelist Tawfiq al-Hakim argued that the political system that emerged out of the 1952 revolution lost its equilibrium after the 1967 defeat, leading to its subsequent collapse. By shaking the ideology of the "dictatorial" regime to its very foundation, the defeat paved the way for the centrifugal forces which would so swiftly dismantle the pan-Arab nationalist edifice in the wake of Nasser's death three years later.

Arab historian Constantine Zurayk, who in the early 1950s published *Ma'na al-nakba* (The meaning of the disaster), a book dissecting the causes behind the loss of Palestine in 1948, revisited the theme of disaster in another book written almost two decades later. Zurayk identified two reasons for the 1967 catastrophe that had befallen the Arabs: scientific underdevelopment and a weak spirit of *asabiyya* or group solidarity. Israel crushed the Arab armies because it was more advanced scientifically and technologically. The Arabs also lost the struggle because they lacked clarity of purpose, which he attributed to divisiveness and fragmentation into warring "nationalist," "socialist," and "reactionary" camps. Zurayk spent a lifetime calling for a transformation of Arab societies along rational and scientific lines, shedding mythology, conspiracy, emotionalism, and illusion. In his view, the real challenge facing the Arabs is *ma'rakat al-hadara*, or the battle of civilization.[54]

Similarly, Moroccan historian Abdallah Laroui views the Six-Day War as a watershed marking the end of an important epoch in Arab history. According to Laroui, pan-Arabism had been a response to the colonial legacy, an ambitious effort to free the Arab world from the clutches of dependency and to achieve real independence. That new historical phase in Arab politics had faced its "Waterloo" during the Six-Day War,[55] exacerbating what Laroui believes was a structural crisis that has yet to be resolved.[56]

According to Laroui, what was needed to overcome the crisis in Arab thought was genuine historical understanding and a willingness to transcend the past, to take what was important from it by "radical criticism of culture, language, and tradition" and to utilize it in the forging of a new future. This process of critical understanding must be guided by the living thought of the age, particularly Marxism if correctly understood, whereby the past is instilled and incorporated into a new system of thought and action.[57] In a similar vein, scholars such as Hisham Sharabi took the defeat as an occasion of soul-searching for new values to replace Arab psychosocial ills.[58] Some of these include family authoritarianism, discrimination against women, and "the slavery of a dominant mode of thinking."[59] Sharabi, an Arab-American academic, argued that obsession with the Arab and Islamic *turath* (heritage) is a symptom of an "inferiority complex" and a self-defense mechanism against the civilized West.[60]

Other Marxists, like the Syrian philosopher Sadiq Jalal al-'Azm and the Egyptian economist Samir Amin, attributed the 1967 defeat to the religious structure of traditional Arab society and the crisis of the modern nation-state. The postcolonial state, they argued, had not settled vital questions of Arab unity and foreign policy, the class nature of the regime, and the corresponding development strategy;

the post-independence state perpetuated traditionalism and backwardness, merely wrapping them in a modernist garb. Unlike Laroui, 'Azm and Amin were not concerned with reconciling past and present or with bridging the divide between *turath* (heritage) and modernity. Rather, 'Azm stressed that the solution to the Arab predicament lies in authentic scientific Marxism and the total rejection of religious thought. Borrowing from Western thinkers like Friedrich Nietzsche and Bertrand Russell, 'Azm contends that attempts to "reconcile" religion and science are doomed, calling such attempts "naive intellectual acrobatics."[61] The Syrian philosopher accused the Arab liberation movement of deliberately obstructing intellectual enlightenment and of sticking to a falsified and medieval transcendental religious *turath* (heritage).[62] Similarly, Amin decried the inherent incapacity of the petit bourgeois nationalist movement of the Nasserist variety to carry out an authentic socialist revolution. Both writers pinned the blame indirectly on Nasser's haphazard policies and his unwillingness to cut the umbilical cord from the referential framework of the past and his petit bourgeois class.[63]

Although not completely agreeing with the Marxist critique of traditional Arab society, Syrian writer Burhan Ghalyoun zeroed in on the crisis of the modern nation-state, particularly the tiny power elite that had remained aloof from the Arab masses. In contrast to the journey of its Western counterpart, which emerged as a means of freeing knowledge and reason from the domination of an elitist and obstructionist theocracy, the Arab secular modernizing elite had been given a privileged position by the state; this elite had affirmed and justified the existing undemocratic and unfair system, "either in the name of progress or the logic of history, but always against the freedom of the ordinary individual."[64]

Ironically, immediately after the Six-Day War, Nasser himself joined this deluge of self-criticism and arrived at conclusions similar to those of many of these thinkers. In a stormy session of the Supreme Executive Committee of the Arab Socialist Union (ASU), its highest decision-making body, which lasted for two nights in early August 1967, Nasser frankly admitted that the war had been disastrous and that it had exposed the failure of the country's closed single-party system. He reminded his colleagues of what citizens were saying in private: "that we are devouring one another and that the system is self-destructing." Change or die, Nasser warned his five shaken council members. He lectured them about how "the state broke down into several power centers: Abdel Hakim's power center, the power center of Zakaria [Mohieddin], al-Sadat's power center, Ali Sabri's power center, and so on."[65] To weather the 1967 defeat storm, Nasser had no qualms about employing religion as a tool to legitimize and mobilize. For example, after the defeat Nasser ordered the appointment of an imam for every unit in the army,[66] and the press, government-controlled, gave space and voice to religiosity and myth such as the cited appearance to Egyptians of the Virgin Mary in a Cairo church in 1968.[67] Critic Ghalyoun pointed out that the rise of political Islam was a by-product of "religious maneuvering," or using religion for political purposes, in which the authorities had participated.[68]

Nevertheless, there is consensus among Egyptian and Arab critics that religion was not a strategic choice for Nasser throughout his presidency. Ansari said that Nasser had always been a pragmatist, preferring a synthesis of different ideological shades, such as materialism, socialism, and Islam.[69] For example, Nasser dismissed claims that attributed the 1967 defeat to a "religious vacuum."[70] As discussed in chapter 4, Nasser used religion to neutralize the country's most important religious institution, al-Azhar, and place the *'ulama* under his control. The nationalization of this key religious institution allowed Nasser to disseminate the state's vision of Islam in an attempt to counteract the Muslim Brotherhood and regional rivals like Saudi Arabia as well. The Nasserist state framed Islam as a religion that was open to progress and that could be included within its project of a new Egyptian modernity; it posited its religious vision in opposition to the "reactionary" model of the Saudis and the Ikhwan, which called for a return to the Islam that had been practiced in the past. Nasser's use of Islam was portrayed more as a cultural trait of the Arabs than as a powerful tool of coercion.

The Transformation?

There is no doubt that the 1967 defeat was a transformational development in regional politics, one that undermined the legitimacy and authority of Nasser's Arab socialism and Arab nationalism. In the eyes of Arabs, the crushing defeat discredited the radical tenets of the thesis of "state and revolution," which had been enunciated by Egyptian leaders at the height of the country's "sacred march" in 1961:

> Egypt as a state and as a revolution. ... If as a state Egypt recognizes boundaries in its dealings with governments, Egypt as a revolution should never hesitate to halt before these boundaries but should carry its message beyond the borders to the people in order to initiate its revolutionary mission.[71]

Egypt's dual role, as a state and as revolution, was no longer tenable after the 1967 defeat. One of the major consequences of the Six-Day War was that Nasser had little choice but to relinquish Egypt's role as a revolutionary vanguard and concentrate on rebuilding his broken army. The survival of the state took priority over Nasser's desire to spread revolution to neighboring Arab countries and topple reactionary rival regimes. As Middle East scholar Adeed Dawisha noted, "The radicals of the 1950s, mainly young modernizing national military officers who embodied the aspirations of the Arab nationalist generation, miserably failed to deliver on that most central of Arab nationalist concerns, the Palestine issue."[72]

This new reality could not have been clearer in the Arab Summit held in Khartoum, Sudan, on August 29, 1967, just a few weeks after the 1967 defeat. The summit of Arab heads of state reached an agreement which saw Egypt focus on rebuilding its army and putting its own house in order, with Saudi Arabia coming to Nasser's financial rescue. The agreement in Khartoum was an explicit acknowledgment of Nasser's retrenchment from the Arab arena and the ascendancy of the logic of the state over that of the revolution. The 1967 defeat resuscitated the primacy of the state system or territorial nationalism. The Arab summit also presaged the 1973 oil crisis by calling on the oil-producing Gulf countries to leverage their petroleum resources vis-à-vis oil consumers, particularly Western governments, to influence the outcome of any future war. Ahmad al-Shuqayri, the first chairman of the PLO, opined that "the Arabs' oil defeated the Arabs," referring to what essentially amounted to Nasser's surrender in the decade-old rivalry between Egypt and the Gulf monarchies and his acceptance of financial dependency on Saudi Arabia.[73] After a meeting with King Faisal, Nasser agreed to withdraw Egyptian troops from war-torn Yemen, while the Saudi ruler promised to stop military aid to the royalists.[74] Abdel Rahman al-Iryani, who served as the president of Yemen from 1967 until 1974, convincingly argued that the Saudis had basically emerged victorious in Yemen since they knew that the Yemeni royalists had enough arms to continue fighting for years without their support.[75]

Nasser's decision to desist from even paying lip service to Egypt's dual role as both state and revolution was a product of necessity, not choice. The destruction of the Egyptian armed forces tied his hands, leaving him with only painful, costly options. After the Khartoum summit, he became increasingly dependent on the economic support of conservative oil-producing states. Just as importantly, the defeat compromised Nasser's revolutionary appeal among supporters and battered his reputation as the leader who would bring deliverance and salvation. The Arab mood darkened, and a sense of uncertainty, doubt, and questioning of authority set in. This disillusionment existed on both the public and the official level, as reflected in the testimony of Nasser's confidant Abdel Latif al-Baghdadi, who met the president on the day of the defeat:

> We felt it was a dream! A nightmare! Can our air forces and ground forces be destroyed in one day? Could not this magnificent power stand thirty-six hours [of fighting]? We went back with our memories to what was happening in the army and the style of leadership ... This is the end of such a regime and of Nasser's gambling with the future of the whole nation in return for a personal glory of himself. This is the end; the end of his injustice.[76]

As Malcolm Kerr noted, Nasser's popularity and moral standing among Arabs had rested on twin pillars: the liberation of Palestine from the Zionist usurpers (unification of the Arab lands) and the liberation of the Arab world from reactionary rulers and their imperialist masters. Whether Nasser had been actually committed to the liberation of Palestine and the unification of Arab lands, he nourished such an image, one that resonated with Arabs from all walks of life:

> Still, ironically enough, it was reputation that mattered in politics; and the fact was that for many Arabs after 1967 Nasir, while still basically respected, was no longer altogether relevant. Whatever miracles he had worked in the past, he had none left for the future. All he could now offer the Arabs was another military defeat, or else a disguised diplomatic surrender. If anyone held the promise of miracles in his hand—and the Arab public lived as always in the hope, if not the expectation, of miracles—it was the Palestinian guerrilla.[77]

With Nasser's "Arab revolution" having run out of steam, Palestinian guerrillas emerged as a new force to carry the revolutionary torch forward. For a fleeting moment, these non-state actors filled the vacuum left by Nasser's discredited elite and captured the Arab imagination. Initially untainted by official ties and power, Palestinian resistance fighters pledged to undo the defeat and recover lost Arab lands and reputation. A critical segment of the Arab nationalist movement abandoned Nasserism, now widely seen as a "petit bourgeois" trend which "had been destined to fail," and espoused Marxist-Leninist principles instead.[78]

It is worth stressing that this wave of self-doubt in the wake of the Six-Day War came predominantly from nationalist, Marxist, and secular quarters, not from figures claiming religious authority or those with an Islamist orientation. After the defeat, many members of the Munazzamat al-Shabab al-Ishtiraki [the Organization of Socialist Youth], the main state-run representative body for students, migrated from Nasserism to Marxism.[79] Even Nasser's own domestic and foreign policy moved in some ways further to the left, uneasily combining a gradual process of economic liberalization in the domestic sphere with an increasing reliance on the Soviet camp.[80] Nasser hoped that the Russians would supply sufficient offensive weapons and expertise to allow Egypt to recover its lost territory from Israel in the future.

Initially, only a very few critics explained the 1967 defeat in religious terms. For example, in his book, *A'midat al-nakba* (The pillars of the disaster), Salah al-Din al-Munajid argued that the Arabs had been defeated because they had "forfeited their faith in God, so He gave up on them."[81] But his was a lone voice in a chorus dominated by pan-Arab nationalists, liberals, and leftists. What accounts for the paucity of the religious trend in the contemporary critiques of the 1967 war, and the dominance of nationalist and secularist writers? In light of this, how does one then explain the religious revival that swept Arab and Muslim lands from the 1970s, and the rise of radically politicized religious groups and movements? This is not merely an academic exercise but is essential to deciphering the causes and variables behind the transformation of Arab politics and the surge of political Islam during the last four decades. One of my key arguments is that there is no direct, straightforward link between the Arab defeat in the 1967 war and the Islamic revival of the 1970s. Notwithstanding the significance of the Arab defeat and its repercussions, there is much more to the rise of political Islam led by the Ikhwan than a single causal event.

Contrary to received wisdom, in the aftermath of the Six-Day War, Islamists were nowhere to be heard or seen in Egypt except in their natural pasture, Saudi Arabia and the Gulf, as well as in Iraq, Syria, Jordan, and beyond. From 1954 onwards Nasser had brutally suppressed the Ikhwan, the most powerfully organized religious and social movement in the Arab world. For almost two decades, the rank and file of this key Islamist movement had wasted away in Egyptian prisons. Furthermore, although the Nasserist state allowed a limited space for nationalists and socialists to vent their grievances after the Six-Day War, it did not tolerate Islamists or their supporters linking the defeat to a perceived abandonment of religion.

However, Nasser's success in marginalizing and weakening the Ikhwan had in part relied on his ability to invoke an appealing ideology which took the wind out of their sails. Since the mid-1950s, he had advanced an ideological narrative stressing dignity, social justice, national independence, economic development, Arab solidarity, and resistance to foreign domination, particularly in Palestine, which appealed to millions of Arabs and Muslims. As Adeed Dawisha put it, it was the general acceptance of this narrative and ideology that allowed Egypt and its president to carry out the country's radical policies and to do so with popular approval:

> Nasser's fiery radicalism fed the anti-colonialist and anti-imperialist orientation of the people. The coincidence of the two phenomena produced perhaps the only true radical mass movement of contemporary Arab history.[82]

This "coincidence" enabled Nasserism, along with similar nationalist ideologies like Baathism, to find "in the hearts and minds of Arabs of that period fertile ground for penetration and growth."[83] Politically and operationally, pan-Arab nationalism climbed on the shoulders of the man on the horseback, particularly Nasser, and thus gained greater public traction and momentum. If Nasser had not adopted Arab nationalism as the ideology of the Egyptian state, it would neither have turned into a rallying cry for the Arab populations nor eclipsed and cast a shadow over political Islamists like the Ikhwan. If the state was so crucial in the ascendance of Arab nationalism, its voluntary withdrawal from that role under Sadat during the 1970s deprived that ideology of the vital means of public support. But by 1970 Arab nationalism had become a mass movement, a greater social force, beyond Nasser and the Egyptian state. Some, like Nafouri and Mohamed Heikal, sought to blame the defeat on actors other than Nasser or on factors other than any inherent weakness in his political project. Some writers even contended that the 1967 defeat consolidated the position of Arab nationalism and Nasser. Gamal al-Baramawy claimed that "Israel had not been able to realize the target behind its aggression; therefore pan-Arabism had become an indubitable reality."[84] Less sentimental and emotional, Lutfi al-Khouli insisted that an ongoing commitment to Arab nationalism remained of utmost importance in the wake of the war, "since the aggression continues, the land occupation remains, plans of expansion are still being carried out and the goals of bringing down progressive Arab regimes have not yet been fully realized."[85]

It is often asked whether Nasser genuinely believed in Arab nationalism or was he simply using it to advance his country's national interests. The question presupposes a clear-cut distinction and a neat divide in Nasser's conduct, which in reality did not exist. For most of his tenure Nasser did not have to choose between the two. Some of Nasser's aides told me that he did not see any contradiction between promoting Arab nationalism and serving Egyptian primary interests. As made clear in chapter 3, first and foremost Nasser was an Egyptian nationalist and a patriot. But by the mid-1950s he had adopted Arab nationalism as a foundation of his regional and international relations, which allowed him to maximize his bargaining position with his Arab rivals and the great powers. While the Baathists advocated demolishing national borders and replacing them with a pan-Arab unitary state, Nasser called for Arab solidarity and Arab cooperation. The breakup of the United Arab Republic (UAR) reinforced his conviction that pan-Arab unity was not feasible till the social and political structures in Arab countries evolved in harmony with each other and reached a comparable level of development. Nasser did not even believe that Arab nationalism and religiosity were mutually exclusive, only that the latter could not serve as a framework for understanding and advancing national interests.[86] But an appropriate question that has received no analytical attention is the extent to which Arab nationalism was driven and fueled by Nasser.

The role of the Egyptian state, along with its charismatic leader, in promoting and popularizing Arab nationalism is critical to understanding and explaining the configuration of social and political forces in the Arab arena during the 1950s and 1960s. As the cultural capital of the Arab world and its center of political gravity, Nasser's

Egypt operationalized the doctrine of Arab nationalism and turned it into a power to be reckoned with. Since it was one of the most powerful weapons in his arsenal, Nasser deployed Arab nationalism to great effect against his domestic and Arab rivals and foreign adversaries.[87]

Pan-Arab intellectuals largely accepted the state's sponsorship of Arab nationalism, assuming that some form of an Arab "Bismarckian Prussia" was required for the achievement of unity. From Sati' al-Hosary to Nadim al-Bitar, pan-Arab intellectuals have consistently sung the praise of states that support unity projects.[88] Although Nasser's project failed, this did not diminish either the significance of his effort or the intensity of pan-Arab feelings, which he unleashed and which persisted after the 1967 defeat. As Fred Halliday has convincingly argued, "It was easy to say that Arab nationalism had later failed. But nationalism is partly a matter of sentiment and a shared sense of collective grievance; neither in August 1990 nor in the aftermath of March–April 2003 would it be said that these feelings had disappeared."[89] Halliday adds that these sentiments and grievances were absorbed within the "dominance of state interest in domestic and international politics." This dominance pushed forward certain ideologies and ensured that "political purpose rather than historical 'substratum' or cultural accuracy determined how these ideologies were formulated."[90]

But the patronage of the state and its sponsorship of Arab nationalism was a double-edged sword. The fortunes and prospects of this pan-Arab ideology became organically and inextricably tied to those of the Egyptian state. When the state and its leader, Nasser, were at the height of their prowess during the 1950s and 1960s, Arab nationalism seemed unstoppable—the wave of the future. In the aftermath of the defeat, Arab nationalism suffered a crippling setback. With Nasser's death in 1970, that ideology was at the mercy of the new ruler of the Egyptian state: Anwar al-Sadat.

By 1970, Arab nationalism had become a mass social movement that acquired its own momentum and had taken on a life of its own, beyond Nasser and Egypt. Nevertheless, the withdrawal of the support of Sadat and the Egyptian state had a crippling effect on Arab nationalism as a political project, though not as a popular sentiment—Arabism or pan-Arabism. Therefore, Arab writers like Ansari set 1970, the year that Nasser died and Sadat succeeded him, as the "benchmark" that heralded the rise of right-wing politics and Islamism in general.[91]

A qualification is in order. I do not imply that there was a void of Islamism before 1970s. The history of the Muslim Brotherhood and the competing visions within the that organization attest to the staying power of political Islam in Egypt. So too do the myriad groups that had, by then, been present in many parts of the Middle East, and had certainly since the 1950s been formulating what we now call an Islamist political agenda. Their continuing presence almost everywhere was certainly visible to many, including foreign diplomatic missions. So striking was this, in fact, that the U.S. National Security Council had a subcommittee on Islam from the mid-1950s; and British documents reveal the voluminous reporting on even the most inconsequential Islamic gathering for fear that it would play into emerging Cold War rivalries. In the 1950s and 1960s, however, Nasser succeeded in clipping the wings of the Islamist movement using not only coercion and domination but also an (attractive) competing vision and ideology. His two-pronged strategy silenced the Islamists and kept them in jail or underground. On its own, the Six-Day War did not bring about transformation in either internal Egyptian politics or internal Arab politics in general.

Conclusion

Nevertheless, the Six-Day War was a catalyst that changed the regional balance of power in favor of pro-American Middle Eastern allies like Israel, Saudi Arabia, and Iran. In the eyes of Egyptians and Arabs, the defeat undermined the authority of Nasser's pan-Arabist regime and temporarily empowered a new generation of non-state Palestinian actors who pledged to be the new standard-bearers and vanguard of the Arab revolution. Rhetorically and literally, Egypt could no longer afford to play a dual role as a state and as a revolution.

It reached a rapprochement with what Nasser had previously labeled the "reactionary" Arab regimes, and it surrendered its revolutionary function to the Palestinian *fedayin*, who, for a fleeting moment after the defeat, captured the Arab imagination.

On the intellectual, ideological, and sociological level, a soul-searching of what went wrong swept the Arab lands. Marx, God, and Kant were called to the rescue—to set things right. A common denominator in the torrent of self-criticism by the intelligentsia focused on the crisis of the modern nation-state, particularly the lack of institutions, and the backwardness of Arab societies and the hegemony of authoritarianism.

Ironically, most of the critiques were internal, part of the broader constituency of Nasser's pan-Arabist regime, not external or adversarial. The defeat undercut the confidence that Nasser's constituency had had in his regime, thus weakening the state and making it vulnerable to external attacks. Disillusioned with Nasserism and Nasser's Arab socialism, Arab nationalists joined Marxist-Leninist organizations.

Beyond that, it would be misleading to argue, as some writers do, that the Six-Day War marked the end of Arab nationalism and the onset of a new epoch, a new ideological framework driven by religious politics that has dominated Arab politics until today. We must be wary of single-factor explanations that ascribe causality to a specific event, regardless of how pivotal that event was. That warning applies to both the 1948 defeat and the 1967 defeat.

The 1948 defeat was the final nail in the coffin of the old regime because Egypt had been ripe for a revolution. The loss of Palestine and the defeat of the Egyptian army accelerated the erosion of the legitimacy and authority of the colonial-sponsored ruling elite. In the 1952 coup, it took fewer than a hundred junior officers to destroy the British-supported monarchy because its hegemony had already been shattered. The consequences of the 1967 defeat must be similarly contextualized. The coming to power of Sadat and his radical change of direction was transformative, particularly Sadat's use of the state to purge the country of Nasser's pan-Arab nationalism and substitute Islam as the public face of his regime. The role of the Egyptian state was pivotal in dismantling the Nasserist power structure and networks, and in marginalizing and weakening Nasser's ideology of Arab socialism. Soon, the Sadat administration also invested important resources in helping to empower religiously based groups, thus tipping the balance of social forces in favor of the Islamists.

After the Six-Day War, writers who wrote the obituaries of Arab nationalism and reported the Islamist resurgence did not fully consider the real drivers that brought about this sociological transformation. These included a concerted effort by the Sadat state, the 1973 October War, the petrodollar revolution, and an alliance between the Egyptian state and the Saudi monarchy.

Yet a counterfactual question is in order: Would not the received wisdom have been turned on its head had Nasser lived beyond 1970 to fight another battle or to resolve the Arab-Israeli conflict? Surely the course of contemporary Arab politics would not have been the same. If Nasser had survived and Sadat had not gained power, it is unlikely that the Ikhwan and other Islamists would have dominated the Middle Eastern landscape and replaced Arab nationalism as an all-powerful ideology. We must look at the role and functions of the Egyptian state before and after the 1967 war, first in advancing pan-Arab nationalism as its official doctrine and then in promoting an alternative ideological narrative based on religion. Time and again the state tipped the balance of power for and against competing social forces, a testament to the enduring hegemony of statism in the postcolonial Arab world.

Chapter 11

Sadat's Coup and the Islamist Revival

ISLAMISM DID NOT JUST burst onto the Arab scene after the exhaustion and weakening of the Nasserist state in 1967. It was not until the 1970s that religiously oriented activists or Islamists openly reappeared on the Arab horizon and began to flex their muscle.[1] The revival of political Islam and the Ikhwan took place after Nasser's death from a heart attack in 1970. The resurgence of the Islamists was aided by Nasser's successor, Anwar al-Sadat, who made a fundamental decision to wrap himself with religious garb and shed the Nasserist legacy. Like its ideological rival, Arab nationalism, political Islam was fueled in considerable part by state patronage and sponsorship.

To understand how the balance of social forces eventually tipped in favor of Islamism, one must also take into account a distinct set of developments which came after the 1967 war and were just as important in shifting political momentum from secular Arab nationalism to Islamism. These included the role played by Sadat in attacking his predecessor's inheritance and legacy. Sadat built his own legitimacy by reaching an informal alliance with Islamists and putting the power of the state in the service of a drive to bring about a sea change in Egypt's economy, politics, and society. Other important factors which energized the Islamists after the 1967 defeat included the increasing wealth and assertiveness of conservative Gulf countries, particularly Saudi Arabia. Millions of Egyptians and Arabs worked in the Gulf in the 1970s and 1980s and returned home not only with money and consumer habits but also with ultraconservative religious values. The petrodollar financed the publications of thousands of religious texts every year which favored a puritanical interpretation of the faith. An alliance of convenience between the Sadat regime and the Saudi monarchy played a key role in reshaping the sociological and ideological landscape of Arab societies. Egypt also felt the impact of the 1979 revolution in Iran, which established an Islamist system grounded in the principle of *wilayat al-faqih,* or the governance of the jurist.[2] Sadat's coming to power and his concerted effort to purge Egypt of Nasser's Arab socialism tipped the scale against Arab nationalism and socialism in favor of the politicization of religion.

Cleansing the Government of Nasserist Elements

From the outset of his rule, Sadat labored hard to cleanse from the Egyptian landscape the very ideology that had powered the revolution from the mid-1950s until 1970. When the Free Officers overthrew the monarchy, they, including Sadat himself, had consolidated their grip on the state by getting rid of the old regime's backers. Similarly, as Egypt's new president, Sadat systematically purged the government of Nasserist loyalists. In less than a year after gaining power, Sadat dismissed most of Nasser's trusted aides and lieutenants from various ministries and institutions and replaced them with his own men. In particular, he carried out a putsch against Nasser's all-powerful inner circle, leveling charges of conspiracy against such figures as Vice President Ali Sabri, General Mohamed Fawzi, and senior ministers and heads of security like Shaarawi Gomaa and chief of staff Sami Sharaf. In one strike in May 1971, Sadat wiped out most of the Nasserists and locked them away behind prison walls. He claimed that the conspiracy included an attempt to assassinate him in an ambush on May 13, 1970.[3] Before Sadat purged the Nasserists, he had held meetings with the armed forces and said, while Fawzi was sitting next to him, "I will not allow centers of power or struggle. If anyone does anything against Egypt I will mince him."[4] Sadat also asserted that his battle against these "centers of power" was intended to bring freedom to the population after years of suffering "from fear, lack of justice, malice, and humiliation and torture," an explicit indictment of his predecessor: Nasser.[5]

Sharaf, who had served as Nasser's powerful chief of staff, said that the moves made by Sadat at this stage amounted to an internal coup intended to wipe out the Nasserist legacy. "Sadat possessed an irrational fear of Nasser and wanted a clean break with the past. We had underestimated Sadat's blind ambition and the length to which he would go to rid Egypt of the Nasserist inheritance. He was willing to go to bed with the devil [the Islamists] to do so."[6] Sharaf is bitter because Sadat persecuted him along with other Nasser loyalists. "I was psychologically tortured and imprisoned for more than ten years in a tiny cell not bigger than two meters, freezing cold in the winter and punishing hot in the summer," Sharaf said angrily. "Imagine Sami Sharaf, who ruled the country at one point, thrown in a dirty and dark jail cell. Imagine how I felt."[7]

Another member of Nasser's inner circle, Mohamed Fayek, who also spent ten years in prison, said that Sadat not only distanced himself from his predecessor but also changed Egypt's internal and external policies. "Sadat's rule marked a rupture in the country's domestic and international affairs. He empowered the Ikhwan and the religious right in general and put all his eggs in America's basket," he said in an interview in his office in Misr al-Jadida. "Sadat had an inferiority complex where Nasser was concerned, and took extreme measures just to show that like Nasser he was also a great leader."[8]

Nasser's daughter Huda, who acted as his private secretary after the Six-Day War, also recalled that Sadat systematically dismantled the networks built by her father and subverted the political system. "Sadat engaged in character assassination of Nasser and allowed the Ikhwan to colonize Egyptian society," Huda, now an academic and activist, told me in one of two lengthy interviews in her flat in Zamalek, an upscale Cairo neighborhood. "Sadat sowed the seeds of religious extremism in Egypt and the Arab nation."[9] In his autobiography, *Al-bahth an al-dhat* (In search of identity), Sadat himself used strong language to indict the legacy of his predecessor. He pinned the blame squarely on Nasser for many of the ills faced by Egypt during his reign and afterwards as well. Sadat accused Nasser of being "preoccupied with the myth associated with his name ... a big myth claiming that he [Nasser] conquered two empires, France and Britain, in 1956 while ignoring the role of [U.S. president Dwight] Eisenhower in turning defeat into victory."[10]

Similarly, from the outset of his presidency Sadat attempted to qualitatively shift Egyptian regional and international relations in a different direction than Nasser's. He sought to cultivate close relations with the United States, by ridding Egypt of the Soviet military presence and moving from the socialist orbit to the American-dominated camp. According to minutes of Sadat's first meeting with U.S. secretary of state William Rogers, in early May of 1971, Rogers and his aides were surprised by Sadat's strong anti-Nasserism and his "Egypt first" approach to foreign policy; he showed little interest in the Palestinians or the Syrians, and focused exclusively on recovering the Sinai for Egypt.[11]

Ideological Reorientation

In September 1970, after Nasser's death and the internal purges carried out by his successor, Sadat radically changed the state's direction from the left to the right and instituted another top-down transformation. This move was formalized in October 1974, when Sadat announced his intention to restructure the country's economy. Moving away from Nasser's policy of state management of the economy, Sadat bet on both foreign and domestic investments and export-oriented industries to grow the economy. He initially aimed to use his *infitah* or "open door" policy to attain his political objectives and tackle the country's deepening economic crisis. However, in the end his plan laid out the foundation for a more consumer-oriented society which made it vulnerable to domestic and foreign interests and international trade fluctuations as well as foreign creditors and donors.

Wahid Abdel Majid, a liberal public intellectual, argues that instead of gradually reforming the Egyptian political system, Sadat delivered the country on a silver platter to "fat cats" and "men of money and religion." Sadat's economic liberalization or open door policy, Maghid told me in an interview in his flat in the upper-middle-class Cairo neighborhood of Dokki, was shallow and chaotic and unaccompanied by real institutional reforms. "This opened Egypt to all kinds of viruses that sapped its strength and made it an easy prey to capitalist and Islamist vultures." [12] He argued that "while Nasser blundered and overestimated Egypt's reach and power, Sadat committed unforgivable sins by taking the country from one extreme to another, causing Egypt to lose its equilibrium and plunge into decline." The country could not cope with two violent shocks in two decades; it needed time and space to adjust. "The cancer started with Sadat and spread throughout society's veins and institutions. With Mubarak putting Egypt in a freezer for decades, the rot has set in. State and society are teetering on the brink of collapse."[13]

In a similar vein, Mohamed al-Sayed Said, a former editor of *al-Badeel*, an online progressive newspaper, accused Sadat of mortgaging Egypt's future to a new breed of corrupt and parasitic businessmen, surrendering its leadership in the Arab world, and turning the country into a dependency of the United States. "Sadat transformed Egypt from a pivotal regional power to a declining power, though Mubarak reduced it to a contractor state."[14]

Re-Islamization of State and Society

Contrary to the dominant narrative in the West, Arab nationalism did not just disappear naturally into the sunset. There was no "end" to

Arab nationalism, as some writers have wrongly suggested.[15] Rather, the shift was gradual, and it was expedited by the Sadat regime, which systematically rehabilitated political Islam as a counterweight to Nasser's Arab nationalism and Arab socialism. Public surveys and polls conducted over the past decades in the Arab region clearly show this process of gradualism.[16] After Sadat had removed senior Nasserist officials from their positions, he turned his attention to society and the need to build a social base in order to consolidate his rule. Religious activists, a big constituency, were particularly suitable to Sadat's goal of distancing himself from Nasser and building his own legacy. Remarkably, the business elite pushed Sadat to pursue an open market policy and provided him with the patronage to tilt the balance of power in favor of the Islamists. In a state that can be best described as clientelist, businesses financed the first Islamist body formed in universities after Sadat's coming to power.[17] It offered students free tickets to go on pilgrimage to Saudi Arabia and staged other activities such as summer camps.[18] The state now openly promoted Islamic activism.

Transition from Arab Nationalism to Islamism

The gradual transition from Arab nationalism to Islamism was obvious if one traces Sadat's words and actions. Initially in speeches, Sadat made an effort to keep up appearances by praising Nasser and embracing Arab nationalism. In a major speech to the ASU after Nasser's death, Sadat said that Egyptians "belong to the Arab nation both historically and by common destiny" and also pledged that Egypt under his leadership would "serve as the vanguard of Arab nationalism." He called Nasser's principles and attitudes "an inexhaustible treasure for us all."[19] Immediately after his selection as president, Sadat also made a commitment in a speech before parliament to "travel the same road as that of Gamal Abdel Nasser" and to "keep intact the socialist gains."[20] Less than two years later, however, he fully distanced himself from the overbearing shadow of Nasser and carried out a palace coup against his successor's legacy.

After Sadat removed Nasser's confidants from their seats of power, he knew he needed to offer an appealing doctrine, an ideology, to serve as an alternative to Nasser's Arab nationalism and socialism. It is important to keep in mind that by the early 1970s, there existed no rival competitive ideologies that could fill the ideological and leadership vacuum left by the departure of Nasser and his inner circle. Since the mid-1950s, the rank and file of the Islamist movement had been either underground or in prison. The Nasserist state had partially dismantled the organizational infrastructure of the Ikhwan and appropriated its functions in society.

In interviews, top jailed leaders of the Ikhwan from the Nasserist era paint a dark portrait of a hellish existence, and hardly anyone says there was any ray of light at the end of the prison tunnels. More than fifteen years of incarceration and suppression left the Islamist organization broken and lifeless, with the exception of some Islamist dissidents in the diaspora. Some of Qutb's ardent disciples, who spent a decade in prison with him, told me that on the morning after the 1967 defeat it dawned on them that this could mean the beginning of the end of the Nasserist state. But they said they had no idea how and when this "end" might come about. One thing is clear: they did not and could not imagine that the winds of political fortune would blow their way and sweep away their cruel tormentors—the Arab nationalists. "None of us could foresee the consequences of Nasser's defeat in 1967 on Egypt's political future," said Ahmed Ra'if, who was imprisoned as part of Qutb's al-Tanzim al-Sirri in 1965. "Although the Ikhwan prisoners celebrated the humiliation of Nasser, they did not expect the Six-Day War to swiftly alter the balance of power inside Egypt."[21]

"The shameful 1967 defeat exposed the bankruptcy of Nasserism and secular nationalism," said Sayyid Eid, Qutb's confidant and soul mate inside and outside prison. "It was a divine punishment." However, when pressed on the question of whether he and other members of the Ikhwan viewed the defeat as the end of their ordeal and of Nasser's state as well, Eid and other incarcerated Islamists said they could not envision such an ambitious scenario because they had been out of circulation for two decades and had lost touch with their social base and constituency, not to mention society at large.[22]

"Remember that beginning in 1954 we [the Ikhwan] were subjected to several waves of oppression and were kept off balance and on the run till the first half of the 1970s," said Ahmed Abdel Majid, a senior lieutenant in Qutb's al-Tanzim al-Sirri. Abdel Majid was sentenced to death with his mentor, but Nasser commuted his sentence to life in prison. "The Nasser regime temporarily silenced the Islamist movement and terrorized its sympathizers into either submission or inaction. But in the deepest depth of our being, we believed that *iman* [faith] would triumph over *kufr* [apostasy in this context]."[23]

Mustafa Mashour, who spent almost a decade in prison and was subsequently elected supreme guide of the Muslim Brotherhood, acknowledged the hegemony of secular Arab nationalism and said he believed that Islam was ultimately bound to return to all Arab lands, including Egypt; it was a matter of time and God's will. However, when asked whether he perceived the 1967 defeat and Nasser's death as a catalyst for the revival of the Islamist movement and the Ikhwan from their prolonged political slumber, he replied, "Not really." He elaborated: "We were not in a position or a state of mind to envision such a comeback, although our faith in God and our Islamic mission never lessened or wavered despite the suffering and humiliation we endured at the hands of Nasser and his thugs."[24]

By 1970 the Egyptian state had almost succeeded in breaking the back of the Islamist movement and consolidating the dominance of relatively secular Arab nationalism. That was the context under which Sadat labored to purge Egypt of Nasser's legacy and remake it in his own image. He released hundreds of Ikhwan prisoners and allowed them to move freely, to organize themselves, and to publish and distribute their publications. During the first half of the 1970s, Sadat gave the broken Islamist movement a new lease on life.[25] Prominent figures released from prison in this period included Omar al-Telmessany, who had spent nearly two decades behind bars before his release in 1971. In 1974 Telmessany became the new supreme guide of the Ikhwan, securing a *bay'a* from the group.[26] Knowing his power over the holder of the highest position in the Ikhwan, in 1980 Sadat invited Telmessany to an *iftar* (the evening meal that breaks the fast each day of Ramadan) along with scholars from al-Azhar. Sadat was furious because *al-Da'wa* magazine, the mouthpiece of the Ikhwan, had savagely criticized him for his Camp David Peace Accords with Israel in the late 1970s. The president lectured Telmessany and gave him a stern warning: "Omar, I still allow *al-Da'wa* to be published without a license. This is against the law, and I turn a blind eye to that. But you went too far, and I can, if I like, apply the law and close this magazine."[27]

Other prominent Ikhwan members permitted to return to their activism in this period included Abbas al-Sissi, who was released in 1974 after having been jailed since 1965. Once out of prison, Sissi got involved in the elections of the Rashid Club, a social club in his hometown of that name in the Beheira governorate, an Ikhwan stronghold.[28] A slate supported by the Ikhwan won all the seats on the board of the club. Sissi also began a "*da'wa* campaign" in the club and outside it, including reprinting and distributing free copies of Ikhwan literature. Comparing and contrasting the conditions for Islamist activism under Nasser and Sadat, Sissi titled one of his books, *Min al-mazbaha illa sahat al-da'wa* (From the slaughterhouse to the horizons of *da'wa*).[29] In addition to social clubs like the Rashid Club, the Ikhwan dominated trade unions and NGOs as well. Unlike Nasser, who had banned all civil society groups, Sadat allowed NGOs and trade unions to work more freely.[30] Sometimes boasting a million members each, these unions offered an important platform to the Islamists as long as they respected red lines and limits set by the Sadat regime.

Visiting notorious Egyptian prisons, the "pious president" spoke solemnly about his opposition to the violation of human dignity of Egyptians and, before the hungry cameras, chipped away with a hammer at their thick walls. He pledged to shut them down and put an end to abuse and torture, implying a radical departure from his predecessor, Nasser. He neglected to remind his audience that he had been a loyal senior official who had done Nasser's bidding from the beginning of the revolution until the end.

Egypt's 1971 constitution also reflected this reorientation, with Article 2 stating that "the principles of Shari'a are the main source of legislation."[31] Political scientist Alieddin Helal called this step unprecedented because "Shari'a has never been mentioned in an Egyptian constitution before." Civil society groups criticized the article as exclusivist and discriminatory in a country where Christian Copts represent 10 percent of the population.[32] This article has survived for more than four decades, even after the January 25 Revolution, despite attempts by some secular groups to remove it from the new constitution,[33] a testament to the durability of the Sadat legacy on Egyptian life.

The State's Use of Islamists against the Nasserist Left

Although Nasser had used al-Azhar as a weapon in his fight against the Ikhwan and the "reactionary" Arab monarchies, Sadat co-opted Egyptian Islamist factions to dismantle Nasserist groups operating at the societal level. Sadat's officials targeted the universities where Arab nationalists and socialists held the upper hand in student unions. Under Nasser, students had only been allowed to organize or participate in activities under the umbrella of youth organizations fully controlled by Hay'at al-Tahrir, the state-run body put in charge following the dissolution of all political parties in 1953.[34] Student activities on campus were also closely observed by security staff who answered directly to the minister of interior.[35] Nonetheless, the period after the 1967 defeat witnessed a marked shift in student politics towards leftist alternatives to Nasserism. Leftist groups dominated university politics in the first half of the 1970s, which represented a challenge for Sadat, who sought to bolster religious activists as a counterweight.

Under Sadat, the state authorities actively supported religious students and cracked down hard on Nasserists and leftists. The struggle for political dominance in the universities was a microcosm of the greater struggle in society at large, in which the state took sides and tipped the balance of social forces in favor of religiously based activists. In his autobiography, *Al-din wa al-thawra fi misr* (Religion and revolution in Egypt), philosopher Hassan Hanafi, who was at that time a junior academic at Cairo University, recalls how the authorities built up religious groups and unleashed them against Nasserists and socialists. The so-called al-Jama'at al-Islamiyya (Islamic Group) imposed a reign of terror on universities under the watchful eyes of Sadat's security forces.[36]

Throughout the 1970s, the Sadat regime played a key role in empowering Islamic-oriented students on campuses and weakening their nationalist and leftist counterparts. A new generation of politically radicalized young religious activists was born, one that subsequently spread its subversive ideas outside the university walls to urban centers, Upper Egypt, and other Muslim lands.[37] In an apparently coordinated coup, Islamists took over the student unions, which would not have been possible if the state had remained neutral, according to Salah Hashim, a founder of al-Jama'at al-Islamiyya. "We were allowed to work without any harassment or detention. He [Sadat] did not even act when there were clashes, as long as they did not target him," Hashim revealed in an interview.[38] The new changes on campuses were very conspicuous, such as separating males from females in classes, including an interval for prayers, modifying curriculums, banning opposition lectures or events, and forbidding music concerts.[39] Scholars and religious activists alike point to Sadat as the one who had given the kiss of life to political Islam, and from then on Qutbian ideas took hold of the imagination of this generation.[40]

In interviews, most Islamists of the 1970s generation concede that Sadat allowed them to participate in the public space and used them as a counterweight to leftists and Nasserists. Montasser al-Zayat, a former member of the militant Islamic Group who was a college student in the 1970s and is now a leading Islamist attorney, acknowledged that the coming to power of Sadat marked a significant shift in the Islamists' fortune. "Sadat's rule was a golden moment for the Islamist movement. He permitted us to organize and recruit followers on campus and outside. We were a healthy generation because we were not persecuted and harassed like our predecessors in the 1950s and 1960s," he said.[41] Ibrahim Za'farani, an Islamist student in the 1970s and now an Ikhwan leader in Alexandria, echoed the point: "Our generation was normal and did not live in fear and underground. We had opportunities that previously our elders never dreamed of because of Sadat's positive approach to the Islamists."[42]

This reorientation from Nasser's Arab nationalism and socialism to Islamism was designed to consolidate Sadat's rule in two ways: first, by undermining his foes who claimed the mantle of Nasserism; and second, by spreading the values of patience and faith, at a time when there were mounting public calls to stage another war against Israel in retaliation for the 1967 defeat.[43] Those who were young religious activists in the 1970s note that from the outset of his rule, the Sadat team leaked reports about abuses committed by Nasser and attempted to discredit Sadat's charismatic predecessor. "These negative leaks opened our eyes to the abuses of the Nasserist era and we knew that Nasser was a dictator," said Seif Abdel Fattah, who is now a prominent Islamist-leaning academic. His verdict is that Sadat was instrumental in weakening the left and fueling the Islamist resurgence, he told me in one of several interviews in Cairo.[44] Hossam Tammam, an Egyptian specialist on the Ikhwan, argued how the Sadat authorities restricted the activities of socialists and leftists, while showing tolerance and encouragement toward religious activities of all colors.[45]

According to religious activists of the 1970s, Sadat also tried to co-opt them and turn them into his own men. "Sadat thought he could rely on us because in his eyes we owed our existence to him and we would not dare challenge his regime and rise up against him; though when we subsequently discovered his lies, we killed him," recalled the Islamist attorney Zayat during a long conversation in his spacious office in Cairo.[46] Seif Abdel Fattah offered a more nuanced viewpoint, noting that religious activists split fifty-fifty in favor of Sadat. "We knew that Sadat was using religion for political ends," he said. "He could not fool us because we were conscious and politicized."[47] It was a reciprocal relationship in which Sadat's interests and those of the Islamists dovetailed. Sadat treated Islamists with "a benevolence that was well reciprocated, as the Islamists 'purged' the universities of anything that smelled of communism or Nasserism."[48]

The October 1973 War and the Petrodollar Revolution

In his effort to marginalize the Nasserists and socialists, Sadat thus sowed the seeds of religious revivalism and radicalism. The relative success of the Arab coalition in the October War of 1973 added momentum and impetus to the religious milieu which had been nourished by Sadat. Unlike the Six-Day War of 1967, the regime and its clerical allies portrayed the 1973 war as a divine victory fought under a religious banner, Allahu Akbar (God Is Great)—although the Sadat regime did not fully deploy the war-cry "Allahu Akbar" until the intensification of its de-Nasserization campaign in 1975. Sadat made sure that his predecessor did not earn any credit for the self-claimed Egyptian victory in the 1973 war, despite Nasser's having rebuilt the army after the 1967 defeat along more professional lines and laid the foundation for the next showdown with Israel.[49] The victory was personalized and internalized; Sadat was depicted as the "hero of war and peace," as he came to be known in Egypt. Only three days after the war started on October 6, the armed forces' information section published a pamphlet for distribution among the troops which framed the conflict in religious terms:

> In the name of Allah, the beneficent, the merciful. Oh, the soldiers of Allah, Prophet [Muhammad] is with us in the battle. One of the pious men saw while asleep that the Prophet, clad in white and accompanied by the Sheikh of al-Azhar, pointed his finger forward and said, 'Come with me to Sinai." It was said that some pious people saw the Prophet walking among soldiers with a smile on his face and an array of light in his surroundings. Oh, soldiers of Allah, it is clear that Allah is with You.[50]

Time and again Egyptians were told that "God and his angels" fought on the side of advancing Egyptian soldiers and helped them triumph over the enemy. The airways were filled with gripping stories about divine intervention on behalf of Sadat's pious green-clad army. For example, the Sadat regime portrayed early gains in the 1973 war as a divine victory: "Prophet [Muhammad]," proclaimed one pamphlet issued by the army three days into the war, "is with us in the battle. It was said that pious people saw the Prophet walking among the soldiers."[51] Shown on television screens praying at mosques, clutching his prayer beads and softly murmuring Allah's name, the "pious president" conveyed a sense of symbolic divergence with his predecessor. Religious programs dominated the airwaves. In Egyptian universities, the Sadat regime backed religious activists against nationalist and leftist students, thus tilting the scales in the former's favor. Nasser's Arab nationalism was criticized as secular or anti-religious because it presupposed that the bonds that tie the Arab people together are language, history, and a sense of belonging, not only religion.

Moreover, during the war, on October 13, the mouthpiece of the state, *al-Ahram*, linked the war with the Battle of Badr (624 CE), a turning point in Muhammad's struggle against the idolaters of Mecca.[52] Indeed, "Badr" was used as the code name for the Egyptian military operation to cross the Suez Canal and seize the Bar-Lev line of Israeli fortifications on October 6, 1973.

This religious framing of the war reflected positively on Sadat himself. Writing again in *al-Ahram*, the Islamic thinker Abdel Moneim Khallaf put it this way:

> It is the hand of God which made Sadat think [of the crossing] and inspired him with the plan of deception. [It was the hand of God] which affected the minds of the Israeli leaders and intelligence bodies, making them hesitant and intrigued and deceived ... [Anwar Sadat] is a godly man cast in the fame of one of those heroic mythical heroes ...[53]

Religious fervor reached new heights. "God and His Prophet" joined the fight and tipped the scales in favor of the virtuous Arabs who had returned to Islam. The Sadat regime, Islamists, and others insinuated that in 1967 God had punished Egypt because it had given up the faith, while in 1973 God rewarded it for re-embracing Islam. The tide had decisively shifted against the Arab nationalist and socialist paradigm. Marking the anniversary of the 1973 war in 1978, *al-Ahram* interviewed the scholar Abdullah al-Nemr, who compared and contrasted the 1967 and 1973 wars in binary terms:

> We came across two experiences; one in which we forgot God ... and the result of this was a bitter *naksa* [in June 1967]. The second [experience] was on 10 Ramadan [October 1973], where we prepared for it with enough *iman* [belief] and spiritual mobilization along with weapons; so the army entered into the fighting with the spirit of the believer and shouting "God is great" ...[54]

Islamists, for their part, backed the narrative of the 1973 war as a divine victory. Abbas al-Sissi, a leading Ikhwan member detained in the Tanzim al-Sirri case in 1965, put it bluntly: "I was released after the Ramadan War, which was a chance for me to tell people about the impact of [the verse] 'God is great' in securing victory."[55] Some even suggest that they were inspired to embrace religion with new vigor in the wake of the war. Zayat, the Islamist attorney, said that the fact that God had endowed Egyptians with victory in October 1973 was the main reason that he committed to "returning to God."[56] Sadat won the war because he raised the slogan "There is no God but God."[57]

The dominance of Saudi Arabia's petrodollar or "petro-purse," which expanded enormously during the 1970s, augmented the religious narrative and fueled it further. If one of the major effects of the 1967 war had been a rise in Saudi influence and assertiveness, this received another major boost with the October 1973 war and the subsequent quadrupling of crude oil prices because of the oil embargo imposed by Arab states during the conflict. Even Nasser had swallowed his pride after the Six-Day War and relied on Saudi money to rebuild his army and finance the costly war of attrition with Israel. At the Khartoum summit in August 1967, Saudi Arabia, Kuwait, and Libya agreed to provide Egypt with around EGP135 million annually until the occupied land and lost revenue had been recovered. Only a month after the Khartoum summit, Egypt began withdrawing troops from Yemen. Checkbook diplomacy allowed the House of Saud to consolidate its authority at home, exercise a greater regional role, and spread its conservative ideas far and wide.

Even more than in Nasser's final years, the close alliance forged by Sadat with the Saudi monarchy had far-reaching consequences on the configuration of social forces in Arab and Muslim societies. Now two pivotal Arab states actively promoted an ideological narrative intrinsically opposed to Nasserism and socialism. The resources and assets of these two powerful regimes were fully deployed in the service of conservative religious narratives and the reinterpretation of contemporary Arab history. Once again the role of the state was critical in spearheading the transition from one ideological paradigm to another.

For instance, in 1971 King Faisal offered a gift of $100 million for the sheikhs of al-Azhar to launch a campaign against "communism and atheism"; most of the gift made it into the coffers of the Sadat regime.[58] In addition to backing the Egyptian state's efforts to promote Islamism and attack Nasserism and communism through its financial support, Saudi Arabia played a direct, active role. According to Mohamed Heikal, King Faisal helped arrange a meeting between Sadat and the Ikhwan leaders, which took place in the autumn of 1971 at Sadat's presidential retreat in Ismailia. Sadat agreed with the attendees that "atheism and communism should be resisted," and offered an alliance with the Ikhwan.[59]

One of the least examined chapters in this unfolding drama is the convergence of interests between the Sadat regime and the House of Saud in creating a religiously oriented constituency: a community of opinion makers, public intellectuals, and clerics. Ideas do not move in a vacuum but are sustained and nourished by material interests and social networks. Since the 1970s, millions of Arabs, including workers, professionals, educators, and writers, found employment opportunities in Saudi Arabia and the small Gulf sheikhdoms and subsequently returned home with monetary savings and a new conservative sensibility and way of life. Some of these Egyptian intellectuals and scholars even stayed in Saudi Arabia and other Gulf sheikhdoms until their deaths; the most prominent among them is Mohamed Qutb, the brother of Sayyid Qutb. Qutb was imprisoned with his brother in 1954 and 1965. Sadat released him in 1972, and Mohamed traveled to and lived in Saudi Arabia until his death in April 2014. While living in Saudi Arabia, Mohamed propagated the concepts that had been developed by Sayyid Qutb before the latter's execution. During his fifty-year stint in Saudi Arabia, Mohamed wrote dozens of books, including *Jahiliyyat al-qarn al-ishreen* (The jahiliyya of the twentieth century), in which he affirmed some of the ideas advanced in his brother's *Signposts*.[60] Mohamed's book was published in Egypt in 1980 and subsequently reprinted many times. Ma'mun Hudaybi, son of Hassan Hudaybi and the supreme guide of the Muslim Brotherhood from 2002 to 2004, also worked in Saudi Arabia's Ministry of Interior before the group recalled him back home.

The conservative social model found in Saudi Arabia migrated with Egyptian returnees. Resistance was futile, according to many activists and scholars who lived in the midst of this ideological transformation. "It was impossible to stem the conservative religious tide that flooded Egypt and other Muslim countries," said Gamil Mattar, a public intellectual. "The petrodollar revolution swept people off their feet and transformed the social landscape. Oil money fueled the rebirth of political Islam at the expense of Arab nationalism and leftist politics."[61] According to Hossam Tammam, a top specialist on political Islam, the Ikhwan greatly benefitted from the rise in oil prices after the 1973 war and the expansion in construction projects in Saudi Arabia because they worked in this sector: that came at a cost, though, an ideological rapprochement with Saudi Wahhabism.[62] For example, Saudi money flowed to Islamic activists in Egyptian universities, providing for the publication and distribution of Salafist books free of charge. Many students went to Saudi Arabia for pilgrimage and even stayed there for long periods.[63] Those returning students brought with them free books promoting an ultraconservative interpretation of the faith.[64] Tammam even asserts that some of these activists turned into followers of Saudi sheikhs like Ibn Baz and al-Uthaymiyan. Official bodies in the Saudi kingdom, such as the association of religious scholars and the Ministry of Endowments, financed the spread of conservative Salafist ideas to Egypt.[65] Salafi influence in Egypt expanded further as thousands of Islamists, released from detention with no job prospects in the country, emigrated mainly to the Gulf and especially to Saudi Arabia.[66] Many Ikhwan leaders also traveled to Saudi Arabia, including Tawfiq al-Shawy, Ali Gereisha, Abdel Moneim Tualib, and Ahmed al-Assal.[67] In doing so, they followed in the footsteps of Ikhwan senior members like Said Ramadan who had earlier found refuge in Qatar and Kuwait following the clampdown by the Nasserist state.[68] When the Ikhwan held an extended meeting in 1973, the first of its kind since 1954, they did so in Mecca, Saudi Arabia. One of the first decisions of the meeting was to reformulate membership of the group's Shura Council, which acts like the Ikhwan's legislature.[69] Three committees were formed in Saudi Arabia (Riyadh, Dammam, and Jeddah) and three others in Kuwait, Qatar, and the United Arab Emirates (UAE), establishing a network which would finance the group's activities.[70] A Qatari member was appointed as the financial controller of the movement's resources.[71]

This ideological penetration of Egypt went unchallenged, with al-Azhar colluding with the Saudi-backed ultraconservative currents because it stood to benefit financially. The Egyptian economy became dependent on remittances mainly from the Gulf, particularly from Saudi Arabia. Remittances flowing through official channels alone from Egyptians working in the Gulf from 1973 until 1983 amounted to $15 billion.[72] These remittances also influenced the level of investments, the rate of inflation, the level of wages, and other macro- and microeconomic gauges of Egypt.[73]

Heikal, who shared with Nasser the dream of an Arab future with no borders, conceded that the rise of the statist, oil-rich countries and the growing respect for the political power of money all made the earlier focus on "revolutionary struggle" a thing of the past.[74] On another occasion, he eloquently played on lexical similarities in Arabic to drive the point home: the *thawra* (revolution) is now replaced with *tharwa* (wealth).[75] In short, the oil revolution trumped the pan-Arab revolution. Saad Eddin Ibrahim, an Egyptian sociologist, said that "Wahhabi ideology fueled by *al-tufra al-naftiyya* [the oil boom] infiltrated Egyptian society in the 1970s and changed peoples' sensibilities, tastes, and values, and even politics. Petrodollars allowed Wahhabism to spread beyond the Arabian Peninsula to the heart of the Arab world and attract a huge following," Ibrahim noted in an interview in his small study at the American University in Cairo.[76] Ibrahim pointed out that direct and indirect petrodollars financed a variety of religious and civil society activities, including al-Azhar University, the oldest and most prestigious institution of Muslim higher learning, lending momentum to a religious revival. Religiosity spread like wildfire in society and the cultural realm, and religious discourse dominated the media and airwaves. "Popular culture was Islamized," added Ibrahim.[77] Ibrahim does not view the Six-Day War in a vacuum or in isolation from subsequent developments, particularly the October 1973 war and the oil boom, which exhausted Nasser's Arab nationalist project and empowered the Islamist current, including the Ikhwan.[78]

"If it was not for Sadat and the petrodollar, Islamists would not have had the resources to spread their influence inside and outside Egypt. ... In the 1970s the merchants of religion had unlimited sums of money at their disposal and the backing of the two most powerful states in the Arab world. We [nationalists] struggled against great odds and fought a losing war," recollected al-Sayyed Yassin, a leading public intellectual and commentator at the Al-Ahram Center for Political and Strategic Studies.[79]

While Saudi Arabia spent plenty of oil money to combat Islamism's rival ideologies outside its borders, other Gulf sheikhdoms abandoned Arab nationalism by focusing on domestic issues. These small sheikhdoms now had enough wealth to "buy off dissent and opposition" and avoid the costs of an expensive ideology like Arab nationalism which could "dilute their newly found wealth."[80] With a newly reinvigorated U.S. security umbrella, including the establishment of military bases, the petroleum-producing Gulf sheikhdoms felt secure enough to enjoy the fruits of oil and gas wealth. "Oil nationalism" clashed with "Arab nationalism" and vanquished it.[81]

The Egyptian liberal Wahid Abdel Majid also stressed the pivotal role played by oil, money, power, and globalization in bringing about the social and political transformation of Arab countries during the 1970s. "Sadat played on people's hopes, fears, and greed to bury Nasserism and portray himself as the leader who would bring about salvation," said Abdel Majid, who does not hide his contempt for Sadat. "The name of his game was religion and the manipulation of religious symbols to restructure social and political space." Abdel Majid contends that Sadat's shortsightedness and recklessness brought ruin to Egypt, as damaging as the 1967 defeat, if not more so.[82]

Regardless of the merits and costs of Sadat's alliance with the petrodollar, his policies transformed the political landscape and the social structure in Egypt and created fertile ground for conservative religious revivalism and Islamism. During the second half of the 1970s, radical religious sensibility reigned supreme, with the Saudi and Egyptian states carrying out a concerted effort to indoctrinate and shape public opinion and using multiple tools and incentives. My goal is neither to overstate Sadat's role in fueling the Islamic revival in the late 1970s and 1980s nor to understate the degree to which Islamic organizations and ideas had been around for a long time. Rather, the analysis aims to show how Sadat's flirtation with Islam, together with his strategic alliance with Saudi Arabia, helped tilt the balance of power in the Islamists' favor.

The prevailing mood in Egypt at the time was further reinforced by the revolution led by Ayatollah Khomeini in Iran, whose success in toppling the shah in 1979 inspired a new generation of Islamists which Sadat had nourished. According to the Ikhwan mouthpiece, *al-Da'wa*, the Iranian revolution offered the lesson "that God's party is victorious regardless of the power of tyrants and the forces that support them."[83] The magazine attacked state-censored media outlets which attempted to portray the new post-shah Iran as reactionary.

Other Islamists also took heart. Fathi al-Shaqaqi, the future founder of the Palestine-based Islamic Jihad, who was living in Egypt at that time, penned a manifesto calling for an Iran-style Islamic solution in the Arab region. Overstepping the boundary of what was considered acceptable by the Sadat regime, Shaqaqi ended up in an Egyptian prison.[84] His case illustrates the rocky and unstable relationship between Sadat and the Islamists in Egypt as tested by developments in Iran. Comparisons between Sadat and the shah were not far from the minds of Islamists, especially as both were in alliance with the United States and both were known for getting closer to Israel. Sadat's decision to offer asylum to the shah following the latter's ouster poured gasoline on a fire raging below the surface.

The second half of the 1970s witnessed a migration of many prominent nationalist and Marxist intellectuals and scholars to the religious camp. Many former leftists and Arab nationalists found in religion solace, refuge, and answers to their pressing questions; they shed their former beliefs for a more "authentic" identity and a cultural project in harmony with the people. These included Adel Hussein, Tariq al-Beshri, Munir Shafiq, Mohamed Ama'ra, Abdel Wahab al-Misiri, Ra'fat Sayyid Ahmed, and Hassan Hanafi. Again, these transformations did not occur overnight and involved a gradual process of adaptation and reorientation. In the case of Tariq al-Bishry, now a prominent jurist with centrist Islamist tendencies, Angela Giordani observes that the 1967 war was not the turning point in his transition from Marxism to Islamism.[85] On the contrary, it took Bishry another ten years to make the transition. He initially blamed the 1967 defeat on the absence of democracy and argued that filling the democracy deficit could have allowed Nasserism to survive because the ideology is in harmony with the values and aspirations of Egyptians. According to Giordani, Bishry's transformation occurred as "he witnessed what is called the *Sahwa al-Islamiyya* (Islamic Revival) when a strong wave of political Islam swayed young generations in Egypt, from activists and intellectuals to university students."[86] Observing this *sahwa*, Bishry "saw the tradition that is required by people as it appears in a traditional garment. Therefore he reformulated the national project to reflect its authenticity."[87] Nevertheless, Bishry believes that there is no ideological contradiction between Islam and Arab nationalism, and that they only differ in "political functionalism," meaning they come from same family tree and same gene pool.[88] Indeed, Bishry's oscillation and conversion sheds further light on the tumultuous journey of both nationalists and religious activists who seem to share a similar foundation myth. This also helps to explain the relative ease by which both migrate from one camp to the other.

Bishry recalled that although he and his generation had been critical of the Ikhwan in the 1950s and 1960s, they had concluded in the 1970s that mining the Islamic heritage was the only way to undo defeat and achieve genuine independence and development. "Our heritage supplied the symbols and framework for popular mobilization and cultural renewal and rejuvenation," he said. "The Islamist movement is an important vehicle to drive this change, and it cannot and should not be excluded and repressed."[89]

Similarly, Adel Hussein is a fascinating example of a hardcore Marxist who turned Islamist during the late 1970s. Although he said he was very critical of the conduct of the Six-Day War and the Nasser regime in general, he still supported Nasser's progressive agenda at home and his foreign policy, particularly the quest for Arab nationalism. More than ever, Hussein said he felt the need to stand by Nasser's side in order to prevent reactionary forces from outflanking the Egyptian revolution and to prepare for the coming fight against Israel.[90] However, in the 1970s and 1980s, Hussein embraced Islam as a more effective form of resistance and liberation than socialism, Marxism, and Arab nationalism. He noted that the Islamist revival was part of a broader societal shift toward religiosity—*al-'awda ila al-usul*, or a return to the fundamentals—throughout the world, not just in the Muslim realm; it is a transnational phenomenon rooted in the struggle between the colonial north and the emancipated south, a struggle that has taken a different direction under a new banner—culture and religion.[91] "Many of us rediscovered Islamic ideology as inspirational to the struggle against foreign domination and the new colonialism, as well as internal liberation. What happened in the 1970s and 1980s is that the cultural divide which had existed between the elite and the masses narrowed greatly because the former returned to its Islamic roots," Hussein told me in an interview at his flat in Misr al-Jadida. "Today there is harmony between the elite and the masses; opinion makers are no longer estranged from popular culture."[92]

Mohamed Ama'ra, another nationalist turned Islamist, agrees with Hussein's thesis that there existed a rift between the secular-leaning elite in the 1950s and 1960s and the pious masses, a rift that tilted the balance of social forces against the religious current. Amara blames these secular intellectuals for diverting the revolution from its rightful path and driving a wedge between the Islamist and nationalist camps. His view is that in the 1970s many public intellectuals reconciled not only with religion but also with Islamism. "Arabism and Islam were no longer estranged," Amara said, implying that his migration to Islam, along with that of others, was natural.[93]

A common thread that runs through the narratives of these nationalists and leftists who found solace in religious heritage and embraced the Islamist current is the urgent need for resistance to triumphant Israel and foreign intrusion. Most say that Islam provides more inspiration and motivation than nationalism and that they came to this realization after the June 1967 defeat and Nasser's death in 1970. "The Nasserist state gradually and inadvertently emptied Arab nationalism of its religious content, which led to public alienation and exhaustion," Bishry argued. "Our goal is to reinstitute Islam in *al-haraka al-wataniya* (the nationalist movement) and rebuild it on a more solid foundation."[94]

Ra'fat Sayyed Ahmed, an activist and researcher who straddles the nationalist-Islamist divide, was more direct. "Resistance to the Zionist enemy and the Americans necessitated marshaling all elements of our power, including the most powerful weapon—Islam—and putting an end to the civil war that weakened the nationalist cause," said Sayyed Ahmed.[95] Before Sadat gained power in 1970, Nasser had already begun to use religious symbolism, such as fate and God's will, to explain Egypt's defeat in June 1967 and to mobilize the masses.

According to Sayyed Ahmed, the Nasserist authorities sent religious caravans to the battlefront to provide a religious education to soldiers and officers. "Although Sadat opened the floodgates to religious politics and activism, the current gained momentum in the late 1960s," he argued during a conversation at his research center in Cairo.[96]

Likewise, Abdel Wahab al-Misiri, an academic and a public intellectual, belongs to this generation of leftists and nationalists who finally reconciled with the religious current in the 1970s. He told me that the Nasserist state committed a strategic blunder by its persecution of religious activists, thus causing a rupture between the nationalist and Islamist movements, a rupture that weakened Egypt's ability to resist its enemies. "Our goal is to bridge the divide between the social strata and build a representative alliance to roll back Zionism and colonialism. We had no choice but to unite in the face of the Zionist aggression."[97]

According to these firsthand testimonies, the Islamist resurgence in the 1970s coincided with the migration of a critical segment of the elite to religious politics. Prioritizing the religious heritage as an effective weapon of resistance and cultural renewal, the new elite provided intellectual legitimacy to Islamists and facilitated the spread of their ideas in Egypt and the Arab neighborhood. Although they did not formally join the Ikhwan and other Islamist groups, public intellectuals like Tariq al-Bishry and Adel Hussein were part of a general trend in the 1970s, one that marked a key shift in the balance of social forces favoring religious politics. There is no doubt that Sadat nourished this religious trend and religiosity and that this, in turn, helped the Ikhwan and Islamists in general gain recruits and expand their base of support, said Seif Abdel Fattah, who was a young religious activist in the 1970s and is now an academic and public intellectual.[98]

Nonetheless, it is now forgotten that the revolt against Nasser's Arab nationalism and socialism first came from *within* the regime's power structure. Despite his best effort to downplay his part in the emergence and consolidation of Nasser's power, from the onset of the Egyptian revolution Sadat had been one of Nasser's loyal associates and had blindly defended the regime's policies. He had dutifully earned the nickname "the yes man" precisely because he hardly ever dissented. During that period, he had shown no mercy towards political Islamists who challenged Nasser's authority and that of the army officers. In fact, Sadat presided over revolutionary courts which persecuted dissidents, especially the Ikhwan. A particularly salient case in point is his involvement as a member of the People's Tribunal formed by the RCC a few days after the apparent attempt on Nasser's life in October 1954 to try those accused of involvement in the allegedly Ikhwan-orchestrated plot. Richard Mitchell, an authority on the early years of the Ikhwan, pointed out that proceedings before the court were farcical: most of the questioning was irrelevant to the crime; the evidence was full of contradictions; and the judges themselves exchanged "petty insults with the witnesses; in most cases the insults came from the court alone."[99] As Mitchell put it: "The audience was allowed, even encouraged, to participate in laughter and ridicule and to jeer at and insult witnesses."[100] Hussein al-Shafei, one of the three judges on the tribunal, admitted that there were "violations" in the court proceedings because the "main purpose was to provide protection to the revolution."[101] The court ordered the execution of seven members of the Ikhwan. Given his key role in the Nasserist regime, Sadat's decision to use the Islamists to counterbalance and weaken the left was perilous. By giving religious activists free rein to target Arab nationalists, leftists, and socialists, Sadat allowed the emergence of various Islamist groups, which spiraled out of his control. Despite Sadat's repeated efforts to distance himself from the Nasserist legacy, Islamists, including many Ikhwan members who had spent time in Nasserist prisons, remained wary of him. They never trusted Sadat, even though they had been willing to work with him to escape persecution and increase their influence.

"We will never forget and forgive Sadat for serving as a member of the Free Officers' court that sentenced seven members of the Ikhwan to death after the so-called assassination attempt on Nasser's life in 1954," Abdullah Rashwan, an Islamist and a pro-Ikhwan attorney who defended the accused, told me. "Sadat was immoral and ruthless."[102] In my conversations with Rashwan, Zayat, and other Islamists, I got the impression that Sadat underestimated the shrewdness and political ambitions of the Islamists, particularly the radical youth, and miscalculated the degree to which he could manipulate them.

The assassination of Sadat by Islamist militants in 1980 should not blind us to his use of the sacred as a political tool to build a constituency that rivaled that of Nasser's Arab nationalism and socialism. Under Sadat, the instrumentalization of religion was a matter of state policy. Ironically, the generation of militant Islamists who turned their guns on Sadat and killed him has taken a second look at his presidency. Although throughout the years, radical religious activists whom I interviewed insisted that they were not creatures of the Sadat regime but were their own men, many now concede that Sadat allowed them to organize, establish a social base of support, and spread their ideas on campuses all over Egypt and beyond.

"Come to think of it, during the Sadat era we were a healthy generation," said Kamal Habib, a founding father of Egyptian Islamic Jihad who, along with a few cohorts, engineered the assassination of the Egyptian president. "We had space and freedom of speech and movement; and unlike our brethren in the Nasserist period we were not harassed and persecuted," reflected the middle-aged activist, who spent more than a decade behind bars and whom I profiled over a period of several months during the 1990s and in 2006–2007. "To be honest with you, the Sadat moment was a golden age for the Islamist movement, and we squandered it away."[103]

Habib is not the only radical Islamist who now reflects nostalgically on the Sadat era. Montasser al-Zayat, a prominent Islamist attorney, confessed that his generation had made a strategic error by rising up against Sadat. "In comparison to Nasser, Sadat was a godsend for the sons of the Islamist movement. He released Islamist activists from Nasser's prisons and contributed to the religious revival that swept the *umma* in the 1970s. If we had had patience and forbearance, we could have gradually transformed Egypt into a truly Islamic society."[104]

In an unprecedented gesture, more than two decades after assassinating Sadat, the leadership of al-Jama'at al-Islamiyya made a formal apology and called the late president a "martyr" because, in their opinion, he protected and defended the faith. A founder of al-Jama'at al-Islamiyya, Najih Ibrahim, who spent twenty-five years in prison after being convicted of killing Sadat, said in a 2011 interview that he regretted the assassination as it wrought more harm than good.[105] Though politically and ideologically costly, al-Jama'at's decision to call Sadat a "martyr" shows that even (former) Islamist militants now recognize Sadat's contribution to their movement, an historic testament to the role of the state in nourishing religious politics in the 1970s.

Overwhelming evidence indicates that Sadat was an enabler who systematically paved the way for religious activists to dominate the public space. Not unlike Nasser, who privileged Arab nationalism and empowered it, Sadat cultivated a religious current. The difference is that Nasser adopted Arab nationalism as his state's official ideology, while Sadat indirectly promoted a religious alternative without formally espousing it. The result was the same: the postcolonial, post-independence state was instrumental in propping up ideologies that allowed it to construct a durable hegemony and consolidate its rule. Conversely, the fortune of these ideas depended on the state's ability to provide social public goods and security.

Conclusion

The Six-Day War did not automatically usher in a dramatic shift from one ideological narrative, pan-Arab nationalism, to another, pan-Islamism. That hypothesis is a simplistic sketch of a much more complex social and political reality. As with Nasser's adoption of Arab nationalism during the 1950s and 1960s, Sadat and his state apparatus played a key role, some would say unwittingly, in the rise and expansion of Islamism. In his effort to rid Egypt of his predecessor's inheritance, al-Ra'is al-Mu'min (the pious president), as Sadat insisted on being addressed, called for the establishment of *dawlat al-'ilm wa al-iman* (the state of knowledge and faith). He helped Islamize political space, as opposed to social space, and systematically dismantled the entrenched main core of the Nasserist ruling group.

First, Sadat got rid of Nasser's all-powerful inner circle by accusing them of conspiracy and imprisoning them. In a further effort to escape Nasser's shadow, Sadat carried out an ideological reorientation from the left to the right. The shift took the form of restructuring the country's economy and pursuing an *infitah* policy which represented a dramatic departure from Nasser's socialism. Sadat's economic program relied on boosting capitalist investment from domestic and foreign investors in a bid to revitalize the Egyptian public sector. This economic conversion went hand in hand with another ideological shift away from secular Arab nationalism to religiosity and even Islamism. Sadat tried to fill the ideological vacuum left by Nasser's death with that of Islam, which resonated with Egyptians. He emphasized his own "pious" character and freed Islamists from Nasserist prisons, then used them to target leftist unions and student groups. The October 1973 war provided Sadat with another impetus to demonstrate his piety and consolidate his public standing at home. The official discourse on the war was suffused with religious imagery and symbolism, depicting Egypt's victory as the sanctification of Sadat's own power. As the pious president, Sadat was the legitimate leader of Egypt and the victory proved it. Finally, Sadat's rapprochement with Saudi Arabia and reliance on Gulf money provided more ideological motivation for his religious framing of politics, considerably influencing Egyptian society. Millions of Egyptians traveled to the Gulf to work, and when they returned to Egypt they had embraced ultraconservative Salafi ideology and espoused its stricter and narrower interpretation and vision of Islam.

Not unlike its ideological nemesis, secular Arab nationalism, had been in the past, the Islamist project was nourished during the Sadat era both by social and ideological mobilization from below and also by top-down backing from the state.[106] The Nasserist state had invested considerable ideological and material resources in elevating and disseminating Arab nationalism at home and across the Middle

East. Turning the tables to consolidate his own rule, Sadat instead began to channel state assets and institutions in support of the Islamists against Arab nationalists and socialists. His alliance with Saudi Arabia, which invested its new wealth in spreading ultraconservative religious norms worldwide in the 1970s and 1980s, further tipped the balance of social forces in favor of the Islamists in both Egypt and the Arab world.

Chapter 12

The Mubarak Era

Keeping the Ikhwan in the Freezer

WHILE THE EXECUTION OF Sayyid Qutb in August 1966 marked the end of one era in the history of the Ikhwan, Qutb's legacy did not by any means die with him. Rather, his influence came to inform significant dynamics in the development of the Ikhwan—the period of Islamist revival under Anwar Sadat in the 1970s and subsequently the careful maneuvering under the regime of Hosni Mubarak from the early 1980s until 2011. Throughout this time, the Ikhwan has been riven by a profound ideological division. On the one hand, the Islamist group has in many ways been dominated by an ultraconservative old guard loyal to the memory of Qutb. On the other, it has seen the emergence of an energetic group of younger, reform-minded figures with a more cosmopolitan and inclusive vision. The two factions have clashed on substantive political, social, and strategic questions, including the status of women, the forms of political activism to be pursued within the political context they face in Egypt, and the appropriateness of coordinating with other, secular-leaning Egyptian opposition groups. Perhaps even more importantly, the old guard and the younger reformers have been at loggerheads over the internal practices of the Ikhwan as an organization; with the reformers calling for a fundamental restructuring to overcome what they see as the autocratic and opaque practices of the old guard.

This conceptual divide contributed to shifts in the balance of power within the Ikhwan in the period after Qutb's death—between the guardians of his legacy and their reformist challengers. By keeping a firm hand on the organization's decision making and maintaining an autocratic rule resistant to change, the ultraconservative leadership was able to undermine the reformists' efforts for greater openness and a more inclusive public policy. Moreover, this internal power struggle fueling the rise of the ultraconservative wing was brought about by various developments, including migration of Ikhwan members to the Gulf for work from the 1970s onwards, the increasing proportion of members hailing from rural parts of Egypt, and alternating periods of relative freedom and repression dealt the Ikhwan by the Egyptian regime.

Divisions in the Ranks after Qutb

As discussed in the previous chapter, Egypt witnessed a religious revival in the 1970s under the leadership of President Anwar al-Sadat. Hoping to use the Islamists as a bulwark against Nasserist and leftist segments of the political opposition, Sadat released the disciples of Sayyid Qutb and other Ikhwan members who had been in jail since the mid-1960s. Upon their release, Qutb's disciples carved a niche for themselves within the Ikhwan and established an ultraconservative center of power at the heart of the organization. Many of those new key power brokers, who included Mustafa Mashour, Ahmed al-Malt, Husni Abdel Baqi, Kamal al-Sananeiry, and Ahmed Hassanein, had previously been part of the paramilitary wings associated with the Ikhwan, such as al-Nizam al-Khass and Qutb's own al-Tanzim al-Sirri.[1] This reactionary core formed a powerful bloc that played a pivotal role in the Ikhwan's exclusive sixteen-member Maktub al-Irshad (Guidance Office), an apparatus tasked with policy making and electing leaders.

In parallel, a loose coalition of younger and more progressive members had also risen within the Ikhwan. Often referred to as "the 1970s generation," they were initially active in radical university groups and joined the Ikhwan in the 1970s. Ironically, those younger, radical elements became important challengers to the ultraconservative Qutbian influences within the Ikhwan. They received support from a few leading older Ikhwan members, including the aforementioned Kamal al-Sananeiry, who distinguished himself as one of the more moderate figures within the Ikhwan's reactionary power bloc. Indeed, as the Ikhwan enjoyed a new lease on life in the 1970s, Qutbians and forward-looking students alike joined the mainstream, moderate line promoted by Hassan al-Hudaybi's successor as supreme guide, Omar al-Telmessany. Released from jail in 1971, Telmessany's close links with the Sadat state helped him expand his influence within the Ikhwan. By the mid-1970s, the mainstream camp had almost succeeded in asserting control over the Ikhwan's ultraconservatives. However, by the end of the 1970s, Sadat's policies, such as the signing of the Camp David peace accords with Israel, coupled with his deepening authoritarianism, led to a breakdown in Ikhwan-state relations.[2] As Sadat clamped down on the opposition in 1981, Telmessany was arrested. The resulting severance of connections between Telmessany and Sadat partially re-empowered the Ikhwan's old guard, launching the organization on a more reactionary and autocratic path. Remembering the moderating role that Telmessany had played, Ibrahim Se'da, the, top editor of the leading state-run newspaper, *al-Akhbar*, mourned his death in May 1986: the loss of the *murshid* (guide) was the nation's loss because he was a man who had acted as "a safety valve serving a group, a people, and a whole nation."[3]

Despite these setbacks, the forward-looking students who had joined the more mainstream wing of the Ikhwan continued their efforts to offset the increasing influence of the reactionary Qutbian power core. This new "reformist" camp sought political transformation through peaceful action and participation in state institutions such as the parliament and professional syndicates. Abdel Moneim Abu al-Futuh, who had joined the Ikhwan in the early 1970s, was part of this movement. Originally, he was a leader in the Jama'at al-Islamiyya, the Islamist movement active on Egyptian university campuses that called for radical change, including overthrowing the *kafir* (atheist) regime. In his memoirs, Abu al-Futuh revealed that he had found the Ikhwan appealing because of the similarities between his own commitment to bringing about change through revolutionary action and the ideologies of the Qutbian wing of the Ikhwan.[4] Abu al-Futuh's radicalism eventually subsided as he was exposed to Telmessany's "reformist" efforts. He even became a high-profile voice within the reformist camp, which earned him a place in the Ikhwan's Guidance Office beginning in 1987. A pediatrician by profession, he was a formidable challenger to the Ikhwan's hardliners until his departure from the Guidance Office in 2009. Prior to his departure from the Ikhwan, I discussed his influence within the movement with his ally Hesham El-Hamamy. "Abu al-Futuh is the leader of the reformist camp within the Ikhwan and has massive support, particularly among the youth," Hamamy said. "But his influence on decision making is minimal because the elders [the ultraconservative old guard] who wield power have sidelined him."[5]

Mukhtar Nouh served as another illustration of the reactionary-reformist divide that increasingly threatened the cohesion of the Ikhwan. Having earned a reputation as a young, energetic activist and an articulate orator in the Syndicate of Lawyers, Nouh first clashed with the old guard in the late 1980s and early 1990s.[6] Despite—or perhaps because of—his popularity among members of the syndicate, the leading figures in the old guard, including Mashour and Mahmoud Izzat, sought to sideline him.[7] Nouh turned to Telmessany for support. According to Tharwat al-Kharabawy, an Ikhwan dissident, on at least one occasion Telmessany was forced to conduct a conversation with Nouh by leaning over and whispering in the latter's ear in order to avoid the watchful eyes of the old guard.[8] Internal distrust and enmity were threatening the cohesion of the

Islamist organization.[9] In the end, Nouh left the Ikhwan and became a staunch public opponent of what he has repeatedly called "the Qutbian branch" within the Ikhwan.[10]

As the reformists' influence increased within the Ikhwan, they began to challenge the de facto hegemony of the old guard that dominated decision making even under Telmessany's leadership. In 1986, for example, Mohamed al-Tahawy, a student of medicine and the brother of renowned novelist Miral al-Tahawy, presented an internal reform initiative. Nothing came of his proposal or of similar initiatives by others; they were simply shelved. Recalling this period, many members of the Ikhwan complained that they had been faced with "a legacy of rigidity in concepts and stiffness in organizational structures."[11]

Despite growing internal discontent and criticism, after the end of Telmessany's tenure in the mid-1980s, the Ikhwan was mostly headed by representatives of the old Qutbian generation. Although in 1986 Telmessany was succeeded by another reformist, Mohamed Hamed Abu al-Nasr, his authority was limited. He was a "weak leader who came from the rear ranks of the group and lacked organizational weight." Nasr's tenure nonetheless allowed for some opening as the group participated in parliamentary elections in 1987 and 1995 and joined a coalition with leftist rivals—the al-A'mal and al-Ahrar parties. In 1996, Nasr was replaced by hawkish Mustafa Mashour, who served as the supreme guide until 2002. Mashour's appointment marked a return to a stricter and more conservative vision of power. He had been an Ikhwan member for some time and his repeated stays in jail inspired respect from other Brothers. Mashour had been arrested in 1954 after the attempt on Nasser's life and was imprisoned again in 1965 during the wider crackdown that occurred following the discovery of Qutb's Tanzim al-Sirri. After Sadat released him in 1971, he reemerged as an influential hardliner within the Ikhwan, and dominated decision making for years. Many inside the Ikhwan argue that as the supreme leader, Mashour and his deputy, Ma'mun Hudaybi, stamped out the "1970s generation" from within the Ikhwan.[12] Members who were part of the reformist camp, including Abu al-Futuh, but also Abu El-Ela Madi, Ibrahim Al-Za'farani, Khaled Dawoud, and many others—all ended up either dissenting or distancing themselves from the organization's activities to escape the wrath of its hawks.

The leverage of the conservatives further increased with the appointment of Ma'mun Hudaybi as supreme guide in November 2002. Ma'mun, the son of Hassan al-Hudaybi, believed in strengthening the Ikhwan through centralized, hierarchical decision making and administration. His line of thought was that "if the group is strong enough, these acts of [internal] dissent would be ineffective." Doubling down, Ma'mun denied that there ever was "anything called the old/new guards in the group. They are false myths made by the hostile conspiratorial press."[13] The new supreme guide exposed an authoritarian streak by summarily dismissing accusations of the Ikhwan's lack of transparency in its leadership selection processes as the work of communists and Zionists:

> Those individuals who raise such issues are viciously cunning. They want us to speak and then instigate the state against us. What if we speak on what we have of *Shura* [consultation] ... would the state then stay silent? [The state] would say: "You are a disbanded group and yet you have a hundred-member council and you have administrations and you make decisions. Undoubtedly, the reason behind raising this issue is to cause a clash between the Ikhwan and the state. The majority of those who raise these issues are Marxists ... and they are causing a *fitna* [sedition] and crises in society ... [and] they are also atheists ... The communist group in Egypt had earlier been founded by the Zionists.[14]

Although Ma'mun's tenure lasted only two years, he cemented the conservatives' control over decision making.[15] For example, in 2001 he appointed Mahmoud Izzat, a well-known hardliner, as secretary general of the Muslim Brotherhood. Izzat's task was to restructure the Ikhwan's administrative offices along more hierarchical and patriarchal lines.[16] Following the end of his tenure, Hudaybi was succeeded by two other Qutbians. Mohamed Mahdi Akef, a hardliner and an icon of the 1950s and 1960s generation, served as the supreme guide from 2004 until 2010.[17] Akef was subsequently followed by Mohamed Badie, another loyal disciple of Qutb, who was sentenced to ten years in prison after the Tanzim al-Sirri was discovered. Selected as the supreme guide in 2010, Badie is currently in prison following his arrest after the clampdown on the Islamist movement in 2013.

The Fault Lines

This decades-old divide between the core reactionary leadership of the Ikhwan and the reformist camp has greatly hindered the institutional development of the organization. Disagreements between the two factions revolve around a wide range of important issues, such as calls for greater transparency and power sharing and the role of women in society. The intransigence of the ultraconservative wing and its dogged refusal to open up the Ikhwan and institute meaningful internal reforms weakened the organization and left it unprepared for and unequipped to cope with the titanic changes unleashed by the January revolution in 2011. The Ikhwan's failure to adopt a more conciliatory stance and a more open mind towards its political rivals was one of the most notable blunders made by the leadership during and after the January revolution. It fed into the fears of the Egyptian public and consequently allowed the military to carry out a counterrevolution and remove the group from power after it had won the 2011 presidential elections. One of the major criticisms leveled against Mohamed Morsi's presidency was his growing autocracy, secrecy, and opaque decision making; similar charges had been internally voiced by many Ikhwan members against their own leadership for some time.

Autocracy

The most contentious and enduring charge leveled by the reformist camp against the old guard is that they are deeply autocratic, controlling the Ikhwan as their own personal fiefdom. Reformists insist that the ultraconservative leaders impose their will in a patriarchal manner by demanding absolute obedience (*al-sam' wa-l-ta'a*), refusing to accept transparency or scrutiny, and brooking no dissent or free thinking. Mohamed Abdel Sattar, who knows the Ikhwan intimately and who spent three years in Mubarak's prisons in the second half of the 1990s, pointed out that within the group's internal hierarchy, loyalty and seniority were placed over creativity and qualification. He explained that promotion to executive posts depended on patrimonial ties and stressed that the Ikhwan remained institutionally fragile because it had not developed formal mechanisms for decision making. As Abdel Sattar put it, the personal superseded the institutional. Moreover, the senior leadership resented younger members who earned a high public profile, often belittling their public engagement and participation as mere grandstanding. In an effort to curb such practices, the old guard fielded mediocre candidates for Parliament and other elections because they are seen as nonthreatening to the status quo: "They fear the emergence of dynamic and charismatic leaders who might challenge their hold on the movement," he said.[18] "After their release from jails in the 1970s, the Ikhwan chiefs dominated the organization and behaved as if [they] had traded a small prison for a bigger one. They inhabited a culture of conspiracy, secrecy, and enmity toward the outside world, and [they] never reconciled with state and society," he said.[19] Abdel Sattar compared this problem to a kind of siege mentality directly related to the conditions under which the movement was forged and evolved over the years. "What you need to understand is that the powers that be in the Ikhwan do not forget and do not forgive," he said. "They modeled their movement along Leninist lines in order to strengthen its resistance against infiltration by the authorities and alien cultural viruses as well."

Abdel Sattar elaborated on the drivers behind the conduct of the Ikhwan leaders, many of whom belonged to the 1960s generation. "To put it bluntly, Ikhwan elders hoped to exact vengeance against the Egyptian state and settle scores with the Nasserist revolution. Long after they gained their freedom, Ikhwan chiefs still view themselves as exiles from society, disinherited and disenfranchised. They thus prioritized the organization's security and survival over genuine reforms. What this meant is that the old guard protected its turf."[20] Overall, Abdel Sattar drew a dark portrait of "closed, secretive, and undemocratic decision making, where a few elders of the 1960s generation decide the destiny of the entire organization." His account echoed others that described how those sheikhs are able to maintain their dominance by using their prolonged imprisonment as a legitimizing tool to ensure that their orders are fully obeyed by younger members, who tend to be humbled by the sacrifices those elders had made.[21]

Comparable sentiments were also expressed by Ahmed Ra'if. In several interviews in his condominium in a suburb outside Cairo in 2007, he explained that he was no longer formally affiliated with the organization.[22] Ra'if prided himself on thinking outside the Islamist box despite having spent years in prison as part of Qutb's al-Tanzim al-Sirri. He conceded that while he still believed in the Islamist project, decades of close encounters with the Ikhwan had made him cynical about the group. "The Ikhwan is a huge machine operated by a single key, a self-enclosed apparatus that defies explanation," he told me. "I know what I am talking about because I have been part of it for the past fifty years. The differing voices you get from Ikhwan members are misleading because they imply diversity and plurality. Not so—the apparatus is impenetrable like a rock for outsiders like you."[23]

Ra'if argued that repression, secrecy, and decades in the underground have deformed the movement. Like Abdel Sattar, he linked this to a siege mentality, in which Ikhwan leaders see themselves as persecuted and estranged from society. This sense of *ghurba*, or alienation and isolation, is deeply entrenched in the political culture of the movement and causes it to be secretive and self-enclosed, distrustful of the outside world and public engagement. Ra'if, who has known every one of the Ikhwan supreme guides since the 1950s, asserted that "the Ikhwan have their special world. The public face of the Ikhwan is a facade. [...] The movement's real strength lies underground, not above ground. Senior leaders are naturally socialized into this culture and they take it for granted."[24] "Go and ask top leaders of the Ikhwan about their budget, elections, and recruitment," he suggested sarcastically before exclaiming, "They never reveal a thing! The Ikhwan world is sealed and classified."[25] In addition to a lack of transparency, Ra'if suggested that Ikhwan leaders failed to recognize the importance of engaging with other groups or reconciling with society in general. "A widespread sentiment exists among the Ikhwan that they have gained the upper hand over the state because of their organizational strength throughout Egypt and the world," Ra'if explained. "'Strength in numbers' is the Ikhwan's motto, which shows shortsightedness and naiveté."[26] In remarks that some would see as a harbinger of events in the two years following the 2011 uprising in Egypt, Ra'if expressed his suspicion that if the Ikhwan were to gain power, they would be unwilling to deal transparently with society or to share authority with others. "My knowledge of the Ikhwan, with their victimhood mentality, tells me that if empowered they would not trust the other or allow him a place at the table. I say this as an Islamist from within the movement. We are on the brink of a catastrophe."[27]

In 1999, I had already confronted Ma'mun Hudaybi with members' accusations of autocratic practices within the Ikhwan during his tenure, but he remained defiant. Although he deigned to offer a denial of sorts—"people who say we are authoritarian are lying; in 1995 we elected a Majlis al-Shura [Guidance Office] and established a legal decision-making body"—he also staunchly defended the movement's demand for obedience from its members. "Yes, we expect members to show obedience because not to do so would sow chaos and confusion in the Ikhwan," he said. "How do you exercise authority if members oppose decisions taken by legitimately elected leaders? Why do critics deny us the right to demand *al-sam' wa-l-ta'a* [absolute obedience] after that?"[28]

Ma'mun's assurances were echoed by another former supreme guide, Mohamed Akef, who belittled my questions related to the dominance of the old guard and the sidelining of the reformists as a figment of their imagination. When I presented him the specific complaints advanced by reformists like Abu al-Futuh, Abdel Sattar, and others, he exploded in anger, saying those who "whisper behind my back are not real Ikhwan." In contrast, he asserted, "My door is open to all members who are disciplined and who regularly communicate with me. Those who do not have themselves to blame. Al-Jama'a [the Ikhwan] is a big organization with twenty-five administrative offices nationwide. I receive reports from every one of them and each office makes decisions about its own locality."[29] Akef's attempt to portray the Ikhwan as decentralized and institutionalized is not fully convincing given the assertion by many members, not just reformists, that decision making is centralized, top-down, and that the movement is highly patriarchal. Even former senior figures such as Mohamed Habib refuted Akef's claims, however. Habib, who was first deputy to Akef, pointed out that Akef himself had broken the rules on at least one occasion, by appointing one member for a senior post without consulting the Guidance Office.[30] Ironically, that appointee was Mohamed Morsi, who later became the president of Egypt.

When I put to Akef the charges by Ikhwan members that the elections are a predetermined ritual and that the candidates are selected in advance by the inner circle, he once again rejected them as lies. "We are not a political party led by one person but an institutionalized *jama'* based on *al-shura* [consultation], and we take that religious duty very seriously," he insisted impatiently. "Like similar institutions elsewhere, we consult among each other and reach decisions by consensus. The personalized factor is not important." Akef even went further by presenting the organization as embracing freedom of speech: "I have given every member the right to speak about the Ikhwan and to promote it ... We carry out internal surveys to find out what members think. There is no disconnect between the leadership and the base."[31]

Despite Ma'mun's and Akef's assurances, there exists a relative consensus among internal critics that the Ikhwan have not made a break with the past either epistemologically or institutionally. According to this viewpoint, the top leadership is still wedded to a worldview nourished on victimhood, fear, and suspicion of the Other. They draw a portrait of an entrenched elite which is weighed down by the demons of the prison camps. Although they insist they seek no vengeance or retribution against their tormentors, Ikhwan leaders of the Qutbian generation have made no steps to reconcile with either the state or society. "The elders have a different take on politics than political scientists," said Ahmed Ra'if. "Us versus the world, a definition born out of decades of confrontation with the authorities. The sheikhs view politics as trench warfare."[32] Ahmed El-'Gouz, a dissenter from the Ikhwan, called this defect "the Ikhwan peculiarity"—a dominant sentiment within the group that "degrades the Other as less qualified or capable of doing what the Ikhwan member can do."[33]

Reformists single out Mahmoud Izzat as one example of one whose mind-set is a major hindrance to the institutional development and democratization of the Ikhwan. Izzat has been a power broker with significant influence over decision making during the last four decades. All of my interviewees conceded that he is at the center of the Ikhwan power structure and that as such he is greatly feared. Coincidentally, he is one the few top Ikhwan leaders who evaded the net cast by the Egyptian authorities following the 2013 crackdown against the movement. There are credible reports that following the incarceration of the supreme guide Badie, Izzat became the de facto leader. His wealth and personal networks have allowed him to accumulate excessive power. Abu El-Ela Madi, who broke with the Ikhwan in 1996 to form the moderate Islamist party al-Wasat, accused Izzat of "acting as a patriarch, granting his blessing and favors to obedient figures and excluding reformists who do not toe the official line and are seen as troublemakers."[34]

Izzat's central role was exposed in the events that took place around the Ikhwan's 2008 internal elections and the subsequent 2009 selection of the new supreme guide. Akef, then the supreme guide, refused to run for a second term after his request to make Essam al-Erian a member of the Guidance Office was rejected, reportedly because of Izzat's opposition.[35] Against demands to postpone the election for six months in order to allow candidates to explain their platforms, Izzat insisted on holding the vote much sooner (before January 2010), allegedly in an attempt to sideline the reformist candidate, Mohamed Habib, who had been a member of the Guidance Office for twenty-four years and was already serving as deputy to Akef.[36] Habib presented a complaint to the guidance committee against what he described as a hasty procedure to elect the leader of the group, but he did not hear back from them. In response, Habib took his battle to the media and threatened to resign.[37] The Ikhwan reacted with another statement confirming the procedure as being in line with the Ikhwan code. Habib resigned and subsequently became one of the staunchest critics of the movement. In a series of articles published in 2015, he exposed Akef as lacking "the strategic mind-set and having limited skills in planning, organization, and management, which allowed the Qutbians to dominate the whole group." Habib also named Izzat as one of those "Qutbians" who facilitated the old guard's control of the Ikhwan.[38]

Habib's distaste for Izzat was shared by Madi, who angrily told me that "autocratic leaders like Izzat, who monopolize power, give the Ikhwan a bad name and prevent it from embracing modernity and a critical sensibility and outlook." Using strong words, he described the Ikhwan as brainless and disconnected from what is happening in the world. In his words, the leadership's fear of change and "unwillingness to nourish an open and inclusive political culture" has led the organization to become a creature that has "the body of a dinosaur with the brain of a bird."[39] As a result of such failings, he suggested, the Ikhwan "frightens away thinkers, theorists, and reformists. It is a graveyard for creative ideas." Noticeably, this criticism has been repeated again and again by other members like Ahmed Ramzy, who blamed the group for the 2013 catastrophe, almost seven years after my interview with Madi, writing that "the Ikhwan is brainless, a group that obeys an order before thinking about it, a policy of herd mentality."[40] Another dissenter, Ahmed El-'ouz, revealed in his memoirs that he left the Ikhwan "in order to allow my brain to escape attempts to freeze it" by the domineering leadership.[41]

Structural Ideological Rigidity

Moreover, reformists argue that the ideological rigidity of the movement inhibits the ability of members to find their place in society, or lack thereof. Although many of the younger members of the Ikhwan are open-minded and forward-looking, the base, as a whole, is as intolerant and reactionary as the top, and perhaps more so, because of the organization's rigid patriarchal and hierarchical structure. Members are co-opted through practices that closely resemble those of paramilitary organizations, meaning that the structure constantly clones itself through a limited process of selection of recruits and indoctrination. The result is that the base is socialized into an insular culture that isolates members from their broader social environment and turns them into robot-like agents. They are taught to always obey their elders and to have blind faith in the group. According to insiders' accounts, the curriculum is permeated with Qutbian terms and references and is designed to inhibit dissent. "The Ikhwan have not abandoned the Qutbian legacy and his ideas still provide inspiration to young members," acknowledged Farid Abdel Khaleq, a former top leader who did not take sides in the internal power struggle. This fixation on Qutbian ideals, he warned, presents a constant risk for young members of being led down the "dead-end" route of taking up arms against the state.[42] Implying that the curricula was at fault for perpetuating an ultraconservative political culture among members, he argued that a substantial revision is urgently needed and instead independent thinking, love of one's country, respect for the Other, and better knowledge of the world should be prioritized. He further contended that the leadership should also emphasize the organization's commitment to moderation and cooperation with other political forces to bring about peaceful change.

Similarly, Abu al-Futuh argued that such co-optation practices risk what he referred to as "postponed violence" being activated in the future. This insular culture of socialization and constant mobilization of the youth, coupled with the political persecution of the Ikhwan, has made them vulnerable and susceptible to engaging in violence, he warned. "We need to demobilize our youth and incubate them against thinking the unthinkable—resorting to violence either defensively or offensively," he said.[43] Abu al-Futuh was particularly wary of the increasing risks of a confrontation between the Ikhwan youth and the state because of a widespread belief among young members that politics is ineffective in dealing with the security services.

In order to avoid such dangers, Ussama Abdel Khaleq, a reformist figure and a son of Farid Abdel Khaleq, called on senior Ikhwan leaders to implement structural reforms: "It is more urgent to design pedagogical and cultural strategies to effect change from the bottom up, and to reward members based more on their contribution to the institution than on their blind loyalty to the leadership; we need to transform the worldview of cadres and the political economy of benefits as a prerequisite for the transformation of the movement," he told me.[44] According to Ussama, the current status quo rewards those members who toe the party line by granting them jobs and economic benefits. This reinforces the dominant structure and culture within the Ikhwan. Rather than being exposed to critical ideas of tolerance, inclusiveness, and citizenship, members are fed a rich diet of blind loyalty to the organization, thus co-opting them and cloning the structure that favors the conservative elites.

As recent complaints by other prominent members who deserted the group after the Arab Spring uprisings in 2011 show, the hardliners who dominate the Ikhwan continue to veto reform initiatives. According to Sameh Eid, a well-known Ikhwan dissident, one of the key sectors used by the hardliners to stall change is to "educate" or brainwash Ikhwan members once they are drawn into the group. Eid described the methods used as "quasi-military ... since it is based on the literature of al-Nizam al-Khass."[45] To support his assertion, Eid cited terms used by the Ikhwan to sum up the values that a "good" Ikhwan member should hold dear, including "*bay'a* [fealty], confidence, obedience, discipline, secretiveness. [We were asked to do] physical exercises such as walking long distances with a limited supply of water and to play martial arts such as karate and kung fu."[46] Published in 2014, these criticisms were a carbon copy of those already leveled by Mohamed al-Tahawy against the Ikhwan in 1986. Ahmed Ban, a leader in the Ikhwan who also dissented in 2011, echoed Eid's claims and denounced ultraconservative ex-members of al-Nizam al-Khass who "have always been keen to control the *tarbiyaa* [education] sector in the Ikhwan from the time they got out of prisons in 1973 until today."[47]

Clientelism and Nepotism

These dynamics of autocracy and insularity go hand in hand with an organizational culture of patronage, clientelism, and nepotism, which guarantees secrecy and lack of accountability and transparency. This culture also allows the leadership to institute harsh punishments for members who challenge or violate the order of things. Sameh Eid cited a case where a member was threatened with separation from his wife and children, who were also Ikhwan members, to dissuade him from opting out.[48] This punishment is particularly harsh because the group's recruitment is in the first place based on "social exclusion" of its members.[49] Thus, subsequently, if a member decides to leave the Ikhwan or is forced out, he also inevitably loses all his social networks, which may also include his family unit. As Eid notes, the Ikhwan leaders threaten an unruly member this way: "If you disobey us, God will punish you in the afterlife and we will punish you in this life."[50]

According to Intisar Abdel Moneim, Ikhwan members who have the right connections receive massive financial support from the group.[51] Ahmed Ramzy, a journalist and former Brother, pointed out that members are linked to each other through a "sacred tie."[52] According to him, promotion within the group is based not only on the degree of religiosity but on closeness to the group's leaders.[53] Ramzy pointed to the organization's media outlets as a case in point: these are a failure because since "trust comes first," editorial posts are given to Ikhwan members only, regardless of their qualification or lack thereof.[54] Ramzy developed his own theory to explain the leadership's aim in its recruitment and indoctrination processes, which he sarcastically labeled the "jelly theory." Their focus, he explains, remains on "cloning members identical to each other who can easily be brainwashed or reconstructed exactly like producing seamlessly patterned jelly cubes."[55]

Other dissenters like Tharwat al-Kharabawy are critical of how social status can lead to internal favoritism. He highlighted the example of Ahmed Seif al-Islam Hassan al-Banna, a grandson of the founder of the movement. In 1992, Banna was selected by the leadership to stand for elections in the Lawyers Syndicate. This was in clear violation of the rules that a candidate should be elected internally before being selected for an external election. His selection, Kharabawy suggested, was made only on the basis of his family background. Further illustrating how economic, social, and family relations contribute to shutting off the Ikhwan from wider society, he described the ideal type of Ikhwan member as a "bird in a golden cage":

> [The Ikhwan member] marries another Ikhwan member, works for an Ikhwan member, makes friends with Ikhwan members, rents or buys a flat from an Ikhwan member, has an Ikhwan neighbor, has an Ikhwan colleague ... She/he ends up living in a circle of Ikhwan insulated from the outside world.[56]

The relationship between material wealth and power within the organization is corroborated by evidence of concentration of resources in the hands of a few leading members, such as Hassan Malek and Khairat al-Shater.[57] In the context of the crackdown on the Ikhwan that followed the ousting of President Mohamed Morsi in 2013, for example, the prosecutor ordered the freezing of no fewer than sixty-six companies owned by Malek and Shater.[58]

When confronted with such charges leveled by the reformists, the Ikhwan old guard tends to mount two kinds of defense. One, they deny the accuracy of the criticism, and two, they defend their prerogative to behave in some of the ways described by the reformists. For example, when I pressed former supreme guide Akef about the Ikhwan's sources of funding for its activities and the lack of financial transparency, he was unapologetic and refused to engage seriously with this line of questioning. When I questioned him about expenditures, he hesitated before irritatedly replying, "We spend what we need." When I asked where these funds come from, he replied, "Those members who are financially fortunate give more. I cannot give you exact figures because we do not have a budget. Every office takes care of its own expenses and every member donates according to his means. We are like a family." When I further pressed Akef on the question of who is in charge of finances and on the size of the annual budget, he was evasive. He claimed that there is no particular person in charge of such matters. In contrast, reformists have told me time and time again that the powerful Mahmoud Izzat, the gatekeeper of the Ikhwan, has firm control of the purse strings.

Coincidently, in response to my questions about the size of the membership of the Islamist movement, Akef curtly suggested that I might seek such information from Izzat instead. This was clearly an effective diversionary tactic, given that my experience with Izzat had been highly negative. As one of the most influential behind-the-scenes figures in the Ikhwan, Izzat shuns the public limelight. He is a man of few words and his preferred playground is closed Ikhwan tea rooms. Though after several Ikhwan members interceded on my behalf, Izzat granted me an interview at the Ikhwan headquarters in the Rawda neighborhood of Cairo in late 2006, he avoided offering substantive answers to most of my queries.

However, Izzat was quick to dismiss the reformers as "sore losers" who "do not speak for the base and have no constituency of their own." In response to the charges of autocracy and lack of transparency, he replied in the same vein as Akef, telling me, "The Ikhwan holds regular elections, practices *shura* [consultation], and is transparent. We have our own mechanisms of selection of morally fit candidates, as opposed to those politically ambitious [individuals]."[59] He equally disputed the idea that hardliners of the Qutbian school have been in control of the Ikhwan since the 1970s, and that they have impaired the development and evolution of the movement. As an example, he pointed to the presence of a plurality of viewpoints in the Guidance

Office and cited the movement's pacts with non-Islamist parties to run candidates in parliamentary elections in the 1990s. Against charges of stagnation and fossilization, he replied, "You can't stop change because it is *sunnat al-hayat* [life's law] and we have endeavored to embrace good changes; but [we] reject foreign influences that corrupt our faith and culture. We do not pay attention to detractors who wish al-Jama'a harm and are envious and full of hate."[60]

Public Policy

Another contentious issue between the old guard and the younger reformers is whether political participation should be practiced through the formal political system or by joining protests and other forms of street politics. These debates have come down to one particularly prominent question: the possible formation of an Ikhwan-affiliated political party. This subject is central to the widening gap between the younger members of Ikhwan and the power core of the ultraconservative leadership, which fears that democratizing the organization would dilute their domination of the decision making and increase the influence of reformists. Abu El-Ela Madi was a witness to this controversy. He told me that from the early 1980s until the late 1990s, the reformers lobbied hard to establish a political party in order to allow the Ikhwan to function legally and to compete openly in the public sphere. "Our goal was to get closer to the concerns and the needs of the Egyptian people and to deepen our engagement with civil society and build a democratic foundation. That is what politics is all about—delivering public goods to the community," he told me.[61]

However, despite the reformists' efforts, Madi explained that Ikhwan leaders kept stonewalling and deferring questions concerning the establishment of a political party. "Most [members of the Ikhwan] had a background in paramilitary networks, such as al-Nizam al-Khass, which was established by *al-murshid* Hassan al-Banna, or the 1965 Tanzim [al-Sirri] of Sayyid Qutb. [They] had serious misgivings about opening up the organization and exposing it to public scrutiny," he pointed out. "They were socialized into an underground mind-set with a preference for hierarchy, secrecy, and closed decision making. They only trusted one another."[62] Consequently, core members of the Ikhwan internalized the culture they had been exposed to from early on and promoted it within the organization. Faced with repeated rejections, Madi said that he and others "gave up on the Ikhwan." As he put it: "We concluded that we could not resist Mubarak's authoritarianism while belonging to an autocratic group. That undermined our credibility as religious activists and the Islamist movement as well."[63]

Madi left the Ikhwan in the mid-1990s and formed al-Wasat in 1996. However, despite the incorporation of secular nationalist demands in its program and the inclusion of the moderate thinker Abdel Wahab al-Messeiry, al-Wasat was denied a license to operate as a political party by the Mubarak regime.[64] The old guard even used the Mubarak regime's refusal to support the foundation of an Ikhwan political party to defend their opposition to initiatives such as Madi's. "If the president [Mubarak] insists on refusing to permit the establishment of an [Islamic] party, we in the group find the step of even proposing to create such a party inappropriate and politically inadequate," Ma'mun Hudaybi said in an interview in 2005.[65] However, despite the Mubarak regime's initial refusal and the Ikhwan's backing of it, al-Wasat eventually secured legal recognition in 2011.[66]

As in Madi's case, other younger reformists were greatly frustrated by the seeming submissiveness of the old guard to the Mubarak regime and their reluctance to consider cooperation with the secular political opposition. They accused senior leaders of refusing to build coalitions with rival political groups in order to forestall the emergence of any social and political movement that could threatens the Ikhwan's supremacy. The core leadership of the Ikhwan, they insist, lacks public consciousness and is not prepared to work with others on an equal footing even in the interest of the common good. Some have even openly accused prominent leaders of working with the state to increase their own power. According to Haytham Abu Khalil, who resigned from the Ikhwan in March 2011 after twenty-two years in the organization, "some leaders of the Guidance Office had taken actions which run against the history of the Ikhwan by colluding with the government in previous elections and agreeing to vote rigging in return for parliamentary seats."[67]

Of all the reformists whom I interviewed, Abdel Sattar was the most scathing in his criticism. He argued that the Ikhwan leaders' refusal to be part of any oppositional civil society coalition came down to the fact that, on some level, they considered a deal with the incumbent authorities to be more profitable than a risky gamble with the opposition. "To gain legalization, Ikhwan leaders desperately and cynically tried to appease the ruler by concluding informal electoral alliances with members of his party against their own candidates and eschewing any public challenge," he said. "Having neither a political imagination nor a moral compass, the elders desired recognition regardless of the costs, including alienation of civil society,"[68] he added before noting that the Ikhwan had ended up damaging and isolating itself in the process. For example, he recalled how senior Ikhwan leaders refused to coordinate action with Kifaya, the protest movement. Established in 2004, Kifaya was heavily involved in a wave of anti-government street protests in the run-up to the 2005 presidential election. Abdel Sattar put the leadership's reaction down to small-minded rivalries and a reluctance to disrupt the status quo. "They [the senior Ikhwan leaders] were petty and envious, fearing that Kifaya could become a political rival," he said. "The old guard put the narrow interest of their organization over the national interest. They didn't want to rock the boat with the old regime."[69]

When in 2007 I pressed Akef on the leadership's refusal to join protests organized by political parties or movements such as Kifaya, he followed the same line of reasoning as Ma'mun had in my 2005 interview with him. "I will not risk the future of al-Jama'a [the group] by defying the Mubarak regime and triggering all-out confrontation. Critics who call on us to protest in the streets do not think about the grave consequences. Unlike other small groups, we, as the biggest organization, act responsibly and measure our actions carefully. We will not give the security forces justification to clamp down harder on us. I have to protect the brothers and the movement," he told me.[70] Akef's tone left no doubt that he had contempt for Kifaya and other political parties. He dismissed them as "*ahzab waraqiyya*," or paper parties, implying that they possess no real social base. In practice, the conservative preference of the Ikhwan leadership for maintaining a compromise with the then incumbent government rather than embarking upon a revolutionary path with uncertain outcomes fragmented the opposition and contributed to extending the life of the Mubarak regime. Despite the best efforts of the reformists, it becomes apparent that the ultraconservatives continued to call the shots within the Ikhwan until the movement was crushed in 2013.

The Role of Women

The views prevalent within each of the reformist and reactionary camps regarding the status of women in society is perhaps what best epitomizes the divide that separates them. In my interviews with Akef and his cohorts, they were adamant that women do not have the right to serve as judges or as heads of state. "A woman president, no way!" Akef exclaimed. Although he contended that "we respect women," he clearly delineated the role of the female subject as being in the private sphere. "Women are builders of men," he said, further emphasizing this trope. "I recall vividly how [my] mother visited me in the military prison in 1965 [following his arrest in connection with the crackdown of that year] and told me, 'Son, stand firm.'" Akef's view of women's role as being exclusively limited to the private sphere was further epitomized by a rhetorical question he asked me: "What happens if a woman is in a meeting and suddenly had her period?" His answer followed: "She would stain the wall and be humiliated." He added, "Women could easily be exploited by unscrupulous men who play on their emotions and lead them astray." It is likely that Akef's view of such strictly defined female-male roles extends to most of the ultraconservative core leadership. Mustafa Mashour had expressed similar sentiments regarding the role of women. In an interview I conducted with him in the late 1990s when he still held the post of supreme guide, he praised women's contribution to society before exclaiming, "How could a woman lead prayers if elected president?"[71]

Privately, the young reformists point to their elders' stance on women and minorities as a general example of the struggle playing out within the Ikhwan to define its public agenda. While they acknowledge that the views held by much of the movement's grassroots membership are as conservative and reactionary as those of the old guard, they decry the unwillingness of the latter to undertake efforts to educate the base about the importance of inclusiveness and gender tolerance. A hopeful sign of change came with the announcement of a reform initiative in March 2004 that explicitly guaranteed equal rights for women in relation to voting, standing for elections, and, crucially, taking up senior positions within the structure of the state. However, this apparent breakthrough, which marked a major shift in Ikhwan policy, was abruptly reversed in 2007 with the announcement of a new political program that reaffirmed the traditional orientation of the organization and reversed the decision to allow women to become judges or to serve as president.[72]

Furthermore, evidence suggests that women were never actually allowed equal opportunities inside the group. Providing backup for this argument, in her autobiography Intissar Abdel Moneim, a former Ikhwan activist, detailed how women who join the Ikhwan are dissuaded from opposing the movement's patriarchal decision-making hierarchy. The group takes this position on religious grounds and on the basis of its principle of *al-sam'a wa-l-ta'a* (blind obedience), Abdel Moneim explained.[73] While women were allowed to stand for elections in 2000 and 2005, it was a reflection of nepotism rather than a genuine change in attitudes on matters of gender, she argued.[74] In 2000, for example, it was Jihan al-Halafawi, the wife of Ibrahim al-Za'frany, a senior Ikhwan figure, who was selected as a candidate. Similarly, Makarem al-Deiry, who was allowed to run as a candidate in 2005, was the widow of the late Ibrahim Sharaf, who had been a member of the Guidance Office and had spent almost a decade in Nasser's and Mubarak's prisons. According to Abdel Moneim, women members of the group were not even consulted on the 2004 reform initiative or the 2007 political program.[75]

However, some Ikhwan leaders blame the lack of female representation on the state's oppressive attitude. "Any man walking in the street is exposed to detention. We even heard threats that women can be detained as well," Ma'mun Hudaybi warned in an interview.[76] Indeed, these fears were not unfounded. In 2005, despite the Mubarak regime's pledge for a democratic and peaceful ballot, security forces used force to disrupt the flow of voters in a constituency where the Ikhwan had chosen a woman to run for office. This wave of violence left 14 killed, 800 injured, and 1,700 imprisoned.[77] Having conducted extensive interviews with a great many members of the Ikhwan over the past two decades, my own reading is that Ikhwan members of all persuasions hold deeply illiberal views on women as a result of patriarchal socialization. While there are important differences in the views held by the old guard and the younger reformists in this regard, ultimately these are a matter of degree rather than fundamentally opposing outlooks.

Many of the criticisms leveled by the reformists against the Ikhwan old guard ultimately boil down to a frustration with their profound conservatism and repeated refusal to envision changing the status quo either politically or in the broader social sphere. This problem had long ago been highlighted by none other than Yusuf Qaradawi, the high-profile religious scholar who is widely considered a spiritual mentor for the Ikhwan. In 1992, Qaradawi authored a book in which he warned the group's leadership against the risk of arriving at "an extremist position," resulting from a habit of "keeping what is traditional and old and resisting what is modern and new."[78] He cautioned that shutting down processes of modernization and *ijtihad*, or independent reasoning, would lead to a brain drain and create a situation where the Ikhwan would lose all but "traditionalist and conservative" elements. Such developments, he warned, would encase the group in "rigidity and sterility."[79] Qaradawi's worst fears did come true, since many reformists, including Hassan al-Baquri,

Mohamed al-Ghazli, and Anwar al-Gindi, have exited the group in protest.[80]

Ruralization of the Ikhwan

From the 1970s onwards, an important shift occurred in the social composition of the Ikhwan. An increasing number of rural and agrarian members, both in the organization's lower ranks and in its top echelons, further entrenched the Ikhwan in a culture of secrecy and insularity. Rapidly socialized into the organization, rural members had fewer chances of opening up to the urban environment and its cosmopolitanism. This dynamic also allowed for the establishment of relationships based on patronage and clientelism, which only fed the members' dependency on the group. By cultivating fear of the Other, the top leadership was able to play on traditional values of kinship and loyalty and successfully forestall potential dissent. In addition to the ruralization phenomenon, the Ikhwan's complex relations with the state was another important driver behind the ultraconservative camp's consolidation of power. Using its alternating conciliatory and confrontational positions vis-à-vis the state, the Ikhwan leadership succeeded in pushing back against the reformists' efforts for change.

In the first decades of the Ikhwan's existence, some of those associated with it claimed that over half of its membership was drawn from rural areas.[81] Although this may have been true, the scholar Richard Mitchell considered that these rural members were generally no more than "a backdrop for the urban activists who shaped the Society's political destiny."[82] Lists of Ikhwan leaders who attended major meetings in the 1930s and 1950s suggest that only a minority came from rural areas.[83] Supporting this assertion, regulations at that time specifically stipulated that nine members of the eleven-man Guidance Office must come from Cairo.[84] Concurring with Mitchell, Nazih Ayubi provided further evidence by examining the composition of the administrative bodies in the Ikhwan. According to Ayubi, "a listing of their consultative Assembly in 1953 showed that out of 1,950 members, all but 22 of them belonged to the *effendiya*. The top leadership of 12 was of a higher educational, cultural, and possibly social level."[85] However, there was a qualitative change in the composition of the Ikhwan's leadership beginning in the 1970s. This decade witnessed socioeconomic transformation which fueled massive emigration from rural to urban areas, with both changes having an unprecedented effect on the Ikhwan. In addition to increased travel to Cairo by young students seeking a university education, the economic liberalization promoted by Sadat widened the opportunities for private-sector companies, most of which were concentrated in urban areas. This led to further emigration from the rural to the urban, specifically Cairo. Furthermore, many Ikhwan members from rural Egypt traveled to the Gulf, especially Saudi Arabia, and returned home rich and more conservative, exercising more influence within the Ikhwan.

The weight of evidence shows that the "overwhelming majority of migrants to urban areas have come directly from their communities of origin, bypassing small and medium-sized towns."[86] This rural migration led to social alienation and radicalization for some of the newcomers.[87] For example, surveys show that "membership of militant Islamist groups in the 1970s and 1980s tended to come from urban areas but with more recent recruits from rural or small town backgrounds."[88] With the increased ruralization of the Ikhwan leadership came new forms of clientelism, whereby officials could be identified with certain provinces in stable patron-client relationships.[89] This social transformation also consolidated patriarchal practices like *al-sam'a wa-l-ta'a* (absolute obedience), thus reinforcing the influence of ultraconservative power brokers such as Izzat.[90] Remarkably, out of the eight supreme guides, only Omar al-Telmessany was born in Cairo, the capital. The rest came from either the upper or lower part of Egypt. A convincing case can be made that Telmessany's open-mindedness and tolerance can be traced to his cosmopolitan "urban" background, which, according to his memoirs, included going to the cinema, dancing the tango and the Charleston, and playing music.[91] His childhood memories stand in stark contrast with those of Ikhwan leaders from "rural" backgrounds like Qutb or Akef.

Researcher Hossam Tammam, a former member of the Ikhwan, suggested that this process of ruralization pushed the group into a dynamic of "re-traditionalization" and widened the gap between conservatives and reformists.[92] In the late 2000s, the ruralization of the organization had a direct impact on the makeup of the movement's Guidance Office. For example, in the 2008–2009 elections four out of five winners of seats were from rural areas.[93] Finally, fifteen members out of the seventeen-member Guidance Office were living in or rooted in provincial areas.[94] This pattern was also reflected in the Shura Council (Consultative Assembly) of the Ikhwan, with a mandatory requirement of twenty-three seats allotted to candidates from the three provincial governorates (Daqahliyya, Sharqiyya, and Gharbia), compared with eleven seats for members from urban Cairo and Alexandria.[95] The leadership also used loopholes to increase the involvement of rural members in the organization, appointing them to positions reserved under the quota for members from the urban areas.[96]

Repression and Counter-reaction

While ruralization is one factor that has contributed to bolstering the position of the old guard, the fortunes of the conservative and reformist factions have also depended in part on the varying force with which the movement as a whole has been repressed by the Egyptian state over the past decades. As will be discussed below, periods of increased state repression tended to benefit the more conservative currents within the Ikhwan. If Sadat's signing of the Camp David Peace Accords, followed by increased state repression towards the end of his tenure, bolstered the position of the ultraconservative faction within the Ikhwan, the subsequent thirty-year rule of Mubarak can be loosely divided into two stages. The first, the 1980s, saw a period of relative accommodation that in the second, from the 1990s up until the January 2011 revolution, gave way to a tenser and more confrontational relationship.

Although the Ikhwan was still officially outlawed in the 1980s, Mona El-Ghobashy has described this period as one of "electoralism and the politics of adaptation" marked by "de facto tolerance."[97] In 1984 the Ikhwan were allowed to put forward independent candidates for the Parliament, thus giving them eight seats. Again in 1987 the Ikhwan participated in the parliamentary elections, winning thirty-six seats after forging an alliance with the liberal Wafd party. In addition to the parliamentary elections, the Ikhwan ran candidates for the elections in the country's professional syndicates and won most of the seats, including the syndicates for doctors, engineers, pharmacists, scientists, and lawyers. The programs of these new Ikhwan-dominated syndicates were not limited to the "Islamicization of Egypt" but rather varied from providing social services for members to boosting the national economy and opposing the normalization of relations with Israel.[98]

Although the Ikhwan offered support to Mubarak throughout the 1980s, the regime nevertheless became increasingly anxious as the group continued to grow in influence. In 1986, for example, the Ikhwan in the medical syndicate in Cairo introduced a subsidized health-care scheme which benefited the families of 43,000 members of the syndicate. The huge number of beneficiaries underlined the real need for quality health care in Egypt and highlighted the deficiencies of the state institutions responsible for the provision of health services. State officials were primarily concerned with the expansion of the Ikhwan while the latter sought to harvest "societal legitimacy," through provision of social welfare and services, into formal legal recognition of the movement's right to operate in Egypt.[99]

As the organization grew in confidence, it became more confrontational towards the Mubarak regime. An important sign of this shift came with the 1991 Gulf War, in which the movement backed Saddam Hussein against the Egyptian regime's involvement in the U.S.-led coalition to expel the Iraqi army from Kuwait.[100] Another turning point came with the earthquake which hit Egypt in 1992, killing hundreds, injuring thousands, and causing devastating damage. While the state authorities were slow to respond to the devastation, the Ikhwan saved the day. It used the professional syndicates' resources to come to the rescue of the earthquake's victims and was able to deliver relief assistance in a more organized and prompt manner than the state.[101] The Ikhwan's organizational power and ability to mobilize both volunteers and resources unnerved Mubarak as he fully understood that this leverage could be politically exploited.[102]

The 1990s thus witnessed more confrontation between the state and the Ikhwan, including waves of state-led security crackdowns against the movement. As tensions intensified, the Ikhwan boycotted the 1990 parliamentary elections because the leadership believed that the state would not allow them to gain any seats. Indeed, the group's suspicions were not far-fetched, as was shown in 1995 when the Ikhwan managed to secure only one seat.[103] Meanwhile, the security forces in charge of the important Ikhwan portfolio became more alarmed by the group's dominance in the syndicates and the growing confidence they exhibited in staging a public demonstration in downtown Cairo.[104] The Mubarak regime also felt threatened by the Ikhwan's control of the 'Amal (Labor) party and became suspicious of its use of the 'Amal newspaper, *al-Sha'ab*, to propagate its messages.[105] The popularity of *al-Sha'ab*, which regularly carried articles by Mashour and other Ikhwan leaders, had skyrocketed, leading the owners to put out two issues per week instead of only one. The newspaper published scathing investigative reports documenting state corruption and patterns of torture by the security forces. The Mubarak regime finally closed it down, suspended the 'Amal party, and used legislation to freeze the activities of the syndicates.[106] A judicial ruling allowing civilians to be tried in military courts further facilitated the regime crackdown and almost 30,000 members were detained between 1995 and 2005.[107]

The old guard within the Ikhwan was able to take advantage of the state-led crackdown to consolidate its internal hegemony. The ascension of the ultraconservative faction over the reformist camp was confirmed with the election of Mustafa Mashour as supreme guide. From then on, the Ikhwan worked hard to create its own "quasi-state" infrastructure. It divided its organizational structure according to the same geographical and administrative areas as the state and appointed "quasi-governors" for each area. It also recruited groups and individuals to build up "points of influence" in order to control civil society institutions and universities. Although the authorities claimed that all these steps were geared towards the gradual enablement of a takeover of the state by the Ikhwan,[108] senior members told me that these actions were designed to protect the movement and ensure its survival if the leadership were to be incapacitated. They insisted that the Ikhwan created multiple power structures in order to give the movement organizational depth and security in case the Mubarak regime decided to dismantle it.

In the following decade, relations between the Ikhwan and the state once again shifted from confrontation to relative accommodation. In the 2000 parliamentary elections, the Ikhwan won seventeen seats and in 2005 it won eighty, but in 2010 it failed to win any. Despite the state's more conciliatory attitude towards the group, the old guard's consolidation of power had enabled the further radicalization of other Islamists. A new breed of radical Islamist saw Mubarak as a *hakem kaffer* (apostate ruler) and called for killing him, a necessary step for the application of the Islamic law.[109] The rise of rival militant Islamist groups, such as Egyptian Islamic Jihad and the Islamic Movement, whose members included Ayman al-Zawahiri, the current leader of Al Qaeda, made the ultraconservative old guard within the Ikhwan appear moderate in comparison. The reformists within the Ikhwan found themselves pressed between the rock of the ultraconservatives inside their own organization and the hard place of a new wave of Islamist militancy outside.

After the September 11, 2001, attacks in the United States, the Mubarak regime instituted reforms which were presented as positive steps towards democratization, including a constitutional amendment providing for presidential elections and a greater space for freedom of speech and protest. The context behind these changes was U.S. pressure on Egypt to liberalize and open dialogue with "moderate"

Islamic groups like the Ikhwan. It was hoped this would allow the country to crack down on "extremist" Islamists.[110] Seeking to get the double benefit of rapprochement both with the Egyptian regime and with the United States, the Ikhwan leadership welcomed the new change in Cairo. Reflecting the new political atmosphere, Mohamed Akef, then the supreme guide, publicly declared an Ikhwan "reform initiative" in a press conference held at the premises of the journalists' syndicate, a governmental institution. The Ikhwan presented its reform initiative to accord with and complement the program of the ruling National Democratic Party at its annual congress in September 2003.[111] Hossam Tammam, a former member of the Ikhwan and a specialist on the group, explains this symbiotic relationship between the state's actions and the rise of Ikhwan reformists:

> The political ground was prepared for a different [reformist] Ikhwan discourse that corresponded with the fever of change sweeping Egypt. That was, therefore, a rare moment signaling the rise of the reformist wing in the Ikhwan and allowing it to boost its position in Egyptian political life amidst a local demand for such a progressive agenda. The conservatives turned a blind eye to these developments as long as they could gain new areas of influence and audience inaccessible traditionally.[112]

Tammam's argument is corroborated by other studies that show that the influence of the reformers in the Ikhwan "has waxed when the government has allowed some form of political participation and waned when the government turned more repressive."[113] Nevertheless, the ultraconservative wing was aware that these reform initiatives were designed more for "external public consumption" than for the group's base.[114]

While the victory of the Ikhwan in the 2005 parliamentary elections was impressive, it proved to be short-lived. To deter the organization, Mubarak reverted to an arrest campaign. About a thousand members were imprisoned, including the influential leader Khairat al-Shater.[115] Opposition groups also decided to exclude the Ikhwan from deliberations and meetings regarding the question of reforms.

At the time, the political environment was characterized by street activism instigated by movements such as Kifaya and smaller groups set up by journalists, workers, and even children, all geared towards seeking political and social change.[116] Against calls from reformist voices, the Ikhwan kept a low profile and refrained from publicly challenging the regime. The old guard even made a conscious decision to appease the authorities and hoped to reach a deal with Mubarak.[117] The regime did not reciprocate, however, and kept the pressure on the Ikhwan. According to Kamal Habib, a former militant Islamist and a specialist on the movement, the Mubarak authorities no longer needed the services of the Ikhwan. While in the 1980s Mubarak used the organization as "a political and intellectual apparatus to besiege" jihadist groups like Islamic Jihad and the Islamic Movement, these had by then been crushed.[118]

The reformists within the Ikhwan felt undermined by the old guard's continued regressive measures. They had hoped that the relaxed political situation of the first half of the 2000s would allow them to advance their forward-looking agenda. In contrast, the ultraconservatives felt that the movement should not lower its guard and engage in risky political ventures with either the regime or the secular opposition.[119] The Ikhwan backpedaled on previous reform initiatives. They justified their move by claiming that these measures had been sanctioned not by the executive leadership but by certain individual members who did not represent official Ikhwan policy. A new draft party platform reversed the reforms that had been announced in the 2004 initiative, such as the declaration that women and Copts were eligible to assume the presidency. With the internal elections in 2008, the ultraconservative wing cemented its dominance over the Ikhwan, weakening the reformists further.

In a way, the periods of repression faced by the Ikhwan provided an ideal environment for the Qutbian old guard to flourish within the Islamist movement. Reformists like Madi and Abdel Sattar point out that the interests of the Mubarak regime and the old guard effectively converged on the issue of keeping the Ikhwan insular and fossilized. On the one hand, Mubarak used the Ikhwan as a *faza'a*, or a threat to internal and external stability, portraying his own political authoritarianism as a necessary evil to deter the Islamists. On the other hand, the Ikhwan old guard countered the reformists' demands to open up the movement and democratize by repeatedly claiming that the organization faced imminent danger due to its being targeted and repressed by the authorities. The leadership prioritized the survival and security of the movement over reforms, transparency, and the democratization of decision making.

The mind-set of the old guard—their preference for security and stability and their opposition to genuine reforms—is reflected in the response of the then supreme guide, Mustafa Mashour, to a question asked in the 1980s by Ahmed Ra'if about what the senior leadership wanted. Ra'if, who belonged to the Ikhwan worldview, recalled Mashour as saying "I want to keep *al-jama'a* [the group] in the freezer for the next twenty years. My goal is to preserve the organization. Everything else is secondary."[120]

According to Ra'if, the strategic goal of the elders within the Ikhwan is simply to "hoard" and co-opt as many members as possible in order to be able to mobilize them when conditions ripen. Senior leaders, added Ra'if, pay lip service to calls emanating from within and without about the need for reforms and transparency; but they do not take action and they resist initiatives that loosen their absolute control. This gap between the Ikhwan's discourse and its action widened in what scholars called the "gray areas," such as Islamic law, violence, pluralism, civil and political rights, women's rights, and religious minorities. Although the Ikhwan supported democratic reforms, the leadership is reluctant to formally endorse equal rights for the Copts, Egypt's native Christian minority.[121] For example, the Ikhwan continues to use its electoral slogan, "Islam is the solution," which has caused consternation among secular forces and the Copts.[122]

Although internal critics blame the authoritarianism of the Mubarak regime for reinforcing the culture of secrecy and paranoia within the Ikhwan,[123] political repression exercised by the authorities is in fact instrumentalized by ultraconservative leaders as an excuse for tightening their grip on the organization. It appears that both worked together to maintain the status quo, benefitting the leadership of the Ikhwan and the state as well. The result is that the conservative core at the center of the organization's power continued to resist change and pursued its aim to keep the Ikhwan in the "freezer" till conditions for a more alternative authentic Islamic vision had ripened. In the end, this strategy did more harm than good since the Ikhwan were caught unprepared when the large-scale popular uprising took Egypt by storm in 2011.

Taking Stock of the Reformist–Old Guard Divide

Since the end of the Sadat era in the early 1980s, the reformists have achieved only limited progress in carrying out their agenda. Mohamed Ali Beshr, another rising star of the 1970s generation, suggests that internal and external pressure has softened and mellowed the attitudes of the old guard on many issues, including the need for a civil state in which sovereignty stems from the will of the people. "No one I know among Ikhwan leaders, young or old, subscribes to Qutb's controversial notion of *hakimiyyat allah* [the sovereignty of God]," said Beshr, whom I met at Ikhwan headquarters while interviewing Abdel Sattar.[124] Beshr, who represents the rise of a technocratic group within the Ikhwan, affirmed that the Islamist movement has evolved and has renounced violence as a tool for bringing about change. Although he conceded that senior leaders still resist providing a public and detailed policy program, the Ikhwan, he points out, has engaged in the political process since the mid-1990s. "The movement is gradually being transformed by political and civic engagement against the wishes of the old guard," he said, "while a new elite is rising, one that is open-minded and does not eschew cooperation with secular and leftist groups."[125] This transformation, Beshr reminded me, was reflected in the performance of reformist Ikhwan MPs in the parliament, where their inquests were dominated by calls for improving education and health sectors, cancelling the Emergency Law, and even protecting the environment.[126]

Beshr's views were in some ways paralleled by those of Abu al-Futuh, although the latter seemed unimpressed with the slow pace of change within the organization. "We have progressed very slowly. The movement is still dominated by regressive tendencies due to the predominance of Bedouin [tribal] thinking and a prison mind-set, both of which have impeded change," he stated.[127] "My generation has attempted to carry out a coup inside the Ikhwan through institutionalization and reforms, but we are besieged internally and externally. We are pressed between a rock of resistance from within and a hard place of repression by the authorities. Reformists of my generation do not have much room to maneuver externally and cannot afford to take big risks," Abu al-Futuh confided.

However, he also noted that gradually the 1950s and 1960s generations and their rigid mind-set are losing their grip on power. Competition for elections in the 1990s and mid-2000s forced Ikhwan leaders to experiment and venture out, to appeal to the public and to reach understandings with differing political and ideological forces. "There is no turning back," noted Abu al-Futuh.

According to Abu al-Futuh, at the time of our interviews, which took place over a period of seven months between 2006 and 2007, reformists actually held a majority of seats in the Ikhwan's Guidance Office. "Reformists are not as powerless as people think. We have the votes. The challenge is to convert our numerical majority into profitable political currency, a challenge that requires further institutionalization and changing of Ikhwan's political culture," he told me.[128] This, however, did not prevent the supreme guide and the inner circle around him from bypassing the formal decision-making process, he lamented, before saying that "to overcome the current *istibdad* [despotism], we have to sustain our public engagement and moderation, and build coalitions with a broad spectrum of opinion in Egypt. The Ikhwan cannot perform the public on its own. Therefore, the way forward is an inclusive nationalist alliance that encompasses the left and the center and the right."[129] Will the senior leadership buy this ambitious road map? "Not yet," said Abu al-Futuh. "*Al-shuyukh* [the sheikhs] put up stiff resistance. But they are fighting a losing battle. [They] own the keys to the past; we own the keys to the future."[130]

"The first decade of the twenty-first century was a watershed for the Ikhwan," agreed Essam al-Haddad, a centrist Ikhwan leader in Alexandria. "We are fully engaged in the political realm and the public debate. Despite being brutally repressed by the security services, the Islamist movement has begun to think seriously about internal reconstruction and reforms."[131] Haddad, a doctor by profession, admitted that the dominance of ultraconservatives at the helm had slowed down the progress and institutional development of the Ikhwan. Nevertheless, he assured me that the balance is shifting: "My generation of the 1970s is establishing itself as a power to be reckoned with. It is a matter of time before we take the reins."

As a leader who was present at the creation of the Ikhwan, Farid Abdel Khaleq emphasized the importance of the current moment. "The Islamist movement is at a critical juncture—either it reforms itself or it collapses," he said. "There is an urgent need to rethink the Islamist discourse and action."[132] In Abdel Khaleq's view, Islamists are obsessed with appearances and rituals, such as beards, dress, and the veil, and spend little effort on substantive issues of governance, political economy, and the real concerns and interests of the people. He was scathing in his criticism of senior Ikhwan leaders who prioritize the unity of the organization and internal group loyalty over reforms and institutionalization; the survival and cohesion of the organization has become a goal in itself, overriding more important dimensions.

In contrast to Beshr and Abu al-Futuh, Abdel Khaleq, who was privy to battles raging within the Islamist movement, was more skeptical about the extent to which the Ikhwan had really transformed over the years. The reforms carried out by the Ikhwan were all talk and no action in regards to transparency and power sharing. In reality little had changed and there was no margin of freedom for reformist members to theorize and debate with one another. On the whole, the Ikhwan had neither democratized nor kept up with rapidly changing realities: "The West is right to label Islamists regressive because we have not constructed a modern progressive vision to tackle our severe problems," he said. "We must learn how to deal with the Other and provide a positive civilizational model of our religion and movement. The question is to how to introduce Islam to people and restructure Muslim narratives to fit the contemporary age."[133] Abdel Khaleq's critique cannot be easily dismissed by the old guard because of his seniority and stature within the Ikhwan and his pivotal historical role. The key problem with the Islamist movement, he stressed, is that it has not bridged the divide between the public realm and the secret realm. This has exacted a heavy toll on its development and growth, keeping one foot underground and another above ground.

According to Abdel Khaleq, the dialectics stem from the influence of two opposing conceptual and ideological models or approaches: Banna versus Qutb, or the reformist versus the revolutionary. "Members are pulled and pushed in two different pedagogical directions. Qutb's worldview continues to inspire the base as well as key senior figures," he said.[134] The way forward is to structurally transform the Islamist movement by being transparent and open, and by putting an end to the split personality that undermines public trust and confidence, Abdel Khaleq noted. "The Ikhwan must work hard to gain credibility with the Egyptian public."[135]

Keeping the Ikhwan in the freezer, Abdel Khaleq told me, would only cause the organization's decline. "My hopes are invested in reformists like my son, Ussama, who are renewing the Islamist movement and making it more dynamic and responsive to peoples' lives," Abdel Khaleq said. "Ussama and his Brothers possess a more inclusive and pragmatic viewpoint than my own generation and are consumed with questions of how to improve the social and economic well-being of Egyptians."[136] He noted that Ussama's generation knows well that abject poverty and unemployment weigh down Egyptians and prevent them from being active citizens. They are more concerned with finding practical solutions to pressing problems like urban slums and youth training than with resurrecting the caliphate, as their fathers were, he explained. Reformists borrow from whatever system provides answers, including the United States, because they want to succeed and deliver the goods, he further noted, though he conceded that they have little influence over Ikhwan decision making: "Slowly but surely, reformists are making inroads and gaining authority within the Ikhwan. But the birth is painful and could even be aborted."[137]

Despite his lobbying for change, Abdel Khaleq said he has no illusions about the difficulties that lie ahead. He conceded that reformists face opposition from influential quarters within the Ikhwan and have yet to develop a program of their own; his son's generation does not have the space and freedom to construct a vision or road map for the future. "Reformists are squeezed between their conservative elders and the security forces, and they feel powerless to take independent initiatives," he said with a sigh. "They face an uphill battle." When asked what is to be done next, Abdel Khaleq's hopes waned as he bluntly told me that "the odds are against transformation of the Ikhwan in my lifetime."[138] "We have not learned from our mistakes and have not developed institutions that allow the organization to avoid the tragedies of the past. Instead of strengthening its defenses before a gathering storm, more often than not the Ikhwan is caught off guard and battered. Calamities have shaped the character and identity of al-Jama'a, though with few lessons learned."[139] Abdel Khaleq's warning darkly foreshadowed the events which would follow in the aftermath of the January 25 revolution in 2011.

I also asked Abdel Khaleq's son, Ussama, his thoughts about the Ikhwan. An engineer by profession, he owns a construction and a domestic airline company. As such, he represents a new influential trend of successful businessmen within the Ikhwan who argue that Islam is good for business and that business is good for promoting moderate Islam. Ussama was direct and self-critical, accusing the old guard of impeding progress and structurally weakening the Islamist organization. "At the heart of the crisis is a knowledge gap among senior leaders who are isolated from the world and who doggedly resist change," he said. "It is imperative that civil ideas are nourished within the Ikhwan in order for the movement to grow its brain and be prepared to govern Egypt in the future."[140] Like other critics, he used a code phrase—"small brain"—to point to the Ikhwan's rigidity and lack of dynamism and open-mindedness.

"I told the supreme guide that we must think outside the box and undertake fundamental change within the movement. This would entail a freer environment for members to air their views and let their voices be heard," he explained. One of the major points which Ussama stressed is the need to provide Ikhwan members with a "civil education" and get them to engage with society at large. He said that the knowledge gap that exists among the rank and file has far-reaching implications for the future of the organization. In contrast to others, Ussama was more concerned about the bottom-up than the top-down, particularly the psychological isolation of ordinary members from civil society. "Many members not only live in the past, self-enclosed and detached from society's natural rhythm, but also in constant fear of persecution and mobilization," he lamented. "We need to nourish a sense of national pride and normalcy among members and civic and cultural engagement. The senior leadership eschews educating the Muslim Brother lest he rebel and join civil society, a fact that exposes the predicament of the education and socialization of young members."[141]

According to Ussama, one of the reasons that the Ikhwan has not democratized internally stems from a self-induced tendency to isolate itself from the outside world and to focus on growing the organization at the expense of institutionalization and transparency. "The problem with Ikhwan leaders is that they do not know what they want and they refrain from taking initiatives that explain their policy agenda to the public," Ussama said. "They are blind and deaf to the primacy of politics and the imperative of public engagement. The biggest challenge facing Islamists is to integrate themselves into the political and public sphere."[142] In Ussama's diagnosis, the ailment resides more in the culture of the Ikhwan and its inertia than in external causes. "The problem is the absence of politics and a political horizon among Ikhwan leaders; they have not developed strategies of governance and a knowledge base to provide them with policy options," he stressed. "Culturally, the Ikhwan is illiterate."[143]

He stressed that the culture of the underground and secrecy must be replaced with the culture of modernity, citizenship, and an inclusive political vision. Ussama's relatively progressive ideas are at odds with the dominant viewpoints within the Islamist organization. He told me that senior leaders get easily agitated by terms and references outside their comfort zone, such as citizenship, civil state, and separation of religion and politics. He said he told the former supreme guide, Mohamed Akef, and his deputy, Mohamed Habib, that religion and politics are already separate and that it is wishful thinking to pretend otherwise. "I argued that the Ikhwan does not possess a political imagination and does not know the meanings of the political," Ussama said with a broad smile. "I told them that they need to train specialists in their respective fields and develop institutional mechanisms to inject fresh blood in the veins of the movement. They should allow young and mid-level talent to assume a leadership role and give the Ikhwan a lift."[144] Did Akef and Habib know that in reality state and religion in Egypt are separate? "Yes, they do but they live in a state of denial and adopt constructive ambiguity on sensitive issues," Ussama said. "Ikhwan leaders must develop a program that resolves contradictions and inconsistencies, and level with young members about what the movement stands for."[145]

If the Ikhwan does not overcome its culture of secrecy and paranoia, it will decline and lose public support, warned Ussama; the future of the movement depends on the renewal of the leadership and ideas and on reconciliation with the outside world. After spending two hours with Ussama, it was clear that he and his generation are not optimistic that new winds of change will sweep the Ikhwan anytime soon. Senior Ikhwan leaders fear change, younger members often say, and resist efforts to reform the organization from within.

Hesham El-Hamamy, a young centrist and a critic of the Ikhwan leadership, was also pessimistic. He acknowledged that the 1980s and the 1990s were two lost decades because the group did not produce a road map, a blueprint that spelled out their philosophical vision, their ideas about the identity of the state that they desire, or relations between government and civil society. Instead, they resisted efforts by reformists like Abu al-Futuh, Abdel Sattar, Madi, Mohamed Ali Beshr, and others to translate and codify their scattered pronouncements on various issues into concrete policy proposals.

He also lamented inflammatory statements by top Ikhwan leaders, such as Akef's insulting proud nationalist Egyptians by saying "*tuz fi misr*" or "Egypt my ass"; or his second in command Mohamed Habib's stating that Copts do not have the right to compete for the presidency, or of Mashour's warning that Copts should not serve in the military because of risks to national security.[146] He also said he was saddened by Ma'mun Hudaybi's boasting that he controls non-governmental associations. In a leaked videotape that went back to a 1992 mass gathering of the Ikhwan, Hudaybi even hinted that the group's al-Gihaz al-Sirri, the Secret Apparatus, is still functioning, contradicting previous denials by the leadership. "We boast of and approach Allah through al-Gihaz al-Sirri," said Hudaybi in the tape.[147] Hamamy attributed such declarations to the immaturity of senior Ikhwan leaders and their desperation "to be heard and to make headlines," in the process "churning out public utterances that provide ammunition to their enemies."[148] According to Hamamy, Ikhwan elders do not appreciate that these statements deepen the public's mistrust of the Islamist movement and damage its standing and reputation.

Hamamy argued that it would take an internal revolution to transform the power structure within. "It is a struggle that has to be fought and won by reformists, even though the odds are against us. For the foreseeable future, the elders will continue to have the upper hand at the cost of stagnation and paralysis for the Islamist movement."[149] The struggle within will determine not only the future of the Ikhwan but also that of Egypt and the Arab region, stated Hamamy emphatically.

Like other reformists, he mainly blamed the old guard for the stagnation of the Islamist movement and the marginalization of the progressive camp. "Although it is present, the reformist current is silenced, repressed, and dispirited. Despondent and frustrated, reformists like Abu al-Futuh bite the bullet and bide their time until the security state recedes," he said. However, he also struck a note of, if not optimism, then defiance: "Sooner rather than later, the reformist generation will rebuild the movement on a more transparent, accountable, and inclusive foundation. The future belongs to us."[150]

Looking more closely into the power struggle between the reactionary and reformist camps within the Ikhwan shows that the old guard's resistance to change has not prevented younger generations from challenging the status quo. The rise of a reformist elite like Abdel Moneim Abu al-Futuh, Mohamed Ali Beshr, and Hesham El-Hamamy promised more moderation, openness, and transparency and the likelihood that the Ikhwan could fruitfully engage with secular rivals. The reformists have pushed back against the entrenched culture of insularity, secrecy, obedience, and autocracy that dominates the ranks. Although they have failed to transform the organization, they have succeeded in advancing the debate and the internal struggle for a more transparent and inclusive agenda. The Ikhwan's participation in the parliamentary elections in the mid-1990s and in 2005 expanded their political appetite, forcing them to consider a public outreach policy and legalization through the establishment of a party.

However, against all those efforts, the old guard has remained an immensely powerful force that has repeatedly prevented any real change from taking place. As we have seen, the consolidation of power by the ultraconservatives was due to the group's rigid organizational structure and strict Qutbian-inspired ideology, a vision that reproduces dominant relations of power within the group in order to produce subjects who are faithfully subservient to the top echelons. By cutting members off from their social networks and blending them into a new Ikhwan-only set of connections, the leadership had won their consent and loyalty. In a way, a relationship of ideological and material co-dependency is established between the leadership and members: the latter's needs for better living conditions, work prospects, and climbing the social ladder make it dependent on the hierarchy of power and clientelism. The leadership's emphasis on disciplinary action to silence dissent clearly shows that control and power are highly prized by the old guard. The idea of the Ikhwan as a traditional family is used to perpetuate subservience and domination, as ordinary members are treated like children who must obey their fathers and elders.

In addition to the internal techniques of control and ideological subject production, political repression also partially allowed the ultraconservatives to keep the lid tightly shut on the movement and to resist carrying out transformative change. The political authoritarianism of the Mubarak regime and that of the Ikhwan old guard were two sides of the same coin; they complemented each other and fed upon one another in order to preserve the supremacy of their respective camps.

Conclusion

The result is that the Islamist movement did not fundamentally evolve and democratize; it also did not develop the internal resilience that would have allowed it to fully engage in Egypt's political life and govern such a complex state and society. These defects largely explain the movement's spectacular downfall in 2013 after the Arab Spring uprisings. The choices made by the Ikhwan leadership proved costly and even catastrophic. Internally ill-equipped and unprepared to face the challenges following the January 25 revolution, Ikhwan leaders did what they know best: bide their time and strike a deal behind closed doors with the new authority represented by the Supreme Council of the Armed Forces (SCAF) headed by General Mohamed Hussein Tantawi. They drew the wrong lessons from history and time and time again bet on the wrong horse. Both the Free Officers in 1952 and the military junta in 2011 initially used the Ikhwan to consolidate their power, but subsequently turned against the Islamist movement.

Perhaps the biggest mistake of the leadership is to conceptualize power only as an end in itself rather than a means to an end. The result is that Ikhwan leaders were unable to come up with a political project that engaged the public imagination and offered a blueprint for the future. This three-decade-long resistance to change has impeded the sociological evolution of the group and reinforced its insular political culture and lack of connection with society at large. The lack of cosmopolitanism and connectivity is a symptom of a greater challenge that afflicts the Ikhwan: deep suspicions of the political and the outside world. Burdened by frequent waves of state repression in the late 1940s, early 1950s, and mid-1960s, or what members call *meh'an* (calamities), the old guard internalized these bitter moments in the history of the movement and developed a defensive and underground mentality.

My conversations and encounters with senior members of the Ikhwan over the past two decades have convinced me that they feel besieged by an intrinsically hostile world. The Ikhwan's influential old guard has never reconciled with the outside world, and feel they live in a state of war. They see enemies lurking everywhere trying to harm the Islamist movement, which allowed the Mubarak regime to portray the Ikhwan as subversive, a threat to national security. The ultraconservatives have been their movement's own worst enemies, alienating important social segments of the population.

The prolonged confrontation with the state has left deep scars on their imagination, scars that have not healed yet. Baptized in the prison camps, this generation has neither forgotten nor forgiven. Instead, the long Islamist-nationalist war has framed the Ikhwan's leadership subjectivity and its priorities as well. Unwilling to or incapable of overcoming this bitter historical legacy, the hardliners in the Ikhwan view the present and the future through the lens of the past. Mashour's intimation that he wants to keep the Ikhwan in the freezer for twenty years reflects a sensibility that prioritizes political survival and organizational expansion at the expense of openness, transparency, and democratization of internal decision making.

In a way, the Ikhwan resembled the authoritarian state in its narrow, top-down decision making with the views of a powerful, reactionary minority prevailing. The Islamist group had not developed transparent, formal institutions that set an exemplary model for governance. A movement that does not internally practice transparency and democracy won't do so externally. While the old guard strengthened the Ikhwan's organizational capacity and expanded its membership, they have not thickened the institutional fabric which would have turned it into a formidable and dynamic political party. The Ikhwan's structural weaknesses were mainly self-inflicted, though repression by the state was a significant contributing factor to the paranoia that infected the leadership of the Islamist movement.

In my interviews, the conservatives within the Ikhwan showed themselves to be hypersensitive to any criticism that targets their power structure or the way they exercise control over the organization. In our meetings, Akef patronizingly called me *habibi*, or buddy, and pointedly lumped together all of those who challenge the wisdom and purity of the Ikhwan leadership—including reformist members of the Ikhwan itself—as misguided or even as conspirators and traitors. Such attitudes reflect a sociological and an epistemological gap between the ultraconservative old guard and the reformist generation, which tends to be more open-minded and at peace with the outside world. As leaders of one of the most powerful social and political movements, Akef, Izzat, and their cohorts do not recognize their responsibilities as potential drivers of transformation in the authoritarian political life of Egypt in particular and the Arab/Muslim arena in general. Whenever they are pressed, they fall back on terms such as "authenticity," "identity," and "Islam" as justification and rationale for postponing efforts to structurally reform the most influential Islamist movement in the region. For the Ikhwan leaders, instead of burying their heads in the sand, trafficking in conspiracy theories, and being captives of the past, the way forward is to take stock of the internal structural defects that hinder the evolution of the movement into a fully fledged pluralistic one. Unfortunately, they had refrained from doing so, even at the risk of bringing ruin to their own organization.

As the January 25 revolution exposed the group's predicament, it became apparent that in choosing to "keep the organization in the freezer," the old leadership had made one of its biggest mistakes to date. The movement was caught off guard, unprepared to engage in the open and active political arena. Ikhwan leaders, true to form, were neither transparent nor truthful and consistent, reinforcing public perceptions about their double-talk and duplicity. Long before the military ousted Mohamed Morsi, a member of the Brotherhood and the first democratically elected president since the 1952 revolution, in 2013, the movement had already lost the trust of important segments of public opinion, including some of those who voted Morsi in. The ability of the military to carry out a relatively successful coup against Morsi stemmed partly from a pattern of blunders committed by the Ikhwan leadership during the January 25 revolution and after, mistakes which estranged many Egyptians from the Islamist movement. When the Egyptian military led by General Abdel Fattah al-Sisi moved against Morsi and the Ikhwan in July 2013, the Islamist movement fell like ripened fruit. The public had already turned against the Ikhwan, which provided additional impetus for the military generals to crush their historical nemesis.

Of course, the security forces and the remnants of the deep state had blocked Morsi's efforts at exercising power, preventing him from controlling key institutions. There had existed entrenched interests in state and society that were determined to undermine the Ikhwan and see them fail. The designs of the anti-Ikhwan coalition were facilitated by Morsi's incompetence and ineptitude as well as the old guard's interference in the management of the presidency. Regardless of the veracity of these claims, many Egyptians believed that the lines were blurred between the Morsi presidency and the Ikhwan leadership, particularly strongman Khairat al-Shater and the supreme guide, Mohamed Badie. Moreover, the inability of Morsi to deliver on his exaggerated promises reinforced public perceptions of the Islamist movement's untrustworthiness and incompetence, providing the military with rationale to militarily crush the Ikhwan.

Like his predecessor Gamal Abdel Nasser, Sisi depicted the Ikhwan as an existential threat to the nation, while portraying the military as a savior and the guardian of the will of the people. As he sought to crush the Islamist movement, Sisi wrapped himself with the mantle of Nasser, reminding Egyptians that he was following in the footsteps of his popular predecessor in preventing the Ikhwan from hijacking the state. As usual, the military sees its raison d'être as defending and protecting the nation.

In contrast, the Ikhwan viewed the removal of Morsi from power and the subsequent wave of repression as an extension of the military's repeated clampdown on the Islamist movement and flouting of the popular will. Not unlike the 1950s and 1960s, Ikhwan leaders accused Sisi and other Egyptian generals of collusion with the United States and other regional powers to dismantle the democratic process and again establish a dictatorship. As before, the Ikhwan leadership vowed to resist the "coup" by the military and to defend the will of the people.

Investing their struggle with ideological and even cultural overtones and painting the other as an enemy of the people, both camps have hunkered down for another confrontational cycle. Both have reawakened the ghosts of the past, even though their deadly struggle has been more about power politics and control than about defending democracy or the state.

Conclusion

THERE WAS NOTHING INEVITABLE about the confrontation between the Ikhwan and the Egyptian state spearheaded by the military in the aftermath of the January 25 revolution in 2011. History does not ineluctably repeat itself, and the historical vendetta between the Islamists and the nationalists could have been laid to rest. However, leadership, historical memory, and circumstance make a big difference, and both sides have become prisoners of their narratives about themselves and each other, discourses invested with cultural and apocalyptic overtones. And so the armistice between the military and the Islamists after the January 25 revolution was short-lived, a tantalizing moment of cooperation in an otherwise strife-filled saga.

In the final analysis, the bitter clash of interests, coupled with a huge deficit of trust, posed an insuperable hurdle to any amicable resolution. Yet each side, drawing on familiar practices from their long confrontation, tried to outmaneuver the other and gain the upper hand. In 1954 and in 2011, the Ikhwan bet on the military as its route to power. In both instances, their gamble backfired badly. The Islamists were no match for the military. They took unwarranted risks, knowing full well the severe consequences of political exposure. The ultraconservative leadership miscalculated monstrously and repeatedly; they plunged headfirst and with eyes wide open into the fray—to little avail. The Ikhwan has again mastered the art of blundering, and it has the enemies to prove it.

Thus, the Ikhwan finds itself at another critical juncture in its eighty-five-year history, besieged and battered and struggling to survive. And though it has faced the wrath of the Egyptian state before, its loss of public stature now aggravates its predicament. The movement might be at a breaking point as the Sisi regime moves to systematically dismantle its widespread social infrastructure, composed of businesses, clinics, schools, and day-care centers. It stands nearly alone in the eye of the storm, exposed to the bruising elements of our times, with dwindling public backing and only poor political options to choose from. There is a real danger that different factions within the Ikhwan will turn on one another and that the movement will be consumed by internecine warfare.

Nevertheless, it is premature to pen its obituary.[1] The Ikhwan is deeply embedded in Egyptian society, with a huge membership and extensive networks of welfare services that touch the lives of millions of Egyptians. Over the decades, the movement has built many local layers and circles of support to shield itself against the state's persistent efforts to eliminate it from roof to root. Even Gamal Abdel Nasser, with his special mix of charisma and popular appeal, could not bridle it, nor could he divest it of its theological and social influence. When Nasser condemned the Ikhwan's leading theoretician and agitator, Sayyid Qutb, to the gallows in 1966, he inadvertently turned Qutb into a "living martyr" and an inspiration for subsequent waves of radicalized religious activists. The political rivalry between Nasser's Arab nationalist supporters and Qutb's Islamists hardened into a titanic clash that has shaped the modern history of the Middle East. It is unlikely, then, that President Sisi's clampdown on the Ikhwan will succeed where Nasser failed.[2] That said, Sisi might trigger a new wave of religious radicalization, like that of the 1970s generation that followed the execution of Qutb, which may spur further internal divisions within the Ikhwan.

Over the past eighty-five years, the Ikhwan has exhibited exceptional resilience, developing social and psychological mechanisms to cope with state persecution and prolonged imprisonment. Indeed, Ikhwan rank and file from the past two decades have told me that they thrive on hardship and that persecution serves to strengthen their resolve, not weaken it. There is an understanding among Ikhwan officials that time spent in jail is a prerequisite for promotion within the movement. The prison experience develops interpersonal ties and common experiences that bind members to one another, and it is part of the ethos of the group as well, creating a kind of *asabiyya*, or group feeling and solidarity. The Ikhwan resembles a tribal organization with informal networks and family (blood) ties which supersede formal institutions. This helps explain the group's internal resilience and its ability to survive in the face of the Egyptian state's ferocious efforts to dismantle it.

Although the nationalists, led by the military, hold the advantage for now, they have not converted their victory over the Islamists into enduring political and social capital. Theirs is a hollow victory. They have delivered neither prosperity nor justice and fairness to the people. The self-anointed nation builders have failed at state building and stripped institutions of their effectiveness. Their visions of progress have often produced the opposite results. Nasser's foundational myth of pan-Arab nationalism has been torn asunder by inter-Arab rivalries and geopolitics. Pan-Arab nationalism did not survive Nasser's death in 1970, and Sadat's vision of economic liberalization opened the floodgates for pervasive state patronage and corruption, giving rise to super-rich "fat cats" who accumulated huge fortunes at the expense of the citizenry. Mubarak, a functionary president, pursued policies reminiscent of Sadat's, which ultimately led to the political and economic emaciation of Egypt. Under Mubarak, Egypt became a broken state.

Sisi, a former general, clothes himself in Nasser's mystique and promises to rescue Egypt from the machinations of the Ikhwan. But he appears to be traveling the same road to nowhere that Mubarak did. As Sisi's first presidential term comes to a thudding close, it is clear that he has not offered Egyptians a captivating strategic vision around which to rally. Instead, he micromanages crisis after crisis. Like his predecessors, Sisi relies heavily on the military and security services to ensure compliance and control and to try to improve the economy. Even more than Nasser, he has turned the fight against the Ikhwan into the raison d'être of his presidency—though Sisi does not possess his predecessor's charisma and public appeal, and he faces deepening social and economic problems at home.

Since the mid-1950s, Arab politics have been polarized, a struggle between Islamists and nationalists. There is no third wave or viable alternative to compete with the ideological hegemony of the Islamists on one hand and the nationalist-military alliance on the other. While the Arab Spring uprisings briefly raised hopes that such an alternative would emerge, those hopes were dashed by collusion between the two sworn enemies. Both the Islamists and the nationalists benefit from the other's existence. The military-dominated state justifies itself by promoting the fear that the Islamists will take over, and the Ikhwan feeds its followers a steady and unnourishing diet of victimhood and visceral hostility toward their nationalist and secularist tormentors. The Qutbian wing within the Ikhwan is still alive and well.

In the wake of the Arab Spring, the Nasserist-Qutbian clash endures and shapes the trajectories of Arab politics. Sisi is wrapped in Nasser's iconic cloak, and he borrows heavily from his predecessor's repertoire to try to discredit and delegitimize the Ikhwan. He has repeatedly reminded Egyptians that the Islamist organization cannot be trusted to be in charge of the state, because its members are not patriots: their primary loyalty lies outside the country's borders. Similarly, the Islamist organization frames its post–Arab Spring ordeal as an extension of a historical vendetta or a conspiracy by the state and its pro-Western patrons against Islamic values and heritage. Sisi is portrayed as Nasser's heir. The only significant difference in today's clash is that Qutb's followers have publicly broken ranks with the Ikhwan, accused it of shedding its Islamic identity, and joined up with extremist groups like the Islamic State and Al Qaeda. From Sinai to Cairo and even beyond Egypt, religious radicals inspired by Qutb wage all-out war against what they call "apostate" and "renegade" regimes. These Qutbians are iconoclasts who seek to bring the temple crashing down on everyone, including the Ikhwan.

Nasser and Qutb must be turning in their graves at the drama unfolding in Egypt and across the Arab region. Nasser would be heartbroken to see Egypt a shadow of its former self, adrift with no ideational anchor to unite the ancient nation. His successors have replaced his doctrine of *qawmiyya* (Arab nationalism) with *wataniyya* (local patriotism), but they must rely on corporate militarism to maintain control. Nasser would criticize his successors for abandoning Arab nationalism, thus leaving ideology to the Islamists and failing to provide both symbolic inspiration and motivation for the Egyptian people and a center of gravity for the region. He would see the Ikhwan's coming to power in 2012 as a consequence of this. Nasser would bemoan the political and economical emasculation of Egypt and its voluntary shedding of its larger-than-life self-image. Qutb would be equally enraged by the naiveté and cynicism of the Ikhwan leadership for joining the polluted political process and for falling into apostasy. He would reproach his disciples who control the decision making for emasculating the Ikhwan ideologically and theologically and for giving up the utopian dream of a Qur'anic state. Qutb would be equally displeased with his self-appointed disciples for distorting his Islamic doctrine by spreading violence and chaos at home and abroad.

Nasser's and Qutb's successors have dominated the social and political scene for sixty years, not only by battling each other but also, sometimes, by collaborating to prevent the rise of third-party competitors and rivals. The Arab world has been unable to overcome the dialectics of Islamism and militarism and to pass into new democratic territory. Will the current round of confrontation break this vicious binary cycle and produce a different political outcome? To what extent has the military hold on state and society been weakened in the aftermath of the Arab Spring uprisings and the inability of military-supported ruling elites to furnish the public goods and to espouse a new political vision? Have the Ikhwan been discredited by their conduct during and after the Arab Spring, especially their brief stint in power? Will the Islamist movement undergo transformation and rebirth and learn from history, or will it repeat the mistakes of the past? What do the Ikhwan's internal dynamics reveal about the future direction of the movement?

Divisions and Defections

Long before the Arab Spring uprising in Egypt and the ouster of the Ikhwan president, Mohamed Morsi, in July 2013, the Islamist movement had suffered serious divisions along generational, ideological, and social lines. The junior and senior members I interviewed exposed authoritarian practices by top leaders and a well-worn ideological rift between a dominant Qutbian faction and a centrist wing. Although centrist and reformist members represented a majority in the Ikhwan, they did not have operative control and could not set its public policy agenda. Decision making was controlled by Qutbian hardliners. Until the Arab Spring uprising, the conservative Ikhwan leadership suppressed any hint of divisions within the group and punished members who dared challenge the official line. The Islamist movement also shielded itself from public scrutiny by avoiding the public arena and broadcasting muddled and contradictory messages regarding its political intentions.

With the fall of Mubarak in February 2011 and the social turbulence that followed, all the contradictions within and without the Ikhwan burst into the open. They publicly exposed the organization as unprepared to govern effectively and transparently. The secretive leadership failed to restructure the movement along democratic lines. Pronouncements by Ikhwan officials contradicted the conduct of its top leaders. From the beginning of the uprising to the toppling of Morsi in July 2013, the Ikhwan placed the interests of the movement ahead of the public good and aligned with the military to gain power. Instead of trusting the vicissitudes of democracy, the Ikhwan leadership chose to be a counterrevolutionary force. Guided by blind ambition, the Ikhwan old guard preferred a profitable partnership with the remnants of the deep state to an unpredictable pact with the people.

From its prolonged confrontation with the Egyptian state the Ikhwan has learned to avoid direct clashes with the authorities and to do whatever it takes to become legal. Proscribed since 1954, it was unable to organize openly, knowing that the state used the law and its organs against it. The conservatives who controlled the organization were ready to strike any deal with the authorities in order to gain legal rehabilitation and official recognition. As the new authority represented by the Supreme Council of the Armed Forces (SCAF) undermined Mubarak, it reached an understanding with the Ikhwan to bring an end to the popular protests that threatened the very foundation of the political system. Both the military and the Ikhwan had a vested interest in moving the struggle from the streets to the ballot box and preserving the status quo. The Ikhwan were rewarded for playing by the rules, winning both a majority of seats in the Parliament and the presidency.

In one stroke, the Islamist organization went from being proscribed to being in charge, at least in theory, of the Egyptian state. An ultraconservative Qutbian wing, opaque and subject to the whims of inflexible old men who had spent years in prison and had developed a bunker mentality, became the de facto leaders of an Egypt abuzz with possibility. Unprepared to govern and facing multilayered social challenges, the group improvised. Ikhwan leaders had spent decades growing the movement while neglecting theory, public policy, and a strategic vision for the country. They had neither a grand political project nor a concrete social agenda, and political rule exposed the group's paucity of ideas. Mohamed Morsi, the man chosen by the Ikhwan leadership for president, personified mediocrity. Morsi, to be blunt, was a political pygmy with limited intelligence and charisma, along with a penchant for making overblown promises and pronouncements. He provided endless material for late-night comedians. During his eventful year in office, a belief spread in Egypt that Morsi was an impotent figurehead and that the real driver behind the presidency was the Ikhwan's supreme guide, Mohamed Badie, and his right-hand strongman, Khairat al-Shater.

After it gained power in 2012, the Ikhwan did not formalize its institutions or dramatically alter its decision-making process. It still lacked transparency and clarity about where authority lies and who was really in charge. Like their nationalist and secularist detractors and foes, the old guard who dominated the Ikhwan saw themselves as victims of a threatening and hostile outside world with enemies lurking everywhere. Morsi's inability to exercise control over key state institutions, particularly the security forces, reinforced the deep-seated fears of Ikhwan leaders that a conspiracy was afoot to deny them the fruits of their electoral victory. Walled in by paranoia and overcome by fear, Morsi and the Ikhwan's top leaders underestimated the depth and gravity of popular discontent and were slow to acknowledge and respond to rising public opposition and resistance. Yes, the security forces, together with the secularists and nationalists, did incite the public and mobilize activists to protest against Morsi and call for his resignation. But Ikhwan leaders did great harm to their cause by burying their collective head in the sand and acting as if the public discontent was solely a sinister plot hatched by their enemies. Once again, as it repeatedly has been over the past century, the top Ikhwan leadership was its own worst enemy.

The blurring of the lines between the Morsi presidency and the Ikhwan reinforced the perceptions of many Egyptians that the Islamist movement was neither competent nor trustworthy. Popular opposition hardened into active resistance, as the security forces and elements of the old regime fed public anger by making sure that Morsi could not exercise control over state institutions. Not unlike 1954, the Ikhwan leaders bided their time and hoped that the storm would blow over, overestimating their strength and resilience and underestimating the military's determination to crush them. For instance, warned by an Arab leader to be on his guard against Sisi, Morsi reportedly said that "al-Sissi is in my small pocket,"[3] an Arabic expression suggesting that Morsi was fully in control of the state apparatus. He was not.

In 2013 the Ikhwan faced greater odds than in 1954 because they failed to offer a development strategy for the struggling Egyptian economy, thereby alienating a large segment of public opinion. If Morsi and the Ikhwan had managed to improve the people's well-being by providing jobs and hope, the Egyptian public would have been more supportive. But the Islamist movement lacked policy ideas and was generally ill equipped to govern. Facing a highly determined and disciplined security apparatus which received pivotal backing from key regional actors, the Ikhwan did what they had often done: nothing.

A perfect storm allowed the army, led by General Sisi, to move against Morsi in July 2013 and end the Ikhwan's brief moment in power. The loss of public trust in Morsi was one of the most important factors that facilitated the military clampdown.

Many Egyptians believed that the Islamist movement was playing a double game, waiting to consolidate its power before hijacking the nation-state. Promoted by the military and the nationalists and secularists, this argument, that the Ikhwan aimed to stealthily replace *al-dawla al-wataniyya*, or the Egyptian nation-state, with an Islamic state, gained popular currency in 2013. It became an anti-Ikhwan rallying cry in Egypt and neighboring Arab countries, as it had been in the mid-1950s and late 1960s. The irony is that after they gained power in 2012, the Ikhwan did not act as a counterforce to the Egyptian state, but instead sought to keep it as it was. Ikhwan members who defected regarded the Mubarak regime and the Morsi regime as two sides of the same coin, and argued that the Ikhwan had been co-opted by the state. The Ikhwan's attitude towards the state changed dramatically after it gained power in 2012: it used co-optation, not coercion, to establish its hold on institutions. Power became an end in itself. Like the nationalists, the Islamists sought to monopolize power at the expense of others, rather than adhere to their traditional ideals or the Islamist project they had claimed to possess.

In the opinion of detractors and some supporters, the Ikhwan's realism exposed the falsity of the whole Islamist project on which the organization has based its legitimacy for almost a century. What the Ikhwan's brief experience in power showed is that "Islamism, the ideology that abolishes the boundaries between this life and the next, found itself, in 2013, face-to-face with the iron curtain that separates the two."[4] In other words, the Ikhwan could no longer even pretend to be pursuing their stated dream of building an "Islamist state" that would resurrect the Islamic caliphate and allow its members to realize their Islamic identity, salvation, and empowerment.[5] After gaining power the Ikhwan acted as a special interest group driven by modernist ideas closer to "a strong, authoritarian developmental state than to classical Islamic political thought."[6] The Ikhwan resembled their nationalist foes in how they conceived of and exercised power. Ahmed Ban, a former leader of the organization, now saw the Ikhwan as being like other special interest groups that lacked a religious identity, and he wondered "how this politics of pure interests and sheer lies relates to honesty, brotherhood, sacrifice among all other sublime meanings in the Ikhwan dictionary?"[7]

Secularists, nationalists, and the security forces saw the Ikhwan's realism in more sinister terms, as part of a strategic calculation to Islamize the Egyptian state. They coalesced around the idea of forcing Morsi out of the presidential palace before this could happen. The Islamist-nationalist fault line was violently resurrected. Both sides depicted the other as an existential threat to the nation and the *umma*. As during the 1950s and 1960s, the struggle was framed in ideational, ideological, and moral terms, not just political ones: it was about the future of the nation and the Islamic community.

The current, deadly conflict between the military and the Ikhwan is bloodier, fiercer, and broader than previous waves. While Nasser's clampdown on the Ikhwan and Qutb's followers in the 1950s and 1960s claimed only a dozen lives, Sisi's confrontation with the Islamist organization has killed thousands. There is now an all-out war between the Egyptian state and the Islamist organization, and both are preparing for a prolonged fight. Incarcerating thousands of Ikhwan officials, including top leaders, Egypt designated the group "terrorist" and has lobbied regional allies to follow suit. In response, the Islamist movement appears broken, leaderless, and on the run. Thousands of junior and senior members have left for exile in Turkey, Qatar, Great Britain, and other European countries.[8] Those remaining in Egypt have gone underground.

Divides have deepened between a de facto leadership in exile that struggles to maintain discipline, cohesiveness, and organizational unity and young cadres inside Egypt who call for military confrontation with the authorities. This rift threatens to tear apart the façade of institutional solidity that the old guard would like the world to believe in. Radicalized and organized, young members have taken matters into their own hands and carried out attacks all across Egypt.[9] It is too early to tell if these attacks are the work of freelancers within the Ikhwan or an organized rogue faction. The Egyptian government makes no distinction between the Ikhwan and extremists like the Islamic State and has unleashed its fury against the entire Islamist movement. There is a real danger that the situation could escalate dramatically if more young Ikhwan members join paramilitary wings, which would be similar to what happened in the 1960s. Within the Ikhwan some agitate for armed confrontation with the state, while others advocate genuine reforms.[10] It is difficult to know the weight and influence of these competing currents and whether the traditional leadership will be able to exercise control over the disparate elements in the diaspora and at home.

One thing is clear: it is unlikely that the Islamist movement will undergo a democratic transformation anytime soon. Historically, when under attack and besieged, Ikhwan leaders hunkered down, trying to weather the violent storm. They prioritized organizational survival and avoided contentious ideological debates and social experimentation. They preferred generalities and vacuous slogans to detailed policy prescriptions and directives. Given the disarray in their ranks and the clampdown by the security forces, it would take a political miracle for senior Ikhwan leaders to engage in self-criticism and reform, though now and then reports do surface regarding internal deliberations.[11] Self-criticism would antagonize young hardliners in Egypt who demand a more militarized approach towards the authorities, not democratization. If history is a guide, the Ikhwan leaders will not acknowledge any mistakes lest they appear weak and wavering before their base. They will bide their time, hoping that the Sisi administration fails in its endeavor to deliver the goods and services, and particularly jobs, to pressed Egyptians. The Ikhwan have survived similarly dire circumstances before. After languishing in Nasser's prison camps from 1954 until his death in 1970, the Ikhwan quickly recovered and revived in the 1970s and 1980s. That experience has shaped the Ikhwan's worldview and their self-definition as well.

In my interviews over the past two decades, Ikhwan officials seem to have internalized Nasser's prison years as a traumatic but purifying and galvanizing experience. They told me tales of the courage and heroism of Ikhwan prisoners who defied Nasser and his security forces and refused to compromise their Islamic ideals. The movement's dominant narrative celebrates the sweat, pain, and sacrifice of Ikhwan members and their stamina, while vilifying Nasser and his prison enforcers. As they see it, ultimately the sacred truths of Islam will triumph over the powerful forces of darkness and apostasy. This conviction is an impediment to critical self-reflection and acknowledgment of what went wrong with the movement. It is difficult to imagine the Ikhwan leadership in exile calling for open and genuine deliberation, which is not part of their political DNA.

The most likely scenario, if Sisi is re-elected for another four-year presidential term in April 2018, as seems plausible, is that the Ikhwan will try to offer feelers to the former general about striking a reconciliation deal—a return to cold peace and coexistence between the state and the Islamist organization. Each side has an interest in its own political survival and in preventing the emergence and consolidation of organized internal challenges to its own leadership.

The New Dissidents

The Ikhwan's conduct between 2011 and 2013 provided dissatisfied members with a moment of "emancipation" at the individual level because they no longer felt guilty for abandoning the group's utopian dream—"Islam is the solution." In their view, the leadership had already abandoned the dream by sacrificing the foundational myth at the altar of short-term political gain.[12] For some members, this dilemma offered a "Columbus discovering America" moment, according to Sameh Fayez, a young member.[13] He says he suddenly felt free to read books outside the Ikhwan curriculum, free of the censorship of the group's leaders.[14]

The Islamist movement now faces reckoning from within, with a new wave of defections and a serious revolt by radicalized young members in Egypt. Although defections are hardly a new phenomenon and have occurred since Hassan al-Banna founded the group, the current, post-2011 wave is bigger in sheer numbers and socially more sophisticated than before. Shying away from the limelight and avoiding a challenge to the Ikhwan's orthodoxy, previous defectors did not impact the group's unity or decision making. In contrast, the post–Arab Spring "dissidents" are more daring in their critique of the leadership's authoritarian ways. Veteran leaders like Ibrahim Za'farani, a member of Ikhwan's Shura Council, or legislative body; Mohamed Habib, the former deputy supreme guide; and Kamal al-Helbawi, the group's spokesperson in the West, either stepped down or were dismissed at almost the same time in 2011–2012. Each has authored autobiographies, regularly written columns in leading newspapers, given television interviews about their personal experiences within the Ikhwan, and backed state-approved political parties.

The portrait of the organization that the new dissidents paint is fundamentally at odds with the Ikhwan's official narrative. The new defectors aim to expose the Leninist-like control that the ultraconservative leaders exercise over the organization as well as the tribalism that cements internal networking among members and their families. Calling into question the foundational myth of the Ikhwan, which revolves around Islamic revival and the building of a new religious community at the center of which is a Brotherhood member, these disgruntled senior officials depict a power-thirsty leadership that is mainly interested in exercising control and protecting its fiefdom: power, politics, and material gains take front seat in the calculations of current Ikhwan leaders.

Moreover, the post-2011 dissidents even criticize Hassan al-Banna, who as a founding figure is regarded as beyond criticism.

For example, Ahmed al-'Gouz, a young Ikhwan member, published an essay based on an imaginary dialogue with Banna in which he questions the founder's key decisions and principles, including the demand for absolute obedience to the leadership and the formation of an armed wing, al-Nizam al-Khass, within the group. "If he [Banna] lives among us today, will he create the Ikhwan in the first place?"[15] Similarly, Ahmed Ban, a leader in the Ikhwan before his resignation in February 2012, took the pioneering supreme guide to task for "engagement in power struggle" and his "approval for the use of force" as well as the "destabilization of the nation-state," along with a long litany of Banna's other mistakes.[16] Sameh Eid, another young dissident, condemned the "illusion of sacredness" invested in Banna, which had been used by the group's ultraconservative leadership to "prevent any internal self-criticism."[17]

By targeting Banna, the new dissidents strike at the Ikhwan's core symbol of ideological legitimacy. Intissar Abdel Mon'im, a member of this generation of dissidents, questions Banna's teachings which she believes "contradicted the theological teachings of the Prophet Muhammad and his caliphs."[18] Abdel Mon'im accuses the group's leaders of manufacturing a "myth" around Banna which they brandish as a sword in their arsenal against rivals.[19] Fayez, another young defector, goes further by claiming that the Ikhwan indoctrinates each member to be a "slave to al-Banna" and his "own religion, setting him as a prophet."[20]

There is undoubtedly a link between the open political environment following the January 2011 revolution and the increasing number of defectors from and dissidents within the Ikhwan. Reformists acknowledge that after Mubarak's removal from power they sensed a golden opportunity to "voice their dissent" and to challenge the culture of absolute obedience and imposed silence that dominates the group. For example, Mohamed Habib, deputy supreme guide and leader in the Guidance Office, the executive body, resigned in July 2011 and accused the group of having tried to abort the January revolution by holding secret talks with Mubarak's confidants while also joining the Tahrir protests demanding regime change.[21]

Abdel Moneim Abu al-Futuh, another veteran in the Guidance Office, left the Ikhwan in March 2011, formed his political party in November 2012, and ran in the May 2012 presidential elections against the group's candidate, Mohamed Morsi. Against the wishes and orders of the Ikhwan leadership, many members joined Abu al-Futuh's al-Tayyar al-Misry (the Egyptian Trend). Similarly, former members such as Sameh Fayez signed on to al-Wasat (the Center), a breakaway party founded by Ikhwan dissidents in 1996 that had been previously banned by the state, and Habib joined al-Nahda (the Renaissance), a party founded by Ibrahim Za'farani.[22]

With the old regime neutralized, the new dissidents felt free to revolt against the dominant power structure within the Ikhwan. They joined a new grouping called Ikhwan Munshawun (Dissident Brothers), which has nationalist overtones. The absence of the oppressive state from 2011 until 2013 encouraged criticism and dissent within the Ikhwan, which represented a serious challenge to the leadership.

Although these defectors and dissidents dented the Ikhwan's public image and standing and even cohesiveness, their activities did not lead to any internal soul-searching or transformative change by the organization. The conservative leadership, blindly ambitious and insular, saw the toppling of Hosni Mubarak and the new freedom more as a golden opportunity to grab power than as a catalyst to overhaul the rusty old organization and open up and democratize its decision making. Intoxicated by the promise of power, Ikhwan leaders like Badie, Shater, and Mahmoud Izzat, the gatekeeper of the group, who controls the purse strings, marched on to the echoes of their empty rhetoric—rhetoric that resonated with their followers but undermined their credibility in the eyes of the public and made them vulnerable to accusations of treachery and even treason by their foes.

Ikhwan leaders did not feel the need to genuinely address the concerns of the reformist wing of their movement or external critics; instead they felt vindicated by developments at home which brought them a step closer to gaining power. The top leadership showed no appetite for real change. In June 2011, the Ikhwan established the Freedom and Justice Party (FJP), whose platform promised to promote freedom and justice, as its name implied. The leadership also promised to separate the *da'wa*, or religious call, from the newly set up political party. Many observers hailed this move by the Ikhwan as transformative, signaling a rupture with the past. The theory that the Islamist organization was progressing and morphing into a modern, multi-vocal political association guided by educated, savvy professionals gained new momentum and traction among Ikhwan watchers.[23] In reality, the change was more cosmetic and superficial than profound and real. There existed no daylight between the *da'wa* and the political wing, or between the movement and the presidency of Morsi, who was supposed to be his own man and the leader for all Egyptians. Morsi, a figurehead who lacked charisma and a solid grounding, was at the mercy of the power brokers within the Ikhwan, particularly the supreme guide, Badie; his right-hand millionaire tycoon, Shater; and Izzat, the powerful chief of staff.

Deadly Embrace

Now that the Ikhwan have lost power, the group's conservative leaders have migrated to their "comfort zone," scattered across the globe and trying to survive state clampdown and repression. With the revival of the authoritarian state, the moral authority of the new dissenters no longer carries the same weight. Now that the Ikhwan is banned and its leaders locked behind bars or in exile, the old guard dismisses the new dissidents as traitors to the cause who are doing the bidding of the Sisi regime; instead, they call for solidarity and unity in the face of state repression.[24] Old mottos like "organizational unity," "steadfastness," and the "Islamic project" are deployed to suppress alternative visions and internal pleas for "self-critical analysis" and forward thinking. The Ikhwan's strategic priority is survival, which in the leaders' view means demanding obedience from members, not agonizing over the road not taken and publicly debating what went wrong.

Strikingly, the Ikhwan faces another kind of revolt. Radicalized younger members are agitating not for internal democratic reforms and open dialogue but for more "militant" measures in order to visit violent "retribution" against the Sisi regime for the overthrow of Morsi and the subsequent clampdown against the Ikhwan.[25] The Ikhwan has sought to appease this faction by co-opting many of its members into central leadership posts.[26] This does not seem to have fully succeeded in convincing the radicalized youth to avoid violent confrontation with the authorities, a path that could spell disaster for the future of the Ikhwan and Egypt as well. The Islamist organization faces reckoning from within and without, with the social space it has relinquished at home now filled by extremist religious politics. Under such severe circumstances, it is doubtful that the Ikhwan can moderate its stance or undertake substantive internal reforms.

In a similar vein, the Sisi government does not tolerate calls by nationalist and secularist allies for de-escalation and reconciliation with the Ikhwan. The authorities have cracked down hard on dissenting nationalist and liberal voices, making sure that there is no serious organized challenge to President Sisi's rule. The government wages war against the Ikhwan, classifying this mainstream group as a terrorist organization on a par with Salafi-jihadists like Al Qaeda and the Islamic State. Like Nasser in the 1950s and 1960s, Sisi aims to crush the powerful Islamist organization and dismantle its social networks, a thorny and costly mission.

The space for free, open debate and political activism is tightly shut, not only between the two warring camps but also within each camp, a toxic situation similar to that of the 1950s and 1960s. All sides are on a war footing, waging trench warfare against each other. Apart from the human and social toll that this six-decade-old violent struggle has exacted, it has radicalized and militarized Arab politics and led to entrenched dictatorships and deeper repression. The Islamist-nationalist fault line remains the single most important impediment to the normalization and institutionalization of political life in Egypt, the most populous Arab state, and other Arab countries. There can be no political transition as long as the Ikhwan, the most influential social movement in the Arab world, and the military-dominated regime are locked in a state of war.

Notes

Preface

1. For example, a book by Christina Phelps Harris, *Nationalism and Revolution in Egypt: The Role of the Muslim Brotherhood* (Stanford, CA: Hoover Institution Publications, 1964), from the time of the peak of Nasser's popularity in the 1960s, shows how the two themes have been integrated in past studies. But recent studies tend to deal with the two themes as distinct developments: see the following critical studies by Tarek Osman, *Egypt on the Brink: From Nasser to the Muslim Brotherhood* (New Haven, CT: Yale University Press, 2010); Said K. Aburish, *Nasser, the Last Arab: A Biography* (New York: St. Martin's Press, 2004); Joel Gordon, *Nasser: Hero of the Arab Nation* (Oxford, UK: Oneworld Publications, 2006); Omar Khalifah, *Nasser in the Egyptian Imaginary* (Edinburgh: Edinburgh University Press, 2017); Carrie Rosefsky Wickham, *The Muslim Brotherhood: Evolution of an Islamist Movement* (Princeton, NJ: Princeton University Press, 2013); Abdullah al-Arian, *Answering the Call: Popular Islamic Activism in Sadat's Egypt* (New York: Oxford University Press, 2014); and Barbara H. E. Zollner, *The Muslim Brotherhood: Hasan al-Hudaybi and Ideology* (New York: Routledge, 2009).
2. Adnan Musallam, *From Secularism to Jihad: Sayyid Qutb and the Foundations of Radical Islamism* (Westport, CT: Praeger Press, 2005); Sayed Khatab, *The Political Thought of Sayyid Qutb: The Theory of Jahiliyyah* (London: Routledge, 2006); John Calvert, *Sayyid Qutb and the Origins of Radical Islamism* (New York: Columbia University Press, 2010); Gilles Kepel, *Muslim Extremism in Egypt: The Prophet and Pharaoh* (London: Al Saqi, 1985); James Toth, *Sayyid Qutb: The Life and Legacy of a Radical Islamic Intellectual* (Oxford: Oxford University Press, 2013); Wickham, *The Muslim Brotherhood.*
3. Author's interview with Ahmed Abdel Majid, Cairo, 7 January 2007.
4. Author's interview with Ahmed Abdel Majid, Cairo, 15 January 2007.

5. Author's interview with Ahmed Ra'if, Cairo, 19 March 2007. Ahmed Ra'if has since passed away.
6. Ibid.

Introduction

1. See a few headlines of Arabic-based newspapers and websites: "Egypt's Future in the Shadow of Nasser"; "Sisi Runs for President in Nasser's Shadow"; and "Egypt Wonders If Army Chief Is Another Nasser."
2. http://www.theguardian.com/world/2013/aug/07/egypt-morsi-nationalist-general-sisi [accessed 21 October 2014].
3. http://alhayat.com/Details/535673 [accessed 22 October 2014].
4. For example, on July 13, 2014, the Ikhwan posted a statement on its website describing its supporters as "the soldiers of God" battling the soldiers of *kufr*. Citing a Qur'anic verse, the statement concluded that the forces of belief would ultimately prevail. See http://www.ikhwanonline.com/Article.aspx?ArtID=193050&SecID=212 [accessed 21 October 2014].
5. Author's interview with Sherif Younis, Cairo, 20 October 2006.
6. Author's interview with Farid Abdel Khaleq, Cairo, 2 October 2006.
7. Michael Barnet, *Dialogues in Arab Politics: Negotiation in Regional Order* (New York: Columbia University Press, 1998). See also M. Barnet's chapter, "Identity and Alliances in the Middle East," in *The Culture of National Security: Norms and Identity in World Politics*, ed. Peter J. Katzenstein (New York: Columbia University Press, 1996).
8. Anissa Haddadi, "Myths, Norms and the Politics of National Identity in the Egypt of Nasser and Qutb: Society Must Be Desired," PhD dissertation at the London School of Economics (work in progress, 2017).
9. Aziz al-Azmeh, *Islams and Modernities* (London: Verso, 2009).
10. Nayef al-Rushaydat, *Gamal Abdel-Nasser fil Mizan* (Beirut: Al-Muassasa al-A'rabiyya leil Derasat wal Nashr, 2003), pp. 57–60. See also Sa'id Abul-Reesh, *Gamal Abdel-Nasser: Akher al-Arab* (Beirut: Markaz Derasat al-Wihda al-A'rabiyya, 2005); James Jankowski, *Nasser's Egypt, Arab Nationalism, and the United Arab Republic* (Boulder, CO: Lynne Rienner Publishers, 2002); Rashid Khalidi, ed., *The Origins of Arab Nationalism* (New York: Columbia University Press, 1993).
11. Peter Johnson, "Egypt under Nasser," *MERIP Reports* 10 (July 1972), pp. 3–14. See also Anouar Abdel-Malek, *Egypt: Military Society; the Army Regime, the Left, and Social Change under Nasser* (New York: Random House, 1968); Gamal Hamad, *Asrar Thawrat 23 Uluu*, 2 vols. (Cairo: Al-Zahraa Leil E'laam Al-Arabi, 2006).
12. See the conceptually and literarily interesting study of Nasser by Omar Khalifah, in which he argues that Nasser has become "a rhetorical device," a trope that connotes specific images constantly invoked whenever he is mentioned: *Nasser in the Egyptian Imaginary* (Edinburgh: Edinburgh University Press, 2016).
13. Author's interviews with Kamal Habib, Cairo, 21 November 2006 and 8 February 2007.
14. Author's interview with Huda Abdel Nasser, Cairo, 21 November 2006.
15. Author's interview with Sami Sharaf, Cairo, 8 February 2007.

16. Author's interview with Khaled Mohieddin, Cairo, 12 December 2016.
17. Author's interview with Mohamed Fayek, Cairo, 26 November 2006.
18. Author's interview with Abd al-Ghafar Shukr, Cairo, 10 October 2006.
19. Ibid.
20. Author's interview with Montasser al-Zayat, Cairo, 20 October 2006.
21. Author's interview with Ibrahim Za'farani, Alexandria, 13 January 2007.
22. Author's interview with Seif Abdel Fattah, Cairo, 20 November 2006.
23. Author's interview with Wahid Abdel Majid, Cairo, 11 January 2007.
24. Author's interviews with Mohamed Abdel Sattar, Cairo, 9 December and 16 December 2006; Ahmed Ra'if, Cairo, 19 March 2007; and Farid Abdel Khaleq, Cairo, 7 December 2006.
25. Author's interview with Ahmed Ra'if, Cairo, 19 March 2007.
26. Author's interview with Mohamed Abdel Sattar, Cairo, 16 December 2006.
27. Author's interview with Ma'mun Hudaybi, Cairo, 13 December 1999.
28. Author's interview with Mohamed Mahdi Akef, Cairo, 22 March 2007.
29. Author's interview with Mohamed Mahdi Akef, Cairo, 24 December 2006.
30. Author's interview with Mahmoud Izzat, Cairo, 24 December 2006.
31. Ibid.
32. Author's interview with Hesham El-Hamamy, Cairo, 14 January 2007.
33. Author's interview with Hesham El-Hamamy, Cairo, 15 January 2007.
34. Eric Hobsbawm, *On History* (UK: Hachette, 2011).

Chapter 1. Egypt's "Liberal Age"

1. This geographical intersection has been described eloquently by renowned Egyptian geographer and scholar Gamal Hamdan, who writes that "judging by land and water, Egypt is African ... Judging by orientation, history, influence and destiny, Egypt is Asian. Therefore, the part of Europe starts at Alexandria, the part of Asia starts at Cairo and the part of Africa starts at Aswan." G. Hamdan, *Shakhsiyyat misr* [Egypt's character], vol. 1 (Cairo: Dar al-Hilal, 1984), p. 45.
2. J. Cole, *Napoleon's Egypt: Invading the Middle East* (Basingstoke, UK: Palgrave Macmillan, 2007), pp. 145–155. For example, Bonaparte "had convened the Egyptian Institute, modelled on the French Institute, as a scientific society that would intensively study Egypt and help with the needs of the army." The establishment of the institute was justified as an attempt "to implant liberty in Egypt" (ibid., p. 145). Napoleon's purported civilizing mission is discernible in his address, in Arabic, to the Egyptian population upon the arrival of his army in the country: "I have not come to you except for the purpose of restoring your rights from the hands of the oppressors." A. R. Al-Jabarti, *Mazhar al-taqdis bi-dhahab dawlat al-faransis* [The holy feature with the disappearance of the French state], vol. 1, collected by 'A. Al-Raziq, R. A. 'Isa, and 'I. A. Hilal (Cairo: Dar al-'Arabi li al-Nashr wa al-Tawz'i, 1998), pp. 101, 105.
3. Within the Mamluk sultanate, the Mamluk elite were considered to have a social status above other civilians.
4. The Circassian people originally come from the North Caucus. In Egypt, they were first linked to the Mamluk dynasty. As more Circassians immigrated to the Ottoman

Empire in the 1850s and mid-1860s, more moved to Egypt. The descendants of the Mamluks and these new immigrants came to form an elite ruling class in Egypt known as the Turco-Circassians.

5. Originally, capitulations were a privilege that a government could extend to the citizens of another country and could abolish as it saw fit. The capitulations of the Ottoman Empire were contracts between the Ottoman Empire and European powers, particularly France.
6. A body of Muslim scholars who are recognized as having specialist knowledge of Islamic sacred law and theology.
7. See S. A. Hanna and G. H. Gardner, *Arab Socialism: A Documentary Survey* (Leiden: E. J. Brill, 1969), p. 51.
8. Ibid., p. 51.
9. A. Hourani, *Arabic Thought in the Liberal Age, 1798–1939* (London: Oxford University Press, 1967), p. 108.
10. Ibid.
11. G. Baer, "Islamic Political Activity in Modern Egyptian History: A Comparative Analysis," In *Islam, Nationalism, and Radicalism in Egypt and the Sudan*, ed. G. R. Warburg and U. M. Kupferschmidt (New York: Praeger, 1983), p. 39.
12. R. Al-Sa'id, *Al-asas al-ijtima'i leil thawra al-urabiyya* [The social basis of the 'Urabi revolution] (Cairo: Maktabat Madbouli, 1967), p. 69. Abduh wrote in November 1881 an article on the meanings of "nationalism," in which he associated the concept with "homeland" based on equality and justice as well as individual rights for every citizen. A. 'A. Mustafa, *Al-thawra al-'urabiyya* [The 'Urabi revolution] (Cairo: Ministry of Culture and Guidance, 1961), pp. 12–13.
13. A. Goldschmidt, "The Egyptian Nationalist Party: 1892–1919," in P. M. Holt, ed., *Political and Social Change in Modern Egypt: Historical Studies from the Ottoman Conquest to the United Arab Republic* (London: Oxford University Press, 1968), pp. 308–309. Goldschmidt called the battle at Tel el-Kebir "the final defeat of the first Egyptian nationalist revolution," especially as nationalists other than 'Urabi made their peace with Khedive Tawfiq, who "managed to cooperate fairly amicably" with the French invaders" (ibid.).
14. A. 'Urabi, *'Urabi: Kashf al-sitar 'an sirr al-asrar fi al-nahda al-misriyya al-mashhura bi al-thawra al-'urabiya* [Unveiling the secret of the secrets on the Egyptian renaissance known as the 'Urabi revolution], vol. 1, ed. A.M.I. Al-Jumi'i, (Cairo: Dar al-Kutub wa al-Watha'iq al-Qawmiyya, 2005), pp. 485–587. Unwillingly and under the pressure of the 'Urabists, Khedive Tawfiq agreed to give legislative powers to the *majlis al-nuwab al-misri* (Egyptian House of Representatives). The council's first session was meant for the government to present the "Basic Law." This Basic Law allowed wide powers for the council, including summoning and questioning ministers and debating the national budget including expenses and revenues; the latter power infuriatedg European creditors who loaned money to the Egyptian government. Wilfrid S. Blunt, a British observer and diplomat, commented in his memoirs that "the three months which followed this notable event were the happiest time, politically, that Egypt has ever known." See W. S. Blunt, *Secret History of the English Occupation of Egypt: Being a Personal Narrative of Events* (New York: Howard Fertig, 1967), p. 116. Historians even argued that the 1881 revolt allowed the Egyptians to participate in their own government for the first time since the Persians conquered

Egypt in 343 B.C., with a constitution and an elected legislature. After three months, the British occupied Egypt, dissolved this council, and cancelled the Basic Law governing its entitlement. It is no wonder that 'Urabi blamed the French and the British for the failure of his rule. See A. 'Urabi, *'Urabi*, vol. 1, pp. 485–487.

15. See T. Abu Arja, *Al-muqatam jaridat al-ihtilal al-britani fi misr* [Al-Muqatam: The paper of the British occupation in Egypt] (Cairo: al-Hay'a al-Misriyya al-'Amma li-l-Kitab, 1997), p. 9; and S. Aziz, *Al-sahafa al-misriyya wa-mawqifuha min al-ihtilal al-ingilizi* [The Egyptian press and its position on the British occupation] (Cairo: Dar al-Kitab al-'Arabi, 1968), pp. 68–69.
16. One such journalist was 'Abdullah al-Nadim, who was imprisoned and sent into exile by the British. Al-Nadim is called "the Journalist of the Nineteenth Century" in Egypt due to his considerable role in founding new influential publications, i.e., *Al-Tankit wal Tabkit*, *Al-Ustadh*, and *Al-Ta'if*. See M. T. A. Allah, *Al-Nadim: Al-tankit wal tabkit* [Al-Nadim: Al-Tankit and Tabkit], intro. A. A. Ramadan (Cairo: Al-Hay'a al-Masriyya al-'Amma li al-Kitab, 1994), pp. 5–6. Unlike Ahmad Lutfi al-Sayyid, Nadim severely criticized Europe's influence, contending that European foreigners always brought with them *al-da' al-afrangi* (the foreign malaise) (ibid., p. 37). In his articles, Nadim urged the Egyptians to reclaim their history and reminisce about "their glory" in order to stand up to any European influences. Nevertheless, Nadim was critical of political and social problems in Egypt, such as the resort to *khurafat* (metaphysical beliefs and unscientific approaches). Yet he insisted that the treatment of these ills be locally done "using herbs grown in the land of my country, and prescribed by the doctors of my country and prepared by pharmacists of my country" (ibid., p. 11). Nadim joined 'Urabi and toured the province of Egypt with him during the 'Urabi revolt. He was described as a vocal orator during these tours. He also played a pivotal role to influence nationalist leader Mustafa Kamil and even convinced the latter to get into journalism (ibid., p. 5). See also A. M. A. Naga, *Al-awda ella al-manfa: Hayat 'abdullah al-nadim* (Cairo: Dar al-Helal, 1969).
17. A. Goldschmidt, *Biographical Dictionary of Egypt* (Boulder, CO: Lynne Rienner, 2000), pp. 101–102.
18. A. Goldschmidt, "The Egyptian Nationalist Party: 1892–1919," p. 320.
19. Ibid.
20. Ibid.
21. A. Goldschmidt, *Historical Dictionary of Egypt* (Plymouth, UK: Scarecrow Press, 2013), p. 124.
22. Y. L. Rizq, "Al-guzour al-tarikhia leil ahzab al-misriyya" [The historical roots of the Egyptian parties], in *Al-ahzab al-misriyya: 1922–1953* [The Egyptian parties: 1922–1953], ed. R. A. Hamed (Cairo: Markaz al-Ahram li-l-Dirasat al-Siyasiyya wa-l-Istratijiyya, 1995), p. 12.
23. A. Goldschmidt, "The Egyptian Nationalist Party: 1892–1919," p. 321.
24. I. Gershoni, *Egypt, Islam, and the Arabs: The Search for Egyptian Nationhood, 1900–1930* (New York: Oxford University Press, 1986), pp. 8–9.
25. S. Tadros, *Motherland Lost: The Egyptian and Coptic Quest for Modernity* (Stanford, CA: Hoover Institution, 2013), pp. 113–114.
26. A. R. Al-Rafi'i, *Mustafa Kamil: Ba'ith al-haraka al-wataniyya, tarikh misr al-qawmi min 1892 ila 1908* [Mustafa Kamil: The generator of the nationalist movement, the national history of Egypt from 1892 until 1908], 5th ed. (Cairo: Dar al-Ma'arif, 1984), p. 265.

27. A. A. R. Mustafa, *Tarikh misr al-siyasi min al-ihtilal ila m'ahada* [The political history of Egypt from occupation to the treaty] (Cairo: Dar al-Ma'ref, 1967), pp. 33–35.
28. Goldschmidt, "The Egyptian Nationalist Party: 1892–1919," p. 321.
29. Mustafa, *Tarikh misr*, p. 50.
30. P. J. Vatikiotis, *The Modern History of Egypt* (London: Butler and Tanner, 1969), pp. 226–227.
31. Goldschmidt, *Historical Dictionary of Egypt*, p. 124.
32. 2 Rizq, "Al-guzour al-tarikhia leil ahzab al-misriyya," p. 35.
33. Ibid. Helmi was the first journalist to be imprisoned for "*al-'aib fi al-dhat al-hakima*" (tarnishing the image of the ruler). The most famous square in Cairo is named after him.
34. Rizq, "Al-guzour al-tarikhia leil ahzab al-misriyya," p. 6. According to 'Abbas, cited here, and other scholars, the Liberal Era ended in 1953, the year in which the Revolutionary Command Council (RCC) issued a decree to dissolve all political parties.
35. When Kamil announced the foundation of his own National Party, for example, some 7,000 people attended the ceremony in Alexandria. The figure was cited by Kamil's party mouthpiece *al-Liwa'*, while rival newspapers put the figure at 5,000. Still, this figure is huge taking into consideration the population figures of this time. Rizq, "Al-guzour al-tarikhia leil ahzab al-misriyya," p. 19.
36. Ibid., p. 36.
37. Ibid., p. 6.
38. Other scholars such as Griffel referred to this causal relationship sequentially. "Following the failure of the *salafiyya* [pioneered by Afghani and Abduh], a younger generation of Muslim activists created a new momentum when they rejected the colonial state as the vehicle for reform." F. Griffel, "What Do We Mean by 'Salafi'? Linking Muhammad 'Abduh with Egypt's Nur Party in Islam's Contemporary Intellectual History," *Die Welt des Islams, International Journal for the Study of Modern Islam* 55, no. 2 (2015): 196. Griffel named Banna as the "archetype" of this new generation and Sayyid Qutb as well because he adopted Banna's attitude towards the state (ibid.).
39. For example, Mustafa Kamil has been described by such scholars as Samuel Tadros as a "romantic nationalist," in contrast with "realist nationalists" like Ahmed Lutfi al-Sayyid. Kamil "preached love of Egypt whilst paying little attention to the contradictions between pro-Islamic, pro-Sultan, and initially pro-Khedive rhetoric, and Egyptian nationalism. This contradiction became more apparent during a 1906 incident" in which Ottoman troops occupied Taba, an Egyptian town in the Sinai peninsula, with a view to enlarging Ottoman access to the Red Sea. S. Tadros, *Motherland Lost: The Egyptian and Coptic Quest for Modernity* (Stanford, CA: Hoover Institution, 2013), p. 112. When British forces stationed in Egypt forced the Ottoman troops to withdraw, the pro-Ottoman Kamil was among those who challenged Britain's right to negotiate Egyptian territory. Faced with the struggle between the British occupier and the Ottoman sultan over Egypt's exact borders, he "supported the Sultan's rights at the expense of Egypt's territorial rights." The incident showed that Mustafa Kamil still harbored what Tadros called "pan-Islamism dreams." It also showed the break between him and Ahmed Lutfi al-Sayyid and other colleagues who sought to define the Egyptian nation in territorial terms. Ibid., pp. 112–114.
40. For example, Zaghloul, in one of his speeches in January 1919, urged liberal constitutionalism as a political mode for Egypt to adopt, and within which the country

had to witness massive economic, administrative, and social reforms guaranteeing respect for "principles of democracy" and "human values." Furthermore, the independence of Egypt should be secured via legally binding and internationally inviolable channels such as the League of Nations to get rid of the British occupation. Zaghloul and his co-nationalists in the Legislative Assembly even sent a letter to U.S. President Woodrow Wilson to obtain the support of the "the US Greater Democracy's man who left his country to spread in the world peace and comprehensive justice." The letter's final line read: "Long Live the US. Long live Dr. Wilson." Furthermore, Zaghloul's liberalism had been obvious in stressing not only that foreigners should remain in Egypt but also that their privileges be guaranteed after independence. The reason, Zaghloul contended, was that those foreigners would be the link with the West and their "springs of science and sources of invention and discovery." The Wafd leader envisaged that Egypt "must be" a member of "Al-Musabaqa al-'Alamiyya" (the International Competition). All quotations from *Mudhakkirat sa'ad zaghloul* [The memoirs of Sa'ad Zaghloul], vol. 7, collected by 'A. A. Ramadan (Cairo: Al-Hay'a al-Misriyya al-'Amma li al-Kitab, 1990), pp. 210–214/2890–2894 (Note: the pages of the publication are double-numbered).

41. P. J. Vatikiotis, *The Modern History of Egypt* (London: Butler and Tanner, 1969), p. 248.
42. *Mudhakkirat sa'ad zaghloul*, pp. 260–262/2940–2942 (Note: the pages of the publication are double-numbered).
43. Encyclopaedia Britannica Online, s.v. "Wafd," http://www.britannica.com/EBchecked/topic/633823/Wafd [accessed 1 November 2013].
44. *Al-dasatir al-misriyya, 1805–1971: Nusus wa tahlil* [The Egyptian constitutions, 1805–1971: Texts and analysis] (Cairo, Markaz al-Tanzim wa al-Microfilm, 1977), pp. 79, 159–160.
45. M. Deeb, *Party Politics in Egypt: The Wafd and Its Rivals, 1919–1939* (London: Ithaca Press for the Middle East Centre, St. Antony's College, Oxford, 1979), p. 124. *Al-dasatir al-misriyya, 1805–1971*, pp. 162–165.
46. J. Berque, *Egypt: Imperialism and Revolution*, trans. J. Stewart (London: Faber, 1972), p. 393. See also H. A. Rashid, *Tarikh nahdat misr al-haditha min Mohamed 'Ali al-Kabeer ella al-rais Gamal Abdel-Nasser, 1801–1960* [The history of modern Egypt's renaissance from Mohamed Ali to President Gamal Abdel-Nasser, 1801–1960] (Beirut: Maktabat al-Fikr al-'Arabi, 1960), pp. 162–163. As the constitution included the country's first electoral law, Egyptians were invited in 1923 and 1924 to elect their MPs. The Wafd swept the elections, capturing 188 out of 215 seats. The king had no choice but to select a rival, the Wafd leader Zaghloul, to form a cabinet. For historical and personal reasons, the king did not enjoy good relations with the Wafd; the crisis peaked in 1942 when British tanks surrounded the royal palace and forced the king to appoint a Wafd government.
47. Deeb, *Party Politics in Egypt*. p. 128.
48. Ibid., p. 126.
49. Ibid., p. 131.
50. Sticking points in Zaghloul's negotiations with the British included his objection to the presence of British posts on the Suez Canal or anywhere else in the country: Deeb, *Party Politics in Egypt*, p. 132. Zaghloul also faced internal opposition both from radical forces within the Wafd and from other political forces such as the Liberal

Constitutionalists, who insisted that there should be no negotiations before evacuation (ibid., pp. 133–135).

51. Ibid., p. 135. When a general election was held in May 1926, the Wafd also won, but Zaghloul, now nearly seventy years old, did not take the post of premiership. Under pressure from Lord Lloyd, the new British high commissioner, Zaghloul agreed to the formation of a coalition government and contented himself with the presidency of the Chamber of Deputies (Parliament). See *Encyclopaedia Britannica Online*, s.v. "Sa'd Zaglul," http://www.britannica.com/EBchecked/topic/655329/Sad-Zaghlul [accessed 4 February 2014].
52. Berque, *Egypt: Imperialism and Revolution*, p. 394.
53. Deeb, *Party Politics in Egypt*, pp. 127, 142. Y. L. Rizq, "An Issue of Identity," *Ahram Weekly Online*, 22–28 November 2001, available from http://weekly.ahram.org.eg/Archive/2001/561/chrncls.htm [accessed 12 February 2014].
54. This is known as the crisis of the Assemblies Law when the British crushed attempts by the Egyptian Parliament to establish a right to public assembly, which would have restricted state powers to suppress demonstrations. A further demonstration of the historical continuity adopted in this book; the 1923 law, which the British employed all attempts to abrogate, remained in operation for seventy years, even after the fall of President Hosni Mubarak in February 2011.
55. Deeb, *Party Politics in Egypt*, p. 128.
56. Ibid., p. 144. Cited from FO 407/206, No. 137, Lloyd to Chamberlain, 22 June 1928.
57. Vatikiotis, *The Modern History of Egypt*, p. 265.
58. Berque, *Egypt: Imperialism and Revolution*, p. 393.
59. The words *fellah* or *fellahin* mean "farmer" or "farmers" and are used to refer to the peasant classes.
60. Vatikiotis, *The Modern History of Egypt*, p. 332.
61. Deeb, *Party Politics in Egypt*, p. 320.
62. I. Gershoni and J. P. Jankowski, *Redefining the Egyptian Nation, 1930–1945* (Cambridge: Cambridge University Press, 1995), pp. 11–12.
63. Israel Gershoni and James P. Jankowski linked these conditions to the rise of a new type of nationalism different from the territorial nationalism which emerged in the earlier decades of the century. This new nationalism, which Gershoni and Jankowski called the "supra-Egyptian" nationalism in the post-1930 period, was based on broader processes of urbanization (identified in the increased population in Cairo and Alexandria), the formation of new occupational groups which are more traditional and less Westernized than the new *effendiyya*, and educational expansion (manifested in rising numbers of literate Egyptians). Gershoni and Jankowski, *Redefining the Egyptian Nation*, pp. 11–12. Indeed, this transformation of nationalism can be taken as a massive historical development since Egyptians have always known only territorial nationalism since throughout the ages based on an identification with a fixed piece of land in which "native Egyptians recognised the existence of a fixed and unchanging territory that was Egypt, which had fixed natural boundaries, and which was separate as a territory even when it was the centre of an empire or amalgamated into an empire as a mere province." A. L. A. Marsot, *A Short History of Modern Egypt* (Cambridge: Cambridge University Press, 1985), p. vii. Marsot even attributed this "territorial" nationalism to the pharaonic times in which Egyptians

had identified themselves as "inhabitants of a fixed and unchanging entity known as Egypt" (ibid., p. 7). The new type of nationalism was massively influential that it had left an impact on the class mobility associated with educational expansion. The father of prominent novelist Nawal Sa'dawi is one case in point as she narrates in her memoirs: N. Sa'dawi, *Awraqi ... Hayati* [My papers ... my life] (Beirut: Dar al-Mustaqbal al-'Arabi, 2004 [vol. 1, 2nd ed.], 2005 [vol. 2, 7th ed.], 2007 [vol. 3, 2nd ed.]), p. 202.

64. Berque, *Egypt: Imperialism and Revolution*, p. 418.
65. Gershoni and Jankowski, *Redefining the Egyptian Nation*, p. 1.
66. Ibid., pp. 1–2.
67. Vatikiotis, *The Modern History of Egypt*, p. 335.
68. Ibid.
69. Ibid.
70. Ibid.
71. Ibid., pp. 336–337.
72. R. A. Hinnebusch, "The Reemergence of the Wafd Party: Glimpses of the Liberal Opposition in Egypt," *International Journal of Middle East Studies* 16, no. 1 (1984): 101.
73. Ibid.
74. Ibid.
75. On 4 February 1942, the British ambassador to Egypt, Sir Miles Lampson, sent tanks to surround the Abdeen Palace and to force King Farouk to sack his ally, Prime Minister Ahmad Mahir, over the latter's lukewarm support for the Allied war effort. In Mahir's stead, Farouk appointed a compliant Wafdist cabinet led by Nahhas, much to the anger of both Mahir and many Egyptians, who saw this as Wafd's collusion with the British occupiers. Furthermore, this crisis embodied personal ambitions and intrigues, as it was meant to satisfy Nahhas's attempts to seek some route to power. See C. D. Smith, "4 February 1942: Its Causes and Its Influence on Egyptian Politics and on the Future of Anglo-Egyptian Relations, 1937–1945," *International Journal of Middle East Studies* 10, no. 4 (1979): 470–472. This narrow-mindedness continued when Nahhas came to power. For example, as al-'Alamayn, the decisive battle for Egypt's future and the world conflict itself, raged within fifty miles of Alexandria, "Nahhas devoted much attention to a violent struggle in his party which resulted in 'Ebeid's expulsion in July" of the same year. Ibid., p. 474.
76. Examples of newly formed parties include the Kutla Sa'diyya Party, founded in 1938 by former Wafd leaders Ahmad Mahir and Mahmud al-Nuqrashi, and the Kutla Wafdiyya, founded in 1942 by one of the Wafd party's most prominent and veteran figures, Makram 'Ebeid, who was to become the secretary of Wafd after the death of Zaghloul. An intellectual and refined orator as well as a prominent representative of the Coptic constituency, 'Ebeid was so influential a figure inside and outside the party that his departure is taken as a turning point in the history of the Wafd. Mahir formed the Kutla Sa'diyya in 1937–1938. By this time he had no relation with the Wafd. Wafd leader Mustafa Nahhas had fired Mahir from the party a few years earlier (after the 1936 agreement signed by the party).
77. The "conscience of the nation" is a concept referred to heavily in the Wafd manifesto published in 1924.

Chapter 2. The Anti-colonial Struggle and the Dawn of Underground Politics

1. P. J. Vatikiotis, *The Modern History of Egypt* (London: Butler and Tanner, 1969), pp. 315–316, 328–329.
2. Ibid., p. 328.
3. Schulze labeled Abduh's movement "Salafiyya" and Banna's "neo-Salafiyya," stressing similarities between both despite the differences. R. Schulze, *A Modern History of the Muslim World* (New York: New York University Press, 2000), pp 18, 90; F. Griffel, "What Do We Mean by 'Salafi'? Connecting Muhammad 'Abduh with Egypt's Nur Party in Islam's Contemporary Intellectual History," *Die Welt des Islams, International Journal for the Study of Modern Islam* 55, no. 2 (2015): 196.
4. C. R. Wickham, *The Muslim Brotherhood: Evolution of an Islamist Movement* (Princeton, NJ: Princeton University Press, 2013), p. 24.
5. R. A. Hinnebusch, "The Reemergence of the Wafd Party: Glimpses of the Liberal Opposition in Egypt," *International Journal of Middle East Studies* 16, no. 1 (1984): 100. These Wafd connections were further widespread across the different regions and classes of the country. "In the rural areas its linkage to the masses was dependent on the personal and patronage ties of Wafd notables to the peasantry. In the cities the Wafd had similar links to all sectors of society: Wafdists dominated the professional associations, the student union, and much of the labour movement; its influence reached, through the effendiyya into the bureaucracy, and through prominent merchant partisans, into the commercial community." Ibid., p. 100.
6. S, Bahr, *Al-aqbat fil hayaa al-siyassiya al-misriyya* [Copts in Egyptian political life] (Cairo: Maktabat a-Anglo al-Misriyya, 1979), pp. 156–157.
7. See S. Botman, *The Rise of Egyptian Communism, 1939–1970* (New York: Syracuse University Press, 1988), p. 20.
8. Hussein admitted the emotional and aesthetic purposes for writing this two-volume work. See the introduction of the first volume, T. Hussein, *'Ala hamish al-sira*, vol. 1., 31st ed. (Cairo: Dar al-Ma'arif, n.d.). The very fact that Hussein wrote Islamic-oriented works has been shocking and contradictory for many detractors and researchers who accused him of always undermining the Qur'an and sarcastically belittling the sayings of Muhammad. See F.H.J. al-Hussayni, *Fikr Taha Husayn fi daw* (al-'Aqida al-Islamiyya, MA: Umm al-Qura University, 2009). Nevertheless, this did not dissuade Hussein from writing other Islamic-oriented works such as *al-wa'd al-haq*, in which he dissected the journey of Islam in supporting weak people and in enhancing individual liberties. See T. Hussein, *Al-wa'd al-haq* (Cairo: Al-Hay'a al-Misriyya al-'Amma Li al-Kitab, 1995).
9. M. H. Haykal, *Hayat Muhammad* (Cairo: Dar al-Ma'arif, 1965), pp. 36–37, 41. Haykal, not to be confused with Mohamed Hassanein Heikal, the seasoned pan-Arab journalist, was the chairman of the Egyptian senate.
10. See 'A. M. al-'Aqqad, *'Abqariyyat Muhammad* (Cairo: Nahdat Misr, 1941).
11. N. Safran, *Egypt in Search of Political Community: An Analysis of the Intellectual and Political Evolution of Egypt, 1804–1952* (Cambridge, MA: Harvard University Press, 1961), p. 140.
12. Vatikiotis, *The Modern History of Egypt*, pp. 324–325.

13. See the official website of Dar-al-Iftaa al-Misriyaa, available from http://www.dar-alifta.org/ViewScientist.aspx?ID=58&LangID=1 [accessed 14 February 2014].
14. J. Jankowski, "Egyptian Responses to the Palestine Problem in the Interwar Period," *International Journal of Middle East Studies* 12, no. 1 (1980): 1–38.
15. Ibid., pp. 1–38.
16. G. H. Talhami, *Palestine and Egyptian National Identity* (New York: Praeger, 1992), p. 36.
17. Ibid.
18. M. H. Haykal, *Mudhakkirat fi al-siyasa al-misriyya* [Memories of Egyptian politics], vol. 3 (Cairo: Dar al Ma'arif, 1978), p. 15.
19. 'A.F.M. El-Awaisi, *The Muslim Brothers and the Palestine Question, 1928–1947* (London: Tauris Academic Studies, 1998).
20. 'A. Salima, *Misr wa al-qadiyya al-filistiniyya* [Egypt and the Palestinian question] (Cairo: Dar al-Fikr li al-Dirasat wa al-Nashr wa al-Tawzi', 1986), p. 48.
21. The Arab Higher Committee was formed in April of 1936, presided over by the mufti of Jerusalem, Amin al-Husayni. In the context of the UN's partition of Palestine, the committee called for a general strike, non-payment of taxes, and the closing of municipal governments (although government employees were allowed to stay at work). It demanded an end to Jewish immigration, a ban on land sales to Jews, and national independence. In September 1937 the British declared martial law, and the Palestinian Arab Higher Committee was dissolved. A few years later, in 1945, the covenant of the League of Arab States, or the Arab League, contained an annex emphasizing the Arab character of Palestine. Accordingly, the league appointed an Arab Higher Executive for Palestine (the Arab Higher Committee), which "included a broad spectrum of Palestinian leaders, to speak for the Palestinian Arabs." On October 3, 1947, after the UN resolution on the partition, the committee called for a general strike. *Enyclopaedia Britannica*, s.v. "Palestine," http://www.britannica.com/EBchecked/topic/439645/Palestine/45070/World-War-II [accessed 1 November 2013].
22. The Egyptian Feminist Union was established by Huda Sha'rawi in 1923 to focus on women's issues such as suffrage, education, and freedom of dress, but Sha'rawi and other female members of the union extended their agenda to broader nationalist causes such as confronting the British occupation and its general consequences. No wonder, that Sha'rawi helped organize the largest women's anti-British demonstration in the 1919 Revolution. See Huda Sha'rawi, *Harem Years: The Memoirs of an Egyptian Feminist* (1879–1924), trans. and ed. M. Badran (London: Virago, 1986). The broad scope of the union's issue areas is, in my view, another example of the nature of Egypt's social groups.
23. Talhami, *Palestine and Egyptian National Identity*, p. 40.
24. Ibid., p. 38, taken from Salima, *Misr wa al-qadiyya al-filistiniyya*, p. 116.
25. Talhami, *Palestine and Egyptian National Identity*, p. 40.
26. A. A. al-Rahman, *Misr wa Falastin* [Egypt and Palestine] (Kuwait: al-Majlis al-Watani li al-Thaqafa wa al-Funun wa al-Adab, 1980), p. 290. Misr al-Fatah was a radical nationalist party that attached pan-Arabism to serving Egypt's national interests, and tied its vision to a "tight Egyptian imperialism ... dedicated to reviving Egypt's glory and creating a great empire comprising Egypt and Sudan." The group

held that "even if Islam is adopted for this [its envisioned] empire, Egyptianness would have the final say, as Egypt would be above all." See ibid., p. 140. The Muslim Brotherhood formed units for jihad and set up a camp in the southern part of Palestine. The Islamist organization promoted the idea that sending its volunteers to Palestine was part of a grand design of jihad by Hassan al-Banna, founder of the Ikhwan, who pledged to the Arab League that he would send "10,000 volunteers for martyrdom in Palestine." See Mahmud 'Abd al-Halim, *Al-Ikhwan al-Muslimun: Ahdath Sana'at al-Tarikh* [Muslim Brotherhood: Events which made history] (Alexandria: Dar al-Da'wa, 1983), p. 412.

27. In several interviews with this author that will be cited in subsequent chapters.
28. Talhami, *Palestine and Egyptian National Identity*, p. 49.
29. Ibid.
30. F. Gerges, "Egypt and the 1948 War: Internal Conflict and Regional Ambition," in *War for Palestine: Rewriting the History of 1948*, ed. E. Rogan and A. Shlaim (Cambridge: Cambridge University Press, 2007), p. 154, taken from M. Naguib, "The War for Palestine," *Al-Masa'* [Cairo daily newspaper], 2 June 1974.
31. Talhami, *Palestine and Egyptian National Identity*, p. 51.
32. Gerges, "Egypt and the 1948 War," p. 154, citing I. Shaqib, *Harb filistin: Ru'ya filistiniyya* [The Palestine war: A Palestinian perspective]. (Cairo: Zahra' li-l-I'lam al-'Arabi, 1986), p. 127.
33. Gerges, "Egypt and the 1948 War," p. 153.
34. M. H. Heikal, *Suqut nizam: Limadha kanat thawrat 23 yulyu lazema* [The fall of a regime: Why the July 23 Revolution was inevitable] (Cairo: Dar al-Shuruq, 2003), p. 210. M. H. Haykal, *Mudhakkirat fi al-siyasa al-misriyya, men July 29, 1937 ella July 26, 1952* [Memories of Egyptian politics: From July 29, 1937, until July 26, 1952], vol. 2 (Cairo: Matba't Misr, 1953), p. 325.
35. Heikal, *Suqut nizam*, p. 210. See also Gerges, "Egypt and the 1948 War," pp. 150–155.
36. G. A. al-Nasser, *Falsafat al-Thawra* [The philosophy of revolution], 9th ed. (Cairo: Dar al-Sha'ab, n.d.), p. 12.
37. Ibid., p. 11.
38. R. P. Mitchell, *The Society of the Muslim Brothers* (Oxford: Oxford University Press, 1969), pp. 180–183. Examples of expansion in membership can be discerned via the growing numbers of members in the different sections of the group; see ibid., pp. 200–205.
39. Ibid., p. 182.
40. Ibid.
41. S. al-Hakim, *Asrar al-'alaqa al-khassa bayna 'Abd al-Nasir wa-l-ikhwan* [The secrets of the special relationship between Abdel Nasser and the Ikhwan] (Cairo: Markaz al-Hadara al-'Arabiyya li-l-I'lam wa-l-Nashr, 1996), p. 8.
42. Heikal, *Suqut nizam*, pp. 213–214.
43. Ibid., p. 191.
44. Ibid., pp. 367–369.
45. Ibid., p. 367.
46. Ibid., pp. 432–433.
47. Ibid., p. 598.
48. H. Kandil, *Soldiers, Spies, and Statesmen: Egypt's Road to Revolt* (London: Verso, 2012), p. 13.

49. A. Abdel-Malek, *Al-mujtama' al-misry wal thawra* [Egyptian society and revolution], trans. M. Haddad and M. Khouri (Beirut: Dar al-Tali'a, 1974), p. 120.
50. Mitchell, *The Society of the Muslim Brothers*, pp. 240–249.

Chapter 3. The Free Officers and the Ikhwan

1. Author's interview with M. H. Heikal, Cairo, 10 December 2006.
2. *Egypt's Liberation: The Philosophy of the Revolution*, often referred to as simply *Falsafat al-Thawra* (Philosophy of Revolution), is a manifesto published in 1955, in which the rationale behind the 1952 revolution is discussed, along with the basis for Nasser's pan-Arabist ideology, which would take Egypt and the region by storm in the mid-1950s.
3. CBC Egypt, interview with Mohamed Hassanein Heikal, video, viewed 10 September 2013, http://www.youtube.com/watch?v=qCBrwEAJehA.
4. M. H. Heikal, *Suqut nizam: Limadha kanat thawrat 23 yulyu lazema* [The fall of a regime: Why the July 23 Revolution was a must] (Cairo: Dar al-Shuruq, 2003), p. 569.
5. Ibid., p. 568.
6. See British and American official diplomatic correspondences at the end of ibid., pp. 569–602.
7. The Royal Sarayya refers to the king's palace, which had been used to exercise massive influence on Egyptian political life, including controlling publicly elected cabinet ministers and indirectly creating loyalist political parties such as al-Sh'ab and al-Itihad.
8. Author's interview with S. Younis, Cairo, 27 October 2006.
9. Author's interview with K. Mohieddin, Cairo, 12 December 2006.
10. S. K. Aburish, *Nasser: The Last Arab* (London: Duckworth, 2004), p. 49.
11. M. Naguib, *Kuntu ra'isan li-misr* [I was the president of Egypt] (Cairo: al-Maktab al-Misry al-Hadith, 1984), pp. 178–180.
12. G. Hammad, *Asrar thawrat 23 yulyu* [The secrets of the July 23 revolution], vol. 1 (Cairo: al-Zahra li-l-E'laam al-'Arabi, 2006), pp. 601–602. Khaled Mohieddin accused al-Sanhouri himself of initiating this drive away from democracy when he and others "adopted the theory that Egypt first needed a revolutionary authority, through progress and mega projects, before thinking of applying political democracy and parliamentarism." K. Mohieddin, *Mustaqbal al-democratiyya fi misr* [The future of democracy in Egypt] (Cairo: Al-Ahali, 1984), p. 22.
13. Naguib, *Kuntu ra'isan li-misr*, p. 169.
14. Ibid., p. 170.
15. G. Hammad, *Asrar thawrat 23 yulyu* [The secrets of the July 23 revolution], vol. 2 (Cairo: al-Zahra li-l-E'laam al-'Arabi, 2006), p. 1047.
16. Ibid., pp. 1048–1049.
17. T. Badawi, *Thawrat 23 yulyu wa-tatawwur al-fikr al-thawri fi misr* [The July 23 revolution and Egypt's revolutionary and intellectual development] (Cairo: Dar al-Nahda al-Arabiyya, 1970), p. 225.
18. Aburish, *Nasser: The Last Arab*, p. 50.
19. K. J. Beattie, *Egypt during the Nasser Years: Ideology, Politics, & Civil Society* (Oxford: Westview Press, 1994), p. 88.

20. A. Hamroush, *Qissat thawrat 23 yulyu: misr wa-l-askariyyun* [The story of the July 23 revolution: Egypt and the military men], vol. 1 (Syria: al-Mawsua'a al-'Arabiyya li-l-Dirasat wa-l-Nashr, 1974).
21. K. Mohieddin, *Wa Alan Atakallam* [And now I am speaking] (Cairo: Ahram, (1992), pp. 271–272.
22. A. Ramadan, *Awraq Yusuf Siddiq* [The memoirs of Yusuf Siddiq] (Cairo: al-Hay'a al-Misriyya al-'Amma li-l-Kitab, 1999), p. 171.
23. Hammad, *Asrar thawrat 23 yulyu*, vol. 2, pp. 1194–1195.
24. Ibid., p. 1195.
25. Ibid., p. 1194.
26. Naguib, *Kuntu ra'isan li-misr*, p. 186.
27. Ibid.
28. Aburish, *Nasser: The Last Arab*, p. 50.
29. Ibid., pp. 50–51.
30. Hamroush, *Qissat thawrat 23 yulyu: Misr wa-l-askariyyun*, vol. 1, p. 322.
31. Naguib, *Kuntu ra'isan li-misr*, pp. 231–233; See also A. Nutting, *Nasser* (London: Constable, 1972), pp. 66–67.
32. J. Gordon, *Nasser's Blessed Movement: Egypt's Free Officers and the July Revolution* (Cairo: American University in Cairo Press, 1992), pp. 133–135.
33. Aburish, *Nasser: The Last Arab*, p. 51.
34. Author's interview with K. Mohieddin, Cairo, 6 December 2006.
35. J. Lacouture and S. Lacouture, *Egypt in Transition*, trans. F. Scarfe (London: Methuen, 1956), p. 168. The Hayaa al-Sa'diyya party had been influential enough to hold half of the seats in cabinets from 1938 (the year of its foundation) until 1952. Cf. A. Khallaf, *Min tarikh misr al-mu'asir: Al-hayaa al-sa'diyya* [From the modern history of Egypt: al-Hayaa al-Sa'diyya] (Cairo: 'Ein li-l-Dirasat wa-l-Buhuth al-Insaniyya wa-l-Ijtima'iyya, 1999), p. 397.
36. K. Keira, *Muhakammat al-thawra* [The trials of the revolution], vol. 1 (Cairo: Maktab Shuun Mahkamat al-Thawra, 1954), p. 38.
37. F. Abdel-Bar, *Mawqif Abd al-Razzak al-Sanhuri min qadaya al-hurriyya wa-l-dimuqratiyya* [The position of Abd al-Razzak al-Sanhuri and the issue of freedom and democracy] (Cairo: al-Nasr al-Dhahabi li-l-Tiba'a, 2005), p. 195.
38. Hamroush, *Qissat thawrat 23 yulyu: Misr wa-l-askariyyun*, vol. 1, p. 282. The coup leaders founded four courts between 1952 and 1954, variably called courts of "treason," "people." and "revolution." T. al-Bishry, *Al-dimuqratiya wa-23 yulyu* [Democracy and the July 23 regime] (Cairo: Dar al-Helal, December 1991), pp. 184, 492.
39. Hamroush, *Qissat thawrat 23 yulyu: Misr wa-l-askariyyun*, vol. 1, p. 282. This is verse 191 in Surat al-Baqara (The Cow).
40. Ibid., p. 283.
41. A. Ramadan, *Abdel Nasser wa azmat maris 1954* [Abdel Nasser and the March 1954 Crisis] (Cairo: Rose al-Youssef, 1976), p. 30.
42. F. Abdel-Bar, *Mawqif Abd al-Razzak al-Sanhuri*, p. 154. The citation is based on the testimony of Abdel-Aziz Kheir al-Deen, another State Council senior judge who took part in issuing the 1952 change of regime judicial edicts, as published in *Akhbar*, 18 September 1975.
43. Author's interview with A. Ra'if, Cairo, 16 December 2006.
44. Author's interview with K. Mohieddin, Cairo, 6 December 2006.
45. Author's interview with M. al-Sabbagh, Cairo, 5 February 2007.

46. Z. Mardini, *Al-ladoudan: Al-wafd wa-l-ikhwan* [The archrivals: The Wafd and the Ikhwan] (Beirut: Iqraa, 1984), p. 128.
47. Ibid.
48. S. Shadi, *Safahat min al-Tarikh: Hassad al-Umr* [Pages from history: A life legacy] (Cairo: Dar al-Tawzi' wa-l-Nashr al-Islamiyya, 2006).
49. H.M.A. Hamouda, *Asrar harakat al-dubbat al-ahrar wa-l-ikhwan al-muslimun* [The secrets of the Free Officers and the Ikhwan] (Cairo: al-Zahraa, 1985), p. 194.
50. A. Mansour, *Hussein al-Shafei: Shahed 'alla 'asr thawrat yulyu* [Hussein al-Shafei: Witness to the era of the July Revolution] (Cairo: Al-Maktab al-Misry al-Hadith, 2004), p. 126.
51. Author's interview with F. Abdel Khaleq, Cairo, 5 October 2007.
52. Author's interviews with A. Rashwan, Cairo, 28 October and 26 November 2006.
53. Mardini, *Al-ladoudan: Al-wafd wa-l-ikhwan*, pp. 83, 86.
54. Naguib, *Kuntu ra'isan li-misr*, p. 169.
55. Author's interview with T. Aclimandos, Cairo, 7 February 2007.
56. Author's interview with K. Mohieddin, Cairo, 6 December 2006.
57. M. Fathi, "Bi-l-tafasil wa-l-video: Abd al-Nasser qaher al-ikhwan wa-yuakid: Kunna nuriduhum an yasiru 'ala tariq sahih wa-lakinnahum umalla" [In detail and in video: Abdel-Nasser the conqueror of Ikhwan [says] that "we wanted them to move down the right path but they are spies"], *Al-Shabab*, 23 July 2013, available from http://shabab.ahram.org.eg/NewsContent/7/147 [accessed 1 October 2013].
58. Mansour, *Hussein al-Shafei*, pp. 131, 128.
59. Mohieddin, *Wa alan atakallam*, p. 208.
60. Mansour, *Hussein al-Shafei*, p. 131.
61. Ibid., p. 137.
62. A. H. al-Baquri, *Baqaya dhikrayat* [Memoirs] (Cairo: Markaz al-Ahram li-l-Dirasat al-Siyasiyya wa-l-Istratijiyya, 1988), p. 124.
63. Author's interview with T. Aclimandos, Cairo, 7 February 2007.
64. Mohieddin, *Wa alan atakallam*, p. 183.
65. P. Woodward, *Nasser* (London: Longman, 1992), p. 34.
66. Author's interview with F. Abdel Khaleq, Cairo, 7 December 2006.
67. Author's interview with K. Mohieddin, Cairo, 6 December 2006.
68. Author's interview with F. Abdel Khaleq, Cairo, 7 December 2006.
69. Author's interviews with K. Mohieddin, Cairo, 12 December 2006; and with F. Abdel Khaleq, Cairo, 7 December 2006; author's interview with K. Mohieddin, Cairo, 6 December 2006; author's interview with F. Abdel Khaleq, Cairo, 7 December 2006.
70. This conclusion is based on the author's interviews with Aclimandos and Mohieddin.
71. Fathi, "Bi-l-tafasil wa-l-video: Abd al-Nasser qaher al-ikhwan wa-yuakid." Ellipsis in original.
72. Author's interview with T. Aclimandos, Cairo, 7 February 2007.
73. Al-Baquri, *Baqaya Dhikrayat*, p. 87.
74. Ibid., p. 93.
75. Cited in R. al-Sa'id, *al-Irhab al-Mutaslim: Limadha? wa-Mata? wa-Ayn?* [Islamized terrorism: Why? When? and Where?], vol. 1 (Cairo: Akhbar al-Youm, 2004), p. 182.
76. B. Lia, *The Society of the Muslim Brothers in Egypt: The Rise of an Islamic Mass Movement, 1928–1942* (Reading, UK: Ithaca Press, 1998), p. 87.
77. R. Mitchell, *The Society of the Muslim Brothers* (Oxford: Oxford University Press, 1993), p. 147.

78. Author's interview with M. al-Sabbagh, Cairo, 4 February 2007.
79. Ibid.
80. Author's interview with M. al-Sabbagh, Cairo, 5 February 2007.
81. K. Mohieddin, *Wa alan atakallam*, p. 196.
82. Ibid.
83. Ibid.
84. Author's interview with M. al-Sabbagh, Cairo, 5 February 2007.
85. A. H. Qandeel, "Al-nasseriyya wa-l-islam: i'adat nazr" [Nasserism and Islam: A review], in *'An al-Nasseriyya wa-l-Islam* [On Nasserism and Islam], ed. A. H. Qandeel (Cairo: 'Ein li-l-Dirasat wa-l-Buhuth al-Islamiyya wa-l-Ijtima'iyya, 1998), p. 42.
86. A. H. al-Baquri, *Baqaya dhikrayat*, p. 121.
87. Author's interview with M. al-Sabbagh, Cairo, 4 February 2007.
88. Author's interview with M. al-Sabbagh, Cairo, 5 February 2007.
89. Author's interview with M. al-Sabbagh, Cairo, 4 February 2007.
90. A. Ashmawi, *Al-tarikh al-sirri li-jama'at al-ikhwan al-muslimun: Mudhakkirat al-Ashmawi akher qadet al-tanzim al-khass* [The Ikhwan's secret history: The memoirs of al-Ashmawi, the last commander of the special apparatus] (Cairo: Markaz Ibn Khaldoun leil Derasat al-Inma'iyya, 1994), p. 19.
91. Ibid., p. 14.
92. Author's interview with A. Rashwan, Cairo, 6 February 2007.
93. Author's interview with F. Abdel Khaleq, Cairo, 7 December 2006.
94. Ibid.
95. Author's interviews with K. Mohieddin, Cairo, 12 December 2006; and M. Fayek, Cairo, 26 November 2006.
96. Author's interview with F. Abdel Khaleq, Cairo, 7 December 2006.
97. Mitchell, *The Society of Muslim Brothers*, p. 127.
98. Hammad, *Asrar thawrat 23 yulyu*, vol. 2, p. 1109.
99. Ibid.
100. Ibid., p. 1101.
101. Ibid., pp. 994–1000. This episode in the power struggle ended in favor of Naguib after the latter was reinstated as president only hours after Nasser and the RCC had issued a decree affirming his resignation. Naguib's return to power came after massive demonstrations in which the Ikhwan actively participated, as well as rebellious acts of objection from some army units.
102. Ibid., p. 1110.
103. See Abdullah Imam's interview with Kamaleddin Hussein, an Islamist member of the RCC known for his links with the Ikhwan, in A. Imam, *Al-unf al-dini fi misr: Abdel-Nasser wa-l-ikhwan al-muslimun* [The religious violence in Egypt: Abdel-Nasser and the Ikhwan] (Cairo: Dar al-Khayyal, 1997), pp. 84–85.
104. Author's interview with S. Sharaf, Cairo, 8 February 2007.
105. A. Imam, *Sami Sharaf: Rajul al-ma'lumat alazi samata tawilan yatahadath li Abdullah Imam: Abdel-Nasser: kaifa hakama misr?* [Sami Sharaf, the man of intelligence who was silent for long now speaks to Abdullah Imam: Abdel-Nasser: How did he rule Egypt?] (Cairo: Dar al-Geel, 1997), p. 136.
106. Ibid., pp. 137–139.
107. Mitchell, *The Society of Muslim Brothers*, p. 138.
108. Ibid.
109. Author's interview with F. Abdel Khaleq, Cairo, 9 February 2007.

110. R. Mitchell, p. 142.
111. A. Nutting, p. 72.
112. Ibid., p. 71.
113. Ibid., p. 72.
114. Ibid., p. 73.
115. A. Imam, *Al-unf al-dini fi misr*, p. 137.
116. Ibid., pp. 124, 134.
117. For the text of Nasser's speech, see G. Abdel Nasser, 26 October 1954, Bibliotheca Alexandria archives, http://nasser.bibalex.org/Speeches/browser.aspx?SID=263&lang=ar [accessed 28 September 2014].
118. Mitchell, *The Society of the Muslim Brothers*, p. 150.
119. A. Nutting, *Nasser*, p. 72.
120. See the speeches of and interviews with Nasser before he signed the treaty, including one on 17 March 1952 in which he pledged a "complete, unconditional British withdrawal from Egypt, in *Khutab wa-tasrehat al-ra'is, Gamal Abdel-Nasser: 1952–1959*, part 1 (Cairo: Sharikat al-I'lanat al-Sharqiyya, n.d.), pp. 20–21.
121. Author's interview with M. al-Sabbagh, Cairo, 4 February 2007.
122. A. Al-Sayyed, *Abdel-Nasser wa-azmat al-dimuqratiyya: Satwet al-zaama wa-junun al-sulta* [Nasser and the crisis of democracy] (Alexandria: Fleming, 2001), p. 77.
123. Author's interview with S. Sharaf, Cairo, 8 February 2007.
124. Author's interview with A. A. Kamal, Cairo, 5 February 2007.
125. Hamouda, *Asrar harakat al-dubbat al-ahrar wa-l-ikhwan al-muslimun*, p. 112.
126. Ibid., p. 194.
127. Author's interview with T. al-Bishry, Cairo, 22 September 2006.
128. Author's interview with K. Mohieddin, Cairo, 6 December 2006.
129. Hamouda, *Asrar harakat al-dubbat al-ahrar wa-l-ikhwan al-muslimun*, p. 112.

Chapter 4. The Birth of the Deep State and Modern Radical Islamism

1. T. al-Bishry, *Al-dimuqratiya wa-23-yulyu* [Democracy and the July 23 regime] (Cairo: Dar al-Helal, December 1991), p. 185.
2. G. Hamad, *al-Hukuma al-Khafiyya fi 'Ahd Gamal Abdel-Nasser* [The secret government in the era of Gamal Abdel Nasser] (Cairo: al-Zahraa, 1986).
3. al-Bishry, *Al-dimuqratiya wa-23-yulyu*, p. 186.
4. A. Imam, *Salah Nasr yatadhakkar: Al-thawra, al-mukhabarat* [Salah Nasr remembers: The revolution and the intelligence] (Cairo: Rose al-Youssef, 1984), pp. 74, 78.
5. A. Abdel-Malek, *Egypt: Société Militaire* (Paris: Editions de Seuil, 1962).
6. R. Kamal, *Thawrat yulyu wa-l-sahafa* (Cairo: Mahmoud al-Gidawi, 1989), p. 73.
7. Ibid.
8. Mohamed Emara, an ardent Islamist, debunked claims that Nasser was secular, showing that he clothed his discourse in religious terms either genuinely or to outmaneuver his religious foes—the Ikhwan. See M. Emara, "Hal kana Abdel-Nasser almaniyyan" [Was Abdel-Nasser a secularist?], in *An al-Nassiriyya wa-l-Islam* [On Nasser and Nasserism], ed. A. Qandil (Cairo: 'Ein li-l-Dirasat wa-l-Buhuth al-Insaniyya wa-l-Ijtima'iyya, 1988), pp. 181–188.

9. Anissa Haddadi, "Myths, Norms, and the Politics of National Identity in the Egypt of Nasser and Qutb: Society Must Be Desired," PhD dissertation at the London School of Economics (work in progress, 2017).
10. Author's interview with F. Abdel Khaleq, Cairo, 2 October 2006.
11. Ibid.
12. Author's interview with F. Abdel Khaleq, Cairo, 2 October 2006.
13. Author's interviews with S. Sharaf, Cairo, 14 December 2006 and 8 February 2007.
14. Author's interview with M. Heikal, Cairo, 10 December 2006.
15. Author's interview with K. Mohieddin, Cairo, 6 December 2006.
16. D. Bonhoeffer, *Conspiracy and Imprisonment, 1940–1945* (Minneapolis: Fortress Press, 2006).
17. See for example R. Mengus, "Dietrich Bonhoeffer and the Decision to Resist," in *Resistance against the Third Reich, 1933–1990*, ed. Michael Geyer and John Boyer (Chicago: Chicago University Press, 1994).
18. A. Gramsci, *Prison Notebooks*, vol. 3 (New York: Columbia University Press, 1991).
19. A. Sampson, *Mandela: The Authorised Biography* (London: HarperCollins, 1999), p. 288.
20. S. Qutb, *Al-shati' al-majhul* [Unknown beach] (Minya, Egypt: Sadiq, 1950), pp. 200–202.
21. Ibid., pp. 121, 126, 157.
22. S. Khatab, *The Political Thought of Sayyid Qutb: The Theory of Jahiliyyah* (London: Routledge, 2006), p. 80.
23. M. H. Haykal, *al-Imbraturiyya al-Islamiyya wa-l-Amakin al-Muqaddasah* [The Islamic empire and the holy lands] (Cairo: Dar al-Hilal, n.d.), p. 34.
24. A. Shalash, *Al-tamarrud 'ala al-adab: Dirasa fi tajribat Sayyid Quṭb* [Revolt against literature: Studies in Sayyid Qutb's experience] (Cairo: Dar al-Shuruq, 1994), p. 5.
25. Khalid later on changed his positions on democracy and on Islam not being a state. For his changes of positions on democracy, see his book *Likay la tahritho al-ardh* (In order not to plow the land, 1955), and for his changes of position on Islam not being a state, see his book *Al-dawlah fi al-islam* (The state in Islam, 1981).
26. S. A. Hanna and G. H. Gardner, *Arab Socialism* (Leiden: E. J. Brill, 1969).
27. Khatab, *The Political Thought of Sayyid Qutb*, p. 81.
28. Ibid., p. 80.
29. Shalash, *Al-tamarrud 'ala al-adab*, pp. 76–77.
30. A. A. Musallam, *The Formative Stages of Sayyid Qutb's Intellectual Career and His Emergence as an Islamic Dā'iyah: 1906–1952* (London: University Microfilms International, 1984), p. 212.
31. Ibid., p. 214.
32. S. Qutb, *Ma'arakat al-Islam wa-l-Ra'smaliyya* [The battle of Islam and capitalism] (Cairo: Dar Al-Shuruq, (1982), pp. 12–17.
33. Ibid.
34. Ibid., p. 25.
35. Ibid., p. 28.
36. See Fethi Benslama, *La Guerre des subjectivities en Islam* (Paris: Nouvelles Editions Lignes, 2015), in which the author provides an psychoanalytic analysis of the role of Islam as a total ideal in Islamist discourses.

37. Qutb, *Ma'arakat al-islam wa-l-ra'smaliyya*, p. 36.
38. Ibid., p. 59.
39. V. Lenin, *What Is to Be Done?*, trans. Joe Fineberg and George Hanna; revisions to translation, introduction, and glossary by Robert Service (London: Penguin Books, 1988).
40. J. Calvert, *Sayyid Qutb and the Origins of Radical Islamism* (New York: Columbia University Press, 2010), p. 231.
41. This was separate both from the Nizam al-Khass faction loyal to Tal'at and the Nizam al-Khass faction loyal to Sanadi.
42. S. Qutb, *Milestones* (Indianapolis: American Trust Publications, 1990), p. 39.
43. Calvert, *Sayyid Qutb and the Origins of Radical Islamism*, p. 231, citing S. Al-Khalidi in *Sayyid Qutb: Min al-milad ila al-istishhad* [Sayyid Qutb: From birth to martyrdom] (Damascus: Dar al-Qalam, 1991), p. 392.
44. Ibid., p. 233.
45. Z. Al-Ghazali, *Ayyam min Hayati* [Days from my life] (Cairo: Dar al-Shuruq, 1980).
46. Qutb, *Milestones*, p. 46.
47. Ibid., p. 50.
48. H. Al-Banna, *Majmu'at rasa'il al-imam al-shahid Hassan al-Banna* [The compiled letters of martyred Imam Hassan al-Banna] (Cairo: Dar al-Tawzi' wa-l-Nashr al-Islamiyya, 1992), pp. 33–56.
49. A. M. Shamuq, *Kayfa Yufakkiru al-Ikhwan al-Muslimun* [How do the Ikhwan think] (Beirut: Dar al-Jil, 1981), p. 98.
50. Ibid., pp. 434–437.
51. M. H. Heikal, *Gharif Al-Ghadab* [The autumn of fury] (Cairo: Markaz al-Ahram li-l-Tarjama wa-l-Nashr, 1983), p. 290.
52. Al-Ghazali, *Ayyam min Hayati*, p. 4.
53. Ibid., p. 5.
54. Ibid.
55. Ibid., p. 58.
56. Ibid., p. 36.
57. Ibid., p. 37.
58. A. Hamouda, *Sayyid Qutb: Min al-Qarya ila al-Mishnaqa* [Sayyid Qutb: From village to gallows] (Cairo: Sina' li-l-Nashr, 1987), p. 181. There is credible evidence to suggest that Hudaybi did not author the book but lent his name and office to it.
59. Author's interview with A. Amara, Cairo, 6 December 2006.
60. Author's interview with H. Hanafi, Cairo, 25 September 2006.
61. Mohamed Habib, "Islam siyassi muatadel … mumken?" [Moderate political Islam … possible?], *al-Masry al-Youm*, 6 September 2014, http://www.almasryalyoum.com/news/details/517470 [accessed 19 November 2015].
62. Hamouda, *Sayyid Qutb*, p. 184.

Chapter 5. Young Gamal Abdel Nasser

1. See the good collection of studies by E. Podeh and O. Winckler, eds., *Rethinking Nasserism: Revolution and Historical Memory in Modern Egypt* (Gainesville: University Press of Florida, 2004).

2. O. Khalifah, *Nasser in the Egyptian Imaginary* (Edinburgh: Edinburgh University Press, 2016).
3. P. Mansfield, *Nasser* (London: Methuen, 1969), p. 4.
4. Ibid., p. 6. Remarkably, the name of the school which Nasser attended in this part of Cairo was El-Nahassin, which means "the coppersmiths."
5. Nasser told David Morgan, a *Sunday Times* reporter: "My mother's death was a tragic event in itself, but losing her this way was a shock so deep that time failed to remedy ... The pain and sorrow I felt back then made me think twice before hurting anyone ever since." Excerpt from their meeting available from http://nasser.bibalex.org/common/pictures01-%20sira_en.htm. Moreover, biographers see the death of Nasser's mother as a pivotal moment in the life of the young man, making him more resilient as an individual who would become the most powerful Arab leader in modern times. According to admiring biographers, from these early experiences, Nasser developed an admirable personality distinguished by bravery, steadfastness, patience, and a talent for leadership. Later, Anwar al-Sadat, Nasser's fellow officer and the person who eventually succeeded him as president, would concede that the Free Officers could not have succeeded as an organization without these personal traits of Nasser. As Sadat noted in a symbolically written letter addressed to his son:
   Oh, my son, the one who brought this constituent body together was your uncle Gamal ... Uncle Gamal had a balanced personality that we [members of the constituent body of the Free Officers] respected and got used to depending on ... We found in his style relief, confidence and depth. (A. Sadat, *Ya waladi haza amuka Gamal* [Cairo: Madbouly, 2005], pp. 99–100.)
6. Available from http://nasser.bibalex.org/common/pictures01-%20sira_en.htm.
7. J. Lacouture, *Nasser* (London: Secker and Warburg, 1973), p. 27.
8. Mahmoud Fawzi has described this "excellent relationship" between Nasser and the Coptic Pope Kerlos. On one occasion, the pope prayed for the recovery of Nasser's sick son, Abdel Hakim, and on another Nasser's children donated their savings to help build the main cathedral, while their father ordered a further donation of half a million pounds to support the construction process from state funds. On one occasion, Nasser told the pope, "Do not come to the presidential palace to see me. Come to my home directly because it is yours." See M. Fawzi, *al-baba Kerlos wa-'Abd al-Nasir* [Pope Kerlos and Abdel-Nasser] (Cairo: Muassat al-Ahram Leil Nashr wal Tawzei, 1998), pp. 59–60. According to Nasser's confidant Mohamed Heikal, Nasser always believed that the Copts had played a significant role in Egypt's history and should be considered equal with the country's Muslims.
9. Mansfield, *Nasser*, p. 20.
10. Available at http://nasser.bibalex.org/images/fi_megalet_alnadah_01.jpg [accessed 23 January 2015].
11. J. Joachim, *Nasser: The Rise to Power* (London: Odhams, 1960), p. 19.
12. The play was even attended by the minister of education, Ahmad Naguib al-Hilaly. The original pamphlet on the performance is available online at http://nasser.bibalex.org/images/fi_almasra7.jpg [accessed January 23, 2015].
13. Author's interview with M. H. Heikal, Cairo, 24 September 2006.
14. Lacouture (in *Nasser*, p. 27) eloquently describes the impact of the capital, where Nasser arrived when he was seven years old: "In Cairo, he [Nasser] would study,

militate, struggle, be arrested, and eventually begin law school before choosing the military profession, not as a caste, but as a means to action."

15. See M. Gasper, *The Power of Representation: Publics, Peasants and Islam in Egypt* (Stanford, CA: Stanford University Press, 2009), p. 19.
16. Ibid.
17. See chapter 1.
18. M. Gasper's *The Power of Representation* examines the peasant question in the nationalist discourse in Egypt.
19. See I. Gershoni and J. P. Jankowski, *Redefining the Egyptian Nation, 1930–1945* (Cambridge: Cambridge University Press, 1995), pp. 100–101.
20. Ibid.
21. See ibid., pp. 2–3.
22. From a letter sent by Gamal Abdel Nasser to his friend Hassan al-Nashaar on 2 September 1935. Available online from http://nasser.bibalex.org/common/MapViewer.aspx?Index=0&lang=ar&dir=non&type=DocHandWrt&activeLink=1&ID=1&path=http://nasser.bibalex.org/Data/PHDocs/high/01_01.jpg [accessed: January 20, 2015]. The letter was written in September 1935, two months before Nasser participated in the student protests against the British rejection of the return of constitutionalism to Egypt. In 1930, the Egyptian monarchy abolished the 1923 constitution, which is seen as the most liberal and democratically oriented charter in the country's modern history.
23. Ibid.
24. As biographer Anthony Nutting observed, "For in almost every speech and interview which [Nasser] gave after he came to rule Egypt, he was to reiterate it as the very first principle of Egyptian and Arab nationalism. Dignity required independence and independence required the final and total elimination of all foreign occupation and interference." In A. Nutting, *Nasser* (London: Constable, 1972), p. 7.
25. Gershoni and Jankowski, *Redefining the Egyptian Nation, 1930–1945*, pp. 3–6.
26. Ibid., p. 4.
27. H.G.A. Nasser, *A Historical Sketch of President Gamal Abdel-Nasser*, n.d., available online from http://nasser.bibalex.org/common/pictures01-%20sira_en.htm (accessed: 21 August 2014).
28. Nutting, *Nasser*, p. 15.
29. Author's interview with K. Mohieddin, Cairo, 6 December 2006.
30. Nutting, *Nasser*, p. 21.
31. Ibid, p. 22.
32. Author's interview with K. Mohieddin, Cairo, 12 December 2006.
33. P. Johnson, "Egypt under Nasser," *MERIP Reports* 10 (1972): 3, quoting A. Sadat, *Revolt on the Nile* (London: Alan Wingate, 1957), p. 53.
34. Gershoni and Jankowski, *Redefining the Egyptian Nation, 1930–1945*, p. 18.
35. Cited in ibid.
36. B.A.R. al-Tikriti, *Gamal 'Abd al-Nasir: Nasha'at wa-tatawwur al-fikr al-nasiri* [Gamal Abdel-Nasser: The creation and evolution of Nasserist thought] (Beirut: Markaz Derasat al-Wihda al-Arabiyya, 2000), p. 113.
37. G. Abdel Nasser, *Falsafat al-Thawra* [The philosophy of the revolution] (Cairo: Matab'i al-Dar al-Qawmiyya, n.d.), p. 16.

38. M. Naguib, *Kuntu Ra'isan li-Misr* [I was the president of Egypt] (Cairo: Al-Maktab al-Misri al-Hadith, 1984), p. 61.
39. A. al-Sadat, *Ya waladi haza amuka Gamal* [My son, this is your uncle Gamal] (Cairo: Madbouly, 2005), pp. 51, 83. Sadat alleged that Nasser formed and led the Free Officers as an organization as of 1942, the same year in which British forces besieged the king's palace. Members of this organization "shared one sentiment; hatred towards the British control of all walks of life either in the army or outside of it," in ibid., p. 83.
40. M. H. Heikal, "Introduction," in G. Abdel Nasser, *Yawmiyyat Gamal 'Abd al-Nasir 'an Harb Falastin* [The diaries of Gamal Abdel Nasser about the Palestine War] (Paris: al-Watan al-'Arabi li-l-Tiba'a wa-l-Nashr, 1978), p. 116. This group was formed at the end of the nineteenth century and was known for its extremism. Its leader, Ahmad Hussein, was accused of involvement in the Cairo fire in January 1952.
41. Ibid.
42. S. al-Hakim, *Asrar al-'alaqa al-khassa bayna 'Abd al-Nasir wa-l-ikhwan* [The secrets of the special relationship between Abdel-Nasser and the Ikhwan] (Cairo: Markaz al-Hadara al-'Arabiyya li-l-I'lam wa-l-Nashr, 1996), p. 8.
43. The Mahdi was the creator of a vast Islamic state extending from the Red Sea to Central Africa and the movement that he founded remained influential in Sudan a century later. As a youth, he moved from orthodox religious study to a mystical interpretation of Islam. In 1881 he proclaimed his divine mission to purify Islam and the governments that defiled it. His extensive campaign culminated in the capture of Khartoum on 26 January 1885. He then established a theocratic state in the Sudan, with its capital at Omdurman. See Encyclopaedia Britannica, s.v. "Al-Mahdi," http://www.britannica.com/EBchecked/topic/358109/al-Mahdi [accessed 10 December 2013].
44. S. al-Hakim, *Asrar al-'alaqa al-khassa bayna 'Abd al-Nasir wa-l-ikhwan*, pp. 9–11.
45. M. 'Abdel-Halim, *Al-ikhwan al-musleemoon: Ahdath san'at al-tarikh* [The Muslim Brotherhood: Events that made history], part 3 (Alexandria: Dar al-Da'waa, 1985), pp. 252–254.
46. Author's interview with A. S. Yassin, Cairo, 12 October 2006.
47. Joel Gordon criticized this tendency as lacking in conceptualization and attributed it to "broad generalizations" in the literature on the 1952 coup. Gordon noted that some historians even limited their field of study to set the July 1952 as a terminating point of the old order, which means they cut links with the threads of these shifts in the Nasserist movement, including the latter's relation with the Ikhwan. J. Gordon, *Nasser's Blessed Movement: Egypt's Free Officers and the July Revolution* (Cairo: American University in Cairo Press, 1992), pp. 10–12. See also R. Takeyh and K. Gvosdev, *The Receding Shadow of the Prophet: The Rise and Fall of Radical Political Islam* (Westport, CT: Praeger, 1992), p. 60. This book sees the disagreement through the prism of these ideological dualisms.
48. Lacouture, *Nasser*. On one occasion, Nasser called the Ikhwan "idiots with no one single clever person in the whole group" and said that they were "spies working for both *Rajie* [backwardness] and for colonialism," in comments on their cooperation with Egypt's Saudi archrivals: in *Khitab Gamal Abdel-Nasser fi Eid al-Wihda*, 22 February 1966 (N.D.). Cairo: Ministry of National Guidance, p. 12.
49. Author's interview with M. Heikal, Cairo, 10 December 2006.
50. S. al-Hakim, *Asrar al-'alaqa al-khassa bayna 'Abd al-Nasir wa-l-ikhwan*, p. 8.

51. Nasser made no mention of this chapter of his life in all of his memoirs, such as *Falsafat al-Thawra*.
52. Author's interviews with K. Mohieddin, Cairo, 6 December and 12 December 2006.
53. Author's interview with F. Abdel Khaleq, Cairo, 2 October 2006.
54. See chapter 2 of this book.
55. Author's interview with K. Mohieddin, Cairo, 6 December 2006.
56. Author's interviews with K. Mohieddin, Cairo, 6 December and 12 December 2006.
57. Ibid.
58. Ibid.
59. Author's interview with K. Mohieddin, Cairo, 6 December 2006.
60. Ibid.
61. G. Abdel Nasser, *Al-haqiqa al-lati eishtaha* [The reality which I lived], part 2 (Cairo: Idarat al-Shu'un al-'Ama li-l-Quwwat al-Musallaha, 1955), pp. 4, 17, 22.
62. Ibid., p. 5.
63. Ibid.
64. Ibid.
65. Ibid., p. 17.
66. Ibid.
67. Ibid., p. 22.
68. al-Tikriti, *Gamal 'Abd al-Nasir*, p. 120, citing W. Wynn, *Nasser of Egypt: The Search for Dignity* (Cambridge, UK: Arlington Books, 1959), pp. 30–35.
69. Nasser, *Yawmiyyat Gamal 'Abd al-Nasir 'an Harb Falastin*, p. 47.
70. F. Fahmy, *'Abd al-Nasir min al-Hisar leil Inqilab* [Abdel-Nasser: From the besiegement to the coup] (Cairo: Muassar Amoun al-Haditha, 1994), pp. 10–13.
71. At one stage, besieged in Falluja and rejecting all calls for surrender by Jewish militants, Nasser recalls clearly thinking: "We are here to defend the honor of our army"; G. Abdel Nasser, *Yawmiyyat Gamal 'Abd al-Nasir 'an harb falastin*, p. 84.
72. Ibid., p. 117. Other scholars and intellectuals agree, taking Egypt's internal interests as the point of departure for the country's adoption, or not, of pan-Arabism. See M. El-Sulh, *Misr wal-Uruba* [Egypt and Pan-Arabism] (Beirut: Al-Muasassa al-'Arabiyya leil derasaat wal Nashr, n.d.)), pp. 22–25. Scholars such as Louis Awad even linked the rise of this pan-Arabism with what he described as Nasser's populist urge: L. Awad, *Aqni't al-Nassiryya al-Saba': Munaqashat Tawfiq al-Hakim and Mohamed Hassanein Heikal* [The seven masks of Nasserism: Debating with Tawfiq al-Hakim and Mohamed Hassanein Heikal] (Cairo: Madbouli, 1987), p. 49.
73. Author's interview with K. Mohieddin, Cairo, 12 December 2006.
74. Nasser, *Falsafat al-Thawra*, p. 64.
75. T.G.A. Nasser, *Zikrayati ma'ahu* (Cairo: Dar al-Shuruq, 2012), p. 27.

Chapter 6. Young Sayyid Qutb

1. See two informative recent biographies of Qutb: J. Toth, *Sayyid Qutb: The Life and Legacy of a Radical Islamic Intellectual* (Oxford: Oxford University Press, 2013), and J. Calvert, *Sayyid Qutb and the Origins of Radical Islamism* (New York: Columbia University Press, 2010).
2. S. Qutb, *Tifl min al-Qarya* [A child from the village] (Beirut: n.p., 1967), p. 21.

3. Ibid., pp. 201–203.
4. Ibid., p. 21.
5. Ibid., p. 22.
6. Ibid., pp. 128, 140–146.
7. Ibid., pp. 140–146.
8. S. Botman, *Egypt from Independence to Revolution, 1919–1952* (New York: Syracuse University Press, 1991), pp. 18–19.
9. Qutb, *Tifl min al-Qarya*, pp. 147–151.
10. A. J. Bergesen, "Sayyid Qutb in Historical Context," in *The Sayyid Qutb Reader: Selected Writings on Politics, Religion, and Society*, ed. A. J. Bergesen (New York: Routledge, 2007), pp. 1–13.
11. M. H. Diab, *Al-Khetab wal ideologia* [Discourse and ideology] (Cairo: Dar al-Thaqafa al-Gadida, 1987), pp. 50, 89–90.
12. Qutb's village roots seem to have caused an identity crisis which followed him into adult life, and all the way until his death in 1966. His novel *Ashwak*, for example, is full of references to an internal conflict between urban principles associated with where he lived in Cairo and rural roots associated with his life in a small Upper Egyptian village. According to prominent novelist Salwa Bakr, Qutb's novel displayed "intellectual double standards" which Qutb and other literary figures of his generation had harbored. H. Mostafa, "Al-Namnam: Ruwayat ashwak ta'kes al-azma al-thaqafiyya wal ibda'iyya le Sayyid Qutb" [Al-Namnam: How the novel *Ashwak* reflects Qutb's crisis of culture and creativity], *Al-Youm al-Saabi'* (26 April 2012), available from http://www.youm7.com/story/0000/0/0/-/662966#.Vnlhm_mLSUk [accessed 10 March 2014]. Qutb's novel also shows his plight between the contrasting worlds of village and town; in it he admitted that part of his conflict was his conservative background, which made his encounters with women so confusing and shocking that he ended up being single all his life: see S. Qutb, *Ashwak* (Cairo: Al-Hayaa al-Misriyya al-'Ama leil Kitab, 2011). The novel was first published in 1947. Remarkably, Qutb's rural background is similar to that of other Ikhwan leaders such as Yusuf al-Qaradawi, seen as the Ikhwan's spiritual leader. Both chose similar titles for their autobiographies, with Qaradawi's *Son from the Village*, and Qutb's *A Child from the Village*.
13. Qutb noted the influence of Taha Hussein on his thinking in the dedication pages of his autobiography.
14. T. Hussein, *Mustaqbal al-thaqafa fi misr* [The future of culture in Egypt] (Cairo: Dar al-Ma'rif, 1996).
15. I. M. Abu-Rabi', *Intellectual Origins of Islamic Resurgence in the Modern Arab World* (Albany: State University of New York Press, 1996), pp. 100–101.
16. For further details on Qutb's "literary battles" with other intellectuals such as Abdel-Rahman al-Rafi'i, see A. Badawi, *Sayyid Qutb* [Sayyid Qutb] (Cairo: Al-Hayaa al-Misriyya al-'Ama leil Kitab, 1992), pp. 203–228.
17. Qutb, *Tifl min al-Qarya*, p. 22.
18. M. Fadlallah, *Ma'a Sayyid Qutb fi fikrihi al-siyasi wa-l-dini* [With Sayyid Qutb in his political and literary thoughts] (Beirut: Mu'assasat al-Risala, 1978), p. 46.
19. A. Musallam, *From Secularism to Jihadism* (London: Praeger, 2005), p. 35; A.B.M. Hussayn, *Sayyid Qutb* (Egypt: al-Mansura, 1986), p. 122.
20. Musallam, *From Secularism to Jihadism*, p. 35.
21. Ibid., p. 36.

22. S. Qutb, "Naqd '*Mustaqbal al-Thaqafa*'" [A criticism of "A criticism of the future of culture in Egypt"], *Sahifat dar al-'lum* 5 (4), p. 69, cited in Musallam, *From Secularism to Jihadism*, p. 36.
23. Musallam, *From Secularism to Jihadism*, pp. 50–53. See also H. Sharabi, *Arab Intellectuals and the West: The Formative Years, 1875-1914* (Baltimore: Johns Hopkins University Press, 1970).
24. A. Shalash, *Al-tamarrud 'ala al-adab: Dirasa fi tajribat Sayyid Qutb* [Rebellion on literature: A study of the experience of Sayyid Qutb] (Cairo: Dar al-Shurouk, 1994), p. 84. M. H. Diab, *Al-Khetab wal ideologia*, p. 94.
25. M. A. Khouri and H. Algar, trans. and eds., *An Anthology of Modern Arabic Poetry* (Berkeley: University of California Press, 1974), p. 9.
26. M. Fadlallah, *Ma'a Sayyid Qutb fi Fikrihi al-Siyasi wa-l-Dini* [With Sayyid Qutb's political and literary thoughts] (Beirut: Mu'assasat al-Risala, 1978), pp. 48–49.
27. R. Al-Naqqash, *Abbas al-Aqqad bayna al-yamin wa-l-yasar* [Abbas al-Aqqad: Between the left and the right] (Riyadh: Dar al-Marikh li-l-Nashr, 1988), p. 31.
28. Musallam, *From Secularism to Jihadism*, p. 36.
29. M. A. Khouri and H. Algar, *An Anthology of Modern Arabic Poetry*, pp. 8–9.
30. Ibid., pp. 8–9; H. al-Maltawi, *Falsafat al-Taqadum enda al-Aqqad: Falsafat al-Tarikh—Mashro' al Nahda* [The philosophy of progress in Aqqad's thinking: The philosophy of history—the renaissance project] (Cairo: Al-Arabi Leil nashr wal Tawzei, 1996), pp. 50–53.
31. The op-ed by Qutb was published in *al-Ahram* on July 10, 1938, under the title "Ideas of a Summer Resort: Dead Beaches." See "Nanshur maqal kadeem le Sayyid Qutb ..." [We publish an old article by Sayyid Qutb ...], *Albedaiah* 11 July 2014), available online at http://www.albedaiah.com/node/53984 [accessed 8 January 2015].
32. M. Abdel Halim, *Al-Ikhwan al-muslimun: Ahdath san't al-tarikh* [The Muslim Brotherhood: Events that made history], vol. 1 (Alexandria: Dar al-Da'wa, n.d.,) pp. 190–191.
33. Ibid., p. 192.
34. Author's interview with S. Younis, Cairo, 20 October 2006.
35. Author's interview with H. Hanafi, Cairo, 25 September 2006.
36. Author's interview with A. M. Al-Shazili, Cairo, 12 January 2007.
37. Shalash, *al-Tamarrud 'ala al-Adab*, p. 83.
38. A. J. Bergesen, ed., *The Sayyid Qutb Reader*, p. 3.

Chapter 7. The Lion of the Arabs

1. "He found himself among people who are not different; even their history and life are organically connected with those of the Egyptian people's history and life. He found himself fighting an enemy who is not only against the Palestinians but all those north and south of Palestine. ... He found himself among fighters from Jordan, Syria, Iraq and Saudi Arabia and all for the sake of a goal which lies outside the limited borders of their countries ... He found that the forces of imperialism which help the Jewish state are the same as those which take control in Cairo, Baghdad, and the Arabian Peninsula." See G. A. Nasser, *Yawmiyyat Gamal 'Abd al-Nasir 'an harb falastin* [The

diaries of Gamal Abdel Nasser about the Palestine War] (Paris: al-Watan al-'Arabi li-l-Tiba'a wa-l-Nashr, 1978), p. 119.

2. G. Abdel Nasser, *Falsafat al-Thawra* [Philosophy of Revolution] (Cairo: Matab'i al-Dar al-Qawmiyya, n.d.), p. 57.
3. J. Lacouture, *Nasser: A Biography*, trans. D. Hofstadter (London: Secker and Warburg, 1973), p. 189.
4. Nasser used "Arabism" as a weapon of choice against his political foes at home. In an interview, he said, "Communists have ceased to be Arabs and sold themselves to foreign influence. They are behaving like tools and agents in Iraq, Syria, and all over the Arab world. We cannot therefore treat them like Arabs." See *President Gamal Abdel-Nasser's Speeches and Press-Interviews: 1959* (Cairo: Maslahat al-Isti'lamat, n.d.). From "Interview granted by President Gamal Abdel Nasser to Mr. R. K. Karanjia on April 17, 1959," p. 548.
5. Author's interview with M. H. Heikal, Cairo, 10 December 2006.
6. Author's interview with K. Mohieddin, Cairo, 12 December 2006. Nasser did not separate his belief in Arab nationalism and his employing this ideology to silence opposition at home. For instance, Nasser always branded the Ikhwan as "collaborators with the imperialists." In a speech at the heart of the Nile Delta during the opening of an extension of the Mehalla Spinning and Textile Factory, he said: "We shall never give any chance to the imperialists to cause disunity, nor will stooges be able to cause dissension as they did in the past. We had experienced partisanship and disunity, and we realized that partisanship was only a means of weakening us and of enabling our enemies to dominate us and place us in their zones of influence ... Our enemies tried in the name of religion, democracy, and other names to break this republic, divide the Arab world, and destroy Arab unity." See http://nasser.bibalex.org/Speeches/browser.aspx?SID=787&lang=ar [accessed 16 December 2015].
7. P. Seale, *The Struggle for Syria: The Study of Post-War Arab Politics, 1945–1958* (London: I. B. Tauris, 1965), p. 325.
8. Ibid.
9. M. H. Heikal, *Sanawat al-Ghalayan* [Years of turmoil] (Cairo: Ahram, 1988), pp. 258, 266.
10. *Arba'una 'aman 'ala al-wihda al-misriyya al-suriyya* [40 years on the Egyptian-Syrian unity] (Cairo: Ahram, 1998), p. 204. The document is the outcome of a seminar held on February 22–23, 1998.
11. Ibid.
12. When elections took place in the United Arab Republic, there were just 250 Baathists among the 9,445 winners of the vote: see K. Deeb, *Tarikh suriya al-mu'asir: Min al-intidab al-faransi hatta sayf 2011* [Syria's modern history from the French protectorate until summer 2011] (Beirut: Al-Nahar, 2011), pp. 185–196.
13. J. Lacouture, *Nasser: A Biography*, trans. D. Hofstadter (London: Secker and Warburg, 1973), p. 186.
14. *President Gamal Abdel Nasser's Speeches and Press-Interviews: 1959* (Cairo: Maslahat al-Isti'lamat, United Arab Republic, n.d.). From "Interview Granted by President Gamal Abdel Nasser to William H. Stringer and published by the *Christian Science Monitor* on Jan. 22," p. 524.
15. 'A. Abul-Nur, *'Abdel-Mohsen Abul Nur Yarwi al-Hakika an Thawrat Yulyu* (Cairo: Maktabat al-Usra, 2003), p. 83.

16. Lacouture, *Nasser*, p. 186.
17. Author's interviews with K. Mohieddin, Cairo, 6 December 2006 and 12 December 2006.
18. Author's interview with M. Heikal, Cairo, 10 December 2006.
19. Although the memoirs of Nasser's wife, Tahia, never make reference to him praying, she does write frequently of his religiosity. She notes that her husband always carried a mushaf, a copy of the Qur'an, in his pocket when leaving the house. On another occasion, he asked his wife to "hurry up and pray the fajr [dawn prayer] before the sun rises." Although it is permitted in Islam to pray the fajr after the sun has risen, Nasser was keen for his wife to make the prayers according to the precise rules. His wife's next sentence in the memoir is: "He showed relief, love, and sympathy." T.G.A. Nasser, *Zikrayati Ma'ahu* [Memories with him] (Cairo: Dar al-Shuruq, 2012), p. 62.
20. For example, Nasser drew a comparison between his socialist democratic project and the Qur'an: "As I said before, we do not have a written book entitled *The Socialist Democratic, Co-operative Society*. History tells us that no one succeeded overnight in preparing a book. God the Almighty gave us the example. He could have given the Koran in one second, but he spent twenty-three years giving us the Qur'an, to give us an example to follow"; available from http://nasser.bibalex.org/Speeches/browser.aspx?SID=787&lang=ar [accessed 16 December 2015].
21. "Khitab al-rais Gamal Abdel-Nasser ba'da salat al-jum'a min al-jam'i al-azhar athna' al-'udwan al-thulathi" [The speech of President Gamal Abdel-Nasser after the *Jumaa* prayers from the Azhar Mosque during the Tripartite Aggression], available from http://nasser.bibalex.org/Speeches/browser.aspx?SID=524 [accessed 22 March 2014].
22. Nasser's religious rhetoric reminded Egyptians of the pivotal role that al-Azhar's religious scholars played in mobilizing public opinion against Napoleon's invasion of the country in 1798 and against British colonialism. Sheikh Kishk, known as a popular preacher for his visceral attacks on Nasser in his mosque speeches, is a case in point. M. G. Kishk, *Wa dakhalat al-khayl al-azhar* [And the horses entered the Azhar], 3rd ed. (Cairo: Al-Zahraa leil I'lam al-Araby, 1990), pp. 239, 344.
23. "Qanun raqam 103 lesanat 1961 beshaan i'adat tanzeem al-azhar wal hayaat allati yashmalluah" [Law No. 103, 1961 on the reorganization of al-Azhar and the affiliated organizations], available from http://www.alazhar-alsharif.gov.eg/Statistics/law [accessed 21 March 2014].
24. A. Morsy and N. Brown, "Egypt's al-Azhar Steps Forward," Carnegie Endowment for International Peace, 2014; available from http://carnegieendowment.org/2013/11/07/egypt-s-al-azhar-steps-forward [accessed: 21 March 2014].
25. M. Al-Bahy, *Hayati fi rihab al-azhar: Taleeb wa ustaz wa wazir* [My life in Azhar: A student, a professor, and a minister] (Cairo, Maktabat Wahba, 1983), p. 76.
26. Ibid., pp. 83, 116–117.
27. Ibid., p. 117.
28. Ibid., p. 116.
29. S.V.R. Nasr, *Islamic Leviathan: Islam and the Making of State Power* (New York: Oxford University Press, 2001), pp. 3–14; N. Ayubi, *Over-Stating the Arab State* (London: I. B. Tauris, 1995), p. 84.
30. Nasr, *Islamic Leviathan*, pp. 13–14.

31. C. J. Beck, "State Building as a Source of Islamic Political Organization," *Sociological Forum* 24, no. 2 (2009): 341–342); Nasr, *Islamic Leviathan*, p. 4.
32. Remarkably Nasser had exposed an understanding of ideas through the same Gramscian-Foucaultian lens: "Ideas have power. Militarily, today, a big power could bring 100,000 troops and occupy us. But if we are imbued with Arab nationalism, those who would invade us must think many times. The invader would need a million men to conquer Egypt today," in *President Gamal Abdel Nasser's Speeches and Press-Interviews: 1959* (Cairo: Maslahat al-Isti'lamat, United Arab Republic, n.d.). From 'Interview Granted by President Gamal Abdel Nasser to William H. Stringer and published by the *Christian Science Monitor* on Jan. 22," pp. 521–525. As to his stance towards Communism, Nasser noted that "it is not in reality a question of ideology or principle but rather of domination and zones of influence. We may cite as an example in support of this assertion that Yugoslavia, a communist country, has become the target of repeated attacks launched against her because she has refused to enter spheres of influence or submit to the domination of the Soviet Union. It is not, therefore, a matter of ideology but rather a question of domination": see *President Gamal Abdel Nasser's Speeches and Press-Interviews: 1959* (Cairo: Maslahat al-Isti'lamat, United Arab Republic, n.d.). From "President Gamal Abdel Nasser's Speech Addressed to Arab Workers Delegations, April 29, 1959," pp. 227–231. Nevertheless, in another speech the same year, he depicted communism as a deadly menace: "If a communist state is set up then all nationalist and patriotic elements would be destroyed or liquidated": see *President Gamal Abdel Nasser's Speeches and Press-Interviews: 1959* (Cairo: Maslahat al-Isti'lamat, United Arab Republic, n.d.). From "President Gamal Abdel-Nasser's Speech in Damascus March 20, 1959," pp. 162–167.
33. Anwar Sadat's policies and use of religion are reviewed in depth in chapter 8 of this book.
34. For the theme of Palestine in all the speeches of Nasser, see *Palestine: Min Aqwal al-Ra'is Gamal 'Abd al-Nasir* [Palestine: From the mind of President Gamal Abdel-Nasser] (Cairo: al-Dar al-Qawmiyya li-l-Tiba'a wa-l-Nashr, n.d.).
35. Ibid., p. 3.
36. Author's interview with M. Fayek, Cairo, 26 November 2006.
37. G. Abdel Nasser, *'Ala Tariq al-Ishtirakiya* [On the road to socialism] (Cairo: al-Dar al-Qawmiyya li-l-Tiba'a wa-l-Nashr Abdel-Nasser, n.d.), p. 15.
38. Author's interview with M. Heikal, Cairo, 24 September 2006.
39. See F. Fanon, *The Wretched of the Earth*.
40. Ibid.
41. It is where the common ground between Fanon and Nasser ends. Fanon had himself warned of the limits of the anti-colonial movement's emphasis on national identity and more precisely of its inscription of totalizing and essentialist conceptions of the nation.
42. Nasser, *Falsafat al-Thawra*, p. 16.
43. Nutting, *Nasser* (London: Constable, 1972), p. 46.
44. Ibid.
45. Ibid., p. 49.
46. Author's interview with K. Mohieddin, Cairo, 12 December 2006.
47. Author's interview with M. Heikal, Cairo, 10 December 2006.

48. Author's interview with M. Fayek, Cairo, 26 November 2006.
49. Nutting, *Nasser*, p. 117.
50. Author's interview with K. Mohieddin, Cairo, 12 December 2006.
51. Nasser, *'Ala Tariq al-Ishtirakiya*, p. 14.
52. Ibid., pp. 15–16.
53. Ibid., p. 16.
54. J. Gordon, *Nasser: Hero of the Arab Nation* (Oxford, UK: Oneworld, 2006), p. 50. See also F. Labib, *Al-shu'yoon wa Abdel Nasser: Al-tahaluf wal muwagaha (1958–1965)* [The communists and Abdel-Nasser: Alliance and confrontation (1958–1965)], part 2 (Cairo: Sharkat al-Tiba' al-'Arabiyya al-Haditha, 1992).
55. Nutting, *Nasser*, p. 118.
56. Hanna and Garner, *Arab Socialism*, p. 114.
57. Ibid., p. 112.
58. In a 1958 speech Nasser hinted at the evolution of the revolution: "When the revolution of July 23 was staged, each one felt it was an Egyptian revolution. Yet alongside this feeling, there was also the feeling that it was an Arab not just an Egyptian revolution, that it sprang from the land, hearts and souls of Arab people, a revolution which would make no alliances with imperialism nor with any foreign force to promote its own ends." In *President Gamal Abdel-Nasser's Speeches and Press-Interviews: 1958* (Cairo: Maslahat al-Isti'lamat, United Arab Republic, n.d.). From "Address by President Gamal Abdel Nasser to yet another Lebanese delegation that arrived at Evacuation Square, Damascus at 1:15 in March 1958," pp. 94–102.
59. Preamble, Constitution of the Republic, January 16, 1956.
60. Author's interview with S. Sharaf, Cairo, 8 February 2007.
61. Author's interview with K. Mohieddin, Cairo, 6 December 2006.
62. Author's interview with M. Fayek, Cairo, 26 November 2006.
63. Author's interview with K. Mohieddin, Cairo, 6 December 2006.
64. M. A. Sadat, *Asrar al-thawra al-misriyya wa bawaethha al-khafiya wa asbabaha al-saychologia* [The secrets of the revolution and its hidden motivations and its psychological causes], intro. by G. Abdel Nasser (Cairo: Al-Dar al-Qawmiyy aleil Tiba'a wal Nashr, 1965), p. 167.
65. B.A.R. Al-Tikriti, *Gamal 'Abd al-Nasir: Nasha'at wa-tatawwur al-fikr al-nasiri* [Gamal Abdel Nasser: The creation and evolution of Nasserist thought] (Beirut: Markaz Derasat al-Wihda al-Arabiyya, 2000), p. 111.
66. Ibid., pp. 111–112, citing A. Hamroush, *Qissat thawrat 23 yulyu: Misr wal-askaryouun* [The story of the July 23 Revolution: Egypt and the army men] (Beirut: Al-Muassassa al-A'rabiyya leil Derasat wal-Nashr, 1974–1978), p. 99.
67. K. Mohieddin, *Wal-Ann atakallam* [And now I am talking] (Cairo: Ahram, 1992), pp. 64–66.
68. Author's interview with K. Mohieddin, Cairo, 12 December 2006.
69. F. Mattar, *Bi-saraha 'an 'Abd al-Nasir* [Frankly about Abdel Nasser] (Beirut: Dar Al-Qadaya, 1975), p. 95.
70. Author's interview with M. H. Heikal, Cairo, 10 December 2006.
71. Ibid.
72. Author's interview with K. Mohieddin, Cairo, 6 December 2006.
73. Author's interview with S. Younis, Cairo, 20 October 2006.
74. Ibid.

75. Anouar Abdel Malek called the Nasserist state the "Officers' Republic": see A. Abdel Malek, *Egypt: Military Society: The Army Regime, the Left, and Social Change under Nasser*, trans. C. M. Markmann (New York. Random House, 1968). Ahmad Hamroush, an official biographer of the revolution, said that the 1952 coup was about "a transfer of power from civilians to the army ... and a move from one class to another": see A. Hamroush, *Qissat Thawrat Yulyu 23: Al-Bahth 'an al-Demoqratiyya* (Cairo: Dar Ibn Khaldoun, 1982), p. 97. Hamroush also exposed Nasser's lack of ideological commitment at the socioeconomic level by moving from "cooperative democratic socialism" in 1950s to "scientific socialism" in the 1960s: see ibid., p. 129.

Chapter 8. The Accidental Islamist?

1. These questions relate to Qutb's position on the separation of religion from literature: see M. Fadlallah, *Ma'a Sayyid Qutb fi fikrihi al-siyasi wa-l-dini* [With Sayyid Qutb's political and literary thoughts] (Beirut: Mu'assasat al-Risala, 1978), p. 48. Another question revolves around Qutb's gradual drive towards Islam after his falling-out with Aqqad, who was known for his secular approach: see A. Shalash, *Al-tamarrud 'ala al-adab: Dirasa fi tajribat Sayyid Qutb* [Rebellion on literature: A study of Sayyid Qutb's experience] (Cairo: Dar al-Shurouk, 1994), pp. 124–125.
2. S. A. Khalidi, *Sayyid Qutb min al-milad ella al-istishhad* [Sayyid Qutb: From birth to martyrdom] (Damascus: Dar al-Qalam, 2010); M. Abdel Haleem, *Al-ikhwan al-muslimun: Ahdath san't al-tarikh* [The Muslim Brotherhood: Events that made history], vol. 1 (Alexandria: Dar al-Da'wa, n.d.), p. 192.
3. S. Qutb, *Ma'alim fil Tariq* [Signposts] (Cairo: Dar al-Shurouk, 1979), p. 131.
4. J. Calvert, *Sayyid Qutb and the Origins of Radical Islamism* (New York: Columbia University Press, 2010), p. 72.
5. Author's interview with A. S. Yassin, Cairo, 18 October 2006.
6. S. Qutb, "Illa ustazana al-duktur Ahmed Amin" [To our master Dr. Ahmed Amin], *Al-Thaqafa*, no. 633 (10 September 1951).
7. A. Musallam, *From Secularism to Jihadism* (London: Praeger, 2005), pp. 89–90.
8. Qutb, "Illa ustazana al-duktur Ahmed Amin."
9. S. Qutb, "Bada al-ma'raka: Al-damir al-adabi fi misr, shuban wa shuyukh" [After the battle: The literary conscience in Egypt, young men and sheikhs), *al-'Alam al-'Arabi*, year 1, no. 4 (July 1947): 52–54; Musallam, *From Secularism to Jihadism*, pp. 89–90.
10. Shalash, *Al-tamarrud 'ala al-adab*, p. 118.
11. Qutb, "Bada al-ma'raka," pp. 52–54; Musallam, *From Secularism to Jihadism*, pp. 89–90.
12. See M. R. Al-Bayoumi, "Qutb bayna al-Aqqad wal Khili" [Sayyid Qutb between Aqqad and al-Khuli], *Al-Thaqafa*, year 3, no. 53 (February 1978).
13. Shalash, *Al-tamarrud 'ala al-adab*, pp. 124–125.
14. Ibid., pp. 116, 126.
15. It was during this period that Egyptians suffered from dire socioeconomic conditions such as food shortages caused by stagnation in grain harvests against the widespread cultivation of cotton. For further information on this, see N. Reynolds, *A City Consumed: Urban Commerce, the Cairo Fire, and the Politics of Decolonization in Egypt* (Stanford, CA: Stanford University Press, 2012), pp. 148–149.

16. H. al-Namnam, *Sayyid Qutb wa thawrat yulyu* [Sayyid Qutb and the July revolution] (Cairo: Mirit, 1999), p. 75.
17. Ibid., p. 76.
18. At the time, Egypt's social fabric had been massively strained by the UN's decision to partition Palestine. Demonstrations and bombings occurred in Egyptian cities with attacks launched on shops owned by Copts and Jews. Reynolds, *A City Consumed*, p. 151. The lack of law and order led to a continuation of public contention with the police, who acted as spectators as the hooligans carried out attacks; the press's inflammatory coverage poured gasoline on a raging fire. Furthermore, student political activism ran high and discontent persisted against the Wafd's signing of the 1936 treaty, which allowed the British a continued presence in Egypt while granting a limited degree of independence to the Egyptians.
19. Reynolds, *A City Consumed*, p. 151.
20. Haykal, a prominent politician and writer during this time, adopted Islam as a lifestyle—shedding his youthful fascination with Western ideas. Before the 1930s, Haykal made no specific references to Islam as the basis of politics in Egypt. Nor did he dwell on religion as having any social function beyond serving the spiritual needs of the masses. In 1910, for example, he declared that religion's key social function is to maintain order among the masses until science could fully satisfy the requirements of humanity. C. D. Smith, *Islam and the Search for Social Order in Modern Egypt: A Biography of Muhammad Husayn Haykal* (Albany: State University of New York Press, 1983), p. 103. This stage of Haykal's life was clear in his book, *Thawrat alla al-Adab* [The literature rebellion], where he showed a pharaonic bent regarding Egypt's identity, via his argument that science and philosophy are essential for human development: see M. H. Haykal, *Thawrat alla al-Adab* (Cairo: Dar al-Maaref, 1983), p. 25. Haykal noted that in its golden days, Islamic civilization was nourished by the ideas of Western civilization: ibid., p. 28. Following his radical shift, however, Haykal advocated a return to the early days of Islam and adoption of those Islamic principles applicable to modern life. In his book *Hayat Muhammad* [The life of Muhammad], he strenuously argued that Islam is superior to Western civilization because in his opinion "there is a great gap between this full right equality before Allah [as Islam advocates] and this equality before the law [human] as advocated by Western civilization in recent eras": M. H. Haykal, *Hayat Muhammad*, 14th ed. (Cairo: Dar al-Maareif, 1977), p. 526. Haykal also argues with reference to Mohamed Abduh's interpretation of the Qu'ran that Islam made reason the judge in everything: ibid., p. 520. As can be seen, there is a serious clash or a contradiction between Haykal's thinking in the first stage of his intellectual journey and the later stage. Professor Charles Smith explains this contradiction as reflecting a conscious choice by Haykal to secure his political and intellectual position, regardless of how irreconcilable his arguments were with each other. According to Smith, Haykal tried to "manipulate public religious fervour, [although at the same time] he worked strenuously during his tenure as a minister of education to block religious incursions into the state educational policy": Smith, *Islam and the Search for Social Order in Modern Egypt*, p. 132.
21. I. M. Abu Rabi', *Intellectual Origins of Islamic Resurgence in the Modern Arab World* (Albany: State University of New York Press, 1996), p. 59.
22. Mark Juergensmeyer, *The New Cold War? Religious Nationalism Confronts the Secular State* (Berkeley: University of California Press, 1993), p. 24.

23. Misr al-Fatat (Young Egypt), established in 1933, is an example of a beneficiary of Islam's functionary role. That party was "both actively and philosophically opposed to the European style of democracy practiced, especially, by Wafd in Egypt, and was aligned ideologically to the Nazi and fascist groups active in Europe at the time." S. Botman, *Egypt from Independence to Revolution*, 1919–1952 (New York: Syracuse University Press, 1991), p. 118. Although Misr al-Fatat was patriotic and militaristic to the extent that it would ask Egyptians to buy just from Egyptian shops and to speak only Arabic, the party leaders also looked back to the past for Islamic glory and cultural renewal. In keeping with this partially Islamic orientation, leaders argued for religion and morality as the guiding principles of life. Selma Botman indicates that the move to religious radicalism came amidst attempts by the party leader, Ahmed Hussein, to broaden Misr al-Fatat's appeal by first targeting secondary school and university students and then mainstream groups, including urban lower- and middle-class adults. Ibid., p. 117. The success of raising this appeal came as the party changed its name to the National Islamic Party in 1940. Ever since, the party's program was "restoring the country's glory and achieving its independence"—a program which allowed its members to win the majority of seats in Wafd's strongholds in universities. A. Abdalla, *The Student Movement and National Politics in Egypt: 1923–1973* (Cairo: American University in Cairo, 1985), pp. 51–53. Equally important, Misr al-Fatat advocated industrial and agricultural reform and change or even materialistic solutions to the local industry such as the Piastre Plan. The party was also known for being "anti-British," organizing riots against the occupiers. Abdalla, *The Student Movement and National Politics in Egypt: 1923–1973*, pp. 51–53.
24. S. Qutb, *al-'Adala al-Ijtima'iyya fi-l-Islam* [Social justice in Islam] (Cairo: Dar al-Shurouk, 1993), p. 17.
25. Abu Rabi', *Intellectual Origins of Islamic Resurgence in the Modern Arab World*, p. 109.
26. Author's interview with H. Hanafi, Cairo, 25 September 2006.
27. Author's interview with A. Assal, Cairo, 12 December 2006.
28. Author's interview with F. Abdel Khaleq, Cairo, 16 October 2006.
29. Namnam, *Sayyid Quṭb wa thawrah yulyu*, p. 40.
30. F. Gerges, *Journey of the Jihadist: Inside Muslim Militancy* (2006), see chapter 4, pp. 143–181; see S. Qutb, "The America I Have Seen: In the Scale of Human Values," in *America in an Arab Mirror: Images of America in Arabic Travel Literature: An Anthology*, ed. Kamal Abdel Malek (Basingstoke, UK: Palgrave Macmillan, 2000), pp. 9–28.
31. S. Younis, *Sayyid Qutb wa-l-Usuliyya al-Diniyya* [Sayyid Qutb and Islamic fundamentalism] (Cairo: Dar Tiba'a, 1995), pp. 144–145.
32. S. Qutb, *Ma'rakat al-Islam wa-l-Ra'smaliyya* [The battle of Islam and capitalism] (Cairo: Dar al-Shurouk, 1993), p. 21.
33. Ibid., p. 19.
34. Ibid., pp. 19, 54.
35. S. Younis, *Sayyid Qutb wa-l-Usuliyya al-Diniyya*, p. 147.
36. S. Qutb, "Jabha wahida" [United front], *al-Liwa al-Jadid*, issue 15 (July 24, 1951), cited in S. Younis, *Sayyid Qutb wa-l-Usuliyya al-Diniyya* [Sayyid Qutb and Islamic fundamentalism] (Cairo: Dar Tiba'a, 1995), p. 148.

37. S. Qutb, "Hadha Huwa al-Tariq ... Harb 'Isabat'" [This is the road: A guerrilla war], *Da'awa* (August 1951), and S. Qutb, "Alan ila al-'Amal," *al-Liwa al-Jadid*, issue 30 (1951), cited in S. Younis, *Sayyid Qutb wa-l-Usuliyya al-Diniyya* [Sayyid Qutb and Islamic fundamentalism] (Cairo: Dar Tiba'a, 1995), p. 148.
38. Author's interview with M. H. Diab, Cairo, 27 October 2006. See also M. H. Diab, *Al-khetab wal ideologia* [Discourse and Ideology] (Cairo: Dar al-Thaqafa al-Gadida, 1987).
39. Author's interview with K. Mohieddin, Cairo, 6 December 2006.
40. See Namnam, *Sayyid Qutb wa thawrat yulyu*, pp. 61–62.
41. Musallam, *From Secularism to Jihadism*, pp. 140–141.
42. S. Qutb, "Istigwab ella al-batal Mohamed Naguib" [An inquiry into hero Mohamed Naguib], *al-Akhbar al-Jadidia*, issue 46 (August 8, 1952), cited in S. Younis, *Sayyid Qutb wa-l-Usuliyya al-Diniyya*, p. 157.
43. See Namnam, *Sayyid Qutb wa thawrat yulyu*, p. 61.
44. Ironically, after large-scale protests in 2013 calling on the military to oust the first legitimately elected president in Egypt's modern history, Mohamed Morsi, a member of the Ikhwan, they similarly justified their action on the basis of "revolutionary legitimacy," condemning critics for labeling what happened a coup.
45. See S. Qutb, "Idrebou wal hadeed sakhin" [Hit while the iron is hot], *al-Da'wa* (21 August 1952), cited in Younis, *Sayyid Qutb wa-l-usuliyya al-diniyya*, p. 179.
46. S. Qutb, "Hazehi al-ahzab gheir qabela leil-baqaa" [These parties are unviable], *al-Akhbar al-Jadida*, issue 1268 (29 September 1952).
47. Ibid.
48. S. Qutb, "Harakat la tukhifana" [Tactics do not scare us], *al-Akbar al-Jadida*, issue 52 (29 September 1952), cited in Younis, *Sayyid Qutb wa-l-usuliyya al-diniyya*, p. 157.
49. Author's interview with M. H. Diab, Cairo, 27 October 2006.
50. S. Al-Masri, *Al-Ikhwan al-Muslimun wal tabaqaa al-'amela* [The Muslim Brotherhood and the working class] (Cairo: Al-Amal leil Nashr, 1992), pp. 76–77, cited in Musallam, *From Secularism to Jihadism*, p. 140.
51. Musallam, *From Secularism to Jihadism*, p. 140.
52. Some controversy exists regarding the Nasser-Qutb connection. According to Ahmed al-Baquri, Nasser told him that Qutb had wanted to be the secretary of Hay'at al-Tahrir but that Nasser had refused to appoint him to the post "lest Qutb should turn the Hay'at into a section of the Muslim Brotherhood": A. H. al-Baquri, *Baqaa dhikrayat* [Memories] (Cairo: al-Ahram, 1988), p. 218. Salah Shadi, a leading Ikhwan figure, has argued that Sayyid Qutb had refused this post: see S. Shadi, *Al-shahidan Hassan al-Banna wa-Sayyid Qutb* [The two martyrs: Hassan al-Banna and Sayyid Qutb] (Mansura, Egypt: Wafa Press, 1988), p. 61. Salah Abdel-Fatah al-Khalidi cited Mohamed Qutb, the brother of Sayyid, as saying that the Revolutionary Command Council (RCC) appointed Sayyid Qutb as its consultant for interior and cultural affairs; Qutb remained in the post for only a few months: see S.A.F. Al-Khalidi, *Sayyid Qutb: al-Shahid al-Hayy* [Sayyid Qutb: The living martyr] (Amman: Maktabat al-Aqsa, 1981), p. 142.
53. Musallam, *From Secularism to Jihadism*, p. 139.
54. S. Qutb, "Min masalaht kebar al-Mulak an Yakhdau leil Thawra" [It is in the interest of the big landowners to succumb to the revolution], *Rose al-Yusuf*, issue 1263.

55. See S. Fayyad, "Sayyid Qutb bayna al-Naqd al-Adabi wa-Jahaliyyat al-Qarn al-'Ishrin" [Sayyid Qutb between literary criticism and the jahiliyya of the 21st century], *al-Hilal* (September 1986).
56. Abdel-Nasser and other Free Officers met in Qutb's house a few days before the 1952 coup, "much to indicate the big role played by Qutb in preparing for the revolution": S.A.F. Al-Khalidi, *Sayyid Qutb: al-Shahid al-Hayy*. [Sayyid Qutb: The living martyr] (Amman: Maktabat al-Aqsa, 1981), p. 140; Author's interview with M. H. Diab, Cairo, 27 October 2006.
57. A. Hamouda, *Sayyid Qutb: Min al-qariyya ella al-mishnaqa, tahqiq wathaiqi* [Sayyid Qutb: From the village to the gallows, a documented investigation] (Cairo: Sina leil Nashr, 1987), p. 111.
58. Author's interview with K. Mohieddin, Cairo, 12 December 2006.
59. According to critic Sherif Younis, Qutb was close to Kamaleddin Hussein, a Free Officer known for his Ikhwan tendencies, who was tasked with "cleansing the ministry of former regime loyalists." Younis unearthed this fact after interviewing the director of the office of the minister of education, Ismail al-Qabbani, at that time. See S. Younis, *Sayyid Qutb wa-l-usuliyya al-diniyya*, p. 154.
60. Ibid., p. 154.
61. Hamouda, *Sayyid Qutb*, pp. 111–112.
62. M. Abdel-Halim, *Al-ikhwan al-muslimun: Ahdath san'at al-tarikh* [The Muslim Brotherhood: Events that made history], vol. 3 (Alexandria: Dar al-Da'wa, n.d.), p. 174.
63. S. Qutb, *Limaza 'adamuni* [Why they executed me] (Riyadh: Al-Sharika al-Saudiyya leil Abhath wal Nashr, 1990), p. 14.
64. Ibid., p. 15.
65. Ibid., p. 16.
66. Ibid., pp. 15–16.
67. S. Qutb, "Nuqtat al-bad" [Starting point], issue 995, *al-Da'wa* (28 July 1952), cited in Younis, *Sayyid Qutb wa-l-usuliyya al-diniyya*, p. 161.
68. S. Qutb, "Al-Shu'ub al-Islamiyya Tazhaf" [Islamic peoples sweep], *Al-Risala*, issue 979 (April 7, 1952), cited in Younis, *Sayyid Qutb wa-l-usuliyya al-diniyya*, p. 161.
69. Author's interview with A. M. Al-Shazili, Alexandria, Egypt, 12 January 2007.
70. Author's interview with A. Abdel Majid, Cairo, 7 January 2007.
71. Diab, *Sayyid Qutb*, p. 101.
72. Ibid.

Chapter 9. Qutb's al-Tanzim al-Sirri

1. Z. Munson, "Islamic Mobilization: Social Movement Theory and the Egyptian Muslim Brotherhood," *Sociological Quarterly* 42, no. 4 (1972): 487–510.
2. The account of the membership levels draws on R. Mitchell, *The Society of the Muslim Brothers* (1973; New York: Oxford University Press, 1993), p. 183.
3. Ibid.
4. Ibid., p. 196.
5. Munson, "Islamic Mobilization," pp. 487–510.
6. Mitchell, *The Society of the Muslim Brothers*, p. 328. The figures are based on *Qadiyat al-Nuqrashi*, official documents housed at the time of Mitchell's research at the Council of State building in Cairo.

7. Munson, "Islamic Mobilization," pp. 487–510.
8. Mitchell, *The Society of the Muslim Brothers*, p. 188.
9. Ibid., p. 189.
10. U.S. Department of State (USDS), Confidential Central Files, Egypt, 1954, #2439, cited in Munson, "Islamic Mobilization," pp. 487–510.
11. Ibid., p. 499. See also M. Abdel Halim, *Al-ikhwan al-muslimun: Ahdath san'at al-tarikh* [The Muslim Brotherhood: Events that made history], vol. 3 (Alexandria: Dar al-Da'waa, 1985), pp. 32–33.
12. Munson, "Islamic Mobilization," p. 499. Mahmoud Abdel Halim, one of the founding fathers of the group, challenged such restrictions as ineffectual since "members of the Ikhwan are tied together with the *habl ellah* [the rope of God] which is more solid than any ties": in Abdel Halim, *Al-Ikhwan al-Muslimun*, vol. 3, p. 32.
13. Author's interview with A. Abdel Majid, Cairo, 10 January 2007.
14. Ibid.
15. Ibid.
16. Author's interview with A. A. Kamal, Cairo, 13 January 2007.
17. M. A. Al-Siman, *Hassan al-Banna: Al-rajul wa-l-fikra* (Dar al-I'tisam, 1978), pp. 32–33.
18. Author's interview with S. Eid, Mansura, Egypt, 20 February 2007.
19. *Fi zilal al-qur'an* [In the shadow of the Qur'an] is a series of works, each being a *tasir* (interpretation and commentary) of a different part of the Qur'an. Qutb wrote some parts before being jailed in 1954, and others during his time in prison. In the parts that he wrote prior to 1954, he focused more on aesthetic and intellectual aspects of Islam, while those written in jail focused on issues that were clearly political and ideological, including *jahiliyya*, revolutionary activism, and the vanguard; see S. Qutb, *Fi Zilal al-qur'an* [In the shadow of the Qur'an], vol. 1 (parts 1–4) (Cairo: Dar al-Shurouk, 2003).
20. S. Al-Khalidi, *Al-manhaj al-haraki fi zilal al-qur'an* [The operational method in *In the Shadow of the Qur'an*], 2nd ed. (Amman: Dar Ammar, 2000), pp. 26–30.
21. Qutb, *Fi zilal al-qur'an*, vols. 1–6, p. 1417.
22. S. Qutb, *Ma'lim fil tariq* [Signposts] (Cairo: Dar al-Shurouk, 1979), p. 17.
23. Ibid., pp. 17–18.
24. Ibid., pp. 149–150.
25. Ibid., pp. 12–19.
26. Ibid.
27. Author's interview with S. Eid, Mansura, Egypt, 30 February 2007.
28. Qutb, *Fi zilal al-qur'an*, p. 1411.
29. Author's interview with S. Eid, Mansura, Egypt, 18 February 2007.
30. Qutb, *Fi zilal al-qur'an*, pp. 1416–1417.
31. Author's interview with S. Eid, Mansura, Egypt, 18 February 2007.
32. Author's interview with A. A. Ashmawi, Daqahliyya, Egypt, 31 December 2006.
33. Author's interview with S. Eid, Mansura, Egypt, 12 February 2007.
34. Qutb, *Ma'lim fil tariq* [Signposts], p. 150.
35. Author's interview with A. M. Al-Shazili, Alexandria, Egypt, 9 February 2007.
36. Author's interview with S. Eid, Mansura, Egypt, 20 February 2007.
37. Qutb, *Ma'lim fil tariq* [Signposts], p. 35.
38. Ibid., p. 81.
39. Although he did not name them, Qutb was referring here to the scholars of al-Azhar. In the 1960s, Nasser placed al-Azhar, the prestigious thousand-year-old institution

and the highest religious authority, under direct state control with a view of "bringing its teachers and pupils into line and illustrating the compatibility between Islam and Nasserist socialism." The Azharis were even given "military uniforms and found themselves marching in step under orders of army officers": G. Kepel, *Jihad: The Trail of Political Islam*, trans. R. Anthony (Cambridge, MA: Belknap Press of Harvard University Press, 2002), p. 53.

40. Qutb, *Ma'lim fil tariq*, p. 35.
41. Ibid., p. 9.
42. I. Taymiyaa, *Fiqh al-Jihad* [The jurisprudence of jihad], ed. Zuheir Shafiq al-Jabi (Beirut: Dar al-Fiqr al-Araby, 1992), pp. 63–64.
43. In Islamic law, *fard al-'ayn* refers to legal obligations that must be performed by each individual Muslim, including prayer, charity, fasting, and pilgrimage. Individual obligation is contrasted with communal obligation (*fard al-kifaya*). See "Fard al-Ayn" in *The Oxford Dictionary of Islam*, ed. J. L. Esposito, *Oxford Islamic Studies Online*, available from http://www.oxfordislamicstudies.com/article/opr/t125/e624 [accessed 7 April 2014].
44. Author's interview with F. Abdel Khaleq, Cairo, 16 February 2007.
45. Ibid.
46. Ibid.
47. Author's interview with S. Eid, Mansura, Egypt, 12 February 2007.
48. Ibid.
49. Author's interview with S. Eid, Mansura, Egypt, 18 February 2007.
50. Author's interview with A. Ra'if, Cairo, 1 December 2006.
51. Author's interview with S. Eid, Mansura, Egypt, 30 February 2007.
52. Author's interview with S. Eid, Mansura, Egypt, 18 February 2007.
53. Author's interview with S. Eid, Mansura, Egypt, 30 February 2007.
54. Author's interview with A. A. Ashmawi, Daqahliyya, Egypt, 30 November 2006.
55. Author's interview with A. A. Ashmawi, Daqahliyya, Egypt, 31 December 2006.
56. Author's interview with A. Abdel Majid, Cairo, 8 January 2007.
57. Author's interview with A. Abdel Majid, Cairo, 13 January 2007.
58. Author's interview with A. Abdel Majid, Cairo, 7 January 2007.
59. Author's interview with A. Musa, Mansura, Egypt, 6 February 2007.
60. Author's interview with A. Abdel Majid, Cairo, 7 January 2007.
61. Author's interview with S. Eid, Mansura, Egypt, 12 February 2007.
62. Ibid.
63. S. Qutb, *Dirasat Islamiyya* [Islamic studies] (Cairo: Dar al-Shurouk, 1967), p. 161.
64. Qutb, *Fi zilal al-qur'an*, p. 414.
65. As an official of the Ministry of Education, Qutb was sent to the United States to study educational administration. This period is taken as a milestone in Qutb's intellectual journey, particularly because of his antipathy towards Western culture and disillusionment with modernism in general. Qutb's letters and articles on his experience in America were brought together in S. A. Al-Khalidi, *Amrika min al-dakhel bi munzar Sayyid Qutb* [America from the inside: From the perspective of Sayyid Qutb] (Damascus: Dar al-Qalam, 1985). Qutb's stay in America sharpened his "sense of clash of civilizations—beleaguered Islam against threatening West": see L. C. Brown, *Religion and State: The Muslim Approach to Politics* (New York: Columbia University Press, 2000), p. 155. In a book published in 1949, before he traveled to the United States, Qutb had praised

America's "social justice" as an example to imitate. In this sense, Qutb's subsequent American experience represented a turning point in his radicalization. See S. Qutb, *Al-Adala Ijtimi'iyya fil Islam* (1949; Cairo: Dar al-Shurouk, 1995).

66. Author's interview with A. Abdel Majid, Cairo, 7 January 2007.
67. Author's interview with S. Eid, Mansura, Egypt, 12 February 2007.
68. Al-Khalidi, *Amrika min al-dakhel bi manzar Sayyid Qutb*.
69. An example of one such forum is the I Am a Muslim Network, available from http://www.muslm.org/vb [accessed 28 March 2013].
70. See M. I. Mabrouk, *Al-islam al-nafi': Al-islam alladhi turiduhu amrika* [The utilitarian Islam: The Islam America wants] (Cairo: Markaz al-Hadara al-'Arabiyya, 2010).
71. Author's interview with A.A.M. Shazili, Alexandria, Egypt, 21 January 2007.
72. Ibid.
73. Ibid.
74. Ibid.
75. Ibid.
76. Ibid.
77. Ibid.
78. Ibid.
79. Author's interview with S. Younis, Cairo, 20 October 2006.
80. Al-Mawdudi was born in India in 1903. The themes of his ideology have become the norm for many Sunni Islamists, including Qutb. *Jahiliyya* and the vanguard are two concepts which Qutb had adopted almost two decades after Mawdudi's publication. For Mawdudi, Islam is "a revolutionary ideology and programme which seeks to alter the social order of the whole world and rebuild it in conformity with its own tenets and ideals": in A. A. Al-Mawdudi, *Jihad in Islam* (Kuwait: International Islamic Federation of Student Organizations, 1980), p. 5. Since Islam is comprehensive, embracing both public and private life, both governments and people can lapse into *jahiliyya*. For him, the *jahiliyya* is not just a historical era that comes to an end with the arrival of the Prophet Muhammad; rather, *jahiliyya* exists in any time and any place in which the divinely ordained community is not realized: L. C. Brown, *Religion and State: The Muslim Approach to Politics* (New York: Columbia University Press, 2000), p. 153. Therefore, Mawdudi called for the realization of "objective Jihad," insisting that Islam "was never a metaphysical proposition; it was a charter of social Revolution": A. A. Al-Mawdudi, *Jihad in Islam*, p. 14. Consequently, Muslims should create and belong to a "Hizb Allah" (party of God), whose task, according to Mawdudi, is to "devour to destroy the hegemony of an un-Islamic system and establish in its place the rule of that social and cultural order which regulates life with balanced and humane laws, referred to by the Qur'an with the comprehensive term 'the word of God'": see ibid., pp. 17–18. Mawdudi is viewed as the "first twentieth-century Muslim thinker to build a political theory around the original break that led to the founding of Islam": Kepel, *Jihad*, p. 35. Unlike Mawdudi, who formed his own political party, Jamaat-e-Islami, in 1941, to play the "vanguard" of the Islamic revolution, Qutb built up "clandestine organisations and transformed the rupture with ungodly society into violent confrontation": see ibid., p. 35. Nevertheless, while Mawdudi was allowed to form his party within the heated, contentious politics of the Indian subcontinent, the Free Officers had in January 1953 issued a law banning all parties.

81. A.A.H. Al-Nadawi, *Al-tafseer al-siyassi leil islam fi miraat kitabaat al-ustaz Abi al-A'laa al-Mawdudi wa al-shahid Sayyid Qutb* [The political interpretation from the perspective of the writings of Mr. Abi al-A'laa al-Mawdudi and martyr Sayyid Qutb] (Cairo: Dar Afaq al-Ghad, n.d.), pp. 53, 66–67, 101.
82. Author's interview with A. A. Ashmawi, Daqahliyya, Egypt, 30 November 2006.
83. Ibid.
84. Author's interview with A. A. Ashmawi, Daqahliyya, Egypt, 31 December 2006.
85. Author's interview with F. Abdel Khaleq, Cairo, 16 October 2006.
86. Ibid.
87. Author's interview with A. Abdel Majid, Cairo, 10 January 2007.
88. Ibid.
89. S. Tarrow, *Power in Movement and Contentious Politics* (Cambridge: Cambridge University Press, 1998), p. 4.
90. Al-Tanzim as a social movement did not need only "social solidarities" to face down "collective challenges"; it also needed "sustained interaction with elites" at the ideational level, according to theorist Sydney Tarrow. Furthermore, ideas offer what Mark Blyth had called a "blueprint" that shapes understanding of a "crisis": see M. Blyth, *Great Transformations: Economic Ideas and Institutional Change in the Twentieth Century* (Cambridge: Cambridge University Press, 2002), pp. 38–41. This "ideational framing" is all the more important in "high-risk" environments: see C. Wickham, *The Muslim Brotherhood: Evolution of an Islamist Movement* (Princeton, NJ: Princeton University Press, 2013), p. 13.
91. J. Calvert, *Sayyid Qutb and the Origins of Radical Islamism* (New York: Columbia University Press, 2013), p. 229.
92. Author's interview with S. Eid, Mansura, Egypt, 18 February 2007.
93. Author's interview with A. M. Shazili, Alexandria, Egypt, 9 February 2007.
94. Ibid.
95. Author's interview with S. Eid, Mansura, Egypt, 18 February 2007.
96. Ibid.
97. Ibid.
98. Ibid.
99. S. E. Ibrahim, "Anatomy of Egypt's Militant Islamic Groups: Methodological Note and Preliminary Findings," *International Journal of Middle East Studies* 12, no. 4 (2006): 423–453. Author's interview with S. E. Ibrahim, Cairo, 19 October 2006.
100. Author's interview with A. M. Shazili, Alexandria, Egypt, 9 February 2007.
101. Author's interview with A. A. Ashmawi, Daqahliyya, Egypt, 31 December 2006.
102. Ibid.
103. Ibid.
104. Author's interview with A. M. Shazili, Alexandria, Egypt, 9 February 2007.
105. Author's interview with A. A. Ashmawi, Daqahliyya, Egypt, 31 December 2006.
106. Ibid.
107. Author's interview with A. A. Aw'd, Mansura, Egypt, 6 February 2007.
108. Author's interview with M. Izzat, Cairo, 11 February 2007.
109. Author's interview with F. Abdel Khaleq, Cairo, 16 October 2006.
110. Ibid.
111. Ibid.

112. Author's interview with A. Abdel Majid, Cairo, 7 January 2007.
113. Author's interview with A. A. Ashmawi, Daqahliyya, Egypt, 21 October 2006.
114. Author's interview with A. Abdel Majid, Cairo, 7 January 2007.
115. Ibid.
116. Ibid.
117. Z. Al-Ghazali, *Ayyam min hayati* [Days from my life] (Cairo: Dar al-Shurouk, 1980), pp. 35–36.
118. Ibid.
119. Author's interview with A. A. Ashmawi, 21 October 2006.
120. Author's interview with S. Sharaf, 14 December 2006.
121. Author's interview with A. M. Shazili, Alexandria, Egypt, 9 February 2007.
122. Author's interview with S. Eid, Mansura, Egypt, 18 February 2007.
123. S. Guhar, *Al-mawta yatakallamun* [The dead speak] (Cairo: al-Maktab al-Misri al-Hadith, 1975), pp. 197–199.
124. Al-Ghazali, *Ayyam min hayati*, p. 183. The Egyptian authorities believed that al-Tanzim was a tool of the Saudi state, though scant evidence exists to suggest that this was indeed the case.
125. Ibid., p. 184.
126. Author's interview with A. M. Shazili, Alexandria, Egypt, 9 February 2007.
127. See Kepel, *Jihad: The Trail of Political Islam*, pp. 33–35; Abu Rabi', *Intellectual Origins of Islamic Resurgence in the Modern Arab World*, pp. 99–166; and H. Kandil, *Inside the Brotherhood* (Malden, MA: Polity Press, 2014), pp. 82–92.

Chapter 10. The Decline of the Nasserist Project

1. A similar version of this chapter appears as "The Transformation of Arab Politics" in *The 1967 Arab-Israeli War: Origins and Consequences*, ed. W. R. Louis and A. Shlaim (Cambridge: Cambridge University Press, 2012), pp. 285–314.
2. Among those scholars who have propagated this point of view, the late Fouad Ajami stands out for his assertion that pan-Arabism "died" with the 1967 defeat. Ajami essentialized the defeat in the 1967 war as the "Waterloo of pan-Arabism." See F. Ajami, "The End of Pan-Arabism," *Foreign Affairs* 57, no. 2 (1978): 355–373. Ajami's rhetoric has resonated with some other analysts inside and outside the Arab region. Nasif Youssef Hitti saw the defeat as "the end of an Arab system with all its values, frames and ideologies" and as causing "a moment of revolutionary re-orientation." See N. Y. Hitti, "Al-'Amal al-'Arabi ba'ada al-Hazimab" [The Arab action after the defeat], in *Harb yunyu 1967 ba'da 30 'aman* [The June 1967 war after 30 years], ed. L. Al-Kholi (Cairo: Ahram, 1997), pp. 196–207.
3. For example, Khalil al-Anani called for a methodological disentanglement of the 1967 defeat and the rise of Islamism since attempts to tie them together had become "outdated" and "unconvincing": see K. Al-Anani, *Al-ikhwan al-muslimun: Shaykhukha tusari' al-zaman* [The Muslim Brotherhood: Senility struggling with time] (Cairo: Maktabat al-Shuroq al-Dawliyya, 2007), pp. 34–35.
4. R. Al-Naqqash, *Naguib Mahfouz: Safahat min mudhakkiratihi wa adwa' jadida 'ala adabihi wa hayatihi* [Naguib Mahfouz: New pages of his memoirs and new highlights on his literature and life] (Cairo: Ahram, 1998), p. 272.

5. R. A. Hinnebusch, *Egyptian Politics under Sadat: The Post-Populist Development of an Authoritarian-Modernizing State* (Cambridge: Cambridge University Press, 1985), p. 35.
6. J. Waterbury, *Egypt of Nasser and Sadat: The Political Economy of Two Regimes* (Princeton, NJ: Princeton University Press, 1983).
7. L. C. Brown, *Religion and State: The Muslim Approach to Politics* (New York: Columbia University Press, 2000), pp. 130–133.
8. Ibid., p. 132.
9. G. Amin, *Qissat al-iqtisad al-misri: Min 'ahd Muhammad Ali ila 'ahd Mubarak* [The story of the Egyptian economy: From the Muhammad Ali era to the Mubarak era] (Cairo: Dar al-Shurouk, 2012), pp. 52–53.
10. Ibid., pp. 52–53, 57.
11. A. Imam, *Salah Nasr yatadhakkar: Al-thawra, al-mukhabarat, al-naksa* [Salah Nasr remembers: The revolution, the intelligence and the naksa] (Beirut: Dar al-Khayyal, 1999), p. 179.
12. Amin, *Qissat al-Iqtisad al-Misri*, p. 64.
13. See G. Shoukri, *Al-thawra al-mudadda fi misr* [The counterrevolution in Egypt], 3rd ed. (Cairo: Al-Ahali, 1987); Y. Elwy, "A Political Economy of Egyptian Foreign Policy: State, Ideology and Modernisation since 1970," unpublished doctoral thesis. London: London School of Economics and Political Science, 2009.
14. S. E. Ibrahim, "al-Hirak al-Ijtim'i wa-Tawzi' al-Dakhl" [The social mobility and the income distribution], in *Al-Iqtisad al-Siyasi li-Tawzi' al-Dakhl fi Misr* [The political economy and income distribution in Egypt], ed. G. Abdel-Khaleq (Cairo: Al-Hay'a al-Misriyya al-'Amma li-l-Kitab, 1993), pp. 609–686.
15. See Elwy, "A Political Economy of Egyptian Foreign Policy: State, Ideology and Modernisation since 1970."
16. Y. Aboul-Enein, *The Egyptian-Yemen War (1962–67): Egyptian Perspectives on Guerrilla Warfare*, 2004, available from https://www.thefreelibrary.com/The+Egyptian-Yemen+War+(1962-67)%3A+Egyptian+perspectives+on+Guerrilla...-a0116585276 [accessed 16 October 2017].
17. S. Sharaf, *Sanawat wa ayyam m'a Gamal Abdel-Nasser* [Years and days with Gamal Abdel Nasser], part 2 (Cairo: Madbouli, 2006), p. 665.
18. On one occasion, the first president of the republic said upon taking over in 1962 that Yemen had "missiles that could destroy the palaces of Raji'iyyaa [Saudi Arabia] in Riyadh": see M. H. Heikal, *Sanawat al-Ghalayan* [Years of turmoil] (Cairo: Ahram, 1988), p. 647.
19. Y. Aboul-Enein, *The Egyptian-Yemen War (1962–67).*
20. Ibid. Noticeably, this Saudi-Egyptian rivalry in Yemen had been disguised in religious and ideological terms. After the Jeddah Agreement between Nasser and the Saudis on August 1965, the Saudis demanded that the transitional government in Yemen be named "the Islamic State of Yemen": see A. Al-Iryani, *Muzakerat al-Rayees al-Qadi Abdel-Rahman Bin Yehia al-Iryani* [Memoirs of President Abdel-Rahman bin Yehia al-Iryani], vol. 2 (Cairo: Al-Hayaa al-Masriyya al-'Ama leil Kitab, 2013), p. 382. Influential Saudi scholar Abdullah Ali al-Qassimi sent a letter in 1965 to Abdel-Rahman al-Iryani, a prominent figure of the revolution who was Yemen's president from 1967 till 1974, warning him that his destiny would be "in hell" because of his cooperation with foreigners: see A. Al-Iryani, *Muzakerat al-rayees al-qadi Abdel-Rahman Bin Yehia al-Iryani*, p. 369. Some sheikhs of Yemeni tribes also called for the creation

of an Islamic state—the same demand by the ousted imam whose royal family had built its political legitimacy on being descendants of Imams Hassan and Hussein, two grandsons of the Prophet Muhammad: see *Sirat al-Imam Mohamed Ibn Yehia Hamededdin, al-musamaa bel-dr al-manthour fi sirat al-imam al-mansour* [The biography of Mohamed Ibn Yehia Hamededdin known as the dispersed pearls in the biography of the victorious imam], collected by M. S. Salhiyya (Beirut: Dar al-Basheer, 1996). In one of his poems, the imam called on all nations to live in harmony according to this Islamic law and avoid *bid'a* (heresies), a reference to nationalism and socialism, which he always vehemently attacked: see A. Al-Baydani, *Azmat al-Umaa al-Arabiyya wa Thawrat al-Yemen* [The crisis of the Arab nation and the Yemen revolution] (Cairo: al-Maktab al-Misri al-Hadith, 1984), p. 192. Iran joined forces with Saudi Arabia against Nasser because the shah felt compelled to provide the Shia Zaydi imam with money. In contrast, Nasser boasted about the unity and solidarity of the revolutionary camp. Speaking in front of a group of Egyptian soldiers in Yemen, Nasser reminded them that their presence there is "evidence of the unity of revolutionary movements in the Arab region": see *Tarikh al-yemen al-mua'sser: 1917–1982* [The modern history of Yemen: 1917–1982], trans. M. A. Al-Bahr (Cairo: Madbouli, 1990), p. 150. Similarly, in a meeting with Yemeni notables, Nasser defended his intervention on religious grounds, arguing that Islam is a religion that calls for freedom, justice, and equality and that Yemen had played the role of propagator of Islam in the past and should play the role of propagator of freedom in the present: see *Tarikh al-yemen al-mua'sser: 1917–1982*, p. 150. While on the same visit to Yemen, Nasser said that Arab socialism is informed by Islamic principles and Arab traditions, such as the Shura Council which has existed since the beginning of Islam: see ibid.

21. Cited in *Tarikh al-yemen al-mua'sser: 1917–1982*, p. 90.
22. Ibid.
23. See M. H. Heikal, *Waqa'i' tahqiq siyasi amama al-mudd'i al-ishtraki* [Documents of the investigations by the public socialist prosecutor] (Beirut: Sharikat al-Matu'at, 1979); M. Doran, "Egypt," in *Diplomacy in the Middle East: The International Relations of Regional and Outside Powers*, ed. L. C. Brown (London: I. B. Tauris, 2001), pp. 97–120.
24. M. H. Heikal, *Sanawat al-Ghalayan* [Years of turmoil] (Cairo: Ahram, 1988), pp. 663, 669.
25. Al-Baydani, *Azmat al-umaa al-arabiyya wa thawrat al-yemen*, p. 150.
26. This conclusion is disputed by senior figures of the Nasser regime: see Sami, *Sanawat wa ayyam m'a Gamal Abdel-Naser*, pp. 652–659.
27. A. Nutting, *Nasser* (London: Constable, 1972), p. 349.
28. Cited in A. Imam, *Al-'unf al-dini fi misr: 'Abdel Nasser wa-l-ikhwan al-muslimun* [Religious Violence in Egypt: Abdel Nasser and the Muslim Brotherhood] (Beirut: Dar al-Khayyal, 1997), p. 186.
29. These MPs include Ahmed Yunus, Ahmed Said, Nawal Amer, and Mustafa al-Rifaei. Ibid., p. 187.
30. A. Mansour, *Hussein al-Shafei: Shahid 'ala al-'Asr Thawrat Yulyu* [Hussein al-Shafei: Witness to the era of the July Revolution] (Cairo: Al-Maktab al-Misri al-Hadith, 2004), p. 174. Ahmed Abdel Majid, a founder of al-Tanzim, enumerated the various "oppression bodies" targeting the Muslim Brotherhood at the time, including (1) the General Investigations Department of the Ministry of Interior; (2) the

Criminal Investigations Department of the Ministry of Interior; (3) the Central Security Department at the Ministry of Interior; (4) the General Intelligence Department, which is part of the presidency; (5) the Administrative Monitoring, which is part of the presidency; (6) the Presidency Security Apparatus supervised by Sami Sharaf; (7) the Military- Police, the Military Criminal Investigations Department; and (8) the Military Intelligence: see A. Abdel Majid, *Al-ikhwan wa-'Abdel-Nasser: Al-qissa al-kamila li-tanzim 1965* [The Ikhwan and Abdel Nasser: The fully story of the 1965 Tanzim] (Cairo: Al-Zahraa leil 'lam al-Araby, al-Maguid, 1991), pp. 42, 57. Salah Nasser did not deny the multitude of these entities, arguing that Nasser had been interested in "turning these bodies upon each other." Nasser sometimes asked some of them to carry out missions outside their purview, such as asking the National Intelligence Body, mainly dedicated to external intelligence, to carry out internal missions: see A. Imam, *Salah Nasr yatadhakkar*, pp. 171, 207.

31. A. Al-Nafouri, *Tawazun al-quwwa bayna al-'arab wa-israel: Dirasa tahliliyya istratijiyya li-'idwan huzayran 1967* [The balance of power between the Arabs and Israel: A strategic analytical study of the July 1967 aggression] (Damascus: Dar al-I'tedal, 1968), p. 16.
32. Y. Heikal, *Falastin qabla wa b'ada* [Palestine before and after] (Beirut: Dar al-elm leil Malayeen, 1971), p. 273.
33. A. Al-Shuqayri, *Al-hazima al-kubra ma' al-muluk wa-l-ru'sa min bayt 'Abdel Nasser ila ghorfat al-'amalyat* [The great defeat: With the kings and presidents from the house of Abdel Nasser to the operations center] (Beirut: Dar al-Awda, 1973), pp. 8–9.
34. A. Hourani, *A History of the Arab Peoples* (Cambridge, MA: Harvard University Press, 1991), p. 300.
35. Ibid., p. 442.
36. Al-Naqqash, *Naguib Mahfouz*, pp. 269–279.
37. G. Tarabishi, *Al-muthaqqafun al-'arab wa-l-turath: Al-tahlil al-nafsi li-'iṣab jama'i* [Arab intellectuals and heritage: A psychological analysis of a collective neurosis] (London: Riad el-Rayyes, 1991), pp. 22, 39–40.
38. T. Al-Hakim, *The Return of Consciousness*, trans. B. Winder (New York: Macmillan, 1985), p. 18.
39. Ibid., pp. 39–40.
40. Ibid., p. 40.
41. Ibid., pp. 52–53. I cited from both the original in Arabic and the English translation.
42. Ibid., pp. 1–73.
43. Ibid., p. 22.
44. Ibid., p. 43.
45. Ibid., p. 44.
46. Ibid., p. 53.
47. I cite this long poem selectively from N. Qabbani, N. *Al-A'mal al-Siyasiyya al-Kamila* [The full political works], part 3, vol. 6 (Beirut: Manshurat Nizar Qabbani, 1993), pp. 71–98, to drive that point home.
48. Ibid., pp. 71–98.
49. Ibid., p. 73.
50. M. J. Al-Ansari, *Al-nassiriyya bi-manzour naqdi: Ay durus leil mustaqbal* [Nasserism from a critical perspective: Which lessons for the future?] (Beirut: Al-Muasassa al-Arabiyya leil Nashr, 2002), p. 151.

51. Written after the Six-Day War, the works of Ansari, Mahfouz, and others do capture the temperaments and sensibilities of Arabs.
52. A. Baha' al-Din, *Isra'iliyyat wa-ma ba'ada al-'Udwan* [Israelites and the aggression and its aftermath], vol. 200 (Cairo: Dar al-Helal, 1967).
53. Y. Al-Hafiz, *Al-hazima wa al-idiulugiyya al-mahzuma* [The defeat and the defeated ideology] (Beirut: Al-Tali'a, 1978).
54. C. Zurayk, *Ma'na al-nakba mujaddadan* [The meaning of the Nakba anew] (Beirut: Dar al-'Ilm lil-Malayyin, 1967), pp. 14, 17. See also C. Zurayk, *Fi Ma'rakat al-hadara* [On the battle of civilization] (Beirut: Dar al-'Ilm lil-Malayyin, 1973).
55. A. Dawisha, *The Arab Radicals* (New York: Council on Foreign Relations Press, 1986), p. 24.
56. A. Laroui, *The Crisis of the Arab Intellectual: Traditionalism or Historicism?* (Berkeley: University of California Press, 1976), pp. 7–9.
57. See A. Laroui, *L'idéologie Arabe Contemporaine: Essai Critique* (Paris: François Maspero, 1977); A. Laroui, *The Crisis of the Arab Intellectual*, pp. 7–9; and Hourani, *A History of the Arab Peoples*, p. 445.
58. H. Sharabi, *Muqademat li derasat al-mujtama' al-araby* [An introduction to studying Arab society], 3rd ed. (Beirut: Al-Dar al-Mutaheda leil Nashr, 1984), pp. 16, 25–29.
59. Ibid.
60. Ibid., p. 122.
61. S. J. Al-'Azm, *Naqd al-fikr al-dini* [A critique of the religious thought], 6th ed. (Beirut: Dar al-Ṭali'ah, 1988), p. 23.
62. Ibid., pp, 9–10.
63. Al-'Azm, *Al-naqd al-dhati ba'da al-hazima*; S. J. Al-'Azm, *Naqd al-fikr al-dini*; S. Amin, *The Arab Nation: Nationalism and Class Struggles* (London: Zed Books, 1978).
64. See B. Ghalyoun, *Ightiyal al-'Aql Mihnat al-Thaqafat al-'Arabiyya Bayna al-Salafiyyat wa al-Taba'iyya* [The closing of the mind: Arab culture between Salafism and loyalty] (Cairo: Maktabat Madbouli, 1990), pp. 198, 240–247, 300; B. Ghalyoun, *Naqd al-Siyasa: al-Dawla wa-l-Din* [A critique of politics: state and religion] (Beirut: Al-Mu'assasa al-'Arabiyya lil Dirasat wa al-Nashr, 1991). For an excellent summary, see Abu-Rabi', *Intellectual Origins of Islamic Resurgence in the Modern Arab World*, pp. 259–261.
65. A. Farid, *Min mahadir ijtima'at 'Abdel Nasser al-'arabiyya wa-l-dawliyya: 1967–1970* [From the minutes of Abdel Nasser's Arab and international meetings] (Beirut: Mu'assasat al-Abhath al-'Arabiya, 1985), pp. 281–306.
66. An interview with a former military and war correspondent of Ahram, Abdu Mubasher, in M. Menshawy, unpublished PhD thesis, "The Role of the State in Re/Constructing War Victory in Egypt," University of Westminster, 2016.
67. S. J. Al-'Azm, *Naqd al-fikr al-dini*, p. 97.
68. Ghalyoun, *Naqd al-siyassa: al-dawla wal-deen*, p. 221.
69. Al-Ansari, *Al-nassiriyya bi-manzour naqdi*, pp. 136–139.
70. Ibid., p. 128.
71. A. Dawisha, *The Arab Radicals*, p. 24.
72. Ibid., p. 12.
73. Al-Shuqayri, *Al-hazima al-kubra ma' al-muluk wa-l-ru'sa min bayt 'Abdel Nasser ila ghorfat al-'amaliyyat*, p. 138.

74. Al-Iryani, *Muzakerat al-rayees al-qadi Abdel-Rahman Bin Yehia al-Iryani*, p. 582.
75. Ibid.
76. A. Al-Baghdadi, *Mudhakkirat 'Abdel-Latif al-Baghdadi*, vol. 2 (Cairo: Al-Maktab al-Misri al-Hadith, 1977), p. 290.
77. M. Kerr, *The Arab Cold War: Gamal 'Abd al-Nasir and His Rivals, 1958–1970*, 3rd ed. (Oxford: Oxford University Press, 1971), p. 135.
78. Cited in A. Dawisha, *Arab Nationalism in the Twentieth Century: From Triumph to Despair* (Princeton, NJ: Princeton University Press, 2003), p. 284. There is no consensus on this conclusion. Manh al-Solh, for one, said that the aftermath of the 1967 defeat lent Nasser the leadership mantle of the Arab region through a public revolution, not through a coup, as had been the case in 1952, after masses of Egyptians rushed into the streets demanding Nasser's reinstatement after his resignation. Solh attributed this popularity effect to the pan-Arab Palestinian cause: see M. al-Solh, *Misr wal-'uruba* (Beirut: Al-Muassasa al-'Arabiyya leil Derasat wal Nashr, 1979), pp. 190–191.
79. *Jil al-sab'inat: al-rawafid al-thaqafiyya wa-l-ijtima'iyya wa-l-siyasiyya* [The generation of the 1970s: The cultural, social, and political streams; a seminar] (Cairo: Markaz al-Fustat wal Derasat fi Misr, 2000), pp. 32–33.
80. Nasser's overreliance on the Soviet Union to rebuild his broken army after the 1967 defeat went hand in hand with a new economic policy trend at home away from socialist economics and toward a more mixed, liberal market. Several measures of economic liberalization were introduced. The March 30, 1968, Manifesto sought to silence the "calls for radicalization" and the "technocratic discourse" of the regime—arguing that the rightward shift was a result of technical soundness, not ideological backwardness. On this point, see Elwy, *A Political Economy of Egyptian Foreign Policy*; Hinnebusch, *Egyptian Politics under Sadat*; Waterbury, *Egypt of Nasser and Sadat*; M. Wahba, *The Role of the State in the Egyptian Economy, 1945–1981* (Reading, UK: Ithaca Press, 1994). Although after the Six-Day War Nasser began the rapprochement with Saudi Arabia, Sadat built a strategic relationship with the Saudis and used it against their common enemies—Nasserists, socialists, and Marxists. That holy alliance was fueled and cemented by the oil revolution, a development that tipped the balance of social forces in favor of religiously based groups.
81. S. Al-Munajid, *A'midat al-nakba: Bahth 'ilmi fi asbab hazimat 5 haziran* [The pillars of the disaster: A scientific study of the reasons behind the June 5 defeat], 2nd ed. (Beirut: Dar al-Kitab al-Jadid, 1968), p. 17. Although Munjid attributed the defeat to the lack of faith in God, he also mentioned other reasons such as scientific backwardness: see ibid., p. 127. Munajid also cited the lack of "pan-Arab solidarity": see ibid., p. 169.
82. Dawisha, *The Arab Radicals*, p. 24.
83. Ibid., p. 12.
84. G. Al-Baramawy, *Hasad al-ayyam al-sitta aw harb 5 yunyu* [The harvest of the six days or the June 5 war] (Cairo: Dar al-Sha'ab, 1969), p. 51.
85. Al-Khouli, *5 yunyu: al-haqiqa wa-l-mustaqbal* [5 June: Truth and the future] (Damascus: al-Mu'assasa al-'Arabiyya li-l-Dirasat wa-l-Nashr, 1974), p. 80.
86. See E. Seifeddawla, *Usus al-Ishtirakiyya al-'Arabiyya* [The rules of Arab socialism] (Cairo: al-Dar al-Qawmiyya li al-Tiba'a wa al-Nashr, 1965).

87. A background point to this question is the simple distinction in foreign-policy analysis between a realist foreign policy that is driven by the pragmatic pursuit of the national interest and uses ideology as subordinate to it. On the other hand, an ideologically based foreign policy prioritizes the pursuit of ideology and, in a sense, subordinates the national interest to it. For Nasser, there was a happy coincidence, at least until the Six-Day War setback, between the Egyptian national interest and pan-Arab nationalist ideology. But even after 1967, when ideology ceased to serve the Egyptian national interest, Nasser did not fully abandon Arab nationalism, though he injected a heavy dose of realism into Egyptian foreign policy. In contrast, Sadat waged all-out war on supporters of Nasser's pan-Arabism and relied on advocates of pan-Islamism to vanquish his nemeses. Utilizing a religiously based ideology as cover for a statist-realist policy, Sadat, more than anyone else, tipped the scales in favor of political Islam (more on this point in the following chapter).
88. See N. Bitar, *Min al-tajzi'a ella al-wihda: Al-qawanin al-asasiya li-tajarib al-tarikh al-wahdawiyya* [From fragmentation to unification: The basic rules of historical unionist experiments] (Beirut: Markaz Dirasat al-Wahda al-'Arabiyya, 1983).
89. F. Halliday, *The Middle East in International Relations: Power, Politics, and Ideology* (Cambridge: Cambridge University Press, 2005), p. 86.
90. Ibid., p. 210.
91. Sharabi, *Muqademat li derasat al-mujtama' al-araby*, p. 162.

Chapter 11. Sadat's Coup and the Islamist Revival

1. Rif'at Sayyed Ahmed drew a map of what he called "Islamist violence." Ahmed concluded that most of these militant groups were founded after Sadat came to power and one of these factions assassinated him in 1981: see S. R. Ahmed, *Quraan wa sayef: Min malafat al-islam al-siyassi* [Qur'an and a sword: From the files of political Islam] (Cairo: Madbouli, 2002), pp. 68–69. See the excellent study on Islamic activism during Sadat's rule: A. Al-Arian, *Answering the Call: Popular Islamic Activism in Sadat's Egypt* (Oxford: Oxford University Press, 2014).
2. The Iranian revolution was even embraced by Nasser's Arab nationalists as an attempt to stand up to the West and the pro-Western shah: see M. al-Solh, *Misr wal-'uruba*, pp. 235–242.
3. A. Sadat, *Al-bahth 'an al-zat* [In search of identity] (Cairo: Al-Maktab al-Misri al-Hadith, 1979), p. 236.
4. Ibid.
5. Ibid., p. 237.
6. Author's interview with S. Sharaf, Cairo, 14 December 2006.
7. Ibid.
8. Author's interview with M. Fayek, Cairo, 26 November 2006.
9. Author's interview with H. Abdel Nasser, Cairo, 21 November 2006.
10. A. Sadat, *Al-Bahth 'an al-zat*, pp. 160–161.
11. A. Condron, "The Nixon Administration between Cairo and Jerusalem, 1969–1974: Concepts, Strategies, and Implementation," a doctoral thesis submitted in the faculty of International Politics, Aberystwyth University, 2015, pp. 111, 154, 246.
12. Author's interview with W. Abdel Majid, Cairo, 11 January 2007.

13. Ibid.
14. Author's interview with M. A. Said, Cairo, 22 October 2006.
15. See F. Ajami, *The Arab Predicament: Arab Political Thought and Practice since 1967* (Cambridge: Cambridge University Press, 1981), pp. 355–373; A. Dawisha, "Requiem for Arab Nationalism," *Middle East Quarterly* 10, no. 1 (2003); H. Khashan, *Arabs at the Crossroads: Political Identity and Nationalism* (Gainesville: University Press of Florida¸ 2000); J. G. Mellon, "Pan-Arabism, Pan-Islamism and Inter-State Relations in the Arab World," *Nationalism and Ethnic Politics* 8, no. 4 (2002): 1–15.; B. Tibi, *Arab Nationalism: Between Islam and the Nation-State* (Houndmills, UK: Palgrave Macmillan, 1980).
16. In 1979 the Arab Unity Studies Centre conducted a poll which found that 78 percent of Arab respondents believed that they were part of "one nation": see S. Ibrahim, *Itigahat al-rai al-'am nahwa mas'alat al-wahda* [Public opinion surveys regarding unity] (Beirut: Markaz Derasat al-Wahda al-'Arabiyya, 1980). Other surveys found that those sharing a belief of belonging to "one Arab nation" were 35 percent of all respondents, but the percentage went up to 44 in 2011 after the "Arab Spring": see Y.M.J. El-Sawany, *Itigahat al-rai al-'am nahwa mas'alat al-wahda* [The trend of public opinion towards the question of unity] (Beirut: Markaz Derasat al-Wahda al-Arabiyya, 2014), pp. 106–107; "Mashru' Qiyas al-Rai al-'am al-'Araby, 2012–2013" [The project of measuring Arab public opinion, 2012–2013], Arab Center for Research and Policy Studies, available from http://www.dohainstitute.org/release/657dc82a-dfa2-4749-9e96-5af5bf20913a [accessed 5 April 2014].
17. F. Rabi', *Al-harakat al-islamiyya fi misr: Min Muhammad Ali ella thawrat 25 janayir* [Islamist movements in Egypt: From Muhammad Ali until the 25 January Revolution] (Cairo: Dar al-I'tisam, F. 2011), p. 81.
18. Ibid.
19 "The Arab World, Israel, Greece, Turkey, Iran," *Summary of World Broadcasts*, part 4, British Broadcasting Corporation, 1970, pp. 3–4.
20 "Bayan al-rais Mohamed Anwar al-Sadat amama majlis al-umma, 7 October 1970" [The statement of President Anwar Sadat in Majlis al-Umma, October 7, 1970], available from http://sadat.bibalex.org/Historic_Documents/Historic_Docs_All.aspx?TabName=Speech [accessed 20 January 2016].
21. Author's interviews with A. Ra'if, Cairo, 1 December and 29 December 2006 and 19 March and 26 March 2007.
22. Author's interviews with S. Eid, Mansura, Egypt, 12 February 2007, 19 March 2007, and 21 March 2007.
23. Author's interview with A. Abdel Majid, Cairo, 14 February 2007.
24. Author's interview with M. Mashour, Cairo, 16 December 1999.
25. H. Hanafi, *Al-Din wa-l-thawra fi misr, 1952–1981: Al-usuliyya al-islamiyya* [Religion and the revolution in Egypt, 1952–1981: Islamic fundamentalism] (Cairo: Maktabat Madbouli, 1989), pp. 62–68.
26. H. Mustafa, *Al-Dawla wal harakat al-islamiyya al-mu'arada: Bayna al-muhadana wa al-muwajaha fi 'ahday al-Sadat wa Mubarak* [The state and Islamist opposition groups: Between compromise and confrontation during the two eras of Sadat and Mubarak] (Cairo: Al-Mahrousa Centre, 1995), p. 204.

27. Cited in M. H. Heikal, *Kharif al-ghadab: Qissat bidayat wa nihayat 'asr Anwar al-Sadat* [The autumn of fury: The beginnings and the endings of the Anwar Sadat era], 2nd ed. (Cairo: Sharikat al-Matbu'at, 1983), pp. 298–299.
28. A. al-Sissi, *Min al-mazbaha ila sahat al-da'wa* [From the slaughterhouse to the horizons of *da'wa*] (Cairo: Dar al-Tib'a, 1987), p. 21.
29. In Islam, *da'wa* literally means a "call" or "invitation," and has contextually been used to refer to a person being "called" to follow Islam. However, it has also acquired new meanings such as "mission" or "propaganda," either religiously or politically.
30. A. Al-Taweel, *Al-mujtama' al-madani wa-l-dawla fi misr: Q19 ila 2005* [The civil society and the state in Egypt: The 19th century until 2005] (Cairo: al-Mahrousa, 2006), pp. 42–43.
31. "The 1971 Egyptian Constitution," English-language version, available at http://www.wipo.int/wipolex/en/text.jsp?file_id=189854 [accessed 16 October 2017]. Furthermore, in 1980, also under the reign of Sadat, the constitution was amended after a referendum on 22 May. Article 2 was amended to make the shari'a "the main source of legislation" instead of "a main source of legislation," as in the 1971 version. For online copies of the original texts as published in the official gazette, see https://matnwahawamesh.wordpress.com/ [accessed 25 March 2015].
32. 'A. Helal, *Al-nizam al-siyasi al-misri bayna erth al-madi wa-afaq al-mustaqbal* [The Egyptian political system: Between the legacy of the past and prospects of the future] (Cairo: Al-Hay'a al-Misriyya al-'Ama li al-Kitab, 2010), pp. 40–41.
33. "The 2014 Egyptian Constitution," the State Information Service, available online from: http://www.sis.gov.eg/Newvr/consttt%202014.pdf [accessed 14 July 2014].
34. H.H.A. Mohamed, *Al-tanzimat al-siyasiyya li-thawrat yulyu 1952* [Political organizations for the July 1952 revolution] (Cairo: Al-Hay'a al-Misriyya al-'Amma li al-Kitab, 2002), p. 183.
35. Ibid., p. 186, taken from L. Awad, "Al-haras al-gam'i marratan ukhra" [The university guard again], *Ahram*, February 1977.
36. Hanafi, *Al-din wa-l-thawra fi misr, 1952–1981*, pp. 65–71.
37. Ibid., p. 67.
38. Ahmed Zaghlul's interview with Salah Hashim, *Islam Online*, 2 October 2011, available from http://islamonline.net/feker/discussion/1880 [accessed 2 July 2014].
39. Rabi', *Al-Harakat al-Islamiyya fi Misr*, p. 81.
40. Ibid., p. 82.
41. Author's interview with M. al-Zayat, Cairo, 20 October 2006.
42. Author's interview with I. Za'farani, Alexandria, Egypt, 13 January 2007.
43. G. Abdel Khaleq, ed., *Al-iqtisad al-siyasi li-tawzi' al-dakhl fi misr* [The political economy and income distribution in Egypt] (Cairo: Al-Hay'a al-Misriyya al-'Amma li-l-Kitab, 1993), p. 133.
44. Author's interview with S. Abdel Fattah, Cairo, 20 November 2006.
45. Author's interview with H. Tammam, Cairo, 7 February 2007.
46. Author's interview with M. al-Zayat, Cairo, 20 October 2006.
47. Author's interview with S. Abdel Fattah, Cairo, 20 November 2006.
48. G. Kepel, *Muslim Extremism in Egypt: The Prophet and Pharaoh* (Berkeley: University of California Press, 1993), p. 71.

49. See M. H. Heikal, *Al-Tariq ella ramadan* [The road to Ramadan] (Beirut: Dar al-Nahar, 1975). Heikal even made the claim that it had been Nasser who set the original 1973 war plan, a claim dismissed by Sadat and his supporters.
50. Ibid., p. 256.
51. Ibid.
52. B. al-Shatei, "Fi zekra badr: Aya wa madad" [On the anniversary of Badr: A verse and support], *Ahram*, 13 October 1973, p. 5.
53. A. Khallaf, "Yawm min ayyam al-lah wa qaid min ragal al-lah" [One of Allah's days and a leader from Allah's men], *Ahram*, 6 October 1974, p. 9.
54. M. Ibrahim, "Al-Qiyam al-Diniyya fi Uktubir wa Ba'da Uktubir" [Religious values in October and after October], *Ahram*, 22 October 1978, p. 13.
55. A. al-Sissi, *Min al-mazbaha ila sahat al-da'wa*, p. 24.
56. M. Al-Zayat, *Al-Jama'a al-islamiyya: Ru'ya min al-dakhil* [The Islamic movement: A vision from the inside] (Cairo: Dar Masr al-Mahroussa, 2005), pp. 33–34.
57. Ibid.
58. M. H. Heikal, *Kharif al-Ghadab: Qissat Bidayat wa Nihayat 'Asr Anwar al-Sadat* [The autumn of fury: The beginnings and the endings of the Anwar Sadat era], 2nd ed. (Cairo: Sharikat al-Matbu'at, 1983), p. 268.
59. Ibid., p. 269.
60. See M. Qutb, *Jahiliyyat al-qarn al-'ishrin* [The ignorance of the twenty-first century] (Cairo: Dar al-Shurouk, 1980).
61. Author's interviews with G. Mattar, Cairo, 23 September and 18 October 2006.
62. H. Tammam, *Tasalluf al-Ikhwan: Ta'akul al-Utruha al-Ikhwaniyya wa-Su'ud al-Salafiyya fi Jama'at al-Ikwan al-Muslimin* [The Salafization of Ikhwan: The demise of the Ikhwan thesis and the rise of Salafism in the Muslim Brotherhood] (Alexandria: Bibliotheca Alexandria, 2010), p. 13.
63. Ibid., p. 15.
64. Ibid.
65. Ibid.
66. Ibid., p. 12.
67. Ibid.
68. See A. B. Al-Uteiby, "Al-ikhwan al-muslimun wa al-hijra wa-l-'alaqaa" [The Muslim Brotherhood: Immigration and the relationship], in *Al-ikhwan al-muslimun wa-l-salafiyyun fi al-khalij* [The Muslim Brotherhood and Salafism in the Gulf], 2nd ed. (Riyadh: Al-Misbar li-l-Dirasat wa-l-Buhuth, 2011), pp. 7–56.
69. 'A. Al-Nifissi, "Al-Ikhwan al-Muslimun: al-Taghreba wa-l-Khata'" [The Muslim Brotherhood: Experiment and error], in *Al-haraka al-islamiyya: Ru'ya mustaqbaliyya, awraq fi al-naqd al-dhati* [The Islamic movement: A futuristic vision, papers in self-criticism], ed. 'A. al-Nifissi (Kuwait: Afaq, 2002), p. 233.
70. Ibid.
71. Ibid.
72. G. Feiler, *Economic Relations between Egypt and the Gulf Oil States, 1967–2000: Petro-Wealth and Patterns of Influence* (Brighton, UK: Sussex Academic Press, 2003), p. 98.
73. Ibid., p. 113.
74. Cited in A. Dawisha, *Arab Nationalism in the Twentieth Century: From Triumph to Despair* (Princeton, NJ: Princeton University Press, 2005). p. 256. See also M. Heikal,

The Sphinx and the Commissar: The Rise and Fall of Soviet Influence in the Middle East (London: Collins, 1978), p. 262.

75. Heikal, *The Sphinx and the Commissar*, p. 262.
76. Author's interview with E. S. Ibrahim, Cairo, 27 September 2006.
77. Ibid.
78. Ibid.
79. Author's interview with S. Yassin, Cairo, 19 October 2006.
80. A. Gogoi and G.I.A. Ghafour, *Arab Nationalism: Birth, Evolution and the Present Dilemma* (New Delhi: Lancer Books, 1994), p. 220.
81. Ibid.
82. Author's interview with W. Abdel Majid, Cairo, December 2007.
83. "Ru'ya Islamiyya" [An Islamic vision], *al-Da'wa*, April 1979, p. 13, cited in J. Cole and R.N.R. Keddie, *Shi'ism and Social Protest* (New Haven, CT: Yale University Press, 1986), p. 254.
84. See F. Abdel Azizi, *Al-Khomeini: Al-hal al-islami wa-l-badil* [Khomeini: The Islamic solution and the alternative] (Cairo: al-Mukhtar al-Islami, 1979).
85. A. Giordani, *Al-Mustashar Tariq al-Bishry wa rihlatuhu al-fikriyya: Fi masar al-intiqal min al-nassiriyya ila al-islam al-siyasi* [Justice Tariq al-Bishry and his intellectual journey: In the course of transition from Nasserism to political Islam] (Alexandria: Bibliotheca Alexandrina, 2011), pp. 8, 17, 19.
86. Ibid., p. 22.
87. Ibid.
88. T. Al-Bishry, *Fil masa'ala al-islamiyya: Bayna al-islam wal-'uruba* (Cairo: Dar al-Shuruouq, 1998), p. 51.
89. Author's interview with T. al-Bishry, Cairo, 22 September 2006.
90. Author's interview with A. Hussein, Cairo, 6 December 1999.
91. Ibid.
92. Ibid.
93. Author's interview with M. Amara, Cairo, 6 December 2006. As Nasser died in January 1970, Amara published a paper a few months later in which he urged reconnection with Islam as an all-inclusive civilization; see M. Amara, "Al-islam wal-qawmiyya wal-'uruba wal-'almaniyya," *Qadaiyya Arabiyya*, issue 12, May 1970, pp. 67–92.
94. Author's interview with T. al-Bishry, Cairo, 22 September 2006.
95. Author's interview with R. S. Ahmed, Cairo, 2 October 2006.
96. Ibid.
97. Author's interview with W. A. Al-Misiri, Cairo, 28 September 2006.
98. Author's interview with S. Abdel Fattah, Cairo, 20 November 2006.
99. R. P. Mitchell, *The Society of the Muslim Brothers* (Oxford: Oxford University Press, 1993), p. 155.
100. Ibid.
101. A. Mansour, *Hussein al-Shafei: Shahid 'ala al-'asr thawrat yulyu* [Hussein al-Shafei: Witness to the era of the July Revolution] (Cairo: Al-Maktab al-Misri al-Hadith, 2004), p. 136.
102. Author's interview with D. Rashwan, Cairo, 26 November 2006.
103. Author's interview with K. Habib, Cairo, 8 February 2007.
104. Author's interview with M. al-Zayat, Cairo, 20 October 2006.

105. N. Ibrahim, "Law 'ada al-umr sa'mn'a ightiyal al-Sadat" [If I could go back in time, I would have prevented the assassination of Sadat], *al-Wafd*, October 7, 2011.
106. Ideology refers here to a theoretical framework which explains how the state attempts to govern using consent, not just force. Accordingly, "ideology" is defined as a set of concepts, systems, and practices which control the minds of individuals. In other words, ideology is necessary for every political or social formation to reproduce the conditions of its production: see L. Althusser, *Essays on Ideology* (1976; London: Verso, 1984), p. 2. Althusser contends that the state has "Ideological State Apparatuses" (ISAs), e.g., the media, the school, and the museum, to guarantee its control: see ibid., pp. 17, 28.

Chapter 12. The Mubarak Era

1. H. Tammam, *Tahawwulat al-ikhwan al-muslimin: Tafakkuk al-idiyulujiya wa-nihayat al-tanzim* [The transformations of the Muslim Brotherhood: The dismantling of the ideology and the end of the organization] (Cairo: Maktabat Madbouli, 2006), pp. 7–8.
2. For further details on the position of al-Telmessany on the peace accords, see O. Al-Telmessany, *La Nakhaf al-Salam wa Laken* [We do not fear peace but we ask questions] (Cairo: Dar al-Tawze', 1992).
3. O. A. Al-Shahat, "Al-Ikhwan" [The Ikhwan], *al-Masry al-Youm*, 7 June 2007, http://today.almasryalyoum.com/article2.aspx?ArticleID=63729 [accessed 20 May 2015].
4. A. Abu al-Futuh, *Abdel Moneim Abu al-Fotouh: Shahid ala tarikh al-haraka al-islamiyya, 1970–1984* [Abdel Moneim Abu al-Futuh: Witness to the Islamic movement, 1970–1984], ed. H. Tammam, intro. T. al-Bishry (Cairo: al-Shurouk, 2010), pp. 65, 70, 95. The militant thinking at the time was dominant with a number of groups having adopted these policies of change by force, leading to the kidnapping of a cabinet minister and an attack on a Cairo-based military academy. For an overview of these groups, see H. Moustafa, *Al-islam al-siyasssi fi misr: Min haraket al-islah ella gama'at al-unf* [Political Islam in Egypt: From the reform movement to the violent groups] (Cairo: al-Mahrousa, 1999), pp 191–228.
5. Author's interview with H. al-Hamamy, Cairo, 13 December 2006. I conducted the interview with Hamamy in 2006, but his warning turned out to be prophetic. In 2009, Abu al-Futuh left the Guidance Office after what some described as a palace coup or a "mini-coup," in which hardliners sidelined moderates and reformists such as Abu al-Futuh and the deputy supreme leader, Mohamed Habib. Afterwards, and in another challenge to the group, Abu al-Futuh insisted on running in the 2012 presidential elections against other candidates, including the Ikhwan's Mohamed Morsi. That many Ikhwan or ex-Ikhwan members joined Abu al-Futuh's campaign and voted for him (he secured a notable 18 percent of the votes) shows how wide the split had become within the Ikhwan.
6. T. Al-Kharabawy, *Qalb al-ikhwan: Mahakim taftish al-jama'a* [The heartland of Ikhwan: The inquisition within the group] (Cairo: Dar al-Helal, 2010), p. 49.
7. Ibid.
8. *Al-Masry al-Youm*, a private newspaper and one of Egypt's most widely circulated dailies, published a claim that the al-Nizam al-Khass had recruited al-Telmessany's

driver, Mahmoud Sharaf, to spy on the supreme guide in order to abort al-Telmessany's reform initiatives; see Al-Shahat, "Al-ikhwan."

9. T. Al-Kharabawy, *Qalb al-ikhwan: Mahakim taftish al-jama'a* [The heart of the Ikhwan: The inquisition within the group] (Cairo: Dar al-Helal, 2010), p. 33.
10. Nouh turned to television as a platform for his opposition. See M. Nouh, "Al-halaka al-ula min kashf al-mastour ma' Mukhtar Nouh" [The first episode of "Unveiling the Hidden" with Mukhtar Nouh], December 20, 2013, YouTube, https://www.youtube.com/watch?v=Rqf2nqViQpQ [accessed 1 August 2014].
11. H. Abu-Khalil, *Ikhwan islahiyun: shihadat muwaththaqa tunshar li-l-marra al-ula 'n tajarib al-islah al-mamnu'a dakhil al-jama'a* [Reformist members of the Muslim Brotherhood: Verified documents published for the first time on the banned reform experiences inside the group] (Cairo: Dar Dawen, 2013), p. 23.
12. Ibid., pp. 26–29.
13. O. Abdel Haq, *Al-Islamiyyin al-Gudud: Ella Ayn?* [The new Islamists: Where to?] (Cairo: Markaz al-Hadaraa al-'Arabiyya, 2005), pp. 96–97.
14. A. Al-Ansari, "Al-ikhwan al-muslimoon: 60 qadiyaa sakhina, muwagaha m'a Ma'mun al-Hudaybi" [The Muslim Brotherhood: 60 hot issues, a confrontation with Ma'mun al-Hudaybi] (Cairo: Dar al-Tawze' wal Nashr, 1999), pp. 46–47.
15. Al-Anani, K., "Perestroika at the Brotherhood," *Ahram Online*, 5 May 2013, http://english.ahram.org.eg/NewsContentPrint/4/0/70701/Opinion/0/Perestroika-at-the-Brotherhood.aspx [accessed 13 November 2014].
16. Ibid.
17. One of the main accusations directed at the Ikhwan leaders is that their thinking is strongly influenced by Sayyid Qutb's subversive ideas, leading to a focus on operational matters at the expense of intellectual and theoretical pursuits. See K. Al-Anani, *Al-Ikhwan al-muslimun: Shaykhukha tusari' al-zaman* [The Muslim Brotherhood: Senility struggling with time] (Cairo: Maktabat al-Shurouk al-Dawliya, 2007), pp. 296–297. Anani contends that Qutb dragged the Ikhwan from Banna's open "reformist Salafism" to an "isolationist, traditional Salafism": see ibid., p. 297. This conservatism has impeded the Ikhwan's ability to come up with edicts regarding the group's position on key issues, including the status of Copts, the hijab, and even forming a political party: see ibid., pp. 138, 297. The current supreme guide of the Ikhwan, Mohamed Badie, was a disciple of Qutb and was sentenced in 1965 for leading a unit of al-Tanzim in Assuit: see S. Eissa, "Hakadha takallama murshid al-ikhwan: Mohamed Badi' 'an mabadi' tanzim 1965: al-mujtama' 'jahili' wa-l-hukuma 'kafira'" [So speaks the guide of the Ikhwan: Mohamed Badie on the principles of the 1965 Tanzim, the *jahili* society, and the "atheist" government], *al-Masry al-Youm*, 11 February 2010, http://www.almasryalyoum.com/news/details/27098 [accessed 8 April 2014]. If anything, there exists a big divide between the Qutbians, or rejectionists, and the accommodationists. This conflict is evident in the writings of dissidents and leaders of the Ikhwan; the most prominent example is Tharwat al-Kharabawi. Kharabawi dedicated the first section of his autobiography to the ideology of Sayyid Qutb in the context of the division which he witnessed and from which he admittedly suffered: see Kharabawy, *Qalb al-Ikhwan*, pp. 1–30. The author repeatedly mentions incidents of bickering with other members on whether Qutbian concepts should be eschewed: see pp. 89–90.
18. Author's interviews with M. Abdel Sattar, Cairo, 9 and 16 December 2006.

19. Ibid.
20. Ibid.
21. A. Ramzy, *Dawlat al-murshid wa sanam al-ikhwan* [The state of the guide and the statue of Ikhwan] (Cairo: Rodiy, 2013), p. 40.
22. Ra'if died on 27 January 2011.
23. Author's interview with A. Ra'if, Cairo, 19 March 2007.
24. Ibid.
25. Ibid.
26. Ibid.
27. Ibid.
28. Author's interview with M. Hudaybi, Cairo, 13 December 1999.
29. Author's interviews with M. M. Akef, Cairo, 24 December 2006 and 22 March 2007.
30. M. Habib, *Al-ikhwan al-muslimun bayna su'ud al-riyasaa wa taakul al-shari'ya* [The Muslim Brotherhood: Between the rise to presidency and the erosion of legitimacy] (Cairo: Al-Magmou' al-Dawliyya leil Nashr wal-Tawzei, 2013), pp. 24–25.
31. Author's interviews with M. M. Akef in Cairo, 24 December 2006 and 22 March 2007.
32. Author's interview with A. Ra'if, Cairo, 19 March 2007.
33. A. Al-'Gouz, *Ikhwani Out of the Box* [Ikhwani out of the box] (Cairo: Dar Dawen, 2011), p. 31.
34. I. Eissa, *'Amim wa-Khanager: 'An Karithat al-Tatarruf fi Misr* [Turbans and Daggers: The catastrophe of extremism in Egypt] (Cairo: Sphinx, 1993), p. 61. Remarkably, al-Wasat loosened up the Ikhwan's uncompromising vision of creating an Islamic state based on shari'a. Rather, the 2004 Wasat party program called for establishing a democratic political system in Egypt within the framework of the Islamic *marji'iya* (a point of reference); see N. J. Brown, A. Hamzawy, and M. Ottaway, "Islamist Movements and the Democratic Process in the Arab World: Exploring the Gray Zones," Carnegie Endowment for International Peace's Democracy and Rule of Law Project, March 2006, p. 18.
35 "Mustaqbal jama't al-ikhwan al-muslimun" [The future of the Muslim Brotherhood], *Aljazeera*, 18 December 2009, http://www.aljazeera.net/programs/without-bounds/2009/12/18 [accessed 8 August 2014].
36. T. Salah, "Mohamed Habib ba'da al-istiqala: Atawaq'a 'an yahkum al-ikhwan misr, wa igraat tasmiyat al-murshid batella' [Mohamed Habib after resignation: I expect the Ikhwan to rule Egypt and procedures to select the [supreme] guide are void], *al-Masry al-Youm*, 1 January 2010, http://www.almasryalyoum.com/news/details/516 [accessed 1 August 2014].
37. A Khatib and T. Salah, "Mohamed Habib yufaji' al-ikhwan bi-bayan yatlub fihi istiqalatahu min jami' manasibihi" [Mohamed Habib surprises the Ikhwan with a statement announcing his resignation from all his posts], *al-Masry al-Youm*, 29 December 2009, http://www.almasryalyoum.com/news/details/34399 [accessed 1 August 2014].
38. M. Habib, "Ghurub al-jamaa" [The sunset of the group], *El Watan News*, 10 October 2015, http://www.elwatannews.com/news/details/819159 [accessed 22 October 2014].
39. Author's interview with A. Madi, Cairo, 5 January 2007.
40. Ramzy, *Dawlat al-Murshid wa Sanam al-Ikhwan*, p. 42.
41. Al-'Gouz, *Ikhwani Out of the Box*, p. 8.

42. Author's interview with F. Abdel Khaleq, Cairo, 9 February 2007. Abdel Khaleq passed away in April 2013.
43. Author's interview with Abu al-Futuh, Cairo, 14 January 2007.
44. Author's interview with U. Abdel Khaleq, Cairo, 9 January 2007.
45. S. Eid, *Tajribati fi saradeeb al-ikhwan* [My experience in the basements of the Ikhwan] (Cairo: Jazeerat al-Ward, 2013), p. 35.
46. Ibid.
47. A. Ban, *Al-ikhwan al-muslimun wa mihnat al-watan wal deen* [The Muslim Brotherhood and the dilemma of homeland and religion] (Cairo: Markaz al-Nil leil Derasat al-istratijiyya, 2013), p. 89.
48. Eid, *Tajribati fi saradeeb al-ikhwan*, p. 42.
49. Ibid.
50. Ibid., p. 41.
51. I. Abdel Moneim, *Hikayati m'a al-ikhwan: Mudhakkirat ukht sabiqa* [My story with the Ikhwan: Memoirs of an ex sister member] (Cairo: al-Hay'a al-Misriyya al-'Amma li-l-Kitab, 2011), p. 145.
52. Ramzy, *Dawlat al-murshid wa sanam al-ikhwan*, p. 40.
53. Ibid., p. 78.
54. Ibid., pp. 70–74.
55. Ibid., p. 39.
56. T. Al-Kharabawy, *Qalb al-Ikhwan*, p. 130.
57. See the Ministry of Justice's breakdown of al-Shater's fortune in 2006: M. Al-Marsafawi, "Bill-arqam ... imbratoriyat Khayrat al-Shater" [In figures ... The empire of Khairat al-Shater], *al-Masry al-Youm*, 13 April 2012, http://www.almasryalyoum.com/news/details/171799 [accessed 12 August 2014].
58. See M. Abdel-Ati, "Al-Iththithmar Tugamed Ashum Al-Shater wa Malek fi 66 shareka wa tasmah bi-istimrar al-Nashat" [The organization of investment freezes the shares of al-Shater in 66 companies and allows the resumption of activities], *al-Masry al-Youm*, 19 July 2014, http://www.almasryalyoum.com/news/details/485460 [accessed: 12 March 2015.] 2015.
59. Author's interview with M. Izzat, Cairo, 24 December 2006.
60. Ibid.
61. Abu El-Ela Madi charges the old guard within the Ikhwan with obstructing efforts to form al-Wasat before 1996—so that he only eventually managed to do so by quitting the Ikhwan and doing it independently. Author's interview with A. Madi, Cairo, 26 September 2006. For further background on of Madi's recruitment and ideological formulation, see A. Madi, *Gamaat al-u'nf al-misriyya wa taawilatiha leil islam: Al-guzur al-tarikhiyya- al-usus al-fikriyya-al-muragaat* [The Egyptian violent groups and their interpretations of Islam: The historical roots, the intellectual bases, the revision] (Cairo: Maktabat al-Shuruouk al-Dawliyya, 2006).
62. Author's interview with A. Madi, Cairo, 30 October 2006.
63. Ibid.
64. Abdel Haq, *Al-islamiyyin al-gudud*, pp. 55–61.
65. Ibid., p. 95.
66. S. el-Karanshawi, "Egypt Court Approves Moderate Islamic Party," *Egypt Independent*, 19 February 2011, http://www.egyptindependent.com/news/egypt-court-approves-moderate-islamic-party [accessed 3 September 2014].

67. Abu Khalil does not say why he waited for so long to tender his resignation. For further details on the statement of resignation, see H. Al-Waziri, "Abu Khalil yastaqeel min al-Ikhwan" [Abu Khalil resigns from the Ikhwan], *al-Masry al-Youm*, 31 March, 2011, http://www.almasryalyoum.com/news/details/122713 [accessed 12 November 2014].
68. Author's interview with M. Abdel Sattar, Cairo, 16 December 2006.
69. Ibid.
70. Author's interview with M. M. Akef, Cairo, 22 March 2007.
71. Author's interview with M. Mashour, Cairo, 13 December 1999.
72. In 2007 the Ikhwan circulated a draft program that might form the basis for a future Ikhwan-affiliated political party. International Crisis Group, "Egypt's Muslim Brothers: Confrontation or Integration?" *Middle East Report 76*, June 2008, https://www.crisisgroup.org/middle-east-north-africa/north-africa/egypt/egypt-s-muslim-brothers-confrontation-or-integration [accessed 17 October 2017].
73. Abdel Moneim, *Hikayati m'a al-ikhwan*, pp. 12, 13, 16.
74. Ibid., p. 180.
75. Ibid., p. 175.
76. Al-Ansari, *Al-ikhwan al-muslimun*, p. 48.
77. Habib, *Al-ikhwan al-muslimun*, p. 22.
78. Y. Al-Qaradawi, *Al-ikhwan al-muslimun: 70 'aman fi al-d'awa wa-l-tarbiya wa-l-jihad* [The Muslim Brotherhood: 70 years of preaching, education and jihad] (Cairo: Maktabat Wahba, 1999), p. 248.
79. Ibid., p. 252.
80. Ramzy, *Dawlat al-Murshid wa Sanam al-Ikhwan*, p. 66.
81. Mitchell, *The Society of the Muslim Brothers*, p. 329.
82. Ibid.
83. Ibid.
84. Ibid.
85. N. Ayubi, *Political Islam: Religion and Politics in the Arab World* (London: Routledge, 1991), p. 81.
86. A. Zohry and B. Harrell-Bond, "Contemporary Egyptian Migration: An Overview of Voluntary and Forced Migration," working paper published in December 2003 by the Development Research Centre on Migration, Globalisation and Poverty.
87. See S. Younis, *Suwal al-hawiya: Al-hawiya w sultat al-muthaqaf fi 'asr ma ba'ada al-hadatha* [The question of identity: Identity and the authority of the intellectual in the post-modern age] (Cairo, Merit, 1999), p. 189.
88. N. Ayubi, *Political Islam: Religion and Politics in the Arab World*, pp. 81–82.
89. Ibid., p. 90.
90. Ibid., p. 88.
91. For full details of Telmessany's background, see his memoirs: O. Al-Telmissany, *Zekrayat La Muzakerat* ([Memories not memoirs] (Cairo: Dar al-Tawzei al-Islamiyya, 2012).
92. Ibid., p. 92.
93. H. Tammam, *Al-ikhwan al-muslimun: Snawat ma qabla al-thawra* [The Muslim Brotherhood: The years before the revolution] (Cairo: Dar al-Shurouk, 2013), p. 84.
94. Ibid., p. 86.
95. Ibid.
96. Ibid.

97. M. El-Ghobashy, "The Metamorphosis of the Egyptian Muslim Brothers," *International Journal of Middle East Studies* 37 (August 2005): 373–395.
98. M. Mouro, *Al-haraka al-islamiyya fi misr an qurb from 1928 until 1993* [The Islamic movement in Egypt in a close-up from 1928 until 1993] (Cairo: al-Dar al-Masriyy aleil Nashr wal Tawzei, 1994), pp. 141–142.
99. H. Al-Awadi, "A Struggle for Legitimacy: The Muslim Brotherhood and Mubarak, 1982–2009," *Contemporary Arab Affairs* 2 (April–June 2009): 214–228.
100. In 2003 the Ikhwan organized a massive protest against the U.S. invasion in the Cairo Stadium, leading its members "into a feeling of victory": see Al-'Gouz, *Ikhwani Out of the Box*, p. 35. However, this demonstration, which was organized in a public location, with the approval of the state, raised questions about whether the Mubarak regime meant to co-opt the group, while at the same time allowing Egyptians to vent their anger against the unpopular U.S.-led war.
101. Ibid.
102. Al-Awadi, "A Struggle for Legitimacy," pp. 214–228.
103. See *Al-ikhwan fi barlaman 2000: Dirasa tahliliyya li-ada nuwab al-ikwan al-muslimin fi barlaman 2000–2005* [The Ikhwan in the 2000 Parliament: An analysis of the performance of the Ikhwan MPs in the 2000–2005 parliament] (Cairo: al-Markaz al-Dawli li-l-I'lam & Markaz al-Umaa li-l-Dirasat wa-l-Tanmiya, 2005).
104. H. Imam, *Al-ikhwan wa-l-sulta: Sira'at damiyya wa-tahalufat sirriyya* [The Ikhwan and authority: Bloody struggles and secret alliances] (Cairo: Markaz al-Hadara al-'Arabiyya, 2005), pp. 77, 92.
105. See *Al-ikhwan fi barlaman 2000*. Imam, *Al-ikhwan wa-l-sulta*, pp. 84–90.
106. See *Al-ikhwan fi barlaman 2000*. Imam, *Al-ikhwan wa-l-sulta*, p. 140.
107. Habib, *Al-ikhwan al-muslimun*, p. 7.
108. In 1992 the Egyptian state unveiled what it called an "enabling" document discovered during a security raid on the Salsabeel Company, owned by Khairat al-Shater, one of the most influential figures in the Ikhwan. The Ikhwan denied the existence of such a document, but several researchers and former members of the Ikhwan—such as Hussam Tammam and Tharwat al-Kharabawy—claimed otherwise. See Tammam, *Tahawwulat al-ikhwan al-muslimun*, and T. Al-Kharabawy, *Sirr al-ma'bad: Al-asrar al-khafiya li-jam'at al-ikhwan al-muslimun* [The secret of the temple: The hidden secrets of the Muslim Brotherhood] (Cairo: Nahdet Masr, 2012).
109. Sayyid Imam al-Sharif, an Islamist leader associated with Zawahiri, wrote a manual titled *Al-'umda fi i'dad al-'udda* in 1987–1988, in which he prioritized jihad against Muslim rulers, whom he called the "living despots," over the other "jihad against Jews" because those rulers "are closer to us and they are also apostates [abandoning Islamic beliefs]": see A. I. Abdel-Aziz, *Al-'Umda fi I'dad al-'Udda* [The essentials of making ready for jihad], http://www.m5zn.com/newuploads/2015/02/18/pdf/4f2fb076fd7d595.pdf [accessed 8 October 2015], p. 342. In this manifesto, Sharif said that jihad against those "apostate leaders" like Mubarak is *fard ayn* (obligatory) on every Muslim who has reached the age of fifteen: see ibid., p. 30. The significance of this manual is that it became a cornerstone of militant Islamists in Egypt and their operational prioritization of the "near enemy" (Muslim rulers) over the "far enemy" (America, Europe, and Israel): see F. Gerges, *The Far Enemy: Why Jihad Went Global* (Cambridge: Cambridge University Press, 2010), p. 14. See also R. S. Ahmed, *Quraan wa sayef: Min malafat al-islam al-sayasi, derasa muwathaqa*

[A Qur'an and a sword: From the files of the political Islam, a documented study] (Cairo: Madbouli, 2002).

110. K. Habib, *Tahawulaat al-Haraka al-Islamiyya wal Isratejiyya al-Amrikiyya* [Transformation of the Islamic movement and the American strategy] (Cairo: Dar Masr al-Mahrousa, 2005), pp. 192–193.
111. N. Antar, "The Muslim Brotherhood's Success in the Legislative Elections in Egypt 2005: Reasons and Implications," EuroMesco paper 51, October 2006.
112. Tammam, *Al-ikhwan al-muslimun*, p. 19.
113. Brown, Hamzawy, and Ottaway, "Islamist Movements and the Democratic Process in the Arab World," p. 19.
114. Tammam, *Al-ikhwan al-muslimun*, p. 19.
115. M. Salah, "Masr tutahim al-ikhwan bi-l-'amal 'ala qalb al-hukm wa-bi-irsal 'anasir ila al-'iraq wa-al-shishan li-l-tadrib" [Egypt accuses the Ikhwan of plotting a coup and sending supporters to Iraq and Chechnya for training], *al-Hayat*, 18 May 2004.
116. See A. A. Hassan, "Al-haraka al-siyasiyya al-gadida: S'ubat al-tagazur al-ijtim'i" [The New Islamic movement: Difficulties of social rootedness], in *Hudud al-islah al-siyasi fi misr* [Limits of political reform in Egypt], ed. A. Thabet (Cairo: Dar Merit, 2007), pp. 223–246.
117. Ibid.
118. Habib, *Tahawulaat al-haraka al-islamiyya wal isratejiyya al-amrikiyya*, pp. 184–185.
119. Tammam, *Al-ikhwan al-muslimun*, p. 61. Sameh Fawzi, an Egyptian Coptic researcher, agreed with Tammam, contending that the lack of a revisionist (progressive) trend in the Ikhwan led to this radicalism in relations with the Copts. However, Fawzi went further by linking the Ikhwan's position on the Copts to the movement's foundational myth of realizing the goal of an "Islamic homeland," which runs counter to the more inclusive "nation-state" homeland: see S. Fawzi, "Al-ikhwan wal aqbat: Qiraa fil masarat" [The Ikhwan and the Copts: A reading in their positions], in *Ghewayat al-sulta wa wahm al-tamkeen*, editor not given [The temptation of authority and the myth of enablement] (UAE: Al-Misbar, 2013), pp. 179–188.
120. Author's interview with A. Ra'if, Cairo, 19 March 2007.
121. Brown, Hamzawy, and Ottaway, "Islamist Movements and the Democratic Process in the Arab World," p. 6.
122. Ibid., p. 13.
123. Mohamed Habib, for one, blamed the authoritarianism of the Mubarak regime on a number of developments inside the group, such as putting too much emphasis on organization, the centralization of power in the hands of the Guidance Office with no accountability to the remaining institutions within the group, and the lack of dynamic interaction and feedback between the leaders of the group and its grassroots: see Habib, *Al-ikhwan al-muslimun*, pp. 15–16.
124. Author's interview with M. Beshr, Cairo, 16 December 2006.
125. Ibid.
126. See *Adwaa alla adaa nuwab al-ikhwan al-muslemeen fi parlaman, 2005–2010* [A highlight on the Ikhwan MPs in Parliament, 2005–2010] (Cairo: al-Markaz al-I'lami leil Kutala al-Barlamaniyya Leil Ikhwan al-Muslemeen, 2010), a newsletter issued by the parliamentary bloc of Ikhwan MPs; no dates are mentioned on the manuscript.
127. Author's interview with A. M. Abu al-Futuh, Cairo, 17 December 2006.

128. Author's interview with A. M. Abu al-Futuh, Cairo, 22 March 2007.
129. Author's interview with A. M. Abu al-Futuh, Cairo, 14 January 2007.
130. Ibid.
131. Author's interview with E. al-Haddad, Cairo, 9 January 2007.
132. Author's interview with F. Abdel Khaleq, Cairo, 19 January 2007.
133. Ibid.
134. Ibid.
135. Ibid.
136. Author's interview with F. Abdel Khaleq, Cairo, 7 December 2006.
137. Ibid.
138. Ibid.
139. Author's interview with F. Abdel Khaleq, Cairo, 19 January 2007.
140. Author's interview with U. Abdel Khaleq, Cairo, 9 January 2007.
141. Ibid.
142. Ibid.
143. Ibid.
144. Ibid.
145. Ibid.
146. In 1997 Mashour, the Ikhwan's supreme guide, argued that Christians should not be allowed to join the army and should, instead, pay *al-jizya* (tribute or taxation) to the government. The statement caused an uproar in Coptic and liberal circles, ultimately prompting Mashour to issue a denial. Other Islamists shrugged off Mashour's opinion as "'his own' viewpoint that does not reflect the group's thought": see K. Dawoud, "Significant Gestures," *Ahram Weekly*, 15 January 2015, http://weekly.ahram.org.eg/News/10168/17/Significant-gestures.aspx [accessed 14 August 2014].
147 "Video nader: Murshid al-ikhwan: Nahnu naftakher wa nataqrab ella allah bil-gihaz al-sirri" [We boast of and approach Allah through the al-Gihaz al-Sirri], 1 May 2013, http://www.youtube.com/watch?v=GD8ltBk5szo [accessed 2 August 2014]. Although the video could not be independently verified, former Ikhwan leader Tharwat al-Kharabawy claimed that the group still has a functional secret apparatus as Hudaybi hinted in the video: Al-Kharabawy, *Sirr al-Ma'bad*.
148. Author's interview with H. El-Hamamy, Cairo, 14 January 2007.
149. Ibid.
150. Ibid.

Conclusion

1. See the critical analysis by Wahid Abdel Majid, leading Egyptian public intellectual, "The Crisis of the 'Ikhwan': Disentangling Myth from Reality," *al-Hayat*, 9 April 2017 (in Arabic).
2. In fact, the Ikhwan wagers that the state clampdown will ultimately gain them public sympathy. The death of the former supreme guide Mohamed Mahdi Akef on 23 September 2017 is a case in point of how the Ikhwan generates public empathy through this correlation between imprisonment and survival. Akef, eighty-nine years old, died in a public hospital where he had been transferred from his prison. Hasm, an armed faction of the Ikhwan which some members have criticized for its adoption of

violence, issued a statement describing Akef as the "the hero and Mujahid, the icon of resistance and the symbol of steadfastness." TV stations loyal to the Ikhwan, beaming out mainly from Qatar and Turkey, increased this sense of victimization by focusing on the way Egyptian authorities rejected repeated requests to provide medical treatment to Akef before his health deteriorated. Akef was buried amid tight security precautions, which also banned any funeral procession afterwards. See "Dafn Mahdi Akef wasta igraat amniya wa hasm taatabruhu al-batal al-muqatel" [Burying Mahdi Akef amid security measures and Hasm considers him the 'hero and mujahid'"], *al-Hayat*, 24 September 2017. Online at http://www.alhayat.com/Articles/24236104 [accessed 18 October 2017].

3. http://www.watanserb.com/2016/07/24 [accessed 23 October 2017].
4. Hazem Kandil, *Inside the Brotherhood* (Malden, MA: Polity Press, 2015), p. 178.
5. Ashraf El-Sherif, 'The Egyptian Muslim Brotherhood's Failures," *Carnegie Endowment for International Peace* (July 2014), p. 14.
6. Ibid.
7. A. Ban, *Al-ikhwan al-muslimun wa mihnat al-watan wal deen* [The Muslim Brotherhood and the dilemma of homeland and religion] (Cairo: Markaz al-Nil leil Derasat al-istratijiyya, 2013), p. 14. This counter-narrative found support in an official Saudi document leaked by Wikileaks, in which Ikhwan leader Khairat al-Shater offered to release Mubarak and not put him on trial in return for $10 billion paid by the Gulf. Sasapost, "Wikileaks: Al-saudiya wal ikhwan al-muslimeen fi masr" [Wikileaks: The Muslim Brotherhood and Saudi Arabia in Egypt], 20 July 2015, http://www.sasapost.com/saudi-cables-and-ikhwan-in-egypt/ [accessed 23 October 2017].
8. In contrast to the 1950s and 1960s, when Saudi Arabia backed the Ikhwan against Arab nationalist Nasser, now the powerful Saudi kingdom is an implacable enemy of the Islamist group and, together with its Arab Gulf partners, provides the Sisi government with billions of U.S. dollars in financial aid. The nationalist-Islamist conflict is playing out on Arab and Middle Eastern streets in Syria, Libya, and beyond, while Turkey and Qatar embrace the Islamists.
9. Egyptian authorities have accused the Ikhwan of setting up a paramilitary wing called Hasm. The group has attacked judges and security posts since it emerged in July 2016. On 20 October 2017, Hasm, a small Islamist faction, claimed responsibility for a devastating ambush against police and security forces which killed at least fifty-nine officers. Egyptian militancy specialists question the authenticity of Hasm and its capacity to carry out such spectacular operations. Although its structure remains hazy, Hasm is led by Ikhwan members who, angered by Sisi's harsh crackdown since 2013, have abandoned the movement's policy of nonviolence. See Declan Walsh and Nour Youssef, "Militants Kill Egyptian Security Forces in Devastating Ambush," *New York Times*, 21 October 2017, and also "Maza taaref an harakat hasm" [What do you know about the Hasm movement], Aljazeera.net, http://www.aljazeera.net/encyclopedia/movementsandparties/2017/2/13 [accessed 18 October 2017].
10. See an internal document by a radical faction within the Ikhwan: Mahmoud Ali, "Al-Akhbar Publishes a New Internal Ikhwan Document: 'A Coup' within the Group," *al-Akhbar*, 19 December 2016 (in Arabic), and Mahmoud Ali, "The Option of Resolution and Reconciliation Diminishes: 'A Coup' within the Group," *al-Akhbar*, 20 December 2016 (in Arabic).

11. "Ikhwan Revisions ... Will They Pave the Way for a Settlement between the Opposition and the Regime?," *Quds al-Arabi*, 12 January 2017 (in Arabic).
12. El-Sherif, "The Egyptian Muslim Brotherhood's Failures," p. 12.
13. S. Fayez, *Janat al-ikhwan: Rehlat al-khuroug min al-gama'* [The Ikhwan paradise: The journey of leaving the group] (Cairo: Al-Tanweer, 2012), p. 16.
14. Ibid.
15. A. al-'Gouz, *Ikhwani out of the box* [Ikhwani out of the box] (Cairo: Dar Dawen, 2011), pp. 44–45.
16. Ban, *Al-ikhwan al-muslimun*, pp. 38, 51–52.
17. S. Eid, *Al-ikhwan al-muslimoon: Al-hader wal mustaqbal, awraq fil naqd al-zati* [The Muslim Brothers: The present and the future; self-critical notes (Cairo: Mahroussa, 2014), p. 90.
18. I. Abdel Mon'im, *Hekayatii ma' al-ikhwan* [My story with the Muslim Brotherhood] (Cairo: Al-Hayaa Al-Misriyya al-'Ama leil Kitab, 2011), pp. 39, 209–210.
19. Ibid., p. 195.
20. Fayez, *Janat al-ikhwan*, p. 18.
21. M. Habib, *Al-ikhwan al-muslimoon bayna so'ud al-riyasaa wa taakul al-shari'ya* [The Ikhwan: Between the rise to the presidency and the erosion of legitimacy] (Cairo: Al-Magmou' al-Dawliyya leil Nashr wal-Tawzei, 2013). See H. Al-Awadi, "Islamists in Power: The Case of the Muslim Brotherhood in Egypt," *Contemporary Arab Affairs* 6, no. 4 (2013): 544. According to leaked documents, flaunting their pragmatism, or rather political cynicism, the Ikhwan promised the military junta running Egypt, the Supreme Council of Armed Forces (SCAF), legal immunity from future prosecution for any crime committed by the security forces during the 2011 uprising, once they are no longer in control of the government. "H: Intel: Muslim Brotherhood on the Move. Sid," Wikileaks, https://wikileaks.org/clinton-emails/emailid/12522 [accessed 23 October 2017].
22. El-Khirbawi, *Qalb al-ikhwan: Mahakem taftesh al-jamaa* [The heart of the Ikhwan: The group's courts of inquisition] (Cairo: Nahdet Masr, 2013), p. 176.
23. M. El-Ghobashy, "The Metamorphosis of the Egyptian Muslim Brothers," *International Journal of Middle East Studies* 37, no. 3 (2005): 373–395.
24. In 2010, a number of young Ikhwan members approached their leaders and proposed an initiative to launch a sweeping pro-change campaign that would open the group to dialogue both internally and externally with other ideological rivals. Called "New Egypt," the project was vetoed by the dominant leadership because, in their opinion, the "Egyptian regime was repressive and clashing with it would be useless."
25. D. D. Kirkpatrick and M. El-Sheikh, "Push for Retribution in Egypt Frays Muslim Brotherhood," *New York Times*, 5 August 2015. Available at http://www.nytimes.com/2015/08/06/world/middleeast/younger-muslim-brotherhood-members-in-egypt-bridle-at-nonviolent-stance.html?_r=0 [accessed 23 October 2017].
26. In 2014, the group reportedly replaced more than 65 percent of its previous leadership. Ahmed Abdel Rahman, a group leader, estimated that the youth account for 90 percent of these replacements. See Bella Hudud program, *Aljazeera Arabic*, 23 April 2015. Available at https://www.youtube.com/watch?v=Yey7EC8cCM8 [accessed 23 October 2017].

Index